Handbook of Relational Database Design

CANDACE C.
FLEMING

BARBARA
VON HALLE

▲▼ **ADDISON-WESLEY PUBLISHING COMPANY**
Reading, Massachusetts ▪ Menlo Park, California
New York ▪ Don Mills, Ontario ▪ Wokingham, England
Amsterdam ▪ Bonn ▪ Sydney ▪ Singapore ▪ Tokyo
Madrid ▪ San Juan

Keith Wollman: Sponsoring Editor
Karen Myer: Production Supervisor
Melinda Grosser for *silk:* Text Designer
Lyn Dupré: Copy Editor
Marshall Henrichs: Cover Designer
Hugh Crawford: Manufacturing Supervisor
Wendy Lewis: Production Coordinator

Teradata and DBC/1012 are registered trademarks of Teradata Corporation. Many of the designations used by manufacturers and sellers to distinguish their products are claimed as trademarks. Where those designations appear in this book, and Addison-Wesley was aware of a trademark claim, the designations have been printed in initial caps or all caps.

The programs and applications presented in this book have been included for their instructional value. They have been tested with care, but are not guaranteed for any particular purpose. The publisher does not offer any warranties or representations, nor does it accept any liabilities with respect to the programs or applications.

LIBRARY OF CONGRESS
Library of Congress Cataloging-in-Publication Data

Fleming, Candace C.
    Handbook of relational database design / by Candace C. Fleming,
    Barbara von Halle.
        p.   cm.
    Bibliography: p.
    Includes index.
    ISBN 0-201-11434-8
    1. Data base management.   2. Relational data bases.   I. Von
Halle, Barbara.   II. Title.
QA76.9.D3F595   1989
005.75′6—dc19   87-27775
                                                              CIP

10 11 12 13 14 15 16 17 18 19 20 MA 959493

PREFACE

This book provides a comprehensive and practical approach to organizing information requirements and designing relational databases. It introduces two (potentially independent) methodologies, logical data modeling and relational database design. Both methodologies are useful because they are applicable to a wide variety of business requirements, independent of specific product implementations, enhanced with examples from real-life experiences drawn from many businesses, and understandable by people with varying skill and experience levels.

The book is intended for use in the classroom as well as in the business world. Its design methodologies build on the tenets of relational theory. Thus, it is a useful teaching aid for graduate-level courses in logical or relational database design. In addition, it emphasizes pragmatic techniques for designing databases using today's (sometimes imperfect) technologies. It permits less than 100 percent compliance with a theoretical model for situations justified by business practices and needs. As such, it is appropriate for business and systems professionals seeking a reference or aid to self-instruction.

LOGICAL DATA MODELING AND RELATIONAL DATABASE DESIGN

Using the *logical data modeling* methodology, the reader can develop a comprehensive and precise representation of information structures, rules, and relationships. This can be done regardless of whether a database implementation (relational or otherwise) is planned. For example, a strategic business systems planner can use the methodology to develop a high-level model of the information used within a business. On the other hand, a database specialist could employ it to build a foundation for product-specific database implementations.

By employing the *relational database design* methodology, the reader can translate a stable logical data model into a set of tuned relational database structures, incorporating mechanisms to enforce associated integrity rules. Most of the relational design steps are illustrated using ANSI SQL or extensions thereof. Consequently, the book's examples apply to a large number of relational products—those demonstrating at least some compatibility with the SQL standard. Product-specific examples are also provided, primarily for IBM's DB2 and Teradata's DBC/1012 because these products present two technologically very different implementations of the relational model. Other products are referenced when they provide useful design alternatives or solutions.

The relational database design methodology can support the development of simple or complex applications. A team of systems professionals can use the methodology to build a sophisticated, perhaps distributed, set of relational databases to support all information requirements of a sizeable enterprise. A business professional who has had little training or experience in systems development or technology can use it to build a small database on a personal computer. The design methodology is intended to accompany and build on a logical data modeling methodology; however, it need not be used exclusively with the logical data modeling approach in this book.

BIRTH OF AN IDEA

The concept of the book was born when two people, having had experience with very different relational products, joined forces to define 15 general rules of thumb for relational database design. The rules of thumb were to address a broad range of relational database products (spanning micros to mainframes) and an equally diverse designer community.

Over the past 2 to 3 years, we collected, organized, and documented personal experience, research, and even arguments surrounding relational database design principles until the initial 15 rules grew into a design methodology including steps, techniques, and examples. The methodology was tested not only at the original sponsoring organization but also at a number of other companies to meet many different objectives using relational technology.

In summary, our intent was to tackle use of a new technology in a practical way, without losing sight of the benefits associated with the underlying theory. Our hope is that the book enables various types of readers to meet differing, but practical objectives associated with logical data modeling and relational technology.

Reader Background	Reader Objectives
Minimal exposure to database concepts	Understand or even define a data model and/or database design
Some database experience	Build competence in data analysis and design (through logical data modeling)
Non-relational database experience	Build relational databases
Some relational experience	Develop complex, large-scale relational databases
Extensive relational experience	Develop a generic relational design approach for databases that may be ported or span product environments

HOW TO USE THE BOOK

The structure of the book is as follows: Part 1 introduces the concepts and principles underlying the design methodologies. It also summarizes the knowledge required for studying subsequent chapters. Part 2 contains the logical data modeling methodology. Part 3 presents the relational database design methodology. The Index of Design Rules serves as a quick reference.

As the book is a *handbook* addressing two full methodologies, you typically will not read it from cover to cover. Instead, you probably will find it most useful to read specific chapters as appropriate. We shall discuss four typical objectives and corresponding paths through the book.

TASK 1: BUILDING A LOGICAL DATA MODEL

If you are building your own logical data model, Part 2 provides a detailed step-by-step procedure. Begin with the introduction in Chapter 2 and proceed to Part 2. Figure 1 depicts your path through the book.

TASK 2: REVIEWING AN EXISTING LOGICAL DATA MODEL (OR ANY ASPECTS THEREOF)

If you are already familiar with other logical data modeling methodologies, read Chapter 2 for a review of concepts and terms used throughout the book. Then, use the Index of Design Rules as a summary of logical data modeling guidelines while conducting your design review. Each guideline references a design step describing a rationale and the techniques for applying the rule. Refer to the chapter that discusses that design step if you need additional details.

If you are not familiar with logical data modeling, read Chapter 2 and proceed to Part 2. Then, refer to the Index of Design Rules while conducting your design review. Figure 2 illustrates your path through the book.

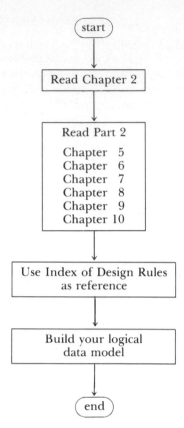

FIGURE 1 How to use this book to build a logical data model.

TASK 3: BUILDING A RELATIONAL DATABASE

If you will be building a relational database, read Chapter 2 to gain an understanding of the logical data modeling concepts and terminology used throughout the book. If you need to review relational database concepts or SQL, read Chapter 3. Review Chapter 4 to obtain an overview of the relational database design philosophy and procedure.

If you already have a logical data model to translate into a relational design, proceed directly to Part 3. If not, read Part 2 and build a logical data model before proceeding to Part 3. Figure 3 shows your path through the book.

TASK 4: REVIEWING AN EXISTING RELATIONAL DATABASE DESIGN (OR ANY ASPECTS THEREOF)

Usually, a logical data model review precedes a relational database design review. If you have not already done so, consider conducting a logical data model review by following the instructions for task 2 in the previous section.

To prepare for a relational database design review, begin with Chapter 2. If you need to review relational concepts or SQL, also read Chapter 3. Then read Chapter 4 to review the relational database design philosophy and procedure, and refer to the Index of Design Rules for guidelines while conducting your design review. Use the references from the rules to design steps to obtain more detail on relational design techniques from Part 3 as needed. Figure 4 shows your path through the book.

ACKNOWLEDGMENTS

We are very pleased to express our gratitude to the many people who made this book a reality. First, we extend our appreciation to the reviewers whose input and insight contributed to the quality of the manuscript: Marilyn Bohl of Digi-

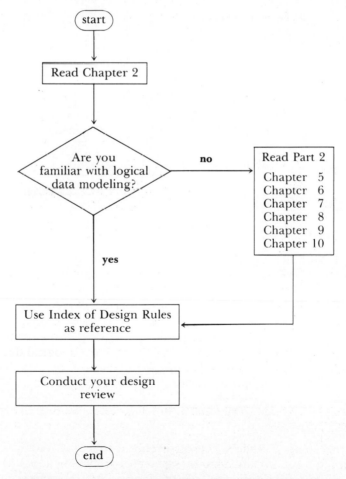

FIGURE 2 How to use this book to review a logical data model.

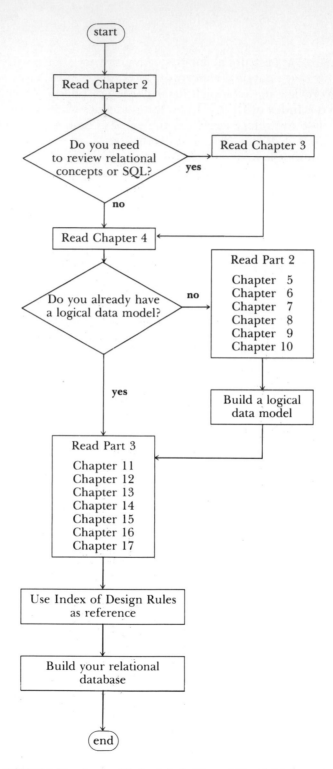

FIGURE 3 How to use this book to build a relational database.

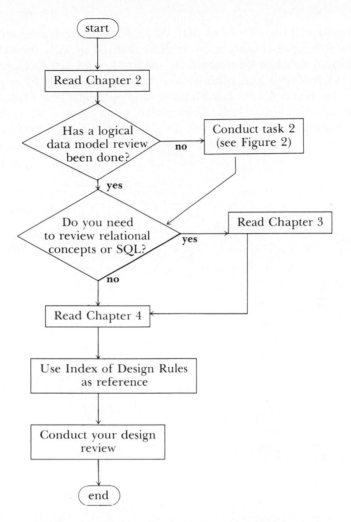

FIGURE 4 How to use this book to review a relational database design.

tal Research, Randell S. Flint, Mary E. S. Loomis of Calma Company, and Helga Spickhoff of IBM SRI. Second, we owe a great deal to our support staff at Addison-Wesley for their cooperation and ever-present professionalism. A very, very special thank-you to our senior editor, Keith Wollman.

This book would not have been possible without the dedication and patience of Martine Londono, who must have typed every chapter at least five times and whose expertise sometimes collaborated two authors' overlapping editing notes into sensible results. In addition, there are many friends whose encouragement we very much appreciate, in particular, that of Mr. Michael Motto.

Finally, we owe a great deal to our devoted husbands: Mike von Halle and Tom Fleming. They sacrificed personal time and increased their shares of home and family responsibilities so that we could dedicate incredible amounts of time to the writing of this book. None of us realized initially the extent of effort and personal sacrifice that would be required. And last but certainly not least, let us acknowledge the roles of our children (in order of appearance): Christopher von Halle, Casey Lee Fleming, and Kenneth von Halle—all born during development of the book. They added some extra challenges and delights to our long working hours. They also informed us (repeatedly and sometimes quite vocally) that maternity leaves have some other purposes than merely the writing of books!

Candace C. Fleming
Barbara von Halle

CONTENTS

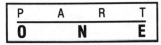

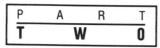

CHAPTER SEVEN   **Add Detail to User Views**   145

CHAPTER EIGHT   **Validate User Views Through Normalization**   179

CHAPTER NINE   **Determine Additional Attribute Business Rules**   213

CHAPTER TEN   **Integrate User Views**   251

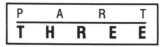

Building and Tuning a Relational Database

P A R T

O N E Introduction

1 Why a Handbook of Relational Database Design?

What is a *Handbook of Relational Database Design*? Let's dissect the title. *Handbook* implies a comprehensive guide for teaching as well as a reference for business professionals. *Relational database* indicates treatment of database technology that is relevant and strategic for the 1980s and 1990s (at least). *Design* implies a procedure for analyzing and organizing data into a form suitable to support business requirements and make use of strategic technology.

Specifically, this book provides a comprehensive cookbook-like approach to uncovering, analyzing, and modeling business information requirements. It also presents a methodology for translating an information model into a stable relational database design.

The idea for this handbook was triggered by four major trends in the evolution of relational technology: (1) increase in commercially available products for relational database management, (2) recognition of relational databases as practical and frequently more desirable alternatives to other database management systems (DBMSs), (3) emergence of relational DBMS products that satisfy a broad range of business requirements (from small-scale read-only applications to large-scale transaction-oriented systems), and (4) increasing involvement of people with limited database background in the design of relational databases.

These trends have moved relational technology out of classrooms and research laboratories into the business world of profit and loss. Consequently, issues of practicality (such as performance requirements, resource constraints, and personnel productivity) have placed new demands on the theoretical relational model and its implementation. As a result, we need a methodology for designing effective, *practical* databases that use today's imperfect relational DBMS products while relying on the limited expertise of available business and systems professionals.

Before introducing the design ideas in the book, we shall look at relational databases from three perspectives: technological, philosophical, and cultural.

The *technological* implications are the best understood and most discussed in the literature. It is common knowledge that relational databases escape many of the limitations imposed by older, more structured DBMS technologies. In fact, relational databases, when designed and implemented appropriately, are able to support a wide variety of access patterns and business needs. Users are able to peruse information in relational databases by asking many different business questions and by employing a variety of adhoc query, analysis, and reporting tools. They want to be assured of valid and consistent answers to their queries without being confused by an overly complex or limiting design. They may choose to start at any piece of information in the database (e.g., customer number) and proceed in any direction in search of other related information, without being constrained by the database design or the DBMS.

The *philosophical* implications of relational technology involve changes in attitude regarding objectives and importance of the database design process itself. Coinciding with, and at least partially due to, the advent of relational technology, effective data management has achieved acceptance as a key competitive business practice. Only an organization that understands the information on which its business is built can effectively employ systems technologies to use that information as a strategic asset. Obtaining an understanding of how information is employed within the business and reflecting that understanding within information systems demand a data-driven approach to systems design. In other words, the goal should be to create databases that are not driven by particular access requirements or technological constraints; the databases should first and foremost reflect the information relationships that are important within the business, independent of any specific usage. Simultaneously, of course, the databases must be user-friendly, maintainable, flexible, meaningful, and accommodating of the future.

The *cultural* aspect of relational technology involves an opportunity to shift, or at least to share, database design responsibilities. Historically, database technology has demanded highly specialized, usually scarce, and rather expensive technical skills. Thus, organizations have employed relatively few database designers, concentrated in centralized support organizations. The limited availability of these designers has severely constrained implementation of database applications.

Relational technology provides an opportunity for greater flexibility. Many aspects of relational design and implementation require lower skill levels than do those of other database technologies. An organization can thus experiment with more distributed and less specialized assignment of database support roles and responsibilities. Still required, however, is a solid methodological framework to enable less experienced designers to select and apply effective design techniques.

This book addresses all three facets of relational technology. It focuses on technological issues by presenting a step-by-step procedure for designing databases that capitalizes on the benefits of relational technology. It endorses the data-driven philosophy in that it includes a logical data modeling methodology for representing information rules and relationships that are independent of specific access requirements. It allows for the cultural flexibility in roles and responsibilities by targeting its design methodology at business professionals and students with varying levels of relational and database experience.

WHAT IS A DESIGN METHODOLOGY?

A *design methodology* is a structured approach for discovering, analyzing, and modeling a set of requirements in a standardized, organized manner. A design methodology thus consists of several key ingredients. Of the eight ingredients listed, the first six are mandatory, and the last two are optional (although also desirable):

1. *Statement of objective,* indicating a starting point (in our case, a loosely defined set of business-information requirements) and a final goal (in our case, a detailed understanding and translation of those business needs to a form suitable for computerized implementation).
2. *Step-by-step procedure* for establishing the objective. Each step should identify the input to the step, a transformation process to be applied to the input, and the resulting output. The steps should include review processes or checkpoints for analyzing, critiquing, and refining interim and final outputs.
3. *Guidelines, or rules of thumb,* that accompany all transformation processes; that is, each step should be reinforced with tips and techniques for dealing with potential choices and challenges.
4. *Standard and consistent documentation techniques* for communicating the procedure and corresponding outputs for each step.
5. *Examples and a case study* to illustrate proper execution of steps, guidelines, and documentation techniques.
6. *Assignment of roles and responsibilities* for performing and reviewing each step in the methodology. Appropriate assignment of roles and responsibilities enables productive sharing of efforts and leveraging of skills and experience of different project members (e.g., users versus data modelers versus database specialists).
7. *Formal course instruction* for transferring the methodology to those people who will apply or review it.
8. *Computer-based tools* to assist in the design process and to capture interim and final documentation.

OVERVIEW OF THE DESIGN METHODOLOGIES IN THIS BOOK

There are two design methodologies in this book: logical data modeling and relational database design. They are integrated in that the second builds on the first, although they can be applied independently.

Logical data modeling is a procedure for representing data requirements in a correct, consistent, and stable format. A *stable* design is one that will service many application requirements over a long period; thus, in addition to being correct and consistent, it must be *sharable* (i.e., it must reflect no bias toward particular access patterns or DBMS considerations). It also must have no unnecessary components and therefore should exhibit minimal redundancy.

The methodology in Part 2 consists of 12 steps for building a logical data model. If they follow these steps, designers are unlikely to misinterpret or unintentionally to omit any aspect of the meaning of the data. In particular, the logical data modeling methodology incorporates discovery and documentation of business rules that define conditions governing integrity of the data.

Relational database design is a procedure for translating the logical data model into an equally stable relational database, using facilities of existing relational DBMSs. Subsequently, the methodology leads designers in tailoring and tuning this pure translation to meet application-specific functionality and performance requirements, while preserving correctness, consistency, and flexibility of the design. The methodology in Part 3 consists of 13 steps to translate the logical data model and to tune the resulting relational database design.

HOW THIS BOOK CAN BE USED AS RELATIONAL TECHNOLOGY MATURES

Relational technology has existed, at least *conceptually*, since Codd's publication of the first paper describing the relational model in 1970. Practically speaking, however, most relational DBMS products are still in their infancy. These products will mature to incorporate more aspects of the relational model, to automate further enforcement of business rules (data integrity constraints), to be more user-friendly, and to provide new and improved performance features.

Wherever possible, this book takes into consideration the advances you can expect in relational DBMS products over the next few years. As appropriate, the design methodology identifies implementation solutions that should be chosen in the ideal world where all desirable facilities are available. Even more important, should those facilities be lacking in your database product, the methodology provides techniques for simulating them or otherwise compensating for their absence in a manner that makes evolution to future product releases an easy, natural progression.

There are still many unknowns relating to relational technology, including a number of key strategic questions. For example,

☐ Which relational DBMS products will survive through the 1990s?

- Which products will evolve to provide important functionality missing to-day (e.g., distributed databases)?
- Which products will evolve to support successfully high-volume, transaction-driven processing needs? Which products will remain focused on the more dynamic end user computing market?

Two points are certain. First, relational technology itself will survive in the form of some set of commercially viable products. Second, the key to gaining the most from relational technology is to begin with a solid relational database design.

C H A P T E R

2 Introduction to Logical Data Modeling

Logical data modeling is a technique for clearly representing business information structures and rules as input to the database design process.

At the heart of logical data modeling is an appreciation of data as a valuable resource for a business organization. Logical data modeling is a philosophy (as well as a technique) for recognizing and documenting the fact that *business data have an existence,* independent of how they are accessed, who accesses them, and whether or not such access is computerized.

Customers place orders

People eat ice cream cones

Some people pay bills on time

Some people do not pay bills on time

Some people do not pay bills at all

These are business facts that you can represent through a logical data model. These facts are true even if there is no current need to produce reports or answer queries about them. By recognizing such facts, identifying those that are significant to a user's business, and developing a corresponding logical data model, you are in a better position to accommodate access requirements through database technology. Even should such facts (or some subset of them) not become components of a database implementation, a logical data model often can help people understand specific aspects of the business.

Part 2 of this book presents a particular methodology for logical data modeling. This methodology has the following characteristics:

☐ It is an entirely *data-driven* process
☐ It encourages *comprehensive understanding* of business information requirements
☐ It enables *effective communication* among designers, developers, and users throughout the design process
☐ It forms the basis for designing *correct, consistent, sharable, and flexible databases* using any database technology

The methodology is entirely *data-driven* in that it seeks to represent types of information used within a business, unbiased by any particular application requirements or technological considerations. For example, in analyzing information required by the customer-services function of a business, you may ask questions like:

☐ What are the major information objects or concepts of interest to that function? (E.g., customers, service requests, service calls, bills, payments.)
☐ What detail information items characterize those major information objects? (E.g., customer number, name, address, telephone number—all of which characterize a customer.)
☐ How are those major information objects or concepts related? (E.g., customers *make* service requests, service calls *are placed to* customers *in response to* service requests, and bills *are sent to* customers *requesting* payments *for* service calls.)

These are facts about the way the business (or some subset of it) operates. They are independent of whether you are designing online or batch systems, providing for monthly summary reports or adhoc queries, using hierarchical, relational, micro or mainframe database technology, or allowing access by customer service clerks or business executives.

These data-driven facts provide an unbiased understanding of how information is employed throughout the business—without consideration of specific processing patterns or usage. By modeling an unbiased understanding of the business's information requirements, you enable greater stability and flexibility within subsequent database design. The database design is more *stable* because its architecture is designed around a thorough understanding of data from a purely business perspective. It is more *flexible* because you are able to tweak the database to meet technological challenges and access priorities while still retaining a faithful representation of the overall business operations. Thus, the logical data modeling methodology focuses on modeling of information requirements from a data-driven perspective first, while allowing for subsequent accommodation of application and technological constraints and priorities.

The logical data modeling methodology discussed in this book facilitates *comprehensive understanding* of the business information requirements. It is a detailed, precise, step-by-step process for producing complete documentation of information requirements. The procedure follows specific guidelines for object representation. It guides you in asking the right questions and recording the answers. It suggests a cookbook-like approach, complete with rules and implementation tips, that will enable even an inexperienced analyst to tackle a complex design problem with confidence.

Equally important, the logical data modeling methodology encourages *effective communication* among designers, developers, and users to achieve and validate this understanding. The methodology relies heavily on diagramming techniques to illustrate information and relationships more clearly and concisely than textual descriptions alone can do. The diagrams are supplemented by text, which itself frequently follows rigorous documentation conventions to convey as much meaning and as little ambiguity as possible. For example, naming guidelines facilitate clear and unambiguous naming of objects while enabling users to converse in terms with which they are comfortable. The diagramming and other documentation techniques are precise and simple enough to be understood even by users who are not trained in data modeling or database design.

Finally, the logical data modeling methodology is a basis for designing *correct, consistent, sharable, and flexible databases* using any database technology. This book discusses relational database design in particular. All the logical data modeling techniques discussed in Part 2, however, are applicable regardless of the type of database technology employed. In fact, you can (and frequently will) apply the logical data modeling methodology even before selecting a database product—due to the data-driven (technology-independent) nature of the methodology. The resultant logical data model is translatable, using any technology, to a database design that is

- □ *Correct*—providing an accurate and faithful representation of the way information is used in the business
- □ *Consistent*—containing no contradictions in the way the information objects are named, defined, related, and documented
- □ *Sharable*—accessible by multiple applications and users to meet varying access requirements
- □ *Flexible*—facilitating additions to reflect new information requirements, "tweaking" to accommodate strengths or weaknesses of a particular implementation approach, and modifications to respond to changes in business operations

There exist many approaches and methodologies for logical data modeling. Some are more formal and more intimidating than are others. The methodology in this book is not so much formal as practical; that is, it is a simplified version of a rigorous, formal treatment. For this reason, the methodology may not address the modeling requirements of every business situation. In the authors' experience, however, it does address the majority of business situations, and it does so in a way that allows even a novice designer confidently and correctly to develop logical data models.

Four complaints are frequently voiced by people who resist the idea of logical data modeling. First, it sounds theoretical (and, therefore, not practical). Second, it seems difficult (what is modeling, anyway? Sounds like an engineering term). Third, it brings with it a world of (sometimes cryptic) terminology. Fourth, who has the time to do it, anyway?

The logical data modeling methodology in this book addresses those objections by its very nature. First, it is straightforward, from the step-by-step procedure to the simplistic diagramming techniques. It does not require (although it might benefit from) automated design tools. Second, it is practical, and it has been used at a number of organizations by professionals of varying experience levels. Third, the terminology is simple, and, wherever possible, is akin to relational terminology (since subsequent design steps in Part 3 are targeted at a relational environment). Fourth, it encourages not only more stable database designs, but also greater productivity in building the designs. Thus, it saves rather than costs time. If this is your first exposure to logical data modeling, you may not fully appreciate this productivity gain until you complete your logical data model (Part 2) and begin actual database design (Part 3).

MAJOR CONCEPTS OF LOGICAL DATA MODELING

Let us take a look at a very simple logical data model, illustrated in Figure 2.1, representing Ron's Real Estate Business. We will use this example to introduce the logical data modeling terminology that we use throughout the book.

What strikes you first? Figure 2.1 is a picture, consisting primarily of boxes and arrows. And even knowing nothing about logical data modeling, you can immediately decipher some important facts about Ron's business:

☐ Ron deals with renters, properties (at least beach properties and mountain properties), and rental agreements. These seem to be the most important objects or concepts—or entities—in the diagram.

☐ Apparently, renters *rent* rental agreements, and properties *are rented to* rental agreements (more or less). Moreover, properties are of *type* beach or mountain. The arrows seem to reflect associations (relationships) between the boxes (entities).

☐ Ron is interested in selected details about each entity. For example, he tracks name, address, telephone number, and maximum monthly rental amount for each renter. He cares how many blocks away the beach is for a beach property, but not for a mountain property. These details are called attributes.

☐ Some attribute names appear above horizontal lines in the boxes—for example, NAME in the RENTER box. These attributes appear to be the most important or most necessary details about the entity. You will learn that

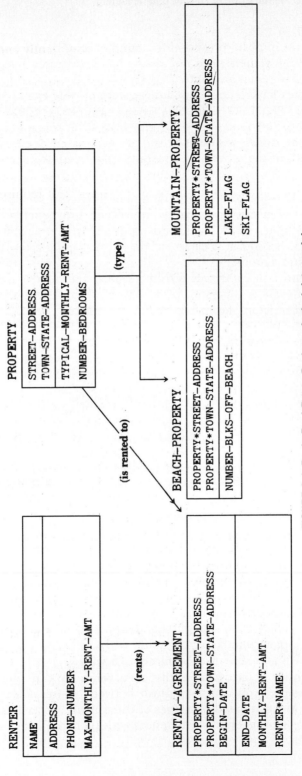

FIGURE 2.1 Ron's Real Estate Business logical data model.

RENTER

NAME
ADDRESS
PHONE—NUMBER
MAX—MONTHLY—RENT—AMT

(rents)

RENTAL—AGREEMENT

PROPERTY*STREET—ADDRESS
PROPERTY*TOWN—STATE—ADDRESS
BEGIN—DATE
END—DATE
MONTHLY—RENT—AMT
RENTER*NAME

PROPERTY

STREET—ADDRESS
TOWN—STATE—ADDRESS
TYPICAL—MONTHLY—RENT—AMT
NUMBER—BEDROOMS

(is rented to)

(type)

BEACH—PROPERTY

PROPERTY*STREET—ADDRESS
PROPERTY*TOWN—STATE—ADDRESS
NUMBER—BLKS—OFF—BEACH

MOUNTAIN—PROPERTY

PROPERTY*STREET—ADDRESS
PROPERTY*TOWN—STATE—ADDRESS
LAKE—FLAG
SKI—FLAG

13

these attributes must be present; for example, renters must have names, whereas perhaps renters need not always have addresses, telephone numbers or monthly rental amounts.

☐ Some attributes have names containing asterisks—for example, RENTER*NAME, PROPERTY*STREET–ADDRESS, PROPERTY*TOWN–STATE–ADDRESS. These attributes seem to refer back to or relate other entities.

☐ The arrows are drawn with one or two arrowheads at one end and have no arrowheads at the other end. Presumably arrowheads carry some meaning.

Without any knowledge of logical data modeling, you are able to interpret quite a lot! Thus, you can immediately appreciate two benefits of the logical data modeling technique. First, it is simple, particularly because it uses uncomplicated diagrams. Second, it is clear—it can express quite a few business facts precisely and unambiguously.

The most important constructs within a logical data model are entities and relationships. An *entity* is a person, place, thing, or concept about which you wish to record facts. Examples in Figure 2.1 are RENTER, RENTAL–AGREEMENT, PROPERTY, BEACH–PROPERTY, and MOUNTAIN–PROPERTY. A *relationship* is an association between two entities. Examples are RENTER *rents* RENTAL–AGREEMENT, PROPERTY *is rented to* RENTAL–AGREEMENT, and PROPERTY is of *type* BEACH–PROPERTY or MOUNTAIN–PROPERTY. In a logical data model diagram, we represent entities by boxes and relationships by arrows.

Entities have a number of properties, all of which we discuss in detail beginning in Chapter 5. For instance, each entity has a name (such as RENTER) and a description (such as "person who obtains the privilege of residing on a specific property according to the terms of a rental agreement"). You can distinguish between entity *sets* (such as all renters) and entity *occurrences* (such as renter Harry Smith and renter Josephine Morgan). All occurrences within an entity set have the same *attributes* or detailed information items (such as NAME, ADDRESS, PHONE–NUMBER, and MAX–MONTHLY–RENT–AMT—all of which are attributes of RENTER).

More formally, an attribute is a fact or nondecomposable (atomic) piece of information describing an entity. *Nondecomposable* means that an attribute represents the smallest unit of information you will want to reference at one time. For example, notice that a renter address is represented as one attribute (ADDRESS), but a property address is represented as two attributes (STREET–ADDRESS and TOWN–STATE–ADDRESS). This design enables the user to easily list all properties in a particular town and state, whereas listing only those renters in a particular town and state may be more difficult.

You can identify a particular entity occurrence by the values of its attributes. For example, you can distinguish between renter Harry Smith and renter Josephine Morgan based on values of their attributes as illustrated in the *sample value listing* (sample entity occurrences with their respective attribute values) in Figure 2.2.

RENTER

NAME (PK)	ADDRESS	PHONE-NUMBER	MAX-MONTHLY-RENT-AMT
Harry Smith	12 Oak Lane, Hopetown, NY 01111	212-984-3158	400
Josephine Morgan	5 Central Ave, Dallas, TX 75080	214-232-7990	650

FIGURE 2.2 RENTER **sample value listing.**

Typically, you do not need all the attribute values to identify a particular entity occurrence. For example, you can identify one particular RENTER by NAME (e.g., Harry Smith or Josephine Morgan). This identifying attribute or set of attributes (NAME in the case of the entity RENTER) is known as a *primary key*. The primary key of PROPERTY is the combination of two attributes, STREET–ADDRESS and TOWN–STATE–ADDRESS. You need both attributes to identify a particular property, because multiple properties may have the same value for STREET–ADDRESS (in different towns) or the same value for TOWN–STATE–ADDRESS (with different street addresses). RENTAL–AGREEMENT has a primary key consisting of three attributes: PROPERTY*STREET–ADDRESS and PROPERTY*TOWN–STATE–ADDRESS (identifying the property) and BEGIN–DATE (identifying the rental period for that property). We write primary key attributes above a horizontal line in the logical data model diagram (as in Figure 2.1) or on the far left above a (PK) designation in a sample value listing (as in Figure 2.2).

Notice you are employing some assumptions about definitions of the attributes as you choose the primary keys. These definitions should be explicitly understood and recorded within the design documentation or data dictionary. A *data dictionary* is a manual or automated repository of information about applications, databases, logical data models, users, and access authorizations (as well as perhaps additional subjects). Without referring to the data dictionary, your assumptions about the model are based on naming conventions used in the logical data model diagram. All entity, relationship, and attribute names are composed of English words, frequently are abbreviated, and usually are connected by hyphens. Abbreviations are used consistently. Moreover, each attribute name includes one word (the *class word*) that indicates the nature of the data represented by the attribute; for example, NAME, ADDRESS, NUMBER, AMOUNT, DATE, FLAG.

Some of the attribute names include the name of another entity as a prefix, followed by an asterisk; for example, RENTER*NAME, PROPERTY*STREET–ADDRESS, PROPERTY*TOWN–STATE–ADDRESS. These attributes are part of a foreign key. A *foreign key* is an attribute or set of attributes that completes a relationship by identifying the associated entity. The term *foreign* conveys the idea that the attribute "belongs" or refers to another "foreign" entity. Thus, RENTER*NAME in RENTAL–AGREEMENT identifies which RENTER is renting the agreement; and PROPERTY*STREET–ADDRESS, PROPERTY*TOWN–STATE–ADDRESS in RENTAL–AGREEMENT identify which PROPERTY is being rented.

BEACH–PROPERTY and MOUNTAIN–PROPERTY share a special type of relationship with PROPERTY, designated by the squared-off arrow connecting the two to PROPERTY. BEACH–PROPERTY and MOUNTAIN–PROPERTY are each *subtypes* of PROPERTY, representing the same real-world object but having slightly different, more specific definitions and characteristics. They also contain the foreign key PROPERTY*STREET–ADDRESS, PROPERTY*TOWN–STATE–ADDRESS, identifying with which PROPERTY each is associated.

Some of the arrows in the diagram are double-headed, whereas others are single-headed. The double-headed arrow represents a *one-to-many* relationship; for example, one RENTER may rent many RENTAL–AGREEMENTs, and one PROPERTY may be rented via many different RENTAL–AGREEMENTs (although not for the same week). A single-headed arrow represents a *one-to-one* relationship; for example, a PROPERTY is listed as a BEACH–PROPERTY or a MOUNTAIN– PROPERTY, but never as more than one.

A full logical data model consists of not only a diagram but also specifications in a data dictionary. For example, we noted that, although there may be multiple RENTAL–AGREEMENTs for the same PROPERTY, they may not be for the same week—or, more generally, they may not be for overlapping time periods. You already know that for two RENTAL–AGREEMENTs on the same PROPERTY (i.e., the same PROPERTY*STREET–ADDRESS, PROPERTY*TOWN–STATE–ADDRESS), the BEGIN–DATEs must be different (because PROPERTY*STREET–ADDRESS, PROPERTY*TOWN–STATE–ADDRESS and BEGIN–DATE constitute a primary key that uniquely identifies a RENTAL–AGREEMENT). However, you need to specify a *business rule* involving END–DATE as well. For example, when you insert a new occurrence of RENTAL–AGREEMENT, the END–DATE must be later than the BEGIN–DATE. Moreover, the END–DATE must precede the BEGIN–DATEs of all existing RENTAL–AGREEMENTs having a BEGIN–DATE later than the new RENTAL– AGREEMENT's BEGIN–DATE, for RENTAL–AGREEMENTs for the same property. Otherwise, the rental agreement is inappropriate and does not make business sense. A database implementation of the model should reject insertion of such an occurrence.

As you can see, such business rules are specifications that preserve the *integrity* of the logical data model by governing which values attributes may assume. True to the data-driven philosophy, you identify business rules without consideration for exactly how the system will produce reports or enforce edit criteria. For now, you are analyzing the data and all their relevant rules, independent of application requirements.

A logical data model therefore incorporates numerous rules about the *integrity* as well as the *structure* of information used within a business. Most of the rules conveyed by the logical data model diagram relate to structure. Other business rules specified within the data dictionary relate to integrity. For instance, the statement, "A RENTAL–AGREEMENT must be for a predefined PROPERTY but may be made by a RENTER who is not yet defined within the database" is a *key business rule* (governing valid relationships between primary and foreign key attributes). "PHONE–NUMBER is a 10-digit numeric attribute" is a *domain business rule* (governing types and ranges of values that attributes may assume). The example we discussed involving END–DATE is actually a type of rule called a *triggering operation* (governing general effects of insert, update, or delete operations on other entities or attributes). Structure and integrity within the logical data model are equally important. It is useless to understand the structure of information within the business without understanding rules pertaining to that information's integrity, and vice versa.

ROLE OF A THREE-SCHEMA ARCHITECTURE

At this point, the experienced reader may be questioning the relationship of a logical data model (supporting one area of the business or one set of business functions) to an integrated model of information used throughout the business. Such an integrated model frequently is called a conceptual model or conceptual schema. Let's digress for a moment to elaborate on this concept.

In 1977, the American National Standards Institute (ANSI/X3/SPARC Committee) developed a set of requirements for effective DBMSs. These requirements were specified in terms of a three-part framework for organizing data managed by a DBMS: (1) the *external schema,* or organization of data as viewed by the user or programmer; (2) the *internal schema,* or data organization as viewed by the DBMS's internal access logic; and (3) the *conceptual schema,* or integrated view of all data employed within the business.

The two methodologies in this book (logical data modeling and relational database design) are consistent with—and, in fact, build on—the ideas in the ANSI/X3/SPARC three-schema architecture. For example, you have just investigated the *external schema* for Ron's Real Estate Business: an organization of data requirements from the perspective of Ron, the owner. You could describe another external schema from the perspective of a property tenant. That external schema might include information about only one rental property, because the tenant cares about only the one property he is renting. It probably would include more details about that one property, such as days for garbage pickup and location of the nearest liquor store.

We have not yet said much about an *internal schema* for Ron's Real Estate Business. In fact, we will show little interest in any aspect of internal schemas throughout the logical data modeling process. Recall the assumption that you may not even have chosen a database technology when you begin your logical data model. Even if you have, you do not want to embed any details in your logical data model about how the DBMS will view the data. In Part 3, you will address how a relational DBMS can represent the data structure and integrity (i.e., an internal schema for a relational DBMS) such that the design effectively supports your external schemas, represented via logical data models.

Let us talk more about a *business conceptual schema* as part of the logical data modeling process. As the integrated view of all the business's data, the conceptual schema is effectively a consolidation of all relevant logical data models. In Part 2, you will learn how to evolve a conceptual schema by consolidating logical data models as they are built. The conceptual schema will help to ensure consistency of multiple logical data models, defined to support different user groups or different areas of the business. Existence of one (although evolving) conceptual schema also will aid in designing shared databases or internal schemas that support multiple external schemas. Finally, the conceptual schema will help to ensure consistency across multiple database implementations or internal schemas (e.g., making use of different technological strengths). Thus, a user

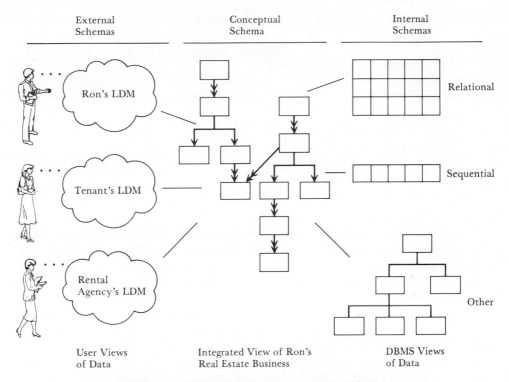

FIGURE 2.3 ANSI/X3/SPARC Three-schema architecture.

can maintain one view (one external schema) of the data regardless of underlying implementations (internal schemas).

Figure 2.3 illustrates the mappings among external, internal, and conceptual schemas.

Our discussion has generalized the ANSI/X3/SPARC definition of a three-schema architecture. ANSI/X3/SPARC defined the three types of schemas in terms of how they should be supported within a given DBMS (e.g., a relational database product). We incorporate the design principles of the three-schema framework to produce logical data models and an integrated business conceptual schema that can be implemented via any (or, indeed, multiple) database technologies. Thus, we are borrowing from ANSI/X3/SPARC not only an architecture for DBMSs but also a specification for effective database design practices.

STEPS IN LOGICAL DATA MODELING

By now, you should be comfortable with many of the concepts embodied by logical data modeling. Let us clarify your understanding by defining a set of criteria for an *optimal* logical data model:

☐ *Structural validity*—consistency with the way the business defines and organizes information

☐ *Simplicity*—ease of understanding even by unskilled people (e.g., by users or by non–systems professionals)

☐ *Nonredundancy*—inclusion of no extraneous information; in particular, representation of any one piece of information exactly once (this may be a subcriterion of simplicity)

☐ *Sharability*—not specific to any particular application or technology; thereby usable by many

☐ *Extensibility*—ability to evolve to support new requirements with minimal effect on existing base

☐ *Integrity*—consistency with the way the business uses and manages information values

Satisfying these criteria requires more than assembling just any combination of boxes, arrows, and labels. Specifically, you will follow a set of *rules* and *steps* for applying those rules that will ensure an optimal logical data model. Chapters 5 through 10 in this book do exactly that. Here, we present a summary of the steps.

Each step is numbered using the convention LDM*n* where LDM denotes logical data modeling and *n* denotes the step number. Within the chapters in Part 2, rules corresponding to each step are numbered LDM*n.m* where *m* denotes the relative rule number within Step *n*. All the rules for logical data modeling are also summarized in the Index of Design Rules for easy reference.

BUILD SKELETAL USER VIEWS (CHAPTER 5)

You build a logical data model by examining one activity or business function at a time. You individually model the information required by each such function, and then integrate the individual models into one composite model. The model or representation of information required by one business function is known as a *user view*. You, as the modeler, define the scope of any one user view. That view may be as narrow as the perspective of one accounting clerk, or it may reflect the perspectives of a group of high-level executives of a business's entire marketing function. Because user views eventually will be combined into a consolidated logical data model, the number and scope of the initial set are entirely at your discretion.

The process of developing a user view is highly interactive at the beginning. You work with one or more users to define the most important elements, comprising a *skeletal user view*. Specifically, you and the users

☐ Identify major *entities* (significant objects of interest)—*Step LDM1*

☐ Determine *relationships* between entities—*Step LDM2*

You name and define the entities and relationships and document them in a data dictionary. You also classify the various types of entities and relationships and diagram them as boxes and arrows. The result is a clear understanding of the most important data requirements and relationships.

ADD KEYS TO USER VIEWS (CHAPTER 6)

The process continues with addition of key detail information items and the first, most important types of business rules. Specifically, you and the users

☐ Determine *primary* and *alternate keys* (identifying properties of entities)— *Step LDM3*
☐ Determine *foreign keys* (identifying properties of relationships)—*Step LDM4*
☐ Determine *key business rules* (rules that govern the effects of insert, delete, and update operations on relationships)—*Step LDM5*

You already understand the concept of primary key—the attribute or set of attributes that identifies particular entity occurrences. *Alternate keys* are alternative choices of identifying attributes that (perhaps arbitrarily) are not chosen to be the primary key. For instance, if you choose NAME as primary key for the RENTER entity in Ron's Real Estate Business, SOC–SEC–NMBR (Social Security number) might be an alternate key.

You also have already learned about foreign keys—the attribute or set of attributes that completes a relationship by identifying the associated entity (for example, RENTER*NAME in RENTAL–AGREEMENT).

Key business rules define conditions under which primary and foreign keys may be inserted, deleted, or updated. You establish one insert rule and one delete rule for each relationship. The insert rule determines valid conditions under which you may insert or update the foreign key in an entity occurrence. The delete rule determines valid conditions under which you may delete or update the primary key referenced by a foreign key. These are the most frequently encountered and typically the most important constraints on insert, delete, and update operations. Because they define rules governing valid existence of particular entity occurrences, they also are called *existence constraints*.

ADD DETAIL TO USER VIEWS (CHAPTER 7)

After identifying all key attributes (primary, alternate, and foreign keys), you

☐ Add remaining *nonkey attributes*—*Step LDM6*

Nonkey attributes are the descriptive detail that users naturally associate with the entities. For example, ADDRESS, PHONE–NUMBER, and MAX–MONTHLY–RENT–AMT are nonkey attributes in the RENTER entity. You associate each attribute with that entity whose entire primary key is required to identify it. (Note that the primary key may be a set of attributes.)

VALIDATE USER VIEWS THROUGH NORMALIZATION (CHAPTER 8)

Step LDM6 relies primarily on an intuitive process of associating attributes with "seemingly" the proper entities. In Step LDM7, you check that process through a more structured, formal technique:

☐   Validate *normalization* rules—*Step LDM7*

Normalization is a body of theory addressing analysis and decomposition of data structures into a new set of data structures exhibiting more desirable properties. Specifically, normalization increases the certainty of achieving an optimal logical data model. Applying normalization principles, you successively examine each entity and its associated attributes for structural redundancies or inconsistencies. Such redundancies or inconsistencies are due to assignment of an attribute to the "wrong" entity (e.g., association of customer credit rating with the ORDER rather than with the CUSTOMER entity). You eliminate such problems by reassigning attributes to more appropriate entities or, in some cases, by decomposing entities into smaller, simpler entities. The result is a model that is at least structurally consistent.

Normalization does not ensure that the model correctly reflects the business meaning of data requirements. Thus, you should employ normalization as a refinement technique (Step LDM7) only after completing a thorough business analysis via the techniques in Steps LDM1 through LDM6.

DETERMINE ADDITIONAL ATTRIBUTE BUSINESS RULES (CHAPTER 9)

Normalization also does not fully address business rules. These should be part of a logical data model to ensure that not only the structure but also the values of the data correctly reflect business operations. Steps LDM3 through LDM5 already have uncovered the most significant business rules—those governing integrity of primary and foreign key attributes. At this point, you identify two additional types of attribute business rules:

☐   Determine *domains* (constraints on valid values that attributes may assume)—*Step LDM8*
☐   Determine *triggering operations* (rules that govern the effects of insert, delete, and update operations on other entities or other attributes within the same entity)—*Step LDM9*

We use the term *domain* to include data type, length, format or mask, uniqueness of values, null support (whether a value must be present), allowable values, default value if applicable, and meaning. Domains verify whether values assigned to an attribute make "business sense." They also help in determining when it makes sense to compare or manipulate values of two different attributes.

We use the term *triggering operation* to refer to the most generalized form of business rule, encompassing domains and key business rules as well as other types of attribute business rules. These operations reflect the user's understanding of all rules that make some sets of data values "correct" and others "incorrect" in the business world. You have seen some examples for Ron's Real Estate Business (e.g., for a given RENTAL AGREEMENT, END–DATE must be later than BEGIN–DATE).

The intent in defining business rules is to clarify all *data-driven* constraints on the data values. In other words, you are defining those rules that always hold true, regardless of any particular processing requirements. Because these rules are application-independent, you define them as part of the data design rather than as part of the application design. If instead you treated them as part of the application, you would have to completely, consistently, and redundantly specify the rules as part of every application accessing the data.

INTEGRATE USER VIEWS (CHAPTER 10)

The final logical design steps combine user views into one consolidated logical data model:

☐ *Combine* user views—*Step LDM10*
☐ *Integrate* with existing data models—*Step LDM11*
☐ *Analyze* for stability and growth—*Step LDM12*

In Step LDM10, you combine user views defined for different business functions or perhaps different user groups into one model. For example, you may define one user view for Ron's Real Estate Business from the perspective of Ron, the owner, as illustrated in Figure 2.1. If Ron also uses rental agencies to assist him in locating potential renters, a different user view can be developed from the perspective of Clancey's Rental Agency, dealing with multiple property owners and additional types of rental properties. Thus, Clancey's user view includes additional entities, subtypes, relationships, attributes, and business rules.

Presumably, in some areas, Clancey's and Ron's user views overlap; in some areas, they may even conflict. In Step LDM10, you consolidate the overlaps, resolve any inconsistencies, and add new, inter-view relationships and business rules to form one composite logical data model.

In Step LDM11, you examine this consolidated logical data model in light of models developed for other purposes. Again, you will discover overlaps and some inconsistencies. Most of these other models may already have been implemented as databases; thus, you may not be able to change the models if you discover errors or omissions now. Your objective is to understand and document relationships (including inconsistencies) among the designs.

You accomplish this task by comparing and defining mappings among the logical data models, specifically through mappings to the *business conceptual schema.* You evolve the conceptual schema by combining the logical data models, merging them two at a time, similar to merging user views. You then identify mappings between each logical data model and the business conceptual schema, including

☐ Differences in names
☐ Operations performed on the conceptual schema to obtain constructs within a particular logical data model
☐ Interrelation of business rules

The existence of a business conceptual schema enables you to have multiple logical data models and multiple database implementations that are consistent with one another and with the business's overall operations, as well as being representative of individual user perspectives.

Finally, in Step LDM12, you consider future business changes that may affect your current logical data model. Those that are significant, imminent, or probable, you incorporate into or at least document with the logical data model. Your goal is to maximize *stability* of the logical data model—to ensure that correctness and usefulness will necessitate few changes over a reasonable period. Most important is to incorporate now, if possible, any changes that affect the business conceptual schema, because these are likely to have major influence on one or more individual logical data models.

Figure 2.4 illustrates all the steps in the logical data modeling process. The result is a simple, clear, sharable, stable model exhibiting minimal redundancy and accurately reflecting both the structure and the integrity of information used within the business.

CRITICAL SUCCESS FACTORS IN LOGICAL DATA MODELING

The logical data modeling methodology described in this book is comprehensive and effective. However, you do not have to apply this methodology exactly as described to develop a good logical design. You may want to customize this methodology to your needs (make it shorter, simpler, applicable to a narrower range of information modeling requirements, or expand it to other analytic or modeling techniques). You may even choose an entirely different logical data modeling methodology. Some characteristics of this or any other methodology are, however, critical to its success. These characteristics must be part of the methodology you choose if you are to end up with an optimal logical data model. Seven such *critical success factors* are as follows:

1. *Work interactively with the users as much as possible.* Hold interactive design sessions in which the users describe their needs and you create a working draft of a logical data model as they speak. Share the model with them; explain what the boxes and arrows mean so that they are confident you

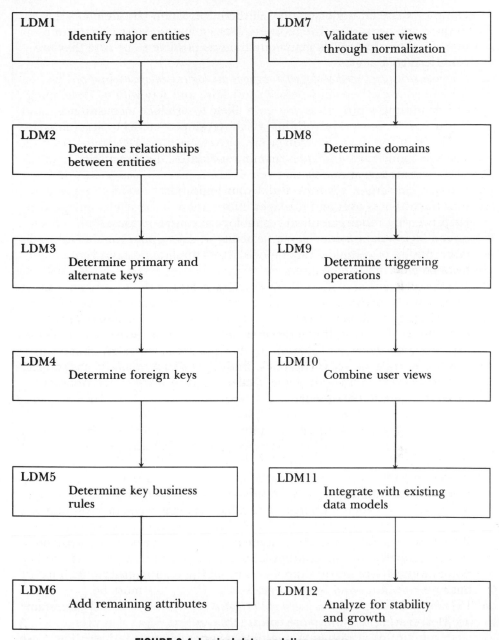

FIGURE 2.4 Logical data modeling process.

and they share an understanding of the information requirements. Listen to their perspectives on the business. Do not impose your own assumptions on them, but ask as many questions as possible to be sure they are considering all angles.

2. *Follow a structured methodology throughout the logical data modeling process.* Choose your methodology before you begin, and stay with it. Developing or customizing a process as you go is likely to produce inconsistencies and confusion. Moreover, retrofitting a half-developed model to accommodate a change in technique is error-prone and wastes time. Determine from the start the modeling steps, rules, naming standards, documentation conventions, techniques, and tools that you will use.

3. *Employ a data-driven approach.* Build your logical data model to represent how the business uses and manages information, unbiased by any particular processing requirements or technological considerations. Only a data-driven logical data model allows flexibility in subsequent tuning and facilitates sharing of common data models across applications and across technological implementations.

4. *Incorporate both structural and integrity considerations in the logical data model.* Addressing structure alone might tell you how to organize records within a database but will not ensure that the data values truly model business operations. Moreover, if you delegate definition of integrity requirements to application developers, you invite incomplete, inconsistent, and even conflicting code across applications. Both data structure and data integrity must be viewed as integral to the database and should be incorporated within the logical data model.

5. *Combine both conceptualization and normalization techniques into the logical data modeling methodology.* Conceptualization is the process of identifying business concepts such as entities, relationships, and keys (Steps LDM1 through 6). Conceptualization is an effective means of ensuring that the model on paper truly represents the use of information within the business. Normalization (Step LDM7) is useful in ensuring that the model is structurally consistent and logical, and has minimal syntactic redundancy. In other words, normalization ensures that all attributes are assigned to the proper entities, assuming that attributes have first been defined and named properly (during conceptualization). Normalization by itself does not address all necessary components of logical data modeling, such as business meanings and business rules.

6. *Use diagrams to represent as much of the logical data model as possible.* Diagrams are clearer, simpler, and more concise than is text. They can present a large amount of information in a precise, unambiguous fashion. They also are effective communication tools for both modelers and users, and they highlight inconsistencies and omissions.

7. *Build a data dictionary to supplement the logical data model diagrams.* Diagrams can communicate a great deal, but they cannot convey everything. Textual

specifications of entity/relationship/attribute definitions and business rules are also needed. If at all possible, use an automated data dictionary tool, whether purchased (such as a commercial data dictionary package) or homegrown (perhaps a relational database, based on a data-driven logical data model). If no automated tool is available, develop a paper-and-pencil repository of relevant documentation.

These critical success factors will be reiterated throughout the methodology in Part 2 of this book. Do not lose sight of them in adapting this or any other methodology to your needs.

BENEFITS AND APPLICABILITY OF LOGICAL DATA MODELS

Now that you understand the constructs and steps involved in logical data modeling, you also should appreciate the benefits. You can see that logical data modeling is a critical prerequisite to effective database design. This, indeed, is the typical application of logical data modeling. Less obvious (but also important), logical data modeling can contribute to the success of certain other endeavors. We shall highlight a few such applications.

☐ *Assessing technological feasibility*—A data-driven logical data model represents data structures, relationships, and rules without any compromises to accommodate technological limitations. The degree to which a particular technological implementation can support all components of the logical data model provides an effective measure of the technology's optimality for related applications.

☐ *Assessing software packages*—In particular, the degree to which the database design of an application software package approximates the logical data model serves as one gauge of the package's ability to meet business requirements.

☐ *Assessing impact of future changes*—A logical data model provides a clear picture of the underlying database design, unobliterated by technological detail. It thus aids significantly in evaluating the effects of changes in business requirements or technology.

☐ *Facilitating end-user access to data*—A logical data model is a business representation of information structures and rules, and can be understood by users. It can provide these users with an intelligible "map" of their data within an end-user computing environment.

☐ *Enabling strategic overview of the business's information needs*—You can apply the logical data modeling process, minus some of its more detailed steps, to building a *strategic data model* or high-level representation of all the business's information requirements. You can think of a strategic data model as a summarized version of the business conceptual schema. The strategic data model can assist in analyzing information interrelationships throughout the business. It therefore can contribute to more effective planning of database and application implementations. For example, it can aid in planning and relating detailed operational systems (those required to run the day-to-day business) and summarized, executive decision-support systems.

☐ *Migrating data from one technology to another*—You can more easily migrate databases from one technology to a newer or more appropriate technology when a current logical data model exists. The model can be translated into a new database implementation. You also can use the logical data model to design extract procedures.

SUMMARY

Logical data modeling is the first phase of an effective database design process. It is a technique for understanding and capturing business information requirements that must be met through a database implementation.

Logical data modeling incorporates such constructs as:

☐ *Entity*—person, place, thing, or concept about which you wish to record information

☐ *Relationship*—fact about or association between two entities

☐ *Attribute*—fact or nondecomposable piece of information describing an entity

☐ *Primary key*—attribute or set of attributes that identifies a particular entity occurrence

☐ *Foreign key*—attribute or set of attributes that identifies the entity with which another entity is associated

☐ *Business rule (key, domain, or triggering operation)*—specification to preserve integrity of the logical data model by governing which values attributes may assume

Chapters 5 through 10 detail 12 steps and associated rules for building a logical data model. They begin with definition of a *user view* or representation of information requirements for one business function, user, or user group. They culminate in integration of user views into one composite logical data model. Multiple logical data models are related via their mappings to a *business conceptual schema,* an integrated logical data model representing all the business's data requirements at their most detailed level.

The steps and rules of the methodology are structured so as to ensure optimality of the logical data model, whereby optimality is defined in terms of structural validity, simplicity, nonredundancy, sharability, extensibility, and integrity.

The major application of the logical data modeling process is as prerequisite to database design, although it also can be useful in several other types of system activities. Of particular interest in this book, an optimal logical data model provides a solid foundation for building and tuning a relational database.

3 | Relational Concepts and SQL

The popularity of relational technology is increasing rapidly. Today, almost every organization is investigating or implementing some form (or multiple forms) of relational technology.

This chapter serves as an introduction to relational concepts, especially as they relate to a design philosophy. It is not our purpose to present a thorough description of relational theory. (More complete coverage on relational theory can be found in C. J. Date, *Relational Database Selected Writings* (Reading, MA: Addison-Wesley Publishing Company, 1986)). Rather, we emphasize important benefits, implications, and product insights that are of value to a relational database designer.

RELATIONAL MODEL OVERVIEW

The relational model is an *intellectual* concept. It is an orderly, predictable, and (for the most part) intuitive approach to perceiving, organizing, and manipulating business data. As such, the relational model is a template for how data appear to a user, how a user performs operations on the data, and how the data behave when they are manipulated. It is important to note that the relational model is an intellectual concept defining *user perception* of data. It does not imply (nor does it address) specific physical or technical approaches for data storage and access strategies.

The relational model was formally introduced by Dr. E. F. Codd in 1970 and has evolved, since then, through a series of writings. So as not to repeat existing and valuable works from Codd and Date, this chapter provides only a brief, albeit important, summary of the model.

First, you should realize that the relational model is a step toward simplicity. Simplicity implies that the model can be described using a few, familiar concepts. Although it *is* true that the relational model has its roots in mathematical set theory, it can be discussed and appreciated by people unfamiliar with such theory. It is precisely this combination of simplicity and solid theoretical foundation that makes the relational model so valuable and long-lasting. The simplicity allows designers, developers, and users to communicate using terms and concepts understood by all. The solid theoretical foundation guarantees that results of relational requests are well defined and, therefore, predictable.

The relational model consists of three components:

1. *Data structure*—organization of the data, as users perceive them
2. *Data manipulation*—types of operations users perform on the relational data structure
3. *Data integrity*—set of business rules that govern how relational data values behave when users perform relational operations

As a database designer, you will concentrate mostly on data structure and data integrity. Data manipulation is important only to understand relational processing in general and your users' access requirements in particular.

DATA STRUCTURE

Relational data are organized into relations. A *relation* is an intellectual concept based on mathematical set theory. For the purpose of this discussion, however, think of a relation as a two-dimensional table with special properties. In fact, to remind you that a relation is a special type of table, we refer to relations as relational tables.

A *relational table* consists of a set of named columns and an arbitrary number of unnamed rows. Each named column is associated with a domain, where a domain (described in more detail in this chapter under *Data Integrity*) is a specification of values that may appear in one or more columns. Figure 3.1 depicts a relational table containing ice-cream VENDOR information. This relational table is shown as having two columns and seven rows. (For this table, there are also two domains: one for each of its columns.)

Relational tables have six special properties that distinguish them from nonrelational (or partially relational) tables. We will describe each property, along with its significance and influence on the design philosophy. As a quick reference, Figure 3.2 summarizes the six properties.

PROPERTY 1: ENTRIES IN COLUMNS ARE SINGLE-VALUED. This property implies that columns do not contain repeating groups. Often, such tables are referred to as

VENDOR

NAME	LOCATION
Mr. Chip	New York
Bean, Inc.	New York
Mrs. Mousse	New Jersey
Mr. Mousse	New Jersey
Sancho	California
Diet-Cream	Colorado
Freeze-It	Alaska

FIGURE 3.1 Ice-cream VENDOR relational table.

"normalized" or as being in "first normal form (1NF)." It is important that you understand the significance and effects of this property because it is a cornerstone of the relational data structure.

Assume you have a table, SUPPLY, containing information about ice-cream flavors supplied by vendors. Further, assume an ice-cream vendor may supply many ice-cream flavors. Using a tabular format, you can represent these flavors in several ways; however, not all such ways are consistent with the single-valued property for relational tables.

One way is to require that each vendor be represented in the table by one row. You can then define a column (FLAVOR*NAME—do not be concerned, at this time, with the column naming convention) in which you place all flavors for a vendor. Figure 3.3 shows such a sample table. Note that multiple flavors for a vendor appear as multiple values in the FLAVOR*NAME column.

This approach is not consistent with the single-valued property of a relational table, because the FLAVOR*NAME column contains repeating groups (namely, several occurrences of ice-cream flavors supplied by a given vendor). Figure 3.3 is, in fact, an undesirable layout because it unnecessarily complicates data manipulation logic. Consider, for example, the complex logic of searching for VENDOR*NAMEs who supply vanilla ice cream. Either the access language must be able to specify a search for a given character string (vanilla) occurring anywhere within a column (FLAVOR*NAME) or the DBMS must be able automatically to detect when such a search is required. Imagine trying to match the FLAVOR*NAME column to values in another table—that could be a complicated

FIGURE 3.2 Special properties of relational tables.

1. Entries in columns are single-valued.
2. Entries in columns are of the same kind.
3. Each row is unique.
4. Sequence of columns (left to right) is insignificant.
5. Sequence of rows (top to bottom) is insignificant.
6. Each column has a unique name.

SUPPLY

VENDOR*NAME	FLAVOR*NAME
Mr. Chip	vanilla, chocolate
Mrs. Chip	avocado, date-nut-cream
Diet-Cream	cottage cheese, skim milk, celery delight

FIGURE 3.3 SUPPLY **table with (columnar) repeating groups.**

request. Some relational operations (such as UNION, described later in this chapter) might not be possible using this table layout.

A variation of this approach is to define a maximum number of FLAVOR*NAME columns corresponding to the maximum number of flavors per vendor. (Ignore, for the moment, the obvious shortcoming—that you must be able to determine this maximum number.) For vendors who do not supply the maximum number of flavors, the corresponding FLAVOR*NAME columns will be set to null (where null means "not applicable"). Figure 3.4 illustrates this alternative and implies that a vendor never supplies more than three flavors at one time (since there are only three FLAVOR*NAME columns).

Although this approach does not specifically violate the single-valued property of a relation, it too is undesirable. This layout contains a subtle implementation of repeating groups—they appear as separate columns. Consider the complexity of this approach. Where do you record an ice-cream flavor for Bean, Inc.? In FLAVOR*NAME1, in FLAVOR*NAME2, or in FLAVOR*NAME3? Or, does it matter? Must a user reference *all* FLAVOR*NAME columns when searching for a particular flavor or when querying all flavors supplied by a vendor? What if Diet-Cream no longer supplies the skim milk flavor? Is celery delight moved over to FLAVOR*NAME2 or is FLAVOR*NAME2 set to null (not applicable)?

The third approach defines one FLAVOR*NAME column and restricts it to one flavor supplied by a vendor. In this case, multiple flavors for a vendor are represented by multiple rows in the table. Figure 3.5 illustrates this concept.

This third approach defines a table that fulfills the single-valued property of a relational table. The basic difference between the first two approaches and

FIGURE 3.4 SUPPLY **table, also with (columnar) repeating groups.**

SUPPLY

VENDOR*NAME	FLAVOR*NAME1	FLAVOR*NAME2	FLAVOR*NAME3
Mr. Chip	vanilla	chocolate	null
Mrs. Chip	avocado	date-nut-cream	null
Diet-Cream	cottage cheese	skim milk	celery delight

SUPPLY

VENDOR*NAME	FLAVOR*NAME
Mr. Chip	vanilla
Mr. Chip	chocolate
Mrs. Chip	avocado
Mrs. Chip	date—nut—cream
Diet—Cream	cottage cheese
Diet—Cream	skim milk
Diet—Cream	celery delight

FIGURE 3.5 SUPPLY **table without (columnar) repeating groups.**

this last one is that the former represent repeating groups across the columns, whereas this one does so down the rows. On initial inspection, Figure 3.5 may seem less intuitive than do the other two. The truth is, however, that the absence of columnar repeating groups simplifies expression and evaluation of relational (and other) operations. Specific advantages are covered later in this chapter under *Significance of Relational Data Manipulation.*

The design approach in this book is heavily influenced by the single-valued property of relational tables. Nearly all the tables you design should conform to this property. You should deviate from this rule (i.e., permit columnar repeating groups) only when you have a strong justification plus a full understanding of the cost (e.g., loss of some relational flexibility).

PROPERTY 2: ENTRIES IN COLUMNS ARE OF THE SAME KIND. In relational terms, this property states that all values in a given column are drawn from the same domain. This means that every value in any given column represents a specific value for the same type of fact about the table. For example, a YEARLY—SALARY column contains only specific yearly salaries and does not (ever) contain addresses, status flags, or even a weekly salary.

This property, too, is significant and useful. First, it simplifies data access in that users can be certain of the type of data contained in a given column. Furthermore, this property simplifies data validation. Because all values in any given column are of the same domain, the domain itself can be defined and enforced.

This property, in conjunction with the first property, gives a relational table a very stable structure. It implies that every row in a relational table has the same "shape;" that is, not only does every row have the same number of columns, but each column contains values drawn from the same domain. As you will see later (under *Data Manipulation*), these properties make it relatively easy to express operations against relational tables.

From a database design perspective, you will always adhere to this property. Each column in your tables will be defined over a domain and will contain only one kind of data element.

PROPERTY 3: EACH ROW IS UNIQUE. Property 3 ensures that no two rows in a relational table are identical; that is, there is at least one column (or, set of columns) the values of which uniquely identify specific rows in the table. As an example, the NAME column in the VENDOR table of Figure 3.1 distinguishes one vendor from another. Such columns are called *primary keys*.

This property guarantees that every row in a relational table is meaningful. Users can refer to a particular row by specifying the primary key value. In the table in Figure 3.5, the primary key consists of two columns (VENDOR*NAME and FLAVOR*NAME) because neither, by itself, identifies a unique row.

This property also will affect your database design. When you design relational databases, you will require that each table have a primary key.

PROPERTY 4: SEQUENCE OF COLUMNS (LEFT TO RIGHT) IS INSIGNIFICANT. Property 4 ensures that no hidden meaning is implied by the order in which columns occur. Moreover, because there is no information implied by a particular sequence of columns, each user can retrieve the columns in any order. Indeed, the same (and different) users can retrieve columns of the same relational table in various sequences. An obvious benefit is that the same table can be shared by many users and can serve a multitude of access requirements. Also, designers are free to change the sequence in which columns are physically stored (perhaps for performance reasons) without affecting the meaning of the data or the formulation of queries by users.

The ability to share data is important. You will want to design relational tables that serve access requirements of various users. Therefore, you will not embed any hidden meaning into the order of columns.

PROPERTY 5: SEQUENCE OF ROWS (TOP TO BOTTOM) IS INSIGNIFICANT. This property is analogous to Property 4, but it applies to rows instead of to columns. The obvious benefit is the ability to retrieve rows of a relational table in any sequence. Thus, the same table can be shared among users even when the users wish to view the rows in different sequences. Further, designers are free to modify the order in which rows are physically stored (perhaps for performance reasons) without affecting the meaning or the users' perceptions of the data.

Again, because you want to design relational tables that can be shared by many users, you will not incorporate hidden meaning into the order of rows. Where a logical sequence of rows is useful for a particular access requirement, you will ensure that the values of one or more columns can explicitly convey this sequencing.

PROPERTY 6: EACH COLUMN HAS A UNIQUE NAME. Think of this property as an extension of Property 4; that is, because the sequence of columns is insignificant, columns are referenced by name and not by position. In general, a column name need not be unique within an entire DBMS environment or even within a given database. However, typically the column name must be unique within the table in which it appears. When we present the design steps, we shall discuss naming conventions for relational tables and columns.

SIGNIFICANCE OF RELATIONAL DATA STRUCTURE

As you can see, there are important reasons for each of the six properties. Together, the properties depict a data structure that is intuitive to users, easy to validate, and flexible with respect to access requirements. To capitalize on the benefits possible with relational data structures, your database designs should deliberately endorse these relational concepts, deviating only where strong justification exists.

There are actually two types of relations. The one discussed so far (with the six properties) is more completely called a *base relation*. We generally refer to base relations as *relational tables* or just *tables*. There is also a second kind of relation, called a *view*. Think of a view as a virtual relation.

A view, like a base relation, is a two-dimensional structure of rows and columns. Whereas a base relation typically corresponds to a stored data structure within a database, a view may relate less directly to stored data values. A view appears to the user (for the most part) to be equivalent to a base relation but in fact reflects the result of one or more relational operations applied to one or more base relations. The data in a view are not stored but rather are dynamically obtained or calculated from underlying tables whenever the view is referenced by a user. The view, thus, automatically reflects any updates applied to data values within the associated tables. In essence, a view serves as a logical "window" through which a user may observe up-to-the-minute data values of relational tables, optionally presented somewhat differently from specifications of the tables themselves.

For example, one view of the ice-cream VENDOR table (Figure 3.1) may consist of only the NAME column. Another view may consist of NAME and LOCATION columns, but only for rows where LOCATION values begin with N. Details on language syntax for creating views and relating them to base relations are discussed in this chapter under *SQL Standard*. Your relational database designs probably will include specification of useful views.

DATA MANIPULATION

The second component of the relational model is data manipulation, or types of operations that users can perform on relational tables. There are two basic types of operations: assignment of relations to other relations (called relational assignment) and manipulation of relations using eight relational operators.

The concept of relational assignment is much like the concept of assignment statements in a program in which the result of an expression is assigned to a variable. The variable in a relational assignment is a relational table, and the expression involves relational tables and relational operations. Thus, you can perform operations on relational tables and assign (perhaps even store) the result to (in) another relational table.

Of more interest to this discussion are the eight relational manipulation operators. Before we discuss each one, observe that all of them have two characteristics in common. First, relational operators both apply to and result in relational tables (i.e., sets of rows and columns). This is known as *set* processing, to be distinguished from *record-at-a-time* (or row-at-a-time) processing. (Note: Most operators in nonrelational data structures reflect record-at-a-time processing. Witness the DL/I GET NEXT or COBOL READ/WRITE operators.) A formal name for this set-to-set processing characteristic is *closure*, meaning that relational operations are closed within the universe of relations. In other words, a relational operation on one or more relations always produces another relation. Even if the result contains one row, it is still a relational table with one row. Thus, result tables also have special (familiar!) properties: most important, entries in columns are single-valued, entries in columns are of the same kind, sequence of columns is insignificant, and sequence of rows is insignificant. Closure implies that relational operators can be applied to results of "previous" relational operations. Hence, users can nest a series of relational operations.

The second common characteristic is that relational operators are unaffected by how the data are stored physically. This emphasizes again that the relational model is an intellectual concept, including its relational operators! Thus, the eight relational operators express functionality without concern for (or knowledge of) technical implementation. An obvious benefit is that relational users apply relational operators without concern for storage and access techniques.

The eight relational operators are select, project, product, join, union, intersection, difference, and division. Each is discussed below.

Select. The *select* operator is sometimes called *restrict* (to distinguish it from the SQL keyword SELECT, described later in this chapter). This operation retrieves a *subset of rows* from a relational table based on value(s) in a column or columns. In other words, rows are included in the result if the values in designated columns match selection criteria of the request. Selection criteria are expressed by means of a comparative operator (such as equals, greater than or less than) and an expression (involving arithmetic operators, Boolean operators, literals, or other column names). Figure 3.6 shows the result when a user selects (or restricts) rows from the ice-cream VENDOR table (Figure 3.1) for vendors located in New Jersey (i.e., rows where the LOCATION column equals the value New Jersey).

Project. The *project* operator retrieves a *subset of columns* from a relational table, removing duplicate rows from the result. Figure 3.7, for instance, projects the LOCATION column from the VENDOR table (Figure 3.1).

VENDOR

NAME	LOCATION
Mrs. Mousse	New Jersey
Mr. Mousse	New Jersey

FIGURE 3.6 Select of VENDOR **table for vendors in New Jersey.**

Product. The *product* operator produces the set of all rows that are a concatenation of a row from one relational table with a row from another (or the same) relational table.

Figure 3.8 illustrates a product of the SUPPLY and VENDOR tables. The result is formed by horizontally concatenating one row from one table (say, SUPPLY table) with every row in the other table (say, VENDOR table) and doing so for each and every row in the first table. This is formally referred to as a Cartesian product.

As you can see, the result of a Cartesian product is not particularly useful. If, however, you apply special criteria to include only those rows that are "related" in some meaningful way, the result has more meaning. Therefore, the Cartesian product is important because it may be an interim step in obtaining a more meaningful result. For example, a Cartesian product may be an interim result when performing a join.

Join. The *join* operator is derived by combining the product and select operators. The join operator horizontally combines (concatenates) data from one row of a table with rows in another or the same table, but does so only when certain criteria are met. The criteria involve a relationship among columns of the joined relations.

FIGURE 3.7 Project of VENDOR **table on** LOCATION **column.**

VENDOR

LOCATION
New York
New Jersey
California
Colorado
Alaska

FIGURE 3.8 Product of SUPPLY **and** VENDOR **tables.**

SUPPLY. VENDOR*NAME	SUPPLY. FLAVOR*NAME	VENDOR. NAME	VENDOR. LOCATION
Mr. Chip	vanilla	Mr. Chip	New York
Mr. Chip	vanilla	Bean, Inc.	New York
Mr. Chip	vanilla	Mrs. Mousse	New Jersey
Mr. Chip	vanilla	Mr. Mousse	New Jersey
Mr. Chip	vanilla	Sancho	California
Mr. Chip	vanilla	Diet—Cream	Colorado
Mr. Chip	vanilla	Freeze—It	Alaska
Mr. Chip	chocolate	Mr. Chip	New York
Mr. Chip	chocolate	Bean, Inc.	New York
Mr. Chip	chocolate	Mrs. Mousse	New Jersey
Mr. Chip	chocolate	Mr. Mousse	New Jersey
Mr. Chip	chocolate	Sancho	California
Mr. Chip	chocolate	Diet—Cream	Colorado
Mr. Chip	chocolate	Freeze—It	Alaska
Mrs. Chip	avocado	Mr. Chip	New York
Mrs. Chip	avocado	Bean, Inc.	New York
Mrs. Chip	avocado	Mrs. Mousse	New Jersey
Mrs. Chip	avocado	Mr. Mousse	New Jersey
Mrs. Chip	avocado	Sancho	California
Mrs. Chip	avocado	Diet—Cream	Colorado
Mrs. Chip	avocado	Freeze—It	Alaska
Mrs. Chip	date—nut—cream	Mr. Chip	New York
Mrs. Chip	date—nut—cream	Bean, Inc.	New York
Mrs. Chip	date—nut—cream	Mrs. Mousse	New Jersey
Mrs. Chip	date—nut—cream	Mr. Mousse	New Jersey
Mrs. Chip	date—nut—cream	Sancho	California
Mrs. Chip	date—nut—cream	Diet—Cream	Colorado
Mrs. Chip	date—nut—cream	Freeze—It	Alaska
Diet—Cream	cottage cheese	Mr. Chip	New York
Diet—Cream	cottage cheese	Bean, Inc.	New York
Diet—Cream	cottage cheese	Mrs. Mousse	New Jersey
Diet—Cream	cottage cheese	Mr. Mousse	New Jersey
Diet—Cream	cottage cheese	Sancho	California
Diet—Cream	cottage cheese	Diet—Cream	Colorado
Diet—Cream	cottage cheese	Freeze—It	Alaska
Diet—Cream	skim milk	Mr. Chip	New York
Diet—Cream	skim milk	Bean, Inc.	New York
Diet—Cream	skim milk	Mrs. Mousse	New Jersey

Diet–Cream	skim milk	Mr. Mousse	New Jersey
Diet–Cream	skim milk	Sancho	California
Diet–Cream	skim milk	Diet–Cream	Colorado
Diet–Cream	skim milk	Freeze–It	Alaska
Diet–Cream	celery delight	Mr. Chip	New York
Diet–Cream	celery delight	Bean, Inc.	New York
Diet–Cream	celery delight	Mrs. Mousse	New Jersey
Diet–Cream	celery delight	Mr. Mousse	New Jersey
Diet–Cream	celery delight	Sancho	California
Diet–Cream	celery delight	Diet–Cream	Colorado
Diet–Cream	celery delight	Freeze–It	Alaska

As an example, one meaningful join involving the VENDOR table and SUPPLY table results in columns from both tables, but only for rows where the values in the NAME column in the VENDOR table are equal to those in the VENDOR*NAME column in the SUPPLY table. The joining column names need not be the same, but the column values should be defined over the same domain. The result of this join is shown in Figure 3.9.

If the join criterion is based on equality (as in Figure 3.9, VENDOR*NAME = NAME), the join is called an *equi-join*. If redundant columns are removed from the result (e.g., by removing one of the vendor name columns in Figure 3.9), the join is referred to as a *natural join*.

Notice that rows in the SUPPLY table (for example, Mrs. Chip rows) having no corresponding vendor name in the VENDOR table do not appear in the join result. Likewise, rows in the VENDOR table (for example, the Mrs. Mousse row) having no corresponding vendor name in the SUPPLY table do not appear in

FIGURE 3.9 Join of SUPPLY **and** VENDOR **tables on equal vendor names.**

SUPPLY. VENDOR*NAME	SUPPLY. FLAVOR*NAME	VENDOR. NAME	VENDOR. LOCATION
Mr. Chip	vanilla	Mr. Chip	New York
Mr. Chip	chocolate	Mr. Chip	New York
Diet–Cream	cottage cheese	Diet–Cream	Colorado
Diet–Cream	skim milk	Diet–Cream	Colorado
Diet–Cream	celery delight	Diet–Cream	Colorado

SUPPLY. VENDOR*NAME	SUPPLY. FLAVOR*NAME	VENDOR. NAME	VENDOR. LOCATION
Mr. Chip	vanilla	Mr. Chip	New York
Mr. Chip	chocolate	Mr. Chip	New York
Mrs. Chip	avocado	null	null
Mrs. Chip	date—nut—cream	null	null
Diet—Cream	cottage cheese	Diet—Cream	Colorado
Diet—Cream	skim milk	Diet—Cream	Colorado
Diet—Cream	celery delight	Diet—Cream	Colorado
null	null	Bean, Inc.	New York
null	null	Mrs. Mousse	New Jersey
null	null	Mr. Mousse	New Jersey
null	null	Sancho	California
null	null	Freeze—It	Alaska

FIGURE 3.10 Two-way outer join of SUPPLY **and** VENDOR **tables on equal vendor names, including unmatched rows.**

the result. Another type of join, known as the *outer join,* includes matched rows and unmatched rows in the result. In the *outer join* result, unmatched rows contain a special notation (representing a null value, meaning value not applicable or unknown) for columns that are inapplicable. A *one-way outer join* includes the unmatched rows from either the SUPPLY or the VENDOR table, depending on user specification. A *two-way outer join* includes unmatched rows from both the SUPPLY and the VENDOR tables.

Figure 3.10 depicts the results of a two-way outer join of these two tables. In this instance, the user wants to know the names and locations of all vendors with the flavors they supply. Notice that there are five vendors in the VENDOR table that do not appear in the SUPPLY table (i.e., Bean, Inc., Mrs. Mousse, Mr. Mousse, Sancho, and Freeze—It). For these vendors, there are null values in the result columns that depict columns from the SUPPLY table. Likewise, there are two rows in the SUPPLY table that do not have matching rows in the VENDOR table (i.e., both for Mrs. Chip). Thus, the result includes null values in these rows for the columns that depict columns from the VENDOR table.

A user can join a table to itself. A common example involves an EMPLOYEE table, as follows:

EMPLOYEE

NUMBER	EMPLOYEE—NAME	DEPT—NUMBER	EMPLOYEE*NUMBER—MANAGES
3	Smith	10	3
10	Jones	10	3
1	Green	10	10

This table has four columns depicting employee numbers, names, department numbers to which employees are assigned, and employee numbers of their immediate managers. (Note the oddity of values in the row for employee 3. Perhaps employee 3 is the CEO, since this employee's immediate manager also is employee 3!) If a user wishes to obtain a list of employee numbers, names, departments and corresponding manager numbers, she can do so quite easily—by merely retrieving all rows and all columns. If, however, the user also wants the name of each employee's manager, the task is a little trickier. To obtain an employee's manager name, the value in the EMPLOYEE*NUMBER–MANAGES column for each employee's row is joined to the value in the NUMBER column for the manager's row. The manager's row also contains the manager's name.

The easiest way to visualize this operation is to imagine joining two tables, each of which is a copy of the other. To illustrate, consider the following two copies of the EMPLOYEE table:

EMPLOYEE–COPYA

NUMBER	EMPLOYEE–NAME	DEPT–NUMBER	EMPLOYEE*NUMBER–MANAGES
3	Smith	10	3
10	Jones	10	3
1	Green	10	10

EMPLOYEE–COPYB

NUMBER	EMPLOYEE–NAME	DEPT–NUMBER	EMPLOYEE*NUMBER–MANAGES
3	Smith	10	3
10	Jones	10	3
1	Green	10	10

Joining these two tables by matching EMPLOYEE*NUMBER–MANAGES from EMPLOYEE–COPYA to NUMBER in EMPLOYEE–COPYB gives the following result:

NUMBER	NAME	DEPT–NUMBER	EMPLOYEE*NUMBER–MANAGES	EMPLOYEE*NUMBER–MANAGES–NAME
3	Smith	10	3	Smith
10	Jones	10	3	Smith
1	Green	10	10	Jones

Union. The relational *union* operator vertically combines (stacks) data in rows of one table with rows in the same or another table, removing duplicates. That is, the union of two relations contains the set of rows belonging in either relation (with duplicates removed).

As an example, given an EAST COAST VENDOR table and a WEST COAST VENDOR table, a union of these tables produces one table containing all rows from both (with duplicates removed, if any). Figure 3.11 shows two such tables and their union.

For the union operation to make sense, the two tables being unioned must have the same "shape"—that is, they must have the same number and type of columns (although the column names need not be identical). Note that you are able to union EAST COAST VENDOR and WEST COAST VENDOR because they meet this restriction.

Another type of union, known as the *outer union,* eliminates this restriction. The outer union results in null values for columns existing in only one table, for rows from the other table. A *one-way outer union* includes unlike columns from only one (either) of the tables; a *two-way outer union* includes unlike columns from both tables. For example, assume the EAST COAST and WEST COAST VENDOR tables each have an additional unlike column, as shown in Figure 3.12. Then Figure 3.12 illustrates a two-way outer union.

Intersection. The *intersection* operator results in rows common to two (or more) relational tables (i.e., rows for which all column values are equal across the two or more tables). For example, the intersection of the MATH CLUB and SKI CLUB tables is the set of rows for students who are members of both clubs, as illustrated in Figure 3.13.

FIGURE 3.11 Union of EAST COAST **and** WEST COAST VENDOR **tables.**

EAST COAST VENDOR

NAME	LOCATION
Mr. Chip	New York
Bean, Inc.	New York
Mrs. Mousse	New Jersey
Mr. Mousse	New Jersey
Sunnyside	Florida

WEST COAST VENDOR

NAME	LOCATION
Sancho	California
Freeze—It	Alaska
Rocky	Colorado
Golden	California

Union of tables

NAME	LOCATION
Mr. Chip	New York
Bean, Inc.	New York
Mrs. Mousse	New Jersey
Mr. Mousse	New Jersey
Sunnyside	Florida
Sancho	California
Freeze—It	Alaska
Rocky	Colorado
Golden	California

EAST COAST VENDOR

NAME	LOCATION	STATUS
Mr. Chip	New York	active
Bean, Inc.	New York	active
Mrs. Mousse	New Jersey	n/a
Mr. Mousse	New Jersey	active
Sunnyside	Florida	active

WEST COAST VENDOR

NAME	LOCATION	OWNERSHIP
Sancho	California	private
Freeze-It	Alaska	public
Rocky	Colorado	public
Golden	California	private

Outer union of tables

NAME	LOCATION	STATUS	OWNERSHIP
Mr. Chip	New York	active	null
Bean, Inc.	New York	active	null
Mrs. Mousse	New Jersey	n/a	null
Mr. Mousse	New Jersey	active	null
Sunnyside	Florida	active	null
Sancho	California	null	private
Freeze-It	Alaska	null	public
Rocky	Colorado	null	public
Golden	California	null	private

FIGURE 13.12 Two-way outer union of EAST COAST **and** WEST COAST VENDOR **tables.**

FIGURE 3.13 Intersection of MATH **and** SKI CLUB **tables.**

MATH CLUB

FIRST NAME	LAST NAME
Dizzy	Frump
Mary	Sue
Joe	Einstein
Squeaky	Jones
Grumpy	Bones

SKI CLUB

FIRST NAME	LAST NAME
Mary	Sue
Alan	Einstein
Dizzy	Frump
Squeaky	Thomas
Grumpy	Bones

Intersection of tables

FIRST NAME	LAST NAME
Dizzy	Frump
Mary	Sue
Grumpy	Bones

Difference of tables

FIRST NAME	LAST NAME
Joe	Einstein
Squeaky	Jones

FIGURE 3.14 Difference of MATH **and** SKI CLUB **tables.**

The intersection operation is actually a special case of a natural join on all columns of both tables. For example, the intersection of the MATH CLUB and SKI CLUB tables also could be defined as a natural join in which the FIRST NAME columns are equal and the LAST NAME columns are equal. Because the join is on all columns, the intersection operator makes sense only when the tables are of the same "shape" (same number and type of columns).

Difference. The *difference* operator results in rows that appear in one relation, but not in another. The difference operator applied to the MATH CLUB and SKI CLUB tables (in that order) retrieves those students who are in the math club but not in the ski club, as illustrated in Figure 3.14. Again, the difference operator makes sense only when the tables are of the same "shape" (same number and type of columns).

Division. Informally, the *division* operator results in column values from one table for which there are other matching column values corresponding to every row in another table. It is best to look at an example.

Consider Figure 3.15. The COMPLETED COURSE table shows courses completed by each student. The RELATIONAL MAJOR table lists courses required for a major in relational theory. Dividing the COMPLETED COURSE table by the RELATIONAL MAJOR table yields a table with two columns: student numbers and names for students who have completed a major in relational theory. Notice that each student number and name in the result (quotient) match two columns in three rows in the COMPLETED COURSE table (dividend) where the other columns of those three rows (course number and name) are identical to the entire RELATIONAL MAJOR table (divisor).

Figure 3.16 summarizes the eight relational operators.

SIGNIFICANCE OF RELATIONAL DATA MANIPULATION

The relational operators define permissible data manipulation functions. They are not a specification for a data access language. Thus, these operators do not require that any particular verbs or other language syntax be implemented within a relational data access language. In fact, a relational access language (e.g., SQL—discussed later in this chapter) need not have explicit verbs for

COMPLETED COURSE **(dividend)**

STUDENT NUMBER	STUDENT NAME	COURSE NUMBER	COURSE NAME
10	Casey	Rel101	Data Structure
10	Casey	Psy101	Schizophrenia
10	Casey	Rel201	Data Integrity
10	Casey	Rel301	Data Manipulation
30	Christopher	Rel101	Data Structure
20	Stephanie	Ped101	Terrible Twos
30	Christopher	Psy101	Schizophrenia
30	Christopher	Rel301	Data Manipulation
30	Christopher	Rel201	Data Integrity

RELATIONAL MAJOR **(divisor)**

COURSE NUMBER	COURSE NAME
Rel101	Data Structure
Rel201	Data Integrity
Rel301	Data Manipulation

Division result (quotient)

STUDENT NUMBER	STUDENT NAME
10	Casey
30	Christopher

FIGURE 3.15 Division of COMPLETED COURSE **table by** RELATIONAL MAJOR **table.**

FIGURE 3.16 Eight relational operators.

1. *Select* (or *Restrict*)—retrieves a subset of rows from a relational table based on value(s) in a column or columns

2. *Project*—retrieves a subset of columns from a relational table, removing duplicates from the result

3. *Product*—produces the set of all rows that are the concatenation of a row from one relational table with a row from another (or the same) relational table

4. *Join*—horizontally combines (concatenates) rows in one table with rows in another or the same table, including only rows which meet some selection criteria relating columns of the two tables

5. *Union*—vertically combines (stacks) rows of one table with rows in the same or another table, removing duplicates

6. *Intersection*—results in rows common to two (or more) relational tables

7. *Difference*—results in rows that appear in one table and not in another

8. *Division*—results in column values in one table for which there are other matching column values corresponding to every row in another table

select, project, join, and so on. Rather, such a language must only support the functionality implied by these operators while screening the user from underlying storage structures and access strategies.

As you can see, the definitions and properties governing relational operators enable powerful and flexible data manipulation. Simplicity and productivity are evident in that there are only eight operators, each operates on and produces entire sets (tables) of data, and users need not be concerned with navigation of data structures or access mechanisms.

In light of these relational operators, let us take a moment to reevaluate significance of the first property of relational tables: entries in columns are single-valued. Consider the ice-cream SUPPLY table in Figure 3.4 (with three FLAVOR*NAME columns), which violates this property.

Imagine the complexity of requesting some of the following operations using this table. To select and project the VENDOR*NAMEs who supply chocolate ice cream, a user must reference three columns instead of one. To join the FLAVOR*NAME column with another column, the user must join each of the three FLAVOR*NAME columns in this table to column(s) in the other table. If columns in the other table also represent repeating groups, the user may have to specify even more complex join criteria.

Now, imagine performing the same operations on the relational table (with only one FLAVOR*NAME column) in Figure 3.5. The first operation requires a select of one FLAVOR*NAME column on the value chocolate and then a project on the VENDOR*NAME column. The join also is simple in that the user need compare only one FLAVOR*NAME column to a corresponding column in the other table.

DATA INTEGRITY

The third component of the relational model is data integrity. Meaningful data within relational tables must comply with certain integrity rules. These integrity rules constrain permissible values within the columns of tables. Indeed, without such constraints, the data may easily assume incorrect, incomplete, or misleading values.

There are two generally recognized rules for data integrity in the relational model, called the entity integrity rule and the referential integrity rule. Other authors frequently refer to additional, miscellaneous integrity rules. For ease of discussion, we classify these miscellaneous rules into a third general rule, domain integrity.

The *entity integrity rule* dictates that no component of the primary key (the column or set of columns the values of which uniquely identify particular rows) accept null values. A null value implies that the value for a given column has not been supplied—that it is either unknown or inappropriate. Because a primary key identifies a unique row in a relational table, its value is always appropriate and should never be unknown.

From a database design perspective, entity integrity is important. It requires that insert, update, and delete operations maintain uniqueness and existence of primary keys. The design steps include identification and enforcement of entity integrity.

The *referential integrity rule* addresses integrity of foreign keys. A foreign key is a column or set of columns in a relational table that serves as a primary key in another table. For example, the VENDOR*NAME column in the SUPPLY table is a foreign key because its values refer to values in the NAME column of the VENDOR table, where the values function as a primary key.

The referential integrity rule states that, if a relational table has a foreign key, then every value of that foreign key either is null or matches values in the relational table in which that foreign key is a primary key.

Referential integrity also is important to database design. Foreign keys serve as the "reference paths" from one table to another. Referential integrity requires that insert, update, and delete operations result in foreign key values that are null or that match existing primary key values. Thus, relationships among tables are preserved and reference paths remain intact. It follows that the design steps must identify and enforce foreign key integrity. The design approach in this book, however, makes special allowances for foreign keys that do not match existing primary keys. For example, a SUPPLY table may include rows for vendors from whom the user used to order ice cream, whereas the VENDOR table may include only currently approved vendors. If, from a business perspective, the nonmatching foreign keys have meaning, you may allow and document exceptions to the referential integrity rule.

We use the term *domain integrity* to mean the integrity rules for *all* columns in a relational table, including primary keys, foreign keys, nonkeys, and so on. (Note: This is not a standard definition for the term *domain integrity*. Rather, it is a convenient term under which to classify miscellaneous integrity rules.) Formally, a *domain* is a logical pool of values from which one or more columns draw their values. In this book, we interpret domain rules to include rules for data type, length, range-checking, default values, uniqueness, nullability, and so on, for *each and every* column. As you can now see, entity integrity and referential integrity are merely special cases of domain integrity. Yet, because they are so important, they are distinguished as separate rules. When designing relational databases, you will identify and enforce domain integrity for every column.

SIGNIFICANCE OF RELATIONAL DATA INTEGRITY

Relational data integrity is logically an integral part of the relational model. Just as the relational model does not provide implementation specifications for data structure and manipulation operators, it also does not dictate how data integrity should be implemented by a given product. It does, however, imply that data integrity should be defined and enforced without involving the user in technical implementation details such as record links or pointers. After all, data integrity rules represent business rules and not technical considerations. The relational model definition also implies that data integrity should be addressed as part of the database implementation and not as part of application implementation. For this reason, definition and implementation of relational data integrity are integral to the design philosophy in this book.

WHAT THEN IS A RELATIONAL DATABASE?

Although the relational model is an intellectual concept, a relational database is a materialization of that concept using DBMS technology. As the words imply, a "relational database" inherits two sets of characteristics, one defining its *relational* aspect and another defining its *database* meaning.

You are now in a position to comprehend the relational aspect. A *relational* database comprises business data that appear to the user to behave according to rules of the relational model. Users perceive the data as a set of tables that obey the six properties of relations, are manipulated via the eight relational operators or their equivalent, and are protected by the relational integrity rules. Because the relational model is well defined, this relational aspect should be consistent across relational products. Presently, however, due to product immaturity, you do not always see complete consistency. (For more on this observation, see *Designing Databases with Today's Relational DBMS Products.*)

The database aspect of relational databases is much more confusing. There is no universal definition of a relational *database* except that it is a computerized structure for storing data that the user regards as relational tables (rows and columns). Beyond that concept, every relational DBMS product relies on its own interpretation of what a database is. To understand better the realm of relational database design, consider three major differences in product-specific definitions of a database: database boundaries, storage and access of relational data, and nonrelational items.

First, each product has its own definition of *database boundary* and of the limitations imposed by this boundary. Consider the following questions as a means of uncovering (subtle and obvious) limitations and implications that may be associated with a relational database boundary:

☐ Can a user access tables from more than one database at one time? For example, can a user join tables from different databases?
☐ Does a database imply storage allocation parameters or limitations?
☐ What security privileges and restrictions apply at a database level?
☐ What limitations are there with respect to executing utilities? Are you restricted to running one utility at a time per database?

☐   How do database boundaries affect locking? Is it possible for a designer to assign tables to a set of databases to minimize or maximize concurrent access?

Second, each product has its own mechanisms for *storing and accessing* relational data. A relational database may consist of sequential files or datasets, linked with pointers, augmented with indexes, or accessed via hash routines.

Third, relational DBMS products usually provide for creation and support of *items other than relational objects;* that is, typically users can associate with a relational database items that are not defined within the relational model. For example, sometimes a user can define macros, procedures, exit routines, access privileges, or user profiles and relate them to specific databases, tables, or columns. Such additional items are useful (in fact, sometimes necessary) when designing relational databases and enforcing data integrity rules.

SQL STANDARD

SQL or Structured Query Language is accepted as an industry standard for a relational data access language. Although not a part of relational model theory, SQL is considered by some people to be equal in importance to the relational model as a foundation for relational DBMS products. SQL as a common relational database language enables consistency across product implementations, at least in the way that users, application developers, and (to some extent) database designers interface with the products. Although internal mechanisms for representing and accessing database structures may differ greatly, a common language allows users to deal with only one syntax for invoking those mechanisms.

SQL, like the relational model definition, has been evolving since the early seventies. In 1986, after several years of development and debate, the American National Standards Institute (ANSI) finally approved definition of a base SQL standard. Proposed extensions to the base standard are still under debate and will undoubtedly evolve for years to come. Since the early eighties, however, SQL has been achieving acceptance as a de facto standard and has prevailed as the database language implemented in most commercial relational DBMS products. SQL's leading competitor has been QUEL, for a long time also widely in use, chiefly through Relational Technology's INGRES. INGRES and most other QUEL-based products, however, have recently adopted SQL-based languages in deference to popular clamor for the SQL standard.

Use of SQL ensures that users perceive data in the form of tables and manipulate data through commands that are equivalent to the set-oriented relational operators. Thus, implementation of SQL implies at least a partial implementation of the relational model. SQL does not ensure full adherence to the relational model, however. In fact, the base SQL standard does not even include constructs for implementation of referential integrity. Thus, it is possible for a product to support SQL and not the full relational model, or to support the relational model and not SQL.

Some strong advocates of SQL consider it as important as or even more important than the relational model as a standard. They point out that a standard SQL can buffer the user from technical implementation details specific to each DBMS product, thereby providing the following benefits:

□ Users (including developers as well as end users) need learn only one language, which they can apply to multiple DBMS products (for example, using their home personal computer, using the office mainframe, or using the volunteer fire department's minicomputer)

□ Applications can potentially be ported from one environment to another, perhaps to accommodate evolving transaction volumes or to service other business sites

□ Applications can even potentially be distributed across multiple environments using different relational DBMS products; for example, ORACLE is advertised as one of the earliest implementations of a distributed DBMS product, enabling close cooperation among different SQL-based relational DBMSs (such as IBM's DB2 and Oracle's ORACLE)

The strongest SQL proponents dismiss the importance of full adherence to the relational model, saying that, as long as users can obtain language consistency across products, details of the underlying data model are not significant. As we pointed out earlier, however, the relational model brings benefits of its own: productivity, flexibility, and highly predictable behavior due to dependence on a well-understood theoretical foundation.

We present an overview of the SQL standard and discuss how it implements each component of the relational model: structure, manipulation, and integrity. The purpose is to establish a basis for presenting examples in subsequent chapters. (A more in-depth treatment of the ANSI SQL standard can be found in C. J. Date, *A Guide to the SQL Standard* (Reading, MA: Addison-Wesley Publishing Company, 1987)). Toward the end of this section are SQL constructs that are not specified by the relational model but are a necessary part of any DBMS language—such as security, transaction management, and programming-language interfaces. We provide only as much detail as you will need to understand subsequent chapters' examples. To this extent, the discussion is generally consistent both with the ANSI standard and also with most commercial products' SQL implementation. When necessary, exceptions to the standard are noted.

DATA MANIPULATION

Although relational data manipulation consists of eight relational operators, SQL data manipulation consists of only four verbs: SELECT, INSERT, UPDATE, and DELETE. In particular, the eight relational retrieval operators are all expressed using SELECT with numerous optional parameters or clauses.

Let's take a brief look at the SELECT statement. It can contain up to seven clauses: SELECT, FROM, WHERE, GROUP BY, HAVING, ORDER BY, and UNION. The SELECT clause lists columns, expressions, built-in functions, or constants that are to be presented in the output.

A sample SELECT clause is:

```
SELECT DEPT, SUM(SALARY)
```

The FROM clause indicates the tables from which data will be retrieved. Extending our SELECT statement to contain a FROM clause results in

```
SELECT DEPT, SUM(SALARY)
FROM EMPLOYEE
```

The WHERE clause contains qualification requirements, as in

```
SELECT DEPT, SUM(SALARY)
FROM EMPLOYEE
WHERE LOCATION='New York'
```

The GROUP BY clause indicates subgrouping for built-in functions:

```
SELECT DEPT, SUM(SALARY)
FROM EMPLOYEE
WHERE LOCATION='New York'
GROUP BY DEPT
```

HAVING eliminates groups from the result. The following example includes in the result only departments the SUM(SALARY) of which is greater than $1,000,000.00:

```
SELECT DEPT, SUM(SALARY)
FROM EMPLOYEE
WHERE LOCATION='New York'
GROUP BY DEPT
HAVING SUM(SALARY) > 1000000.00
```

The ORDER BY clause specifies the columns (either by name or by position within the SELECT clause) the values of which should determine the sequence in which rows are to be presented. To retrieve the results of your SELECT statement in sequence by DEPT, you would specify

```
SELECT DEPT, SUM(SALARY)
FROM EMPLOYEE
WHERE LOCATION='New York'
GROUP BY DEPT
HAVING SUM(SALARY) > 1000000.00
ORDER BY DEPT
```

The UNION clause invokes the relational union operator; for example,

```
SELECT DEPT, SUM(SALARY)
FROM EMPLOYEE
WHERE LOCATION='New York'
GROUP BY DEPT
HAVING SUM(SALARY) > 1000000.00
UNION
SELECT COMMITTEE, SUM(COMMISSION)
FROM VOLUNTEER
WHERE LOCATION='New York'
GROUP BY COMMITTEE
HAVING SUM(COMMISSION) > 50000.00
ORDER BY 1
```

We give SQL syntax for each of the relational manipulation examples described earlier, illustrating the eight basic relational manipulation operators. Each example references the appropriate figure (earlier in the chapter) diagramming the operation's results.

The SQL syntax conforms to the SQL standard except for some of the special characters (hyphen, asterisk) used in data names. The SQL standard supports only uppercase letters, digits, and underscores in data names. We incorporate other special characters to simplify cross-references between logical data model names and relational data names. Moreover, many product implementations support additional (nonstandard) special characters.

```
SELECT NAME, LOCATION FROM VENDOR
WHERE LOCATION='New Jersey'
```

This statement invokes the *select* or *restrict* operation, selecting only those rows (NAME and LOCATION columns) in the ice-cream VENDOR table for which the value of the LOCATION column is New Jersey. Figure 3.1 contains the VENDOR table and Figure 3.6 shows the result of the select operation.

```
SELECT DISTINCT LOCATION FROM VENDOR
```

This statement requests the *project* operation, retrieving distinct values for the LOCATION column in the VENDOR table. Figure 3.7 illustrates the result. The DISTINCT parameter eliminates any duplicate rows from the result, consistent with the definition of project.

```
SELECT VENDOR*NAME, FLAVOR*NAME, NAME, LOCATION FROM SUPPLY, VENDOR
```

This statement implies the *product* operation, concatenating each row from the SUPPLY table (VENDOR*NAME and FLAVOR*NAME columns, Figure 3.5) with all rows from the VENDOR table (NAME and LOCATION columns, Figure 3.1). Figure 3.8 illustrates the result. A product is recognized in SQL by the presence of multiple tables in the FROM clause.

```
SELECT VENDOR*NAME, FLAVOR*NAME, NAME, LOCATION FROM SUPPLY, VENDOR
    WHERE VENDOR*NAME=NAME
```

This statement results in the *equi-join,* imposing a select operation on the product where the vendor name columns (VENDOR*NAME and NAME) are equal. The result of the equi-join is shown in Figure 3.9. Again, note that there are multiple tables in the FROM clause.

```
SELECT VENDOR*NAME, FLAVOR*NAME, LOCATION FROM SUPPLY, VENDOR
    WHERE VENDOR*NAME=NAME
```

This statement reflects the *natural join,* eliminating the redundant column (NAME) from the equi-join (thus imposing a project on a select on a product). The result of the natural join is similar to the diagram in Figure 3.9, with the NAME column eliminated.

This is a good place to introduce the concept of a subquery. You can think of a *subquery* as a nested SELECT statement. A sample subquery is as follows:

```
SELECT VENDOR*NAME, FLAVOR*NAME FROM SUPPLY
    WHERE VENDOR*NAME IN
    (SELECT NAME FROM VENDOR)
```

This statement is a *noncorrelated subquery* implying that the relational DBMS first evaluates the "inner" SELECT (giving the result of Mr. Chip, Bean, Inc., Mrs. Mousse, Mr. Mousse, Sancho, Diet-Cream, Freeze-It). It uses the result of the "inner" SELECT as input to the "outer" SELECT. The result of this subquery is similar to Figure 3.9 (equi-join of SUPPLY and VENDOR tables) but includes only two columns (VENDOR*NAME and FLAVOR*NAME).

Note that the request could have been expressed as a join query:

```
SELECT VENDOR*NAME, FLAVOR*NAME FROM VENDOR, SUPPLY
    WHERE VENDOR.NAME=SUPPLY.VENDOR*NAME
```

If your result is to contain columns from multiple tables (as is not the case in the previous example), you must use a join query, specifying both tables in the FROM clause. If the result is to contain columns from only one table (as is the case in the previous example), you can code either a join query or a subquery. The choice usually is one of preference, or possibly of performance if the optimizer for a given product evaluates joins differently than subqueries (for example, generates different access strategies to obtain the results).

```
SELECT NAME, LOCATION FROM EAST-COAST-VENDOR
    UNION
SELECT NAME, LOCATION FROM WEST-COAST-VENDOR
```

This statement implies the *union* operation, listing all rows in either the EAST-COAST-VENDOR or the WEST-COAST-VENDOR tables. Figure 3.11 illustrates the operand tables and the result.

```
SELECT MATH-CLUB.FIRST-NAME, MATH-CLUB.LAST-NAME
    FROM MATH-CLUB, SKI-CLUB
    WHERE MATH-CLUB.FIRST-NAME=SKI-CLUB.FIRST-NAME
    AND MATH-CLUB.LAST-NAME=SKI-CLUB.LAST-NAME
```

This statement reflects the *intersection* operation, retrieving two columns (FIRST—NAME and LAST—NAME) from the MATH—CLUB table for rows in which the values of those two columns are common to both the MATH—CLUB and the SKI—CLUB tables (see Figure 3.13). Note that, since the column names are common to both tables, they are prefixed by the appropriate table name.

There is another way in SQL to request an intersection. This second way involves two new concepts: *correlated subquery* and EXISTS. In the following intersection example, there are two (nested) SELECT statements.

```
SELECT MATH—CLUB.FIRST—NAME, MATH—CLUB.LAST—NAME
     FROM MATH—CLUB
     WHERE EXISTS
     (SELECT SKI—CLUB.LAST—NAME FROM SKI—CLUB
     WHERE MATH—CLUB.FIRST—NAME=SKI—CLUB.FIRST—NAME
     AND MATH—CLUB.LAST—NAME=SKI—CLUB.LAST—NAME)
```

In this example, you may notice something strange about the inner (second) SELECT statement. Although its FROM clause references only the SKI—CLUB table, its WHERE clause also references the MATH—CLUB table. Thus, this is a correlated subquery. A *correlated subquery* is a SELECT statement the value of which depends on some parameter that receives its value from an "outer" SELECT. Thus, a relational DBMS evaluates a correlated subquery once for each qualifying value(s) of the "outer" SELECT.

Let us analyze conceptually how the relational DBMS evaluates this example. First, it retrieves a row that qualifies for the first SELECT. In this case, it selects two columns from any row in the MATH—CLUB table. Next, it evaluates the second SELECT, using the previous result of the first SELECT as input parameters. In this case, it searches the SKI—CLUB table for values in the FIRST—NAME and LAST—NAME columns that match the values it has just retrieved from the MATH—CLUB table. The EXISTS indicates that, if such a match is found, the relational DBMS should include the two values from the MATH—CLUB table in the result. If no match is found, those values are not included in the result. Next, the relational DBMS chooses another row that satisfies the first SELECT and again evaluates the second SELECT, using the new values as input parameters. The process continues until each FIRST—NAME and LAST—NAME in the MATH—CLUB table, having matching rows in the SKI—CLUB table, have been included in the final result.

```
SELECT MATH—CLUB.FIRST—NAME, MATH—CLUB.LAST—NAME
     FROM MATH—CLUB
     WHERE NOT EXISTS
     (SELECT SKI—CLUB.LAST—NAME FROM SKI—CLUB
     WHERE SKI—CLUB.FIRST—NAME=MATH—CLUB.FIRST—NAME
     AND SKI—CLUB.LAST—NAME=MATH—CLUB.LAST—NAME)
```

This statement requests the *difference* operation, retrieving columns FIRST—NAME and LAST—NAME from the MATH—CLUB table for those students appearing in the MATH–CLUB table but not in the SKI–CLUB table. Figure 3.14 illustrates the result. The example uses a correlated subquery with a NOT EXISTS. In this case, the values from the first SELECT (i.e., FIRST–NAME and LAST–NAME from the MATH–CLUB table) are included in the result only if there are no rows returned for the second SELECT; that is, the result includes FIRST–NAME and LAST–NAME of MATH–CLUB rows for which there are no matching rows in the SKI–CLUB.

```
SELECT DISTINCT STUD-NUMBER, STUD-NAME FROM CPT-COURSE C1
     WHERE NOT EXISTS
          (SELECT COURSE-NUMBER FROM RELAT-MAJOR
          WHERE NOT EXISTS
               (SELECT COURSE-NUMBER FROM CPT-COURSE C2
               WHERE C2.STUD-NUMBER=C1.STUD-NUMBER
               AND C2.STUD-NAME=C1.STUD-NAME
               AND C2.COURSE-NUMBER=RELAT-MAJOR.COURSE-NUMBER
               AND C2.COURSE-NAME=RELAT-MAJOR.COURSE-NAME))
```

This statement expresses the *division* operation. Figure 3.15 illustrates the dividend, divisor, and quotient tables. The example introduces another new construct: the alias. C1 in the first SELECT and C2 in the third SELECT are known as *aliases* because they are merely alternate names for the CPT–COURSE table.

Let us take a closer look at this (rather complex) SQL statement. Eventually, it retrieves all students (eliminating duplicates—DISTINCT) from the CPT–COURSE table who have completed all courses listed in the RELAT–MAJOR table. It does so using two correlated subqueries. The outermost query chooses a student row within the CPT–COURSE table (establishing alias C1 as a future reference to this row). The next (middle) query chooses a course row within the RELAT–MAJOR table. Finally, the innermost query examines student rows in the CPT–COURSE table (using alias C2 to refer to these CPT–COURSE rows, as distinguished from the outermost query's C1 CPT–COURSE rows). Specifically, the innermost query checks whether there is a student row in the CPT–COURSE (C2) table that has the same student number/name as the selected student (from C1—outermost SELECT) and the same course number/name as the selected course (from RELAT–MAJOR—middle query). In everyday language, the innermost query determines whether the student has taken the course. The middle query returns any courses for which the innermost query fails, implying that the student has not taken the course. The outermost query returns all students for whom no courses were returned by the middle query (implying, instead, that the student has taken all the courses).

Most SQL statements are fairly intuitive. As the statements get more complex and nest more parameters (as in the last example), you must concentrate harder to decipher the meaning. Yet little additional syntax is used.

Notice that SQL is generally, although not totally, faithful to the principles of the relational manipulation operators discussed previously. In particular, SQL commands operate on entire sets of data (tables of rows and columns) and likewise produce sets of rows and columns. The results, however, need not be relations (e.g., may contain duplicate rows). Also, details of physical addressing and access mechanisms are hidden from the user and do not affect command syntax.

If physical addressing and access mechanisms were not hidden from the user, then, to join the VENDOR and SUPPLY tables, the user would need to specify in what order rows should be accessed, retrieved, or discarded in forming the result. Instead, the user specifies only *what* is to be done, not *how* to accomplish it. The user doesn't even care whether or what indexes exist (at least insofar as SQL syntax is concerned).

SQL actually includes many additional functions and options that are not inconsistent with, yet are not explicit within, the relational model. We discuss a few of these. Other SQL functions are not discussed here because they are less relevant to examples used within this book.

SELECT * retrieves *all* columns from a specified table for rows that meet conditions stated in the WHERE clause (if present).

```
SELECT * FROM VENDOR

SELECT * FROM VENDOR WHERE LOCATION='Alaska'
```

The SQL SELECT command does not automatically eliminate duplicate rows from the result. For example, the first SELECT command in the following example results in two occurrences of New Jersey because there are two vendors from New Jersey in the VENDOR table. The DISTINCT option eliminates duplicates. Thus, the second SQL command results in only one occurrence of New Jersey.

```
SELECT LOCATION FROM VENDOR

SELECT DISTINCT LOCATION FROM VENDOR
```

The ORDER BY clause sequences results based on values of the column(s) specified. Note that, since there is no inherent order associated with rows of a table or view, leaving off the ORDER BY clause results in an unpredictable (even changeable) ordering.

```
SELECT NAME, LOCATION FROM VENDOR
     ORDER BY NAME, LOCATION
```

The GROUP BY clause defines the boundaries of an aggregate function such as COUNT, SUM, MIN, MAX, or AVG. The following SQL command returns vendor name and count of flavors supplied by (grouped by) each vendor.

```
SELECT VENDOR*NAME, COUNT (FLAVOR*NAME) FROM SUPPLY
     GROUP BY VENDOR*NAME;
```

As illustrated through examples in this chapter, conditions in the SQL WHERE clause may involve arithmetic expressions (+, −, *, /, and so on), comparative operators (<, >, =), aggregate functions, AND/OR/NOT operators, and IN lists. For instance,

```
SELECT NAME FROM EMPLOYEE
      WHERE CURRENT-SALARY  <  (PRIOR-SALARY + 10000)
      AND JOB-CODE NOT IN ('Laid-off', 'Sabbatical')
```

The INSERT statement adds a new row of data to a table. Unless the command specifies otherwise (as in the second example that follows), data values must be listed in the same order as the order in which the columns were defined (through the CREATE TABLE statement, described in the next section, *Data Structure*).

```
INSERT INTO VENDOR
      VALUES ('Weight-Up', 'Florida')

INSERT INTO EAST-COAST VENDOR
      (NAME, STATUS)
      VALUES ('Weight-Up', 'active')
```

The second INSERT example (INSERT INTO EAST-COAST-VENDOR) allows specification of column values in a different order, or specification of values for only some of the columns. Because the LOCATION column is not specified, a null value will be inserted into that column (assuming the definition of the LOCATION column permits null values).

The following statement performs a multirow insert into the VENDOR table by copying selected rows from the EAST-COAST-VENDOR table.

```
INSERT INTO VENDOR
      SELECT NAME, LOCATION
      FROM EAST-COAST-VENDOR
      WHERE STATUS='active'
```

The UPDATE statement modifies data values within one or more columns and one or more rows.

```
UPDATE EAST-COAST-VENDOR
      SET STATUS='active'
      WHERE LOCATION='New York'
```

The DELETE statement deletes the values of one or more rows. Not supplying a WHERE clause (as in the second example below) causes deletion of all rows in the entire table. The table definition still exists, however. A DROP TABLE statement (discussed in the next section, *Data Structure*) deletes the table definition.

```
DELETE FROM EAST-COAST-VENDOR
      WHERE STATUS IS NULL

DELETE FROM WEST-COAST-VENDOR
```

So far, you have seen examples of four SQL data manipulation verbs representing the four functions you can perform on data values: retrieval, insertion, update, and deletion. Most SQL implementations also include three data definition verbs—CREATE, DROP, and ALTER (of which only CREATE is addressed by the SQL standard) and some additional verbs representing miscellaneous control functions. In total, however, there are few verbs. This simplicity is possible because of the absence of "how-to" syntax in the SQL language; that is, the language specifies *what* function is to be performed with no mention of *how*.

DATA STRUCTURE

The *data definition* components of most SQL implementations enable definition of tables and views, including their creation, modification, and destruction. (Surprisingly, the base SQL standard supports syntax for table and view creation only). The following are examples of typical SQL data definition syntax:

```
CREATE TABLE VENDOR (NAME CHAR(20) NOT NULL, LOCATION CHAR(15))

ALTER TABLE VENDOR ADD FLAVOR-COUNT INTEGER

DROP TABLE VENDOR
```

The first statement creates a VENDOR table structure with two columns, NAME and LOCATION. Note that the table structure is defined but is empty of data values. The second statement adds another column, FLAVOR-COUNT, to the VENDOR table. The third statement destroys the VENDOR table, including its definition and data values.

Products differ in their support for various data types (such as character, integer, binary, string, or decimal) and other column parameters. Product-specific parameters may include NOT NULL (value must always be specified), UNIQUE (value is unique within the column), DEFAULT (default value when no value is specified), RANGE (minimum and maximum values), and FORMAT (e.g., display of leading zeros or dollar sign). The base SQL standard incorporates NOT NULL and UNIQUE. Some other parameters are under discussion as extensions to the base standard.

Products typically support additional (nonstandard) statement types and parameters (e.g., CREATE DATABASE, CREATE TABLESPACE) to define further implementation options. Such constructs address physical tuning techniques such as indexing, space allocation or assignment, locking granularity, and recovery mechanisms. For example, many products support indexing of one or more columns through a CREATE INDEX statement:

```
CREATE UNIQUE INDEX XVENDOR-NAME ON VENDOR(NAME)
```

Existence or nonexistence of an index (or other physical implementation options) is transparent to the user who phrases an SQL command to access data. Presence of an index may affect performance but does not alter the result of a query. (An exception is that, if the query does not specify an ORDER BY clause, existence or nonexistence of an index may influence the sequence of rows returned).

Tables created by the CREATE TABLE statement are called *base tables* (or more simply, just *tables*), meaning they generally correspond to stored data structures. Most SQL implementations (as well as the SQL standard) also support views. Recall that a *view* is a logical "window" through which users can observe the results of one or more relational operations dynamically applied against one or more base tables.

Let us consider some examples of views:

```
CREATE VIEW VEND-LOC AS SELECT LOCATION FROM VENDOR

CREATE VIEW VEND-ALASKA AS SELECT NAME, LOCATION FROM VENDOR
    WHERE LOCATION = 'Alaska'

CREATE VIEW VEND-SUPPLY AS SELECT LOCATION, FLAVOR*NAME FROM VENDOR,
    SUPPLY WHERE NAME = VENDOR*NAME
```

The first view presents to a user a (virtual) table called VEND-LOC containing only the LOCATION column. The second view contains two columns (NAME, LOCATION), but rows for only those vendors located in Alaska. The third view contains two columns (LOCATION, FLAVOR*NAME) drawn from the two tables VENDOR and SUPPLY based on matching their respective vendor name columns. Views may even contain columns that do not exist at all in any tables but are derived from existing columns (e.g., SUM, MAX, COLUMNA + COLUMNB).

The syntax for defining a view incorporates syntax for relational manipulation operations (e.g., SELECT LOCATION FROM VENDOR). Essentially, any retrieval operations that can be applied to tables (select, project, join, union, and so on— defined via SQL SELECT commands) logically can be used to define a view (although some products impose certain restrictions). In fact, most SQL SELECT statements can be turned into view definitions simply by prefixing the words CREATE VIEW viewname AS.... Here, the .... represents an SQL SELECT statement.

Because a view, like a table, is a two-dimensional structure of rows and columns, operations that can be applied to a table can also be applied to a view. For example, just as you think of a subset of rows or columns of a table (select or project operation), you also can think of a subset of a view. Thus, the operand(s) in the FROM clause of an SQL SELECT command may be a table, or a view, or combination of both. In fact, often a user need not know whether the SQL FROM clause refers to tables or views. Therefore, a more complete definition of a *view* is a logical window for the result of operations applied to one or more base tables or views. From your knowledge of the nature of relational operators, you can appreciate the wide variety of potential views.

Because views do not represent (but rather are derived from) stored data structures, certain update operations on views may not always make sense. For example, consider the following view, illustrated in Figure 3.17:

VEND—LIST

NAME	LOCATION	COUNT—FLAVOR
Mr. Chip	New York	2
Diet—Cream	Colorado	3

FIGURE 3.17 VEND—LIST **view.**

```
CREATE VIEW VEND—LIST (NAME, LOCATION, COUNT—FLAVOR)
     AS SELECT NAME, LOCATION, COUNT (FLAVOR*NAME)
     FROM VENDOR, SUPPLY
     WHERE NAME = VENDOR*NAME
     GROUP BY NAME, LOCATION
```

This view contains three columns: NAME (from the VENDOR table, equal to VENDOR*NAME in the SUPPLY table), LOCATION (from the VENDOR table), and a derived column COUNT—FLAVOR. COUNT—FLAVOR is equal to the count of FLAVOR*NAMEs for each vendor (i.e., for each grouping of rows by NAME, LOCATION).

Suppose a user tried to update the COUNT—FLAVOR column in the VEND—LIST view. How would the DBMS reflect that update in the underlying SUPPLY table—what flavor would it add or delete? Or, suppose a user tried to update NAME in VEND—LIST. Should that cause an update of NAME in the VENDOR table (Figure 3.1), of VENDOR*NAME in the SUPPLY table (Figure 3.5), or of both? Because of these anomalies, most products do not support updates on (at least certain types of) views, particularly views involving aggregate operations or joins.

We can restate three important facts about views. First, the data values are stored only once (i.e., in tables), regardless of how many views are defined to contain them. Second, views reflect up-to-the-minute data values, because views are materialized (from tables), at the time a user accesses them. Third, for the most part, users are unaware of whether they are accessing tables or views, because users can invoke the same operations using the same SQL syntax against either. A notable exception occurs in the case of updates; some update operations do not make sense for views and thus are not permitted. Products vary in the restrictions they place on view update operations.

From a database design perspective, views as well as tables are important. The book points out valuable uses for views: to shelter users from some table design changes, to provide tailored security and authorization, and to simplify end-user access.

To recap, SQL data structures consist of tables and views, corresponding to stored and virtual relations, respectively. The base SQL standard includes syntax for creation of tables and views. SQL product implementations provide additional syntax, allowing a user to alter and drop tables, to modify (in some products) and drop views, and to define other implementation options (e.g., space management, access mechanisms, and locking granularity).

DATA INTEGRITY

The previous description of the relational model presented three integrity rules: entity, referential, and domain integrity. The SQL standard does not yet explicitly support these constructs. Some of the design guidelines in this book will address how to enforce integrity rules even when the DBMS does not provide automated facilities for doing so. The SQL standard does include some functions that in effect implement some pieces of the integrity rules, and we discuss these functions here.

Recall that the entity integrity rule requires that components of the primary key (unique identifier) for a table not be null. Whereas the SQL standard does not support definition of a primary key as such, it does incorporate the notions of unique and not-null constraints within the CREATE TABLE statement. For example,

```
CREATE TABLE SUPPLY (VENDOR*NAME CHAR (20) NOT NULL,
                     FLAVOR*NAME (15) NOT NULL,
                     UNIQUE (VENDOR*NAME, FLAVOR*NAME))
```

This standard SQL syntax enforces the properties (uniqueness and existence) of the primary key VENDOR*NAME, FLAVOR*NAME.

The referential integrity rule requires that foreign keys either be null or match values of corresponding primary keys in related tables. The base SQL standard does not recognize the concept of a foreign key and provides no simple mechanisms for enforcing referential integrity. Proposed extensions to the standard addressing this requirement are under discussion. For now, application code typically is required to enforce referential integrity, although some products support (nonstandard) DDL syntax for partial automated enforcement. Design guidelines in Part 3 discuss techniques for addressing this shortcoming in current product implementations.

Domain integrity addresses rules for ensuring validity of any column value. The SQL standard does not yet explicitly acknowledge a domain as an object in its own right (i.e., as a logical pool of values from which one or more columns draw their values). However, both the SQL standard and current SQL implementations generally provide mechanisms for enforcing domain constraints over a single column. For instance, the SQL standard supports DDL enforcement of data type, length, null support, and uniqueness. Some product implementations support additional domain constraints, such as minimum/maximum/default values. On the other hand, neither the SQL standard nor product implementations are satisfactory today in supporting rules that relate columns. For example, DDL syntax is unlikely to support specification of a rule stating that a COUNT—FLAVORS column in the VENDOR table must be equal to or greater than the count of FLAVOR*NAMEs for a particular VENDOR*NAME in the SUPPLY table. Cross-column domain rules (as well as some single-column domain rules) typically must be enforced through application code. Again, design guidelines in Part 3 discuss techniques for supplementing products' limited domain integrity features.

The SQL standard and SQL product implementations will evolve over the next few years to support more effectively definition and enforcement of integrity rules. Thus, the task of satisfying business requirements for data validation will become easier. Where possible, the design guidelines in Part 3 are defined to be consistent with anticipated product trends, especially in the area of integrity. Thus, while addressing "holes" in today's DBMS products, you will apply techniques that should be more automated but not made obsolete by future product releases.

OTHER SQL CONSTRUCTS

SQL deals with environmental issues that have nothing to do with the relational model. We discuss those that are related to concepts in this book.

The GRANT command (included in the base SQL standard) authorizes selected users' (e.g., CASEY, CHRISTOPHER, LEE) to perform selected functions (e.g., SELECT, UPDATE, INSERT, DELETE, GRANT, or ALL functions) on selected tables, views, or columns. The REVOKE command (not included in the base SQL standard) revokes such authorizations.

```
GRANT SELECT ON VENDOR TO CASEY
GRANT SELECT, UPDATE ON VENDOR, SUPPLY TO CHRISTOPHER
GRANT ALL ON SUPPLY TO LEE
REVOKE DELETE ON SUPPLY FROM MICHAEL
```

COMMIT and ROLLBACK syntax enable termination of a transaction (sequence of SQL statements) such that the effects of all (COMMIT) or none (ROLLBACK) of the statements are reflected in the database. These are included in the SQL standard. Implicit and explicit COMMIT/ROLLBACK logic is required to support with integrity user-controlled error recovery as well as automated management of concurrent users.

```
COMMIT WORK
```

```
ROLLBACK WORK
```

In some products, there are SQL parameters or statements that specify lock sizes and duration. Employing such parameters or statements, a user can direct a DBMS to restrict access to an entire table, a row, or some other physical grouping of data while that user is performing updates.

The SQL standard also includes syntax to enable invoking set-oriented SQL functions from within record-at-a-time programming languages (such as COBOL). The following syntax defines a *cursor*, VENDORS, which serves as a placemarker for stepping through the multiple rows resulting from an SQL SELECT command.

```
EXEC SQL
     DECLARE VENDORS CURSOR FOR
          SELECT NAME, LOCATION FROM VENDOR
          WHERE LOCATION = 'New Jersey' OR 'New York'
END-EXEC

EXEC SQL
     OPEN VENDORS
END-EXEC

EXEC SQL
     FETCH VENDORS
     INTO :NAME, :LOCATION
END-EXEC
```

The OPEN VENDORS statement initiates retrieval of the data and positions the cursor at the beginning of the result set. The FETCH VENDORS statement transfers the next row of the result into program variables (delineated by product-specific syntax, such as colons prefixing variable names). Each SQL statement is bracketed by EXEC SQL and END-EXEC, so that a precompiler can extract the syntax for later processing by the optimizer. Note that the EXEC SQL and END-EXEC syntax is not explicitly specified by the SQL standard. Rather, this syntax is representative of the way that products support embedding SQL statements directly into the text of a host language program for extraction by a preprocessor.

In this book, you learn to capitalize on the functionality of SQL to maximize benefits achievable with a relational database implementation. The design steps generally disregard implementation details peculiar to particular environments, except where such details are of special interest or value. Techniques for use of cursors and related programming-language logic are of little interest to database designers, so this book does not address them in detail.

DESIGNING DATABASES WITH TODAY'S RELATIONAL DBMS PRODUCTS

Relational DBMS products in the marketplace today adhere to the relational model and to the SQL standard to widely varying degrees. As you have seen, the properties of the relational model enable database design productivity (ease in building design) and flexibility (ease in changing design). They also enable productivity for developers in that access is set-oriented and is independent of storage structures. Moreover, the SQL language standard enables consistency across products and thereby productivity (minimal learning curves) and flexibility (ease in moving designs from one product to another or even implementing designs using multiple products). Relational DBMS products that significantly compromise the relational model or the SQL standard do so at the expense of important benefits.

Products that fail to adhere to all properties of the relational model lack desirable functionality and thus are likely to be less effective in meeting business requirements. Frequently, database designers or application developers must make up for product shortcomings by building additional relational model support into the database or application design. This extra effort may be time-consuming and costly, yet pays off in added design flexibility, usefulness, and longevity.

Alternatively, sometimes a relational DBMS product adheres closely to the relational model but is inadequate in providing other DBMS functionality, such as enabling high concurrent access or achieving acceptable performance levels. In this case, the developer may have to tune the database or application to overcome DBMS limitations. Nonjudicious tuning, however, may risk the flexibility and longevity that are hallmarks of a fully relational design.

You are probably beginning to appreciate that developing an effective relational design entails a combination of building on the features of a good relational DBMS and adhering to properties of the relational model itself. The methodology in this book is intended to help you do exactly that. The design methodology assumes that you are working with a product that is generally, but perhaps not fully, relational. That is, your DBMS enables users to perceive their data as tables (and perhaps views) of columns, rows, and values, meeting some (but perhaps not all) of the six relational properties. It asumes that your product supports some (but probably not all) of the eight relational manipulation operators and enables partial (but definitely not full) automated enforcement of integrity rules. The methodology provides techniques and design guidlines to assist you (1) to achieve a relational design that can satisfy your users' information requirements and accurately reflect rules and relationships that characterize use of information within the business, (2) to capitalize on the strengths of the relational model that are present in your product, and (3) to simulate or build features that counterbalance shortcomings of your DBMS. You will evaluate alternatives for addressing design criteria, such as performance, security, and concurrent access, without undue sacrifice of the simplicity, productivity, and flexibility accorded to the relational model.

It is inconceivable that a book on relational database design could address specific technical details for all relational DBMS products. However, the design procedures in this book serve as a valuable starting point for use of any (fully or partially) relational DBMS. In fact, for many such products and many requirements, applying the guidelines in this book will result in an excellent design. However, if performance is critical or if a specific requirement challenges the limits of a given product, additional product-specific tuning may be necessary.

Throughout the book, there are examples and extensive case studies. Some of the case studies illustrate two relational products: IBM's DB2 and Teradata's DBC/1012. These are only two of the many relational products available in mainframe, mini, and micro environments. However, these products serve as good examples for three reasons. First, they represent two very different implementations of relational DBMSs (including hardware and software implementations). Second, they are capable of handling large and small data volumes and can be used for requirements of varying complexity. Third, both support SQL, accepted as the industry standard for a relational data access language.

More specific information on each product is readily available should you decide to pursue more technical details. Please note that our choice of these products does not imply that they are (or are not) superior to other products currently on the market.

SUMMARY

In this chapter, we have presented an overview of the relational model and of SQL to establish a foundation for the discussion of relational design techniques in subsequent chapters. The three components of the relational model are

□   *Data structure*—organization of data into two-dimensional *tables,* or *relations* of rows and columns
□   *Data manipulation*—eight relational operators, known as select (restrict), project, product, join, union, intersection, difference, and division
□   *Data integrity*—business rules governing the valid values that may be assumed by a relational data structure; specifically, entity, referential, and domain integrity rules

The chapter covered implementation of the relational model via SQL, acknowledged as the evolving industry standard for a relational data access language. SQL implements relational data structures via tables and views; relational manipulation operators via the SELECT verb; and relational integrity rules in part by less well-defined mechanisms, such as table creation parameters, indexes, and application coding techniques.

Finally, the chapter touched on the challenges posed by designing relational databases using today's relational DBMS products. The remainder of the book will expand on these themes: how to achieve the theoretical simplicity, integrity, and productivity associated with the relational data model while making use of the pragmatic technologies available today.

C H A P T E R

4 Introduction to Relational Database Design

Relational database design is a process for transforming a logical data model into a relational database. Typically, the relational database must reflect the logical data model. For example, the relational design should preserve the properties of stability and sharability that characterize the logical data model. The challenge is to design a relational database that also offers acceptable functionality and performance.

Let us take a moment to reflect on the scope of the relational database design methodology in Part 3. The methodology addresses relational implementation of each and every construct of the logical data model. These include not only structural constructs (entities, relationships, attributes) but also integrity constructs (primary keys, foreign keys, domains, and other business rules). An underlying theme is the continuing dominant role of a data-driven design philosophy. Consistent with this philosophy, Part 3 views the scope of the database design project as encompassing all data-related design issues that may affect multiple applications or access requirements.

Let us consider that idea carefully. Concepts that are not specific to a particular application include all the data-driven business rules defined as part of the logical data model to govern integrity of data values. Sometimes, you can enforce these rules via built-in DBMS facilities (e.g., data type specifications in the database definition). Frequently, however, the business rules may require development of application code (e.g., to enforce a rule about the relationship between two attributes). The methodology in this book addresses enforcement of all business rules that are not application-specific as part of the database design process, even if they must be implemented via application code.

There are four benefits of continuing this data-oriented philosophy through the relational design process:

1. *Data integrity.* When you enforce business rules through one integrated approach, the database is less vulnerable to contamination.
2. *Productivity.* You are enforcing business rules completely and consistently, yet with minimal overhead. Specifically, you are at least defining and possibly implementing each business rule only once for the database, rather than once per application.
3. *Maintainability.* As the business evolves, you are able to respond to changes in business rules more quickly and easily, because you have defined and implemented the rules consistently.
4. *Evolution.* As relational DBMS products evolve to provide better automated facilities for enforcing business rules, you can easily migrate from this consistent, integrated implementation approach to take advantage of new facilities.

In the end, you will measure the success of your relational databases by how easily they accommodate a multiplicity of needs: different types of users, various access patterns and requirements, and changing business and technological issues. The databases are more likely to support these various needs if the database design is founded on a data-driven philosophy.

The relational database design methodology presented in Part 3 has three major characteristics. First, it is *data-driven* in that it builds on a logical data model and integrates enforcement of business rules into the database design process. Second, it also is *process-oriented* in that it acknowledges requirements to "tweak" a relational database design to meet specific functionality and performance objectives. In particular, it encourages an understanding of critical access, response time, throughput, and concurrency requirements. Third, it is largely *product-independent* in that the steps provide a basis (or, at least, a starting point) for building relational databases using any relational DBMS product.

MAJOR CONCEPTS OF RELATIONAL DATABASE DESIGN

Let us revisit the simple logical data model from Chapter 2. It depicts Ron's Real Estate Business; it is repeated in Figure 4.1 for your convenience.

Recall the major components of a logical data model: entities, primary keys, foreign keys, attributes, relationships, and business rules. Recall, too, major constructs of the relational data model: relational tables (much like entities?), primary keys, foreign keys, columns (much like attributes?), and integrity rules—entity, referential, and domain (much like business rules?). It is no coincidence that the logical data modeling methodology in Part 2 uses terminology

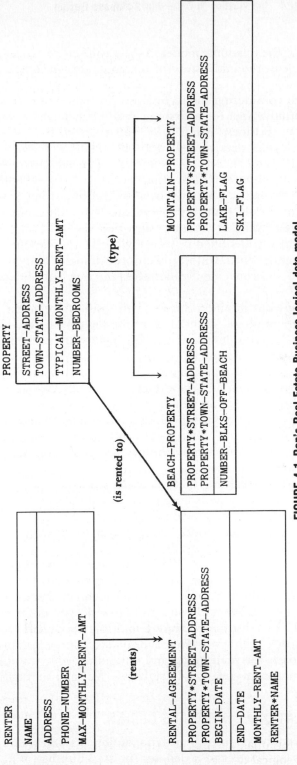

FIGURE 4.1 Ron's Real Estate Business logical data model.

similar to that of the relational model. As you will see, the concepts also are similar, causing at least the initial steps of relational design to be a straightforward process.

Before even considering the techniques presented in this book, you probably have an intuitive feel for a first-cut relational database design to support Ron's Real Estate Business. Most likely, you envision five tables (one for each entity in your logical data model): RENTER, PROPERTY, RENTAL–AGREEMENT, BEACH–PROPERTY, and MOUNTAIN–PROPERTY. The RENTER table, for example, would have four columns representing NAME, ADDRESS, PHONE–NUMBER, and MAX–MONTHLY–RENT–AMT. Thinking back to the important properties of relational tables, you would probably investigate how to enforce such properties. For example, you probably would ensure that the primary key of each table (conveniently already identified in your logical data model!) is unique and does not allow null values. Next, you would enforce domains and other data integrity rules (which are also conveniently identified in your logical data model as business rules!).

By following your intuition this far, you would have accomplished the first of two major design phases: translation of the logical data model into a preliminary relational database design. Once you have your preliminary design, you would probably begin to wonder whether, in fact, it is the best design possible. By merely translating the logical data model into corresponding relational components, have you missed any important ingredient? Are all user queries and transactions feasible with this database design? Will they be efficient? These questions bring you to the second phase of relational database design: tuning the preliminary design. You may try a few techniques—possibly define some indexes, or perhaps duplicate some columns in two or more tables to speed processing of particular data requests.

You are probably realizing that relational database design involves few new ideas, once you have an understanding of logical data modeling and relational concepts (plus perhaps some previous experience with database design). In fact, having a stable logical data model makes it easy to develop a preliminary relational database design.

Of course, had you first read Part 3, you would have proceeded in a more rigorous and systematic manner, referencing guidelines for each step. Part 3 would have guided you in some of the more technical issues, such as: How do you assign names to tables and columns? How do you enforce business rules? How should tables be distributed among multiple databases? How and when do you calculate space utilization? Part 3 provides a more comprehensive, cookbook-like approach for reinforcing and extending your intuitive ideas as you design, tune, and review relational databases. We shall summarize the steps.

STEPS IN RELATIONAL DATABASE DESIGN

Each step is numbered using the convention RDD*n* where RDD denotes relational database design and *n* denotes the step number. Within the chapters in Part 3, rules corresponding to each step are numbered RDD*n.m* where *m* denotes the relative rule number within Step *n*. All the rules for relational database design are also summarized in the Index of Design Rules for easy reference.

TRANSLATE THE LOGICAL DATA STRUCTURE (CHAPTER 11)

As you presumed in your intuitive process, database design begins with translation of the logical data model. Initially, this process occurs independently of any investigation of access patterns, transaction volumes, or even security requirements. You translate components of the logical data model into relational objects that are visible in some way to users (e.g., tables, columns, and mechanisms for supporting business rules).

You begin by translating the logical data structure in Chapter 11. Specifically, the steps are:

☐ Identify *tables—Step RDD1*
☐ Identify *columns—Step RDD2*
☐ Adapt data structure to *product environment—Step RDD3*

The chapter contains sample SQL for defining relational structures.

TRANSLATE THE LOGICAL DATA INTEGRITY (CHAPTER 12)

The second phase of the translation process is to enforce the logical data integrity constraints or business rules. The steps are

☐ Design for business rules about *entities—Step RDD4*
☐ Design for business rules about *relationships—Step RDD5*
☐ Design for additional business rules about *attributes—Step RDD6*

Recall that current relational products are lacking in options for enforcing business rules. Chapter 12, therefore, discusses some alternative implementation mechanisms, with advantages and disadvantages of each. It includes an overview of proposed ANSI SQL extensions that address some (although not all) integrity requirements.

Figure 4.2 illustrates a relational table for RENTER. Note how closely the diagram resembles the sample value listing in Figure 2.2 on page 15. Various codes positioned below each attribute name designate the use of implementa-

FIGURE 4.2 RENTER **relational table.**

RENTER

NAME (UIX)	ADDRESS	PHONE–NUMBER	MAX–MONTHLY– RENT–AMT
Harry Smith	12 Oak Lane, Hopetown, NY 01111	212–984–3158	400
Josephine Morgan	5 Central Ave, Dallas, TX 75080	214–232–7990	650

tion options, selected now or in later design steps. For example, (UIX) beneath NAME indicates implementation of a unique index on the NAME column. When translating the RENTER entity to this relational table, you choose an appropriate table name, column names, data types, validation checks, and so on.

TUNE BY ESTABLISHING STORAGE-RELATED ACCESS MECHANISMS (CHAPTER 13)

Finally, you turn to tuning the relational design. Tuning efforts are primarily concerned with facilitating specific access requirements. Frequently, proper tuning can make the difference between a successful and an unsuccessful relational database implementation. For that reason, this book devotes four chapters (Chapters 13, 14, 15, and 16) to tuning techniques. These chapters present tuning options in a deliberate sequence—the sequence in which you should apply these techniques to maximize benefits yet minimize problems for existing user communities.

Your first tuning efforts should address effective use of access mechanisms provided by your relational DBMS. Techniques include use of scans, clustering, hashing and indexes. There are several reasons to begin here.

First, access mechanisms in relational products are (should be!) transparent to users. Chapter 3 explains that users need never specify via language syntax the access mechanisms the relational DBMS is to use in satisfying a given query. That decision is left to the product's optimizer. Thus, you as the designer can introduce changes in the access mechanisms without necessitating changes in application code or in users' use of SQL (or other) commands.

Second, as a designer, you need to become familiar with the performance benefits and implications of various access mechanisms. Particularly during your first design project using a given product, you need to experiment with access mechanisms early so that you will be able to leverage the performance strengths and weaknesses of your product. Get a feel for limits to the performance afforded by facilities within your DBMS before trying to push those limits by modifying your design.

Chapter 13 specifically discusses access mechanisms that rely on and benefit from choice of storage options for each table. Three steps are involved:

☐ Tune for *scan* efficiency—*Step RDD7*
☐ Define *clustering* sequences—*Step RDD8*
☐ Define *hash* keys—*Step RDD9*

To apply these steps to Ron's Real Estate Business, you must understand more about his processing requirements. Suppose Ron indicates that some of his requirements are as follows:

1. Given renter name, return her address.
2. Given renter name, return her telephone number.
3. Given a monthly rental figure, return the names of all potential renters willing to pay that rent.
4. List all properties with all associated detail information.

5. List properties that will be unrented as of a specific date, in descending order of monthly rental amount.

You investigate alternatives for optimizing cost and performance tradeoffs for each of these requests. Requests 1 and 2 involve direct, random access to individual rows; perhaps hashed access can be most efficient. Request 3 involves qualification on a range of values (which renters are willing to pay maximum monthly rental amounts equal to or greater than some specified figure?). Perhaps storing RENTER rows in sorted sequence by MAX–MONTHLY–RENT–AMT can accelerate processing of this request. However, you cannot both hash and cluster the RENTER table; thus, what compromises should you consider? How quickly can the DBMS scan the entire table? How quickly can the table be sorted? Which requirement is more important? What are its performance objectives? Its performance constraints?

Request 4 entails joins of PROPERTY with BEACH–PROPERTY and PROPERTY with MOUNTAIN–PROPERTY. Can you speed up access by storing the rows in sequalification on a range of values (which renters are willing to pay maximum monthly rental amounts equal to or greater than some specified figure?). Perquence by primary key? Are the tables small enough to rely on internal DBMS scanning and sorting? Will indexes help?

Request 5 involves scanning the RENTAL–AGREEMENT table. Can you speed up access by physically storing the rows in a particular sequence (with or without an index)? Which sequence? END–DATE? BEGIN–DATE? A concatenation of both dates? In ascending or descending order? Or, is it better to store the rows in sequence by MONTHLY–RENT–AMT?

TUNE BY ADDING INDEXES (CHAPTER 14)

Chapter 14 completes the discussion of access mechanisms by addressing indexes. It examines at length the rules, benefits, and costs associated with one step:

□ Add *indexes*—Step RDD10

Indexes usually are optional access mechanisms that can complement scanning, clustering, or hashing. Indexes can significantly increase the ratio of rows returned to rows searched to satisfy a query by (1) enabling direct access to individual rows, thereby eliminating table scans; (2) reducing the span of rows searched when a scan is required; (3) avoiding a sort of table rows (most useful when a small percentage of rows is required in sorted order); and (4) eliminating table access altogether if required columns are stored as part of the index.

Where might indexes help in the implementation supporting Ron's Real Estate Business? What about request 4? Perhaps indexes on the primary key of PROPERTY and on the foreign (also primary) keys of BEACH–PROPERTY and MOUNTAIN–PROPERTY will facilitate the required join. How about request 5? How quickly can the DBMS scan the RENTAL–AGREEMENT table? How does access time improve if you build an index on BEGIN–DATE? On END–DATE? On both dates? What if you build one index on a concatenation of both dates?

Suppose Ron is unsure of other processing requirements. You might proceed with your tuning by assuming that he will need to join tables, most likely via primary-to-foreign key reference paths. You might consider an index on each foreign key. Where a given foreign key is a component of a primary key (e.g., PROPERTY*STREET–ADDRESS and PROPERTY*TOWN–STATE–ADDRESS in the RENTAL–AGREEMENT table) and that primary key already has an index on it (perhaps to enforce uniqueness), you can investigate whether the primary-key index can also be used to facilitate foreign-key access. Maybe the sequence of columns in the index should be altered. Perhaps a new index—one built solely on the foreign key—is needed.

TUNE BY INTRODUCING CONTROLLED DATA REDUNDANCY (CHAPTER 15)

The next group of tuning techniques (in Chapters 15 and 16) involves altering the relational database structure to accommodate functionality and performance requirements. Changing the database structure raises two important issues. First, you introduce deviations from the stable logical data model. Such deviations frequently add complexity or detract from flexibility. Second, structural database changes, although implemented for tuning purposes, are nevertheless visible to users. For example, assume you duplicate a column in another table to avoid joining the two tables. Users and programmers must know that the column appears in both tables and specifically that a join is no longer necessary. Obviously, such tuning efforts affect command syntax used by users and within programs.

These two issues are significant, and they discourage extensive structural modifications. Chapters 15 and 16 guide you in deciding when modifications are necessary. They also assist you in documenting such design changes and ensuring that data integrity is still adequately addressed (i.e., not unintentionally sacrificed).

Chapter 15 contains one step.

☐   Add *duplicate* data—*Step RDD11*

The chapter addresses uses for various types of duplicate data. For example, you may add columns that are exact copies or derivations of other columns. You may also introduce "repeating" columns that represent multiple occurrences of the same attribute. Further, you may replace unwieldy primary or foreign keys by shorter "contrived" columns. Finally, you may add "extra" columns or rows to facilitate functionality requirements such as the outer join.

Suppose a frequent online query in Ron's Real Estate Business involves retrieving the address of a rental property with the name and telephone number of the current renter. This query requires a join of the RENTER and RENTAL–AGREEMENT tables. One option for eliminating the join, and thereby improving performance of this query, is to duplicate the renter's PHONE–NUMBER in RENTAL–AGREEMENT. Consider, however, the cost associated with the data redundancy. Extra storage is required to store each PHONE–NUMBER once for the associated RENTER plus once for each related RENTAL–AGREEMENT. Additional business rules are required to ensure synchronization of the duplicate data whenever PHONE–NUMBER is updated. Finally, user queries must know when accessing PHONE–NUMBER from RENTAL–AGREEMENT is more efficient than accessing PHONE–NUMBER from RENTER, and vice versa. Thus, you must weigh these costs against the performance benefits for the aforementioned and perhaps other queries.

TUNE BY REDEFINING THE RELATIONAL DATABASE STRUCTURE (CHAPTER 16)

Chapter 16 presents reasons and alternatives for redefining the original tables and columns. It consists of two steps:

☐　Redefine *columns—Step RDD12*
☐　Redefine *tables—Step RDD13*

Long textual columns may be candidates for redefinition into one or more shorter columns. Moreover, foreign keys are sometimes redefined to reference alternate rather than primary keys. Chapter 16 presents pros and cons for such alternatives.

Chapter 16 also discusses motivations and techniques for eliminating, duplicating, segmenting (or splitting), and combining tables. The result is a database design in which the tables no longer correspond in a one-to-one manner to the entities of your logical data model.

For Ron's Real Estate Business, suppose Ron discovers that his most active properties are his beach properties. Thus, 90 percent of the time when he needs information about properties, he joins the PROPERTY table with the BEACH–PROPERTY table. As Ron's business grows and the number of properties increases, he discovers that performance of this join degrades (in spite of having indexes on foreign keys and storing rows in foreign-key sequence!). As a designer, you note that the only reason Ron joins these tables is to determine how far from the beach the properties are. You may decide to combine the PROPERTY table with the BEACH–PROPERTY table to avoid this join. The resulting PROPERTY table has five columns instead of four. The BEACH–PROPERTY table no longer exists.

Chapter 16 discusses some negative implications of this action. Specifically, the PROPERTY table becomes larger (one more column for each row). Second, you have increased the occurrences of nulls, because rows representing mountain properties have no value for the attribute NUMBER–BLKS–OFF–BEACH. Third, the relational database is no longer consistent with the logical data model (five entities, but four tables). Fourth, enforcement of business rules pertaining to property deletions is more complex in that a delete of a beach property requires a delete of only the PROPERTY table, whereas a delete of a mountain property requires deletes of both the PROPERTY and the MOUNTAIN–PROPERTY

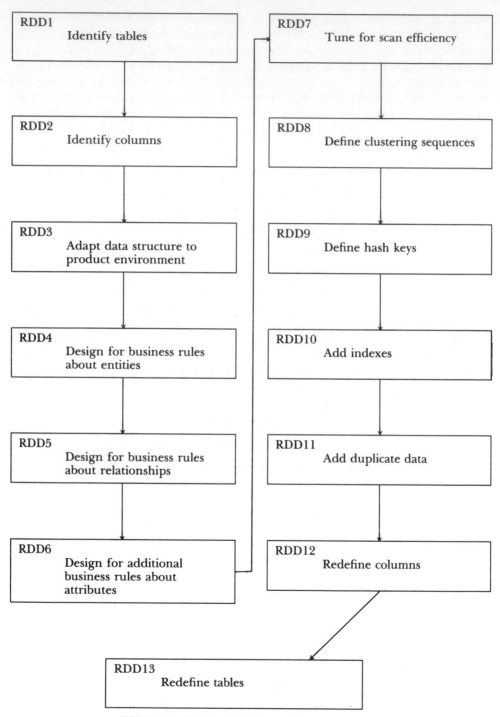

FIGURE 4.3 Relational database design process.

tables. Fifth, users must recode existing commands that reference the BEACH–PROPERTY table so that the commands now refer to the PROPERTY table.

Figure 4.3 depicts all the steps in the relational database design process.

SPECIAL DESIGN CHALLENGES (CHAPTER 17)

Chapter 17 addresses special design considerations that may require additional attention and planning. As such, it is a collection of special-interest topics rather than of design steps. The topics include the following:

☐ *Provide for access through views*—details useful and detrimental use of views.

☐ *Establish security*—examines various ways of providing security within a relational DBMS.

☐ *Cope with very large databases*—outlines special design considerations that apply when developing tables with millions of rows or storing multi-gigabytes (a gigabyte is 10^9 bytes) of data.

☐ *Assess and accommodate change*—addresses planning for potential modifications to your database design.

☐ *Anticipate relational technology evolution*—highlights some of the technology advances you can expect that may influence your database designs.

CRITICAL SUCCESS FACTORS FOR A RELATIONAL DATABASE DESIGN METHODOLOGY

There are many ways to go about designing relational databases. You need not follow exactly the steps in this book. At the very least, you will want to supplement these steps with product-specific techniques for your environment and with other practical tips you learn through experience.

Whether applying, developing, or adapting a relational database design methodology, you will want to ensure that your approach meets the following key criteria, or *critical success factors:*

1. *Provide a step-by-step procedure.* Include guidelines to assist a novice designer. Supplement these steps with organizational standards addressing naming conventions, documentation, and resource utilization. Also provide a list of contacts for education and support.

2. *Evaluate roles and responsibilities carefully.* In some cases, people with minimal (or no) database design experience may develop initial relational database designs. These people will need exposure to concepts, a methodology, and access to more experienced designers. The more experienced designers should critique and tune preliminary designs and choose among proposed design alternatives.

3. *Clearly distinguish between generic and product-specific design techniques.* This allows the methodology to span product environments. It is quite likely that your organization will host a set of relational products. For each generic

design step, you can add guidelines or implementation tips that address product-specific options.

4. *Provide a data dictionary.* The dictionary should capture definitions for the relational database and related objects and especially should provide a cross-reference from the logical data model to relational constructs.

5. *Base the methodology on a logical data model.* Do not assume that designers will automatically build logical data models first. Make a logical data model a prerequisite, if only by using terminology in your relational design steps that demands the application of logical data modeling concepts.

6. *Provide for database design reviews.* Establish checkpoints throughout the design process when designers can or must solicit opinions and insights from other people. Support design review sessions with design documentation produced by the data dictionary or relational DBMS, and with standard forms (preferably computer-based) containing additional relevant design information.

7. *Include both structural and integrity considerations in the relational database implementation.* Enforce business rules as part of an integrated data-driven process rather than by individual applications or users. Define standards for enforcing these rules in a controlled and integrated fashion within your environment.

8. *Use a database diagramming technique to illustrate the relational database design.* Convey similarities between the logical data model and the relational database design by similarities in diagramming constructs. Also convey in the relational diagram use of tuning techniques such as indexes, hashed access, and duplicate data.

These critical success factors are integral to the methodology of Part 3.

BENEFITS AND APPLICABILITY OF A RELATIONAL DATABASE DESIGN METHODOLOGY

A relational database design methodology provides several benefits. First, it *promotes early usability* of a new relational DBMS or related product, especially by encouraging development of prototypes. Second, it *removes fear and doubt* from the minds of first-time designers. Third, it *communicates common and proven approaches* for solving functionality and performance challenges. Fourth, it *promotes consistent documentation and effective communication* of design alternatives and justifications.

Moreover, a relational database design methodology is applicable under many circumstances:

☐ *Developing preliminary or prototype databases.* In this instance, you probably need only to translate the logical data model and choose access approaches. You can omit many technical and product-specific tuning steps.

☐ *Developing production databases.* Here you need all steps of a relational database design methodology, with additional product-specific techniques.

☐ *Assessing maturity of relational DBMS products.* You can evaluate a DBMS by considering how effectively you are able to perform each step of a design methodology using that DBMS for a given set of user requirements. Compare multiple DBMSs by determining for which products you must do the most work (e.g., develop the most customized code). This comparison will indicate which products enable maximum satisfaction of design requirements and with what degree of ease.

☐ *Evaluating applicability of automated design tools.* You can evaluate a design aid by analyzing the degree to which it automates the steps and guidelines of a good relational database design methodology. The methodology should provide an effective benchmark of the product's ability to meet your design needs.

☐ *Establishing a basis for database design reviews.* When a standard step-by-step design process is used, database design reviews are more straightforward because all participants are grounded in common design approaches and goals.

SUMMARY

Relational technology can serve as an important asset within an organization, especially if used to build relational databases that serve a variety of business needs. To be used most effectively, relational technology requires a data-driven design approach.

In this chapter, you learned that data-driven relational database design is composed of two phases. The first, translation of the logical data model, preserves the logical structure and integrity of the data. The second phase, tuning, refines a preliminary relational design to accommodate performance and functionality objectives.

Specifically, this chapter provided an overview of the data-driven relational design methodology detailed in Part 3. The methodology is complete with step-by-step procedures and supporting rules of thumb. Use of these steps and guidelines will increase productivity of relational database designers. Further, it may assist them in avoiding disasters and less severe (albeit more common) errors. The methodology encourages use of consistent and proven approaches for resolving technical issues. It also provides practical techniques for meeting functionality and performance challenges posed to today's (and tomorrow's) relational database products.

P A R T

T W O

Building a Logical Data Model

5 Build Skeletal User Views

The first five steps of logical data modeling focus on building a *skeletal user view*. What is a skeletal user view?

First, a *user view* is a model or representation of data requirements for one user, where "one user" typically implies "one business function." For example, one business function may be production of paychecks for employees who are paid hourly, or generation of customer invoices. You will eventually combine all such user views into one integrated logical data model (as described in Chapter 10).

Second, a *skeletal* user view contains only the most important aspects of data requirements for the business function, without all of the supporting details. That is, a skeletal user view typically does not contain *all* data elements or specifications of valid values for all data elements. At this stage, you are concentrating on identifying and clearly representing the most important characteristics of the user's data requirements, without getting bogged down in detail.

In logical data modeling terminology, a skeletal user view consists of

Entities

Relationships

Primary keys

Alternate keys

Foreign keys

Key business rules

These terms may not be meaningful to you yet, but we will define them as we proceed through this and the next chapter.

The most common use for a skeletal user view is as input into design of a database. Figure 5.1 depicts how the steps for building a skeletal user view (Steps LDM1 through LDM5, presented in Chapters 5 and 6) fit into this book's methodology for relational database design. Skeletal user views may also be used for other purposes, such as designing a prototype or creating a strategic data model.

A *prototype* is a trial, partial implementation of a database or application; for example, an implementation representing one skeletal user view. A prototype

FIGURE 5.1 Relational design methodology steps.

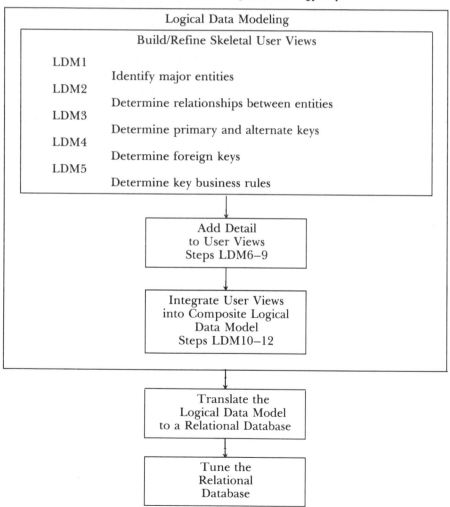

generally is built to enable user interaction with a "live" test system early in the design process. It thus has the primary purpose of solidifying requirements through live experimentation. Subsequently, the prototype can be expanded into a final solution or, alternatively, discarded in favor of building a better system from scratch.

A *strategic data model* is a high-level representation of all of the business's information requirements. Its primary purpose is to assist in understanding all information used by the business, thereby enabling more effective planning of database and application implementation. Because a strategic data model is a high-level overview, skeletal user views provide appropriate input.

Essential to building a skeletal user view is active end-user participation. The data analyst must work with the end user to understand information requirements underlying the user's business function. How is this accomplished? First, the user assembles samples of relevant reports, forms, memoranda, job descriptions, procedural narratives, and existing information systems documentation. Meanwhile, the analyst becomes familiar with existing related systems (if possible, based on the status of existing documentation!) and relevant planning documents such as strategic business, systems, or data plans.

Following this preparatory work, a practical approach is to conduct a series of interactive workshops. Typically, two to five users participate and are responsible for understanding and communicating information requirements in business terms. One, or preferably two, data analysts chair the workshops while asking questions to solicit required information from users. The data analysts lead workshop participants in defining and documenting an accurate, intuitive, clear, and simple (i.e., minimal) data model.

Other possible workshop participants include the application analyst, database designer, and enterprise data administrator. The *application analyst* assumes responsibility for understanding and designing processing flows and user interfaces. For example, the application analyst designs screens, batch reports, and transaction flows. The *database designer* is charged with converting the logical data model (output of the interactive design workshops) to a technically feasible product-specific implementation. The *enterprise data administrator* manages the overall architecture of information requirements for the entire enterprise. The enterprise data administrator usually is the keeper of the strategic data model and the coordinator of interfacing individual logical data models to the strategic model.

Each of these roles may be assigned to various job functions within the business, depending on training, skills, organization, and project complexity. For example, in some organizations and for some projects, the same person may assume both end-user and data-analyst roles. (This presumes that you train end users in the basic steps of logical data modeling). Or one person may assume both data-analyst and application-analyst roles.

The number of participants in an interactive design workshop should never exceed 10 and should preferably be kept to 6 or less. Limit attendees at the workshops to *active* participants only (i.e., no managerial observers). Such guidelines minimize inhibitions and maximize interaction of those involved in the workshop.

Typically, the data analyst is responsible for understanding and directing use of the logical data modeling methodology. At minimum, the data analyst must be comfortable with the steps of the logical data modeling process, a supporting diagramming technique, a complementary data-naming convention, and an associated documentation procedure or tool. The data analyst leads other participants in gaining an understanding of and applying these techniques as appropriate.

The scope of the design workshops (and therefore of the resultant skeletal user view) is dependent on many variables, including the complexity of the business function, the number of users involved, and the skill and experience of the data analyst. A novice data analyst should attempt to deal with a fairly simple requirement (such as the data needed for one ad hoc query) and with only one or two users at a time. A more experienced data analyst may deal with a more complicated business function (such as generation of purchase orders) and with several users. Because you will eventually combine user views into one composite logical data model, scoping of initial user views is primarily a matter of preference and should be commensurate with the skill level of the data analyst.

Logical data modeling is an iterative process. Although it is presented in this book as a procedural activity, be aware that knowledge gained in one step may alter decisions made in a previous step. Likewise, sometimes you will find yourself guessing the outcome of subsequent design steps to get started on an early design step. Thus, use the steps as a framework, but do not be afraid to revisit and challenge the evolving design in light of new insights.

STEP LDM1: IDENTIFY MAJOR ENTITIES

The first step in developing a skeletal user view is to define the major objects in which the user is interested. These major objects are called *entities*. They may be real, tangible items (e.g., students) or more abstract concepts (e.g., a department). For example, a user may envision a marketing database containing information about customers, products, orders, shipments, invoices, and payments. For this user, there are six entities.

Employee, paycheck, branch office, and disease may all be entities, depending on the user's requirements and the user's view of the world. Figure 5.2 lists some possible entities for a manufacturing organization. Be aware that your initial entity list may expand as you proceed through the design steps. Or, you may later reject some initial entity choices.

The task of identifying entities is far more difficult to describe than to do. One way to get started in a logical data modeling workshop is the following:

1. Have the user describe the business activities verbally. As the user speaks, make a list of information items referenced (e.g., employee name, em-

Customer

Product

Part

Manufacturing process

Plant

Order

Shipment

Invoice

Payment

Return

Employee

Supplier

Equipment

Lawsuit

Budget

FIGURE 5.2 List of possible entities in a manufacturing organization.

ployee number, Social Security number, department code, department
name). Use a blackboard or flipchart so that the user can see what you are
writing.

2. Look for major objects (people, places, or concepts) of interest, which you
   can reflect in your list as major groupings of information items. (For instance, you can group employee name, employee number, and Social Security number with the object, or entity, employee). Work with the user in
   identifying an initial list of possible entities.

3. Be prepared to adjust this initial list of entities as you proceed with subsequent logical data modeling steps. At this time, you are merely seeking a
   starting point for design; you will have many opportunities to refine or
   scrap entirely your initial conclusions.

Essential to identifying entities is to group them into *entity sets* or *entity types*
based on similarities in definition and properties. For example, you would
group purchase order #013, purchase order #014, and so on into one entity
set called "purchase order." All members or occurrences of the entity set
"purchase order" have the same generic definition (e.g., a purchase order is a
document that records a request for purchase of goods or services). All purchase order occurrences also have similar properties (for instance, each purchase order occurrence has the same detailed information items: purchase order number, vendor identification, product code, number of units, dollar
amount, and date issued). Of course, you have not really defined all these properties yet. When you do, the definitions will serve as a validation check for your
choice of entity sets.

In this book, the term *entity* refers to an entity set (e.g., purchase order). The term *entity occurrence* refers to one particular member of an entity set (e.g., purchase order #013).

You can divide some entities into *subtypes* having slightly different, more specific definitions and properties. For example, you might divide purchase orders into "canceled purchase orders," "completed purchase orders," and "open purchase orders." Establishing subtype entities allows you to associate shipment information with "completed purchase orders" and cancellation details with "canceled purchase orders."

Formally, entity X is a *subtype* of entity Y, and entity Y is a *supertype* of entity X, if and only if:

1. X (e.g., "completed purchase order") and Y (e.g., "purchase order") represent the same object in the real world (e.g., an actual purchase order)
2. X has all of the properties of Y plus some additional properties of its own (e.g., "completed purchase order" contains all generic "purchase order" information plus shipment information)
3. For every occurrence of X, there also exists exactly one occurrence of Y— although the converse need not be true (e.g., every "completed purchase order" corresponds to one general "purchase order," but each general "purchase order" need not be a "completed purchase order")

The user probably deals with many entities in a business day. Your goal in developing a skeletal user view is to select only those entities of interest to the business function being described by this model. Otherwise, you will spend too much time building your logical data model.

RULE LDM1.1

Name, define, diagram, and document *entities* in the data dictionary (or design documentation).

As you identify entities, assign them names that are meaningful and intuitive to the user. You will refer to entity names frequently during the logical data modeling process so you should use simple and short names (e.g., less than 20 characters). Subtype names should incorporate a reference to the associated supertype. Thus, you might call the purchase order entity ORDER and the subtypes COMPLETED–ORDER, CANCELED–ORDER, and OPEN–ORDER.

(There are more specific rules on naming conventions in Chapter 6, for use when you begin to assign names to other kinds of data objects. Some of the rules in Chapter 6 also may assist in choosing entity names. For now, just follow the general guidelines given here—it is usually simple to name entities. If necessary, you can revise your entity names later.)

You should define entities in terms familiar to the user. In fact, it often is appropriate to give the user responsibility for determining definitions. Be sure definitions are sufficiently complete to distinguish one entity from another.

Record entity names, definitions, and associated descriptive information in a data dictionary. A *data dictionary* is a manual or automated repository of information about applications, databases, and logical data models. Include an identification of the specific user view (by a number or name). Document the expected number of occurrences of the entity. This information will be useful when you integrate user views (Chapter 10) and translate the logical data model to a database design (Part 3).

Naming conventions should be in place and *documented* prior to the beginning of a modeling workshop. These conventions may take into consideration the facilities or constraints of an automated data dictionary tool. They may also reflect the guidelines used for existing systems and data models. Include rules about use of abbreviations (which we will discuss in Chapter 6). Having a well-defined set of naming conventions beforehand saves time in determining existing names and creating new ones.

Now begin your logical data model diagram. A *logical data model diagram* is a pictorial representation of the logical data model that serves to clarify information relationships and enhance communication. Entities are the first items to be placed on your diagram. Show entities (including subtypes and supertypes) as boxes. Write the name of each entity above the top-left corner of the box. Indicate the expected number of occurrences above the top-right corner of the box. Figure 5.3 shows a diagram of some entities for a manufacturing organization.

An automated data dictionary tool will enable faster and easier access to logical data model information. It may even generate the logical data model di-

FIGURE 5.3 Diagram of some entities for a manufacturing organization.

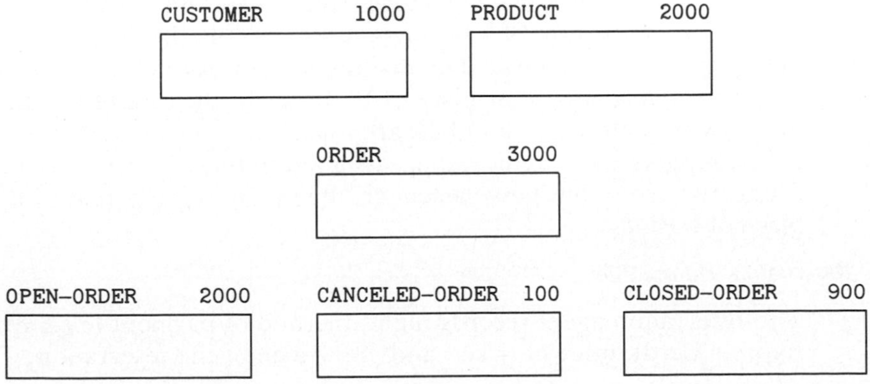

agrams. Its facilities may influence the types of descriptive information that you collect and the nature of the diagrams that you show to the user.

C A S E   S T U D Y

This book contains examples for each step in the design process for several hypothetical business applications. One of these is Moon Launch Enterprise, which markets moon junkets to the business or vacationing traveler in the year 2010. Users want a system to support scheduling and managing Moon Launch space trips. We will expand the details of the enterprise as needed to support our design examples.

Your first data modeling work session for this case study is with the passenger reservations agent of Moon Launch Enterprise. This agent is responsible for placing reservations for business and vacationing passengers. Of course, a given passenger can be a business passenger for some trips and a vacation passenger for others. The details follow. The sentences are numbered for easy reference.

1. *Passenger Information*

   a. Moon Launch assigns all passengers identification numbers within their respective countries (e.g., in the United States, the identification number may be the Social Security number). The numbers used for each country vary in size and may include special characters (e.g., Social Security number contains two hyphens).

   b. There may be a future need to record the passenger's age, in case Moon Launch Enterprise decides to offer special fares by age (e.g., children's fares). For now, fares differ only on the basis of credit-rating discounts.

   c. Each passenger has a last name, first name, middle name (perhaps), and title (e.g., Mr., Mrs., Msr., Señor).

   d. Each passenger has a mailing address for tickets and a mailing address for billing. In the case of a business passenger, the mailing address for billing is place of business. The mailing address for tickets can be either personal residence or place of business. In the case of vacation passengers, both tickets and bills are mailed to personal residence.

   e. All passengers have credit ratings assigned to them by Moon Launch Enterprise. For a business passenger, the credit rating is that of the place of business.

2. *Reservation Information*

   a. The reservation agent records flight, method of payment (e.g., World Express Card), price of ticket, and entry date of the reservation. The agent also records his own Moon Launch employee identification number with the reservations.

b. To calculate ticket prices, the agent checks each passenger's credit rating and applies the following discounts to the base price:

Credit rating	Discount
A	− 20%
B	− 10%
C	0%
D	+ 10%

(Note: Credit Rating D is for undesirable passengers.)

c. All seats are nonsmoking and have no windows.

There is more information in this narrative than is needed for this step. However, never refuse input from a user! It may be useful in subsequent steps.

One interpretation of the primary entities of interest for managing reservations is

```
PASSENGER
BUSINESS-PASSENGER
VACATION-PASSENGER
BUSINESS
RESERVATION
FLIGHT
CREDIT-RATING
```

After interviewing reservation agents and analyzing reservation forms, you can establish definitions for the entities:

PASSENGER	Person in whose name one or more flight reservations are booked.
BUSINESS-PASSENGER	Subtype of PASSENGER. Person traveling on business and therefore associated with a company (BUSINESS).
VACATION-PASSENGER	Subtype of PASSENGER. Person traveling while on vacation. Not affiliated with any company (BUSINESS) for the purpose of this trip.
BUSINESS	Company affiliated with one or more passengers (i.e., with at least one BUSINESS-PASSENGER).
RESERVATION	Planned (booked) passage of a particular PASSENGER on a particular FLIGHT for a particular date.
FLIGHT	Scheduled Moon Launch junket (flight number associated with flight at a given time of day).
CREDIT-RATING	Qualification applied to passengers or businesses to determine amount of discount applied to standard fare.

The entities you (or some other analyst) might have identified could be slightly different. For example, you may have listed COUNTRY, TICKET, and

SEAT as potential entities. Perhaps you would not have included CREDIT–RATING. Later steps in the design process will capture more detail and will tend to drive multiple analysts toward similar (although not necessarily identical) solutions. In fact, as you proceed through the design steps, it becomes important to capture formally as much detail as possible. The more detail, the less room there is for conflicting analyst and user interpretations.

At this point, prompt the users for some approximate volumes. Solicit input from multiple users, because one user may not be knowledgeable about all volumes or may have a limited interpretation of volumes. Lead each user through each entity, asking questions such as: How many flights are scheduled per day? How many go to the moon and how many return? Does this imply *x* flights per week? What about weekends and holidays?

For Moon Launch, our consolidated user input is as follows:

☐ Moon Launch schedules four flights each day: two to the moon and two returning.

☐ One hundred seats are available on each flight. On average, 75 percent are booked. Another 10 percent are booked and canceled. Also, eight crew members attend each flight.

☐ Approximately 50 percent of the passengers on each flight are vacationing and fly Moon Launch an average of 1.05 times per year (round trip, of course). The rest are on business and fly Moon Launch an average of three times per year.

☐ Approximately 3000 passengers book both vacation and business trips within the same year.

☐ Moon Launch deals regularly with about 1000 businesses. From each, an average of six employees per year fly. Another 2000 companies are on file; their employees fly less regularly.

☐ Moon Launch uses four credit ratings: A, B, C, and D.

Document average yearly volumes for each entity in your model as follows:

4 FLIGHTs	4 flight numbers (4 flights/day)
124,100 RESERVATIONs	(75 seats/flight + 10 cancellations/flight) × 1460 flights/year Crew members do not book reservations
26,071 VCTN–PASSENGERs	0.50 × 109,500 uncanceled reservations ÷ 1.05 round trip reservations/year ÷ 2 reservations/ round trip flight
9,125 BSNSS–PASSENGERs	0.50 × 109,500 uncanceled reservations ÷ 3 round trip reservations/year ÷ 2 reservations/ round trip flight
32,196 PASSENGERs	26,071 VCTN–PASSENGERs + 9,125 BSNSS–PASSENGERs − 3000 overlap

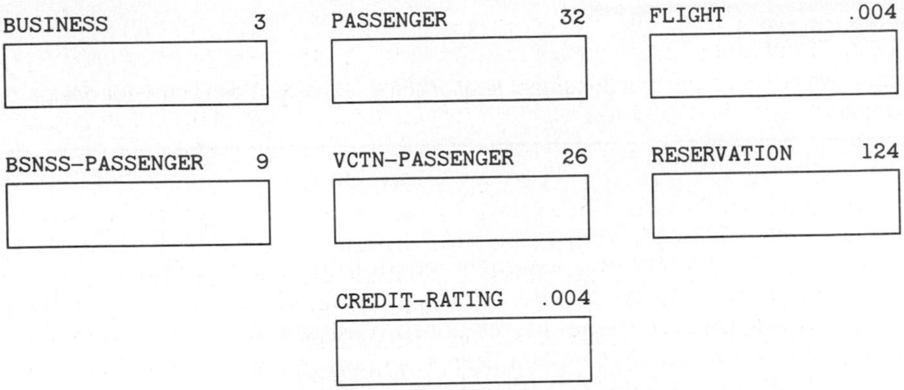

BUSINESS 3	PASSENGER 32	FLIGHT .004

BSNSS–PASSENGER 9	VCTN–PASSENGER 26	RESERVATION 124

CREDIT–RATING .004

Entity Volumes: Annual averages in 000s

FIGURE 5.4 Moon Launch passenger reservations logical data model; Step LDM1.

3000 BUSINESSes   1000 regular + 2000 on file

4 CREDIT–RATINGs   A + B + C + D

A logical data model diagram reflecting the results of Step LDM1 is shown in Fig. 5.4. Note the shortening of some entity names by selective adoption of abbreviations. Not shown is the necessary clarifying data dictionary or design documentation. This should include entity definitions, volumes, and user view references.

STEP LDM2: DETERMINE RELATIONSHIPS BETWEEN ENTITIES

The next step in the logical data modeling process is to identify relationships. A *relationship* is a fact about, or association between, two entities.

Relationships sometimes are difficult to uncover. You need to listen carefully to your users. Typically, a verb or preposition connecting two entities implies a relationship. It may help if you think of relationships as being of three types:

1. *Existence* relationships (for example, employee *has* children)
2. *Functional* relationships (for example, professor *teaches* students)
3. *Event* relationships (for example, customer *places* orders)

It is not necessary to identify or record a type (i.e., existence, functional, or event) for each relationship. The types serve only as an aid for you.

RULE LDM2.1

Name, define, diagram, and document *relationships* in the data dictionary (or design documentation).

As you did for entities, assign to relationships names that are relatively short (preferably less than 20 characters), meaningful, and intuitive to the user. A useful guideline is to name the relationship using a verb in the present tense, as in: purchase order *contains* line items. (Again, more detail on naming conventions is given in Chapter 6. If necessary, you can revise your choice of relationship names later.)

A relationship has a direction and a cardinality ratio. The *direction* indicates which of the two entities involved in the relationship is the "from" entity (referred to as the *parent*) and which is the "to" entity (referred to as the *child*). For example, the relationship *teaches* is from the professor (the parent entity) to the student (the child entity). The relationship *places* is from the customer (parent entity) to the order (child entity). Of course, had you said "An order is placed by a customer" you might initially have considered order to be the parent and customer to be the child. As you study the different kinds of relationships (over the next few pages), you will learn other guidelines for establishing the parent–child direction of a relationship.

The *cardinality ratio* of a relationship defines the expected number of related occurrences for each of the two entity types. For example, a 1 : 2 ratio associated with the purchase order *contains* line items relationship indicates that, for each one purchase order, there are typically two line items. We will consider three types of relationships based on cardinality ratios: one-to-one (1 : 1), one-to-many (1 : N), and many-to-many (M : N)(Fig. 5.5).

A *one-to-one* or *1 : 1 relationship* associates each entity occurrence with, at most, one occurrence of the related entity type. For example,

A school *is managed by* (at most) one dean (a school may be managed by zero or one dean)

A dean *manages* (at most) one school (a dean may manage zero or one school)

The direction of a 1 : 1 relationship is (for now) arbitrary. You may choose either entity as the parent and treat the other as the child.

A *one-to-many* or *1 : N relationship* associates each occurrence of the parent entity with zero, one, or many occurrences of the child entity. Conversely, each occurrence of the child entity is associated with exactly one occurrence of the parent entity. For example,

One-to-One (1 : 1)

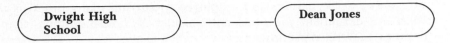

One-to-Many (1 : N)

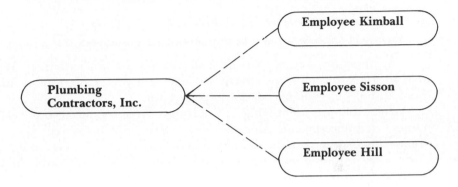

Many-to-Many (M : N)

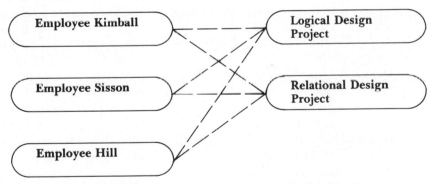

FIGURE 5.5 Types of relationships based on relationship cardinality ratios.

A business *employs* many employees (a business may employ zero, one or many employees). (Note: We may want to require that a business employ at least one employee or else fold. We shall say more about such rules in Chapter 6.)

An employee *is employed by* exactly one business (assuming the user says so!)

The direction of a $1:N$ relationship is from the entity occurring once to the entity occurring potentially many times. Thus, in our example, business (occurring once) is the parent, and employee (occurring many times) is the child. With this definition, you need not consider $N:1$ relationships (simply invert them to $1:N$ relationships).

A *many-to-many* or *$M:N$ relationship* associates each occurrence of the parent entity with zero, one, or many child occurrences, and conversely each child occurrence with zero, one, or many parent occurrences. For example,

An employee *is assigned to* potentially many projects

A project *has assigned to it* potentially many employees

The direction of an $M:N$ relationship also is (for now) arbitrary. We will return to $M:N$ relationships shortly to suggest a preferable way of addressing them and of determining relationship direction.

While you are identifying relationships, you should record relationship names, definitions, and associated descriptive information in the data dictionary. As always, state the definition in business terms familiar to the user. Include other information, such as identification of the parent and child entities (thereby the direction of the relationship).

In addition, document the typical cardinality ratio of the relationship, describing the ratio of parent to child entity occurrences. This information will be useful later when you combine user views into one composite logical data model and when you subsequently transform the logical data model into a database design. Note that cardinality ratios should be consistent with the expected numbers of entity occurrences, determined in Step LDM1. Thus, this step provides an opportunity to validate your initial results for Step LDM1.

In your logical data model diagram, indicate a relationship between entities by drawing a line between the boxes for the parent and child entities. Write the name and cardinality ratio of the relationship in parentheses near the line. Place an arrowhead pointing in the direction of the relationship at the end of the line, touching and pointing to the child entity. Add a second arrowhead for a $1:N$ relationship to denote multiple cardinality of the child.

For example,

Here, DEAN is parent and SCHOOL is child. The single arrowhead connotes direction only.

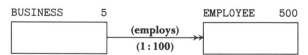

In this $1:N$ relationship, BUSINESS is the parent entity and EMPLOYEE is the child. The double arrowhead pointing to EMPLOYEE indicates both that the relationship is in the direction of BUSINESS *to* EMPLOYEE and that EMPLOYEE may occur multiple times.

We have deliberately omitted discussion of diagramming $M:N$ relationships. Representation of $M:N$ relationships becomes extremely complex as you proceed in the logical data modeling process. Transformation of an $M:N$ relationship into a database design also can be complex, given that many database systems today do not directly support $M:N$ relationships. Accordingly, simplify your task at this point by translating each $M:N$ relationship into a new entity type and two $1:N$ relationships.

For example, transform the $M:N$ relationship

Employee *is assigned to* many projects

Project *has assigned to it* many employees

to a new entity called ASSIGNMENT. Relate this new entity ASSIGNMENT to each of the former entities EMPLOYEE and PROJECT through two $1:N$ relationships:

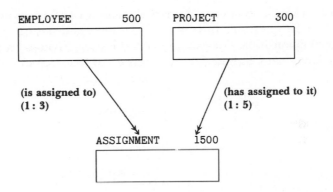

Give each of the $1:N$ relationships its own name, its own cardinality ratio, and its own double arrowhead designating direction and its $1:N$ nature. You may discover that the new relationships are harder to name and seem less intuitive to the user (e.g., employee *is assigned to* assignment). Rest assured that the increased design simplicity will be well worth the apparent confusion in data names.

Notice that you have not lost any information in this transformation. In fact, you have made it easier to represent each piece of information on the diagram. In addition, this representation will be easier to transform to a database design.

RULE LDM2.2

Classify relationships as being either *one-to-one (1 : 1)* or *one-to-many (1 : N)*. For simplicity, reduce each *many-to-many (M : N)* relationship to a new entity type and two 1 : N relationships.

Identifying relationships, as contrasted with identifying entities, frequently requires more skill and more probing on the part of the data analyst. The list of data objects generated by the user at the beginning of an interactive workshop is not likely to include an exhaustive list of relationships. You, as the data analyst, can try this technique:

1. Look for verbs or verb derivatives in the list of objects. (Frequently, the user mentions these verbs, but the data analyst at first is not sharp enough to record them. Be attentive!)
2. Add to the initial (possibly sketchy) list of relationships by asking the user questions regarding possible additional associations between identified entity types.
3. Using a flipchart or blackboard, draw the entities and relationships *while* asking the user questions to verify the existence and nature (1 : 1, 1 : N, M : N) of relationships. For example, tell the user, "You say a purchase order may have many line items? I will represent that like so:"

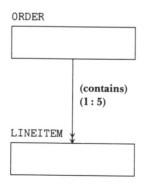

"Now let me just explain and verify what I have drawn. A purchase order may have many line items, right? (About five, did you say?) This double-headed arrow pointing to line item indicates just that. My understanding is that a given line item is associated with exactly one purchase order—is that correct? That is what this diagram says."

4. As you encounter *M : N* relationships, immediately break each one down into a new entity type and two 1 : N relationships. For example, if the user

initially indicates that a purchase order is for multiple products, but a product may appear on multiple purchase orders, then you have an $M:N$ relationship. Define a new entity type (such as line item) and relate it to both purchase order and product through $1:N$ relationships:

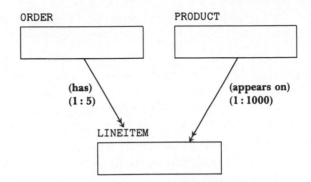

The small extra time it takes to do this now *with* the user will reduce complexity and confusion later in the design process.

5. Add entity occurrence numbers and relationship cardinality ratios as you go. Gaining even an approximate understanding of volumes now will help you and the user to understand the boxes and arrows in the diagram.

6. Verbally discuss definitions for each entity and relationship. If possible, assign someone to take notes. Have the user review and refine these definitions after the meeting.

In determining data volumes (i.e., entity occurrence numbers and relationship cardinality ratios), you must make some explicit assumptions regarding the meaning of the numbers. For example, entity occurrence numbers may designate expected volumes of entity occurrences on initial startup of the system, average volumes after some initial period, peak volumes for a system with high update activity, or maximum possible volumes over the life of the system. Similarly, relationship cardinality ratios may designate startup, average, minimum, maximum, or peak ratios.

The assumptions you choose will depend on the nature of the system and possibly on limitations of products being used in implementation. For example, if you expect data volumes to be large, you may be concerned about maximums due to capacity limitations. Or, in the case of a high-activity online system, you may concern yourself more with peak volumes. Where performance or capacity are likely to be important, you may wish to obtain average and maximum volumes. Document these assumptions and modify your diagramming conventions accordingly.

The following diagram is a suggested expanded technique for documenting more specific entity volumes and minimum/mean/maximum relationship cardinality ratios:

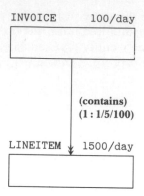

Here, the user receives an average of 100 invoices each day, including a minimum of 1, mean of 5, and maximum of 100 line items per invoice, for an average total of 1500 line items per day.

SPECIAL TYPES OF RELATIONSHIPS

Several commonly encountered types of relationships deserve special mention:

- ☐ Complex (relationships among three or more entities)
- ☐ Potentially redundant
- ☐ Categories (subtype–supertype relationships)
- ☐ Bill-of-materials (recursive or self-relationships)

We will deal first with simplifying complex relationships. Until now we have addressed only *binary relationships*, or associations between exactly two entity occurrences. A *complex relationship* is an association among three or more entity occurrences requiring all three (or more) entity occurrences to be present for the relationship to exist. An example of a complex relationship is the sale of a car by a salesperson to a customer. Think of this sale as an association among car, salesperson, and customer, requiring occurrences of all three entity types for the relationship to exist:

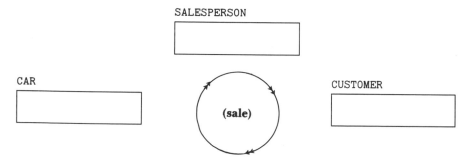

Obviously, drawing this complex relationship is not easy, and the result is probably not exceptionally enlightening! Worse, as you proceed with your design, this type of relationship becomes difficult to evaluate and refine and probably impossible (in most database systems) to transform directly to a database design.

RULE LDM2.3

For simplicity, reclassify a *complex relationship* as an entity, related through binary relationships to each of the original entities.

For example, you can simplify the car-sale *complex relationship* by establishing instead a new entity called SALE. Relate SALE to each of the original entities via binary relationships.

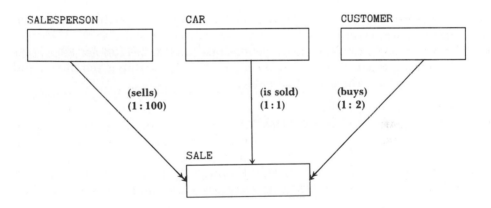

Next, let's consider the possibility of redundant relationships in our logical data model. A *redundant relationship* is a relationship from one entity to a second entity, where the relationship is equivalent in meaning to another chain of one or more relationships beginning at the first entity, perhaps continuing through some intermediate entity, and terminating at the second entity. You should eliminate redundant relationships to keep the logical data model clear and simple.

Consider the following example:

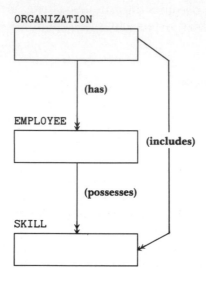

Is the relationship ORGANIZATION *includes* SKILLs redundant? If the skills that you would obtain using this relationship are exactly the same as the skills you would obtain using the other two relationships (ORGANIZATION *has* EMPLOYEEs and EMPLOYEE *possesses* SKILLs), then the former relationship is redundant and should be removed. The simplified model is

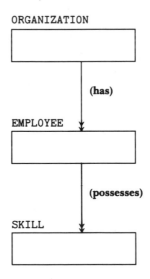

RULE LDM2.4

Eliminate *redundant relationships* from the logical data model.

___

There are three reasons for eliminating redundant relationships from your logical data model. First, redundant relationships are unnecessary and therefore add useless complexity to the model. Second, they may mislead an analyst into interpreting them as nonredundant (i.e., as multiple relationships having different meanings). Third, inclusion of redundant relationships may lead to incorrect placement of information items in the logical data model. For instance, when you add keys for each relationship in Step LDM4, existence of a redundant relationship may result in one too many such keys.

To identify potentially redundant relationships, look for entities that participate as children in both a relationship and a relationship chain originating from the same entity. Then ask whether the relationship is redundant with the relationship chain or whether the two represent potentially different associations in the real world.

Note that it is perfectly plausible to have multiple, nonredundant relationships (with different meanings) between the same two entity types. For example,

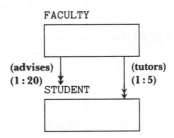

This diagram tells you that a FACULTY member may *tutor* many (average of 5) STUDENTs. Likewise a FACULTY member may *advise* many (average of 20) STUDENTs. Moreover, the relationships are *not* redundant (as you can see from the cardinality ratios). Even more important, a FACULTY member need not (yet may) serve as advisor to the same students she tutors, and vice versa.

A third special type of relationship deals with supertypes and subtypes and the grouping of subtypes into categories.

RULE LDM2.5

Establish 1 : 1 relationships between *supertypes* and *subtypes*. Establish a special type of 1 : 1 relationship, known as a *category*, between a supertype and a set of mutually exclusive subtypes.

A *subtype* is a subset of another entity (*supertype*) where occurrences of both designate the same object in the real world, but the subtype has additional, more specific properties. Let us examine an example of subtypes associated with a supertype. Consider the entity (supertype) EMPLOYEE with three subtypes: executives, monthly paid management, and hourly paid staff. Each subtype occurrence and its associated supertype (e.g., the executive William T. Partel and the employee William T. Partel) represent exactly the same object in the real world. Thus, there is a 1 : 1 relationship between the subtype and the supertype. Moreover, if the subtype exists at all, then the supertype must exist (i.e., if William T. Partel exists as an executive, then he must also exist as an employee). We diagram the 1 : 1 relationships between supertypes and subtypes as shown in Fig. 5.6.

The name of the 1 : 1 relationship between supertype and subtype can be the piece of information that determines membership in the particular subtype. In the example, *status* of EMPLOYEE determines whether the employee is an executive, a monthly paid manager, or an hourly paid staff member.

Frequently, you can group subtypes into sets of mutually exclusive subtypes known as *categories*. In our example, if an employee cannot simultaneously be both an executive and a monthly paid manager (or any other combination of two subtypes), then the subtypes make up a category based on employee status. Now, not only is there a 1 : 1 relationship between EMPLOYEE and each of the

FIGURE 5.6 Supertype–subtype relationships.

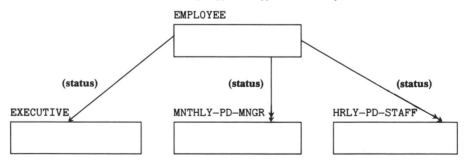

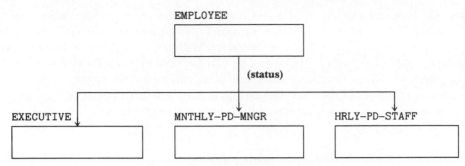

FIGURE 5.7 Supertype–category relationship.

three subtypes EXECUTIVE, MNTHLY–PD–MNGR, and HRLY–PD–STAFF, but also there is a 1 : 1 relationship between EMPLOYEE and the entire category based on status. In other words, a given EMPLOYEE occurrence relates to only one instance of the combination (category) of EXECUTIVE, MNTHLY–PD–MNGR, and HRLY–PD–STAFF. You can diagram this more restrictive 1 : 1 relationship as shown in Fig. 5.7.

Note that Figures 5.6 and 5.7 represent slightly different information. Figure 5.6 shows 1 : 1 relationships between EMPLOYEE and *each* of EXECUTIVE, MNTHLY–PD–MNGR and HRLY–PD–STAFF, permitting, for example, the employee William T. Partel to be simultaneously an executive, a monthly paid manager, and an hourly paid staff member. Figure 5.7 shows a 1 : 1 relationship between EMPLOYEE and the *entire category* based on status, meaning that William T. Partel may be either an executive or a monthly paid manager or an hourly paid staff member, but he cannot be more than one of these simultaneously.

You can relate a given supertype to multiple categories that are independent of one another as shown in Figure 5.8. Here, there are two 1 : 1 relation-

FIGURE 5.8 Supertype–multiple categories relationships.

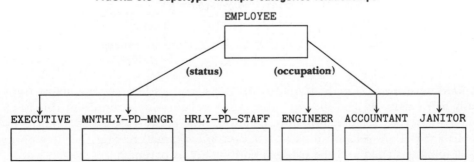

ships: (1) between EMPLOYEE and the category based on employee status, and (2) between EMPLOYEE and the category based on employee occupation. According to the model in Figure 5.8, the employee William T. Partel may be both an executive and an engineer. However, he can be neither both an engineer and an accountant, nor both an executive and a monthly paid manager.

One final special type of relationship is a bill-of-materials relationship. A *bill-of-materials relationship* is an association between occurrences of the same entity type. For example,

$(1:N)$ An employee *manages* many employees
         An employee *is managed by* one employee

$(M:N)$ A part *is composed of* many parts
         A part *comprises* many parts

The bill-of-materials relationship gets its name from bill-of-materials data structures in manufacturing applications (i.e., the breakdown of manufacturing assemblies into parts, parts into subparts, and so on). The recursive nature of bill-of-materials relationships requires some special considerations, if such relationships are to be accommodated in both logical data modeling and subsequent database design.

Consider a $1:N$ example:

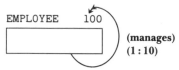

EMPLOYEE   100

(manages)
(1 : 10)

Represent this bill-of-materials relationship as a $1:N$ relationship from and to the same entity. Thus, an EMPLOYEE *manages* many other EMPLOYEEs. An EMPLOYEE *is managed by* one EMPLOYEE. A given EMPLOYEE *manages* an expected 10 EMPLOYEEs.

Now consider an $M:N$ example. An intuitive diagram representing an $M:N$ bill-of-materials diagram is as follows:

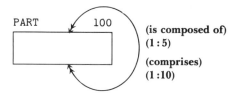

PART   100

(is composed of)
(1 : 5)

(comprises)
(1 : 10)

A PART *is composed of* many (typically 5) PARTs, and a PART *comprises* many (typically 10) PARTs. As you did for other $M:N$ relationships, represent this $M:N$ bill-of-materials relationship by creating a new entity called COMPONENT. Establish two $1:N$ relationships (*is composed of, comprises*) having the new entity COMPONENT as child and the original entity PART as parent.

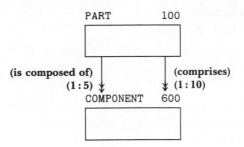

RULE LDM2.6

Represent a *1 : N bill-of-materials relationship* as a 1 : *N* relationship from and to the same entity. Represent an *M : N bill-of-materials relationship* by creating a second entity type and relating it to the original (now parent) entity type through two 1 : *N* relationships.

Notice the similarity to the representation of other *M : N* relationships (refer to Rule LDM2.2). You are representing an *M : N* bill-of-materials relationship in exactly the same way: by transforming it to a new entity type and two 1 : *N* relationships having the original entity types as parents. It just so happens that the original (now parent) entity types are the same (in this example, PART).

The new entity COMPONENT represents occurrences of the relationship between PART (as "comprisor") and PART (as "comprisee"). The volume associated with COMPONENT, therefore, is the total number of associations that exist between any two PARTs.

Relationships are among the hardest concepts to grasp in logical data modeling. Relationships may seem an obvious concept in the real world (obviously, data objects relate to one another—that is what information is all about). Nonetheless, clearly understanding, communicating, and representing each aspect of a relationship is a nontrivial undertaking.

The ability to identify relationships is indispensable for a competent data analyst. We build databases to record information and to represent relationships among information. Thus, the database cannot effectively model and support the business unless you first understand and accurately capture the information relationships in the logical data model. It is for this reason that we stress such precision in diagramming relationships in the model. You will see that *identifying and understanding the entities and relationships in the model is the most important part of the entire design process!*

CASE STUDY

You can now add relationships to the logical data model for the Moon Launch passenger reservations user view, as shown in Fig. 5.9. Note the following points:

1. BSNSS–PASSENGER and VCTN–PASSENGER are *subtypes* of PASSENGER. Each relates to PASSENGER through a 1:1 relationship. They do not together constitute a category because the same PASSENGER can be both a BSNSS–PASSENGER and a VCTN–PASSENGER.
2. Each BSNSS–PASSENGER is employed by exactly one BUSINESS. The businesses that deal most frequently with Moon Launch (1000 companies according to our user) book an average of six employees per year (or 6000 BSNSS–PASSENGERs) on flights. The other 3000 BSNSS–PASSENGERs come from the 2000 other companies on file. (Of course, we will document this

FIGURE 5.9 Moon Launch passenger reservations logical data model; Step LDM2.

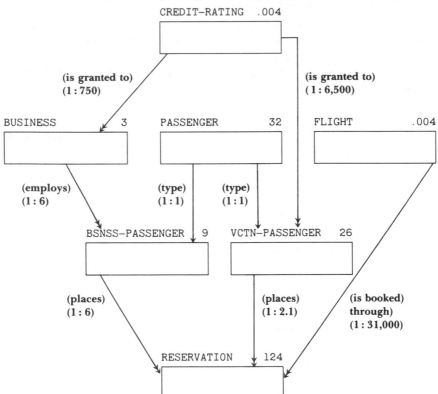

Entity Volumes: Annual averages in 000s

explanation of the ratio for the BUSINESS *employs* BSNSS–PASSENGER relationship in our data dictionary.)

3. Moon Launch applies CREDIT–RATINGs to BUSINESSes and to VCTN–PASSENGERs. They distribute the four credit ratings (A, B, C, and D) fairly evenly.

4. Each RESERVATION is for one FLIGHT and one BSNSS–PASSENGER or one VCTN–PASSENGER. Of course, each PASSENGER and each FLIGHT have many RESERVATIONs.

5. You may not have identified the entity RESERVATION initially. If not, you may have tried to define $M:N$ relationships between BSNSS–PASSENGER and FLIGHT and between VCTN–PASSENGER and FLIGHT. You then would have resolved the $M:N$ relationships by creating the entity RESERVATION.

6. RESERVATION relates to BSNSS–PASSENGER and to VCTN–PASSENGER, rather than to PASSENGER. If RESERVATION related only to PASSENGER, it would be unclear whether a particular RESERVATION was for business or vacation (e.g., whether we should apply a business or individual credit rating).

7. BSNSS–PASSENGERs fly Moon Launch an average of 3 round trip flights (and thus, place 6 reservations) per year. VCTN–PASSENGERs fly an average of 1.05 times per year (and thus, place 2.1 reservations per year).

8. An average of 85 reservations (75 seats + 10 cancellations) are booked for each flight, 365 days per year, or 31,000 total reservations are made per flight each year.

SUMMARY

We have introduced a number of new concepts in this chapter. We review them here.

A *user view* is a model or representation of data requirements for one business function. You eventually will combine user views into one integrated logical data model to provide the basis for database design. You start by defining *skeletal user views*, which contain only the most important data requirements. Specifically, skeletal user views include entities, relationships, primary and alternate keys, foreign keys, and key business rules. In this chapter, you identified entities and relationships.

An *entity* is a person, place, thing, or concept about which you will record information. You may divide entities into *subtypes* that have more specific definitions and additional properties. You can define several subtypes for one *supertype*. As the first step of logical data modeling, you identify, name, define, and diagram entities (including subtypes and supertypes) of interest to the business function being modeled.

A *relationship* is a fact about or association between two entities. As the second step of logical data modeling, you identify, name, define, and diagram relationships between entities.

You classify relationships as *one-to-one (1 : 1)* or *one-to-many (1 : N)*. For simplicity, you reduce each *many-to-many (M : N)* relationship to a new entity type and two 1 : *N* relationships.

All relationships in the model are *noncomplex* (i.e., associate exactly two entity occurrences) and are *nonredundant*. *Categories* (sets of mutually exclusive subtypes) and *bill-of-materials relationships* (associations between two occurrences of the same entity type) may be present. You treat *M : N* bill-of-materials relationships like other *M : N* relationships; you reduce them to a new entity type and two 1 : *N* relationships.

The concepts of entities and relationships are fundamental to the processes of logical data modeling and of database design. They represent critical elements in understanding the user's data requirements.

EXERCISES

5.1 List at least four advantages gained by developing a logical data model before attempting to design a database.

5.2 How does a skeletal user view differ from a full user view? From an integrated user view?

5.3 What are the primary responsibilities of a data analyst with respect to building a logical data model?

5.4 For the Moon Launch case study, how would you alter the logical data model diagram if a passenger were always either associated with a business or considered to be vacationing (but never both)?

5.5 For the Moon Launch case study, how would you alter the logical data model diagram to show a TICKET entity, where a TICKET may or may not be issued for a reservation?

5.6 The passenger reservations agents represent only one user group for Moon Launch Enterprise. Another user group is the baggage tracking and control department. When passengers check their luggage, a baggage clerk records the passenger identification (country name and passenger code), flight number, destination, date of departure, and unique baggage number (generated by the system). Should a piece of luggage be temporarily misplaced, another clerk fills out a "lost-luggage report," which contains the following information: flight number, date of departure, passenger identification, passenger name, passenger address, passenger telephone number, baggage number, description of bag, itemized list of contents of bag (numbered sequentially), and value of bag including contents. Perform Steps LDM1 and LDM2 for baggage tracking and control.

5.7 A third user group in Moon Launch Enterprise is the space shuttle maintenance control group. A space shuttle controller assigns specific space shuttles to flights. Each space shuttle has a serial number, a model number, an age, and a date of last inspection. Each space shuttle also is assigned a captain. Captains are not permitted to head more than one space shuttle at a time. A given space shuttle can be assigned to many flights and a given flight can be assigned to many space shuttles (one per date). A flight is identified by a flight number and associated with a departure place and time and a destination place and time. As Moon Launch adds new types of space shuttles to the fleet, the controller records the model number, seat capacity, and fuel capacity. Perform Steps LDM1 and LDM2 for the space shuttle maintenance control business function.

6 Add Keys to User Views

The third step in building the logical data model is to begin adding detail information items, or attributes. An *attribute* is an atomic unit of data about an entity. It is a fact or nondecomposable piece of information describing an entity. You cannot further decompose an attribute (e.g., purchase order number) into smaller constituents (e.g., individual digits) without losing the meaning of the attribute. Attributes, therefore, are the most detailed units of information about the entity that a user will want to reference.

For example, employee number, employee name, and employee address may each be attributes of the entity employee, depending on the user's view of data requirements. In another user view including the employee entity, you might define different attributes, such as department number, employee number, last name, first name, middle initial, street address, city, state, and zip code. These differences will be resolved when you integrate user views (Chapter 10).

STEP LDM3: DETERMINE PRIMARY AND ALTERNATE KEYS

The first attributes that you add to the logical data model are primary and alternate keys. They serve to distinguish more clearly the meanings of the entities.

A *candidate key* is an attribute or minimal set of attributes that uniquely identifies a specific occurrence of an entity. A "minimal" set of attributes implies that you cannot discard any attribute in the set without destroying the

115

uniqueness property. If a candidate key consists of more than one attribute, it is known as a *composite key*.

For example, the attribute employee number may uniquely identify a particular employee; if so, it is a candidate key for the entity employee. Social Security number may be another candidate key for employee. In some environments, employee name also may be a candidate key; in other environments, employee name is not a candidate key because multiple employees may have the same name. Perhaps employee name combined with date of birth constitute a (composite) candidate key—but only if neither employee name nor date of birth by itself is sufficient to identify an employee uniquely.

You must choose one of the candidate keys to serve as a primary key. A *primary key* is an attribute or minimal set of attributes that not only uniquely identifies a specific occurrence of the entity (i.e., is a candidate key), but also exists for every occurrence of an entity.

For example, you may choose employee number as the primary key of employee, if it is true that every employee has an employee number. Alternatively, in an environment where employee numbers are not assigned until after date of hire, you might more appropriately choose Social Security number as the primary key, if it is true that every employee has a Social Security number. Of course, the situation may be such that each of several candidate keys exists for every occurrence of an entity. This would be true if every employee had both an employee number and a Social Security number. In this case, you still must choose one of these to be a primary key for the entity.

RULE LDM3.1

Choose one *primary key* for each entity.

Candidate keys that you do not choose to be the primary key are called *alternate keys*.

RULE LDM3.2

Identify *alternate keys* for each entity.

Identification of primary and alternate keys is important for three reasons. First, that they are unique for each occurrence of an entity is a business rule about the entity. Second, that at least the primary key and perhaps some alternate keys are always present for each occurrence of an entity is another business rule. Moreover, the existence of a primary key guarantees that you have a way of referencing any given occurrence of an entity. Third, the user frequently references primary and alternate keys in the real world when asking questions or relating information. Thus, primary and alternate keys may later provide effective mechanisms for implementing efficient access paths in the database design.

It is possible for two or more composite candidate keys to overlap. Consider a line item entity. Two candidate keys might be order number plus line item number and order number plus part number (if a given order has only one line item per specific part number).

For *subtypes,* identification of the primary key is easy: The primary key is the same as the primary key of the associated supertype. (Recall that the subtype and supertype designate exactly the same object in the real world.)

RULE LDM3.3

Choose the primary key of an entity that is a *subtype* of another entity (known as a *supertype*) to be the same as the primary key of the supertype.

RULE LDM3.4

Name, diagram, and document primary and alternate keys in the *data dictionary* (or design documentation).

Document primary and alternate keys in the data dictionary by including the attribute name, business description, and associated entity. Sometimes, you may wish to assign a number as well as a name to each attribute, perhaps to accommodate restrictions imposed by an automated data modeling tool.

You should follow a naming convention in naming primary and alternate keys (and, of course, all other attributes). This naming convention should enable development of meaningful names and assist in identification of redundant or vaguely specified attributes. It may need to conform to constraints for an automated data dictionary or data modeling tool.

RULE LDM3.5

Establish *naming standards* that facilitate assignment of clear, descriptive, intuitive, and unique names to attributes (and to entities and relationships).

Naming standards should facilitate *clarity* (i.e., they should produce unique and descriptive names) and *usability* (i.e., they should be intuitive to the user or designer). Avoid assigning the same name to two objects with different meanings.

Synonyms (different names used to refer to the same object) also are undesirable during logical data design. Recall that the objective of logical data modeling is to achieve full understanding of the business meaning of the data. Assigning multiple names to the same object adds confusion.

Brevity (without sacrificing clarity) and *consistency* in data names also are important.

RULE LDM3.6

For brevity and simplicity, use *standard abbreviations* in data names. Be consistent: Always or never abbreviate a given word.

Develop a standard list of abbreviations for use across your organization. If an acceptable abbreviation for a word exists within or outside of your organization, use it. In the absence of accepted abbreviations, establish guidelines for forming abbreviations, such as (1) retaining only the first *n* letters of the word being abbreviated, or (2) retaining only consonants (i.e., removing all vowels). Once you establish a standard abbreviation for a word, always use it. That is, do not intermix use of the full word with even its standard abbreviation. And, of course, document standard abbreviations and general rules on forming them in the data dictionary to encourage adherence.

Take care to develop naming standards that *work for your organization*. Both designers and users should feel comfortable with the standards. In particular, customize your lists of abbreviations to the types of data you will be naming.

A suggested convention for attributes is:

EntityName.Modifier(s)-Classword

$\uparrow$ $\uparrow$

period   dash

Example: `EMPLOYEE.LAST-NAME`

The entity name serves as a prefix. Frequently, when it is clear to which en-tity an attribute belongs (as, for example, on a logical data model diagram), you may not explicitly show the "EntityName." component of the attribute name.

The *class word* indicates the general purpose of the attribute and should be chosen from a previously specified (and well-documented) collection of class words. Ideally, an organization should adopt a standard set of class words that are relevant to the data within its business. Some class words may be industry-wide. Further, some class words may be specific to a given project. Commonly used class words include `AMOUNT`, `UNIT`, `CODE`, `DATE`, `HOUR`, `PERCENT`, `CON-STANT`, `COUNT`, `NAME`, `NUMBER`, `TEXT`, `ADDRESS`, and `TIME`. Class words should be defined clearly so that the analyst knows when to use each of them. (Our definitions appear throughout the case study).

You also can include one or more modifying words in the attribute name as needed to establish a meaningful and unique name. Examples of primary keys and their respective names are in Figure 6.1.

Sometimes, the same attribute is part of the primary keys for both parent and child entities of a relationship. For example, consider the following rela-tionship:

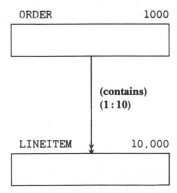

Purchase orders *contain* line items. The primary key of purchase order (`ORDER`) is the purchase order year and purchase order number (`ORDER.YEAR-DATE`, `ORDER.NUMBER`). The primary key of a purchase order line item (`LINEITEM`) is line item number within purchase order, and thus is the combination of pur-chase order year, purchase order number, and line item number.

Entity	Entity Name	Primary Key
Customer	CUSTOMER	CUSTOMER.NUMBER
Vendor	VENDOR	VENDOR.NUMBER
Purchase order	ORDER	ORDER.YEAR—DATE plus ORDER.NUMBER
Product	PRODUCT	PRODUCT.CODE
Customer call	CUSTCALL	CUSTCALL.DATE plus CUSTCALL.TIME
Salesperson	SALESREP	SALESREP.LAST—NAME

FIGURE 6.1 Examples of primary keys.

You will see that it is important to remember the originating entity for an attribute. Thus, when an attribute originates in another entity (a parent), you will add that originating entity's name to the prefix of the attribute name, followed by an asterisk (*). For example, you can name the composite primary key of LINEITEM as follows:

```
LINEITEM.ORDER*YEAR—DATE
LINEITEM.ORDER*NUMBER
LINEITEM.NUMBER
```

Here, the asterisk indicates that two of the attributes originate in another entity (i.e., appear in a parent entity). The name immediately before the asterisk (e.g., ORDER) indicates in which entity the attribute originates.

In the logical data model diagram, write the names of the primary key attributes inside the entity box and above a horizontal line. Write alternate key attribute names inside the box and below the line. Add the designation (AKn) after each attribute constituting the nth alternate key within an entity. The assignment of n to AKn is not important other than to associate multiple attributes of one alternate key. Thus, it does not matter which alternate key is AK1, which is AK2, and so on. In fact, if a given attribute is part of multiple, overlapping alternate keys, it will have multiple (AKn) designations.

For example,

```
EMPLOYEE                1000
NUMBER
SOC—SEC—NUMBER   (AK1)
NAME        (AK2) (AK3)
BIRTH—DATE       (AK2)
HIRE—DATE        (AK3)
```

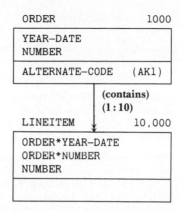

Notice that the "EntityName." prefix has been eliminated, since it is obvious from the diagram. For example, in the LINEITEM box, you see only NUMBER instead of LINEITEM.NUMBER, and ORDER*NUMBER instead of LINEITEM.ORDER* NUMBER. Also, in the EMPLOYEE entity, there are three alternate keys. SOC–SEC– NUMBER, NAME plus BIRTH–DATE, and NAME plus HIRE–DATE. This implies, of course, that you cannot employ two people with the same name who are born on the same day or are hired on the same day.

C A S E   S T U D Y

Review the Moon Launch case study from Chapter 5. Primary keys are chosen as follows:

PASSENGER

Because Moon Launch assigns all passengers identification numbers by their respective country, you can identify a given passenger by knowing both country and identification number. The country is identified by an attribute called PASSENGER.COUNTRY–NAME. (COUNTRY is a modifier. NAME is a class word.) The passenger identification number is PASSENGER.CODE. We use CODE instead of NUMBER because we have no guarantee that identification number is numeric. (CODE is a class word we use to indicate a set of numeric, alphabetic, or special symbols associated with a meaning.)

BSNSS–PASSENGER

This is a subtype of PASSENGER. The primary key is the same as for PASSENGER, prefixed by PASSENGER* to indicate the originating entity. Thus, you have PASSENGER*COUNTRY–NAME plus PASSENGER*CODE. (Or, using the full form for attribute names, BSNSS–PASSENGER.PASSENGER*COUNTRY–NAME plus BSNSS–PASSENGER.PASSENGER*CODE. The names are getting a bit unwieldy here—you can see how abbreviations come in handy!)

VCTN–PASSENGER	Similar to BSNSS–PASSENGER.
BUSINESS	The user has not indicated how a business is identified. A follow-up conversation reveals that each business must have a unique name within a country. Therefore, the primary key is BUSINESS.COUNTRY–NAME plus BUSINESS.NAME.
FLIGHT	Your user has not been specific as to how flights are identified. A little probing elicits the information that each flight has a unique number. Thus, the primary key is FLIGHT.NUMBER.
RESERVATION	This one is a bit tricky. Moon Launch assigns a given reservation to a specific business or vacation passenger for a given flight on a given day. Therefore, the primary key is RESERVATION.PASSENGER*COUNTRY–NAME, RESERVATION.PASSENGER*CODE, RESERVATION.FLIGHT*NUMBER, and RESERVATION.DEPARTURE–DATE.
CREDIT–RATING	Credit ratings are identified by a code (A, B, C or D). The name for the primary key is CREDIT–RATING.CODE.

Note that we have used four class words. They are defined and documented in the data dictionary as follows:

CODE—set of numeric, alphabetic, or special symbols associated with a meaning

NUMBER—numeric designation

NAME—character data (English or other language) representing a name

DATE—special format (*cc/yy/mm/dd*) denoting a calendar date

There do not appear to be any alternate keys. However, after further conversation with the agent, you discover that Moon Launch assigns a confirmation number to each reservation. RESERVATION.CONFIRMATION–NUMBER is an alternate key for RESERVATION.

The expanded logical data model is shown in Figure 6.2.

IMPLEMENTATION TIPS AND TECHNIQUES

Typically, identification of primary keys is intuitive for users. They are accustomed to using pieces of paper to represent most objects in their business world. (For example, the sales department uses Pendaflex file folders to record customers. Or, three-part purchase-order forms filed in several departmental file drawers represent purchase orders.) Usually these manual documents already have some identifying features (for example, customer number, purchase order number).

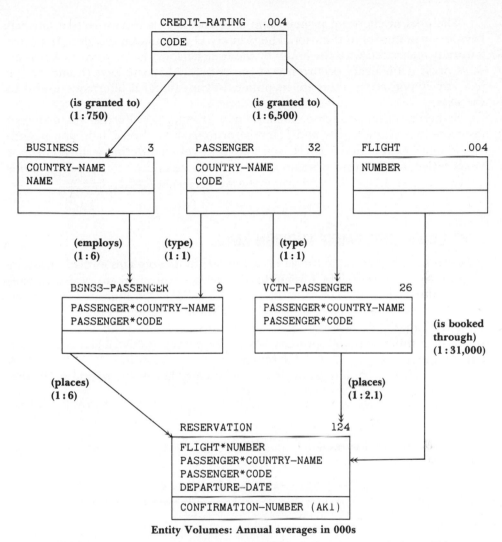

FIGURE 6.2 Moon Launch passenger reservations logical data model; Step LDM3.

The harder question may be determining whether to include a parent's primary key as part of a child's primary key. For example, are order numbers unique, or do you require the combination of customer number and order number for uniqueness? Is invoice number unique, or do you need the combination of supplier name and invoice number for uniqueness? Refer to the relationships on the logical data model diagram as you ask such questions to help the user consider all possibilities.

The goal in choosing primary and alternate keys is to ensure that all such keys are meaningful to the user. The primary key should be the identifier most naturally associated with the entity by the user (as long as the primary key is always present for every occurrence of the entity). Alternate keys should not be just any hypothetical alternate identifier, but meaningful alternates useful to the user.

Sometimes users disagree on choice of a primary key. Further discussion of the meanings of the entity and potential primary keys should help you negotiate an agreement. Alternatively, you may find yourself defining different user views reflecting different primary keys for the same entity. You will resolve this conflict in Step LDM10, when you integrate user views (Chapter 10).

STEP LDM4: DETERMINE FOREIGN KEYS

A *foreign key* is an attribute (or set of attributes) that completes a relationship by identifying the parent. The foreign key is placed in the child entity and equates to the primary key of the related parent. The term *foreign* indicates that the attribute refers to, belongs to, or originates in another, foreign entity.

For example, to represent the relationship SUPPLIER *sends* INVOICE, show supplier number as both a primary key in the parent (SUPPLIER) and a foreign key in the child (INVOICE). To represent the relationship COMPANY *employs* EMPLOYEE, show company name as both a primary key in the parent (COMPANY) and a foreign key in the child (EMPLOYEE).

RULE LDM4.1

For each relationship in the logical data model, identify the *foreign key*.

Identification of foreign keys is important for three reasons. First, foreign keys represent business rules among entities in the logical data model. Second, although explicitly identifying foreign keys within your logical data model may seem redundant (i.e., relationships already imply presence and identification of foreign keys), you gain more insight by doing so. For starters, you must decide whether or not a foreign key also is part of the primary key of the child entity in the relationship. You also must assign the foreign key a meaningful name (one that indicates its foreign property). Moreover, careful designation of foreign keys allows you to reexamine choice of parent and child, potential relationship redundancies, and supertype/subtype designations. The third reason is that explicit identification of foreign keys facilitates database design steps. This is especially true when building relational databases, because foreign keys serve as the primary reference mechanism among relational tables.

It is important that you propagate primary keys (rather than alternate keys) as foreign keys. Use of alternate keys as foreign keys in the logical data model is incorrect for two reasons. First, it adds unnecessary complexity, especially if some relationships are defined using primary keys and some using alternate keys. Second, some alternate keys may accept null values (whereas a primary key cannot, because it must be present for every occurrence of the entity). Thus, use of an alternate key as a foreign key sometimes causes the foreign key to be null, even though the associated primary key is nonnull, thereby rendering the relationship incomplete.

RULE LDM4.2

Name, diagram and document foreign keys in the *data dictionary* (or design documentation).

Document a foreign key in the data dictionary by including its name, its business meaning, the relationship with which it is associated, and possibly its identifying number (for convenience).

Foreign keys deserve special consideration in a naming convention. The analyst (during design) and the user (during ad hoc access) will reference foreign keys frequently; thus, it is desirable to highlight the foreign property of such keys.

A useful naming convention is to extend the one introduced earlier. Consider the following format for a foreign key name:

EntityName.ParentEntityName*Modifier(s)-Classword

      ↑   ↑   ↑

    period   asterisk   dash

Here, "ParentEntityName*" is added to the prefix. For example,

Parent Entity	Primary Key	Child Entity	Foreign Key
SUPPLIER	SUPPLIER.NUMBER	INVOICE	INVOICE.SUPPLIER*NUMBER
COMPANY	COMPANY.NAME	EMPLOYEE	EMPLOYEE.COMPANY*NAME
SCHOOL	SCHOOL.NAME	DEAN	DEAN.SCHOOL*NAME

You already know (from Step LDM3) that a foreign key also may constitute part of the primary key of the child. For example, SUPPLIER*NUMBER is needed to identify INVOICE and thus, in the INVOICE entity, is both a foreign key and part of the primary key.

Recall that there can be more than one relationship between the same two entities (Step LDM2). For example, consider the two relationships PROFESSOR *teaches* CLASS and PROFESSOR *grades* CLASS. If a given class may have one professor who teaches and a different professor who grades, then these are two different relationships. Thus, the CLASS entity will have two foreign keys, each referencing a different PROFESSOR. To distinguish between the two professors, add the relationship name as a modifying word after the class word in the foreign key name. Thus,

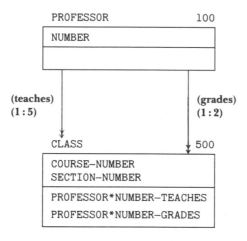

Even when there is only one relationship between two entities, adding the relationship name to the foreign key name for clarity is always correct. It is *required*, however, only when there are two or more relationships between the same two entities. (Note that this naming convention implies that the last component of an attribute name need not be a class word. Sometimes, it is a relationship name. Use of a given design tool may require or suggest a specific sequence of components in an attribute name.)

The diagramming notation for a foreign key is to place its name within the box for the associated child entity. The foreign key goes above the horizontal line when it is part of the primary key and below the horizontal line otherwise. Optionally, you may add the designation (FK*n*) after each attribute constituting the *n*th foreign key within an entity (similar to the convention for designating alternate keys). Again, assignment of *n* to FK*n* is meaningless except to associate multiple attributes of a foreign key. Because foreign keys also can be identified by comparing the primary keys of related parents, you may omit the (FK*n*) designation in favor of greater simplicity in your diagram.

Note that you are collecting attributes below the line. So far, these include alternate keys and also foreign keys that are not primary keys. For an example, see Figure 6.3.

Now we can test your understanding of foreign keys by looking at some special situations: cascading foreign keys, 1:1 relationships, subtypes and categories, and foreign keys that are in part primary and in part not primary keys.

CASCADING FOREIGN KEYS

A *cascading foreign key* is a foreign key that appears in several levels of children (i.e., it is inherited through the primary keys of several levels of parents). For an example see Figure 6.4. We shall check the placement and naming of foreign keys in each entity in this diagram.

ORDER is the child of two relationships: CUSTOMER *places* ORDER and PRODUCT *appears on* ORDER. Thus, ORDER has two foreign keys, corresponding to the primary keys of its two parents: CUSTOMER*NUMBER and PRODUCT*CODE. Because (in this example) you uniquely identify an order by order number within customer, CUSTOMER*NUMBER (along with ORDER.NUMBER) goes above the line, whereas PRODUCT*CODE goes below the line.

Now, an ORDER *is billed through* INVOICEs. INVOICE has one foreign key (composed of two attributes—CUSTOMER*NUMBER and ORDER*NUMBER) representing this relationship and corresponding to the primary key of the parent. Note that the prefix of each foreign key name is the *originating* parent's name. (Thus, CUSTOMER*NUMBER does *not* become ORDER*CUSTOMER*NUMBER—your names would rapidly get extremely long if you carried along prefixes for a whole chain of parents!) The foreign key (CUSTOMER*NUMBER, ORDER*NUMBER) is written

FIGURE 6.3 Primary keys, alternate keys, and foreign keys.

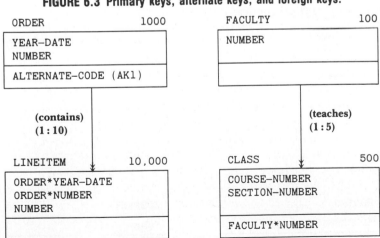

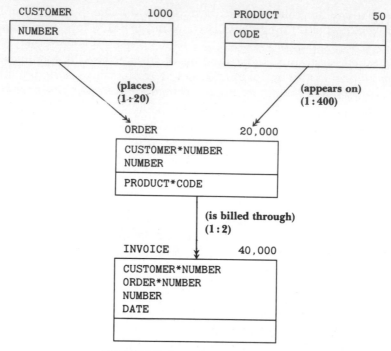

FIGURE 6.4 Cascading foreign keys.

above the line in INVOICE, because you uniquely identify invoices by invoice number and date within order. Notice that PRODUCT*CODE is *not* a foreign key in INVOICE because it is not part of the primary key of a parent to INVOICE.

ONE-TO-ONE (1:1) RELATIONSHIPS

Consider the following alternative representations of the 1:1 relationship COMPANY *has* HDQTRS or HDQTRS *services* COMPANY:

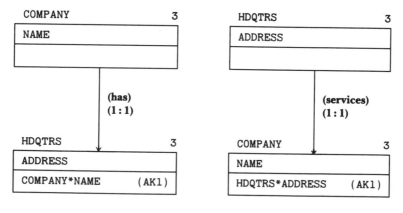

Recall that the direction of most 1:1 relationships (exceptions being sub-types and categories) is arbitrary (Step LDM2). Whichever entity you choose to be the child will contain a foreign key. (Probably the child should be whichever entity seems most dependent on the other—imagining that the parent may exist alone, but the child requires the parent. If neither one intuitively fits this characterization, then the choice is arbitrary.)

Adding the foreign key to both entities is incorrect, because doing so would be redundant or would imply two different relationships. Remember you are developing a *minimal* logical data model, where every element is necessary (that is, not redundant) to reflect the data requirements accurately. The foreign key is required only in the child. Therefore, it would be incorrect to draw

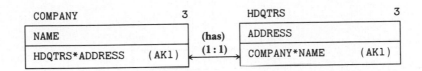

1:1 relationships have some unusual properties. For example, the foreign key serves to identify uniquely the child entity (as well as the parent entity, for which it is a primary key). Thus, in a 1:1 relationship, the foreign key is also a candidate key (typically an *alternate key* although possibly even a primary key) of the child. This implies that you may have already identified some of these foreign keys in Step LDM3.

SUBTYPES AND CATEGORIES

Recall that the primary key of a subtype (or category) is the same as the primary key of its associated supertype, because subtype and supertype designate the same object in the real world:

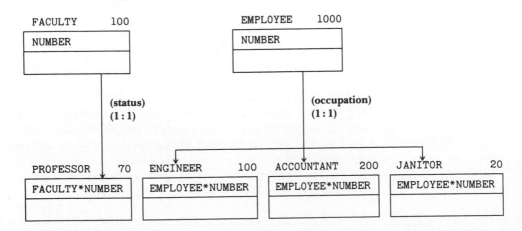

The primary key of the subtype is, of course, also a foreign key and follows the naming conventions for the latter. The foreign key cascades to any children of the subtype:

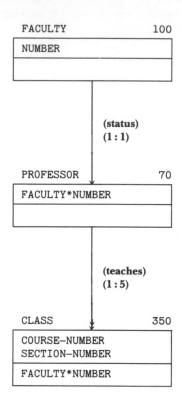

FOREIGN KEYS THAT ARE IN PART PRIMARY AND IN PART NOT PRIMARY KEYS

Consider the diagram on the following page.

The foreign key in DEPT is DIVISION*NUMBER (from DIVISION *has* DEPTs). If you uniquely identify a department by department number within division, DIVISION*NUMBER also is part of the primary key of DEPT and is written above the line.

The foreign key in EMPLOYEE may seem confusing. First, the foreign key is DIVISION*NUMBER, DEPT*NUMBER (from DEPT *includes* EMPLOYEEs). However, if an employee is uniquely identified by employee number within division, only DIVISION*NUMBER is part of the EMPLOYEE primary key and is written above the line. DEPT*NUMBER, on the other hand, is *not* part of the primary key of EMPLOYEE and is written below the line. Note that you still need both attributes because both are needed to identify the employee's department.

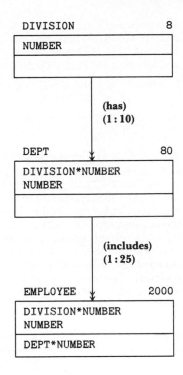

C A S E   S T U D Y

Refer to the logical data model diagram developed thus far for Moon Lāunch Enterprise (Figure 6.2). To identify and add foreign keys, we investigate the entities and their corresponding relationships.

CREDIT–RATING	No foreign keys. (CREDIT–RATING is not a child in any relationship.)
PASSENGER	No foreign keys.
BUSINESS	Add CREDIT–RATING*CODE as a foreign key in BUSINESS, representing the relationship CREDIT–RATING *is granted to* BUSINESS.
BSNSS–PASSENGER	Its primary key is a foreign key, since BSNSS–PASSENGER is a subtype of PASSENGER.
	You need a second foreign key representing the relationship between BUSINESS and BSNSS–PASSENGER. Therefore, add BUSINESS*NAME. But what about BUSINESS*COUNTRY–NAME? Is this the same attribute as PASSENGER*COUNTRY–NAME? If so, you don't want to show it twice. (Remember, your goal is a minimal, least-redundant model). You must ask the user

the following: Can a business passenger be a citizen of one country and work for a business in another country? Your user says yes. Therefore, these attributes are not the same, and you add BUSINESS*COUNTRY-NAME.

VCTN-PASSENGER   Its primary key also is a foreign key, since VCTN-PASSENGER is a subtype of PASSENGER.

Also, add CREDIT-RATING*CODE as a second foreign key.

FLIGHT   No foreign keys.

RESERVATION   The primary key of RESERVATION already includes foreign keys representing its relationships with FLIGHT and BSNSS-PASSENGER or VCTN-PASSENGER. Notice that the foreign key PASSENGER*COUNTRY-NAME, PASSENGER*CODE represents *either* the relationship with BSNSS-PASSENGER *or* the relationship with VCTN-PASSENGER. You can show a common foreign key because both BSNSS-PASSENGER and VCTN-PASSENGER have the same primary key. What if their primary keys differed? Then you would identify a business reservation differently from a vacation reservation and would need to define two different entities (e.g., BSNSS-RESERVATION and VCTN-RESERVATION).

The evolving logical data model is shown in Figure 6.5.

STEP LDM5: DETERMINE KEY BUSINESS RULES

Up to now, you have concentrated mostly on evolving the logical *data structure*. You have identified entities and relationships and have begun to define attributes. You started with determining primary and foreign keys, which serve to identify entities and relationships. You now proceed to define *data integrity*, or that part of your logical data model that will ensure the correctness and consistency of data values.

Of course, you have already begun to address integrity issues through definition of a primary key for each entity. The definition of a primary key includes two *business rules* governing the integrity of entities: (1) a primary key must exist for each occurrence of the entity, and (2) the primary key is unique for each occurrence of the entity.

Alternate keys also address integrity issues for an entity. Definition of an alternate key implies one and perhaps two business rules about entity integrity: (1) each alternate key value, if known, is unique for each occurrence of the entity, and (2) perhaps, but not necessarily, the alternate key value must exist for each occurrence of the entity.

These business rules about entities ensure that the entities in your data model correctly and consistently reflect the real world. For example, if EMPLOYEE.NUMBER is the primary key of EMPLOYEE, these rules ensure that no

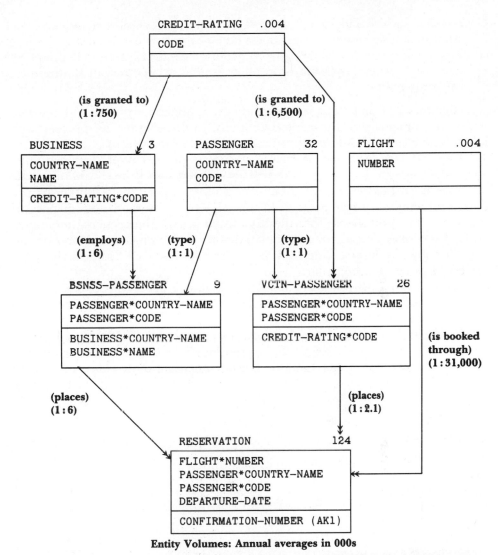

Entity Volumes: Annual averages in 000s

FIGURE 6.5 Moon Launch passenger reservations logical data model; Step LDM4.

employee lacks an employee number and, moreover, that no two employees have the same employee number (just as in the real world).

In addition to the entity business rules, you define three more types of business rules:

□ *Key business rules*—which specifically address integrity of relationships. These rules govern the effects of insert, delete, and update operations on relationships (i.e., what are the effects of changing primary or foreign key values?)

◻ *Domains*—which address integrity of attributes in general and are constraints on the values that attributes (key or nonkey) may assume.
◻ *Triggering operations*—which govern general effects of insert, delete, update, and retrieval operations on other entities or on other attributes in the same entity.

Chapters 7, 8, and 9 discuss identification of nonkey attributes and determination of domains and triggering operations. In this chapter, we proceed with key business rules (those that specifically address relationships).

Like primary keys and alternate keys, foreign keys imply business rules about data integrity. However, the rules associated with primary and alternate keys are fixed (addressing uniqueness and null support, by definition of primary and alternate keys). Foreign keys imply one or more of a set of possible business rules. You choose the rules that fit your users' business requirements.

A *key business rule*, then, defines conditions under which a primary or foreign key may be inserted, deleted, or updated. These key business rules (referred to as relationship insert/delete constraints) typically represent the most important constraints on insert, delete, and update operations. They also are sometimes called *existence constraints*, because they define the valid existence of a particular entity occurrence.

The user, with help from the data analyst, must define the key business rules. These rules should reflect the operations of the user's business, organization, or function. By understanding and documenting these rules, you will be able to design a database that accurately preserves integrity of data relationships to reflect the real world with validity.

INSERT RULES

The *insert rule* determines valid conditions under which you may insert a child entity (or update its foreign key); that is, what restrictions do associated parent entities impose when you insert the child?

RULE LDM5.1

Identify one *insert rule* for each relationship.

We classify insert constraints into six types:

◻ *Dependent*—Permit insertion of child entity occurrence only when matching parent entity occurrence already exists.
◻ *Automatic*—Always permit insertion of child entity occurrence. If matching parent entity occurrence does not already exist, create it.

□ *Nullify*—Always permit insertion of child entity occurrence. If matching parent entity occurrence does not exist, set foreign key in child to *null*.

□ *Default*—Always permit insertion of child entity occurrence. If matching parent entity occurrence does not exist, set foreign key in child to a previously defined *default value*.

□ *Customized*—Permit insertion of child entity occurrence only if certain customized validity constraints are met.

□ *No Effect*—Always permit insertion of child entity occurrence. No matching parent entity occurrence need exist, and thus no validity checking need be done.

For each relationship in the logical data model, define an insert constraint by asking the user appropriate business questions. For example, consider the relationship SUPPLIER *is issued* ORDERs:

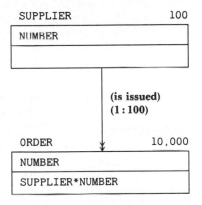

When the user places a new order with the supplier, what rules are in force? In other words, what constraints should govern the insertion or foreign key update of the child entity ORDER? Six possibilities exist:

1. The user must issue the order to an existing supplier (*dependent* insert rule).
2. The user may issue the order to an existing or new supplier. If the supplier is new, the user adds that supplier to the approved list of suppliers (*automatic* insert rule).
3. The user must either issue the order to an existing supplier or record the order without any supplier specification (*nullify* insert rule).
4. The user must either issue the order to an existing supplier or place it with Jones, Inc., the default supplier (*default* insert rule).
5. The user must issue orders to a supplier who has no more than four orders currently outstanding (*customized* insert rule). There are, of course, many possible customized insert rules.
6. The user may issue orders even to suppliers not on the approved list. No validity checking is necessary (*no effect* insert rule). Someone should monitor these supplier numbers.

DELETE RULES

The *delete rule* determines valid conditions under which you can delete a parent entity (or update its primary key); that is, what restrictions do associated child entities impose when you delete the parent?

RULE LDM5.2

Identify one *delete rule* for each relationship.

Six types of delete constraints govern valid deletion of a parent entity (or update of its primary key):

☐ *Restrict*—Permit deletion of parent entity occurrence only when there are no matching child entity occurrences.
☐ *Cascade*—Always permit deletion of parent entity occurrence and cascade the deletion to any matching child entity occurrences (i.e., delete all matching child entity occurrences).
☐ *Nullify*—Always permit deletion of parent entity occurrence. If any matching child entity occurrences exist, set their foreign keys to *null*.
☐ *Default*—Always permit deletion of parent entity occurrence. If any matching child entity occurrences exist, set their foreign keys to a previously defined *default value*.
☐ *Customized*—Permit deletion of parent entity occurrence only if certain customized validity constraints are met.
☐ *No Effect*—Always permit deletion of parent entity occurrence. Matching child entity occurrences may or may not exist, and thus no validity checking need be done.

For each relationship in the logical data model, define a delete constraint by asking relevant business questions. For example, continuing your analysis of the SUPPLIER *is issued* ORDERs relationship, what rules should govern termination of a supplier? In other words, what constraints should govern the deletion or primary key update of the parent entity SUPPLIER? Again, there are six possibilities:

1. The user may not terminate suppliers if the supplier has outstanding orders (*restrict* delete rule).
2. The user cancels any outstanding orders when terminating a supplier (*cascade* delete rule).

3. The user retains outstanding orders on file after terminating a supplier, but updates the orders to reflect their unassigned status (*nullify* delete rule).
4. The user reassigns outstanding orders to Jones, Inc., the default supplier, after terminating the original supplier (*default* delete rule).
5. The user does not immediately terminate suppliers with outstanding orders, but instead flags them for review at a subsequent date (*customized* delete rule). Again, there are many possible customized delete rules.
6. The user terminates suppliers regardless of whether the supplier has outstanding orders. No validity checking is necessary (*no effect* delete rule). Someone should monitor these supplier numbers.

GUIDELINES FOR DEFINING INSERT AND DELETE CONSTRAINTS

For the most part, users must define insert and delete rules to correspond to the way they view their business. However, you can offer some guidelines that stem from the objective of maintaining simplicity, intuitiveness, and consistency throughout the logical data model.

RULE LDM5.3

Avoid the use of *nullify* insert or delete rules. Favor *default* rules instead.

A *null value* is a special value designating "value unknown" or "not applicable." It is *not* the same as a zero or blank value. For example, a null invoice number is not the same as a zero invoice number; a null invoice number probably means that the user has not yet assigned the invoice an identifying number, whereas zero may be a valid invoice number.

Different database systems (particularly different relational products) treat null values inconsistently. Moreover, nulls frequently yield unpredictable or unintuitive results. These problems and their implications will be discussed further in Part 3. For now, try to avoid them by defining default values in place of nulls.

Special circumstances (also discussed in Part 3) may warrant use of null values regardless of the potential problems. However, there are some situations for which a null value is *never* appropriate.

RULE LDM5.4

Never define a *nullify* insert or delete rule when the foreign key also is part of the primary key of the child entity.

Recall that, by definition, a primary key must be present and uniquely identifies an occurrence of an entity. Further, the primary key must be a minimal set of identifying attributes, implying that you cannot discard any attribute from the primary key without destroying its uniqueness property. Obviously, then, no component of the primary key can be null (which would be tantamount to discarding that attribute). Therefore, when a foreign key also is part of the child entity's primary key, it cannot be null.

A special case of this rule occurs with *subtypes,* for which the primary and foreign keys are one and the same.

RULE LDM5.5

Always define the *insert rule* for a supertype–subtype (or supertype–category) relationship as a tailored version of either *automatic* or *dependent* (tailored to enforce the 1 : 1 relationship). Define the *delete rule* for such relationships as *cascade.*

Recall that a subtype and its corresponding supertype designate exactly the same object in the real world. A subtype by definition cannot exist unless its corresponding supertype also exists. Moreover, deleting a supertype that has a subtype logically implies that the subtype also should be deleted. The 1 : 1 supertype–subtype relationship (or in the case of categories, the 1 : 1 relationship between supertype and category of subtypes) requires additional validity checking when a subtype occurrence is inserted. This check should ensure that there is no other child occurrence (within the subtype or category) with the same foreign key value.

C A S E   S T U D Y

When you review the Moon Launch passenger reservations agent's description, you find that there is no mention of anything resembling insert or delete business rules. Therefore, you need to prompt the user for more information. The agent tells you the following:

Moon Launch accepts only those business passengers whose businesses already are in its file.

When Moon Launch drops a business from its files, it stops servicing employees of that business.

When passengers not on file call for reservations, the agent adds the passengers to the file. The agent adds both general and business or vacation passenger information at the same time. If a business passenger's business is not on file, the passenger is not added.

Moon Launch never deletes a passenger who has a current reservation.

Passengers may place reservations for valid flights only.

Whenever Moon Launch cancels (or replaces) a flight, it flags all associated reservations in order to mail out notices.

Moon Launch has already established four approved credit ratings (A, B, C, and D). If Moon Launch ever decides to alter the codes for these credit ratings, you could potentially have to update every business and every vacation passenger to reflect the revised codes.

The corresponding insert/delete rules are as follows:

Parent	Child	Child Insert Rule	Parent Delete Rule
CREDIT–RATING	BUSINESS	dependent	customized
CREDIT–RATING	VCTN–PASSENGER	dependent	customized
BUSINESS	BSNSS–PASSENGER	dependent	cascade
PASSENGER	BSNSS–PASSENGER	automatic	cascade
PASSENGER	VCTN–PASSENGER	automatic	cascade
BSNSS–PASSENGER	RESERVATION	automatic	restrict
VCTN–PASSENGER	RESERVATION	automatic	restrict
FLIGHT	RESERVATION	dependent	customized

Notice that Rule LDM5.5 dictates the *cascade* delete rule for the PASSENGER *type* BSNSS–PASSENGER and PASSENGER *type* VCTN–PASSENGER relationships.

Also notice that some interrelationships are inherent in these business rules. For example, what if you tried to delete a business for which some employees hold current reservations? The delete rule for BUSINESS *employs* BSNSS–PASSENGER is *cascade*. However, the delete rule for BSNSS–PASSENGER *places* RESERVATION is *restrict*. Thus, you would reject deletion of that business until its employees held no more current reservations.

IMPLEMENTATION TIPS AND TECHNIQUES

Many logical data modeling methodologies address definition of the *structure* of data, but largely ignore data *integrity*. Yet, logical data model structures are of absolutely no value unless users also can be sure of the integrity of information maintained within the structures.

Traditional methodologies typically leave definition of integrity constraints or business rules to *application* development rather than to *database* development. Treating business rules as an application-driven requirement raises three dangers. First, users may define the business rules too narrowly, reflecting only the needs of the immediate application. Second, multiple users interested in different applications may have different perspectives on business rules. Thus, they may define inconsistent or even conflicting business rules as part of the application specifications. (Of course, they may also define inconsistent business rules as part of different user views; however, you resolve these conflicts in Step LDM10.) Third, maintaining correctness and consistency across business rules implemented via multiple applications may be extremely difficult (or impossible) to accomplish as applications evolve and new applications arise.

Many business rules are in fact *data-driven* (i.e., inherent to the meaning of the data) rather than *application-driven* (i.e., inherent to the way the data are processed). Define them, therefore, as an integral part of the logical data model.

SUMMARY

In this chapter, you completed development of a skeletal user view. You probably have sufficient design detail to begin prototyping. You have completed your design activities if you are interested in only a high-level skeletal model. More likely, you will continue with the later design steps to refine and eventually to implement a complete and detailed database design. We review what you have learned so far.

A *candidate key* is an attribute or minimal set of attributes that uniquely identifies a specific occurrence of an entity. If composed of a set of attributes, it also is known as a *composite key*. You choose one candidate key to serve as a *primary key*, ensuring that the primary key always exists for every occurrence of the entity. The remaining candidate keys are known as *alternate keys*.

You name primary and alternate keys using the following convention:

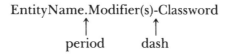

You place them on the logical data model diagram. Primary keys go above a horizontal line drawn through the box for the entity. Alternate keys go below the horizontal line.

A *foreign key* is an attribute or set of attributes that completes a relationship by identifying the parent. In a logical data model diagram, you write the foreign key in the box for the child entity, above the horizontal line if it is part of the child's primary key and below the horizontal line otherwise.

The foreign key of the child corresponds to the primary key of the parent.

You name the foreign key using a special format with an asterisk to highlight the key's foreign property:

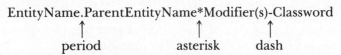

EntityName.ParentEntityName*Modifier(s)-Classword

period   asterisk   dash

If multiple relationships exist between the same pair of entities, you add the relationship name to the foreign key name as a modifying word.

There are four special cases of foreign keys:

1. A cascading foreign key appears in (cascades to) several levels of children (i.e., it is inherited through the primary keys of several levels of parents).
2. In a 1 : 1 relationship, a foreign key appears (only) in the entity chosen (perhaps arbitrarily) as the child. Because the foreign key equates to a primary key in the parent and a 1 : 1 relationship exists between parent and child, the foreign key also is a candidate (probably alternate) key for the child.
3. The primary key of a subtype or category also is a foreign key.
4. A foreign key may consist in part of primary key and in part of nonprimary key attributes.

A *key business rule* defines conditions under which you may insert, update, or delete a primary or foreign key. Key business rules are the first of three types of business rules that you will define to govern data *integrity* in the logical data model (i.e., ensuring correctness and consistency of the data values in a database).

You define one insert rule and one delete rule for each relationship in the logical data model. The *insert rule* determines valid conditions under which you may insert a child entity (or update its foreign key). The *delete rule* determines valid conditions under which you may delete a parent entity (or update its primary key).

The six types of insert rules are *dependent, automatic, nullify, default, customized,* and *no effect.* The six types of delete rules are *restrict, cascade, nullify, default, customized,* and *no effect.*

The users define insert and delete rules to correspond to their view of the business. In general, avoid use of a *nullify* rule in favor of a *default* rule. In particular, a *nullify* rule is never valid when the foreign key also is part of the primary key of the child entity.

The insert rule for a supertype–subtype (or supertype–category) relationship must be either *automatic* or *dependent* (tailored to enforce the 1 : 1 relationship). The delete rule for this type of relationship must be *cascade.*

EXERCISES

6.1 Discuss reasons why every entity must have a primary key.

6.2 Your logical data model diagram represents relationships in two ways: lines connecting entities and foreign keys. Are both necessary? Discuss pros and cons of having each without the other.

6.3 Based on your knowledge of insert and delete rules for primary and foreign keys, discuss possible update rules for foreign keys.

6.4 Suppose Moon Launch Enterprise decides to identify each passenger by a unique international passenger code. How does this affect your logical data model diagram?

6.5 For the RESERVATION *is issued* TICKET relationship (added in Exercise 5.5), assume that primary, alternate, and foreign keys are as follows:

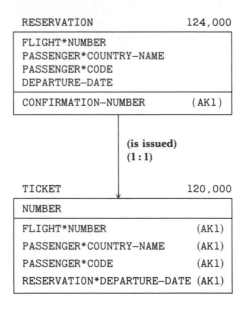

The passenger reservations agent tells you that a ticket cannot be issued unless the passenger holds a reservation. On the other hand, if a reservation is canceled, the passenger may choose to hold on to the ticket, since it may be redeemed for cash or credit. Of course, Moon Launch's records must show the ticket associated with the (now-canceled) reservation, while the physical ticket remains in the hands of the passenger. Identify insert and delete rules for the relationship shown in the diagram.

6.6 Perform Steps LDM3 through LDM5 for the baggage tracking and control department. Refer to Exercise 5.6 for a description of the user view. You will find clues to primary keys there.

A baggage agent provides you with the following additional information. An agent cannot check a piece of luggage unless he associates it with a valid passenger and with a reserved flight. The agent must associate the description of lost luggage contents with a specific piece of (checked) luggage. Whenever Moon Launch locates a piece of lost luggage and returns it to its owner, an agent deletes the luggage record from the system, along with all content descriptions. If a passenger cancels a reservation for which he has already checked luggage (quite rare), the Moon Launch agent flags the luggage information as "canceled".

6.7 Perform Steps LDM3 through LDM5 for the space shuttle maintenance control group. Review their initial information specifications (Exercise 5.7). Also consider the following information, provided by a space shuttle captain. Moon Launch identifies each captain by an employee number or by a name. Moon Launch never adds a space shuttle vehicle to its inventory until it has valid model and serial numbers. If the controller tries to delete information about a general shuttle model when there still exist shuttle vehicles for this model, the system should flag both general model and specific vehicle information as obsolete. If the controller adds a shuttle vehicle without assigning a captain, the system should automatically assign the default captain number of 99 (99 indicating automatic pilot—no human pilot). When Moon Launch fires or retires a captain, the system should assign the associated space shuttles to automatic pilot. (The assumption is, of course, that every space shuttle has automatic pilot capability.) The controller cannot assign a shuttle vehicle to a flight unless both the shuttle and the flight exist and are valid. When Moon Launch cancels a flight, the system should automatically cancel its associated shuttle assignments. The controller cannot delete any shuttle vehicle currently assigned to flights.

7 | Add Detail to User Views

In Chapters 7, 8, and 9 you complete the process of constructing user views. This entails four steps:

- Add remaining attributes or detail data items to the entities—*Step LDM6*
- Validate normalization rules, ensuring that you have correctly associated attributes with entities—*Step LDM7*
- Determine domains, or constraints on the values that attributes can assume—*Step LDM8*
- Determine other attribute business rules, governing the effects of retrieve, insert, update, and delete operations on other attributes in the same or different entities—*Step LDM9*

At the end of this process, you will have completely analyzed and represented data requirements for one business function, as perceived by one user or one group of users. You have not yet worried about reconciling this (possibly biased and certainly incomplete) view of the world with other views. You will concern yourself with integrating multiple logical views only after ascertaining the accuracy, completeness and consistency of each individual user view. Figure 7.1 shows the relationship of the steps in these chapters to the full methodology presented in this book.

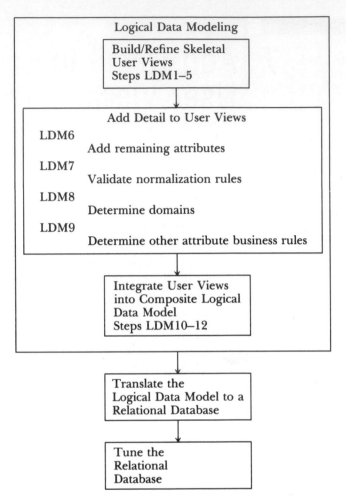

FIGURE 7.1 Relational design methodology steps.

STEP LDM6: ADD REMAINING ATTRIBUTES

Step LDM6 adds remaining attributes to your logical data model. An *attribute* is a fact or nondecomposable unit of information about an entity. Examples of attributes are shown in Figure 7.2.

You already know three types of attributes: primary keys, alternate keys, and foreign keys. You understand their role in *identifying* entities and relationships. Now you determine additional *nonidentifying* (or *nonkey*) attributes, which add clarifying details about entities.

RULE LDM6.1

Associate each *attribute* with the entity the entire primary key of which is necessary and sufficient to identify or determine it uniquely.

Another way of stating Rule LDM6.1 is that you should place attributes within that entity for which they are *dependent* on the entire primary key. That is, a particular value of the primary key determines the values of all other attributes (called *nonkey* attributes) in the entity (being dependent on the primary key). Moreover, no subset of the primary key determines any nonkey attribute.

Consider the attribute customer name and the entities in the following diagram. Assume customer name cannot be a primary key because multiple customers may have the same name. Thus, it is a nonkey attribute, but for which entity? Because the primary key CUSTOMER.NUMBER is necessary *and sufficient* to identify customer name, you should assign customer name to the CUSTOMER entity.

FIGURE 7.2 Examples of attributes.

Entity	Attribute	Type of Attribute
SUPPLIER	SUPPLIER.NAME	Primary Key
	SUPPLIER.ADDRESS	Nonkey
	SUPPLIER.CREDIT-TERMS	Nonkey
PART	PART.NUMBER	Primary Key
	PART.NAME	Nonkey
	PART.SIZE	Nonkey
SUPPART	SUPPLIER*NAME	Primary + Foreign Key
	PART*NUMBER	Primary + Foreign Key
	SUPPART.UNIT-AMOUNT	Nonkey
	SUPPART.DOLLARS-PER-UNIT-AMOUNT	Nonkey
ORDER	ORDER.YEAR-DATE	Primary Key
	ORDER.NUMBER	Primary Key
	SUPPLIER*NAME	Foreign Key
	PART*NUMBER	Foreign Key
	ORDER.UNITS-AMOUNT	Nonkey

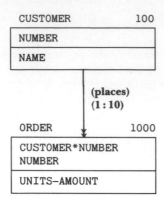

Another example is amount of order. This is a nonkey attribute of ORDER because CUSTOMER*NUMBER and ORDER.NUMBER, which together make up the primary key of ORDER, are both required to determine uniquely amount of order.

Two corollary rules provide further guidance for placement of attributes.

RULE LDM6.2

Place nonkey attributes as *high* as possible in the logical data model (as long as the primary key of the entity uniquely identifies the attribute).

The word *high* in Rule LDM6.2 means that you should associate an attribute with a related parent entity (conceptually placed *higher* on the diagram) instead of with a child entity, whenever it makes sense to do so. Consider the following example:

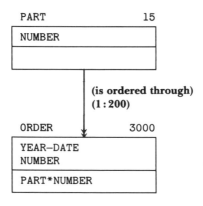

Where should you place part name? Following the guideline to place attributes as high in the diagram as possible, you will associate part name with PART instead of with ORDER (since PART is the parent and ORDER is the child). Note, of course, that PART.NUMBER (primary key of PART) does in fact uniquely identify part name.

This technique of placing attributes as high in the model as possible tends to reduce redundancy. For example, thinking ahead to physical implementation, storing part name with PART rather than with ORDER means that you store a given part name only once. If instead you placed part name in ORDER, you would store it once for each ORDER in which it appeared. Less redundancy in the database simplifies the task of performing updates while maintaining consistency of data values.

RULE LDM6.3

If an attribute in an entity depends on the primary key but is *multivalued* (i.e., may have multiple values for one particular value of the primary key), reclassify the attribute as a new child entity type. If unique, that attribute constitutes the primary key of the new child entity. If not unique, that attribute plus the primary key of the original (now parent) entity constitute the primary key of the new child entity.

Consider the purchase order entity:

```
ORDER                    50
┌─────────────────────────┐
│ NUMBER                  │
├─────────────────────────┤
│                         │
└─────────────────────────┘
```

A purchase order can have one or more line item numbers appearing on it. Thus, given a purchase order, you can *determine* one or more line item numbers. Is line item number an attribute of ORDER? Line item number would be a *multivalued* attribute of ORDER because line item number is not *uniquely* determined by purchase order number.

Instead, remove line item number to a new child entity, LINEITEM:

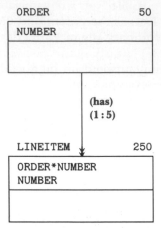

In this case we assume LINEITEM.NUMBER is not unique; that is, multiple ORDERs may be associated with the same LINEITEM.NUMBER value. Thus, the primary key of LINEITEM consists of the primary key of ORDER (ORDER*NUMBER) plus the originally multivalued attribute line item number (LINEITEM.NUMBER).

For now, you are employing a basically intuitive technique in associating attributes with entities. In the next step of the logical data modeling process, you will learn a more refined technique known as *normalization*. At that time, you will define more precisely what is meant by "correct" association of attributes with entities. You will discover, however, that most of the time this intuitive analysis (following Rules LDM6.2 and LDM6.3) leads you to correct results.

Attributes typically appear in a user's list of data items as nouns followed by the words "of entity-name." For example, *name* of supplier, *number* of purchase order, and *color* of part probably are all attributes of the corresponding entities. Sometimes you can recognize attributes by the presence of possessive adjectives, such as supplier's *name* or employee's *address*. Sometimes the possessive adjective is implied, as in part *color* or purchase order *number*.

RULE LDM6.4

Name, diagram, and document attributes in the *data dictionary* (or design documentation).

You are already familiar with a general naming convention for attributes:

EntityName.Modifier(s)-Classword

or, for a foreign key:

EntityName.ParentEntityName*Modifier(s)-Classword

Document attributes in the data dictionary, including such information as attribute name, description, length, type, and associated entity (or entities in the case of a foreign key). Also note whether the attributes are primary, alternate, or foreign keys.

Classifying attributes and associating them with the proper entities are not always straightforward tasks. We shall examine a more complex example.

A user describes the information appearing on a purchase order:

Year

Number

Part number

Part name

Supplier name

Part size

Unit quantity in which the part may be ordered

Dollar quantity associated with unit quantity

Number of units ordered

Supplier's address

Credit terms

Figure 7.3 shows how an analyst associates each of the attributes with an entity, names the attributes, and places them on the logical data model diagram. We shall examine this analysis.

SAMPLE ATTRIBUTE DEFINITIONS

Year	Date (i.e., year) of purchase order, needed to identify a purchase order, and therefore a part of the primary key. It is called ORDER.YEAR-DATE, associating it with entity ORDER. YEAR is a modifying word. DATE is a class word. (Recall that the prefix ORDER. does not appear on the logical data model diagram because it is obvious from the placement of the attribute.)
Number	Number of purchase order, also needed to identify a purchase order (purchase orders are identified by number within year). Therefore, also part of the primary key of purchase order. It is named ORDER.NUMBER, associating it with entity ORDER.
Part number	Number of part appearing on purchase order. Identifying attribute, therefore primary key, of part. Also identifies

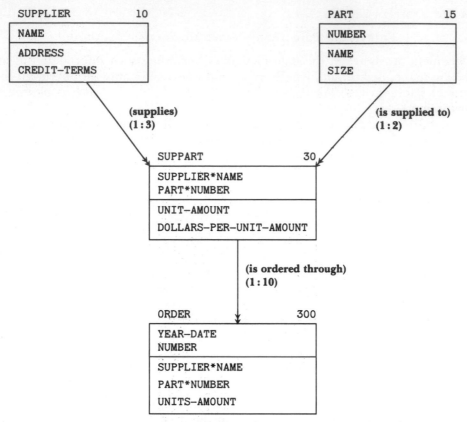

FIGURE 7.3 Association of attributes with entities.

parent in relationship (PART *is ordered through* ORDER) and therefore is a foreign key in purchase order. It is named PART.NUMBER in entity PART and PART*NUMBER (notice the naming convention for foreign keys) in entity ORDER.

Part name   Name of part. Provides further detail describing the PART entity. Not required in the ORDER entity (since the foreign key PART*NUMBER, corresponding to the primary key of PART, already identifies the PART related to ORDER). It is named PART.NAME to associate it with entity PART.

Supplier name   Name of supplier. Identifying attribute and therefore primary key of the SUPPLIER entity. Also required as foreign key in the ORDER entity, identifying which SUPPLIER is related to a particular ORDER. It is named SUPPLIER.NAME as primary key in SUPPLIER, and SUPPLIER*NAME as foreign key in ORDER.

Part size	Detail information characterizing the entity PART. It is named PART.SIZE as a nonkey attribute of PART.
Unit quantity	Unit quantity in which the user may order a part from a particular supplier. Detail information determined by the combination of part number and supplier name. It is called SUPPART.UNIT-AMOUNT as a nonkey attribute of entity SUPPART (having primary key SUPPLIER*NAME, PART*NUMBER). Note that initially you might be tempted to make this an attribute of the $M:N$ relationship between PART and SUPPLIER (a part is supplied by many suppliers, and each supplier supplies many parts). You should resolve this $M:N$ relationship by creating a new entity SUPPART.
Dollar quantity	Dollar quantity in which a user may order a part from a particular supplier. Also determined by combination of part number and supplier name. It is named SUPPART.DOLLARS—PER—UNIT—AMOUNT as a nonkey attribute of entity SUPPART.
Units ordered	Quantity of units ordered on a particular purchase order. It is named ORDER.UNITS—AMOUNT as a nonkey attribute of ORDER.
Supplier's address	Address of supplier, determined by supplier name. It is called SUPPLIER.ADDRESS as a nonkey attribute of SUPPLIER.
Credit terms	Credit terms extended by supplier, determined by supplier name. It is called SUPPLIER.CREDIT—TERMS as a nonkey attribute of SUPPLIER. Note that, if credit terms also varied by part, then you would associate the attribute with SUPPART. If credit terms further varied by order based on additional factors (such as mood of the salesperson), then you would associate the attribute with ORDER. If credit terms strictly depended on PART.NUMBER, SUPPLIER.NAME, and a fixed factor (such as season), then both season and credit terms would be multivalued attributes of SUPPART and would be removed to a new entity SUPPARTCRED (child of SUPPART) with primary key SUPPARTCRED. SUPPLIER*NAME, SUPPARTCRED.PART*NUMBER, and SUPPARTCRED.SEASON—NAME.

Notice this example assumes that a given purchase order can list only one part. Where can you see that assumption? Recall that you classified PART*NUMBER as an attribute (in fact, a foreign key) of ORDER. Therefore, the primary key of ORDER (YEAR—DATE, NUMBER) uniquely determines one PART*NUMBER (according to Rule LDM6.1). What if, instead, a customer could use one purchase order to request multiple parts? That is, what if PART*NUMBER were a multivalued attribute of ORDER? (This is, in fact, the way most purchase order systems operate.) Then, you would define a new entity type (for example, LINEITEM) with a different (more specific) primary key (for example,

ORDER*YEAR–DATE, ORDER*NUMBER, LINEITEM.NUMBER) that uniquely identifies a particular part on a purchase order.

You may have observed from the example that you associate each attribute with exactly one entity (specifically that entity the primary key of which uniquely identifies the attribute) with the one exception of *foreign keys*. Foreign keys are the only attributes associated with multiple entities—as a primary key in the parent, and as a foreign key in the child, of a relationship.

In developing a logical data model diagram and associating attributes with entities, it frequently is helpful to test the model's validity against sample instances of data values. An extension of the diagramming convention accommodates *sample value listings,* or representations of sample instances of an entity. For example:

Logical Data Model

PART

NUMBER
NAME
SIZE–TEXT

Sample Value Listing

PART

NUMBER (PK)	NAME	SIZE–TEXT
135	screw	hundreds
278	fabric	bolts
813	wrench	dozens

In the sample value listing, each row represents one sample occurrence of the entity. For convenience, place primary key attributes to the left and add (PK) to denote them as a primary key. You also can add (AK*n*) below attributes comprising the *n*th alternate key. Likewise, you can add (FK*n*) below foreign key attributes.

Identifying, naming, defining, and diagramming the remaining attributes is largely an intuitive and sometimes even an obvious process. However, a few specific questions and issues crop up frequently and merit some guidelines.

ATTRIBUTES VERSUS ENTITIES

Sometimes a particular data item appears to be either an attribute or an entity, depending on user perspective. For instance, is color an *attribute* of part or an *entity* in itself?

As an entity, color may itself have other, more descriptive attributes, such as a chemical formula detailing color composition, a technical name given to the formula, or a customer-oriented name used for advertising purposes.

As an attribute, color is a *nondecomposable* piece of detail about a part; it does not consist of more detailed attributes.

In case of doubt, the user is the final arbitrator. The logical data model should reflect the user's perceptions of entities (i.e., objects about which he wants to record information) and attributes (atomic units of detailed information characterizing an entity). Of course, you may need some interpretive skills to decipher and translate the user's intentions!

ATTRIBUTES THAT DESCRIBE RELATIONSHIPS

Our definition of attributes clearly associates them with entities. What about an attribute that appears to describe a relationship? For example, consider the relationship MAN *marries* WOMAN. Possible attributes of the relationship *marries* are date, place, and presiding official. Obviously, the diagramming convention does not easily facilitate associating attributes with relationships. (There is a reason for that: As you proceed first with logical design and later with database design, you will discover that handling attributes that describe relationships is unnecessarily complex. Better to avoid the situation!) Generally, if you find yourself trying to hang attributes off a relationship, you have probably misclassified the relationship; that is, it probably should be an entity.

RULE LDM6.5

If there are attributes that seem to describe a relationship (rather than an entity), *reclassify* the relationship as a new entity and as child to each of the original two entities.

In our example of MAN *marries* WOMAN, redefine the relationship *marries* as an entity MARRIAGE. MARRIAGE will become child to both MAN and WOMAN. You can now associate attributes with this new entity:

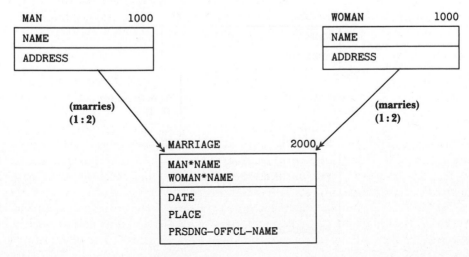

Note that, in this example, the similarity of the entities MAN and WOMAN should cause you to question whether they are two entities or only one. Perhaps a better interpretation would define one entity, PERSON, with an $M:N$ bill-of-materials relationship (*marries*). You would then decompose the $M:N$ relationship into a new entity MARRIAGE related to PERSON through two $1:N$ relationships.

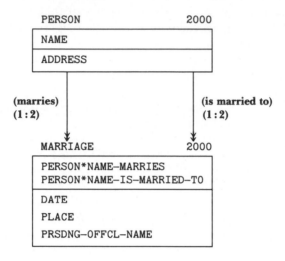

Also note that both of these scenarios assume that people may wed multiple times. What if you assume a truly monogamous world in which people marry only once? Then you have

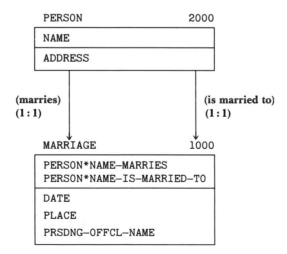

Here MARRIAGE represents a 1 : 1 bill-of-materials relationship that you have re-classified as an entity because of its associated attributes.

In either case ($M:N$ or $1:N$), your model supports the restriction that no one can marry the same person more than once (based on choice of primary key for MARRIAGE). What if you wanted to allow remarriages? Then, you must add date to the primary key. What if the same two people can marry twice on the same date? Then, you will need yet another attribute in the primary key.

Furthermore, currently the model allows for marriages of men to men or of women to women. If you wish to define MARRIAGE as always being between MAN and WOMAN, you can represent MAN and WOMAN as subtypes of PERSON.

Thus, even the seemingly simplest logical data model examples often turn out to be not so simple on closer inspection.

ENCODED ATTRIBUTES

A common practice is to use codes to represent other, more meaningful data values. For example, state abbreviations or codes might represent state names (NJ for New Jersey, TX for Texas, and so on). Or, numeric codes (1, 2, 3, 4, . . .) might represent product colors (such as Boysenberry Blue, Raspberry Red, Sugar Plum Lavender, and Midnight Violet in a cosmetics application). People typically use codes because codes save storage, reduce the number of characters that must be typed in data entry, or conform to coding schemes used in prior applications. Some people use codes just from habit—and some use them to confuse everyone (otherwise known as job security)! During the logical data modeling process, the analyst should avoid such practices.

RULE LDM6.6

Avoid representing attributes in *encoded form* (e.g., 01 = red, 02 = blue) unless the codes are user-defined and are meaningful within the industry or business area.

There are several reasons for *avoiding* use of encoded attributes. First, codes often are unintuitive to users. The objective of logical data modeling is to achieve a clear representation of the *user's* (not the analyst's) view of the data requirements.

Second, introduction of codes requires establishing additional (lookup) entities in the logical data model. The lookup table of codes becomes a new entity that is parent to all entities containing the coded value (Figure 7.4). The logical data model can rapidly degenerate into a messy spider's web if you proliferate

Desirable: Without Encoded Attributes

Logical Data Model | **Sample Value Listing**

PRODUCT   100

PRODUCT

NUMBER	
COLOR–NAME	
PRICE–AMOUNT	

PRODUCT

NUMBER (PK)	COLOR–NAME	PRICE–AMOUNT
66	Raspberry Red	10.00
23	Sugar Plum Lavender	25.00
91	Boysenberry Blue	130.00

Undesirable: With Encoded Attributes

Logical Data Model | **Sample Value Listing**

COLOR   10

COLOR

CODE	
NAME	

COLOR

CODE (PK)	NAME
01	Raspberry Red
02	Sugar Plum Lavender
03	Boysenberry Blue

(characterizes)
(1:10)

PRODUCT   100

PRODUCT

NUMBER	
COLOR*CODE	
PRICE–AMOUNT	

PRODUCT

NUMBER (PK)	COLOR*CODE	PRICE–AMOUNT
66	01	10.00
23	02	25.00
91	03	130.00

FIGURE 7.4 Logical data models with and without encoded attributes.

use of codes. To maintain reasonable order and clarity in the model, avoid unnecessary use of codes.

Third, under some implementation options, use of codes may complicate end-user queries considerably. The user must constantly match data against a lookup table. Although you may decide you need codes when you implement your database, for now leave all options open and do not prejudge possible tradeoffs.

Finally, typically use of codes assumes certain data- or processing-implementation solutions. For example, the analyst assumes that x amount of space will be saved or that some existing set of application programs will not need modifications. These are possibly valid, but premature, assumptions. You should address them later, during database and application design, when you consider all such issues together. Right now, you are addressing the inherent logical properties of the data, independent of any database design or of any particular application processing requirement.

Possible exceptions to Rule LDM6.6 occur when the codes have significant *business meaning* to the user. A shoe business is likely to use codes (4, 5, 6, . . .) rather than actual dimensions to designate shoe sizes. In this case, the codes are more familiar to the user than are the translations. In general, the analyst must exercise judgement about use of codes and above all must be wary of using them just due to habit or because of processing considerations. Furthermore, take care to avoid codes that are intuitive to one user group but meaningless to others.

RULE LDM6.7

Do not include processing-oriented *flags* as attributes in the logical data model.

A processing-oriented *flag* is an attribute that signals whether some computer process has taken or should take place (e.g., just updated or to be printed). It represents no business meaning independent of the computer system.

For example, consider an APPLY-RAISE-FLAG for the SALARY entity in a payroll application. The system is supposed to "turn on" the flag to mark employees who have received a raise, so that the nightly batch run can then recalculate all these people's benefits and pay deductions. At least two assumptions are embedded in the definition of this flag: (1) the system will update benefits and pay deductions in batch, and (2) identification of employees receiving raises will occur at a different time.

These are *processing-oriented* assumptions that you may or may not want to make when you design application processes. When building a logical data model, focus solely on the inherent logical properties of the data. Thus, do not include these processing flags in your logical data model.

Frequently, existing record layouts, used as input to your logical data modeling process, contain processing-oriented flags. As you can see, it would be incorrect merely to translate each field from the existing record layout to an attribute in your logical data model diagram. Thus, you cannot assume that computer-system records are equivalent to entities, fields to attributes, or pointers to relationships within your logical data model.

RULE LDM6.8

If you must represent attributes in encoded form for business reasons, keep the coded values *mutually independent.*

If you establish overlapping coded values, you will be likely to make user queries unnecessarily complex. Consider the following example:

Code	Meaning
WM	weekly paid, managerial employee
WP	weekly paid, professional employee
BM	biweekly paid, managerial employee
BP	biweekly paid, professional employee

To list all weekly employees, a query must search for two codes: WM and WP.

It is preferable to define two distinct encoded attributes (assuming the users insist that you use codes at all):

Pay Code	Meaning	Level Code	Meaning
W	weekly	M	managerial
B	biweekly	P	professional

DERIVED DATA

Derived data are attributes that you can determine by applying an algorithm to some other attribute(s). For example, the sum of all employees' salaries, count of employees within each department, and net product price (gross price less discount) are all derived attributes.

RULE LDM6.9

Optionally represent *derived data* as attributes within the logical data model when they have a significant business meaning, but indicate that they are derived.

Although derived attributes add redundancy (and perhaps unnecessary complexity) to the model, often they are significant to the user. Because of this significance, you may justify including such attributes in your logical data model, but not without special consideration.

For example, examine the following sample value listings:

ORDER

NUMBER (PK)	CUSTOMER*NUMBER	TOTAL—AMOUNT
1	15	500.00
2	24	630.00

LINEITEM

ORDER*NUMBER (PK)	NUMBER (PK)	PART*NUMBER	AMOUNT
1	1	533	100.00
1	2	645	400.00
2	1	768	200.00
2	2	871	430.00

The corresponding logical data model (excluding the related CUSTOMER and PART entities) is:

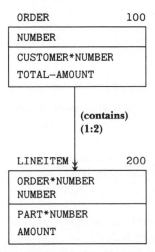

TOTAL—AMOUNT is in fact redundant because it equals the sum of the AMOUNT attribute values for LINEITEM entities related to a specific ORDER. Your objective is to develop a *minimal* logical data model, with no unnecessary or redundant components. Inclusion of TOTAL—AMOUNT on the diagram can be misleading if you do not indicate that this attribute is derived (hence, redundant). That is, a database designer or application developer may not recognize its dependency on another attribute and the need to maintain that dependency to ensure consistency of data values.

A clearer diagram denotes TOTAL–AMOUNT as derived. For example, add the designation (d) following derived attributes:

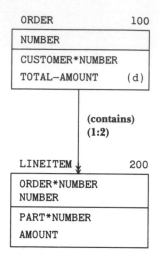

You should also document formulas for derived attributes in the data dictionary (for example, TOTAL–AMOUNT is equal to the sum of the AMOUNT values in LINEITEMs associated with the specific ORDER).

PLACEMENT OF ATTRIBUTES IN SUBTYPES, SUPERTYPES, AND CATEGORIES

Recall that a *subtype* and *supertype* designate exactly the same object in the real world. However, a subtype represents a subset of the supertype (for example, EXECUTIVE is a subtype of EMPLOYEE). A *category* is a set of one or more mutually exclusive subtypes (for example, EXECUTIVE, MONTHLY–PAID, and HOURLY–PAID make up one category based on payroll type).

A category is said to *span* its associated supertype if and only if every supertype is associated with a subtype occurrence within the category. A category may or may not span a supertype (i.e., there may be supertype occurrences with no associated subtype occurrence).

Sometimes, the user identifies an attribute (for example, PAYROLL–CODE) that determines membership in a particular subtype. This attribute is known as a *subtype identifier*. Note that such an attribute is not required, but it is frequently identified as having business meaning to the user. If identified, this attribute is at least partially redundant because its meaning already is conveyed by the existence of category or subtype relationships. Therefore, you need to define business rules synchronizing the values of the subtype identifier with occurrences of the corresponding subtypes. To facilitate defining these business rules (addressed in Step LDM9), we introduce the next rule.

RULE LDM6.10

Use a special designation for *subtype identifiers* in the logical data model.

In the following example, PAYROLL–CODE is a subtype identifier for the *payroll-type* category. PAYROLL–CODE is flagged with the (s) notation.

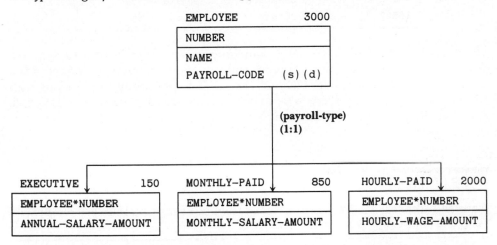

PAYROLL–CODE also is flagged as a derived attribute (d). PAYROLL–CODE is derived because the user indicates it can assume values designating *only* the subtypes EXECUTIVE, MONTHLY–PAID, and HOURLY–PAID. Thus, PAYROLL–CODE is *wholly* redundant, because it can be determined from the subtype relationships.

Consider, however, the following example:

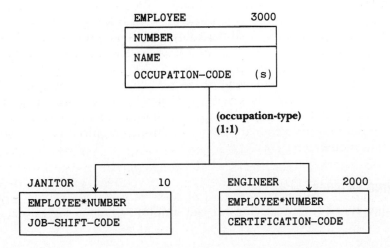

A sample value listing for EMPLOYEE is

EMPLOYEE

NUMBER (PK)	NAME	OCCUPATION–CODE (s)
24352	Smith	janitor
18719	Barnabas	engineer
44531	Champion	executive
19822	Gordon	contractor

Here a value of OCCUPATION–CODE sometimes is associated with a subtype occurrence (i.e., if janitor or engineer) and sometimes is not (e.g., if executive or contractor). Therefore, OCCUPATION–CODE is not wholly redundant with the subtypes and is not flagged as derived in the logical data model. It is still, however, flagged as a subtype identifier.

RULE LDM6.11

Place attributes that are common to all occurrences of a supertype entity in the *supertype* rather than in each of its associated *subtypes*.

Rule LDM6.11 is consistent with Rule LDM6.2, that you should place attributes as high in the logical data model as possible. Rule LDM6.11 has the effect of minimizing redundancy; when feasible, the attribute appears in the least number of entity types. On the other hand, if the attribute occurs in only some of the subtypes within a category, associate it with those subtypes. Moreover, even if the attribute occurs in all the subtypes but would be null in supertypes *not* associated with a subtype (i.e., the category does not *span* the supertype), place the attribute in the subtypes.

You are nearly done! Following these guidelines, you should have (95 to 98 percent of the time) correctly placed attributes in entities. You will reevaluate such placement in the next step (Chapter 8). For now, let us make sure that you truly have defined the minimal number of entities required in this view of the logical data model.

COMBINING ENTITIES

Remember that you are striving for the simplest, minimal logical data model.

Thus, wherever you can, combine entity types *without introducing redundancy* and *without sacrificing clarity or business meaning*. We discuss four guidelines for simplifying the logical data model by combining entities.

RULE LDM6.12

In general, *combine* entities with the same primary key into one entity. Exceptions include entities with truly distinct business meanings.

Frequently, two entities with the same primary key represent the same object in the real world. For example,

```
CONTRACTOR                        CONSULTANT
┌─────────────────────┐         ┌─────────────────────┐
│ NAME                │         │ NAME                │
├─────────────────────┤         ├─────────────────────┤
│ ADDRESS-TEXT        │         │ PHONE-NUMBER        │
└─────────────────────┘         └─────────────────────┘
```

Do the primary keys in these two entities have the same meaning and represent the same object (i.e., is contractor a synonym for consultant)? If so, a simpler view is

```
      CONSULTANT
    ┌─────────────────────┐
    │ NAME                │
    ├─────────────────────┤
    │ ADDRESS-TEXT        │
    │ PHONE-NUMBER        │
    └─────────────────────┘
```

Of course, the user must determine whether in fact the two objects are the same and can be combined into one entity. Clues include the entity volumes (are there always corresponding occurrences of both objects?) and business rules (are the insert and delete rules consistent for relationships involving the objects?). For instance, the RESERVATION and TICKET entities below have the same primary key but different conditions for existence (i.e., different entity volumes). Thus they represent different objects with truly distinct business meanings.

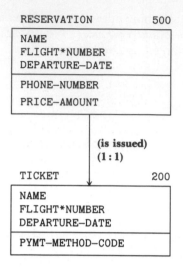

Sometimes when two entities represent different objects (perhaps with different attributes and relationships) yet have the same primary key, they may be subtypes of a not-yet-defined supertype. For example,

PRIVATE–RESIDENCE	COMMERCIAL–BUILDING
STREET–ADDRESS TOWN–ADDRESS STATE–ADDRESS	STREET–ADDRESS TOWN–ADDRESS STATE–ADDRESS
STYLE–CODE HOUSE–SIZE BEDROOM–COUNT BATHROOM–COUNT YARD–SIZE	TYPE–CODE BUILDING–SIZE GROUNDS–SIZE ROOM–COUNT TENANT–COUNT

PRIVATE–RESIDENCE and COMMERICAL–BUILDING have some different (and some similar) attributes, although they share the same primary key. Thus, perhaps they are subtypes of a supertype PROPERTY.

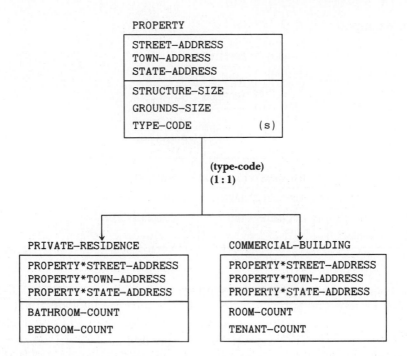

In this diagram, some attributes of PRIVATE–RESIDENCE and COMMERCIAL–BUILDING have become attributes of PROPERTY (i.e., the primary keys; HOUSE–SIZE and BUILDING–SIZE, which are renamed STRUCTURE–SIZE; YARD–SIZE and GROUNDS–SIZE, which are called GROUNDS–SIZE; and STYLE–CODE and TYPE–CODE, which are called TYPE–CODE). TYPE–CODE is flagged as a subtype identifier but is not denoted derived. (Apparently TYPE–CODE conveys information that is beyond that indicated by the subtypes; that is, TYPE–CODE can assume multiple values for each subtype.) Moreover, by establishing a category, you indicate that a given property cannot be both a private residence and a commercial building. You would, of course, validate all these assumptions with the user.

You may discover other opportunities for combining entities by examining all the subtypes initially identified by the user. Are they truly distinct entities?

RULE LDM6.13

In general, *combine* into one subtype all subtypes having the same attributes and the same relationships. (Possibly include a new attribute representing the distinction among the original subtypes.)

For example,

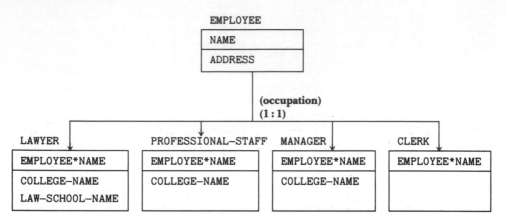

It may make more sense (and be simpler) to combine PROFESSIONAL–STAFF and MANAGER into one subtype. The combined subtype, PROFESSIONAL, would contain the common attribute COLLEGE–NAME and one additional attribute POSITION–TITLE–NAME designating staff or manager:

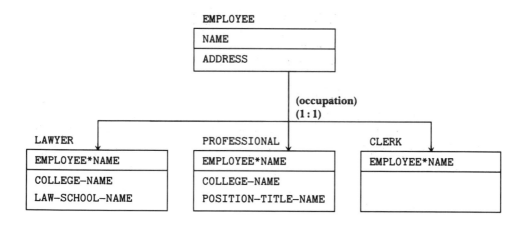

Of course, if you had already defined an attribute representing member-ship in a particular subtype (for example, a derived subtype identifier OCCUPATION–CODE in the supertype EMPLOYEE), you generally would not need a new attribute (such as POSITION–TITLE–NAME). However, the subtype identifier (OCCUPATION–CODE) no longer would be derived, since it would now convey additional information (specifically, manager versus staff designation) beyond that indicated by membership in a subtype.

Once you have consolidated subtypes as much as possible, look for opportunities to combine supertypes with subtypes. Your original purpose in identifying subtypes was to highlight *subsets* of an entity having business significance and typically differentiated by additional attributes or relationships. However, you may find that some of these subsets are not truly meaningful.

RULE LDM6.14

In general, *combine* with its associated supertype any subtype that spans the supertype.

For example, consider this diagram:

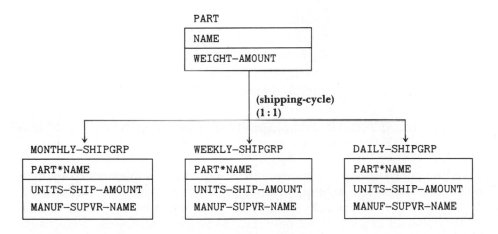

First, note that MONTHLY-SHIPGRP, WEEKLY-SHIPGRP, and DAILY-SHIPGRP all have the same attributes and participate in the same relationships. Thus, following Rule LDM6.13, combine them into one subtype SHIPGRP. This entity includes one new attribute SHIP-CYCLE-TEXT designating the distinctions among the original subtypes MONTHLY-SHIPGRP, WEEKLY-SHIPGRP, and DAILY-SHIPGRP (assuming PART did not originally include a similar, derived subtype identifier SHIP-CYCLE-TEXT).

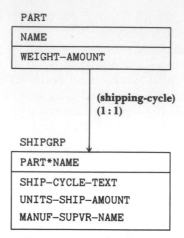

Now, *if* SHIPGRP spans PART (i.e., for every PART there exists an associated SHIPGRP), you no longer have any reason to distinguish SHIPGRP from PART. Instead, following Rule LDM6.14, combine the supertype (PART) with its subtype (SHIPGRP):

```
             PART
             ┌──────────────────────┐
             │ NAME                 │
             ├──────────────────────┤
             │ WEIGHT—AMOUNT        │
             │ SHIP—CYCLE—TEXT      │
             │ UNITS—SHIP—AMOUNT    │
             │ MANUF—SUPVR—NAME     │
             └──────────────────────┘
```

Notice that, if SHIPGRP did not span PART, combining the two would cause some PART occurrences to contain null values for the attributes SHIP—CYCLE—TEXT, UNITS—SHIP—AMOUNT, and MANUF—SUPVR—NAME. Since null values add complexity to the model and to subsequent implementation, do not consolidate a supertype/subtype when the subtype does not span the supertype.

Finally, a user occasionally will identify entities that have business meaning but that contain key attributes only (i.e., no nonkey attributes). Such entities also are candidates for consolidation.

<hr />

RULE LDM6.15

In general, *combine* entities containing no nonkey attributes with their child entities (if any).

<hr />

For example,

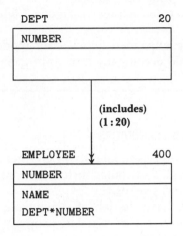

Because you have already represented department number in the EMPLOYEE entity, and because apparently the user requires no additional information about DEPT, you may as well combine the two entities:

Now DEPT–NUMBER is no longer a foreign key.

Note that we refer to this technique as combining two entities, and not as eliminating one entity. Had you merely eliminated the DEPT entity, the EMPLOYEE entity would still (incorrectly) show DEPT*NUMBER as a foreign key.

Be aware that some other user view may contain additional information about department (such as DEPT–NAME and DEPT–LOCATION) and thus may include the entity DEPT. Indeed, every nonkey attribute in a particular user view may be a foreign key in some other user view. You will accommodate these different representations in Step LDM10.

You have now completed the process of adding attributes to the user view using primarily intuitive techniques. In Step LDM7, you will check your results by applying a more rigorous and precise procedure known as *normalization*.

CASE STUDY

Let us look once again at what the passenger reservations agent has said about Moon Launch Enterprise (see Chapter 5). Figure 7.5 lists, names, and classifies the information items.

Figure 7.6 shows the expanded logical data model diagram for this user view. Naturally, you would accompany it by appropriate data dictionary or design documentation.

IMPLEMENTATION TIPS AND TECHNIQUES

Attributes are the easiest objects to identify in an interactive logical data modeling workshop. For example, attributes include the column headings the user wants to see on reports and screens.

You, as data analyst, have the job of structuring the user's identification and definition of attributes so that you can properly associate them with the correct entities. Ask yourself these questions:

☐ Is an attribute identified by the *whole* primary key of some previously defined entity? Do you need to establish a new entity type, not yet mentioned by the user?

☐ Is the user agreeing with your placement of each attribute as high in the model as possible? If not, are you sure you are comprehending the user's intended definition of the attribute? For example, you may think that CURRENT–ACCOUNT–BALANCE belongs with the ACCOUNT entity. If the user wants to record a history of CURRENT–ACCOUNT–BALANCE as it changes from hour to hour, however, perhaps CURRENT–ACCOUNT–BALANCE belongs instead with a TRANSACTION entity.

☐ Do subtypes and supertypes seem to present more confusion than they are worth? You should be seeing this payoff: If attributes and relationships truly differ across subtypes, you have places in which to record those differences. If not, then perhaps you should combine (eliminate) the subtypes.

☐ Does the user want to include derived data? If so, accommodate the need, but flag the attributes as derived. Also, take time to capture correct definitions of the derivations.

☐ Are naming standards confusing to the user or taking up too much time? Stop and agree on a standard list of abbreviations and class words. This list will help you to be consistent as well as more productive.

SUMMARY

In this chapter, you completed the detailed data structure of your preliminary user view by adding nonkey attributes to the logical data model. In Steps LDM3

FIGURE 7.5 Moon Launch passenger reservations—Classification of information items.

Paragraph	User Term	Assigned Name	Classification
1a	passengers	`PASSENGER`	entity
	identification numbers	`PASSENGER.CODE`	primary key of `PASSENGER`
	within their respective countries	`PASSENGER.COUNTRY-NAME`	primary key of `PASSENGER`
1b	passenger's age	`PASSENGER.AGE-YEARS`	nonkey attribute of `PASSENGER`
	fares	`FLIGHT.STANDARD-FARE-AMOUNT`	nonkey attribute of `FLIGHT`
	—	`FLIGHT`	entity (existence implied by user through mention of fares)
	credit rating	`CREDIT-RATING`	entity
	credit rating discounts	`CREDIT-RATING.DISCOUNT-AMOUNT`	candidate key (probably alternate key) of `CREDIT-RATING`
	special fares	`RESERVATION.FARE-AMOUNT(d)`	derived nonkey attribute of `RESERVATION` (equals (one minus `CREDIT-RATING.DISCOUNT-AMOUNT`) times `FLIGHT.STANDARD-FARE-AMOUNT`)
	—	`RESERVATION`	entity (implied by user)
1c	last name	`PASSENGER.LAST-NAME`	nonkey attribute of `PASSENGER`
	first name	`PASSENGER.FIRST-NAME`	nonkey attribute of `PASSENGER`
	middle name	`PASSENGER.MIDDLE-NAME`	nonkey attribute of `PASSENGER`
	title	`PASSENGER.TITLE-NAME`	nonkey attribute of `PASSENGER`
1d	place of business	`BUSINESS`	entity
	—	`BUSINESS.COUNTRY-NAME`	primary key of `BUSINESS` (discovered in follow-up conversation with user)
	—	`BUSINESS.NAME`	primary key of `BUSINESS` (discovered in follow-up conversation with user)
	business passengers	`BSNSS-PASSENGER`	entity—subtype of `PASSENGER`
	in the case of a business passenger, the mailing address for billing information is place of business	`BUSINESS.BILLING-ADDRESS`	nonkey attribute of `BUSINESS`

(continued)

FIGURE 7.5 (continued)

Paragraph	User Term	Assigned Name	Classification
	mailing address for tickets can be either	BSNSS-PASSENGER.TICKET-ADDRESS	nonkey attribute of BSNSS-PASSENGER
	personal residence	PASSENGER.ADDRESS	nonkey attribute of PASSENGER
	vacation passengers	VCTN-PASSENGER	entity—subtype of PASSENGER
1e	for business passengers, credit rating is that of the place of business	BUSINESS.CREDIT-RATING*CODE	foreign key in BUSINESS
	all passengers have credit ratings	VCTN-PASSENGER.CREDIT-RATING*CODE	foreign key in VCTN-PASSENGER
	credit ratings	CREDIT-RATING.CODE	primary key of CREDIT-RATING
2a	flight	FLIGHT.NUMBER	primary key of FLIGHT
	desired flight for reservation	RESERVATION.FLIGHT*NUMBER	foreign key in RESERVATION
	———	RESERVATION.DEPARTURE-DATE	implied
	method of payment	RESERVATION.PAYMENT-CODE	nonkey attribute of RESERVATION
	price of ticket	RESERVATION.FARE-AMOUNT (d)	derived nonkey attribute of RESERVATION (see paragraph 1b)
	date of entry of the reservation	RESERVATION.ENTRY-DATE	nonkey attribute of RESERVATION
	employee identification numbers	RESERVATION.AGENT-NUMBER	nonkey attribute of RESERVATION
2b	ticket prices	RESERVATION.FARE-AMOUNT (d)	derived nonkey attribute of RESERVATION (see paragraph 1b)
	credit rating code	CREDIT-RATING.CODE BUSINESS.CREDIT-RATING*CODE VCTN-PASSENGER.CREDIT-RATING*CODE	primary or foreign keys (see paragraph 1e)
2c	base price	FLIGHT.STANDARD-FARE-AMOUNT	nonkey attribute of FLIGHT
	all seats are nonsmoking	———	does not provide any useful information, so not included
	all seats have no windows	———	does not provide any useful information, so not included

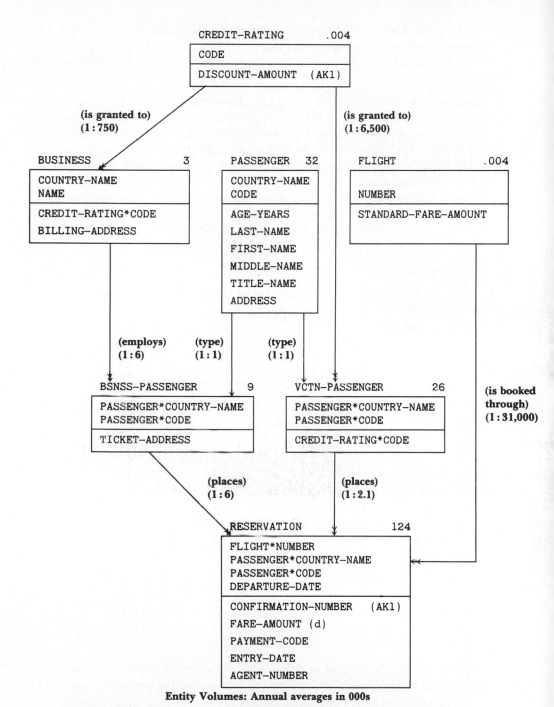

Entity Volumes: Annual averages in 000s

FIGURE 7.6 Moon Launch passenger reservations logical data model; Step LDM6.

and LDM4, you had already identified *key* attributes in the model: *primary keys* and *alternate keys,* which identify entities, and *foreign keys,* which complete relationships by identifying the parent. We recapitulate the rules for dealing with remaining attributes.

1. Associate each attribute with that entity the entire primary key of which is necessary and sufficient to identify it. Moreover, place the attribute as high in the logical data model as possible (i.e., place the attribute in a parent rather than in a child entity whenever appropriate). Reclassify multivalued attributes as child entities. In other words, *make every nonkey attribute dependent on the (primary) key, the whole key, and nothing but the key.*
2. Name attributes according to an organizational naming standard that facilitates clear, descriptive, intuitive, and unique names. A suggested naming standard for attributes in the logical data model is as follows:

   EntityName.Modifier(s)-Classword

   or, for foreign keys:

   EntityName.ParentEntityName*Modifier(s)-Classword
3. Diagram attributes by placing them inside the appropriate entity box. Primary keys go above a horizontal line, and all other attributes go below the line:

   EMPLOYEE

NUMBER
NAME
TOWN–NAME
PHONE–NUMBER

4. Use *sample value listings* to help illustrate the meanings of entities and attributes. For example,

   EMPLOYEE

NUMBER (PK)	NAME	TOWN–NAME	PHONE–NUMBER
02435	Conway	Richardson	658–2308
19786	Law	Sugarland	843–1111
55518	Thomas	Garland	761–2238

5. If there are attributes that describe a relationship, reclassify the relationship as an entity. Relate the new entity to the original two entities as the child in two new relationships.

6. Avoid *encoded attributes* unless the codes have a significant meaning to the user. Above all, do not include processing-oriented flags that have no meaning outside of a computer system. If codes are necessary, keep their values mutually independent.
7. Optionally include *derived data* in the logical data model when such attributes have business significance. However, flag them as derived and document their derivations.
8. Flag *subtype identifiers* denoting membership in a particular subtype. If they are wholly redundant with the existence of subtypes, also flag them as derived.
9. Place attributes common to all supertype occurrences in the supertype rather than in the subtypes. Place attributes that are unique to subtypes in the appropriate subtypes.
10. Combine entities when doing so does not result in loss of meaning. Thus, in general, combine (1) entities with the same primary key (with the exception of subtypes, supertypes, and other entities with truly distinct business meanings); (2) subtypes with the same attributes and relationships (with the possible addition of one new attribute designating the original subtype distinctions); (3) subtype and supertype, when the subtype spans the supertype; and (4) parent and child entities when the parent has no nonkey attributes.

EXERCISES

7.1 Define *nonkey attribute*. What is meant by Rule LDM6.2, that nonkey attributes be placed as *high* as possible in the logical data model? Why is this rule important?

7.2 Why might you include derived attributes in your logical data model even though they may be a form of redundant data?

7.3 Why is it inappropriate merely to translate existing record layouts to entities, field definitions to attributes, and pointer information to relationships within the logical data model?

7.4 Suppose a user for Moon Launch Enterprise is interested in a data item representing the total number of reservations for a given flight. How can you represent this in your logical data model?

7.5 Suppose Moon Launch Enterprise decides to implement a single credit-rating scheme applying to all its passengers (rather than maintaining credit ratings for businesses). How does your logical data model change?

7.6 Perform Step LDM6 for the baggage tracking and control department of Moon Launch Enterprise (see Exercises 5.6 and 6.6 for descriptions of the user view). In addition, suggest five or six other attributes that you think the user might need. (Verify them with the user, of course.) Add them to your logical data model diagram.

7.7 Perform Step LDM6 for the space shuttle maintenance control group (see Exercises 5.7 and 6.7 for user requirements). Suggest five or six additional attributes that the user might consider, and add them to the logical data model.

C H A P T E R

8 Validate User Views Through Normalization

In Step LDM6 you associated attributes with entities by following a set of intuitive rules. *Normalization* is a formalization of those intuitive rules. Normalization is a body of theory addressing analysis and decomposition of data structures into a new set of *relations* (flat data structures) that exhibit more desirable properties.

STEP LDM7: VALIDATE NORMALIZATION RULES

You normalize a data structure to ensure internal consistency, minimal redundancy, and maximum stability. Yet, normalization neither results in loss of information, nor introduces spurious information.

A fully normalized data model is an *optimal* logical data model in the sense that it best meets the logical data design objectives of correctness, consistency, simplicity, nonredundancy, and stability. If you were to translate a logical data model directly into a database design, with no tailoring or tuning for particular application requirements or performance, a normalized design would provide the following advantages:

1. *Minimize amount of space required to store the data.* Normalization precludes storing data items in multiple places (except for foreign keys).
2. *Minimize risk of data inconsistencies within the database.* Because you store data items only once whenever possible, you run minimal risk of data values becoming inconsistent.

3. *Minimize possible update and delete anomalies.* Storing multiple copies of the same data item raises concerns in an update or delete operation: How should the other copies be affected? Similarly, associating an attribute with the wrong entity can cause accidental loss of information during updates or deletes. There are examples of these potential problems later in the chapter. Normalization avoids such possibilities.

4. *Maximize stability of the data structure.* Normalization assists in associating data attributes with entities based on the inherent properties of the data rather than on particular application requirements. Thus, new application requirements are less likely to force changes in the database design.

Because the normalization process is based solely on the meaning of the data, it does not consider particular processing needs. Thus, a fully normalized database design (i.e., prior to any tailoring or tuning) may not be an optimal database design. For instance, it may not meet performance objectives. Later you may choose to reevaluate and perhaps to tailor the design (for example, by selectively introducing controlled redundancies) to favor particular processing priorities. However, you will avoid any such tuning until *after you complete the full normalization process,* so that you can evaluate all potential tuning options to-gether.

Normalization provides a formalized set of techniques for performing some of the intuitive analyses discussed in Step LDM6. However, normalization can only verify *structural correctness and consistency* of the data model. It cannot vali-date *accuracy* of the model in reflecting the business meaning of the data. Thus, it is applied here as a check of the consistency of a data model built through the more intuitive business analysis discussed in Steps LDM1 through LDM6.

Some data modeling methodologies are based almost entirely on normaliza-tion transformations. In these methodologies, designers use normalization rules successively to refine relations and to eliminate structural redundancies and in-consistencies. The designers do not use any business modeling concepts such as entities or relationships. These methodologies may result in a model that is structurally correct but that incompletely represents the business meaning of the data requirements. In this book, normalization serves as one technique among others in a full analytic methodology.

Normalization includes several steps to reduce successively the logical data model to "more desirable" data structures, each exhibiting greater consistency, less redundancy, and improved stability. The results of these normalization steps are known as first, second, third, Boyce/Codd, fourth, and fifth normal forms.

You will look most closely at first, second, and third normal forms, which are easiest to understand and most important. These three normal forms were the originals defined by E.F. Codd in early papers on normalization theory. Usually, third normal form is adequate to ensure a correct, consistent, and nonredundant logical data model.

Boyce/Codd normal form is a more refined and precise redefinition of third normal form. It is called Boyce/Codd because it was developed by Boyce and Codd and evolved subsequent to the development and popular acceptance of Codd's third normal form.

Fourth and fifth normal forms are quite complex, and, in fact, data models that are in third normal form usually (although not always) also are in fifth normal form. Fourth and fifth normal forms evolved to address shortcomings identified in the lower-level normal forms. Fifth normal form is the ultimate normal form. Thus, you need not fear having to master sixth, seventh, or *n*th normal forms in another few years.

Bear in mind that this chapter presents the various forms of normalization in a step-by-step process to facilitate your understanding of each form and of its benefits and shortcomings. In reality, it is probably unimportant for you to remember the definition of each. (If asked, you can always look them up.) Rather, you should understand the characteristics of a desirable (and still practical) normal form (i.e., perhaps only third), because you will want to ensure that your logical data model possesses these characteristics. Moreover, as you gain experience, you will not necessarily dissect your logical data model step by step into progressively more stable normal forms. Rather, you will be able intuitively to recognize and correct flaws in your logical data design to bring it directly to third normal form without explicitly analyzing violations of particular normalization rules.

The discussions in this chapter do not have the precision and rigor of a full treatment of normalization theory. Such treatment is not required to impart the basics that you need for data design. Instead, the material is presented in a commonsense fashion, to be more applicable to the average database designer.

FIRST NORMAL FORM

First normal form addresses organizing data as "flat" structures with no repeating groups.

RULE LDM7.1

Reduce entities to *first normal form* (1NF) by removing repeating or multivalued attributes to another, child entity.

First normal form requires that each entity occurrence have a fixed number of single-valued attributes. That is, an entity in first normal form does not contain repeating groups. Each attribute is atomic and has a unique meaning and name.

An example of an entity not in first normal form is an EMPLOYEE entity that includes dates and amounts for the last three paychecks (i.e., repeating, multi-valued attributes):

```
        EMPLOYEE            1000
      ┌─────────────────────────┐
      │ NUMBER                  │
      ├─────────────────────────┤
      │ NAME                    │
      │ TOWN-TEXT               │
      │ PAY-DATE                │
      │ AMOUNT                  │
      │ PAY-DATE                │
      │ AMOUNT                  │
      │ PAY-DATE                │
      │ AMOUNT                  │
      └─────────────────────────┘
```

A sample value listing is

EMPLOYEE

NUMBER (PK)	NAME	TOWN-TEXT	PAY-DATE	AMOUNT	PAY-DATE	AMOUNT	PAY-DATE	AMOUNT
01245	Fleming	W. Orange	9/2/85	200	9/9/85	200	9/16/85	250
78612	Von Halle	Morristown	9/2/85	165	9/9/85	168	9/16/85	193
39826	Conway	Simsbury	9/2/85	350	9/9/85	350	9/16/85	350

The repeating attributes are PAY-DATE and AMOUNT. Note that these attributes might have three different names (such as PAY-DATE-ONE, PAY-DATE-TWO, and PAY-DATE-THREE), but they are still considered to be repeating if the attributes have essentially the same meaning.

To reduce the EMPLOYEE entity to first normal form, remove repeating attributes to a new, child entity called PAYCHECK as follows:

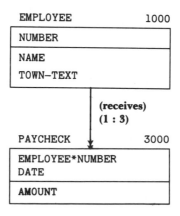

Now there are no repeating (or multivalued) nonkey attributes in either EMPLOYEE or PAYCHECK, as shown in the sample value listings:

EMPLOYEE

NUMBER (PK)	NAME	TOWN—TEXT
01245	Fleming	W. Orange
78612	Von Halle	Morristown
39826	Conway	Simsbury

PAYCHECK

EMPLOYEE*NUMBER (PK)	DATE (PK)	AMOUNT
01245	9/2/85	200
01245	9/9/85	200
01245	9/16/85	250
78612	9/2/85	165
78612	9/9/85	168
78612	9/16/85	193
39826	9/2/85	350
39826	9/9/85	350
39826	9/16/85	350

Actually, first normal form requires that repeating groups be represented down the rows rather than across the columns. (This property should sound familiar—it was discussed in Chapter 3 as one of the properties of a relation.) Moreover, you achieve this property by applying exactly the same technique as that described in Rule LDM6.3, which calls for removing multivalued attributes from entities. First normal form is simply a formal name for the result. Rule LDM6.3 is an intuitive guideline for achieving first normal form.

Achieving first normal form in logical data design is important for three reasons: (1) it adds simplicity to the logical data model (simpler data structures), (2) it gives you the ability to apply further normalization techniques, and (3) it gives you the ability to transform the logical data model to any database structure without sacrificing functionality. For example, the data manipulation operators in a relational data model (discussed in Chapter 3) function correctly with a database in first normal form.

SECOND NORMAL FORM

Second normal form refines the data model a little further. It addresses decomposition of first normal form structures so that the full primary key is necessary to identify all associated attributes.

RULE LDM7.2

Reduce first normal form entities to *second normal form* (2NF) by removing attributes that are not dependent on the *whole* primary key.

Second normal form requires that each nonkey attribute in a first normal form entity be fully dependent on the entire primary key.

Recall that a primary key is a *minimal* set of attributes required to identify uniquely each occurrence of an entity. A *nonkey attribute* is any attribute that is not part of the primary key. Second normal form prohibits assignment of nonkey attributes to entities where a subset of the primary key can determine the nonkey attribute.

For example, consider the following line item entity:

LINEITEM

| ORDER–NUMBER |
NUMBER
VENDOR–NAME
VENDOR–TOWN–NAME
PRODUCT–CODE
PRODUCT–AMOUNT

A sample value listing indicates that the entity is probably not in second normal form:

LINEITEM

ORDER–NUMBER (PK)	NUMBER (PK)	VENDOR–NAME	VENDOR–TOWN–NAME	PRODUCT–CODE	PRODUCT–AMOUNT
124	1	Smith	Madison	145	50
124	2	Smith	Madison	83	63
138	1	Jones	Boston	9762	119
138	2	Jones	Boston	19	253
138	3	Jones	Boston	81	18

Notice that VENDOR–NAME and VENDOR–TOWN–NAME have the same values for every line item on a given purchase order. Imagine how tedious it would be to change the vendor on a purchase order. The DBMS would have to modify VENDOR–NAME and VENDOR–TOWN–NAME for every line of the purchase order. Moreover, imagine the difficulty of establishing a purchase order with no line items (for example, a purchase order authorizing expenditure of dollars without specifying line items). You would have no way of associating a vendor with such a purchase order.

The problem is that VENDOR–NAME and VENDOR–TOWN–NAME probably do not depend on the whole primary key. They are determined by a subset of the primary key—namely, ORDER–NUMBER. Thus, remove them to a (new or existing) parent purchase order entity (ORDER) having primary key ORDER.NUMBER:

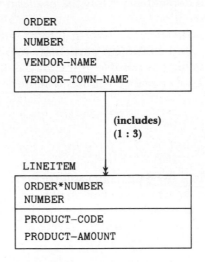

The new sample value listings are

ORDER

NUMBER (PK)	VENDOR–NAME	VENDOR–TOWN–NAME
124	Smith	Madison
138	Jones	Boston

LINEITEM

ORDER*NUMBER (PK)	NUMBER (PK)	PRODUCT–CODE	PRODUCT–AMOUNT
124	1	145	50
124	2	83	63
138	1	9762	119
138	2	19	253
138	3	81	18

Note the reduced redundancy.

You see how a sample value listing is required to identify the presence of this type of redundancy. You are unlikely to recognize the redundancy by examining the logical data model diagram alone. However, a sample value listing is not sufficient to identify the presence of a redundancy. Verification by the user of data dependencies and relationships also is required. For example, you deduced above that ORDER–NUMBER determines VENDOR–NUMBER and VENDOR–NAME by examining five sample rows. It is possible that these rows merely capture a coincidence and that a sixth or seventh sample row would contradict the presumed dependency. Only the user can verify that such dependencies hold without exception.

You typically will achieve second normal form intuitively, following the guidelines presented in Step LDM6. In particular, recall Rule LDM6.2, which says to place attributes as high as possible in the logical data model. By applying this rule, you naturally tend to place attributes where they depend on the whole primary key.

THIRD NORMAL FORM

Third normal form refines the data model still further. It addresses elimination of *transitive dependencies* in which nonkey attributes depend not only on the whole primary key but also on other nonkey attributes (other than alternate keys).

RULE LDM7.3

Reduce second normal form entities to *third normal form* (3NF) by removing attributes that depend on other, nonkey attributes (other than alternate keys).

Third normal form requires that each nonkey attribute in a second normal form entity depend on the *entire* primary key (as required for second normal form) and *nothing but* the primary (or alternate keys).

Consider the purchase order entity again:

ORDER

NUMBER
VENDOR–NAME
VENDOR–TOWN–NAME

with sample value listing:

ORDER

NUMBER (PK)	VENDOR–NAME	VENDOR–TOWN–NAME
124	Smith	Madison
138	Jones	Boston
221	Johnson	Los Angeles
253	Madley	Houston
391	Jones	Boston
511	Johnson	Los Angeles
624	Thomas	New Orleans
836	Smith	Madison

VENDOR–TOWN–NAME is always the same for a given VENDOR–NAME regardless of ORDER.NUMBER. This should raise three questions. First, what happens when vendors relocate? Do you change their towns on every outstanding purchase order, or should the purchase order reflect a vendor's location as of date of issuance? Second, will the user ever want to know the location of a vendor to whom no purchase orders have been issued? Where should you store that information? Third, if you archive or delete purchase orders after a certain period, should the user risk losing information about where the vendor is located?

The problem is that VENDOR–TOWN–NAME, although uniquely determined by the primary key ORDER.NUMBER, probably also depends on a nonkey attribute, VENDOR–NAME. Third normal form addresses such anomalies by removing VENDOR–NAME and VENDOR–TOWN–NAME to a (new or existing) parent entity, VENDOR. VENDOR*NAME becomes a foreign key in ORDER:

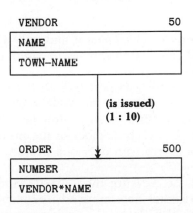

Notice the reduced redundancy.

Here again, user verification of data definitions and dependencies is required to ascertain third normal form compliance or violations. For example, consider the first question we raised: What happens when vendors relocate? Should a purchase order reflect vendor location as of date of issuance? If so, then VENDOR–TOWN–NAME in ORDER depends not on VENDOR–NAME but only on ORDER.NUMBER, and is appropriately placed in the ORDER entity. Does the user also want to track the vendor's current location? If so, then you have two attributes: ORDER.VENDOR–TOWN–NAME (appropriately associated with the ORDER entity) and VENDOR.CURRENT–TOWN–NAME (within the VENDOR entity).

Third normal form generally results from the intuitive practice of placing attributes as high in the logical data model as possible (Rule LDM6.2). Thus, the formal definition of third normal form—elimination of transitive dependencies—should merely check your analysis up to this point.

BOYCE/CODD NORMAL FORM

Boyce/Codd normal form addresses elimination of potential redundancies when there are multiple, composite, overlapping candidate keys. In this case, *depending on your choice of primary key,* you may not have spotted all potential problems when applying the rules associated with first, second, and third normal forms.

RULE LDM7.4

Reduce third normal form entities to *Boyce/Codd normal form* (BCNF) by ensuring that they are in third normal form for any feasible choice of candidate key as primary key.

An entity is in *Boyce/Codd normal form* if and only if all attributes are determined only by each full candidate (primary or alternate) key, and *not* by any subset of a candidate key.

Consider a PROJECT entity composed of the attributes PROJECT.NUMBER, PROJECT.MEMBER–NAME, and PROJECT.ADVISOR–NAME. Assume that (1) each project has many members; (2) a given person may be a member of several projects; (3) for each project, each member of the project works with only one advisor; (4) each advisor works with only one project; and (5) a given project may have several advisors.

There are two candidate keys for the PROJECT entity: project number and member name, which together determine advisor name, or advisor name and member name, which together determine project number. Either candidate key can be chosen as primary key with the other functioning as alternate key. We call these alternatives ASSIGNMENT1 and ASSIGNMENT2:

ASSIGNMENT1

PROJECT–NUMBER
MEMBER–NAME (AK1)
ADVISOR–NAME (AK1)

or

ASSIGNMENT2

ADVISOR–NAME
MEMBER–NAME (AK1)
PROJECT–NUMBER (AK1)

Notice that ASSIGNMENT1 is in third normal form: ADVISOR–NAME depends on the *entire* primary key (PROJECT–NUMBER plus MEMBER–NAME) and on *nothing but* the primary key. ASSIGNMENT2, however, is *not* in third normal form: PROJECT–NUMBER depends on a subset of the primary key, ADVISOR–NAME alone. You can more clearly see the redundancies associated with this structure by inspecting a sample value listing:

ASSIGNMENT1 or ASSIGNMENT2

PROJECT–NUMBER	MEMBER–NAME	ADVISOR–NAME
101	Johnson	Brown
101	Michaels	Brown
101	Stewart	Graham
492	Johnson	Thomas
492	Altman	Thomas
492	Michaels	Andrews

Observe that, if Brown marries and changes her name to Browning, you must update her name in two places. (Multiple updates to reflect a single piece of information should be required only in the case of a foreign key—the only permissible attribute redundancy in a minimal logical data model.) Moreover, if Stewart resigns from project 101, you lose the information that Graham advises that project. These are the same update anomalies you have tried to eliminate through second and third normal forms. In fact, if you choose MEMBER–NAME and ADVISOR–NAME as the primary key (ASSIGNMENT2 design alternative), the problems show up immediately.

A better implementation that eliminates the redundancy is as follows:

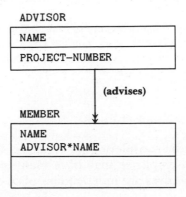

ADVISOR

NAME
PROJECT–NUMBER

(advises)

MEMBER

NAME
ADVISOR*NAME

These entities are both in third normal form. Also, each has only one candidate key. Thus, they are in third normal form for *any* feasible choice of primary key and they satisfy the rules for Boyce/Codd normal form as well.

This less redundant solution, however, has its own problems. You lose the information (business rule) that, on a given project, each member works with only one advisor. In other words, nothing stops you from associating a particular member with more than one advisor on the same project. You need to enforce this business rule through a *customized insert constraint* (i.e., key business rule as discussed in Chapter 6) governing valid insertions of MEMBER and updates of the foreign key MEMBER.ADVISOR*NAME. Specifically, the customized insert constraint must reference a nonkey attribute (PROJECT–NUMBER) of ADVISOR.

Despite this problem, Boyce/Codd normal form is preferred over the older third normal form definition because it reduces redundancy in logical design. However, you must support the normalized entities and relationships with a set of integrity constraints to ensure a comprehensive and consistent logical data model.

FOURTH NORMAL FORM

Fourth normal form addresses recognition and separation of independently multivalued attributes constituting a composite primary key. Probably, you will perform this step intuitively at the very beginning of the design process simply by recognizing and distinguishing among independent repeating groups. However, first-through third normal form definitions do not explicitly address this rule.

RULE LDM7.5

Reduce Boyce/Codd normal form entities to *fourth normal form* (4NF) by removing any independently multivalued components of the primary key to two new parent entities. Retain the original (now child) entity only if it contains other, nonkey attributes.

We clarify this rule by considering an example. Consider an entity representing the fact that an employee may have many skills and many job objectives. The skills and objectives are independent of one another:

EMPLOYEE–SKILL–OBJECTIVE

| NAME |
| SKILL–NAME |
| OBJECTIVE–TEXT |

EMPLOYEE–SKILL–OBJECTIVE

NAME (PK)	SKILL–NAME (PK)	OBJECTIVE–TEXT (PK)
Fleece	accounting	more money
Fleece	accounting	prestige
Fleece	public speaking	more money
Fleece	public speaking	prestige

The problem with this structure is that you must repeat each objective for each skill. Adding a new skill for Fleece, for example, requires two updates to associate Fleece's two objectives with the new skill.

Clearly, a better solution is

EMPLOYEE–SKILL

| EMPLOYEE–NAME |
| SKILL–NAME |

EMPLOYEE–OBJECTIVE

| EMPLOYEE–NAME |
| OBJECTIVE–TEXT |

with sample value listings:

EMPLOYEE–SKILL

EMPLOYEE–NAME (PK)	SKILL–NAME (PK)
Fleece	accounting
Fleece	public speaking

EMPLOYEE–OBJECTIVE

EMPLOYEE–NAME (PK)	OBJECTIVE–TEXT (PK)
Fleece	more money
Fleece	prestige

The original entity remains as a child of the two new entities *only* if it has additional nonkey attributes. For example, suppose the user distributes merit awards recognizing combinations of skills and job objectives. Figure 8.1 illustrates a full logical data model including such an AWARD entity. Figure 8.2 illustrates a sample value listing for AWARD.

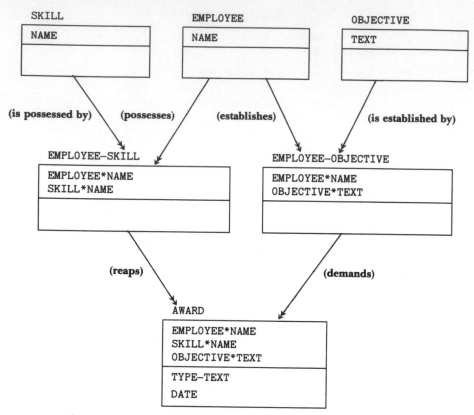

FIGURE 8.1 Logical data model for skills, job objectives, and merit awards.

FIGURE 8.2 Sample value listing for AWARD.

AWARD

EMPLOYEE*NAME (PK)	SKILL*NAME (PK)	OBJECTIVE*TEXT (PK)	TYPE–TEXT	DATE
Fleece	accounting	more money	10% merit raise	1/1/82
Fleece	accounting	prestige	announcement about CPA	1/1/84
Fleece	public speaking	more money	$1000 bonus	1/1/85
Fleece	public speaking	prestige	thank you letter	1/10/86

FIFTH NORMAL FORM

Fifth normal form addresses cyclic dependencies that warrant decomposition of an entity into three or more equivalent entities (i.e., representing the same information) with less redundancy. Fifth normal form differs from the lower-level normal forms in that it requires *simultaneous* decomposition into three or more smaller entities, rather than *repeated* decompositions into two smaller entities (as you did in first through fourth normal forms). Partially for this reason, you may have difficulty recognizing when an entity is in fourth yet not in fifth normal form. For the same reason, the rule for decomposing entities to fifth normal form is less than obvious.

This brief discussion defines the final (fifth) normal form. However, because fifth normal form is complex and unintuitive, it is less useful than first through third or even fourth normal form in database design. Typically, if you achieve third normal form in your design, you are doing well enough. Thus, read this section as a challenge, and do not be discouraged if you feel confused.

RULE LDM7.6

Reduce fourth normal form entities to *fifth normal form* (5NF) by removing pairwise *cyclic dependencies* (appearing within composite primary keys with three or more component attributes) to three or more new parent entities.

A *cyclic dependency* occurs in a composite primary key composed of attributes A, B, and C, if, whenever pairwise associations of particular values of A and B (A1, B1), B and C (B1, C1), and C and A (C1, A1) are all present within three or fewer entity occurrences—as for example in (A1, B1, C2), (A2, B1, C1), and (A1, B2, C1)—then the same values of A, B, and C (A1, B1, C1) also occur together within one entity occurrence. An example will help to clarify this statement, although fifth normal form *is* complex.

Consider a relationship among buyers, vendors, and products as follows:

> Whenever a particular buyer A buys from vendor B who makes product C, *and* buyer A is responsible for buying product C, *then* buyer A buys product C from vendor B.

Notice that this conclusion does *not* automatically follow. That is, you must determine from the user whether such a rule applies. For example, Bloomingdale's buyers may be responsible for buying jeans and may even buy from Jordache (manufacturer of jeans and sneakers). However, they may choose to buy only sneakers from Jordache and to buy jeans from Calvin Klein (another jeans manufacturer).

For this discussion, assume a business rule that dictates that any jeans buyer who buys a product from Jordache in fact buys jeans from Jordache. This is a cyclic dependency, established by the unique rules of a particular business. Consider the following data model:

```
              BUYING
        ┌─────────────────────┐
        │ BUYER*NAME          │
        │ VENDOR*NAME         │
        │ PRODUCT*NAME        │
        ├─────────────────────┤
        │ UNITS—AMOUNT        │
        └─────────────────────┘
```

with sample value listing:

BUYING

BUYER*NAME (PK)	VENDOR*NAME (PK)	PRODUCT*NAME (PK)	UNITS—AMOUNT
Ann	Jordache	Jeans	100
Ann	Jordache	Sneakers	250
Sue	Jordache	Jeans	310
Ann	Liz Claiborne	Blouses	150
Sue	Liz Claiborne	Blouses	400

Now suppose suddenly Liz Claiborne adds jeans to her product line. Following our business rule, because Ann and Sue both buy from Liz Claiborne, and Ann and Sue both buy jeans, and now Liz Claiborne sells jeans, now both Ann and Sue must buy jeans from Liz Claiborne. Thus, two updates (at least) are required to add the information that Liz Claiborne sells jeans.

A better design would decompose BUYING into three entities reflecting the pairwise associations: BUYVEND, VENDPROD, and BUYPROD. Or, if BUYING has other nonkey attributes (such as units purchased), establish the three new entities as parents of BUYING:

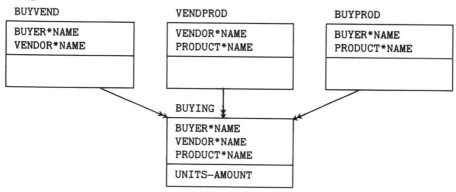

This solution, however, presents other problems in that (similar to Boyce/Codd normal form) some information about cross-entity business rules no longer appears in the data structure and must be recorded elsewhere in the data model. For example, if you replace the BUYING entity entirely by the BUYVEND, VENDPROD, and BUYPROD entities (i.e., because there are *no* other non-key attributes associated with BUYING), then you lose any explicit association of buyer with vendor and product together. You must represent in some other way the business rule stating that all such associations are valid. On the other hand, if you keep the BUYING entity because of the presence of nonkey attributes, then you have accomplished little through the three new entities. They represent no new information, and you still have insert rules that require insert of two BUYING entities for (Ann, Liz Claiborne, jeans, some amount) and (Sue, Liz Claiborne, jeans, some amount) when Liz Claiborne adds jeans to her product line—that is, when you add the VENDPROD entity (Liz Claiborne, jeans).

These anomalies serve to reemphasize the importance of incorporating business rules as well as a normalized data structure into your logical data model. Normalization by itself may yield an incomplete representation of information requirements.

Fifth normal form is *theoretically* important as the final normal form. Like first through fourth normal forms, it is targeted at removing redundancies based on project and join dependencies. Recall that projects involve selecting subsets of attributes from entities. Joins involve matching and combining attributes across entities. The definition of fifth normal form is sufficiently general to address all possible project or join redundancies not resolved by first through fourth normal forms. As such, it also is called the *projection–join normal form* and is the ultimate in normal forms with respect to projects and joins.

However, fifth normal form is complex, usually is unintuitive, typically is difficult to understand, and frequently is not particularly useful. Thus, it is a relatively low-priority part of a pragmatic design methodology.

ADDITIONAL NORMALIZATION CONSIDERATIONS

We add a few cautions against overzealous (potentially incorrect) application of normalization concepts.

RULE LDM7.7

In general, *do not split* fully normalized entities into smaller entities.

In other words, do not overnormalize. For example, consider the fully normalized SUPPLIER entity:

```
         SUPPLIER
        ┌─────────────────────────┐
        │ NAME                    │
        ├─────────────────────────┤
        │ ADDRESS                 │
        │ CREDIT–TERMS            │
        └─────────────────────────┘
```

Breaking SUPPLIER apart into two smaller entities SUPADDRESS and SUPCREDIT (which are also normalized) does not violate any normalization rules.

```
   SUPADDRESS                     SUPCREDIT
  ┌──────────────────┐          ┌──────────────────┐
  │ NAME             │          │ NAME             │
  ├──────────────────┤          ├──────────────────┤
  │ ADDRESS          │          │ CREDIT–TERMS     │
  └──────────────────┘          └──────────────────┘
```

In fact, if you break every entity into a set of entities, each consisting of only the primary key and one nonkey attribute, you do not violate any normalization rules. However, you introduce additional entities and unnecessary complexity to the logical data model. You may even mislead someone into believing that you have completed a security or performance analysis. Thus, for now in the logical data modeling process, decompose entities until you reach third normal form (or fifth, for the ambitious data analyst) and no further! In other words, strive for third to fifth normal form with the least number of entities.

Notice that Rule LDM7.7 is essentially equivalent to Rule LDM6.12. In general, combine entities with the same primary key into one entity. A major exception, pointed out in the discussion of Rule LDM6.12, is subtypes. Subtypes reflect a difference in business meaning of two entities that have the same primary key. Thus, it is appropriate to separate subtypes into different entities. Note that normalization theory does not explicitly recognize subtypes, because normalization does not address business meanings or concepts such as entities. Normalization deals with only structural validity and consistency, as embodied in associations and dependencies among attributes.

The methodology in this book balances consideration of business meanings and structural consistency. *First,* base your model on business concepts such as entities. *Subsequently,* apply normalization theory to verify structural validity and consistency of your entities.

RULE LDM7.8

Reevaluate the normalized data model in light of *insert and delete rules* and *timing considerations.* Introduce additional attributes or entities if necessary to prevent temporal integrity anomalies (loss of data due to historical events and timing differences).

For example, consider the supplier–purchase order relationship:

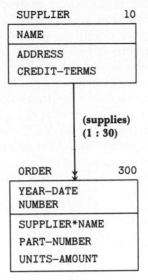

Suppose the delete rule for SUPPLIER is *no effect* (i.e., you may delete the parent SUPPLIER entity with no effect on existing child ORDER occurrences). Then how would you find the address or credit terms of the supplier for an old purchase order?

Or suppose a supplier moves, resulting in update of the address. Do users need to remember the address on past purchase orders?

Possible solutions to these dilemmas are as follows:

1. Accept the loss of data. Clearly, you can choose this alternative only if users have no need to access or remember "old" supplier addresses.
2. Add a SUPPLIER–ADDRESS attribute to ORDER. Maintain supplier address as redundant data in both entities (until the address changes, when only the SUPPLIER entity is updated). Or, store a null or default value in the SUPPLIER–ADDRESS attribute in ORDER until the address changes; then record the historic address in ORDER. (No true redundancies here, but it is complicated.) In either case, you need customized ORDER insert and SUPPLIER delete rules.
3. Establish HISTORIC–SUPPLIER and CURRENT–SUPPLIER subtypes of SUPPLIER. Maintain historic addresses in HISTORIC–SUPPLIER. Again, you need a customized delete rule for CURRENT–SUPPLIER to trigger creation of an HISTORIC–SUPPLIER occurrence (which will inherit all relationships to old ORDERS—also complicated).

None of these solutions is really good. Probably, the last option best reflects the business meaning and therefore is your best choice in the logical data model. However, processing and performance requirements should play a part in making the choice. Accordingly, you will revisit this issue in database design when you review all application requirements and built-in facilities of your database product to tune the design where appropriate.

These examples again caution you to make normalization only one technique within a comprehensive design methodology. Normalization is neither the full nor always the right answer to a database design problem. Other factors must be incorporated into the logical data model.

Moreover, as we pointed out earlier, normalization produces a design with least redundancy but with potentially undesirable performance. During database design, you may choose to denormalize (i.e., introduce redundancy) selectively to tailor the design to particular processing requirements. It is important, however, that you first complete a fully normalized logical data model. In this way, you can be *cognizant* of introducing redundancy into the database and can *manage* it through additional customized insert and delete rules. We discuss this idea in Part 3.

CASE STUDY

Another Moon Launch Enterprise user view addresses the needs of Moon Launch's gourmet chef, Philippe.

Philippe prepares a tantalizing assortment of delicacies for each Moon Launch shuttle flight. He provides for each flight a choice of three meals, selected from his menu of 25. Each meal includes an entrée, a salad, and a dessert. On each flight, he offers a vegetarian platter, a seafood platter, and the chef's choice (standard meal option).

Passengers have the option of reserving their meal choice in advance of the flight; for example, when they book their reservation. A reservation agent records the passenger code, name, and meal preference only when the preference is a seafood or vegetarian platter. The chef ensures that each flight carries enough standard meals for all passengers who have not requested special meals in advance.

The chef also records in the system the number of standard, vegetarian, and seafood meals he is ordering for each scheduled flight. The system should automatically maintain a count of total reservations booked. Moreover, whenever a passenger reserves a special meal in advance, the system should automatically ensure that (1) the numbers of vegetarian and seafood meals ordered are still sufficient to meet all advance bookings (if not, the number ordered is incremented by five), and (2) the number of standard meals ordered is changed to the number of reservations for which special meals are *not* booked, plus a reserve of 10.

Figure 8.3 illustrates the initial logical data model diagram developed in an interactive work session with Philippe. It includes three entities: (1) FLIGHT, containing information about the meals offered on a given flight, (2) FLIGHT–SCHEDULE, providing information about the numbers of reserva-

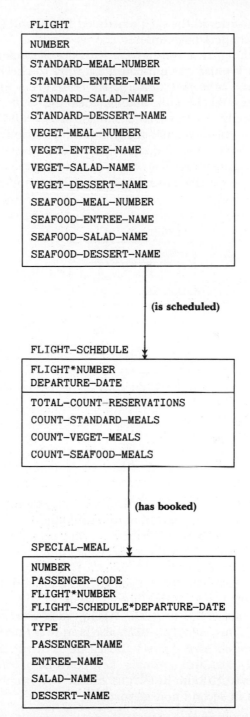

FIGURE 8.3 Moon Launch meal assignments, unnormalized; Step LDM7.

tions and meal types ordered for each scheduled flight, and (3) SPECIAL–MEAL, recording which passengers have ordered special meals.

Do you see anything intuitively wrong with the placement of some of the attributes? Probably! We use our normalization rules to check your thinking.

Is each entity "flat," or in first normal form? (Does each entity have a fixed number of attributes, each with unique meaning and name?) Consider FLIGHT—this one looks tricky. Are STANDARD–MEAL–NUMBER, VEGET–MEAL–NUMBER and SEAFOOD–MEAL–NUMBER really different attributes having unique meanings? Likewise, what about the entrée, salad, and dessert attributes? True, they do have different meanings—so what you have is probably acceptable. Alternatively, you could treat them as repeating attributes and pull them out into a new child entity, as in

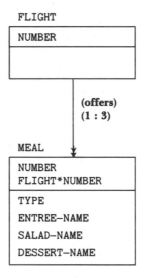

Note, however, that now you need a new attribute, MEAL.TYPE, designating whether the meal is standard, vegetarian, or seafood.

For now, we keep the original diagram, which seems acceptable—placing the three meal types within FLIGHT. Since each attribute has a unique meaning, FLIGHT is in first normal form.

Now consider FLIGHT–SCHEDULE. Each attribute has a unique meaning and name, so FLIGHT–SCHEDULE is in first normal form.

Finally, what about SPECIAL–MEAL? Again, each attribute has a unique meaning and name. Thus, SPECIAL–MEAL also is in first normal form.

Is each entity in second normal form? (Do all of its attributes depend on the whole primary key?) FLIGHT's primary key consists of only one attribute, FLIGHT.NUMBER. Every attribute in FLIGHT can be determined by the primary key. Thus, FLIGHT is in second normal form.

The primary key of FLIGHT–SCHEDULE is FLIGHT*NUMBER and DEPARTURE–DATE. Each attribute in FLIGHT–SCHEDULE is a count for a given scheduled flight, determined by FLIGHT*NUMBER and DEPARTURE–DATE. Thus, FLIGHT–SCHEDULE is in second normal form.

The primary key of SPECIAL–MEAL is NUMBER plus PASSENGER–CODE plus FLIGHT*NUMBER plus FLIGHT–SCHEDULE*DEPARTURE–DATE. This entity poses two problems: PASSENGER–CODE alone determines PASSENGER–NAME, and SPECIAL–MEAL.NUMBER alone determines TYPE, ENTREE–NAME, SALAD–NAME, and DESSERT–NAME. We can pull each set of attributes out into a new parent entity. The resultant diagram is shown in Figure 8.4. Note that the primary key of the remaining child entity (called RESERVED–MEAL) is FLIGHT*NUMBER, FLIGHT–SCHEDULE*DEPARTURE–DATE, and PASSENGER*CODE, which together determine SPECIAL–MEAL*NUMBER.

Are the entities in third normal form? (Are there any transitive dependencies, through which one nonkey attribute depends on another?) Considering the FLIGHT entity, each MEAL–NUMBER clearly determines its respective ENTREE–NAME, SALAD–NAME, and DESSERT–NAME. Pulling each set of attributes out into a new parent entity, you produce the version in Figure 8.5.

The FLIGHT–SCHEDULE entity basically appears to be in third normal form. There may be a complex formula relating the four nonkey attributes, depending on how Philippe determines his initial numbers of orders. However, we do not have enough information to define such a formula, and the formula probably would be too complicated to be useful anyway.

PASSENGER, SPECIAL–MEAL, and RESERVED–MEAL all are in third normal form.

Are the entities in Boyce/Codd normal form? (Or, are they in third normal form for any appropriate choice of primary key?) Based on the information we have, no entity has any alternate keys. You might consider ENTREE–NAME to be a possible alternate key for each MEAL entity. Even if so, each is in third normal form regardless of whether you choose X–MEAL.NUMBER or X–MEAL.ENTREE–NAME as a primary key. Thus, all entities are in Boyce/Codd normal form.

Are the entities in fourth normal form? (Does any primary key contain independently multivalued components?) The first composite primary key is in FLIGHT–SCHEDULE: FLIGHT*NUMBER plus DEPARTURE–DATE. These are not independently multivalued (i.e., you do not associate all flight numbers with all departure dates). A similar analysis holds for the composite primary key in RESERVED–MEAL. Thus, all entities are in fourth normal form.

Are the entities in fifth normal form? (Are there any cyclic dependencies in composite primary keys composed of three or more attributes?) The only three-part composite primary key appears in RESERVED–MEAL: FLIGHT*NUMBER, FLIGHT–SCHEDULE*DEPARTURE–DATE, plus PASSENGER*CODE. There are no hidden cyclic dependencies here. Thus, all entities are in fifth (ultimate) normal form.

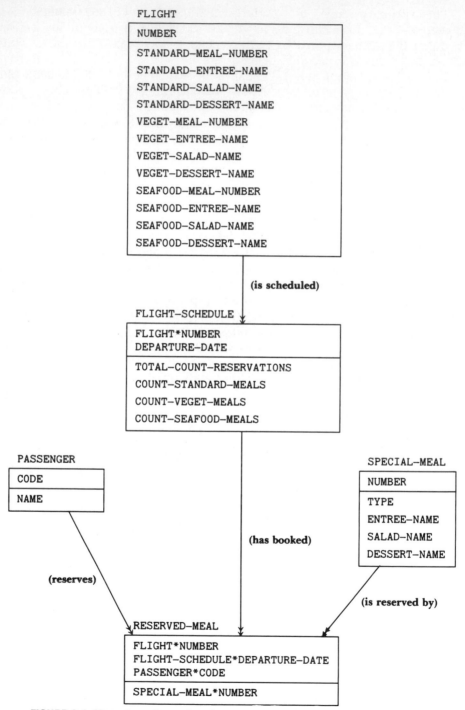

FIGURE 8.4 Moon Launch meal assignments, second normal form; Step LDM7.

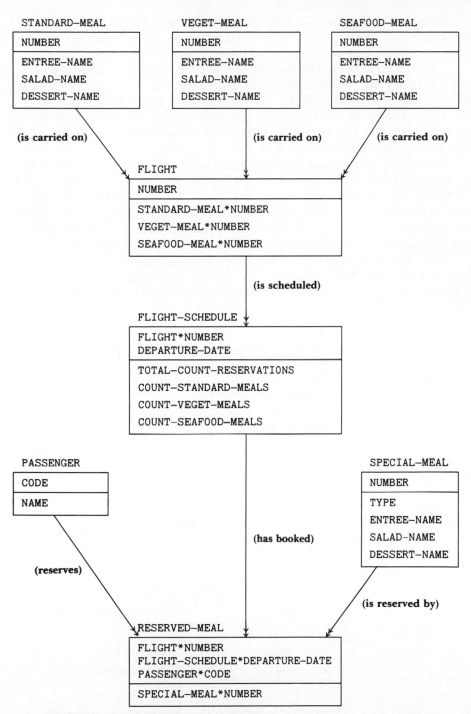

FIGURE 8.5 Moon Launch meal assignments, third normal form; Step LDM7.

Now let us examine your fully normalized user view (Figure 8.5) in light of two final questions: (1) Have you overnormalized (Rule LDM7.7)? (2) Do you need to denormalize at all due to timing differences (Rule LDM7.8)?

A symptom of overnormalization is existence of multiple entities having the same primary key. What about STANDARD–MEAL, VEGET–MEAL, SEAFOOD–MEAL, and SPECIAL–MEAL, all of which have the primary key X–MEAL.NUMBER?

These look a bit like categories of a MEAL entity. You could draw the hierarchy as shown in Figure 8.6. This structure is *normalized* (as is the one in Figure 8.5), but is it *practical?*

We can try using some intuitive guidelines for combining entities (Chapter 7, Rules LDM6.12 through LDM6.15). For example, according to Rule LDM6.15, we should combine entities containing no nonkey attributes with their child entities. SPECIAL–MEAL has no nonkey attributes (since you replaced the SPECIAL–MEAL.TYPE attribute by defining subtypes VEGET–MEAL and SEAFOOD–MEAL). So consolidate parent and children, as in Figure 8.7.

Now, can we combine the three subtypes into one entity (Rule LDM6.13)? No, all have the same attributes, but *different* relationships. VEGET–MEAL and SEAFOOD–MEAL are involved in relationships with RESERVED–MEAL, and

FIGURE 8.6 MEAL entity with hierarchy of categories.

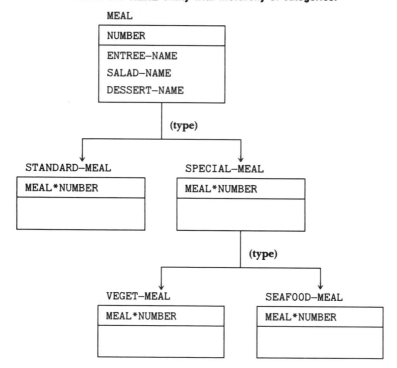

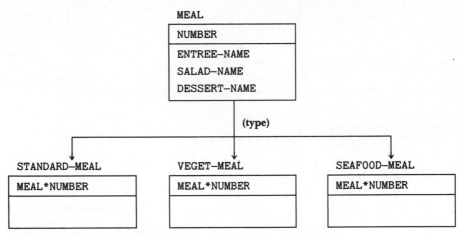

FIGURE 8.7 MEAL entity with one category.

STANDARD–MEAL is not. Thus, we cannot combine the entities any further. The resultant logical data model is shown in Figure 8.8.

Finally, do you have any potential integrity anomalies due to timing differences in updates? For example, suppose the chef Philippe decides to change the meals offered on a particular flight, effective January 1. If you happen to update FLIGHT in November to reflect January 1 meals, you lose the information about what meals Philippe is offering on FLIGHT–SCHEDULE with November and December departure dates. Thus, you should consider carrying redundant MEAL*NUMBER attributes in FLIGHT–SCHEDULE (not desirable) or alternatively adding EFFECTIVE–DATE to the primary key of the FLIGHT entity (could be complicated).

Let us just assume updates occur so that you do not have to worry about these problems. Then, Figure 8.8 truly portrays your final and fully normalized logical data model for meal assignments.

IMPLEMENTATION TIPS AND TECHNIQUES

Normalization is *not* something you want to explain to your user. There should be no need for your user to understand normalization, because intuitive techniques applied properly accomplish the same objectives. Normalization is the data analyst's "hip-pocket" tool for checking this intuitive analysis. Keep normalization concepts in the back of your mind as you guide an interactive design session. Then test your design after the work session by applying normalization rules to check for errors.

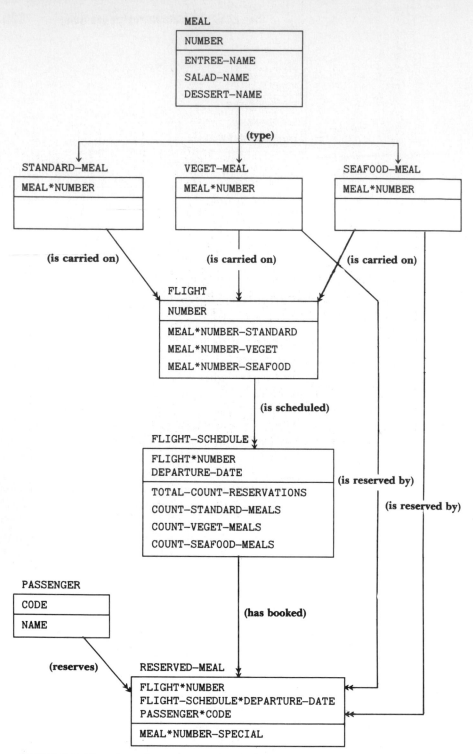

FIGURE 8.8 Moon Launch meal assignments, final normalized user view; Step LDM7.

What do normalization rules say about including derived values in the logical data model? For example, consider the following entity:

PRODUCT

CODE
NAME
PRICE–IN–DOLLARS
PRICE–IN–POUNDS   (d)

Is PRODUCT in third normal form?

☐ It is a flat data structure with no repeating groups, so it is in first normal form.

☐ Its primary key consists of one attribute that determines all nonkey attributes; thus, the entity is in second normal form. (No attributes depend on a subset of the primary key.)

☐ It does include a transitive dependency: PRICE–IN–DOLLARS determines PRICE–IN–POUNDS, and vice versa. Thus, it is *not* in third normal form.

You can *derive* PRICE–IN–POUNDS from PRICE–IN–DOLLARS (or you can derive PRICE–IN–DOLLARS from PRICE–IN–POUNDS). Similarly, many derived attributes are special cases of transitive dependencies. As such, they are prohibited by the third normal form rule, although you may keep them in your model and denote them as derived attributes.

What about the following example?

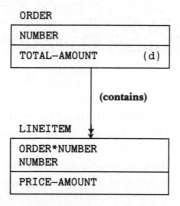

These entities are in third normal form. Yet, you can derive TOTAL–AMOUNT from the sum over PRICE–AMOUNT. TOTAL–AMOUNT is a derived attribute and therefore is redundant.

Normalization helps you discover redundancies only within entities, not across entities. You need other techniques (such as identifying derived data and employing a naming standard to assign unique names) to eliminate or to denote redundancies across relations.

What about a user view in which all attributes appear to be aggregate values, yet are not derived from one another? For example, consider a sales system that monitors monthly sales by product by customer. A possible entity in this system is

MONTHLY–SALES

CUSTOMER–NUMBER
PRODUCT–CODE
MONTH–NAME
UNITS
DOLLARS
DISCOUNT–DOLLARS

Probable formulas for two seemingly derived attributes are:

$$\text{MONTHLY–SALES.DOLLARS} = \text{UNITS} \times \text{price-per-unit}$$

$$\text{MONTHLY–SALES.DISCOUNT–DOLLARS} = \text{UNITS} \times \text{price-per-unit}$$
$$\times \text{discount-per-unit}$$

If price-per-unit and discount-per-unit appear elsewhere in your data model (perhaps in a PRODUCT entity), then MONTHLY–SALES.DOLLARS and MONTHLY–SALES.DISCOUNT–DOLLARS clearly are derived (and therefore are redundant) and should be so denoted. Assume, however, that the user has *not* identified price-per-unit or discount-per-unit as attributes in this user view. In that case, *do* you have any redundancy? Should we suggest the attributes price-per-unit and discount-per-unit as "base" attributes of another (probably PRODUCT) entity and then denote MONTHLY–SALES.DOLLARS and MONTHLY–SALES.DISCOUNT–DOLLARS as derived? Or should you just ignore attributes not mentioned by the user, since they are outside the scope of this user view (in which case you actually have no derivations and no redundancies)?

At this point, the straightforward answer is to record the attributes as the user has identified them. (Thus, show MONTHLY–SALES.DOLLARS and MONTHLY–SALES.DISCOUNT–DOLLARS and do *not* denote them as derived attributes.) However, document in the data dictionary possible derivations from other attributes outside the scope of this user view. You can decide later exactly what attributes you will store as part of the database design. At that point, you will consider two factors: (1) What attributes do other user views in this data model require? (i.e., do other user views include price-per-unit and discount-per-unit attributes, or do they also reference only the monthly figures?) (2) What type of performance does the user need? (is there time to calculate monthly figures when needed?)

This analysis could ultimately lead you to implement an entire database of seemingly derived data. For example, a profit-analysis database for senior management may consist solely of aggregate revenue, profit, and loss data, derivable from base attributes outside the scope of the data model. The derivations recorded for these aggregate figures may become specifications for an extract facility that loads the profit-analysis database. The extract facility may draw from source databases under other DBMSs or on other computer systems.

Is such a profit-analysis database normalized? It certainly is. Yet, it undoubtedly includes some planned data redundancies (e.g., across source and extract databases). These redundancies occur *across* rather than *within* entities. Therefore, normalization does not detect, eliminate, or control them.

In summary, normalization is a powerful technique for detecting and controlling many types of redundancy. However, it does not satisfactorily address all design problems.

SUMMARY

Normalization is a body of formal theory for analysis and decomposition of data structures into relations exhibiting more desirable properties.

A *normalized* data model is optimized with respect to consistency, simplicity, nonredundancy, and stability. It may not, however, fully reflect the business meaning of the data. You require other techniques, such as analysis of *entities, relationships,* and *integrity constraints,* to complement normalization in a full logical data modeling methodology.

A normalized data model also may not meet all database design objectives, such as performance optimization. You will need additional design steps (as discussed in Part 3) to tailor the design for performance and processing requirements. At that point, you may choose to introduce *controlled* data redundancy (i.e., selectively to *denormalize* the model) to achieve desired performance. However, typically denormalization introduces integrity problems that you must resolve through other mechanisms. Fully normalizing the data model *first* ensures that you see the problems raised by selective denormalization and address them appropriately.

Formal application of normalization entails several steps that successively reduce the logical data model to more desirable forms (known as *n*th normal forms).

First normal form (1NF) requires that each entity have a fixed number of attributes, each with a unique meaning and name. You achieve first normal form by removing to a child entity any repeating or multivalued attributes, thereby organizing the data as "flat" structures.

Second normal form (2NF) requires that each nonkey attribute in a first normal form entity depend on the entire primary key. You achieve second normal form by removing to a parent entity any attributes dependent on only a subset of the primary key.

Third normal form (3NF) requires that each nonkey attribute within a second normal form entity depend on the entire primary key and nothing other than the primary (and alternate) keys. You achieve third normal form by removing to a parent entity any attributes exhibiting *transitive dependencies* (i.e., nonkey attributes that depend on other nonkey attributes, where these other attributes are not alternate keys).

Boyce/Codd normal form (BCNF) requires that all attributes depend on only the full candidate keys (primary and alternate keys) and do not depend on any subset of a candidate key. You achieve Boyce/Codd normal form by assuring that an entity is in third normal form for any feasible choice of candidate key as primary key. (For many logical data models, third normal form is equivalent to Boyce/Codd normal form.)

Fourth normal form (4NF) requires that the primary key of a third normal form entity contain no independently multivalued attributes. You achieve fourth normal form by removing any pair of such attributes to two new parent entities. (Many data analysts attain fourth normal form instinctively in the process of achieving third normal form.)

Fifth normal form (5NF) requires that the primary key of a fourth normal form entity contain no pairwise cyclic redundancies. A *cyclic redundancy* occurs in a composite primary key of three or more attributes (A, B, C) if whenever entity occurrences (A1, B1, C2), (A2, B1, C1) and (A1, B2, C1) occur, then (A1, B1, C1) also is present.

In nearly all logical data models, reaching third normal form is sufficient and is equivalent to reaching Boyce/Codd normal form, fourth normal form, and fifth normal form. Thus, if you are confused about levels beyond third normal form, do not worry! The highest three levels are minutely more desirable and need be attempted only by the advanced design analyst.

There are two final rules about normalization. First, do not overnormalize. In other words, do not continue splitting entities apart once you have reached third normal form (unless you are reducing them to fourth normal form or fifth normal form). Follow the rules suggested in Step LDM6 to minimize the number of entities and to combine entities wherever doing so makes business sense without compromising third normal form (or fifth normal form). Second, look for the need to add attributes or entities to avoid potential loss of data associated with historical events or timing differences. Also add customized insert and delete rules to maintain integrity.

EXERCISES

8.1 Some logical data modeling methodologies begin with and rely solely on normalization techniques for developing a user view. Where does normalization fit into the logical data modeling methodology in this book? What aspects of a logical data model are not adequately addressed by normalization alone? What additional techniques are used in the methodology in this book?

8.2 Which design rules from Chapter 7 specifically address normalization techniques (but from a more intuitive approach)?

8.3 Which normal forms may not necessarily be accommodated by following the design rules in Chapter 7?

8.4 In the Moon Launch case study, Philippe decides to calculate the number of calories for each meal (for dieting passengers). During a design session, he indicates (not knowing normalization rules) that calories are associated with RESERVED–MEAL. Where would normalization rules dictate that calories be placed? Comment on the advantages and disadvantages of placing calories with STANDARD–MEAL, SEAFOOD–MEAL, and VEGET–MEAL.

8.5 Suppose Moon Launch Enterprise decides that Philippe must record the wholesale cost for each meal (so that they can control his expensive tastes). There are separate costs for each entrée, salad, and dessert. How is the logical data model affected?

8.6 Look at the user view you developed for baggage tracking and control (Exercises 5.6, 6.6, and 7.6). Is it fully normalized? Are there any potential information losses due to update timing considerations? (Hint: The baggage agents said that, when a passenger cancels a reservation, they mark as "canceled" the records for any baggage already booked. Are there any anomalies here?)

8.7 Reexamine the user view you developed for space shuttle maintenance control (Exercises 5.7, 6.7, and 7.7). Is it fully normalized? (Hint: Reexamine primary keys. Are all component attributes necessary? Also reexamine nonkey attributes. Do any attributes appear to be redundant? Might the space shuttle controller have improperly *directed* you to store redundant data?)

8.8 Study your Moon Launch passenger reservations user view (Figure 7.6). Did you make any errors here? Is the user view fully normalized?

C H A P T E R

9 Determine Additional Attribute Business Rules

In Chapter 6, you began defining *business rules* about data—rules governing *integrity* (correctness and consistency) of data values. You began by defining *key business rules,* which address validity of update operations on primary and foreign key attributes. In this chapter, you complete your definition of business rules by including more generalized rules governing update (and sometimes even retrieval) operations on any key or nonkey attribute.

For the sake of this discussion, we classify additional attribute business rules into two types: (1) *domains,* or constraints on the valid values that attributes may assume, and (2) *triggering operations,* or rules that govern the effects of insert, delete, update, and (less frequently) retrieval operations on other entities or on other attributes within the same entity.

We use these terms to facilitate a step-by-step approach to uncovering more business rules. As you will see, however, many business rules span both domains and triggering operations. The distinction is not important. Rather, it is important that you have a procedure for uncovering all business rules.

STEP LDM8: DETERMINE DOMAINS

A *domain* is a set of valid values for an attribute. More precisely, it is a pool of logical or conceptual values from which one or more attributes draw their values.

For example, consider the set of United States zip codes. This set may constitute the domain for attributes such as EMPLOYEE.ZIP–ADDRESS (for firms that employ U.S. residents), RESIDENT.ZIP–ADDRESS (for residents of towns within the United States), or BRANCH–OFFICE.ZIP–ADDRESS (for firms with branch offices in the United States).

Think of a domain as a new construct in your logical data model—much like a special-purpose set of separate entities. Because domains describe the valid set of values for an attribute, existence of domain definitions (separate from attribute definitions) allows you to determine more easily whether certain DML operations (e.g., comparison of two attributes) make sense.

There are two ways to go about defining domains and assigning them to attributes. One way is to define domains up front and then associate each attribute in your logical data model with the appropriate predefined domain. The other way is to assign domain characteristics (e.g., data type and length) to each attribute and then (perhaps) to determine domains by identifying similar groupings of domain characteristics.

Unfortunately, many existing dictionaries, design tools, and database systems do not provide for definition of domains as a separate construct. Thus, typically you will be forced to apply the second approach: assign domain characteristics to attributes without formally defining the domains themselves. The next few pages assume this (more usual, although perhaps less desirable) approach and discuss how to assign domain characteristics to attributes such that you can detect when two or more attributes share or overlap domains. Subsequently, the *Implementation Tips and Techniques* section provides more information on defining domains explicitly.

FIGURE 9.1 Payroll application entities.

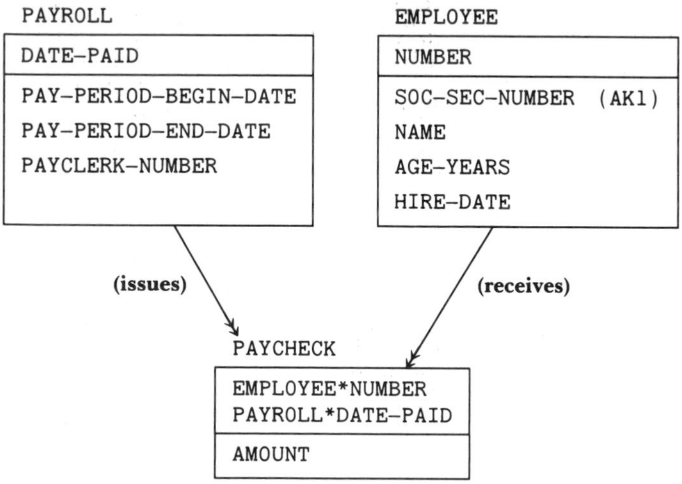

RULE LDM8.1

Associate each attribute with a *domain* or with a set of domain characteristics.

For example, consider the payroll application entities illustrated in Figure 9.1. You can define domain characteristics for each attribute as follows:

Payroll Entity

DATE–PAID
data type: date
format: cc/yy/mm/dd
range: 19/50/01/01–19/99/12/31
meaning: date when paychecks are issued
allowable values:Wednesday or Friday date based on 1950–1999 calendar
uniqueness: unique
null support: nonnull
default: equal to date inserted

PAY–PERIOD–BEGIN–DATE
data type: date
format: cc/yy/mm/dd
range: 19/50/01/01–19/99/12/31
meaning: date for beginning of pay period
allowable values: first or sixteenth date of month within 1950–1999 calendar
uniqueness: nonunique
null support: nonnull

PAY–PERIOD–END–DATE
data type: date
format: cc/yy/mm/dd
range: 19/50/01/01–19/99/12/31
meaning: date for end of pay period
allowable values: fifteenth or last date of month within 1950–1999 calendar
uniqueness: nonunique
null support: nonnull

PAYCLERK–NUMBER
data type: numeric
length: 2 digits
range: 20–50
meaning: payclerk number at firm AC/DC identifying payclerk responsible for payroll on this date
uniqueness: nonunique
null support: nonnull

Employee Entity

NUMBER
data type: numeric
length: 4 digits
range: 1000–7999
meaning: employee number at firm AC/DC

	uniqueness: unique *null support*: nonnull
SOC–SEC–NUMBER	*data type*: character *format*: numeric plus hyphens, mask nnn-nn-nnnn *meaning*: employee Social Security number at firm AC/DC *uniqueness*: if nonnull, must be unique *null support*: may be null
NAME	*data type*: character *length*: 35 characters *format*: alphabetic plus commas/period/blanks, as in C . . . C, C . . . C, C. *meaning*: employee name at firm AC/DC *uniqueness*: nonunique *null support*: nonnull
AGE–YEARS	*data type*: numeric *length*: 2 digits *range*: 18–65 *meaning*: employee age at firm AC/DC *uniqueness*: nonunique *null support*: may be null
HIRE–DATE	*data type*: date *format*: cc/yy/mm/dd *range*: 19/50/01/01–19/99/12/31 *meaning*: date when employee is hired *allowable values*: Monday through Friday date based on 1950–1999 calendar *uniqueness*: nonunique *null support*: nonnull

Paycheck Entity

EMPLOYEE*NUMBER	*data type*: numeric *length*: 4 digits *range*: 1000–6999 *meaning*: employee number receiving paycheck at firm AC/DC *uniqueness*: nonunique (as long as composite primary key EMPLOYEE*NUMBER, PAYROLL*DATE–PAID is unique) *null support*: nonnull
PAYROLL*DATE–PAID	*data type*: date *format*: cc/yy/mm/dd *range*: 19/50/01/01–19/99/12/31 *meaning*: date when paycheck is issued *allowable values*: Wednesday or Friday date based on 1950–1999 calendar *uniqueness*: nonunique (as long as composite primary key EMPLOYEE*NUMBER, PAYROLL*DATE–PAID is unique) *null support*: nonnull

AMOUNT

data type: numeric
format: 2 decimal places
range: 0–15,000
meaning: dollar value of paycheck
uniqueness: nonunique
null support: nonnull

Domains are important specifically because they (1) verify that values for an attribute (via inserts or updates) make "business sense," (2) ascertain whether two occurrences of the same value in two different attributes denote the same real-world value, and (3) determine whether various data manipulation operations (such as joins or unions in a relational database system—discussed in Chapter 3) are logical or make "business sense."

For example, domain characteristics (specifically, range) for EMPLOYEE. AGE–YEARS prevent you from adding to the firm's roster an employee who is 3 years old. Moreover, domain characteristics for EMPLOYEE.AGE–YEARS and PAYROLL.PAYCLERK–NUMBER, even though similar in data type and length, clearly are different in meaning (not to mention range and null support). Thus, the values 22 for AGE and 22 for PAYCLERK–NUMBER represent different real-world values.

Finally, domain characteristics indicate that it is probably illogical to join (match) records based on values of EMPLOYEE.AGE–YEARS and PAYROLL. PAYCLERK–NUMBER, or values of EMPLOYEE.NUMBER and PAYCHECK.AMOUNT, even though it might appear to be possible based on data type or length alone. It does make sense, however, to join (match) records based on the values of EMPLOYEE.NUMBER and PAYCHECK.EMPLOYEE*NUMBER. These attributes have a number of domain characteristics in common (i.e., same data type, same length, overlapping ranges, and similar meanings). It also makes sense to compare values of EMPLOYEE.HIRE–DATE and PAYCHECK.PAYROLL*DATE–PAID to ensure that employees do not receive paychecks prior to their hire date.

The typical types of domain characteristics that may be associated with an attribute are as follows:

Domain Characteristics	**Examples**
data type	integer decimal character
length	5 digits 35 characters
format (mask)	nnn-nnn-nnnn (e.g., telephone number) nnn-nn-nnnn (e.g., social security number) cc/yy/mm/dd (e.g., date)
allowable value constraints (e.g., range)	$0 < x < 50$ X in ('dog,' 'cat,' 'bird') X in set of valid employee numbers PK—component of primary key (the composite of which must be unique)

	AK—component of alternate key (the composite of which must be unique) FK—component of foreign key, which must obey key business rules
meaning	dollar value of purchase order street address purchase order identification number
uniqueness	unique nonunique
null support	nulls allowed nulls disallowed
default value (if any)	default of zero default of 'coach class' default equals two times current salary default equals current date

Some characteristics of a domain are *independent* of the entity to which the attribute belongs. For example, data type and length should be the same for a particular attribute throughout the logical data model, regardless of the entities with which the attribute is associated. Similarly, some aspects of allowable value constraints and meaning may apply regardless of entity. For instance, the domain of DATE–PAID is such that, in all entities (e.g., in PAYROLL and PAYCHECK), it has data type of "date," meaning of "date when paychecks are issued" (possibly with further qualifications), mask "cc/yy/mm/dd," range "19/50/01/01–19/99/12/31" (possibly qualified further), and allowable values equal to valid Wednesday and Friday dates within a 1950–1999 calendar (possibly with additional constraints).

On the other hand, some characteristics of a domain may *depend* on the entity to which an attribute belongs. Frequently, uniqueness, null support, default value, and some aspects of meaning and allowable values for an attribute vary by entity. For example, the domain of DATE–PAID also varies depending on the entity. In the PAYROLL entity, PAYROLL.DATE–PAID is a primary key and thus must be unique. In the PAYCHECK entity, PAYROLL*DATE–PAID need not be unique (since many employees can be paid on the same date), although the composite primary key (EMPLOYEE*NUMBER, PAYROLL*DATE–PAID) must be unique. Both PAYROLL.DATE–PAID and PAYCHECK.PAYROLL*DATE–PAID must be nonnull. As another example, assume the attribute PAYROLL*DATE–PAID is added to the EMPLOYEE entity, reflecting the date of the last paycheck received by a particular employee. (Actually, EMPLOYEE.PAYROLL*DATE–PAID is both a foreign key reflecting a relationship between PAYROLL and EMPLOYEE and a derived attribute equal to the last PAYROLL*DATE–PAID in a related PAYCHECK entity.) EMPLOYEE.PAYROLL*DATE–PAID may be null for new employees who have not yet received any paychecks. Moreover, EMPLOYEE.PAYROLL*DATE–PAID has the same allowable value constraints as PAYROLL.DATE–PAID, but also is restricted to values within 1 year of the current date (since you do not keep information about retired or former employees in the EMPLOYEE entity).

RULE LDM8.2

Document the domain or set of domain characteristics for each attribute in the *data dictionary* or design documentation. Include *data type, length, format* or *mask, allowable value constraints, meaning, uniqueness, null support,* and *default value* if applicable.

Document domain characteristics in two parts. For each attribute, independent of the entity to which it belongs, describe its *generic* domain characteristics: data type, length, format or mask, allowable value constraints, and meaning. In addition, for each entity in which an attribute appears, describe uniqueness, null support, default value (if applicable), additional format parameters, additional constraints on allowable values, and additional semantic characteristics (or aspects of meaning).

Thus, a given attribute in an entity inherits the generic domain for that attribute. Other characteristics of the attribute's domain are specific to its appearance in the given entity. Describe domain characteristics using a sufficiently structured syntax that you can recognize when two or more attributes have the same or similar domains. This allows you to determine when it makes sense to perform operations involving different attributes.

PRIMARY KEYS

As you already know, primary keys are attributes that possess special qualities. Hence, they have special domain considerations. Although you have already identified primary keys and their inherent properties, this is a good place to highlight (and in the process, revalidate) primary key definitions in light of domain specifications.

RULE LDM8.3

Define *domains for primary keys* to be consistent with the following rules:

- [ ] Primary keys are unique
- [ ] Components of composite primary keys are not unique
- [ ] Neither primary keys nor primary key components may be null
- [ ] Both primary keys and primary key components may accept default values (as long as primary key uniqueness still holds)

Primary keys must be unique by definition. For example, EMPLOYEE.NUMBER must be unique within EMPLOYEE; and the combination of EMPLOYEE*NUMBER plus PAYROLL*DATE-PAID must be unique within PAYCHECK.

However, components of primary keys are not defined as unique. In fact, if one component were unique, it would be incorrect to choose that component in conjunction with other components as the primary key. By definition, a primary key is a *minimal* set of attributes required to identify an entity. If only one of those attributes were needed to determine uniqueness, the other components would be unnecessary (i.e., choice of primary key would not be minimal). Consider EMPLOYEE*NUMBER and PAYROLL*DATE-PAID, the composite primary key of PAYCHECK. Neither component by itself is unique within PAYCHECK. A given employee may receive multiple paychecks (for different dates) and a given date typically is associated with many paychecks (for many employees).

Primary keys cannot be null because, by definition, primary key values must be present in every occurrence of an entity to identify the occurrence uniquely. Furthermore, if one component of a composite primary key were allowed to be null, that attribute would not be a required part of the primary key (i.e., the primary key would not be minimal). Thus, primary key components must be nonnull.

Primary keys may be permitted to assume default values. This property is most logical when the default value is based on some formula (e.g., current date or an expression involving another attribute) rather than being a fixed value. Since primary keys must be unique, only one occurrence of the primary key may contain a fixed default value at any given time. Usually, default primary keys make little sense. For example, it probably is not meaningful to assign a default employee number to a new employee, or a default order number to a new order. More frequently, components of composite primary keys may accept default values. For example, in the PAYCHECK entity, PAYROLL*DATE-PAID may default to current date without violating uniqueness of the composite primary key, PAYROLL*DATE-PAID plus EMPLOYEE*NUMBER.

ALTERNATE KEYS

Again, you are already aware of alternate keys. Their special properties can be highlighted and revalidated in the form of domain specifications.

RULE LDM8.4

Define *domains for alternate keys* to be consistent with the following rules:

☐   Alternate keys are unique

- □ Components of composite alternate keys are not unique
- □ Both alternate keys and alternate key components may be null (although use of default values is preferred)
- □ Both alternate keys and alternate key components may accept default values (as long as alternate key uniqueness still holds)

Recall that an *alternate key* is another candidate key that uniquely identifies each occurrence of an entity. The alternate key (perhaps arbitrarily) was not chosen as the primary key of the entity, however, possibly because the user considered a different candidate key to be more intuitive. Thus, alternate keys, like primary keys, must be unique. Alternate key components, also similar to primary keys, are not unique.

Because alternate keys are not chosen to be primary keys in your model, you may choose to relax the constraint that alternate key values always be present. Thus, alternate keys, unlike primary keys, may accept null values (as may components of composite alternate keys). Consider, for example, SOC-SEC-NUMBER in the EMPLOYEE entity. Perhaps the firm always assigns an employee number immediately on hiring a new employee, but employees need not supply a Social Security number until shortly before receiving the first paycheck. For this reason, you must choose EMPLOYEE.NUMBER as primary key and classify EMPLOYEE.SOC-SEC-NUMBER as an alternate key. Thus, EMPLOYEE.SOC-SEC-NUMBER may be null for a short while—after new employees are hired and before they are paid.

On the other hand, recall that, in general, use of nulls is undesirable because nulls frequently are unintuitive to the user. (Later, you will understand other implications of specifying use of nulls, depending on your database product.)

Consider substituting default values for use of nulls. Like primary keys, alternate keys and alternate key components may accept default values. Of course, only one occurrence of an alternate key may contain a fixed default value at any given time, due to the alternate key uniqueness property.

FOREIGN KEYS

The special properties of foreign keys also can be validated while you define domains.

RULE LDM8.5

Define *domains for foreign keys* to be consistent with the following rules:

- Data type, length, and format (mask) of foreign key components must be the same as data type, length, and format of corresponding primary key components in parent entities
- Uniqueness property for foreign keys must be consistent with relationship type (i.e., 1:1 relationship implies unique foreign key, 1:*N* relationship implies nonunique foreign key)
- Null support, default values, and allowable value constraints for foreign keys must be consistent with key business rules (insert/delete constraints), but may include additional constraints as needed

---

You already know that data type, length, and format (generic domain characteristics) for an attribute should be the same throughout the logical data model. This implies, in particular, that data type, length, and format of foreign key attributes should be consistent with those of corresponding primary key attributes. For example, EMPLOYEE.NUMBER should be defined as numeric and four digits both as a primary key in EMPLOYEE and as a foreign key in PAYCHECK.

You already determined the uniqueness property for foreign keys when you defined the relationship cardinality (1:1, 1:*N*). The relationship EMPLOYEE *receives* PAYCHECK is 1:*N*; thus, EMPLOYEE*NUMBER is not unique in PAYCHECK. Consider a 1:1 relationship, however, such as PAYCHECK *has* STUB. In this case, the foreign key in STUB (EMPLOYEE*NUMBER plus PAYROLL*DATE−PAID) should be unique. In fact, the foreign key of a 1:1 relationship is always an alternate key (and possibly even a primary key); thus, it must always be unique.

You have already constrained many of the other domain characteristics for foreign keys through your key business rules. For example, insert rules of *automatic* or *dependent* and delete rules of *cascade* or *restrict* (as discussed in Chapter 6) indicate that foreign key values must be a subset of corresponding primary key values. Insert/delete rules of *no effect* indicate that no such constraint is present. *Default* or *nullify* rules define existence of a default value or indicate that nulls are allowed.

Of course, additional constraints may be imposed on the foreign key domain, independent of the key business rules. For example, EMPLOYEE.NUMBER as a primary key in EMPLOYEE is restricted to a range of 1000 to 7999. Assume the relationship EMPLOYEE *receives* PAYCHECK is associated with a *cascade* delete rule and a *dependent* insert rule. Then, EMPLOYEE*NUMBER as a foreign key in PAYCHECK also must not exceed the range 1000 to 7999. However, the user may impose the additional constraint that employees identified by numbers greater than or equal to 7000 are volunteer employees and receive no paychecks. Thus, you further restrict the range of foreign key EMPLOYEE*NUMBER in PAYCHECK to 1000 to 6999. Ideally you should not embed hidden meanings in the definition of an attribute, like those implied by this definition of the domain of EMPLOYEE.NUMBER. However, sometimes the real world has already embedded hidden meanings in its domains, and you must model that world—not mold it!

Most of Rule LDM8.5 constrains domains of entire foreign keys (which are composed of groups of attributes in the case of composite foreign keys). Component attributes of composite foreign keys may by themselves have different (although not conflicting) domain characteristics. For example, a component of a composite foreign key in a 1 : 1 relationship need not be unique, as long as uniqueness of the full foreign key still holds.

DERIVED ATTRIBUTES

Recall that the values of *derived attributes* are determined by applying an algorithm to some other attribute(s). For example, in Figure 9.2, there is a derived attribute PAYCHECK–AMOUNT–TOTAL in the PAYROLL entity, where PAYCHECK–AMOUNT–TOTAL is equal to the sum of AMOUNTs for all PAYCHECK entities with a corresponding PAYROLL*DATE–PAID.

FIGURE 9.2 Derived attribute in PAYROLL.

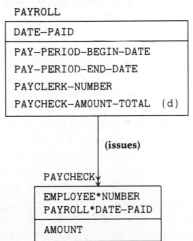

RULE LDM8.6

Define *domains for derived attributes* to be consistent with the following rules:

☐   Allowable value constraints must include the derivation algorithm
☐   Data type must be the same as data type for the source attribute(s) unless specified otherwise by the derivation algorithm
☐   Meaning must be defined using the derivation algorithm and source attribute(s) meaning

In our example, domain characteristics for PAYCHECK.AMOUNT and the derived attribute PAYROLL.PAYCHECK–AMOUNT–TOTAL are as follows:

PAYCHECK.AMOUNT

data type: numeric
format: 2 decimal places
range: 0–15,000
meaning: dollar value of paycheck
uniqueness: nonunique
null support: nonnull

PAYROLL.PAYCHECK–AMOUNT–TOTAL

data type: numeric
format: 2 decimal places
range: ≥ 0 (no upper limit)
derivation algorithm:

SUM(PAYCHECK.AMOUNT)
WHERE PAYCHECK.PAYROLL*DATE–PAID
= PAYROLL.DATE–PAID

meaning: total dollar value of paychecks issued on this date
uniqueness: nonunique
null support: nonnull

SUBTYPES, SUPERTYPES, AND CATEGORIES

Recall that a subtype is an entity representing a subset of another entity (known as a supertype) and is associated with all of the supertype's properties plus some additional ones. Typically, a subtype has a slightly more specific definition and additional attributes than does its supertype, and also potentially can have additional business rules. For example, in Figure 9.3 AUTO is a subtype of VEHICLE because (1) AUTO and VEHICLE designate the same object in the real world— therefore, all the attributes of VEHICLE (CODE, SALES–YEAR, DESCRIPTION–TEXT, WHEEL–COUNT, and so on) also characterize AUTO; and (2) AUTO has additional attributes such as REGISTRATION–FEE–DOLLARS and MAXIMUM–PASSENGER–COUNT.

Further, a subtype has the same primary key as its corresponding supertype because both designate the same object in the real world. Of course, you denote

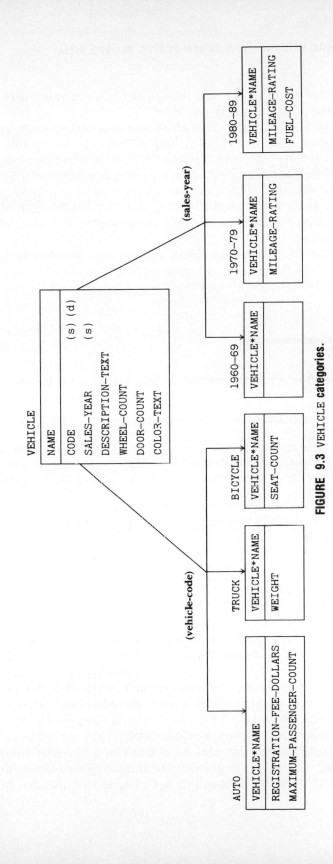

FIGURE 9.3 VEHICLE categories.

the primary key of a subtype as a foreign key, since it references the primary key of its corresponding supertype.

Also recall that a category is a set of one or more mutually exclusive subtypes. In Figure 9.3, AUTO, TRUCK, and BICYCLE make up one category of VEHICLE. Frequently, the user identifies a subtype identifier, which is an attribute that determines membership in a particular subtype of a given category. For example, VEHICLE.CODE identifies subtype membership for the category comprised of AUTO, TRUCK, and BICYCLE. VEHICLE.SALES—YEAR identifies subtype membership for another category composed of 1960–69, 1970–79, and 1980–89 subtypes.

The domain for the primary key of a subtype must reflect its dual nature as both primary and foreign key. In addition, the domain of a subtype primary key has a special dependency on the subtype identifier.

RULE LDM8.7

Define the *domain for a subtype primary key* (which is also a foreign key) to be a subset of the domain for the associated supertype primary key. Specifically,

☐ Data type, length and format must be the same as those for the supertype primary key
☐ Allowable value constraints must be based on the subtype identifier (whether the subtype identifier is explicitly represented in the logical data model or not)
☐ Meaning must be similar to that of the supertype primary key but based on the subtype identifier
☐ Uniqueness must be specified (for the entire primary key)
☐ Nonuniqueness must be specified for component attributes in the case of a composite primary key
☐ Nulls must be prohibited (both for the entire primary key and for component attributes)
☐ Default values can be specified as appropriate

We consider the implications of Rule LDM8.7 for our example. The domains for AUTO.VEHICLE*NAME, TRUCK.VEHICLE*NAME, and BICYCLE.VEHICLE* NAME all must be defined as subsets of the domain for VEHICLE.NAME. The subset definitions in this case refer to values of the subtype identifier VEHICLE.CODE (which is a derived attribute because it is wholly redundant with existence of the subtypes—see the discussion of Rule LDM6.10 in Chapter 7).

The domains for 1960–69.VEHICLE*NAME, 1970–79.VEHICLE*NAME, and 1980–89.VEHICLE*NAME must also be defined as subsets of the domain for VEHICLE.NAME. The subset definitions for this category map to groupings of values of VEHICLE.SALES—YEAR (which is a subtype identifier but not a derived attribute because it identifies a specific sales year and not just a decade, as indicated by the subtype).

Examples of these domain definitions are as follows:

VEHICLE.NAME
data type: alphabetic
length: 35 characters
format: embedded with blanks
meaning: name of vehicle
uniqueness: unique
null support: nonnull

TRUCK.VEHICLE*NAME
data type: alphabetic
length: 35 characters
format: embedded with blanks
range: = VEHICLE.NAME WHERE VEHICLE.CODE='T'
meaning: name of truck vehicle
uniqueness: unique
null support: nonnull

1970–79.VEHICLE*NAME
data type: alphabetic
length: 35 characters
format: embedded with blanks
range: = VEHICLE.NAME
WHERE 1970 ≤ VEHICLE.SALES–YEAR ≤ 1979
meaning: name of 1970–79 vehicle
uniqueness: unique
null support: nonnull

OTHER ATTRIBUTES

Domains for all other attributes in the logical data model should reflect rules defined by the user. Typically, such rules include allowable value constraints as well as data type, length, format, and meaning. Default value (if applicable), prohibition against nulls (typically), and specification of nonunique (for attributes that are neither primary keys nor alternate keys) are also generally included.

CASE STUDY

We shall reexamine the Moon Launch passenger reservations user view. The logical data model developed in Chapter 7 is repeated in Figure 9.4.

Assign domain characteristics to each attribute. Draw on what the user has already told you about passengers and reservations (refer to the case study specifications in Chapters 5 through 7). Prompt the user for any additional information you require.

Figure 9.5 illustrates a partially completed form for documenting generic domain characteristics that are *independent* of the entities: data length, data

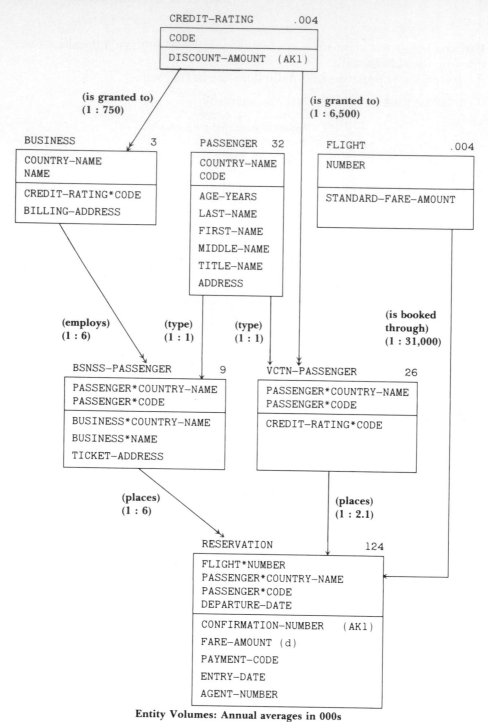

Entity Volumes: Annual averages in 000s

FIGURE 9.4 Moon Launch passenger reservations logical data model; Step LDM8.

type, format, allowable values, and meaning. Notice the form shows independent domain characteristics for primary keys and nonkey attributes only. You
do not need to define independent domain characteristics for foreign keys, because they are the same as those of corresponding primary keys.

In some cases, it may seem that you are defining exactly the same set
of independent domain characteristics multiple times. This occurs when the
same logical attribute appears in several entities, but is not (yet) identified
as a foreign key. For example, BUSINESS.COUNTRY–NAME and PASSENGER.
COUNTRY–NAME probably should draw their values from the same domain.
This may be a clue that BUSINESS.COUNTRY–NAME and PASSENGER.COUNTRY–
NAME really may be foreign keys, referring to an as-yet-undefined entity
COUNTRY.

Other questions will surface as you probe the user's domain definitions. For
example, the user defined PASSENGER.AGE–YEARS as part of the PASSENGER entity. Is age recorded only when passengers are first added to the file, or must
age be updated every time passengers place reservations? Should there be an
additional EFFECTIVE–DATE attribute associated with AGE–YEARS? Should the
AGE–YEARS attribute be associated with RESERVATION instead, or does it make
sense to record it at all? Perhaps BIRTH–DATE would be more appropriate.

In defining the domain of BSNSS–PASSENGER.TICKET–ADDRESS (with allowable values "B," indicating that tickets should be mailed to the business address,
and "P," indicating that tickets should be mailed to the personal residence), you
see that this attribute really does not represent an ADDRESS at all. Rather, it represents a FLAG, where FLAG is a class word defined as a one-character code allowed to assume only two values (e.g., on/off, or in this case "B"/"P"). Thus, for
clarity, you rename the attribute to BSNSS–PASSENGER.TICKET–ADDRESS–FLAG.

Figure 9.6 illustrates a form for documenting domain components that *depend* on (or are *specific to*) the entities to which attributes belong. Notice that included as part of "Entity-Specific Meaning and Allowable Values" is an indication of whether attributes participate in a primary, alternate, or foreign key.
You can use abbreviations to designate key participation as follows:

(PK)	primary key—attribute is used to identify this entity; must be unique and nonnull
(PK component)	primary key component—combination of this attribute with other primary key components must be unique; must itself be nonunique and nonnull.
(AK)	alternate key—attribute may be used to identify this entity; must be unique if nonnull, but may be null
(AK component)	alternate key component—combination of this attribute with other alternate key components must be unique if nonnull; must itself be nonunique but may be null
(FK) or (FK component)	foreign key or foreign key component—values must be consistent with relationship type and insert/delete/update rules

Attribute Name	Data Type, Length, and Format	Allowable Values	Meaning
CREDIT-RATING.CODE	1 character	A, B, C, D	code determining which discount to apply to base price of ticket
CREDIT-RATING.DISCOUNT-AMOUNT	signed numeric, 2 digits	-20, -10, 0, +10	percentage amount of discount to apply to base price of ticket, depending on CREDIT-RATING.CODE
BUSINESS.COUNTRY-NAME	alphabetic, 25 characters (may include blanks/periods)	—	name of country in which business is located
BUSINESS.NAME	alphabetic, 30 characters (may include blanks/periods/commas)	—	name of business
BUSINESS.BILLING-ADDRESS	alphanumeric, 60 characters (may include blanks/periods/commas)	—	business mailing address for billing, including street/P.O. box/city/state/zip/country
PASSENGER.COUNTRY-NAME	alphabetic, 25 characters (may include blanks/periods)	—	name of country of which passenger is a citizen
PASSENGER.CODE	alphanumeric, 25 characters (may include blanks/hyphens/periods)	—	identification number for passenger, as used by country of citizenship
PASSENGER.AGE-YEARS	numeric, up to 3 digits, mask zz9	0-110	age of passenger as of date of purchase of most recent ticket
PASSENGER.ADDRESS	alphanumeric, 60 characters (may include blanks/periods/commas)	—	mailing address for personal residence of passenger, including street/P.O. box/city/state/zip/country; used as mailing address for tickets and billing for vacation passengers; optionally used as mailing address for tickets for business passengers
BSNSS-PASSENGER.TICKET-ADDRESS-FLAG	alphabetic, 1 character	B or P	indicator of whether tickets should be mailed to business address (value B) or personal residence (value P)

FIGURE 9.5 Moon Launch passenger reservations logical data model; Step LDM8, entity-independent domain characteristics (selected attributes only).

Attribute Name	Uniqueness	Null Support	Default Value	Entity-Specific Meaning and Allowable Values
CREDIT–RATING.CODE	Y	N	—	(PK)
CREDIT–RATING.DISCOUNT–AMOUNT	N	N	—	(AK)
BUSINESS.COUNTRY–NAME	N	N	—	(PK component)
BUSINESS.NAME	N	N	—	(PK component)
BUSINESS.CREDIT–RATING*CODE	N	N	C	(FK)
BUSINESS.BILLING–ADDRESS	N	N	—	—
PASSENGER.COUNTRY–NAME	N	N	—	(PK component)
PASSENGER.CODE	N	N	—	(PK component)
PASSENGER.AGE–YEARS	N	Y	—	—
PASSENGER.ADDRESS	N	N	—	—
BSNSS–PASSENGER.PASSENGER*COUNTRY–NAME	N	N	—	(PK component) (FK component)
BSNSS–PASSENGER.PASSENGER*CODE	N	N	—	(PK component) (FK component)
BSNSS–PASSENGER.BUSINESS*COUNTRY–NAME	N	N	—	(FK component)
BSNSS–PASSENGER.BUSINESS*NAME	N	N	—	(FK component)
BSNSS–PASSENGER.TICKET–ADDRESS–FLAG	N	N	B	—

FIGURE 9.6 Moon Launch passenger reservations logical data model; Step LDM8, entity-specific domain characteristics (selected attributes only).

Of course, you may define other types of allowable value constraints, specific to the entity. For example, allowable value constraints for RESERVATION.FARE–AMOUNT (flagged as derived by the (d) notation in the logical data model, Figure 9.4) should include a derivation algorithm. The domains illustrated in Figure 9.6 include no such constraints.

IMPLEMENTATION TIPS AND TECHNIQUES

In the case study, we defined domain characteristics separately for each attribute. Consequently, we may have difficulty determining whether domains for two different attributes coincide or overlap (and thus whether operations involving those attributes make sense). To answer that question easily, we need a fairly systematic coding convention for recording domain characteristics. Particularly if we are using an automated data dictionary, we want to record domains to facilitate automated detection of similarities and overlaps.

This objective is easy to meet for comparison of data types and lengths. Most data dictionaries and database systems have a well-defined syntax for defining at least selected data types and lengths, such as character (10), integer (3), decimal (10, 2), and so on.

You probably will need to define standards for additional data types and for common formats or masks, such as date (cc/yy/mm/dd), telephone (nnn-nnn-nnnn), name (————, ————, —.), and so on. You also probably will need to formalize standards for defining allowable value constraints.

An alternative option, as we mentioned at the beginning of this chapter, is to define explicitly a set of domains and then to associate the appropriate domain with each attribute. In this way, multiple attributes can be explicitly associated with the same general or entity-independent domain. For example, Figure 9.7 illustrates an explicitly defined hierarchy of general, entity-independent, and entity-specific domains associated with DATE–PAID attributes (e.g., PAYROLL.DATE–PAID and PAYCHECK.PAYROLL*DATE–PAID). Characteristics of the general domain are inherited by the entity-independent domain, the characteristics of which in turn are inherited by the entity-specific domain.

If you define domains explicitly, you should, of course, develop standard naming conventions for domains. For example, you may establish a general domain for each class word in your model and use the class word as the domain name (e.g., DATE in Figure 9.7). For entity-independent domains, you might use

FIGURE 9.7 Hierarchy of domains.

General domain	DATE *data type:* date *mask:* cc/yy/mm/dd *range:* calendar date within 1950–1999 calendar *meaning:* calendar date (century/year/month/day)
Entity-independent domain	DATE–PAID *allowable values:* Wednesday or Friday DATE within 1950–1999 *meaning:* date when paychecks are issued
Entity-specific domain	PAYROLL.DATE–PAID *uniqueness:* unique *null support:* nonnull *default value:* date of insertion *meaning:* date of this payroll
Entity-specific domain	PAYCHECK.PAYROLL*DATE–PAID *uniqueness:* nonunique (composite PK EMPLOYEE*NUMBER, PAYROLL*DATE–PAID must be unique) *null support:* nonnull *allowable values:* (PK component) *meaning:* date of this paycheck

a generic attribute name (with no entity name prefix—e.g., DATE–PAID in Figure 9.7). Of course, sometimes the generic attribute name is not meaningful. For example, the name of an entity-independent domain for CUSTOMER.NAME probably must include the word CUSTOMER. Options include CUSTOMER–NAME, CUSTOMER NAME, CUSTOMER.NAME. For entity-specific domains, it is probably best to use the full attribute name including the entity name prefix, as in PAYROLL.DATE–PAID and PAYCHECK.PAYROLL*DATE–PAID.

Implementation considerations become more complex when you define all domains explicitly. However, you are likely to see attempts to implement explicit domain constructs in future design methodologies, design tools, and DBMSs as the theory of logical data modeling (and of the relational model) evolves.

STEP LDM9: DETERMINE OTHER ATTRIBUTE BUSINESS RULES (TRIGGERING OPERATIONS)

A final type of business rules is triggering operations. *Triggering operations* are rules that govern the validity of insert, delete, update, and (less frequently) retrieval operations, including the effects of these operations on other entities or on other attributes within the same entity. Triggering operations actually encompass domains and insert/delete rules as well as all other forms of attribute business rules. Triggering operations are treated here as a separate step specifically to capture business rules that do not fall into previous sets of rules, or that you may have overlooked.

The following are examples of user rules that define triggering operations:

1. A customer may not have an outstanding total balance due of more than $1000 (total across all unpaid orders)
2. A firm cannot exceed the credit allowed by each of its suppliers (across all outstanding orders with that supplier)
3. The planned delivery date for a customer order must be at least 1 week after the date the order is placed
4. Units requested on a customer order must be a multiple of the number of units per package for that product
5. All customer orders must include at least one line item (i.e., must specify at least one product being ordered)
6. A counter is kept of total number of telephone calls received from customers to date this year; when order information is updated due to a customer telephone call, this counter must be incremented—it must never decrease in value

RULE LDM9.1

Define for all business rules *triggering operations* that maintain integrity and consistency of attribute values.

Triggering operations may reflect several types of constraints:

☐ *Constraints involving attributes across multiple entity types or occurrences.* For example, triggering operation 1 constrains the sum of balance due attributes across multiple customer order occurrences. Triggering operation 2 constrains the sum of balance due attributes across multiple supplier order occurrences to be less than the credit allowed in the supplier entity. Also, triggering operation 4 compares the attribute for number of units ordered on a customer order occurrence versus the units per package attribute on the product occurrence. Triggering operation 5 constrains the relationship between a customer order occurrence and associated line item occurrences. The *key business rules* or *insert/delete constraints* that you identified in Step LDM5 (Chapter 6) are a subset of this type of triggering operation.

☐ *Constraints involving two or more attributes within the same entity.* For example, triggering operation 3 compares the order date and delivery date attributes within a customer order entity.

☐ *Constraints involving an attribute or entity and an external parameter.* Triggering operation 6 ensures that the value of the calls-received counter always is higher than its previous value.

Triggering operations have two logical components: (1) the *trigger*, or the event and condition that cause the operation to take place (e.g., update of a particular attribute under a particular set of circumstances triggers . . .); and (2) the *operation*, or the action triggered (e.g., reject the update when specified circumstances hold true, or initiate another update to a related attribute).

It is best to be as systematic as possible in defining and documenting logic for triggering operations to facilitate implementation during a later phase. Some database environments may even enable automatic enforcement of triggering operations (automated code generation and execution), given clear and systematic logic specification.

RULE LDM9.2

Document all triggering operations in the *data dictionary* or design documentation. Include documentation about the *trigger:*

☐　Event that initiates the triggering operation (i.e., insert, update, delete, or retrieval)

- □   Object of event (i.e., name of entity and/or attribute being modified or accessed)
- □   Condition under which the triggering operation is initiated

Also include documentation about the *operation:*

- □   Action to take place (such as reject event or trigger related event)

For example, assume that the six business rules described at the beginning of Step LDM9 apply to the customer–supplier logical data model illustrated in Figure 9.8. You would document triggering operations as shown in Figure 9.9.

Note that at this time you are defining only triggering *logic.* You are not yet concerned with implementation or execution efficiency. You will tune for potential performance problems later, in Part 3. For example, the logic for trig-

FIGURE 9.8 Customer–supplier logical data model.

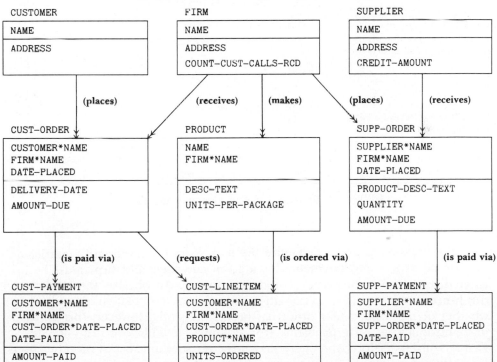

User Rule	Event	Entity Name	Attribute Name
1. Customer may not have outstanding total balance due of more than $1000 with given firm	INSERT	CUST–ORDER	–
	UPDATE	CUST–ORDER	AMOUNT–DUE
2. Firm cannot exceed credit allowed by supplier	INSERT	SUPP–ORDER	–
	UPDATE	SUPP–ORDER	AMOUNT–DUE
3. Planned delivery date for customer order must be at least 1 week after date order is placed	INSERT	CUST–ORDER	–
	UPDATE	CUST–ORDER	DELIVERY–DATE
4. Units on customer order must be multiple of units per product package	INSERT	CUST–LINEITEM	
	UPDATE	CUST–LINEITEM	UNITS–ORDERED
5. Customer orders must include at least one line item	INSERT	CUST–ORDER	–
	DELETE	CUST–LINEITEM	–
6. Keep count of customer calls received	UPDATE	FIRM	COUNT–CUST–CALLS–RECD

FIGURE 9.9 Customer–supplier triggering operations.

géring operations 1 and 2 in Figure 9.9 may seem extraordinarily inefficient because all orders and payments for a given customer and firm must be inspected every time you insert or update an order. An obvious way to reduce this processing is to add a special attribute to the CUST–ORDER entity, indicating whether or not a particular order has been fully paid. However, this solution may introduce its own problems (for example, it adds overhead to CUST–PAYMENT inserts). Moreover, there may be better solutions based on other user

Condition	Action
total of AMOUNT-DUE across all CUST-ORDER entites (including new CUST-ORDER) for this CUSTOMER*NAME and this FIRM*NAME, minus total of AMOUNT-PAID across all CUST-PAYMENT entities for this CUSTOMER*NAME and this FIRM*NAME, exceeds $1000	reject the insert
total of AMOUNT-DUE across all CUST-ORDER entities (including new CUST-ORDER) for this CUSTOMER*NAME and this FIRM*NAME, minus total of AMOUNT-PAID across all CUST-PAYMENT entities for this CUSTOMER*NAME and FIRM*NAME, exceeds $1000	reject the entire update transaction
total of AMOUNT-DUE across all SUPP-ORDER entities (including new SUPP-ORDER) for this SUPPLIER*NAME and this FIRM*NAME, minus total of AMOUNT-PAID across all SUPP-PAYMENT entities for this SUPPLIER*NAME and this FIRM*NAME, exceeds CREDIT-AMOUNT in SUPPLIER entity for this SUPPLIER*NAME	reject the insert
total of AMOUNT-DUE across all SUPP-ORDER entities (including new SUPP-ORDER) for this SUPPLIER*NAME and this FIRM*NAME, minus total of AMOUNT-PAID across all SUPP-PAYMENT entities for this SUPPLIER*NAME and this FIRM*NAME, exceeds CREDIT-AMOUNT in SUPPLIER entity for this SUPPLIER*NAME	reject the entire update transaction
DATE-PLACED +7 > DELIVERY-DATE	reject the insert
DATE-PLACED +7 > DELIVERY-DATE	reject the update
UNITS-ORDERED ÷ PRODUCT.UNITS-PER-PACKAGE for this PRODUCT*NAME is not an integer	adjust UNITS-ORDERED to nearest multiple of PRODUCT.UNITS-PER-PACKAGE
UNITS-ORDERED ÷ PRODUCT.UNITS-PER-PACKAGE for this PRODUCT*NAME is not an integer	adjust UNITS-ORDERED to nearest multiple of PRODUCT.UNITS-PER-PACKAGE
no associated CUST-LINEITEM also being inserted	reject the insert
last CUST-LINEITEM associated with CUST-ORDER	delete associated CUST-ORDER
new value ≤ old value	reject the update

requirements. Thus, postpone any tuning (in particular, avoid definition of attributes that assume certain processing solutions—see Rule LDM6.7, Chapter 7) until all the information requirements are fully understood and are reflected in the logical data model.

Also notice that triggering operations implied by user rule 5 are quite similar to the key business rules (insert and delete constraints) discussed in Chapter 6. In fact, Chapter 6 focused on rules governing valid *deletes of parent entity oc-*

currences (such as CUST–ORDER) and *inserts of child entity occurrences* (such as CUST–LINEITEM). These are the most frequently encountered and typically the most important constraints on relationships. Yet, triggering operations incorporate all other, possibly less common types of constraints, including rules governing valid *inserts of parent entity occurrences* and *deletes of child entity occurrences.* User rule 5 is an example of these less frequently encountered constraints.

Again, whether you refer to a business rule as a key business rule, a domain rule, or a triggering operation rule is not important. The concepts are discussed separately only to highlight different types of rules that are possible and that you must consider while you prompt the user with questions. Specific questions about each relationship, attribute, and entity should elicit at least key business rules and domains. Miscellaneous user comments and insightful questions should identify other triggering operations.

In general, there is no systematic way of discovering triggering operations. In a few special cases, however, triggering operations are required. We discuss these situations next.

DERIVED ATTRIBUTES

Naturally, the domain of a derived attribute depends on the value of some other (source) attribute(s). Thus, you must define triggering operations to ensure consistency of source and derived attributes after update operations.

RULE LDM9.3

Define *triggering operations* for all attributes that are *sources for derived attributes,* such that update of a source attribute triggers update of the derived attribute.

For example, consider the customer–supplier logical data model in Figure 9.8. For the sake of this discussion, assume there is a flag in CUST–ORDER indicating whether a particular order has been fully paid. This flag might be added as a (derived) attribute because it is a data item on existing documents with which the user is familiar. Perhaps it appears on current reports or is otherwise maintained by the user's department.

each parent entity (supertype). In particular, you followed two guidelines. First, the insert rule must be *automatic* or *dependent,* tailored to enforce the 1 : 1 relationship. Thus, insert of a subtype should take place only when a corresponding supertype is present (or is being inserted). Second, the delete rule must be *cascade.* Thus, delete of a supertype must cascade to delete any associated subtype.

However, these insert and delete rules are not sufficient. You typically also require a "child delete" constraint for subtypes.

RULE LDM9.4

Typically define *triggering operations for subtypes* such that, when a subtype occurrence is deleted, the corresponding supertype also is deleted.

Consider the VEHICLE category comprised of AUTO, TRUCK, and BICYCLE (in Figure 9.3). Deletion of the AUTO occurrence where VEHICLE*NAME='BUICK' should automatically trigger deletion of the corresponding VEHICLE occurrence since the two represent the same object (an automobile) in the real world.

An exception to Rule LDM9.4 may apply when a subtype or associated category does not span the supertype and reflects a condition of existence of the entity (supertype) occurrence. For example, consider a STUDENT supertype with subtype HONOR–STUDENT. A particular HONOR–STUDENT occurrence exists only as long as the student remains on the honor roll. The STUDENT occurrence is retained, however, even if the student's grades slip (assuming he does not leave the school).

RETRIEVAL TRIGGERS

Less frequent but also possible are triggering operations initiated by read access to an entity or attribute. For example, for security purposes, you may log an audit trail entry whenever anyone accesses an employee salary attribute. This triggering operation can be documented as follows:

Event	Entity Name	Attribute Name	Condition	Action
SELECT	EMPLOYEE	SALARY–AMOUNT	–	insert (User–Id, Current–Date) into SALARY–ACCESS–LOG

TIME-INITIATED TRIGGERING OPERATIONS

All the rules discussed thus far have been *data-driven* triggering operations, triggered by events involving *access or change of data.* Another type of rule is *time-driven* triggering operations, triggered by *time-initiated events.*

Consider the customer–supplier logical data model in Figure 9.8 and, in particular, the CUST–PAYMENT entity

CUST–PAYMENT

| CUSTOMER*NAME |
| FIRM*NAME |
| CUST–ORDER*DATE–PLACED |
| DATE–PAID |
| AMOUNT–PAID |

Suppose the domain of CUST–PAYMENT.DATE–PAID is constrained to include only values within the last year. Customer payments older than 1 year are deleted, archived, or perhaps copied elsewhere (e.g., for partial payments made over 1 year ago on orders that are still not closed). To enforce this domain rule, you need a triggering operation that is time-initiated. This operation is triggered by change in time, represented by update of a current date/time variable within the system. Thus, time-initiated triggering operations are actually a subset of data-driven triggering operations.

RULE LDM9.5

Define *triggering operations for time-initiated integrity constraints.* Specify the event initiating the operation (i.e., the trigger) as a change in a system current date/time variable.

In our example, you document the triggering operation as follows:

Event	Entity Name	Attribute Name	Condition	Action
UPDATE	system variable	current date	current date > CUST–PAYMENT.DATE–PAID + 1 year	delete CUST–PAYMENT

APPLICATION-SPECIFIC OPERATIONS

Data-driven (including time-driven) triggering operations are independent of any particular application. They are required to maintain consistency among values of attributes represented in the logical data model.

Other operations are *application-driven*—initiated by application transactions (external events) rather than by data-related events. For example, when a customer calls to place an order (application event), the customer service agent must insert a CUST–ORDER occurrence (resultant operation). These operations are necessary to maintain consistency between values in the data model and those in the real world. However, such operations are highly application-dependent. They are also more prone to change as the business evolves the way it operates. For example, insertion of CUST–ORDER occurrences may start out as a batched group of transactions entered nightly. It may evolve to an online operation occurring throughout the day, perhaps with several different operational components involving several users.

Do not focus on these application-driven operations now. You are concerned solely with operations required to maintain consistency and integrity *within* the logical data model. The data-driven operations prevent corrosion and contribute to the *stability* of the logical data model over time. However, application-driven requirements will be important when you assess and tune the *performance* of the database design (Part 3).

C A S E   S T U D Y

Refer again to the Moon Launch passenger reservations logical data model in Figure 9.4.

Further discussion with the user (including some insightful probing from the analyst) elicits these additional business rules about Moon Launch attributes:

1. If, 24 hours before a scheduled flight, fewer than 10 reservations have been made, flight status changes to "canceled" (to be communicated as "probable cancellation" to any inquiring would-be passenger). From then until 2 hours before the flight, any modifications to the reservation list (additions or cancellations) may affect flight status. (If fewer than 10 reservations are active at any time between 24 and 2 hours before scheduled departure, flight status is "canceled." If new reservations increase the total to 10 or more, flight status is "as scheduled.") At 2 hours before departure, flight status is made final, which determines whether or not that flight will depart.

2. Any passenger holding an active reservation on a flight that is finally canceled (i.e., it does not depart) is granted a 50-percent credit on any one future round-trip Moon Launch flight (in addition to a full refund).

3. An additional discount is available to business passengers. (You learn of this discount from the manager of business invoicing. The passenger reservations agent, who provided the initial information, was unaware of this discount.) If five or more passengers representing the same business (i.e., a branch of the same company located within the same country) book reservations on the same flight, each passenger receives an additional 10-percent discount. If cancellations cause total number of reservations from that company to fall below five, the discount is revoked.

User Rule	Event	Entity Name	Attribute Name
1. 24–2 hours before flight departure, a decrease in reservations to fewer than 10 triggers cancellation of flight; an increase in reservations to 10 or more reactivates flight	DELETE	RESERVATION	–
	INSERT	RESERVATION	–
2. Grant a 50% credit on any future round-trip flight to passengers holding reservations on flights that are finally canceled	UPDATE	system variable	current date and time
	INSERT	RESERVATION	
3. Five or more business passengers from the same company (and same country) booked on the same flight receive an additional 10% discount	INSERT	RESERVATION	–
	INSERT	RESERVATION	–
	DELETE	RESERVATION	–
4. When decreasing standard flight fare, also reduce fares on reservations already booked (but not yet used) for that flight	UPDATE	FLIGHT	STANDARD–FARE–AMOUNT
5. Ripple increased discounts in credit-rating schedule through existing booked (but unused) reservations	UPDATE	CREDIT–RATING	DISCOUNT–AMOUNT
6. Reflect changes in business name in all (current and historical) passenger records	UPDATE	BUSINESS	NAME

FIGURE 9.11 Moon Launch passenger reservations logical data model; Step LDM 9, triggering operations.

Condition	Action
remaining count of RESERVATIONs for this FLIGHT*NUMBER and DEPARTURE–DATE is less than 10, and 2 hours < (RESERVATION. DEPARTURE–DATE//FLIGHT.DEPARTURE– TIME minus current date//time) < 24 hours	set FLIGHT–SCHEDULE.STATUS–CODE to 'CANCEL'
increased count of RESERVATIONs for this FLIGHT*NUMBER and DEPARTURE–DATE is 10 or more, and 2 hours < (RESERVATION. DEPARTURE–DATE//FLIGHT.DEPARTURE–TIME minus current date//time) < 24 hours	set FLIGHT–SCHEDULE.STATUS–CODE to 'ACTIVE'
current date//time = RESERVATION. DEPARTURE–DATE//FLIGHT.DEPARTURE.TIME minus 2 hours, and associated FLIGHT. STATUS–CODE='CANCEL'	increment PASSENGER.CANC–CREDIT–COUNT by 1 for each related PASSENGER*COUNTRY–NAME and PASSENGER*CODE
PASSENGER.CANC–CREDIT–COUNT > 0 for this PASSENGER*COUNTRY–NAME and PASSENGER*CODE	decrement PASSENGER.CANC–CREDIT–COUNT by 1; also apply 50% discount to RESERVATION.FARE–AMOUNT
increased count of RESERVATIONs for this FLIGHT*NUMBER, DEPARTURE–DATE, BUSINESS*COUNTRY–NAME, and BUSINESS*NAME = 5	apply additional 10% discount to all RESERVATIONs for this FLIGHT*NUMBER, DEPARTURE–DATE, BUSINESS*COUNTRY–NAME and BUSINESS*NAME
increased count of RESERVATIONs for this FLIGHT*NUMBER, DEPARTURE–DATE, BUSINESS*COUNTRY–NAME, and BUSINESS*NAME = 6 or more	apply additional 10% discount to just this new RESERVATION
decreased count of RESERVATIONs for this FLIGHT*NUMBER, DEPARTURE–DATE, BUSINESS*COUNTRY–NAME, and BUSINESS*NAME = 4	increase fares on remaining RESERVATIONs for this FLIGHT*NUMBER, DEPARTURE–DATE, BUSINESS*COUNTRY–NAME, and BUSINESS*NAME by 11%
new value < old value	reflect decrease in all RESERVATION.FARE–AMOUNTs for this FLIGHT*NUMBER and DEPARTURE–DATE > current date
new value > old value	reflect increased discount in all RESERVATION.FARE–AMOUNTs for this CREDIT–RATING*CODE and DEPARTURE–DATE > current date
—	reflect change in BUSINESS*NAME for all associated BSNSS–PASSENGERs

4. When the standard fare for a flight decreases, all fares for reservations already booked on that flight also must change. If the standard fare increases, reservations already booked are not affected.
5. If the schedule of credit ratings and associated discounts changes, increased discounts should ripple down to booked reservations. Decreased discounts affect future reservations only.
6. If a business decides to change its name, this change should appear on all records for passengers from that business.

The triggering operations defined by these user rules are shown in Figure 9.11. Note the following observations about the translation of each user rule into triggering operations:

☐ *User rule 1*—This rule indicates the need for a new attribute—in FLIGHT called DEPARTURE-TIME. It also indicates a need for a new entity FLIGHT-SCHEDULE, with primary key FLIGHT*NUMBER, DEPARTURE-DATE, and nonkey attribute STATUS-CODE. Finally, it points out the need for access to a current date-time variable in the system.

☐ *User rule 2*—This rule defines a time-driven triggering operation. In other words, it occurs at a particular time, relative to the value of an attribute (FLIGHT.DEPARTURE-TIME) defined on the domain of time. User rule 2 indicates another new attribute: PASSENGER.CANC-CREDIT-COUNT. It also indicates that RESERVATION.FARE-AMOUNT, although derived through an algorithm, is not wholly redundant and thus is required in the logical data model after all.

☐ *User rule 3*—The complexity of these triggering operations stems from the requirement to apply (or to revoke) an additional 10-percent discount only when the count of reservations made by a particular business reaches (or drops below) five. Note that revoking the 10-percent discount implies increasing discounted fares by 11 percent. As an example, if the standard fare is $100, a 10-percent discount reduces it to $90. To revoke the discount, the fare must be increased by $10, or 11 percent (after rounding) of the $90.

☐ *User rule 4*—This rule involves an external constraint—comparing the old and new values of FLIGHT.STANDARD-FARE-AMOUNT.

☐ *User rule 5*—This is similar to user rule 4.

☐ *User rule 6*—This rule specifies how changing part of a primary key value should affect related foreign keys. Again, our discussion of key business rules in Chapter 6 concentrated on the effects of deleting (rather than inserting) parent entities. Updating a primary key can be equated to first deleting a parent occurrence and then immediately inserting another occurrence.

Figure 9.12 illustrates the Moon Launch passenger reservations user view with the additional attributes identified in Steps LDM8 and LDM9.

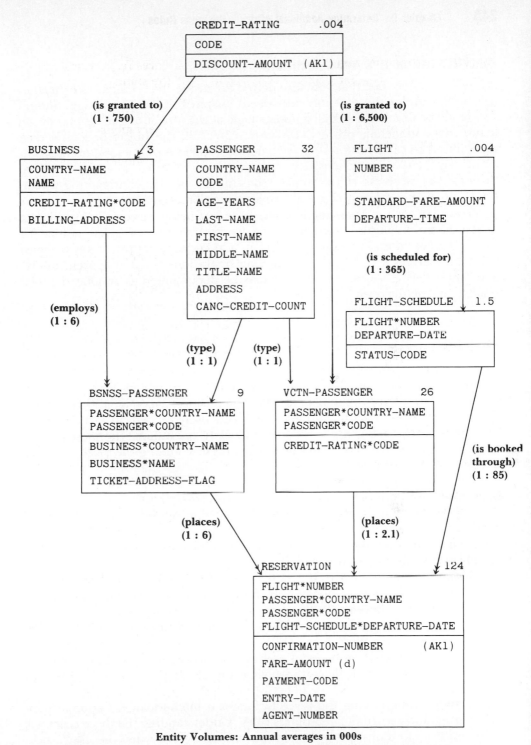

CREDIT-RATING   .004

CODE
DISCOUNT-AMOUNT   (AK1)

(is granted to)
(1 : 750)

(is granted to)
(1 : 6,500)

BUSINESS   3

COUNTRY-NAME NAME
CREDIT-RATING*CODE BILLING-ADDRESS

PASSENGER   32

COUNTRY-NAME CODE
AGE-YEARS LAST-NAME FIRST-NAME MIDDLE-NAME TITLE-NAME ADDRESS CANC-CREDIT-COUNT

FLIGHT   .004

NUMBER
STANDARD-FARE-AMOUNT DEPARTURE-TIME

(is scheduled for)
(1 : 365)

FLIGHT-SCHEDULE   1.5

FLIGHT*NUMBER DEPARTURE-DATE
STATUS-CODE

(employs)
(1 : 6)

(type)
(1 : 1)

(type)
(1 : 1)

BSNSS-PASSENGER   9

PASSENGER*COUNTRY-NAME PASSENGER*CODE
BUSINESS*COUNTRY-NAME BUSINESS*NAME TICKET-ADDRESS-FLAG

VCTN-PASSENGER   26

PASSENGER*COUNTRY-NAME PASSENGER*CODE
CREDIT-RATING*CODE

(is booked
through)
(1 : 85)

(places)
(1 : 6)

(places)
(1 : 2.1)

RESERVATION   124

FLIGHT*NUMBER PASSENGER*COUNTRY-NAME PASSENGER*CODE FLIGHT-SCHEDULE*DEPARTURE-DATE
CONFIRMATION-NUMBER   (AK1) FARE-AMOUNT (d) PAYMENT-CODE ENTRY-DATE AGENT-NUMBER

Entity Volumes: Annual averages in 000s

FIGURE 9.12 Moon Launch passenger reservations logical data model; Step LDM9.

247

IMPLEMENTATION TIPS AND TECHNIQUES

By now, you may feel that you have delved far inside the boundaries of *application* design under the (possibly misnamed) auspices of *database* design. Should you really be discussing detailed update logic at the attribute level as part of the logical data modeling process? *Definitely.* After all, the object of logical data modeling is to capture *structural and integrity components* of data requirements as accurately and comprehensively as possible. These components (defined through key business rules, domain constraints, and other triggering operations) must be consistent across all applications that access the data.

You may wish to show some or all of the business rules on the logical data model diagram. Simple extensions to the diagramming notation may suffice for some types of rules. For example, you can add codes to represent key business rules and certain other types of triggering operations (such as "parent insert" and "child delete" rules). Other rules may be documented as annotated explanations on the diagram.

SUMMARY

In this chapter, you refined the integrity of your logical data model by adding to the business rules already defined. Specifically, you added definition of domains and triggering operations to the key business rules identified in Step LDM5. The three types of business rules are closely related; in fact, key business rules and domains are subsets of triggering operations, the most general form of business rule. Thus, how do you distinguish among the three concepts, and why should you do so?

Key business rules are triggering operations involving primary and foreign keys. They are defined as particular types of events (namely, delete/update of primary keys or insert/update of foreign keys) that, under particular types of conditions (existence or nonexistence of a related primary or foreign key value), trigger particular types of actions (e.g., *cascade* of delete to child, *automatic* insert of parent, or reject operation entirely).

Domains are another (overlapping) subset of triggering operations governing values that any (key or nonkey) attribute may assume. Domains also can be defined in terms of events (in this case, insert of an entity or update of an attribute) that, under particular conditions, trigger acceptance or rejection of the insert or update operation.

Triggering operations in general address the actions triggered by any event (retrieval, update, insert, delete) involving any attribute under any given circumstances.

Distinguishing among the three facilitates a methodological approach for discovering and recording all business rules. Understanding the three types will help you ask questions, probe for details, and recognize when the user articulates a business rule. Once you have identified a business rule, however, its classification as key business rule or domain or general triggering operation (or any two or all three) is unimportant. Your goal is to define and document all integrity constraints relating to your model as accurately and thoroughly as possible.

EXERCISES

9.1 The term *domain* is first introduced in Step LDM8. Yet, implicitly you have been dealing with domain constructs in earlier steps. What domain characteristics have you already defined? In what steps of the logical data modeling methodology did you do this?

9.2 List some standard data types that you might want to see supported by your data dictionary, design tool, or DBMS.

9.3 Explain why triggering operations are discussed as part of the logical data model rather than as part of the application-processing design.

9.4 Define three explicit domain hierarchies for the Moon Launch case study (refer to Figure 9.7 for an illustration).

9.5 Moon Launch Enterprise records information about passengers who request flight reservations and about passengers who merely request information (but do not reserve flights). In particular, Moon Launch marketing wants the system to track potential passengers who have never actually made reservations. One approach is to add a FIRST–RESERVATION–PENDING–FLAG to the PASSENGER entity (where PASSENGER is redefined to include both actual and potential passengers). Document some triggering operations that may be needed to preserve integrity of such a flag.

9.6 Define domains for the following attributes in the baggage tracking and control user view: PASSENGER.HOME–PHONE–NUMBER, RESERVATION.DEPARTURE–DATE, BAGGAGE.RESERVATION*DEPARTURE–DATE, BAGGAGE.NUMBER, and LOST–BAGGAGE.BAGGAGE*NUMBER. Follow the format used in the Moon Launch case study for recording entity-independent and entity-specific domains. Make assumptions where necessary regarding data types, lengths, and formats.

Also define triggering operations reflecting the following business rules: (1) if luggage that has been reported lost is not located within 90 days, the "lost luggage report" is deleted from the system, and (2) the baggage agent adds $3 to the passenger's fare for each piece of luggage checked after the first two pieces (which are checked free of charge).

9.7 Define domains for the following attributes in the space shuttle maintenance control user view: FLIGHT.DEPARTURE–TIME, SHUTTLE–TYPE.OBSOLETE–FLAG, SHUTTLE–VEHICLE.OBSOLETE–FLAG, SHUTTLE–VEHICLE.SERIAL–NUMBER, and SHUTTLE–ASSIGNMENT.SHUTTLE–VEHICLE*SERIAL–NUMBER. Follow the format used in the Moon Launch case study for recording entity-independent and entity-specific domains. Make assumptions where necessary regarding data types, lengths, and formats.

Also define triggering operations reflecting the following business rules: (1) whenever a general shuttle model is marked obsolete (meaning it will be phased out within the next year), all shuttle vehicles of that model type also are marked obsolete; and (2) once a shuttle vehicle reaches 8 years of age, its retirement date is set to the end of the current calendar year.

10 | Integrate User Views

Through the steps in Chapters 5 through 9, you have developed fully detailed user views. Each user view models information requirements for one business function, group of related users, or individual user. Each user view should be correct, comprehensive, and unambiguous—*from the perspective of that business function or that user.*

Each user view represents one (almost surely *incomplete*) understanding of the business. Without doubt, you will find inconsistencies as well as overlaps among multiple user views. You now face the imposing task of putting views together, merging overlaps, resolving inconsistencies, and producing a composite logical data model. This may be the most difficult task in the entire logical data modeling process because it requires both *analytical skills,* for identifying different representations of the same fact and reconciling incompatibilities, and *interpersonal skills,* for persuading individuals to communicate and negotiate agreement.

This task also may be the most important in the logical data modeling methodology because it achieves a representation of the business's information requirements that is *independent of any particular user, business function, or application*—a chief goal of your work.

Developing and verifying a composite, integrated logical data model requires three steps:

☐ Combine user views—*Step LDM10*
☐ Integrate with existing data models—*Step LDM11*
☐ Analyze for stability and growth—*Step LDM12*

In Step LDM10, you merge user views for different users or subactivities within the scope of your logical data modeling task. For example, suppose the scope of your current logical data model is employee-related information. You may have three user views, one for the payroll department, one for the employee benefits department, and one for the management development department. Now you will combine those user views. What entities and relationships do they have in common? How similar are the definitions, attributes, and business rules? If you simply add everything together into one logical data model diagram and data dictionary, do you have any inconsistencies? Are there cross-view relationships or missing business rules?

Step LDM11 looks beyond the scope of this logical data model to examine logical data models built previously or perhaps concurrently. For example, suppose there are models for customer and stockholder information: How do these models relate to yours? Are there incongruencies? Are some of the entities the same, and, if so, are their definitions and business rules complete and consistent? For example, how do all three logical data models handle the case of an individual who is simultaneously an employee, a customer, and a stockholder? Is it important for the business to be able to identify that fact? Are, perhaps, new relationships or categories required to convey this possibility?

Step LDM12 contemplates the future, thereby predicting significant business changes that *may* occur, and for which perhaps you should plan now. Recall that another critical objective of your logical data model is to produce a *stable* and extensible representation of the business's information requirements. You want a model that will not be drastically affected by time or by new application requirements. All steps until this point have focused on achieving stability with respect to current business requirements. In Step LDM12, you try to increase that stability still further. You extend the context of the logical data model to include facts about the business that you do not know for sure, but can project with reasonable certainty.

At the conclusion of Steps LDM10 through LDM12, you will have a clear, accurate, comprehensive, integrated, and stable model of the business's information requirements (at least within a reasonably defined scope). You are then finally in a position to address database design.

STEP LDM10: COMBINE USER VIEWS

Your objectives in combining multiple user views are

☐   To represent the views accurately in a composite logical data model
☐   To eliminate redundancies
☐   To resolve any inconsistencies across views
☐   To add any new, inter-view relationships and business rules

You accomplish this step through several substeps:

1. Integrate entities and associated business rules (primary keys and alternate keys)
2. Integrate relationships and associated business rules (insert/delete constraints)
3. Integrate attributes and associated business rules (domains and triggering operations)

In practice, you mix and iterate these substeps as appropriate.

It is best to work with only a few user views at a time, gradually building up to one integrated logical data model. In fact, it may be easiest to combine exactly two views with each iteration of the process. For simplicity, in this chapter, we look at only two user views at a time.

INTEGRATION OF ENTITIES

Your purpose in integrating entities is to combine entities that in fact represent the same business object, while retaining or adding subtypes, supertypes, and categories as appropriate.

RULE LDM10.1

When combining user views, *merge entities* with the same primary key and equivalent primary key domains. Include in the merged entity all attributes from the original entities (eliminating redundant attributes).

Generally, entities with the same primary key represent the same real-world object and should be combined. For example, assume one user view includes a CUSTOMER entity, and another user view includes a CLIENT entity, as shown in Figure 10.1. The primary key of one is CUSTOMER.NUMBER, and the primary key of the other is CLIENT.CODE. Discussion with the user elicits the conclusion that CUSTOMER and CLIENT are, in fact, the same real-world object; furthermore, CUSTOMER.NUMBER and CLIENT.CODE are *synonyms* having different names but identical meanings and drawing their values from the same domain. Thus, CUSTOMER and CLIENT are one entity and are combined as such.

In Figure 10.1, CUSTOMER becomes the name of the new, combined entity. In selecting a name for a new, combined entity, choose the name that is more widely accepted or that more accurately conveys the full (new) meaning of the entity. You may wish to record the discarded name (CLIENT) as an alias or synonym in the design data dictionary.

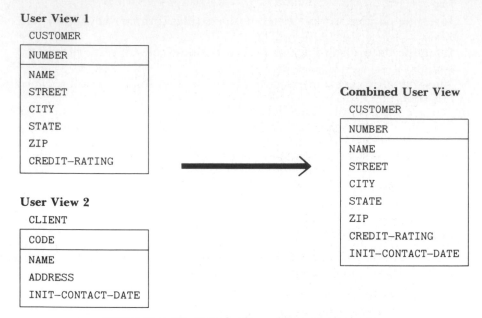

FIGURE 10.1 Combining entities with same primary key.

In Figure 10.1, the primary key is named CUSTOMER.NUMBER and CLIENT.CODE is eliminated as being redundant with CUSTOMER.NUMBER.

You also must adjust the definition of the merged CUSTOMER entity to encompass both definitions of the original CUSTOMER and CLIENT entities. Finally, you must resolve any inconsistencies between volumes for the original two entities and reflect a consensus volume for the new CUSTOMER entity.

More formally, you merge entities having the same primary key and *equivalent primary key domains*. Equivalent domains are domains encompassing generally the same logical pool of values, with perhaps some differences in data type, length, or format. If two domains are equivalent, you should be able to derive one from the other. Consider, for example, these two domains:

$$010,020,030,040$$

and

$$10, 20, 30, 40$$

Each includes the same logical values and is fully derivable from the other. Thus, they are *equivalent* if they are equal in other domain constraints—specifically, uniqueness rules, null support, default value, and business meaning.

Assume that the CUSTOMER.NUMBER attribute in user view 1 (Figure 10.1) actually has a domain consisting of values 010, 020, 030, . . . , 090. CLIENT.CODE in user view 2 has a domain consisting of values 10, 20, 30, . . . , 90. If the user considers the *meanings* of these domains to be synonymous, then the domains may be equivalent. In merging the CUSTOMER and CLIENT entities, you must choose one domain for the primary key CUSTOMER.NUMBER: either 010, 020, 030, . . . , 090 or 10, 20, 30, . . . , 90.

Attributes in the combined entity include any attribute that was in one or both of the original entities. In some cases, the same logical attributes may be represented in different forms in the original two entities. For example, an attribute may have the same meaning but different names or data types in the original two entities (as in the case of CUSTOMER.NUMBER and CLIENT.CODE). Alternatively, one or more attributes in one entity may be derivable from one or more attributes in the other entity. (For instance, CLIENT.ADDRESS appears to be the concatenation of STREET, CITY, STATE, and ZIP within the CUSTOMER entity). For now, intuitively merge attributes when it seems appropriate, to minimize redundancy. (Thus, in Figure 10.1, CLIENT.ADDRESS is represented by the STREET, CITY, STATE, and ZIP attributes within CUSTOMER.) Later in this chapter, we discuss more formal techniques for identifying when and how attributes should be integrated.

Note that you are *not* combining subtypes or supertypes from the same user view, even though they have the same primary key. Subtypes and supertypes have different primary key domains because subtypes represent different subsets of the corresponding supertype. Moreover, in Chapter 7 (Rules LDM6.13 and LDM6.14), there are guidelines for combining supertypes and subtypes when there is insufficient business motivation to define them as separate entities. Assuming you have already applied those guidelines, each user view depicts the supertypes, subtypes, and categories required to convey business meanings fully. You do not, therefore, consider eliminating these entities, since doing so results in loss of meaning.

On the other hand, you may need to combine subtypes or supertypes across user views. Use primary key domains as your guide. Combine those entities from different user views having primary keys that are similar in allowable values and other domain constraints.

For example, Figure 10.2 shows a VEHICLE entity in user view 1 with subtypes AUTO, TRUCK, and BICYCLE. User view 2 includes an AUTOMOBILE entity. All five entities have primary keys meaning vehicle name, but their primary key domains are defined differently. Since the primary key domains for AUTO and AUTOMOBILE are equivalent, you merge those entities in the composite model.

The combined entity is called AUTOMOBILE; it has primary key VEHICLE*NAME. It includes attributes from both original entities. Note, however, that one of the attributes in the original AUTOMOBILE entity (DESCRIPTION-TEXT) already is represented in the supertype VEHICLE. Thus, it is eliminated from the combined AUTOMOBILE subtype. (Again, formal techniques for when and how to combine, eliminate, and otherwise integrate attributes appear later in this chapter).

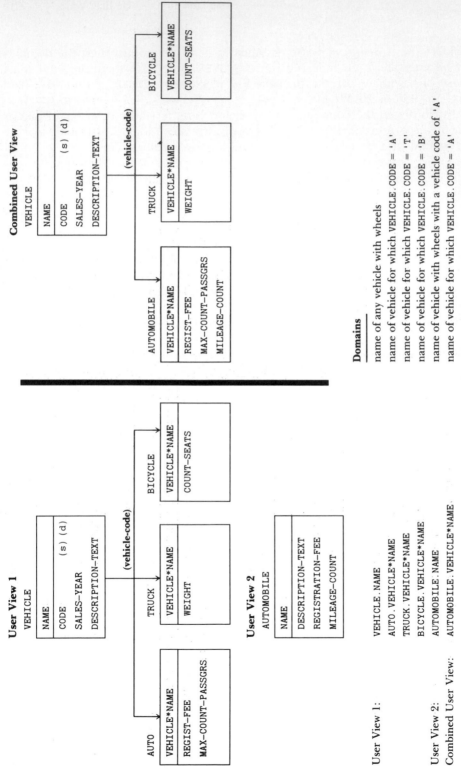

FIGURE 10.2 Combining entities with supertype or subtype based on primary key domain.

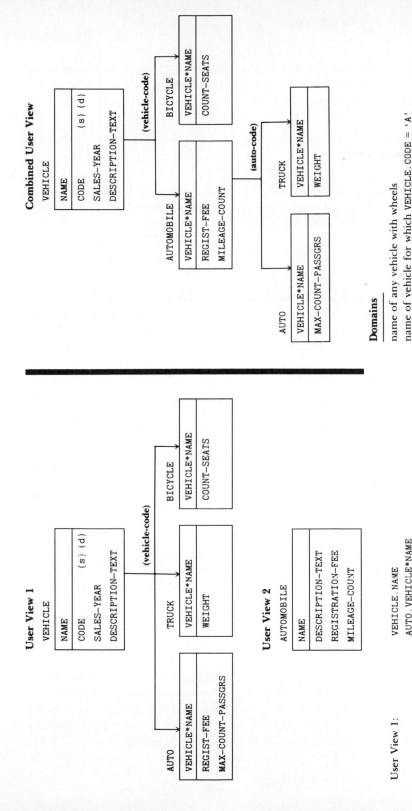

FIGURE 10.3 Creating new subtypes or supertypes based on primary key domain.

Domains

name of any vehicle with wheels
name of vehicle for which VEHICLE.CODE = 'A'
name of vehicle for which VEHICLE.CODE = 'T'
name of vehicle for which VEHICLE.CODE = 'B'
name of vehicle with wheels with a vehicle code of 'A' or 'T'
name of vehicle for which VEHICLE.CODE = 'A' or 'T'
name of vehicle for which VEHICLE.CODE = 'A'

User View 1:   VEHICLE.NAME
                  AUTO.VEHICLE*NAME
                  TRUCK.VEHICLE*NAME
                  BICYCLE.VEHICLE*NAME

User View 2:   AUTOMOBILE.NAME

Combined User View: AUTOMOBILE.VEHICLE*NAME
                      AUTO.VEHICLE*NAME

Suppose instead that the primary key domain for AUTOMOBILE in user view 2 differs from all the primary key domains defined in user view 1. Then, you may have an additional subtype of VEHICLE, as illustrated in Figure 10.3.

RULE LDM10.2

When combining user views, establish a *supertype–subtype relationship* between entities with the same primary key, where one primary key domain is a subset of the other. Eliminate from the new subtype any attributes that are also in the supertype.

In Figure 10.3, the primary key domain for AUTOMOBILE (vehicle code = 'A' or 'T') in user view 2 is not equivalent to any primary key domain in user view 1. However, it is a subset of the primary key domain for VEHICLE in user view 1. Thus, the combined user view establishes AUTOMOBILE as a new subtype of VEHICLE. The DESCRIPTION–TEXT attribute is eliminated from AUTOMOBILE because it already appears in the supertype VEHICLE. Moreover, the primary key domains for AUTO (vehicle code = 'A') and TRUCK (vehicle code = 'T') in user view 1 are each subsets of the primary key domain for AUTOMOBILE (vehicle code = 'A' or 'T') in user view 2. Thus, the combined user view establishes AUTO and TRUCK as subtypes of AUTOMOBILE. The REGIST–FEE attribute is eliminated from AUTO because it already appears in the supertype AUTOMOBILE.

RULE LDM10.3

When combining user views, establish a *common supertype* to relate two entities with

☐   The same primary key
☐   Primary key domains that differ in allowable value constraints but are otherwise equivalent

For example, in Figure 10.4, user view 1 includes a PROFESSIONAL entity with primary key PROFESSIONAL.NUMBER. User view 2 includes a MANAGER entity with primary key MANAGER.NUMBER. The meaning of these primary keys is the same (employee identification number), although their domains differ in range specification. That is, PROFESSIONAL.NUMBER draws its values from employee

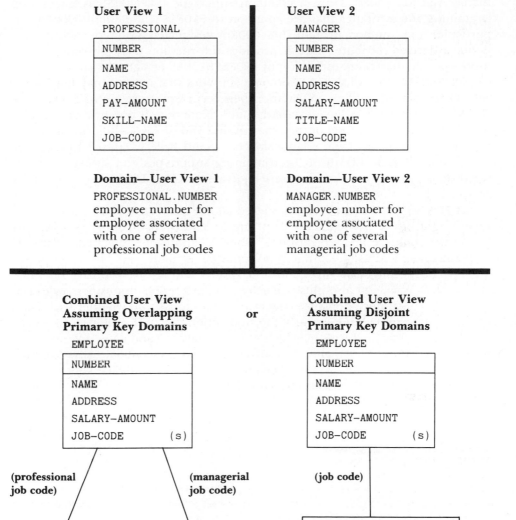

FIGURE 10.4 Integrating entities with overlapping or disjoint primary key domains.

numbers associated with professional job codes, and MANAGER.NUMBER draws its values from employee numbers associated with managerial job codes.

In addition, the set of professional job codes is different from the set of managerial job codes. Thus, a common supertype (EMPLOYEE) is established containing the attributes that are common to PROFESSIONAL and MANAGER. In particular, the common attribute JOB-CODE is designated a subtype identifier. It is not a derived attribute, since it provides information (i.e., job code) that is more specific than mere indication of PROFESSIONAL or MANAGER status.

PROFESSIONAL and MANAGER become subtypes that may or may not constitute a category, depending on whether their occurrences are mutually exclusive (i.e., their primary key domains are disjoint). Note that, if one primary key domain were actually a subset of the other, Rule LDM10.2 would dictate establishing one supertype–subtype relationship (as would Rule LDM10.3 followed by application of Rule LDM6.14 for combining supertypes and subtypes). If instead their primary key domains were equivalent, Rule LDM10.1 would call for merging the entities.

If PROFESSIONAL and MANAGER shared all the same attributes, separate subtypes might not be needed at all. Applying Rules LDM6.13 and LDM6.14, perhaps they could be merged into one subtype or into one EMPLOYEE entity. If PROFESSIONAL and MANAGER shared no common attributes, establishing a supertype EMPLOYEE might be superfluous (as you would see by applying the same rules). Of course, you also must consider any differences in business rules (insert/delete constraints, domains, triggering operations), and whether such rules could be represented more clearly through supertypes and subtypes.

There is one final case in which entities may be candidates for merging: when their primary keys, although different, serve as candidate keys for each other. This occurs when two user views depict different candidate keys to be the primary key of what is actually the same entity.

RULE LDM10.4

When combining user views, *merge entities* the primary keys of which serve as candidate keys for each other. Include in the merged entity all attributes from the original entities (eliminating redundant attributes).

For example, Figure 10.5 illustrates an EMPLOYEE entity with primary key EMPLOYEE.NUMBER in user view 1 and a STAFF entity with primary key STAFF.SOC-SEC-NUMBER in user view 2. Users indicate that both employee

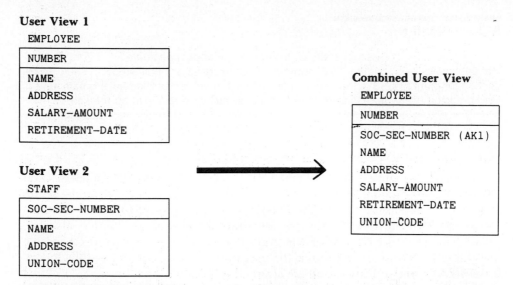

FIGURE 10.5 Combining entities the primary keys of which are candidate keys for each other.

number and Social Security number are valid candidate keys for either one of these entities. In fact, each may have been identified as alternate keys within the original user views. Thus, merge the two entities, choose one primary key (e.g., employee number), and identify the other candidate key (e.g., Social Security number) as an alternate key of the merged entity (designated by (AK1) in Figure 10.5).

RULE LDM10.5

When combining user views, include without change (i.e., do not merge) all *entities with different primary keys.*

Rule LDM10.5 covers the general case of including in the combined user view all distinct entities from the original user views. In Figure 10.2, you include not only the merged entity AUTOMOBILE but also all other entities (VEHICLE, TRUCK, BICYCLE) from the original user views. Attributes for these nonmerged entities in the combined user view are the same as those in the original user views.

RULE LDM10.6

When combining user views, retain all *business rules about candidate keys* from the original user views (e.g., primary and alternate key uniqueness and null support). Allow an exception for primary keys in the original user views that are reclassified as alternate keys in the combined user view: Consider whether the no-null constraint can be relaxed.

Consider Figure 10.5 again. In general, EMPLOYEE.NUMBER and EMPLOYEE.SOC–SEC–NUMBER in the combined user view should retain business rules defined in the original user views. However, because EMPLOYEE.SOC–SEC–NUMBER is now an alternate key, it no longer must be present in every occurrence of the entity (i.e., it can be permitted to assume null values). On the other hand, if the user indicates that SOC–SEC–NUMBER is always present, retain the no-null constraint.

INTEGRATION OF RELATIONSHIPS

When entities are integrated (merged), relationships between them also are candidates for integration. For example, in Figure 10.6, the CUSTOMER and PRODUCT entities in the combined user view represent merged entities. Thus, the relationships from the original user views (CUSTOMER *orders* PRODUCT and CUSTOMER *is shipped* PRODUCT) also should be merged if they have the same meaning.

RULE LDM10.7

When combining user views, *merge relationships* between entities where the entities themselves are the results of merging, but only when such relationships convey the same meaning. Apply to the resultant merged relationship a cardinality incorporating cardinalities of the original source relationships. If the resultant relationship is many-to-many ($M:N$), resolve it by defining a new entity type and two one-to-many ($1:N$) relationships.

Figure 10.6 illustrates the most typical case: CUSTOMER *orders* PRODUCT and CUSTOMER *is shipped* PRODUCT are both $1:N$ relationships. Assuming the relationships have the same meaning, they can be merged into a $1:N$ relationship. If

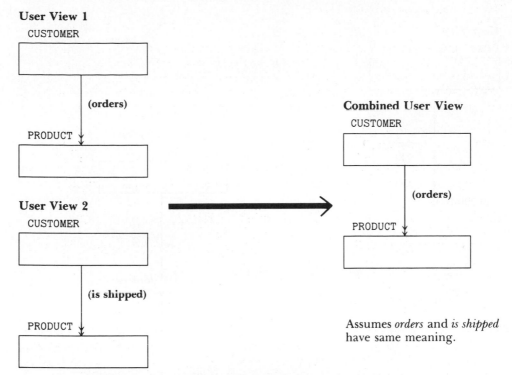

FIGURE 10.6 Merging equivalent one-to-many (1 : *N*) relationships.

they were both 1 : 1, they would be merged into a 1 : 1 relationship. If one relationship were 1 : 1 and the other 1 : *N* (still assuming they have the same meaning), they would be merged into a 1 : *N* relationship.

Figure 10.7 illustrates the case in which CUSTOMER *orders* PRODUCT is 1 : *N* and PRODUCT *is shipped to* CUSTOMER is 1 : *N* (i.e., both relationships are 1 : *N* but in opposite directions). The merged relationship initially is an *M* : *N* relationship. Rule LDM10.7 instructs you to resolve new *M* : *N* relationships as you did previously—by creating a new entity type and two 1 : *N* relationships.

It is possible, of course, that user view 1 and user view 2 contain different relationships with different meanings associating the merged entities CUSTOMER and PRODUCT. For example, the relationship CUSTOMER *orders* PRODUCT may represent orders placed, regardless of whether they are ever shipped. CUSTOMER *is shipped* PRODUCT may represent shipments, regardless of whether an order is ever placed. Both are 1 : *N* relationships in the same direction but with different meanings. If this is the case, include both relationships in the combined user view and assign different names, as shown in Figure 10.8. Moreover, include in

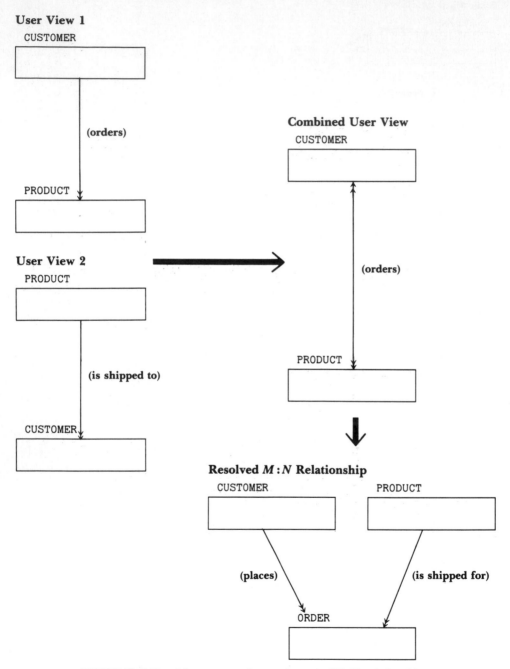

FIGURE 10.7 Resolving a merged many-to-many (*M* : *N*) relationship.

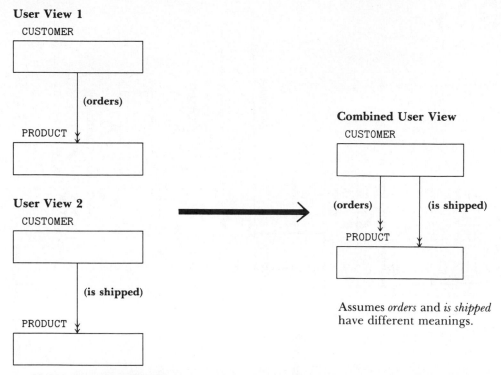

FIGURE 10.8 Integrating user views with nonequivalent one-to-many (1 : *N*) relationships.

the merged child entity (PRODUCT) two foreign keys with role names reflecting the two relationships with CUSTOMER (e.g., PRODUCT.CUSTOMER*NUMBER−ORDERS and PRODUCT.CUSTOMER*NUMBER−IS−SHIPPED).

RULE LDM10.8

When combining user views, initially include without change (i.e., do not merge) all *relationships with different meanings*. Then identify and eliminate any *redundant relationships*.

In Figure 10.9, the combined user view includes two entities (CUSTOMER and PRODUCT) which each represent merged entities. However, at first glance there are no merged relationships, because only user view 1 includes a relationship

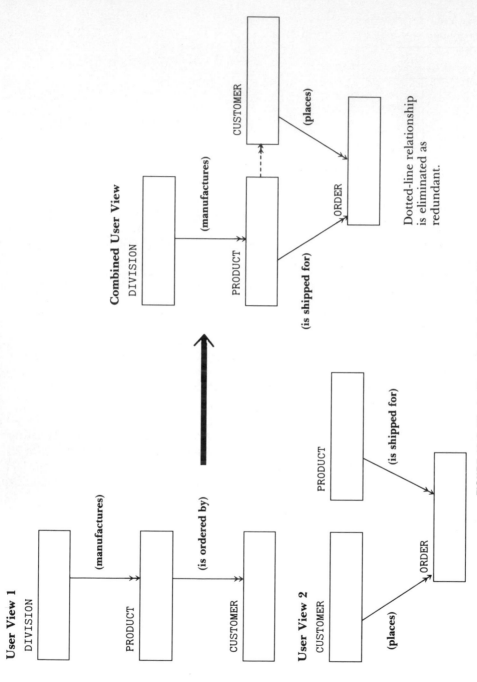

FIGURE 10.9 Eliminating redundant relationships.

between the two merged entities. Closer examination reveals that user view 2 actually includes an $M:N$ relationship between CUSTOMER and PRODUCT, represented via the entity ORDER, and two $1:N$ relationships (CUSTOMER *places* ORDER and PRODUCT *is shipped for* ORDER). Thus, PRODUCT *is ordered by* CUSTOMER (from user view 1) is redundant and should be eliminated.

Note that, if the relationship in user view 1 were PRODUCT *is most preferred by* CUSTOMER ($1:N$, since each CUSTOMER prefers only one PRODUCT), its meaning would be different. It would not be redundant and it would not be eliminated from the combined user view.

RULE LDM10.9

When combining user views, look for *missing relationships* between entities originating in different user views. Add these relationships to the combined user view.

For example, in Figure 10.10, the initial combined user view contains one merged entity (PRODUCT) and no merged relationships. After further analysis, including discussions with users, you discover an inter-view relationship between DIVISION and PRODUCT–MANAGER. In fact, in user view 2, PRODUCT–MANAGER may have already carried a reference to a primary key, alternate key, or even nonkey attribute of DIVISION; for instance, it may have included the attribute DIVISION–NAME. Because DIVISION was not identified as an entity in user view 2, however, DIVISION–NAME was not recognized as (or replaced by) a foreign key. Now adding the relationship DIVISION *employs* PRODUCT–MANAGER requires that another relationship, DIVISION *manufactures* PRODUCT, be eliminated as redundant (if, of course, the division *employing* the manager is the same as the division *manufacturing* the manager's products).

You already have added some inter-view relationships during entity integration, when you identified new supertype–subtype and supertype–category relationships (Rules LDM10.2 and LDM10.3).

RULE LDM10.10

Correct all *foreign keys* in a combined user view to reflect the primary keys (rather than the alternate keys) of parent entities.

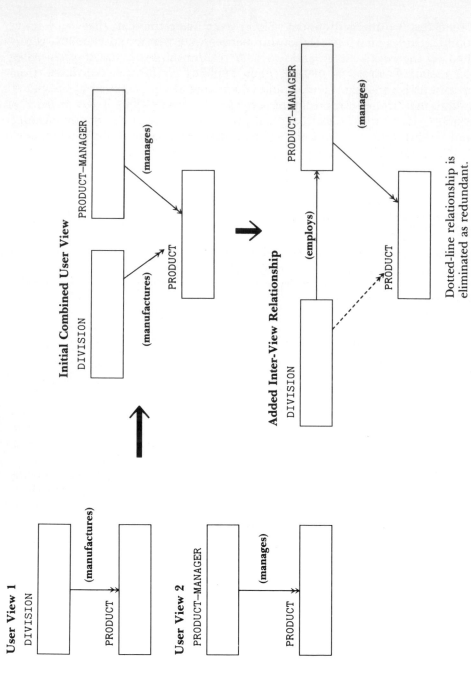

FIGURE 10.10 Adding inter-view relationships.

Applying Rule LDM10.4 (merging entities the primary keys of which serve as candidate keys for each other), you may have merged entities that originally had different primary keys, each primary key serving as a candidate key for the other. You then reclassified one of the original primary keys as an alternate key. Now, you must change any foreign keys referencing the newly classified alternate key to reflect the primary key instead. In Figure 10.11, for example, the foreign key for the PAYCHECK entity in the combined user view is EMPLOYEE*NUMBER rather than EMPLOYEE*SOC–SEC–NUMBER because EMPLOYEE*NUMBER is now the primary key for the EMPLOYEE entity.

FIGURE 10.11 Correcting foreign keys to reflect primary keys.

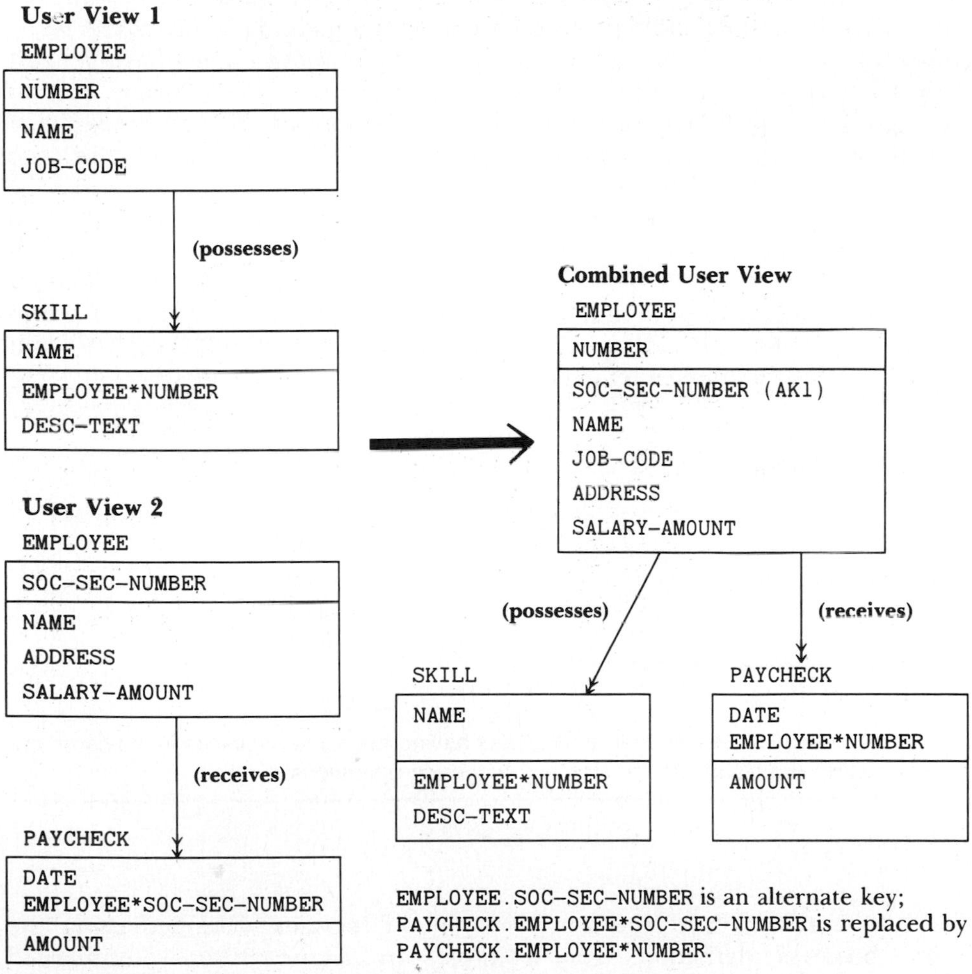

EMPLOYEE.SOC–SEC–NUMBER is an alternate key;
PAYCHECK.EMPLOYEE*SOC–SEC–NUMBER is replaced by
PAYCHECK.EMPLOYEE*NUMBER.

RULE LDM10.11

When combining user views, initially include *key business rules* (insert/delete constraints) as defined in the source user views. Add key business rules for new relationships. Then evaluate for inconsistencies. Resolve through discussions with users.

As you build the combined user view, insert/delete constraints initially may be inconsistent for two reasons: (1) relationships in the combined view may be the result of merging relationships that had different key business rules, and (2) relationships involving a common merged entity may have inconsistent key business rules. An example of the first case is the merging of CUSTOMER *places* ORDER having a *restrict* delete rule and CUSTOMER *is shipped* ORDER having a *cascade* delete rule. Perhaps the business rules for the merged relationship need to be negotiated. Or, perhaps the users' disagreement over business rules is a clue that these are, in fact, different relationships with different meanings; i.e., the CUSTOMER who places an ORDER (perhaps the customer's home office) may be different from the CUSTOMER to whom that ORDER is shipped (such as a branch office). An example of the second case might be the integration of CUSTOMER *places* ORDER with a *cascade* delete rule, and ORDER *includes* LINEITEMs with a *restrict* delete rule. Incorporating both of these rules means that you must purge all of a CUSTOMER's LINEITEMs before you can drop the CUSTOMER off the mailing list. Is this the users' intent? Or are these rules inconsistent?

INTEGRATION OF ATTRIBUTES

Integration of attributes is largely intuitive. Merge any two attributes having equivalent meanings in the same (perhaps previously merged) entity.

RULE LDM10.12

When combining user views, *merge attributes* having the same meanings in the same entity. Reconcile or union their domains and triggering operations.

Two attributes have the same meaning if they are described using the same business definition. For example, in Figure 10.1, you merged CUSTOMER.NUMBER and CLIENT.CODE because they have the same definition.

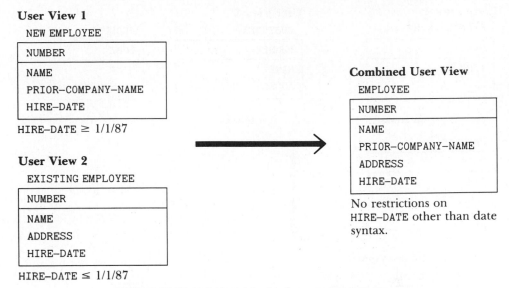

User View 1

NEW EMPLOYEE

NUMBER
NAME
PRIOR–COMPANY–NAME
HIRE–DATE

HIRE–DATE $\geq$ 1/1/87

User View 2

EXISTING EMPLOYEE

NUMBER
NAME
ADDRESS
HIRE–DATE

HIRE–DATE $\leq$ 1/1/87

Combined User View

EMPLOYEE

NUMBER
NAME
PRIOR–COMPANY–NAME
ADDRESS
HIRE–DATE

No restrictions on
HIRE–DATE other than date
syntax.

FIGURE 10.12 Unioning domains for merged attributes.

You reconciled their lengths and formats by selecting one domain to be the domain of the new primary key.

In Figure 10.12, NEW–EMPLOYEE and EXISTING–EMPLOYEE in user views 1
and 2 can be merged into one entity EMPLOYEE because they have the same
primary keys. You also could have established NEW–EMPLOYEE and
EXISTING–EMPLOYEE as subtypes of a new supertype EMPLOYEE. After discussion, however, users indicate that *all* the same attributes characterize both
entities and both entities are involved in the same relationships. Thus, the entities are better combined into one entity. The domain for HIRE–DATE in NEW–
EMPLOYEE is dates after and including 1/1/87; the domain for HIRE–DATE in
EXISTING–EMPLOYEE is dates prior to and including 1/1/87. When you merge
NEW–EMPLOYEE and EXISTING–EMPLOYEE, you must union the domains for
HIRE–DATE to include dates before, including, and after 1/1/87. You must also
combine or, if necessary, reconcile any triggering operations involving the
merged attributes.

RULE LDM10.13

When combining user views, eliminate or flag *derived attributes.*

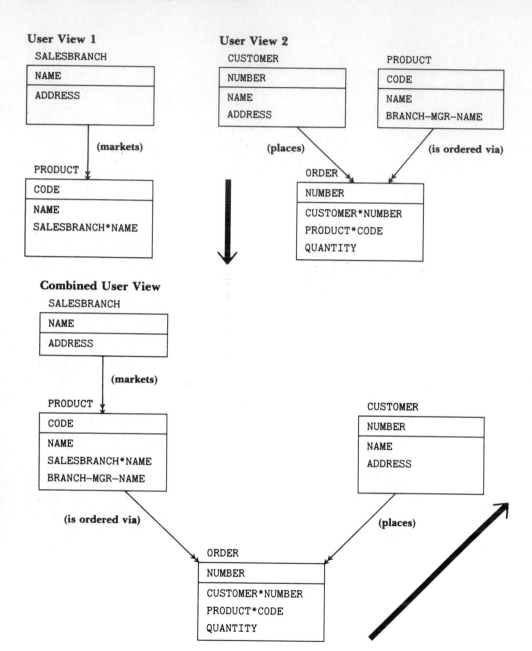

Normalized Combined User View

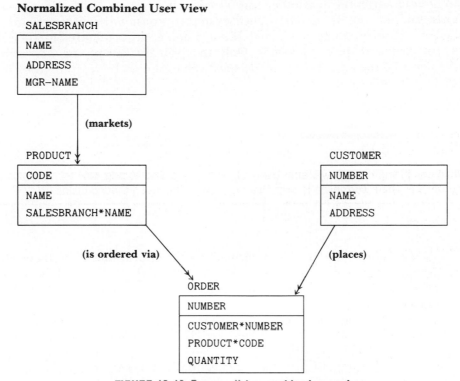

FIGURE 10.13 Renormalizing combined user view.

Attributes in one user view may be derivable from one or more attributes in the combined user view. In Figure 10.1, CLIENT.ADDRESS is derived from the concatenation of CUSTOMER.STREET, CUSTOMER.CITY, CUSTOMER.STATE, and CUSTOMER.ZIP. CLIENT.ADDRESS therefore is eliminated from the combined user view. Alternatively, you could have included CUSTOMER.ADDRESS and flagged it as derived (documenting the derivation algorithm, of course).

Derived attributes in the combined user view may appear in the same entity as their source attributes (as in this example) or in different entities. An example of the latter is two user views where user view 1 tracks dollar amount of orders at the line item level (LINEITEM.AMOUNT), and user view 2 tracks dollar amount of orders at the customer level (CUSTOMER.TOTAL–LINEITEMS–AMOUNT). CUSTOMER.TOTAL–LINEITEMS–AMOUNT in user view 2 can be derived from LINEITEM.AMOUNT in user view 1 and thus is eliminated (or flagged as derived) in a combined user view.

A special case of derived attributes is encoded attributes. Look for *encoded* attributes in one user view, such as STATE–ABBREV–CODE (NJ, TX, and so on) and *decoded* attributes in another user view, such as STATE–NAME (New Jersey, Texas, and so on). If you find such examples, consult the users regarding whether one form can be eliminated. If not, a new entity is required to associate the encoded and decoded values. Only the primary key of the new entity (whether it be the encoded or the decoded value) should be referenced by foreign keys in other entities.

RULE LDM10.14

When combining user views, after merging, eliminating, and adding new relationships as appropriate, again *normalize* to eliminate any newly introduced redundancies.

One example of the need to renormalize is the appearance of both encoded and decoded attributes (e.g., STATE–ABBREV–CODE and STATE–NAME) in a combined user view. You resolve this redundancy by creating a new STATE entity associating the two.

Figure 10.13 shows a second example involving the merging of two PRODUCT entities. As a result, PRODUCT is no longer in third normal form. PRODUCT.BRANCH–MGR–NAME is dependent on the foreign key PRODUCT.SALESBRANCH*NAME. Thus, MGR–NAME migrates upward into the parent SALESBRANCH entity.

RULE LDM10.15

After combining user views, reexamine attributes to identify *changes in domain characteristics* such as null support. Consider establishing subtypes or categories to reduce occurrences of nulls.

So far, you have combined entities based on common primary keys and equivalent primary key domains. Generally, you included in the combined entity all attributes from the original entities. The combined entity may have attribute domains that are slightly different from the original domains, since the combined entity may represent a broader range of real-world occurrences. For example, some attributes originally defined as nonnull may now assume null values for some occurrences. It may be appropriate to define new subtypes to reduce the instance of nulls.

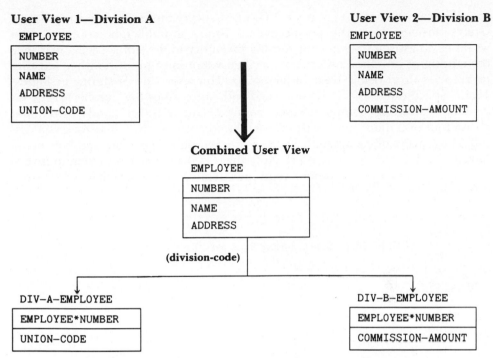

FIGURE 10.14 Establishing new subtypes to minimize occurrences of nulls.

In Figure 10.14, there are initially two user views. Employees in user view 1 are in division A, and employees in user view 2 are in division B. When you combine these entities into one EMPLOYEE entity, users indicate that UNION–CODE for division B employees will be null. Likewise, COMMISSION–AMOUNT for division A employees will be null. To avoid proliferation of nulls, you may decide to create subtypes of EMPLOYEE, as shown.

When establishing new subtypes, remember to flag any subtype identifiers (Rule LDM6.10) and to denote them as derived if they are wholly redundant with the category or subtype relationship. In Figure 10.14, if the combined entity EMPLOYEE included an attribute DIVISION–CODE, that attribute would be flagged as a subtype identifier. If it could assume only the values 'A' or 'B,' it also would be flagged as derived.

C A S E   S T U D Y

The case study in this chapter deals with Gran's Grocery Store. This will provide an opportunity to gain experience in modeling a different type of business.

We examine two user views for Gran's Grocery Store. The first represents Gran's business from the perspective of Gran's granddaughter Cecilia, who works as an assistant buyer replenishing inventory in the store. Cecilia manages the cutting of purchase orders for specified volumes of products when existing inventories drop below their order points. Her user view is shown in Figure 10.15. Specifically, Cecilia is concerned with store aisles (by number), with inventory (including computer-based count of quantity on hand, price, and reorder information), and with orders placed with vendors for stock (specifically, how many of each item have been ordered on a given date and how many have been shipped for that order). Note that Cecilia identifies an item in inventory by a combination of vendor code plus item code (primary key) or by store code (alternate key).

FIGURE 10.15 Gran's Grocery Store assistant buyer user view.

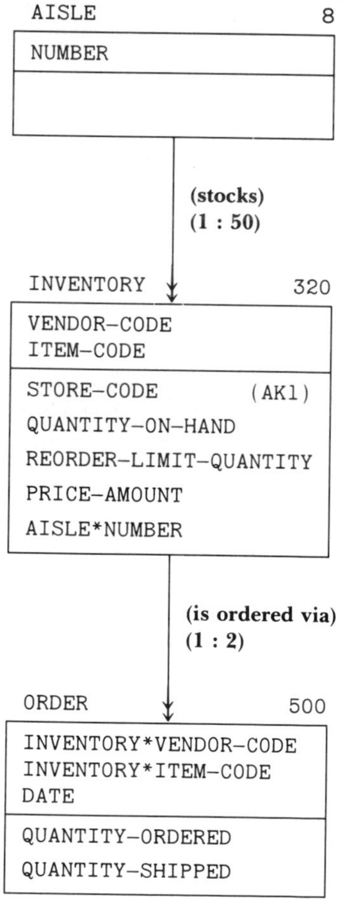

```
AISLE                      8
┌─────────────────────────┐
│ NUMBER                  │
├─────────────────────────┤
│                         │
└─────────────────────────┘

            (stocks)
            (1 : 50)

INVENTORY                 320
┌─────────────────────────┐
│ VENDOR-CODE             │
│ ITEM-CODE               │
├─────────────────────────┤
│ STORE-CODE      (AK1)   │
│ QUANTITY-ON-HAND        │
│ REORDER-LIMIT-QUANTITY  │
│ PRICE-AMOUNT            │
│ AISLE*NUMBER            │
└─────────────────────────┘

            (is ordered via)
            (1 : 2)

ORDER                     500
┌─────────────────────────┐
│ INVENTORY*VENDOR-CODE   │
│ INVENTORY*ITEM-CODE     │
│ DATE                    │
├─────────────────────────┤
│ QUANTITY-ORDERED        │
│ QUANTITY-SHIPPED        │
└─────────────────────────┘
```

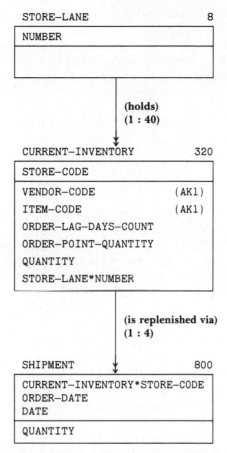

FIGURE 10.16 Gran's Grocery Store shipments manager user view.

The second user view models information needed by Grandpa, Gran's ship-ments manager. Grandpa tracks receipt of shipments and verifies that they gen-erally are within a prespecified lag period following issuance of order. Grand-pa's user view is depicted in Figure 10.16. As you can see, Grandpa is interested in store lanes (identified by number), in the status of current inventory includ-ing computer-based count and reorder information, and in shipment informa-tion. Note that Grandpa identifies an item in inventory by store code (primary key) or by a combination of vendor code plus item code (alternate key).

Gran would like her inventory-management functions to be consistent in the way they define and report information. Therefore, let's integrate these two user views into one composite logical data model.

Your discussion with Grandpa and Cecilia leads you to conclude that AISLE.NUMBER and STORE–LANE.NUMBER represent the same real-world objects designated via the same numbering scheme. In fact, aisles in the store are labeled (for customer reference), and these labels are the numbers used by both Grandpa and his granddaughter.

Thus, AISLE and STORE–LANE have the same primary key with equivalent primary key domains. Applying Rule LDM10.1, you merge AISLE and STORE–LANE into one entity and name it AISLE, the term used by most people (including Grandma and her customers):

AISLE   8

NUMBER

You also document STORE–LANE as an alias (to aid in communicating with Grandpa).

The CURRENT–INVENTORY and INVENTORY entities require further investigation. The primary key of each is an alternate key for the other. This suggests two possibilities. Are CURRENT–INVENTORY and INVENTORY the same entity (applying Rule LDM10.4)? Or, could CURRENT–INVENTORY be a subtype of INVENTORY (applying Rule LDM10.2)? After investigation, you determine that there is only one kind of inventory (after all, Gran's Grocery Store does not record past and future inventories). Thus, you merge the entities into one and name it INVENTORY. Again, you may document CURRENT–INVENTORY as an alias (for Grandpa). Further, you choose the combination of VENDOR–CODE plus ITEM–CODE to be the primary key because it is more commonly used (e.g., by Grandma). STORE–CODE becomes an alternate key (again, for Grandpa). The foreign key in INVENTORY is named AISLE*NUMBER.

Fortunately, the entity volumes for INVENTORY and CURRENT–INVENTORY and for AISLE and STORE–LANE are consistent. But what about the relationships AISLE *stocks* INVENTORY and STORE–LANE *holds* CURRENT–INVENTORY? They have generally the same meaning but different cardinality ratios (1 : 50 versus 1 : 40). Grandpa indicates that 40 is the average and 50 is the maximum number of inventory items per aisle. Since you are reflecting average cardinality ratios in your diagram, you choose to show 1 : 40 for the merged relationship (Rule LDM10.7), but you make a note of the upper limit of 50 in your data dictionary.

You can further consolidate some of the attributes in the merged entity INVENTORY. Specifically, both REORDER–LIMIT–QUANTITY and ORDER–POINT–QUANTITY represent the count at which Gran orders more of a given item in inventory. Therefore, you merge these attributes into one ORDER–POINT–QUANTITY (to appease Grandpa) and document REORDER–LIMIT–QUANTITY as a synonym. Similarly, you merge the attributes QUANTITY and QUANTITY–ON–HAND, choosing QUANTITY–ON–HAND as the attribute name and QUANTITY as an alias (which also makes Grandpa happy).

Thus far, your consolidated logical data model appears as follows:

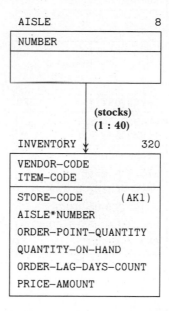

Applying Rule LDM10.5, you add without change the ORDER and SHIPMENT entities, each of which has a different primary key. You also add their relationships to INVENTORY (Rule LDM10.8). However, the foreign key in SHIPMENT (INVENTORY*STORE–CODE) reflects an alternate rather than primary key of INVENTORY. Applying Rule LDM10.10, you replace it by INVENTORY* VENDOR–CODE plus INVENTORY*ITEM–CODE, as shown in Figure 10.17.

Now, are you missing any new, inter-view relationships (Rule LDM10.9)? ORDER.DATE and SHIPMENT.ORDER–DATE sound suspiciously alike. Examination of attribute definitions indicates that they are, indeed, the same; thus, SHIPMENT contains a foreign key (INVENTORY*VENDOR–CODE, INVENTORY*ITEM– CODE, ORDER*DATE) representing a relationship that you choose to call ORDER *is filled via* SHIPMENT. But then the relationship INVENTORY *is replenished via* SHIP– MENT must be eliminated (Rule LDM10.8), because it is redundant with INVEN– TORY *is ordered via* ORDER and ORDER *is filled via* SHIPMENT. Your refined logical data model is as shown in Figure 10.18.

You need to determine a cardinality ratio for ORDER *is filled via* SHIPMENT. Gran's granddaughter indicates that she tracks the last two orders per item in inventory (i.e., the cardinality ratio of INVENTORY *is ordered via* ORDER is 1:2). Grandpa indicates that he tracks as many as four shipments per item (the cardinality ratio of INVENTORY *is replenished via* SHIPMENT is 1:4). Further discussion results in agreement that the four shipments relate to the last two orders outstanding; thus, cardinality of ORDER *is filled via* SHIPMENT is 1:2. Note that not

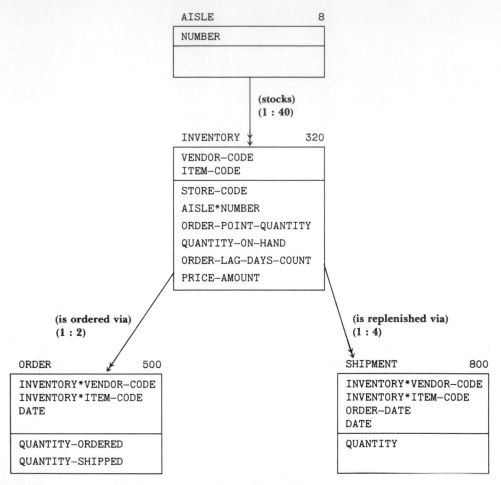

FIGURE 10.17 Evolving combined logical data model.

every item in inventory is reordered (depending on sales activity); therefore, entity volumes for ORDER and SHIPMENT are less than the maximums implied by the relationship cardinality ratios.

Finally, Grandma points out that ORDER.QUANTITY-SHIPPED is derived from SHIPMENT.QUANTITY (since it is the sum of QUANTITY values for all SHIPMENTS associated with an ORDER). For now, you choose to retain ORDER.QUANTITY-SHIPPED in the model but flag it as derived (Rule LDM10.13).

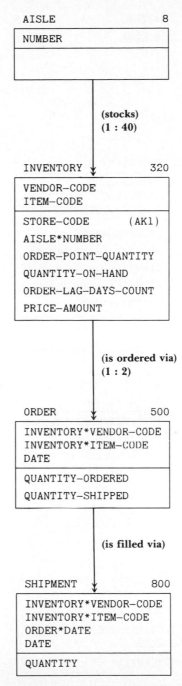

FIGURE 10.18 Combined logical data model with more refinements.

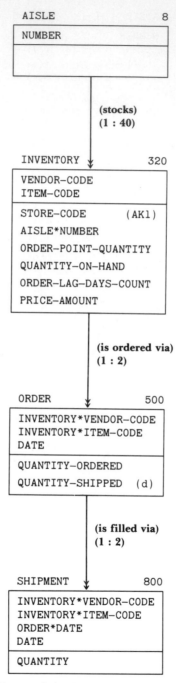

FIGURE 10.19 Gran's Grocery Store inventory-management logical data model.

We shall not discuss the details of insert/delete rules, domains, and other triggering operations. You should, however, evaluate and integrate all such business rules as per Rules LDM10.6, LDM10.11, LDM10.12, and LDM10.15. The composite logical data model diagram is shown in Figure 10.19.

IMPLEMENTATION TIPS AND TECHNIQUES

Until now, much of the logical data model can be developed most effectively in interactive user workshops. However, the first cut at Step LDM10 is best undertaken by the analyst alone. If different analysts designed different user views, the analysts should exchange logical data model diagrams and dictionary documentation for individual review at first. An interim design review session with developers (but not with users) might be held next. At this session, the developers should discuss, question, and generally challenge the preliminary composite logical data model. Someone should record questions that require more information from the users. Finally, the developers should hold a design review with the users.

Expect that several iterations of these design reviews may be needed. The reviews are meant to identify questions about and inconsistencies in the model. Thus, leave ego and pride of ownership outside the door! On the other hand, careful design of the model prior to the review sessions minimizes group time expended on technicalities such as unnormalized entities or incorrect foreign keys. The reviewers, whether developers or users, should concentrate primarily on whether business meanings are correctly, completely, and consistently reflected in the model.

Bringing other analysts, perhaps unfamiliar with the proposed logical data model, into the review sessions may identify questions about consistency with existing databases or other data models. Those questions lead to Step LDM11.

STEP LDM11: INTEGRATE WITH EXISTING DATA MODELS

Recall from Chapter 2 that a *business conceptual schema* is an integrated logical data model representing all data employed within the business. Step LDM11 evolves the conceptual schema by integrating your new logical data model with existing ones. If a conceptual schema already exists for the organization, this step should be relatively easy. In this case, you integrate your logical data model with an existing conceptual schema. This process is fairly similar to integration of two user views.

More frequently, no conceptual schema exists. Instead, you face what may seem an onerous task: analyzing your logical data model vis-à-vis existing databases (which may not have associated logical data models) and other proposed logical data models representing other business functions. In this case, the integration step may be particularly challenging, yet it is an important factor contributing to usefulness and longevity of databases resulting from your design work.

Typically, you cannot be as flexible as you were in view integration now that you are evaluating existing models or databases. There will be inconsistencies, at least in data names and scope of attributes included within the entities. You probably do not have the option of changing existing models or databases. Yet, you do not want to constrain your new logical data model unjustly, by the limitations and perhaps errors of existing designs. Your purpose, then, is not to reconcile all differences, but merely *to understand and document relationships (including, if necessary, inconsistencies) among the various designs.*

Achieving this objective requires access to more than the code that defines an existing database. Just imagine examining a COBOL data definition or a database control block module. How would you infer which fields in the file relate to attributes in your logical data model? How records relate to entities? Whether relationships are implemented consistently with your model? It would be extremely difficult! Rather, you must evaluate the logical data models represented by the database implementations. If an existing database is not founded on a logical data model, you must develop one. A logical data model is necessary to communicate the *business meaning* associated with, but not readily apparent from, a database structure.

RULE LDM11.1

Integrate databases by comparing and defining mappings among the underlying logical data models.

Depending on the scope of the integration effort, the logical data models need not include all the details discussed in Chapters 5 through 9. For instance, you may decide to map models at the entity and relationship level only. Doing so implies you *are* mapping primary and foreign keys, since they *identify* entities and relationships and thus are fundamental to those mappings. However, you exclude nonkey attributes and related business rules from the scope of your integration effort.

The logical data models being compared must be based on similar (although not necessarily identical) methodologies. For example, major constructs within the logical data models, such as entities, relationships, attributes, and keys, must be translatable across the models.

Building a logical data model for a database originally designed without one is a nontrivial effort. Therefore, requiring logical data models as input into the integration process can be a significant barrier to performing any integration at all. On the other hand, integrating without a logical data model may result in a mapping of physical (versus business) relationships and may ignore potential conflicts in business meaning.

Of course, as you compare logical data models, you will discover differences. Yet, each existing logical data model is correct in representing a particular aspect of the business. Therefore, your goal in integration is not to resolve all differences, but to ensure that the models do not conflict or, at minimum, to document any potential conflicts. To accomplish this goal, you integrate each logical data model with, and thereby will evolve, one business conceptual schema. If each logical data model can be mapped to (thus, is consistent with) the conceptual schema, then in turn each must be consistent with one another.

RULE LDM11.2

Evolve the *business conceptual schema* by integrating and incorporating each new logical data model that is developed.

If at first no conceptual schema exists, create one by merging the first two logical data models selected for integration. Continue to extend the conceptual schema by successively merging with the combined user view each new logical data model. In this way, the conceptual schema evolves to represent an integrated view of all business data in their most detailed form.

As you integrate a new logical data model into the conceptual schema, attempt to modify that model *only* if it so conflicts with the conceptual schema that it cannot be merged into it. For example, suppose the new logical data model includes a contradictory entity definition or a conflicting business rule. Then it actually contradicts some other logical data model. One of the logical data models must be changed to enable integration of both within one conceptual schema. If neither logical data model can be changed (e.g., because both reflect existing database implementations), then at minimum you must recognize and document the fact that one of the models reflects an incorrect understanding of the business. (Perhaps a future design project should be scheduled to correct this problem.)

Because the conceptual schema is built by merging logical data models, it should be possible to derive each logical data model from the conceptual schema. Specifically, the following types of transformation operations should suffice:

Name substitutions—replacement of entity, relationship, and attribute names in the conceptual schema by other names specific to a logical data model

Relational manipulation operations—such as select, project, join, and union (discussed in Chapter 3)

Attribute derivation algorithms—such as changing the unit of measure, combining two or more attributes, or otherwise summarizing attribute values

Entity aggregation algorithms—enabling a collection of dissimilar entities within the conceptual schema (e.g., SHELF and BOOK) to be viewed as one summary entity in a particular logical data model (e.g., LIBRARY)

Additional qualification of business rules—such as more specific constraints on domains or triggering operations within the context of a particular logical data model

---

RULE LDM11.3

Identify the *mappings* between each logical data model and the business conceptual schema. Document these mappings in the data dictionary, including:

☐ Naming differences
☐ Operations performed on the conceptual schema to obtain a specific logical data model, such as selects, projects, joins, or aggregations of entities and summarization or other derivations of attributes
☐ Interrelation of business rules, such as additional constraints applied by a particular logical data model to the domains or triggering operations defined within the conceptual schema
☐ Actual conflicts between a particular logical data model and the conceptual schema, such as contradictions in data definitions or business rules

---

In summary, you integrate your logical data model with existing models and databases by integrating it into the business conceptual schema. In the process, extend the conceptual schema as necessary to incorporate new entities, relationships, attributes, and business rules at their most detailed level. Apply the same integration techniques that you used in merging user views. Modify a logical data model *only* if it conflicts with the conceptual schema such that they cannot be integrated. Then document mappings between the conceptual schema and the logical data model in the form of well-defined transformation operations (where the logical data model is different but consistent) along with notes that highlight actual contradictions (where the logical data model must remain inconsistent with the conceptual schema).

This approach facilitates maximum flexibility within each logical data model, reflecting the perspective of a particular business function. Yet, it ensures fundamental consistency at the most detailed level of information representation across the business. It also calls for documenting differences (e.g., synonyms, attribute derivations, entity transformations, and actual conflicts) such that the business meanings peculiar to each logical data model are equally well defined and clearly understood.

CASE STUDY

Figure 10.20 illustrates two logical data models supporting different aspects of Gran's Grocery Store business:

1. *Checkout LDM*—defining information required and generated at the checkout counter. At Gran's Grocery Store, automated scanners read product codes from purchased products and feed the correct prices and discounts to the cash registers. At the same time, the system records purchase transactions and adjusts computer-based inventories to reflect purchases made. Transactions are logged in this system for 1 year and then archived.

2. *Shelf-stock LDM*—defining information required and generated when stocking store shelves. The stock staff fills the aisles of frozen bins and dry goods shelves with products. They track physical count of inventory on a monthly basis. If the count for a given product drops below a prespecified order point, the stock staff notifies the assistant buyer (Gran's granddaughter Cecilia) that a new order should be placed for that product.

Let's integrate these models with the inventory-management logical data model, developed earlier in this chapter. Recall that the inventory-management model supports the needs of Grandpa and Cecilia in managing inventory, including recording of orders and shipments. Cecilia monitors the computer-based inventory count (automatically maintained via the checkout counters and the shipment deck) to determine when inventory must be replenished. Cecilia also adjusts the computer-based inventory count when necessary based on physical stock counts supplied monthly by the stock staff. Grandpa verifies that shipments are reflected properly within the computer-based inventory count.

In surveying these logical data models (and imagining the appropriate accompanying data dictionary information), you see a number of similarities and overlaps. Clearly some common naming standards have been applied, which makes the job of understanding the interrelationships and inconsistencies easier. However, a number of questions still arise in comparing the logical data models:

1. There seems to be some relationship, not clearly specified, between AISLE in the inventory-management model and FROZBIN and SHELF in the shelf-

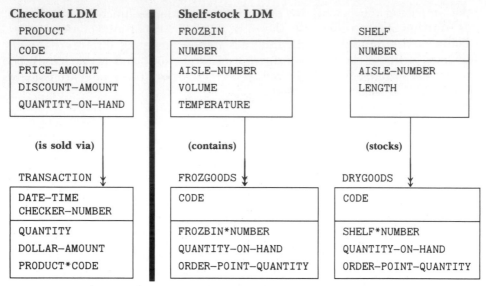

FIGURE 10.20 Gran's Grocery Store functional logical data models.

stock model. According to the stock staff's description, AISLE seems to be an *aggregation* of several FROZBIN and SHELF occurrences with the same AISLE–NUMBER value.

2. PRODUCT and INVENTORY appear to represent the same entity, although different candidate keys have been chosen as primary keys.
3. FROZGOODS and DRYGOODS appear to constitute a category of PRODUCT (alternatively called INVENTORY).
4. The QUANTITY–ON–HAND attributes in the checkout, shelf-stock, and inventory-management logical data models appear to describe two different real-world constructs: computer-based inventory count and physical inventory count. The similarities in data names are confusing and misleading.
5. The PRICE–AMOUNT attributes in the checkout and inventory-management logical data models probably have different meanings: store selling price in the checkout model versus vendor price in the inventory-management model. You need to verify this assumption with the users.

Figure 10.21 depicts a conceptual schema for Gran's Grocery Store that is the result of merging the three logical data models in Figures 10.19 and 10.20 while applying the rules and techniques discussed in Step LDM10. For example, new supertype–category relationships have been established, data names reconciled, and derived data eliminated as appropriate. Each of these transformations is tracked to document the mappings between the logical data models and the conceptual schema, as highlighted in the following descriptions.

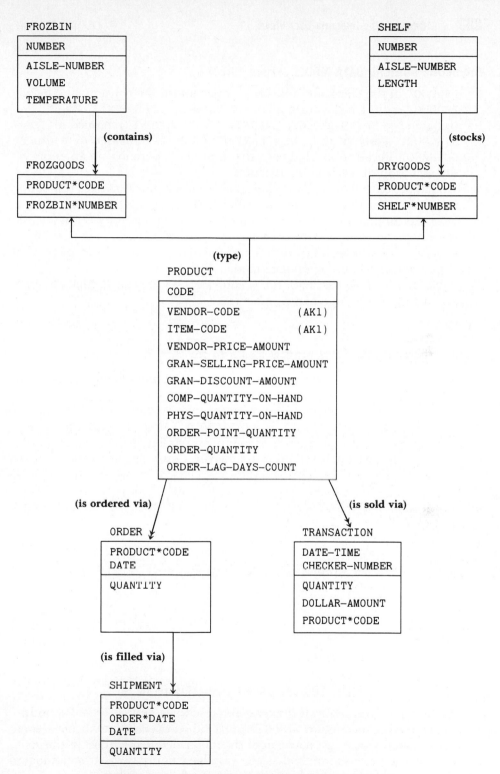

FIGURE 10.21 Gran's Grocery Store conceptual schema.

CHECKOUT LOGICAL DATA MODEL (Figure 10.20)

☐   PRODUCT in the checkout model is a projection of the conceptual schema PRODUCT entity on the attributes CODE, GRAN–SELLING–PRICE–AMOUNT (renamed to PRICE–AMOUNT), GRAN–DISCOUNT–AMOUNT (renamed to DISCOUNT–AMOUNT), and COMP–QUANTITY–ON–HAND (renamed to QUANTITY–ON–HAND). Recall from Chapter 3 that a project operation on an entity is the inclusion of a subset of attributes.

☐   TRANSACTION is equivalent to the conceptual schema TRANSACTION entity, selected on (or restricted to) values for DATE–TIME that are within the past year. Recall that a select (or restrict) operation on an entity is the inclusion of only those entity occurrences that meet some criteria. Note that this transformation results in a different domain for TRANSACTION.DATE–TIME within the checkout logical data model.

☐   PRODUCT *is sold via* TRANSACTION is equivalent to the conceptual schema relationship of the same name.

SHELF-STOCK LOGICAL DATA MODEL (Figure 10.20)

☐   FROZBIN and SHELF are equivalent to the conceptual schema FROZBIN and SHELF entities.

☐   FROZGOODS is a join of the conceptual schema PRODUCT and FROZGOODS entities over the PRODUCT.CODE and FROZGOODS.PRODUCT*CODE attributes. Remember, a join operation on two entities combines the attributes of both entities usually based on matching the values of one or more attributes in each entity. This join then has been projected on the attributes CODE, FROZBIN*NUMBER, PHYS–QUANTITY–ON–HAND (physical inventory count, renamed QUANTITY–ON–HAND in the shelf-stock logical data model), and ORDER–POINT–QUANTITY.

☐   DRYGOODS is a join of the conceptual schema PRODUCT and DRYGOODS entities over the PRODUCT.CODE and DRYGOODS.PRODUCT*CODE attributes. This join has then been projected on the attributes CODE, SHELF*NUMBER, PHYS–QUANTITY–ON–HAND (physical inventory count, renamed to QUANTITY–ON–HAND in the shelf-stock logical data model), and ORDER–POINT–QUANTITY.

☐   The logical data model relationships are equivalent to conceptual schema relationships of same name.

INVENTORY-MANAGEMENT LOGICAL DATA MODEL (Figure 10.19)

☐   AISLE is an *aggregation* of the conceptual schema entities FROZBIN and SHELF having a common AISLE–NUMBER value. (Recall that an *aggregation* relationship enables a collection of dissimilar detailed entities in the conceptual schema to be viewed as one summary entity in a particular logical data model.) AISLE is not reflected in the conceptual schema because it would be redundant with FROZBIN and SHELF. Only the most detailed entities are represented in the conceptual schema. Within the inventory-management logical data model, AISLE is projected on one attribute, AISLE–NUMBER (renamed to AISLE.NUMBER).

☐ INVENTORY is the conceptual schema PRODUCT entity, renamed to INVENTORY, with VENDOR–CODE and ITEM–CODE (a conceptual schema alternate key) as a composite primary key, and projected on the attributes shown in Figure 10.19. PRODUCT.CODE has been renamed to INVENTORY.STORE–CODE (in the logical data model an alternate, rather than primary key). PRODUCT.COMP–QUANTITY–ON–HAND has been renamed to INVENTORY.QUANTITY–ON–HAND, and PRODUCT.VENDOR–PRICE–AMOUNT has been renamed to INVENTORY.PRICE–AMOUNT. The foreign key INVENTORY.AISLE*NUMBER references the aggregate entity AISLE.

☐ ORDER is the conceptual schema ORDER entity, with foreign key changed to reflect the primary key of its parent, INVENTORY*VENDOR–CODE and INVENTORY*ITEM–CODE. QUANTITY has been renamed to QUANTITY–ORDERED, and QUANTITY–SHIPPED has been added as a derived attribute.

☐ SHIPMENT is the conceptual schema SHIPMENT entity, with foreign key changed, similarly to ORDER.

☐ AISLE *stocks* INVENTORY *aggregates* the conceptual schema relationships FROZBIN *contains* FROZGOODS, SHELF *stocks* DRYGOODS, and PRODUCT *type* FROZGOODS or DRYGOODS (category relationship). Other logical data model relationships are equivalent to the like-named conceptual schema relationships.

Note that no changes are required in the functional logical data models. The models are consistent with one another (i.e., with the conceptual schema) after some well-defined transformations have been applied.

Suppose, instead, that the shelf-stock logical data model included the entities shown in Figure 10.22. This model defines AISLE–NUMBER as a primary key of SHELF. Thus, according to this model, AISLE–NUMBER is unique within SHELF, and there is one SHELF occurrence per AISLE–NUMBER. Based on the stock staff's description of the entity SHELF, you know this assumption is false. An aisle may have multiple shelves. If you do not discover this error while building the shelf-stock logical data model, you will discover it when attempting to integrate that model with the conceptual schema (assuming the conceptual schema is correct). Since this is an error in the shelf-stock model's representation of real-world business rules, you should attempt to negotiate a change to that model. If the shelf-stock logical data model represents existing databases and thus cannot be modified, document its inconsistency with the real world (and, hence, conceptual schema).

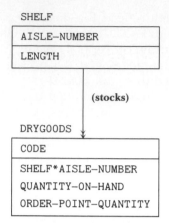

FIGURE 10.22 Revised shelf-stock logical data model, shelf identified by aisle number.

STEP LDM12: ANALYZE FOR STABILITY AND GROWTH

Throughout your analysis of business requirements to this point, you concentrated on the present. As the analyst, in fact, one of your chief responsibilities has been to keep the user focused on present business needs, avoiding speculative "what if" meanderings and other flights of fancy. In this last step of logical data modeling, however, you will give imagination its head and broaden your scope to include the "maybes."

What could change in the logical data model due to changes in the way the business operates or in the way the users view the world? For example,

- Might any new entities and relationships arise that affect existing entities by the addition of new foreign keys?
- Might the cardinality of any existing relationships change? For instance, might any $1:N$ relationships become $M:N$, necessitating introduction of a new child entity and two $1:N$ relationships?
- Might any primary keys be replaced, due to change in uniqueness or null properties, affecting foreign keys in related entities?
- Might new categories or subtypes arise?
- Might new attributes arise, or might existing ones be changed or eliminated?
- Might business rules—insert/delete constraints, domains, or triggering operations—change?
- Might entity volumes increase or decrease?

RULE LDM12.1

Incorporate into or at least document with the logical data model *changes that are imminent, significant, and/or probable,* for further evaluation during database design or future logical data modeling projects.

The stability and extensibility of your logical data model depend on your ability to solicit and predict potential new or changing requirements. Most important are potential changes to the conceptual schema, for two reasons:

1. Potential conceptual schema changes also may affect other logical data models (already implemented, under design, or to be developed in the future).
2. Changes that do not affect the conceptual schema therefore affect only the transformations from the conceptual schema to a particular logical data model (for example, derived attribute definitions, entity aggregations, or other transformations). These transformation changes usually are far easier to implement than are conceptual schema changes (particularly using a relational database system, as you will see in Part 3).

You may or may not choose actually to incorporate potential changes into the logical data model diagram at this time. For example, these changes may be extensions (such as new entities or attributes) that can be added without changing the meanings already represented by the model. Or, they may reflect changes in the business's use of information that cannot be integrated into a model reflecting the business today. At minimum, you should note the potential changes, reasons, and probabilities in the data dictionary documentation accompanying your model. Such notes may prove to be important factors affecting immediate database design decisions (Part 3) as well as future logical data model (and consequent database) modifications.

C A S E   S T U D Y

Consider three potential changes within Gran's Grocery Store that may affect the existing conceptual schema (Figure 10.21) as well as the three logical data models (Figures 10.19 and 10.20).

1. *Gran's assistant buyer (her granddaughter Cecilia) decides to maintain a history of vendors and addresses.* This is both a change in the operation of the busi-

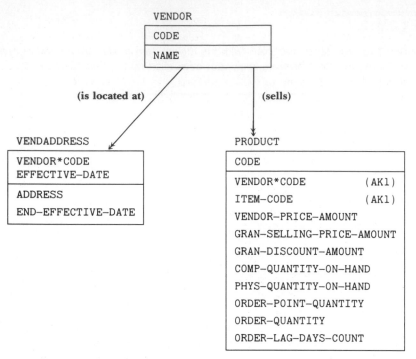

FIGURE 10.23 Gran's Grocery Store conceptual schema with vendors.

FIGURE 10.24 Gran's Grocery Store conceptual schema with drygoods on multiple shelves.

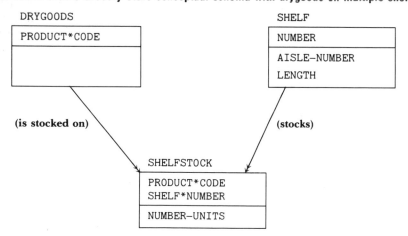

ness (since Gran herself never kept a history of vendor addresses before) and a change in the way a user (in this case Cecilia) views the business. Since previously vendor addresses were not represented in the conceptual schema at all, you have at least one new entity. In fact, Cecilia indicates that vendors may have multiple addresses over time; thus, you have two new entities. Changes required in the conceptual schema are shown in Figure 10.23. In addition to incorporating the new entities VENDOR and VENDADDRESS, you must rename PRODUCT.VENDOR*CODE to reflect its new foreign key property.

2. *Gran's shelf stockers decide to stock dry goods on potentially more than one shelf (to accommodate special sales).* Thus, the SHELF *stocks* DRYGOODS relationship becomes $M:N$. The effect on the conceptual schema is shown in Figure 10.24. Note that the foreign key SHELF*NUMBER, originally in DRYGOODS, moves to a new child entity.

3. *Cecilia begins ordering products from multiple vendors and thus expands the product identification code to include vendor code.* This represents a change in the primary key of PRODUCT in the conceptual schema, with a rippling effect on foreign keys in FROZGOODS, DRYGOODS, ORDER, SHIPMENT, and TRANSACTION. Figure 10.25 illustrates the changes required in the conceptual schema.

Note that establishing PRODUCT.CODE plus PRODUCT.VENDOR*CODE as the new primary key of PRODUCT implies that both are required to determine all nonkey attributes within PRODUCT (GRAN–SELLING–PRICE–AMOUNT, COMP–QUANTITY–ON–HAND, and so on). Suppose instead PRODUCT.CODE still sufficed as primary key; that is, PRODUCT.CODE alone sufficed to determine the nonkey attributes. Then the effect of ordering products from multiple vendors would be an $M:N$ relationship between PRODUCT and VENDOR. You would resolve this $M:N$ relationship by creating a new child entity (PRODUCT–ORDER) and two $1:N$ relationships (from PRODUCT to PRODUCT–ORDER, and from VENDOR to PRODUCT–ORDER). You then must evaluate whether TRANSACTION and ORDER are related to PRODUCT–ORDER (thus have foreign key PRODUCT*CODE, VENDOR*CODE) or to PRODUCT (thus have foreign key PRODUCT*CODE).

IMPLEMENTATION TIPS AND TECHNIQUES

Review of a logical data model for stability and growth is most effectively accomplished via an interactive design review session to which you invite practically everyone (e.g., designers, users, and perhaps other reviewers not involved with earlier design phases).

For example, you may hold all questions about the future until a design review held near the conclusion of the logical data modeling project. At this de-

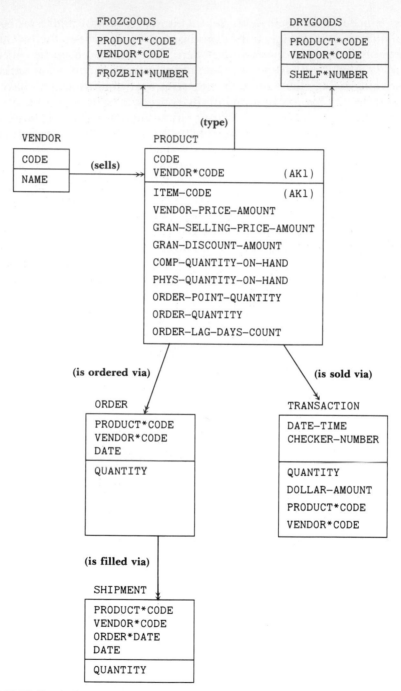

FIGURE 10.25 Gran's Grocery Store conceptual schema with product identified by product code plus vendor code.

sign review, first the principal data modeling analyst should present an overview of the logical data model diagram and accompanying definitions. The analyst should explain how the logical data model reflects the users' requirements as stated during earlier interviews. All participants—users and other analysts—should be urged to ask questions to ensure understanding and agreement. You should then open the floor to speculation about the future: What in the business might someday cause the logical data model to change? An appointed secretary should note all ideas. Initially, no ideas should be thrown out; you should encourage all participants to exercise their imaginations. Eventually, when the stream of ideas diminishes, discussion should begin as to the probability and potential significance of each suggested change. Those changes that are imminent, significant, or probable should be incorporated into the logical data model documentation.

You also may consider holding similar reviews, although smaller in scope, throughout the course of the logical data modeling project (e.g., at the conclusion of each related group of user views). Frequently, such brainstorming may surface previously overlooked, existing requirements, as well as potential changes.

SUMMARY

This chapter has completed the logical data modeling process by integrating individual user views into one composite logical data model that is consistent with other logical data models within the business.

In Step LDM10, you combine multiple user views into one logical data model. You apply the following guidelines:

- ☐ Merge entities with the same primary key and equivalent primary key domains
- ☐ Establish new supertype–subtype relationships to relate entities with the same primary key and primary key domains that include subset, disjoint, or partially overlapping allowable value specifications but that are otherwise equivalent
- ☐ Merge relationships between entities that have been merged when the relationships convey the same meaning
- ☐ Include entities with different primary keys and relationships with different meanings
- ☐ Eliminate redundant relationships and add missing (inter-view) relationships
- ☐ Merge attributes with equivalent meanings within the same entity
- ☐ Eliminate or flag derived attributes
- ☐ Renormalize
- ☐ Incorporate all business rules; evaluate for inconsistencies; reconcile or union

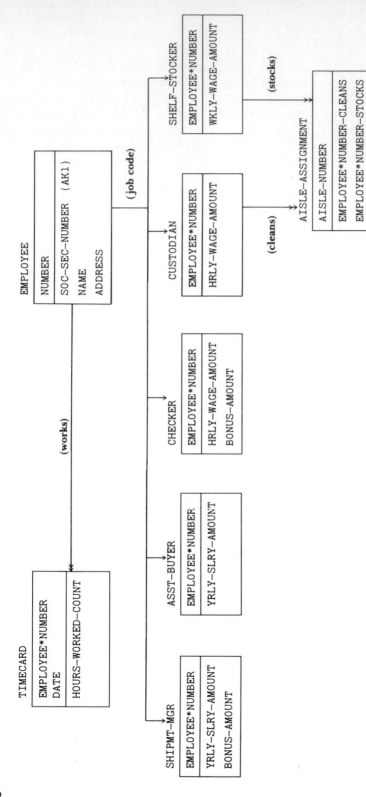

FIGURE 10.26 Gran's Grocery Store payroll logical data model.

In Step LDM11, you evaluate existing databases and other logical data models for conflicts or inconsistencies. You apply the following principles:

☐ Integrate databases by comparing and defining mappings among underlying logical data models

☐ Evolve the *business conceptual schema* by integrating and incorporating each new logical data model that is developed; a conceptual schema is an integrated logical data model representing all the business's data requirements (structure, meaning, and integrity constraints) at the most detailed level

☐ Define and document mappings between the business conceptual schema and each logical data model; mappings may include naming differences, transformation operations on the conceptual schema, interrelation of business rules, and actual conflicts.

Finally, in Step LDM12, you examine scenarios for possible future business changes that might affect the logical data model. You document any imminent, significant, or probable changes for further evaluation during database design or subsequent logical data modeling projects.

EXERCISES

10.1 Why is combining user views one of the most difficult tasks in the logical data modeling process?

10.2 Discuss the differences between combining user views and integrating multiple (perhaps existing) logical data models.

10.3 Step LDM12 calls for documenting anticipated changes in business data requirements. Discuss why it may be advisable to reflect such changes in a logical data model (and conceptual schema) before attempting to incorporate them into existing database designs.

10.4 Merge the payroll logical data model in Figure 10.26 into the conceptual schema for Gran's Grocery Store.

10.5 Evaluate the conceptual schema for Gran's Grocery Store in light of the following anticipated business changes: (1) Gran plans to buy an additional cash register—when she does, she will want to track the cash register on which transactions are rung; (2) Cecilia wants to begin tracking where inventory is stocked by identifying not only aisle number but also north or south side of the aisle; and (3) Gran plans to begin monitoring vendor performance. As part of this last task, Gran wants to track the dates on which orders are shipped by vendors, as well as the dates on which orders are received at her store.

10.6 Combine the Moon Launch passenger reservations user view (Figure 9.12) and the baggage tracking and control user view (Exercise 7.6).

10.7 Combine the user view for Philippe (Moon Launch's gourmet chef—Figure 8.8) with the Moon Launch passenger reservations user view (Figure 9.12).

PART

THREE

Building and Tuning a Relational Database

11 | Translate the Logical Data Structure

Chapters 11 and 12 deal with the first phase of relational database design, called the translation process. The *translation process* is a step-by-step procedure for transforming each component of the logical data model into a corresponding relational implementation. The result of the translation process is the *preliminary design*.

The steps in the translation process presume that you are starting with an integrated logical data model. This assumption means that the difficult decisions have already been made: how to group attributes into data structures, how to relate data structures, and how to define business rules to ensure that data stored within data structures are valid and consistent. You addressed these issues in developing a logical data model. In fact, if you have not yet addressed these questions—if you are attempting to begin relational database design before establishing a logical data model—you will end up building some version of a logical data model as the first steps of your relational design. It is far better that you consciously develop a complete, correct, consistent logical design up front. That is, build a comprehensive logical data model incorporating all the constructs discussed in Part 2. Then turn to translating the model into a relational database design.

The translation process has the following characteristics:

☐ It is simple
☐ It is faithful to the structure and integrity of the logical data model
☐ It builds on the simplicity, productivity, and flexibility advantages of relational database technology

☐   It is largely independent of any particular choice of relational database management system (DBMS)

☐   It is data-driven (i.e., processing-independent)

The translation process is *simple* because it is a straightforward, step-by-step procedure for representing each component of the logical data model as a relational database construct. Only basic relational database knowledge is required. You consider only requirements that are reflected in the logical data model, thereby excluding specific processing requirements (for now). In fact, if your logical data model is complete and consistent (as it should be if you followed the methodology in Part 2), you will find the translation process to be almost mechanical. One of the benefits attributed to relational database technology is the reduced technical complexity and effort of database design. This productivity gain, however, may not be realized without a comprehensive, high-quality logical design.

The translation process is *faithful* to the logical data model because it yields a database design that is entirely consistent with the logical design. The translation process addresses each logical data model component (the logical data structure and associated integrity properties) in a straightforward manner.

The translation process *builds on relational technology* because the step-by-step procedure is specific to relational environments. Further, it capitalizes on features that are common to all (or nearly all) relational database products.

The translation process is largely *independent of any particular choice of relational product* in that most of the process can be applied using any relational DBMS. Product-specific commentary assumes only general knowledge of your particular product environment. In fact, you can do much of the translation analysis before selecting your relational DBMS. When you are unsure of your product's facilities, you can make a note to investigate prior to implementation. The results of your investigations may even assist in choosing among products.

The translation process is *data-driven* (or processing-independent) because it ignores performance considerations and special requirements that may call for sophisticated tweaking or tuning. You address these issues later (Chapters 13 through 17). For now, focus on accurately capturing and addressing all requirements reflected in the logical data model via a preliminary relational database design.

Like the underlying logical data model, a relational database consists of two components: (1) data structure, and (2) data integrity. Logical data model constructs that primarily address data structure are entities, attributes, and relationships. In this chapter, you define the structure of a relational database by translating these logical constructs into corresponding relational constructs. Specifically, you define relational tables and columns.

The logical data model also includes business rules addressing data integrity (e.g., primary keys, foreign keys, and insert/delete rules). In Chapter 12, you define the integrity properties of a relational database by translating these logical business rules into relational database constructs. Specifically, you add rule parameters to your table definitions plus unique indexes, macros, programs, and perhaps other items.

At the conclusion of the translation process, you have a preliminary relational design that reflects all components of the logical data model. In fact, you could even implement this design as is, before incorporating any of the tuning techniques discussed in subsequent chapters. If you chose to disregard tuning options, essentially you would be delegating all tuning responsibility to the DBMS. You would be providing the DBMS with a design that is truly application-independent and allowing the DBMS to default or dynamically to choose appropriate tuning options based on its assessment of processing requirements. Thus, the translation process is itself a "submethodology" addressing totally data-driven relational database design.

In reality, however, relational products are not perfect and may not be able to meet all performance or functionality requirements through a totally data-driven design. Thus, most likely, you will also apply the tuning steps discussed in Chapters 13 through 17.

Figure 11.1 illustrates the six steps of the translation process as covered in Chapters 11 and 12.

FIGURE 11.1 The translation process.

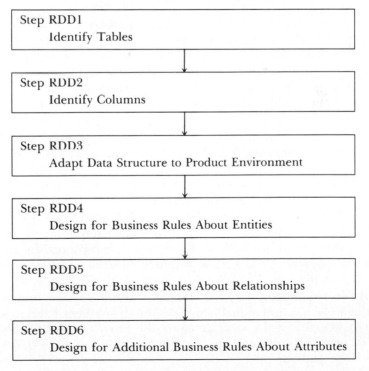

Step RDD1
    Identify Tables

Step RDD2
    Identify Columns

Step RDD3
    Adapt Data Structure to Product Environment

Step RDD4
    Design for Business Rules About Entities

Step RDD5
    Design for Business Rules About Relationships

Step RDD6
    Design for Additional Business Rules About Attributes

STEP RDD1: IDENTIFY TABLES

Recall that, in a logical data model, an *entity* is a person, place, thing, or concept about which information is recorded (e.g., EMPLOYEE, DEPARTMENT, PAYCHECK). In a relational environment, a *table* is a collection of rows, where each row has the same columns. Therefore, an entity is a *logical* object. A table is a *relational* object. The starting place for relational database design is to translate each entity into a relational table.

RULE RDD1.1

In general, identify one *table* for each entity.

For example, the following ANSI SQL syntax begins the definition of tables representing the entities CUSTOMER, INVOICE, and LINEITEM:

```
CREATE TABLE CUSTOMER ...
CREATE TABLE INVOICE ...
CREATE TABLE LINEITEM ...
```

Every relational DBMS supports definition of tables through its data definition language (DDL)—although the syntax might vary somewhat from the ANSI SQL standard shown here. It is not necessary, therefore, to consider other implementation options. (As you proceed through the translation steps, you will see that, for most steps, you have a choice of implementation options. The option you select will depend on your DBMS and the effort you are willing to invest in a faithful representation of your logical data model.)

Initially, make no attempt to combine several entities into one table or to segment one entity into multiple tables. You have distinguished among particular entities in the logical data model for *business reasons*. That is, users think of each entity as representative of a distinct business object. Each entity has a business definition, a particular identification (primary key), descriptive attributes, and a set of relationships with other entities. For these reasons, represent each entity as a separate relational table. You investigate deviations from this rule later, only after achieving a faithful translation that captures the meaning of the logical data model. More details on potential deviations are presented in Chapters 15 and 16.

Remember that supertypes and subtypes are themselves entities. Thus, translate these also into relational tables. Although subtypes have an identification (primary key) that is the same as that of the supertype, each subtype entity may have its own attributes and may participate in relationships different from those of the supertype. Again, for these reasons, represent each subtype entity as a separate relational table.

Your logical data model may also contain several entities that are not subtypes but have the same primary key if such entities represent distinct business objects (e.g., RESERVATION, TICKET) identified by the same primary key (e.g., RESERVATION–NUMBER). Translate each of these entities into a relational table.

RULE RDD1.2

Name and document each relational table in the catalog or *data dictionary*. If feasible, incorporate the entity name within the table name while accommodating specific product restrictions. Cross-reference each table to the entity it represents.

TABLE NAMES

Assign to each table a meaningful name according to accepted naming standards or guidelines. Naming standards should include rules for abbreviations and synonyms. As much as possible, establish relational naming standards that are consistent with your logical data naming standards (e.g., use consistent abbreviations). However, you may have to accommodate restrictions imposed by a particular DBMS, data dictionary, or design tool.

Generally, strive for names that are intuitive to users of the relational objects. In particular, end users are likely to have more direct access to relational objects than they did to nonrelational objects. In Chapter 17, you will see the desirability of providing end-user access only through *views* (logical table definitions) and not directly through tables. If you follow that approach, you may legitimately define table names that will be intuitive to database designers and data administrators rather than to end users. (You will choose view names to be intuitive to end users.) The table name should still convey the entity name, but may also convey other meaningful information: project or database name, area of business, status (production or test), version (1, 2), and so on.

DATA DICTIONARY OR CATALOG SUPPORT

Relational DBMS *catalogs* are built-in system tables that, somewhat like data dictionaries, provide information required by the DBMS about the objects it manipulates. The catalogs of most relational DBMS products automatically record some information about tables. However, such information typically is limited to data needed by the DBMS to operate. There is additional information that a database analyst, designer, or administrator may find useful. Full data dictionary or catalog documentation about tables should include descriptive design detail and relevant database maintenance specifications.

At this point in the design process, you should record

☐ Table name
☐ Table description
☐ Creator or owner
☐ Synonym(s)
☐ Test or production status
☐ Version or copy
☐ Source (if original data reside elsewhere)
☐ Cross-reference from each table to its corresponding entity (particularly if the association is not obvious from the table name)

In later design steps, you will want to add information about

☐ Related columns
☐ Assignment to relational databases
☐ Physical storage characteristics (storage device, and so on)
☐ Access mechanisms
☐ Use of other tuning techniques
☐ Load and refresh (i.e., periodic reload) processes
☐ Backup and recovery procedures
☐ Reorganization parameters
☐ Associated data maintenance and integrity audit routines
☐ Purge routines
☐ Security restrictions
☐ Other details specific to your environment

The designer (perhaps following organizational guidelines) must determine how to record information that is not captured automatically by the catalog of a given relational DBMS. One approach is to extend the DBMS catalog into a more comprehensive data dictionary by creating additional catalog-like tables. To do so, begin by developing a logical data model depicting table information that you wish to document. (Why not follow steps in Part 2?) Then describe the relationships to data already stored in the catalog. For example, you may define new entities representing logical data modeling constructs such as entities, relationships, and business rules, including how they relate to relational implementation constructs; routines associated with maintaining data integrity, such as standard data maintenances routines, integrity audit routines, and purge routines; tuning options chosen to tweak performance; and database maintenance utility parameters and associated documentation.

After completing a comprehensive, data-driven logical design, translate your data dictionary model to a relational implementation following the methodology presented in Part 3. Finally, create *views* (logical table definitions, as described in Chapter 3) to integrate (e.g., join) original catalog tables with your extensions. The views will create the appearance of one integrated set of tables containing both built-in and extended catalog information. Most catalog users (whether developers or end users) will be oblivious of whether particular information is documented in the standard DBMS catalog or has been added through your dictionary extensions. Obviously, however, you must provide mechanisms for capturing the information that is not built into the catalog.

An alternative for addressing data dictionary requirements is to implement a totally separate (perhaps nonrelational) data dictionary facility. This alternative requires implementing mechanisms to synchronize the built-in DBMS catalog and a standalone data dictionary. For instance, you may need procedures to refresh your data dictionary periodically with extracts from the relational DBMS catalog. This alternative sacrifices up-to-the-minute currency and guaranteed accuracy (as provided by views of the "live" DBMS catalog) in favor of perhaps greater functionality at lower cost (as afforded, for example, by a purchased data dictionary software package).

C A S E S T U D Y

Figure 11.2 reviews the entities in the Moon Launch passenger reservations logical data model. There are eight entities (including supertypes and subtypes). Therefore, there are eight relational tables in the preliminary database design:

☐ BSNSS
☐ PSSGR
☐ BSNSS–PSSGR

FIGURE 11.2 Moon Launch passenger reservations logical entities.

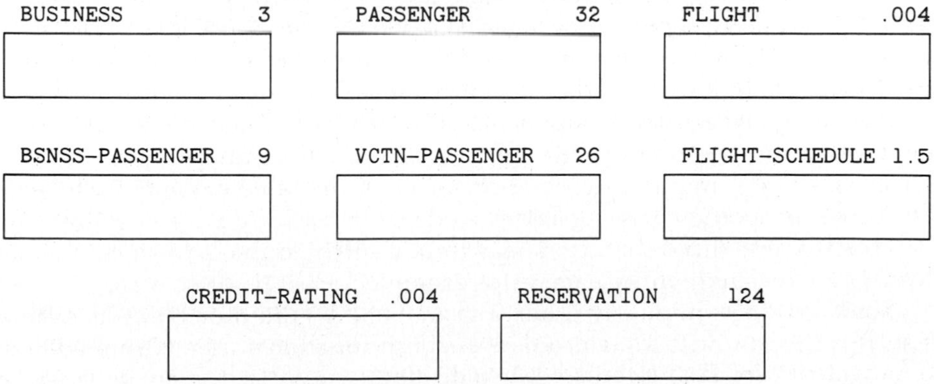

BUSINESS 3	PASSENGER 32	FLIGHT .004
BSNSS–PASSENGER 9	VCTN–PASSENGER 26	FLIGHT–SCHEDULE 1.5
CREDIT–RATING .004	RESERVATION 124	

Entity Volumes: Annual averages in 000s

- □   VCTN–PSSGR
- □   FLIGHT
- □   FLIGHT–SCHDL
- □   RSVTN
- □   CRDT–RTNG

As you can see, you are likely to need additional abbreviations (typically formed by dropping vowels) to shorten your table names. Many products require reasonably short table names; also, short yet meaningful table names are more convenient for designers and users. If you abbreviate a word in one table name, consistently use the same abbreviation in other table names.

IMPLEMENTATION TIPS AND TECHNIQUES

If possible, establish organization-wide standards or recommended naming conventions for relational tables prior to initiating database design. If standards are lacking or incomplete, develop a set of guidelines for your project so that, at least across these logically related tables, names are meaningful and consistent.

One factor affecting table naming conventions is the naming length restrictions imposed by particular products. For instance, in IBM's DB2 relational DBMS, table names cannot exceed 18 characters; in Teradata's DBC/1012 DBMS, table names can be 30 characters. Despite the preference of programmers and end users for short names, choose somewhat longer names if necessary to convey the full meaning of the object (in this case, the table) being named. You also may create synonyms using shorter, more user-friendly names. Chapter 17 discusses use of views to support synonyms. Alternatively, your DBMS may extend ANSI SQL to support synonyms as part of the table definition (CREATE TABLE statement).

Other potential constraints on names are product restrictions on use of special characters or reserved words. For instance, most SQL products do not permit an object (e.g., table) to be named ORDER, since ORDER is a keyword for specifying ORDER BY. Thus, you must rename an ORDER (purchase order) entity to a PORDER table (or some other nonreserved word).

As mentioned earlier, components of a table name may convey the entity name, status (test or production), version (current, 1, 2), and project or owner. For example, you might assign one character of the table name to each of the last three properties with standard codes for each (e.g., P = Production, T = Test). These three characters may form a suffix to the corresponding (and possibly abbreviated) entity name—for example, DPT–T2C, EMPL--P1C.

Some products implicitly prefix a table name by the user ID of its creator. If such is the case with your product, establish functional user IDs (in addition to individual user IDs) to be used by individuals authorized to create tables. In this way, you associate tables with a business function or project, rather than with a specific individual who may leave or transfer within the organization.

The functional user IDs might conform to a standard that includes project, status, or version as part of the creator's user ID. This convention enables you to use the same table name (without the prefixed user ID) across various environments (test versus production, payroll versus personnel application projects, version 1 versus version 2, and so on).

In general, it is good practice to save a copy of the DDL that creates relational tables (indeed, all relational objects). In this way, not only do you have an informal audit mechanism, but also you facilitate recreation of such objects should the need arise (e.g., to move objects among systems, or to recreate objects in the event of inadvertent or necessary object drops). Of course, you will also need naming conventions for files containing your DDL.

STEP RDD2: IDENTIFY COLUMNS

You can think of a row in a table as a record of related data items. The related data items are called *columns*. You must identify the columns in each table.

RULE RDD2.1

In general, identify one *column* in the appropriate table for each attribute of an entity.

You assigned attributes to entities in the logical data model based on their business definitions and associated dependencies. Now represent the attributes in your preliminary relational database design as columns in the appropriate tables.

For example, using ANSI SQL syntax, you can define columns in a table to represent attributes in the CUSTOMER entity as follows:

```
CREATE TABLE CUSTOMER (BRANCH-CODE . . . ,
                       NUMBER . . . ,
                       NAME . . . ,
                       ADDRESS . . . ,
                       CREDIT-RTNG-CODE . . . )
```

Again, every relational DBMS supports DDL syntax to define columns in a table. Consideration of other implementation options is therefore unnecessary.

Notice that in establishing columns for *foreign key* attributes, you are effectively translating the logical data model *relationships* into relational database constructs. Recall that, in a logical data model, foreign keys (as well as arrows) represent relationships. In the relational database design, you similarly represent relationships by columns corresponding to foreign keys.

In your preliminary relational design, you aim for absolute consistency with the logical data model. Therefore, foreign keys should be the *only* columns appearing in more than one table (just as they are the only attributes appearing in more than one entity).

RULE RDD2.2

Do not define *multiple attributes* as one (composite) column in a table.

Occasionally, you may be tempted to define two or more closely related attributes as one column in a table, particularly if the users often (or always) reference these attributes together. For instance, you might consider defining a composite employee identification column EMPL–ID–CODE as DDnnn where DD is a department code (representing departments AP, AR, CS, MN, and PY) and nnn is an employee number within the department (for employee numbers 100 through 399). There are several dangers in doing this.

Most important, you may lose some of the functionality associated with data manipulation commands provided by the product (i.e., the commands in its language). For example, if the EMPL–ID–CODE column actually consists of two logical attributes, DEPARTMENT–CODE and EMPLOYEE–NUMBER, defining both of these attributes as one column may make the following operations difficult or impossible to perform (e.g., using SQL): range-checking of the employee number (SQL BETWEEN syntax), ordering or sorting of the employee numbers (SQL ORDER BY syntax), and grouping of the employee numbers (SQL GROUP BY and HAVING syntax). (Note: If your relational product supports text manipulation operators (e.g., substring and concatenation operators), or if the product supports a COBOL-like "redefines" facility, you may be able to perform these functions. However, performance considerations associated with either feature may discourage its use. For example, some products cannot use indexes when searching on substrings or concatenated columns.)

Another disadvantage of combining attributes into one column is the requirement that each column be defined as one data type, even if its component attributes are logically different data types. In the example, you would have to define the entire employee identification column as character, even though employee number itself is numeric. Thus, you lose the ability to rely on the DBMS to verify that the employee number contains only numeric values. More subtly, DBMS optimizers, in choosing access paths, make assumptions about the potential range of values in a column. For example, an optimizer, on evaluating a range specification (BETWEEN, <, >), may assume all combinations of character data in estimating access possibilities. If the data actually are numeric, such assumptions are incorrect and may lead to less efficient access paths.

A third disadvantage is that you typically cannot define an index on an attribute constituting only part of a column (since a relational DBMS builds each index on one or more columns). Of course, a particular relational product might be intelligent enough to use the column index to satisfy queries qualified on leading characters (e.g., leading component attributes) of the column (for instance, WHERE EMPL-ID-CODE LIKE 'AP%%'). However, a product will be less efficient in using a column index for queries involving only trailing characters (or trailing component attributes in the selection criteria, as in WHERE EMPL-ID-CODE LIKE '%%199'). Indeed, many products will not use an index at all in processing the latter query.

RULE RDD2.3

Name and document each column in the catalog or *data dictionary*. If feasible, incorporate the attribute name within the column name while accommodating specific product restrictions. Cross-reference each column to the attribute it represents.

COLUMN NAMES

A column name must be unique within a table. In general, it should be similar to the name of the attribute it represents. However, whereas attribute names frequently are long (because they convey meaning and role of the attribute), product-specific naming restrictions may require use of more cryptic names for columns. Thus, as for tables, you may need to increase your use of abbreviations or deploy synonyms for columns to shorten names further. As much as possible, remain consistent with (while adding to and in some cases even shortening) abbreviations established by your logical data naming conventions.

Most relational DBMS products define a full column name to consist of the table name, followed by a separator (such as a period), followed by the user-defined column name.

Preferably, your column naming standard should resemble your logical attribute naming standard and should support inclusion of the following naming components:

- ☐ Table name (which may be implicitly assumed by the DBMS)
- ☐ Originating table (for foreign key columns)
- ☐ Class word (specifying general nature of column—e.g., DATE, AMOUNT)
- ☐ Modifying words (providing further description as required)

The table name and originating table name components may be followed by special separator symbols to highlight their meaning. For instance, extending the logical data naming standard described in Part 2:

TableName.ParentTableName*ModifyingWord(s)-ClassWord

$\quad\uparrow\qquad\qquad\qquad\uparrow\qquad\qquad\qquad\qquad\uparrow$

$\quad$period$\qquad\qquad\quad$asterisk$\qquad\qquad\qquad$dash

Other separators may be substituted (such as # for *) if, for example, your product does not permit asterisks in column names. If your product prohibits any special separators (e.g., it allows only dashes or underscores), you may have to standardize the sequence of words within a name. Or, you might allocate a specific number of characters to each name component to distinguish table name, parent table name, and class word.

Consider, for example, that EMPL.ID-NUMBER is the column name for the primary key of the EMPL (employee) table, where ID is a modifying word and NUMBER is a class word. The foreign key in the PRJCT (project) table may have one of the following names (all including EMPL to designate the originating table):

PRJCT.EMPL*ID-NUMBER	* highlights the column as a foreign key
PRJCT.EMPL#ID-NUMBER	# highlights the column as a foreign key
PRJCT.EMPL-ID-NUMBER	the fact that EMPL is the name of another table (and perhaps the position of the word EMPL within the name) highlight the column as a foreign key

As mentioned previously, in Chapter 17 you evaluate use of views rather than tables to support direct end-user access. When defining columns in views, you can assign column names that are meaningful and intuitive to the end user. Therefore, when defining columns in the actual underlying tables, you may choose to make the column names meaningful to the database designers and to data administrators (rather than to end users).

DATA DICTIONARY OR CATALOG SUPPORT

The catalogs of most relational DBMS products contain only information that the DBMS itself requires. An analyst typically desires additional information about columns. Useful documentation for columns includes:

- Column name
- Column description
- Cross-reference of each column to a corresponding attribute (particularly if the association is not obvious from the column name)
- Synonym(s)
- Source
- Type of column (primary key, alternate key, foreign key, nonkey)
- Stored data type and length

- ☐ Uniqueness property
- ☐ Null support property
- ☐ Sample values
- ☐ Default value
- ☐ Allowable value constraints (range, discrete values, and so on)
- ☐ Default print format
- ☐ Update routine(s) (if applicable)

You can record the first five items now. You will document the remainder during subsequent design steps. Options for facilitating capture of this information (if the DBMS catalog does not automatically support all the items) are the same as options for documenting tables: establishing additional catalog-like tables or implementing a separate data dictionary facility.

RULE RDD2.4

Diagram relational tables, columns, and selected implementation options in a format that aids understanding of the design by users and by developers.

Ideally, a diagram of the relational database design is generated from an automated data dictionary. It should be a concise, graphical representation depicting the types of information stored in the database and the critical implementation options employed. Preferably, it should illustrate the relationships between the relational database design and an underlying logical data model. However, this last objective may require that the relational design resemble a logical data model. If you choose tuning options that cause your relational design to deviate significantly from the logical data model, diagramming relationships between the two may be complex.

For now, of course, your design closely approximates your logical data model. Thus, you can extend your logical data model diagrams and your sample value listings to indicate selected implementation options. The exercises at the end of appropriate chapters provide insight into diagramming conventions.

C A S E   S T U D Y

Refer back to Figure 9.12 to review the attributes in the Moon Launch passenger reservations logical data model. For each attribute in an entity, establish a column in the corresponding table. Retain the same names as much as possible while conforming to product restrictions. For example, consider the RSVTN table, corresponding to the RESERVATION entity. Establish columns as follows:

```
FLIGHT#NMBR
PSSGR#CNTRY_NAME
PSSGR#CODE
FLT_SCHDL#DPT_DATE
CNFRMTN_NMBR
FARE_AMT
PYMT_CODE
ENTRY_DATE
AGNT_NMBR
```

The column names above illustrate naming conventions you might adopt for IBM's DB2. Note the following points:

1. Column names cannot exceed 18 characters (consistent with the ANSI SQL standard). Therefore, abbreviations are used more abundantly than in the logical data model. Whenever an abbreviation seems relatively clear, it is used in place of the corresponding word. This convention increases the likelihood that other column names (not yet created but possibly including the same words) will not exceed the length restriction.
2. Hyphens (-) are not permitted, but underscore characters (_) are allowed in DB2 (as in the ANSI SQL standard). Thus, all hyphens in logical attribute names are replaced by underscores.
3. Asterisks (*) are not permitted, but pound signs (#) are. Thus, asterisks are replaced by pound signs. (The ANSI SQL standard does not permit any special characters. Thus, using ANSI SQL, some other convention must be used to designate foreign keys.)

Sample value listings can effectively supplement the use of descriptive column names in conveying the types of data stored in a table. For example, a sample value listing for the BSNSS_PSSGR table is depicted in Figure 11.3.

FIGURE 11.3 BSNSS_PSSGR **relational table sample value listing.**

BSNSS_PSSGR

PSSGR# CNTRY_NAME	PSSGR#CODE	BSNSS# CNTRY_NAME	BSNSS#NAME	TCKT_ ADDRS_ FLAG
France	146523	France	Gourmet Chefs, Inc.	B
Portugal	XTF-9146	Spain	Bullfighters Corp.	P
USA	059-11-2874	USA	Pharm Ops, Inc.	B
Canada	591-XV-11	USA	Shipping Co.	B

IMPLEMENTATION TIPS AND TECHNIQUES

So far, your relational tables look exactly like the entities in your logical data model. The columns have a one-to-one correspondence to attributes in entities. You may already be questioning such an exact translation under one or more of the following circumstances:

1. What about *derived* attributes? Should you establish columns for those as well—and won't they consume extra storage and impose additional update overhead? Yes indeed! For now, however, if you chose to represent them in the logical data model, also include them in the relational table. A final decision requires analysis of processing requirements and consequent cost versus performance tradeoffs. You consider those tradeoffs in Chapter 15 when you examine possible deviations from the logical data model.

2. What about *combining some tables,* or even *breaking some tables into component tables* to simplify or speed up some processing requirements? Again, defer making any such changes until you have thoroughly analyzed their effects (Chapter 16).

3. What about *redefining some columns*—for example, changing a foreign key column to reference an alternate rather than primary key, thereby reducing the need for joins to obtain the alternate key? This can be a useful technique, but once again calls for assessment of all processing requirements and all possible tuning options. Thus, defer it until later in the process (Chapter 16).

STEP RDD3: ADAPT DATA STRUCTURE TO PRODUCT ENVIRONMENT

Steps RDD1 and RDD2 translate the logical data model to relational tables and columns, independent of particular relational DBMS implementations. The final step in translating the structure adapts that structure to your product environment. This step is not really required to design your relational database "on paper"; thus, you may defer this step until later in the design process. It is necessary, however, before beginning implementation.

The concepts underlying relational tables and columns are fairly consistent across relational products: A column is an addressable unit of data (a field) and a table is a group of columns. Actual implementation of tables and columns, however, involves some highly product-specific considerations. For example, how is a table stored in a database? Are the columns physically adjacent and stored in left-to-right order? How is space allocated to the rows? Are all rows stored together, and is contiguous space reserved for subsequent row inserts? How many tables and what other items constitute a database? In fact, what is a relational database in your product environment? Moreover, what units in a database (or across databases) are accessible to and potentially locked by a given query—one or more tables, rows, or other items?

You will refine the answers to these and other questions as you tune your database design to accommodate particular processing requirements and performance objectives. However, some consideration of these issues would be required to implement even a preliminary, untuned design.

SEQUENCING COLUMNS IN TABLES

Generally, the ordering of column names in your table definition (SQL CREATE TABLE syntax) establishes the sequence of columns in storage. From a user's perspective, ordering of columns in a relational table is arbitrary. A user can retrieve the columns in any order (e.g., by varying the sequence of column names specified in an SQL SELECT clause). The ability to retrieve columns in any order is a consequence of the relational model, which dictates that there be no meaning implied by any particular sequencing of columns.

You, however, must choose a left-to-right sequence for storing columns when you define a table. Product-specific considerations may favor choosing one sequence over another.

RULE RDD3.1

Define left-to-right *sequencing of columns* in a table to optimize product-specific storage utilization and performance.

For example, a given product may require that you define variable-length columns as the rightmost columns of a table. Or, a product may allow you to define columns in any sequence, but may manage storage utilization more efficiently (e.g., minimize free space fragmentation) when variable-length columns are all at the far right of table rows. Or, a product may be more efficient in performing update operations when all variable-length columns are stored at the end (on the right) of rows. You should examine effects of column sequence in your product environment and construct your DDL to establish the most efficient sequence.

RULE RDD3.2

Require users and programs to *explicitly name* (and therefore *sequence columns*) to be returned by a query; i.e., discourage use of SQL SELECT * syntax (or equivalent). Also discourage INSERT commands that do not specify column names.

Consider the following SQL syntax:

```
SELECT column1, column2, column3 FROM tablename
```

This command requests three columns in a specified order, regardless of the sequence in which columns are stored. In contrast, consider the following syntax, also supported by ANSI SQL and most product implementations:

```
SELECT * FROM tablename
```

This syntax returns all columns for a table in the order in which they are stored (typically defined by a CREATE TABLE command).

Suppose you subsequently decide to change the CREATE TABLE sequence of columns and to reload the table, based on product storage or performance considerations. Or, you may be adding new columns, whether at the end of the rows (through an ALTER TABLE command) or between existing columns (by modifying the CREATE TABLE command). Queries specifying SELECT * will return different results; they may even cause an abend in a calling program that expects the former results.

Similarly, ANSI SQL INSERT syntax does not require specification of column names. An INSERT command may assume the column sequence specified by the CREATE TABLE command, as in:

```
INSERT INTO tablename
     VALUES (column1value, column2value, column3value)
```

Suppose you subsequently change the CREATE TABLE command to alter the sequence of columns. INSERT commands that assume the previous column sequence may no longer work. Worse, they may insert values into the wrong columns. Avoid the problem by specifying column names in INSERT commands as shown:

```
INSERT INTO tablename (column1name, column2name, column3name)
     VALUES (column1value, column2value, column3value)
```

MAPPING TABLES INTO DBMS STORAGE

When defining a table to a DBMS, you must define not only the columns composing the table but also the parameters affecting allocation and management of storage. For example, you must determine (or allow the DBMS to default):

☐ *Primary space*—the initial amount of (typically contiguous) space allocated for the table
☐ *Secondary space*—additional space to be allocated after using up (perhaps some of) the primary space
☐ *Free space*—that portion of space that is not filled with data during initial load of the table

RULE RDD3.3

If feasible, allocate *primary space* large enough to contain the entire table.

Frequently, the relational DBMS cannot allocate secondary space that is physically adjacent to primary space. Thus, access to data in secondary space may be less efficient. Wherever possible, avoid any allocation of secondary space by defining sufficient primary space to hold all or most of the rows in a table, including projected growth.

RULE RDD3.4

If feasible, allocate *free space* to accommodate all anticipated row inserts and updates that may occur after table load or reorganization.

Free space, if available, is used for new rows inserted into a table. Free space also can accommodate updates that increase row size (e.g., through increasing length of values in variable-length columns or sometimes through replacing nulls by nonnull values). Appropriate placement of free space may enable the DBMS to optimize placement of data for efficient access, and may increase efficiency of insert and update operations (i.e., by minimizing DBMS activity to find or create available space).

Typically, free space specifications determine distribution of free space after table reorganizations as well as initial table load. You may want to specify different free space parameters for a reorganization as opposed to a load. Moreover, you should schedule reorganizations to optimize availability and distribution of free space. For example, try to schedule reorganizations after periods of intense insert/update activity to reduce free space fragmentation and to allocate additional free space.

ASSIGNING TABLES TO DATABASES

Recall from Chapter 3 that a relational *database* has a product-specific meaning. To the users, a relational database is simply a collection of relational tables. To a designer, the definition of a database may have additional implications; for example, relating to security, space allocation, or limitations on data access. In some products, a database is a logical unit for backup, restore, recovery, or reorganization. Sometimes, definition of databases may affect lock management, concurrent access, or effects of certain utilities on data availability.

At one extreme, you can combine all tables into one relational database. At the other extreme, you can assign each table to its own database. You must consider implications in your particular DBMS environment to choose some variant on these extremes.

RULE RDD3.5

In general, assign to one *database* tables representing entities that are closely related in business meaning.

Remember that entities are business objects of interest to the user(s). Entities that are closely related in business meaning usually are characterized by high *affinity*. In other words, they are frequently accessed together. They also are typically maintained to the same degree of currency and thus are backed up, restored, and perhaps even updated together. Collecting such closely related entities into one database usually aids access efficiency and simplifies support.

RULE RDD3.6

When different groups of users consistently access different sets of tables, consider separating those sets by placing them in *separate databases*. This may facilitate greater concurrency or data availability, and may avoid database size limitations.

In some products, database boundaries are related to concurrency and availability limitations. For instance, DDL statements may lock all tables in the database until the change is completed, with the result that all other access to the database is blocked. Moreover, some utilities (e.g., backup or restore) may operate against all tables in a database or may run against only one table at a time in a given database. Thus, establishing separate databases for tables that are rarely accessed together may improve concurrency or availability.

Some relational DBMSs limit size of a database in terms of number of tables, amount of storage, or length of descriptive information defining the database. Separating tables that are rarely accessed together may reduce the effects of such size limitations.

On the other hand, some DBMS products (e.g., Britton-Lee IDM, SQL/DS, INGRES) do not allow users to access more than one database in one query. For such products, you may want to assign as many tables as possible to the same database (e.g., establish one test and one production database, or establish one database for each division). This maximizes capabilities for multi-table access and, therefore, for *data sharing* among users.

RULE RDD3.7

Assign to each database a meaningful *name* that conveys general business meaning (grouping of entities) and conforms to product-specific restrictions.

In many products, databases are or can be made transparent to end users. In other words, end users may access tables without specific reference to databases. Other products require that users explicitly issue "open database" commands or prefix table names by database names. In the latter case, keep the database names intuitive. Optionally (particularly if database names need be referenced only by designers or by database administrators), you can incorporate additional information into your naming conventions, such as test versus production status, version, or number.

RULE RDD3.8

Document information about databases in the catalog or *data dictionary*.

Most relational DBMS catalogs automatically record some information about databases (e.g., name, associated tables, perhaps size, name of creator, or date created). You may want to record additional information, such as location, description, primary user or owner, security administrator, or database administrator.

Note that many relational DBMSs define databases to include other types of items, in addition to tables. For example, a given DBMS may associate views, users, macros, other types of procedures, indexes, hash algorithms, or other items with databases. Generally, you associate items related to particular tables with those tables' respective databases. However, guidelines in this area depend on the DBMS in question.

SETTING DATABASE LOCKING PARAMETERS

Locking is the mechanism whereby a DBMS controls data integrity during concurrent access (simultaneous access by multiple users) to the same data. Essentially, when one user or application begins to *read* the data, the DBMS obtains a *read-lock* on the data. This allows other users to read the data, but prohibits them from updating the data. When one user or application begins to *update* the data, the DBMS obtains a *write-lock* on the data. This prevents any other users from updating or reading the data until the lock is released.

A lock obtained by the DBMS has several properties:

☐ *Amount of data that is locked*—A lock may lock multiple tables, one entire table, a storage unit containing a subset of a table (e.g., one block), or a single row of a table.
☐ *Mode of the lock*—A lock may facilitate read-only access or update access. Read-only locks can be shared with other readers. Update locks cannot be shared with any other users.
☐ *Duration of the lock*—A DBMS may hold a lock for the duration of an operation or command, or it may hold the lock throughout an entire transaction or program. Further, in some products, a DBMS may hold a lock only while it reads a row or physical block; that is, individual read locks (as opposed to update locks) may be held for less than the duration of a command or transaction.

Different relational DBMSs have different locking mechanisms. Some are more sophisticated than others are. Some products allow the database designer to choose or tailor locking options and some do not.

RULE RDD3.9

If feasible, set *database locking parameters* to effect locking of the least amount of data for the shortest duration.

Isolate the effects of locks to maximize concurrent access. Opt for locks on small amounts of data for durations that are as short as possible without risking data integrity.

Some products support specification of locking options at multiple levels, such as database, table, program. In the absence of application-specified locks, table or database locking parameters prevail. Set the most generally applicable locking options (e.g., at the database or table level) to promote maximum concurrency. Override these options in specific applications when more pervasive locks are necessary.

IMPLEMENTATION TIPS AND TECHNIQUES

Techniques for this step depend on your particular product and the importance of product-specific options to your requirements. When using products with few alternatives or when implementing designs that do not challenge the performance and functionality limits of a product, you may not have much to do in this step. On the other hand, for a product with many options or for a challenging design, you will spend a lot of time in this step. Hints on how to proceed follow.

1. *Understand how your product associates a relational table with a physical storage structure.* Determine whether executing a DDL statement to create a table automatically generates appropriate physical storage structures (e.g., datasets or files). Or, do you need to define such structures explicitly?
2. *Learn the physical layout of table rows for your product.* If possible, obtain diagrams of your product's internal storage layout for table rows. These will highlight product-specific details and efficiencies. For example, what data types are available, and how is each stored? What is the overhead associated with columns allowing null values or columns that vary in length? How much storage space is wasted when row sizes are small? When they are large? What is the maximum number of rows that will fit in a physical block?
3. *Determine the meaning of "database" in your product.* Learn the obvious and subtle boundaries imposed by the concept of database. In particular, do you need to be concerned with assigning tables to more than one database?
4. *Identify locking parameters that can be specified by the database designer.* Determine whether such parameters exist and how they affect performance and concurrency. Determine, too, whether you can easily alter such parameters as you gain a better understanding of your product and user needs.

CASE STUDY

Step RDD3 is product-specific. Rather than providing a case study illustrating the myriad possibilities, let us discuss IBM's DB2 DBMS, a very popular product. If you are using another product, you can probably gain some insight by studying DB2 considerations.

DB2 DATA STRUCTURES

ASSOCIATION OF RELATIONAL TABLES WITH STORAGE STRUCTURES. A DB2 table is assigned to an object called a *tablespace*, which generally correlates to a dataset (i.e., file). You can allow DB2 automatically to create tablespaces and datasets for you. Or, you can explicitly define them. You will, of course, need to establish naming conventions for tablespaces and datasets, even though such constructs are transparent to users. You may, for instance, want to include in tablespace names information pertaining to chargeback. Perhaps a tablespace name should identify not only the tables stored in it, but also the cost center to which the storage costs are to be charged.

DB2 allows for specification of primary, secondary, and free space when defining a tablespace.

PHYSICAL LAYOUT OF TABLE ROWS. DB2 tables consist of physical blocks (called pages), which are generally 4K bytes in length. There are three types of pages in DB2 tablespaces: a header page, a space map page, and data pages. A data page can hold a maximum of 127 rows. Each row has 8 bytes of overhead associated with it. Descriptions of these page layouts are available in IBM manuals and course materials.

A general recommendation is to store columns in the following sequence:

Fixed length and not null

Fixed length and null

Variable length and not null

Variable length and null

This sequence involves the least CPU overhead when accessing the leftmost columns (although such overhead—relating to nulls or variable-length columns—probably is fairly insignificant in light of other tuning options that reduce I/O). A nullable column contains an extra byte to indicate its null status. Even when a column value is null, space is still reserved for the full column—thus, use of nulls does not save space. A variable-length column contains 2 extra bytes indicating its length. If it is also nullable, it contains 3 extra bytes: 1 byte indicating null status and 2 bytes specifying column value length.

MEANING OF "DATABASE". DB2 SQL can reference tables from multiple databases. In fact, the SQL never specifically indicates which database is involved (DB2 determines that from its catalog). Thus, assignment of tables to databases is transparent to users. Considerations for grouping tables into databases include:

☐ Degree of affinity (Whether the tables are related in business meaning and whether they are accessed together—questions addressed by Rules RDD3.5 and RDD3.6.)

☐ Distribution of access privileges and security administration responsibilities (Because, with DB2, some privileges and responsibilities can be "bundled" by database.)

☐ Distribution of technical support responsibilities (Because, with DB2, some maintenance activities—such as backup, recovery, and reorganization—can be "bundled".)

☐ Potential for locking contention (For example, during DDL operations, an entire DB2 database is locked from most other access. You may wish to isolate, in their own databases, tables that are frequently changed using DDL commands. In particular, you may consider creating one database per user, or per group of users, if users are allowed to create and drop their own tables. Creating separate databases will minimize the locking contention that creation and dropping of "personal" tables might otherwise have.)

LOCKING PARAMETERS. A designer specifies the size of locks when creating a DB2 tablespace. This lock size pertains to all users of the tablespace unless escalated by the DB2 system (to minimize locking overhead) or by a LOCK TABLE statement in a program. The options for lock size include: TABLESPACE, PAGE, and ANY. For ANY, DB2 starts with PAGE locks and escalates to TABLESPACE locks when certain locking limits are reached. In general, specify LOCKSIZE TABLESPACE for tables that are read-only (since tablespace locks incur less overhead, and, for read-only tables, tablespace locks will not restrict required access). For tablespaces that will be updated, specify ANY, thereby allowing DB2 to escalate as it sees fit. You can modify the lock size parameter through an ALTER statement.

Other locking parameters (e.g., when locks are obtained and released) are set at DB2 BIND time (BIND is the process whereby access paths are selected). Such locks are typically the responsibility of application developers rather than of database designers. Yet, as a designer, you may want to review them.

SUMMARY

In this chapter, you translated the structure of the logical data model into a preliminary relational database design. The design is preliminary in that you made no attempt to tailor or tune it to accommodate specific functionality, performance, or (for the most part) DBMS product requirements. In fact, you have not even studied access requirements or performance criteria.

The translation process begins by creating a relational table for each entity. You include tables for each subtype and supertype. Thus, initially you have a one-to-one correspondence between the number of boxes (entities) in your logical data model and the number of tables in your preliminary relational design.

Next, you assign columns to each table such that each attribute for an entity in the logical data model becomes a column in the corresponding table. Therefore, each table contains columns for its primary key, any alternate keys, any foreign keys, and all nonkey attributes. At this point, the tables in your preliminary design are normalized, since your logical data model is normalized.

The final step in translating the structure adapts it to a particular relational DBMS. You examined four issues: (1) sequencing of columns, (2) mapping of tables into DBMS storage, (3) assigning of tables to databases, and (4) setting of database locking parameters.

Chapter 12 translates the integrity properties of the logical data model into relational constructs. Your goal will be to preserve the logical structure and its integrity in their entirety, preferably using automated implementation mechanisms.

EXERCISES

11.1 List three major logical data model constructs that primarily address data structure. Discuss how they relate to relational objects.

11.2 Why is the process of translating a logical data model to a relational database design described as data-driven and processing-independent?

11.3 Discuss why you should not consider deviating from the logical data model during the translation process.

11.4 Draw a logical data model diagram depicting information to be stored in a data dictionary about tables. Include in your model the following: table name, table description, creator's user ID, creator's name, database name, database description, synonyms, test or production status, version or copy identification, actual/scheduled production date, processor identification, source, and cross-reference to entity.

Assume the following: (1) a table is uniquely identified by knowing the user ID of the creator and the table name, (2) a particular version of a table is identified by its full table name (user ID of creator plus table name) plus test or production status plus version or copy number, and (3) tables and entities map to one another with an $M:N$ relationship, although in this chapter you have created one table per entity.

For extra credit: Relate this diagram to the information stored in your relational DBMS catalog.

11.5 Extend your logical data model from Exercise 11.4 to include information about columns, specifically: column name, column description, cross-reference to attribute, synonyms, source, type (primary key, alternate key, foreign key, nonkey), stored data type and length, uniqueness, null support, sample values, default value, allowable value constraints, default print format, and update routine. Assume that there is only one data source for a column.

For extra credit: Relate this diagram to your product's catalog.

11.6 Suggest modifications to the logical data model diagramming conventions in Part 2 to depict a relational database design. Show a sample diagram for the passenger reservations tables. Refer to Figure 9.12 for the logical data model.

11.7 For the Moon Launch Enterprise case study, assume that security will be administered decentrally by designating a security officer in each of the user groups; that is, you can create a set of security officers (e.g., USERADM1, USERADM2). How, then, might you assign tables to relational databases?

11.8 Assume that different sets of passenger reservations tables will be supported technically (e.g., backed up, recovered, reorganized) by different functions within the organization (e.g., a decentralized organization for database administration). How might you assign tables to databases to support this requirement? What other technical support considerations might influence how you group tables into databases?

12 | Translate the Logical Data Integrity

Chapter 12 completes the translation process. It examines implementation options for enforcing business rules about

- Entities—*Step RDD4*
- Relationships—*Step RDD5*
- Attributes—*Step RDD6*

STEP RDD4: DESIGN FOR BUSINESS RULES ABOUT ENTITIES

As part of logical data modeling, you identified two types of business rules about entities. These rules define the primary and alternate keys for an entity.

To review, a *primary key* is an attribute or minimal set of attributes that uniquely identifies an occurrence of a given entity. The primary key must exist for all occurrences of the entity. That is, it must never contain null values. Enforcing the properties of primary keys is important in your relational implementation if you are to achieve a faithful and complete translation of your logical data model.

RULE RDD4.1

Enforce logical properties (uniqueness, minimality, and disallowance of nulls) of the entity's *primary key* through the relational implementation.

Different relational database products provide various mechanisms for enforcing these logical properties. We describe options that may be available, in order of preference and with associated advantages and disadvantages.

OPTION 1 FOR ENFORCING PRIMARY KEY PROPERTIES: DBMS DATA DEFINITION LANGUAGE (DDL)

As an example of option 1, the following syntax represents a proposed extension to the ANSI SQL standard to support primary key specification:

```
CREATE TABLE CUSTOMER (BRANCH-CODE...,
                       NUMBER...,
                       NAME...,
                       ADDRESS...,
                       CREDIT-RTNG-CODE...,
                       PRIMARY KEY (BRANCH-CODE,NUMBER))
```

Ideally, a PRIMARY KEY clause should be mandatory. It is not mandatory in the proposed ANSI SQL extension, thereby allowing for compatibility with the base SQL standard and upward compatibility in product implementations. A mandatory PRIMARY KEY clause would reflect the rule that every entity must have a primary key. Since a table represents an entity (or at least—as you shall see—a derivation of one or more entities), every table likewise should have a primary key. The primary key guarantees a method of identifying a particular row in a table.

By definition, a primary key must be unique and nonnull. Moreover, since it is a minimal set of identifying attributes, if it is composite, each component must be nonunique. (That is, if one component is unique, then the other components are not necessary to guarantee uniqueness. Thus, the combination of components is not a minimal set of identifying attributes.) The PRIMARY KEY syntax ideally should activate automatic enforcement of these properties by the DBMS. (In fact, the proposed ANSI SQL PRIMARY KEY clause implies only uniqueness, not existence and not minimality.)

Advantages of a DDL PRIMARY KEY specification include:

□ Option is easy to implement
□ Implementation mechanism is transparent to users
□ Integrity checks on uniqueness, minimality, and nulls disallowance (if automated by the PRIMARY KEY clause) are difficult or impossible to circumvent; that is, a user cannot override these restrictions without altering the table definition (e.g., via an SQL ALTER TABLE command)
□ Option eliminates manual efforts by users to enforce primary key properties (i.e., you need not rely on the user to "do it correctly")

Be sure you understand the distinction between the *primary key* of your table and a *primary index* or other *primary access mechanism*. You define the primary key and enforce its properties to preserve data integrity. The primary key implies nothing about access patterns. In other words, whether or not a user ever references the primary key in query selection criteria (e.g., in the SQL WHERE clause), you still must define and enforce primary key properties as part of ensuring validity of data values.

On the other hand, you may later (in Chapters 13 and 14) define a primary index or other primary access mechanism (such as clustering or hashing). The primary or favored access mechanism represents the most efficient way of accessing the table for most requests. Thus, it typically reflects access requirements rather than data integrity rules. Sometimes, the primary access mechanism is built around the primary key, but only when access by primary key is frequent or important. If access by primary key is infrequent or unimportant, the primary access mechanism is built around other columns (e.g., foreign keys, nonkeys, or partial primary keys).

OPTION 2 FOR ENFORCING PRIMARY KEY PROPERTIES: DOMAIN DEFINITION TECHNIQUES

You can enforce at least some primary key properties (uniqueness, disallowance of nulls) through a product's domain capabilities. Options and examples for enforcing domains are discussed as part of Step RDD6. For primary keys, you will typically use DDL to specify nonnull, and either DDL or a unique index to specify uniqueness. Automated enforcement of nonuniqueness of primary key components (in the case of a composite primary key) may not be possible (see discussion of enforcing nonuniqueness under Step RDD6). Therefore, be sure the user has defined a minimal primary key in the first place.

Advantages of using domain techniques to enforce primary keys are the same as those identified for option 1. Disadvantages include the following:

☐ Each property of the primary key must be separately defined and enforced

☐ Use of indexes to enforce uniqueness introduces potential performance and administrative overhead (more details are discussed under option 2 for Step RDD6)

☐ Use of custom-tailored code, if required (e.g., to enforce minimality for a composite primary key) requires programming resources and may introduce performance overhead

Determine how optimally to enforce primary key properties for your specific DBMS. If you have not yet selected a relational DBMS product, evaluate the relative effectiveness of alternative products in enforcing primary key properties. Lack of automated support, via DDL or unique indexes, may be a compelling factor discouraging selection of a given product.

RULE RDD4.2

If an entity has an *alternate key,* enforce the logical properties (uniqueness, minimality, and, if applicable, disallowance of nulls) of the alternate key through the relational implementation.

To review, an *alternate key* is an attribute or minimal set of attributes that, if present, uniquely identifies an occurrence of an entity. However, you chose another attribute or set of attributes to be the primary key. If an entity has an alternate key, the properties of this key are an important component of the business data's integrity. Again, determine how optimally to enforce these properties using a given DBMS. Implementation options are similar to those available for primary keys.

RULE RDD4.3

Document primary and alternate keys for each relational table in the catalog or *data dictionary,* including mechanisms for enforcing the keys' properties.

If your relational DBMS supports designation of primary and alternate keys via DDL, then it will automatically document such keys in its catalog. Unfortunately, many relational DBMSs lack such DDL syntax. If so, you will have to decide how to document these keys and corresponding enforcement mechanisms.

Preferably, designers, data administrators, and end users all should be able to determine primary and alternate keys by accessing the catalog or data dictionary. Programs also should be able to access the dictionary (which requires an automated implementation) to enforce primary and alternate key properties or to detect violations of these business rules.

It is desirable to incorporate into your relational database diagrams indication of primary and alternate key support. (This is addressed further in the exercises.)

C A S E   S T U D Y

Refer to Figure 9.12 (p. 248) for primary keys of all entities in the Moon Launch passenger reservations logical data model. If your product supports

BSNSS__PSSGR

PSSGR# CNTRY__NAME (PK)	PSSGR#CODE (PK)	BSNSS# CNTRY__NAME	BSNSS#NAME	TCKT__ ADDRS__ FLAG
France	146523	France	Gourmet Chefs, Inc.	B
Portugal	XTF-9146	Spain	Bullfighters Corp.	P
USA	059-11-2874	USA	Pharm Ops, Inc.	B
Canada	591-XV-11	USA	Shipping Co.	B

FIGURE 12.1 BSNSS__PSSGR **sample value listing.**

specification of primary keys, add the appropriate syntax to your DDL. For example,

```
CREATE TABLE RSVTN (FLIGHT#NMBR...,
                    PSSGR#CNTRY_NAME...,
                    PSSGR#CODE...,
                    FLT_SCHDL#DPT_DATE....,
                    CNFRMTN_NMBR...,
                    FARE_AMT...,
                    PYMT_CODE...,
                    ENTRY_DATE...,
                    AGNT_NMBR...,
                    PRIMARY KEY (FLIGHT#NMBR,
                                 PSSGR#CNTRY_NAME,
                                 PSSGR#CODE,
                                 FLT_SCHDL#DPT_DATE))
```

If necessary, use techniques for defining domain constraints (instead of or in addition to PRIMARY KEY specifications) to enforce uniqueness and to restrict nulls. Again, examples of syntax for enforcing domain constraints are discussed as part of Step RDD6.

You will probably choose not to automate enforcement of primary key minimality due to the difficulty of enforcing nonuniqueness. Rather, be sure your user understands the minimality rule and has defined the primary key appropriately.

You will want to add primary key (PK) and alternate key (AKn, for columns constituting the nth alternate key) designations to the sample value listing diagram for each relational table. For example, Figure 12.1 depicts the design of the BSNSS_PSSGR table to this point.

IMPLEMENTATION TIPS AND TECHNIQUES

Many products (e.g., IBM's DB2, Teradata's DBC/1012, MUST's NOMAD) require definition of a unique index to enforce uniqueness. Although generally you implement indexes as *access mechanisms* to improve performance of specific data requests (see Chapter 14), do not consider indexes defined to enforce data integrity optional. Lack of a unique index, in the absence of any other mechanism that enforces uniqueness, can result in incorrect data values (as well as possibly inefficient access). On the other hand, nonunique indexes (addressing performance) may be defined or not, depending on your assessment of cost and performance tradeoffs.

STEP RDD5: DESIGN FOR BUSINESS RULES ABOUT RELATIONSHIPS

In the logical data model, you also defined business rules about relationships (otherwise known as insert, delete, and update constraints). In Step RDD5, you translate these business rules into relational constructs.

RULE RDD5.1

Enforce *business rules about relationships* (key attribute insert, delete, and update constraints) through the relational implementation.

Providing support for relationship business rules means maintaining the appropriate references from foreign keys to primary keys. This is generally known as *referential integrity*. Options for establishing this support vary significantly depending on the relational DBMS product. We discuss the options in order of preference.

OPTION 1 FOR ENFORCING RELATIONSHIP BUSINESS RULES: DBMS DATA DEFINITION LANGUAGE (DDL)

This option presumes DDL support for defining primary keys (option 1 under Step RDD4). The following is sample SQL syntax for defining foreign keys, proposed as an extension to the ANSI SQL standard:

```
CREATE TABLE INVOICE
      (NUMBER...,
       CSTMR*BRANCH-CODE...,
       CSTMR*NUMBER...,
       AMOUNT...,
       PRIMARY KEY (NUMBER),
       FOREIGN KEY (CSTMR*BRANCH-CODE, CSTMR*NUMBER) REFERENCES CUSTOMER)
```

Here the foreign key (CSTMR*BRANCH-CODE, CSTMR*NUMBER) references the primary key (BRANCH-CODE, NUMBER) of the parent CUSTOMER table. Implied by the foreign key definition is a parent delete/update rule of *restrict* (parent CUSTOMER cannot be deleted nor its primary key updated if it has matching child INVOICE) and a child insert/update rule of *dependent* (child INVOICE cannot be inserted nor its primary key updated unless a matching parent CUSTOMER exists).

A second set of proposed extensions to the ANSL SQL standard supports more variety in parent delete and update rules. Possible DELETE and UPDATE actions are RESTRICT, CASCADE, SET NULL, and SET DEFAULT. For example,

```
CREATE TABLE INVOICE
           (NUMBER...,
            CSTMR*BRANCH-CODE...,
            CSTMR*NUMBER...,
            AMOUNT...,
            PRIMARY KEY (NUMBER),
            FOREIGN KEY (CSTMR*BRANCH-CODE, CSTMR*NUMBER)
               REFERENCES CUSTOMER
               ON DELETE SET DEFAULT
               ON UPDATE CASCADE)
```

This example shows a parent delete rule of SET DEFAULT (on delete of parent CUSTOMER, set foreign key of INVOICE to default value) and a parent update rule of CASCADE (on update of parent CUSTOMER primary key, set foreign key of INVOICE to new value). The child insert/update rule is still an implied *dependent*.

Missing from the proposed ANSI SQL extensions is support for the following types of business rules (which you may have defined in your logical data model): (1) parent delete/update *no effect* rule, (2) parent delete/update *customized* rule, and (3) any child insert/update rule other than the implied *dependent*.

Lack of support for *no effect* reflects adherence to a property underlying the relational model—that a foreign key must *always* refer to an existing primary key value or be set to null. Nevertheless, in our experience, a *no effect* rule is sometimes required and practical. For instance, you might remove customers from the approved CUSTOMER table but still track their outstanding invoices in the INVOICE table.

A *customized* action is for business rules that cannot be described by the standard keywords. For instance, CUSTOMIZED (routine-name) could specify invocation of a customized routine to flag all associated unpaid INVOICEs as uncollectible whenever a CUSTOMER is deleted.

Finally, standard keywords representing child insert/update rules (to override the implied *dependent*) are clearly desirable.

Advantages of enforcing relationship business rules using DDL syntax include:

☐ Option is easy to implement (particularly in the case of standard business rules that can be represented by keywords; coding of routines to implement customized rules requires a little more work)

☐ Implementation mechanism is transparent to users

☐   Integrity checks are difficult or impossible for users or programs to circumvent; circumvention requires altering the data definition or, in the case of a customized business rule, altering a routine

☐   Option eliminates manual effort by users to enforce the business rule (i.e., you need not rely on the user to "do it correctly")

OPTION 2 FOR ENFORCING RELATIONSHIP BUSINESS RULES: TRIGGERING OPERATION IMPLEMENTATION TECHNIQUES

The techniques for option 2, with associated advantages and disadvantages, are discussed as part of Step RDD6. Generally, they involve writing data maintenance routines or relying on the users to enforce the rules manually. Since many relational DBMSs do not yet support DDL syntax for referential integrity, you will probably need to rely on such mechanisms.

Evaluate the importance of each key business rule, the DDL features of your relational DBMS, and the cost and availability of programming resources. Then, choose how and whether to automate full referential integrity as specified in your logical data model. If you can easily automate only selected integrity constraints with your database product, and if it is acceptable for the user manually to enforce some of the business rules, you may decide against programming enforcement of all rules.

RULE RDD5.2

Document foreign keys for each relational table in the catalog or *data dictionary*, including techniques used to enforce related business rules.

If your relational DBMS supports designation of foreign keys through DDL, then it will automatically document them in its catalog. If not, you will need to document them in your data dictionary (e.g., catalog extension).

You also will want to document the mechanisms for enforcing foreign keys, especially if not enforced using DDL. For example, if you enforce an insert rule through a macro, document the macro name, macro creator, input parameters, and instructions for invocation. Furthermore, cross-reference the macro to the business rule that it implements.

It also is advantageous to include documentation on foreign key support in your relational database diagram. (Again, see exercises for more insight here.) Optionally, you can instead or also include such information on forms (or screen layouts in the case of an automated data dictionary).

C A S E   S T U D Y

Consider the key insert/delete rules for the Moon Launch passenger reservations logical data model, developed in Chapter 6 and repeated in Figure 12.2. What problems might you have in implementing these rules using ANSI SQL DDL syntax?

1. The *dependent* child insert rules can be implied through definition of foreign keys. The *automatic* child insert rules, however, cannot be supported; thus, you probably would redefine them as *dependent* and institute procedures to ensure that update/insert of a parent always precedes update/insert of a corresponding child.
2. The *cascade* and *restrict* parent delete rules can be implemented by the syntax ON DELETE CASCADE and ON DELETE RESTRICT. The *customized* rules, however, are not supported by ANSI syntax. User-written routines probably are required to implement parent delete operations associated with customized business rules.
3. Parent update rules are not explicitly specified in Figure 12.2. One possible implication is that parent updates are treated like parent deletes; i.e., since a primary key update involves deleting the former primary key value, apply the parent delete rule. However, it is not necessarily true that the parent delete rule and parent update rule are the same. For example, you may have a *cascade* parent delete rule for the relationship from CUSTOMER to INVOICE (ON DELETE CASCADE) to handle writeoffs of bad customers. But you may restrict updates of a customer's primary key as long as that customer has any outstanding invoices (ON UPDATE RESTRICT). Or, on update of the customer's primary key, you may want to delete (rather than update) all associated invoices, or leave the invoices as they are. Note that the ANSI SQL extensions do not address these latter circumstances— other implementation options must be employed.
4. Likewise, child update rules are not specified in Figure 12.2. The proposed ANSI SQL FOREIGN KEY syntax implies that all child update rules are *dependent*. That is, if a foreign key of a child is updated, its new value must match an existing primary key in the parent or be null. Any other rules require other enforcement mechanisms.

Key business rules that are not supported by DDL syntax must be implemented by options available for general triggering operations, discussed in the next step.

You may add designation of foreign keys to your relational table diagrams as shown in Figure 12.3. Here FKn denotes columns constituting the nth foreign key. Optionally, you might also add designation of parent and child delete/insert/update rules by associating with the foreign keys appropriate codes to designate corresponding rules. Note that even parent delete/update rules must

Parent	Child	Child Insert Rule	Parent Delete Rule
CREDIT-RATING	BUSINESS	dependent	customized
CREDIT-RATING	VCTN-PASSENGER	dependent	customized
BUSINESS	BSNSS-PASSENGER	dependent	cascade
PASSENGER	BSNSS-PASSENGER	automatic	cascade
PASSENGER	VCTN-PASSENGER	automatic	cascade
BSNSS-PASSENGER	RESERVATION	automatic	restrict
VCTN-PASSENGER	RESERVATION	automatic	restrict
FLIGHT	RESERVATION	dependent	customized

FIGURE 12.2 Moon Launch passenger reservations key insert/delete rules.

BSNSS_PSSGR

PSSGR#CNTRY_NAME (PK, FK1)	PSSGR#CODE (PK, FK1)	BSNSS#CNTRY_NAME (FK2)	BSNSS#NAME (FK2)	TCKT_ADDRS_FLAG
France	146523	France	Gourmet Chefs, Inc.	B
Portugal	XTF-9146	Spain	Bullfighters Corp.	P
USA	059-11-2874	USA	Pharm Ops, Inc.	B
Canada	591-XV-11	USA	Shipping Co.	B

FIGURE 12.3 BSNSS_PSSGR sample value listing.

be documented by associating them with the foreign key (rather than with the parent's primary key). This requirement reflects the association of insert/delete/update rules with *relationships* (represented in relational tables by foreign keys). The exercises illustrate possible diagramming conventions for these rules.

IMPLEMENTATION TIPS AND TECHNIQUES

SQL product implementations, like the ANSI SQL standard, have been slow to provide DDL support for referential integrity. Moreover, in the absence of a standard, those products that provide referential integrity support define their own syntax for (typically some subset of) possible business rules.

Let us consider one example, the early implementation of referential integrity within MUST Software International's NOMAD DBMS. NOMAD uses the terminology MASTER to refer to a table and ITEM to refer to a column. The following is an excerpt from NOMAD's database definition syntax:

```
MASTER INVOICE KEYED NUMBER...;
    ITEM NUMBER...;
    ITEM CSTMR_KEY MEMBER'CUSTOMER'...;
    ITEM AMOUNT...;
```

The KEYED keyword defines the primary key for the table (actually, the primary index or primary means of access, but for now assume for simplicity that the two are the same). The MEMBER keyword defines CSTMR_KEY as a foreign key referencing the primary key of CUSTOMER. (Since this is actually a composite key, additional parameters, not shown here, are needed to redefine CSTMR_KEY into its component attributes.) The MEMBER parameter requires that, on insert, an ITEM value must be null (NOMAD's NOTAV, meaning "not available") or match a key value in the corresponding parent table; for example, on insert of INVOICE, CSTMR_KEY must be null or match a value of the key of CUSTOMER. Thus, specification of MEMBER has the same effect as the *dependent* child insert rule implied by a FOREIGN KEY definition in the extensions to the ANSI SQL standard. However, MEMBER does not enforce the *restrict* parent delete rule also implied by the proposed ANSI SQL FOREIGN KEY syntax.

A more recent version of NOMAD adds explicit support for other parent delete/update rules, as illustrated by the following:

```
MASTER CUSTOMER KEYED BRNCH_CD_NMBR...;
    ITEM BRNCH_CD_NMBR...;
    ITEM NAME...;
MASTER INVOICE KEYED NUMBER...;
    ITEM NUMBER...;
    ITEM CSTMR_KEY...;
    ITEM AMOUNT...;
RULE CSTMRINV REFERENCES CUSTOMER USING CSTMR_KEY
    UPDATE CASCADE NOWARN
    DELETE CASCADE NOWARN;
```

This example establishes CASCADE parent delete and parent update rules for the relationship from CUSTOMER to INVOICE. Interestingly, NOMAD's implementation requires a name for the rule, which might be viewed as a name for the relationship.

Referential integrity is not an entirely new concept surfacing with relational database systems. Hierarchical as well as CODASYL database systems have always automated some aspects of referential integrity. For example, a hierarchical database mandates parent delete rules of *restrict* or *cascade* (depending on product implementation) and child insert rules of *dependent.* In other words, in a hierarchical database, deletes of all child occurrences occur whenever (or before) a parent is deleted, and inserts of any child for which no parent exists are rejected.

Relational DBMSs, as contrasted with hierarchical, provide greater flexibility in two ways. First, multiple parents can be defined for a given child (i.e., any table may contain multiple foreign keys). Second, additional referential integrity rules (such as *default, nullify,* or even *no effect* or *customized*), if valid, can be supported without database structural changes.

STEP RDD6: DESIGN FOR ADDITIONAL BUSINESS RULES ABOUT ATTRIBUTES

In the logical data model, you defined business rules governing the integrity of attributes. These rules apply to all attributes (not just to primary keys and foreign keys). Specifically, they include rules about domains and triggering operations.

RULE RDD6.1

Enforce *business rules about attributes* (domains and triggering operations) through the relational implementation.

Implementing domain support for each column means enforcing the following:

- ☐ Data type
- ☐ Length
- ☐ Format or mask
- ☐ Allowable value constraints (range, discrete values, and so on)
- ☐ Uniqueness
- ☐ Null support
- ☐ Default value (if applicable)

Enforcing triggering operations means establishing mechanisms to enforce all remaining business rules associated with the logical data model. These rules call for *triggering* integrity-related *actions* as a result of *events* (retrieval, insert, update, or delete operations) under specified *conditions*.

The techniques used to enforce domains and triggering operations vary based on (1) facilities provided by the DBMS product, (2) cost and difficulty associated with use of these facilities to enforce the business rules automatically, and (3) feasibility or desirability of users' enforcing the rules via manual techniques. We discuss options that may be available, in order of preference and with associated advantages and disadvantages.

OPTION 1 FOR ENFORCING DOMAINS AND TRIGGERING OPERATIONS: DBMS DATA DEFINITION LANGUAGE (DDL)

In the case of domains, ideally you would like explicitly to define a domain and to associate it with various attributes. Such syntax is not supported by the ANSI SQL standard. However, you might imagine the following syntax:

```
CREATE DOMAIN EMPLOYEE-NAME CHAR(30)
ASSIGN TO NAME IN EMPLOYEE DOMAIN EMPLOYEE-NAME
```

The first statement defines a domain called EMPLOYEE-NAME as a pool of values of data type CHAR and length equal to 30. The domain EMPLOYEE-NAME is then associated with column NAME in the table EMPLOYEE.

More typically with today's relational DBMS products, such a domain cannot be defined. Rather, individual *domain characteristics* are defined for each column as part of the CREATE TABLE command. For example, using ANSI SQL syntax,

```
CREATE TABLE EMPLOYEE (NAME CHAR(30) NOT NULL,
                       DEPT*NAME CHAR(10) NOT NULL,
                       SALARY DECIMAL (5),
                       UNIQUE (NAME, DEPT*NAME))
```

This syntax defines an EMPLOYEE table with three columns: NAME, DEPT*NAME, and SALARY. Data types and lengths are provided for all three. NAME and DEPT*NAME are nonnull and together form a combination that must be unique. These two properties imply that NAME and DEPT*NAME together probably constitute the primary key for the EMPLOYEE table. Of course, more desirable DDL would include a PRIMARY KEY clause as in the proposed ANSI SQL extension where there can be only one such clause per table.

Other proposed ANSI SQL extensions add support for default values and other domain characteristics. For example,

```
CREATE TABLE EMPLOYEE
     (NAME CHAR(30) NOT NULL,
      DEPT*NAME CHAR(10) NOT NULL
          CHECK DEPT*NAME IN ('RESEARCH  ', 'INFOSYSTEM'),
      SALARY DECIMAL(5) DEFAULT (20000)
          CHECK SALARY BETWEEN 10000 AND 99000,
      UNIQUE (NAME, DEPT*NAME))
```

This syntax defines a default value for SALARY and some allowable value constraints for DEPT*NAME and SALARY.

Advantages of enforcing attribute business rules using DDL wherever feasible include the following:

☐ Option is easy to implement
☐ Implementation mechanism is transparent to users
☐ Integrity checks are difficult or impossible for users or programs to circumvent; that is, circumvention requires altering the data definition, perhaps with an SQL ALTER TABLE command
☐ Option eliminates manual effort by users to enforce such business rules

A particular relational DBMS product is likely to support DDL for only selected domain characteristics. Moreover, very few products provide DDL for general triggering operations, other than domains and perhaps some referential integrity rules. Typically, you are driven to less desirable implementation options.

OPTION 2 FOR ENFORCING DOMAINS (SPECIFICALLY UNIQUENESS): UNIQUE INDEXES

Many products support creation of unique indexes rather than specification of UNIQUE within the CREATE TABLE statement to enforce uniqueness. For instance,

```
CREATE TABLE EMPLOYEE (NAME CHAR(30) NOT NULL,
                       DEPT*NAME CHAR(10) NOT NULL,
                       SALARY DECIMAL (5))
CREATE UNIQUE INDEX EMPID
    ON EMPLOYEE (NAME,DEPT*NAME)
```

In fact, products that support specification of UNIQUE as part of the CREATE TABLE statement may be implementing an index as the enforcement mechanism. Requiring the designer to create an index is slightly less desirable, because the designer must establish procedures ensuring that the index is always present (i.e., has not been dropped) whenever the unique columns are inserted or updated.

Advantages of enforcing uniqueness via a unique index include the following:

☐ Option is relatively easy to implement
☐ Implementation mechanism is transparent to users
☐ Integrity check is difficult for users or programs to circumvent; specifically, circumvention requires dropping the index
☐ Option eliminates manual effort by users to enforce uniqueness

Disadvantages include the following:

☐ Index overhead affects performance of loads, inserts, updates, deletes, reorganizations, and recoveries

☐ Procedures are required to ensure unique indexes are always in place for inserts and updates of indexed columns (e.g., if indexes are dropped for table reorganizations, they must be recreated before commencement of update activity)

Most relational DBMS products support either option 1 (UNIQUE DDL parameter) or option 2 (unique index) to enforce uniqueness. Either option implies an enforcement mechanism that is basically automated by the relational DBMS and therefore is acceptable.

You might ask, what about enforcing nonuniqueness? For example, consider the challenge of enforcing primary key minimality—the property that no subset of the primary key is unique, or that every component attribute must be nonunique. Not specifying UNIQUE (or not defining a unique index) is insufficient by itself to enforce nonuniqueness; that is, not enforcing uniqueness is *not* equivalent to enforcing nonuniqueness. Very few (to our knowledge, *no*) products provide an easy-to-use, automated mechanism for enforcing *non*uniqueness.

On the other hand, consider that values in a relational table capture a point-in-time subset of real-world information. Thus, database values typically do not reflect the universe of values attributes may assume. At a given time, values in a column may all be unique, whereas the attribute represented by the column may not always be unique. Thus, enforcing nonuniqueness, depending on how a table is loaded, inserted, updated, and otherwise maintained over time, may be inappropriate anyway.

OPTION 3 FOR ENFORCING DOMAINS AND TRIGGERING OPERATIONS: STANDARD MAINTENANCE ROUTINES FOR EACH TABLE

For domain characteristics and triggering operations that cannot be implemented through DDL or indexes, you may choose to custom-tailor code in the form of *standard maintenance routines*. There are two kinds of standard maintenance routines: those invoked by Data Manipulation Language (DML) update operations (thereby enforcing domains or triggering operations as users perform updates), and those invoked for read-only tables prior to or after load (thereby enforcing domains or triggering operations independent of user access—in fact, users do not update these data). Both should trigger related actions and reject any transactions that conflict with business rules.

Advantages of either kind of maintenance routine include the following:

☐ Option eliminates (or at least reduces, depending on implementation mechanism) manual effort by users to enforce attribute rules.
☐ Implementation mechanism (depending on the relational DBMS product and its programming facilities) may be nearly transparent to users. Degree of transparency depends on whether the DBMS supports one or both of the following two implementation modes. In the first, maintenance routines can be automatically invoked via user exits from the relational DBMS

whenever a given column is updated. In this way, users and programmers continue to use the product's native DML and load utilities. In the second, maintenance routines can be invoked easily by a user or program via pseudo-commands—macro names or other apparent extensions, from a user perspective, to the existing data manipulation language. In this way, users do not use the product's native language, but instead use commands similar in syntax for specific operations, such as insert, delete, update, or load of a given table. The pseudo-commands actually invoke the operations while enforcing related business rules.

Disadvantages of embedding rule enforcement in standard maintenance routines include the following:

☐ The standard maintenance routines, used in place of or in addition to native update and load operations, may affect performance of table inserts, updates, and loads.

☐ Circumvention of integrity checks (depending on implementation mechanism) probably is feasible and possibly is relatively easy. For example, if a user finds a way to execute the native DML (e.g., an UPDATE command), he may bypass use of a macro or other maintenance routine intended to enforce update integrity.

☐ Programming is required. Amount of effort associated with the programming requirement will depend on (1) whether the routines can be coded entirely in SQL or whether they require a procedural programming language (and how easy or difficult that programming language is), (2) whether the routines can be written to access parameters and rules in the data dictionary or catalog (thereby improving development and maintenance productivity), and (3) how difficult it is to establish security such that these routines provide the only means of updating tables.

You probably will have to resort to this option to enforce at least some domain characteristics and most triggering operations, given the limitations of the DDL supported by today's relational products. For some read-only tables, executing validation routines as part of or prior to the load process may in fact be more efficient than using DDL or unique indexes.

Whether you employ routines that complement update DML or routines that complement load of read-only tables, there is some possibility of circumvention. Consider implementing standard *integrity audit routines* as well. Execute these routines on a periodic basis to detect any data inconsistencies that may have escaped or bypassed your standard table maintenance routines.

Deciding how to integrate all integrity support using standard maintenance routines can involve some highly product-specific considerations. For example, you must determine how many routines to implement, how to relate or override integrity checks implemented by different routines, and how to choose and even mix product-specific implementation alternatives. For now, concentrate primarily on specifying the logic that must be included as part of these routines (i.e., business rules that cannot be enforced directly using DDL or establishing indexes). Some implementation tips for integrating integrity support are provided at the end of this chapter.

OPTION 4 FOR ENFORCING DOMAINS AND TRIGGERING OPERATIONS: MANUAL ENFORCEMENT BY THE USERS

If automated integrity capabilities are weak, or if other reasons prevent you from electing options 1, 2, or 3, you must resort to manual enforcement. Manual enforcement implies that users are responsible for performing insert, update, and delete operations according to business rules. There is no automatic enforcement—the entire burden of ensuring integrity rests with the users. Obvious disadvantages are the following:

☐ Option requires manual effort by the users, and thus creates more work for them
☐ Integrity checks may be easily circumvented
☐ Option may require implementation of inappropriate or complex security schemes

Consider potential security issues raised by manual enforcement. For example, a user may be authorized to delete customers from the approved CUSTOMER table, but not authorized to delete INVOICEs. Yet, if the business rule for the CUSTOMER–INVOICE relationship is a parent delete rule of *cascade*, and if a user is manually enforcing this rule, that user must be permitted to delete rows from both tables. Automated enforcement of the business rule may (depending on the relational DBMS product) eliminate this problem. For example, the user may be authorized to use a maintenance routine that deletes rows and enforces rules triggering related deletes. Yet, the user may not be authorized to issue native DELETE commands.

Manual enforcement of business rules may be appropriate for read-only tables. For such tables, automated integrity checks (e.g., unique indexes or maintenance procedures) may impose unnecessary overhead. In this case, "manual enforcement" may consist of user verification of input data before or after the load.

RULE RDD6.2

Document in the catalog or *data dictionary* business rules about attributes, including techniques used to enforce them.

This documentation aids designers in implementing and maintaining automated enforcement mechanisms. Programs (e.g., standard maintenance and integrity audit routines) may even access these specifications (if in automated form) to enforce rules or detect potential violations. Equally important, good documentation assists users in remembering and, if necessary, manually enforcing the business rules.

For example, assume you properly documented an index, the purpose of which is to enforce uniqueness. If a user's update is rejected due to duplicate primary key values, the user should be able to check the dictionary to review what columns are required to be unique. Moreover, a designer is unlikely to drop the index (e.g., in favor of other better-performing tuning mechanisms) without at least considering the effect on data integrity.

In general, you need not specify domains and triggering operations on your relational database diagram—these rules probably are too detailed. Recall that your logical data model diagram does not depict them. Rather, you may want to design additional forms (or screen layouts, in the case of an automated data dictionary) to document enforcement mechanisms.

RELATIONAL IMPLEMENTATION OF NULL VALUES

Part of enforcing domain characteristics is enforcing nonnull constraints. Because nulls have some properties that are peculiar to relational DBMS products, a few comments are in order regarding their behavior and how to handle them in a relational environment.

Recall that a null value is a special value meaning "information unknown" or "attribute inapplicable." If you followed the logical design methodology in Part 2, you already minimized (although perhaps not entirely eliminated) occurrence of nulls in your logical data model by using default values (rather than nulls) for foreign keys that may reference nonexistent primary keys (Rule LDM5.3), and by defining subtypes when nonkey attributes may not exist for all occurrences of an entity.

A null is not equivalent to a zero or a blank or any other value. Its representation is product-specific, but must be such that the relational DBMS can distinguish nulls from all known (i.e., nonnull) values. Null values can add complexity, unpredictability, and possible inconsistencies to a database implementation. Different relational products represent and manipulate null values in different ways. Some relational products do not support nulls at all.

In products that do support null values, nulls often do not behave as users might expect. Also, results of operations involving nulls may be inconsistent across products. We discuss four examples.

First, nulls may give unexpected results when used in *comparisons*. For instance, in the ANSI SQL standard, all the following expressions evaluate to *condition unknown* rather than to *true* or *false:*

Question	Result		
	Yes	*No*	*Unknown*
Is a null = a null			X
Is a null = a nonnull			X
Is a null <> a null			X
Is a null <> a nonnull			X
Is a null > a null			X
Is a null > a nonnull			X
Is a null < a null			X
Is a null < a nonnull			X

Accordingly, a request involving the clause WHERE NAME <> 'MARGARET' does *not* return rows for which the NAME column contains a null value, since it is not true that a null (e.g., value of NAME column) does not equal a nonnull (such as the constant 'MARGARET'). Moreover, the syntax WHERE NAME = NULL is not even permissible, since the concept of selection criteria involving a null equal to anything (null or nonnull) is not supported.

On the other hand, the ANSI SQL standard does treat nulls as being equal for purposes of ordering, grouping, and elimination of duplicates (SQL ORDER BY, GROUP BY, and DISTINCT syntax).

To add to the confusion, some products that do not conform to the ANSI SQL standard take the more intuitive (but theoretically incorrect and inconsistent) approach of treating a null and a nonnull as unequal. They may treat two nulls as either equal or unequal (neither choice being exactly intuitive or consistent with the definition of *null*—"value unknown"). Obviously, the same queries involving null values in different products can produce different results. For instance, given the selection criteria WHERE NAME <> 'MARGARET', a product that treats nulls as unequal to nonnulls will return rows where NAME is null.

Second, null values may give unexpected results when used in *join* operations. Assume a product evaluates the expression null = null as either unknown (the ANSI standard interpretation—nulls are neither equal nor unequal) or false (nulls are treated as being unequal). Then joins over columns that allow null values will exclude from the result any rows in which the joined columns are null (i.e., null values will not match up to other null values).

Consider an example. Suppose you are generating a list of form letters to send to employees, based on the employee's selection of a profit-sharing plan. Figure 12.4 illustrates the tables involved. You might try the following query:

```
SELECT EMPLOYEE.NAME, LETTER.CODE
    FROM EMPLOYEE, LETTER
    WHERE EMPLOYEE.PLAN-CODE=LETTER.PLAN-CODE
```

The results will exclude employees who have not yet selected any profit plan (i.e., EMPLOYEE.PLAN-CODE is null as for Smith) even if you have defined a form letter for those delinquent employees (i.e., LETTER.PLAN-CODE is null). That is, null values in EMPLOYEE.PLAN-CODE will not match null values in LETTER.PLAN-CODE.

EMPLOYEE

NAME	DEPT	PLAN–CODE
Jones	Research	2
Smith	Systems	null
Green	Accounting	14

LETTER

PLAN–CODE	CODE
2	101
14	1221
3	93
null	0

FIGURE 12.4 Tables for generating employee form letters.

Third, some *aggregate operations* on columns where such columns allow nulls may not work as expected. An aggregate operation on a column summarizes a set of values for that column. Aggregate operations include SUM, COUNT, AVG, MIN, and MAX (for sum, count, average, minimum, and maximum). The ANSI SQL standard disregards nulls when applying aggregate operators to columns that allow nulls. Thus, SUM(SALARY) yields the sum of salaries for employees who have (nonnull) salaries. Similarly, COUNT(SALARY) yields the count of only those employees with (nonnull) salaries.

So far, this behavior seems logical and intuitive. However, the following points illustrate anomalies that may arise:

☐ Summing down a column (e.g., SUM(SALARY)) disregards nulls, yet summing across a row (e.g., SALARY + COMMISSION) always results in a null value if any of the operands is null. Thus, SUM(SALARY) + SUM(COMMISSION) probably is not equal to SUM(SALARY + COMMISSION) if either SALARY or COMMISSION allows null values.

☐ COUNT(*) (where the asterisk specifies that all rows are to be counted; see Chapter 3), oddly enough, *does* include even all-null rows in its count.

☐ AVG(SALARY) equals SUM(SALARY) divided by COUNT(SALARY), but probably does not equal SUM(SALARY) divided by COUNT(EMPLOYEE.NUMBER), or SUM(SALARY) divided by COUNT(*), if SALARY allows null values.

Fourth, to accommodate the special behavior of nulls, *special operators* are required. For example, ANSI SQL syntax includes the operators IS NULL and IS NOT NULL to enable testing of null values (since =NULL and <>NULL are not permissible syntax). Moreover, some products provide special aggregate operators allowing the user to control how nulls are handled (e.g., NOMAD supports COUNT(SALARY), which excludes nulls, and NUMBER(SALARY), which includes nulls).

Avoiding nulls where possible minimizes all these problems and generally increases the simplicity and intuitive behavior of your relational implementation.

RULE RDD6.3

In general, do not permit *null values* for any column.

At minimum, attempt to avoid use of nulls for the following types of columns:

☐ Primary keys, which are frequently used in comparisons and joins. Plus, of course, primary keys should never be null due to their identifying nature. Recall the business rules for primary keys.

☐ Foreign keys that are frequently used in comparisons and joins. Recall Rule LDM5.3, which promotes use of default values in place of null values for foreign keys.

☐ All other columns that may be involved in query selection criteria (SQL WHERE syntax).

☐ Numeric columns, *unless* the product's manner of treating nulls in arithmetic calculations is what users expect and cannot easily be simulated without nulls. For instance, recall that nulls may be automatically excluded from a SUM or AVG operation. Moreover, a sum across two or more columns may be set to null if any operand is itself null.

In summary, any decision to allow null values for a column should be made carefully. It requires understanding of the users' requirements and expectations and of the product's treatment of nulls. Various factors may necessitate different implementations for different database products. A multi-DBMS implementation (for example, spanning both a mainframe and a personal computer environment) may rapidly generate inconsistencies and extreme complexity where nulls are involved. If you can avoid nulls entirely, do so and eliminate confusion.

Most relational DBMS products allow you to prohibit nulls via DDL (i.e., through the CREATE TABLE syntax illustrated earlier). If, however, a value may be unknown, you may prefer to define a default value.

RULE RDD6.4

In the relational implementation, favor use of *default values* over null values.

Default values, unlike nulls, typically yield expected results when used in comparisons or joins (as long as you know what the default value is and consider its effect on an operation). On the other hand, treatment of default values when performing built-in functions may require special consideration.

RULE RDD6.5

Automate assignment of *default values,* if feasible.

Some database products support specification of default values through DDL. Others require the analyst to implement user exits, macros, other types of programs, or manual user procedures—the implementation options already discussed for enforcing domain characteristics.

RULE RDD6.6

When defining *default values for foreign keys,* establish a corresponding primary key occurrence containing a matching value.

Establish a matching primary key occurrence to facilitate joins on primary/foreign key combinations. For instance, consider again the tables for generating employee form letters in Figure 12.4. Suppose you replace null values for EMPLOYEE.PLAN–CODE by the default value 'N/A'. You must also establish a LETTER row in which LETTER.PLAN–CODE equals 'N/A' in order to include employees with no profit-sharing plan (e.g., Smith) in the results of the query:

```
SELECT EMPLOYEE.NAME, LETTER.CODE
    FROM EMPLOYEE, LETTER
    WHERE EMPLOYEE.PLAN–CODE=LETTER.PLAN–CODE
```

RULE RDD6.7

When using default values, establish special mechanisms as needed to ensure correct execution of *aggregate operations.*

Default values can contribute to misleading results from aggregate operators (AVG, SUM, COUNT, and so on) unless the designer explicitly codes procedures to recognize defaults. For example, assume you have established the value −1 as a default (meaning value unknown or inapplicable) for a SALARY column. Then the following SQL query produces a meaningless result:

```
SELECT AVG(SALARY) FROM EMPLOYEE
```

Rows containing the value −1 for SALARY should be excluded from the AVG operation. Either of two tactics will achieve that result. You can apply the AVG operation to a view SAL−EMPLOYEE containing rows only for salaried employees, as in

```
CREATE VIEW SAL-EMPLOYEE AS
    SELECT * FROM EMPLOYEE
    WHERE SALARY <> -1
SELECT AVG(SALARY) FROM SAL-EMPLOYEE
```

Or, you can define a special routine (SQL macro or other type of program) that averages SALARY for rows where SALARY <> 1, such as

```
PROCEDURE AVGSAL
    SELECT AVG(SALARY) FROM EMPLOYEE
    WHERE SALARY <> -1
CALL AVGSAL
```

Either of these options requires that users specify they want average salary for salaried employees only (either by selecting from a special view or by invoking a special procedure). Or, equivalently, either option makes *explicit* an assumption that the users were already making *implicitly*: that indeed the users want to include only salaried employees in the average.

INTEGRATING INTEGRITY SUPPORT

In Steps RDD4 through RDD6, you probably identified a number of integrity rules that your product does not support through DDL or unique indexes. Thus, you may consider enforcing some or all of these rules through custom-tailored user code.

RULE RDD6.8

Enforce business rules about tables and columns through *standard maintenance routines,* always executed in place of or in addition to native DML update commands, when the DBMS table definition cannot enforce these rules automatically.

Support integrity requirements through a minimal set of standard routines, rather than by creating routines for each individual requirement. How many routines is a "minimal" set? We consider three alternatives.

First, you can create *one maintenance routine per table* to handle all inserts, deletes, and updates to that table. The advantages of this approach include that users (or programmers) call *one* routine, no matter what change they are making to a table. A simple naming standard is helpful, such as UPDATE–TABLENAME. Disadvantages include that, in current relational products, insert, delete, and update syntax are all different. Moreover, relational update commands typically apply to specified columns as well as rows (e.g., UPDATE table1 SET column1 = value1 WHERE column2 = value2). Thus, establishing one maintenance routine per table requires a fairly complex parameter scheme. The parameter scheme must indicate desired operation (insert, update, delete), desired rows, and (for update) desired columns. The one-routine approach also is likely to affect efficiency of at least update operations (due to interpretation and substitution of parameters) and probably of inserts and deletes as well.

Second, you can create *one insert and one delete routine per table, plus one update routine per column*. Advantages include that each routine performs one operation (insert, update, or delete) and is therefore simpler. Each routine also requires a more limited parameter set. Since there is less deciphering to do, the routines are likely to be more efficient. Disadvantages include that users (or programmers) must remember the names and call interfaces of many more routines. An appropriate naming standard may minimize this difficulty—for instance, INSERT–TABLENAME, DELETE–TABLENAME, and UPDATE–COLUMNNAME. A second disadvantage is the potential inefficiency of calling multiple update routines when updating more than one column within a table.

Third, you can create *one insert, one delete, and one update routine per table*. Advantages include that, again, each such routine performs only one operation. Thus, the routines are simpler, involve fewer parameters, and may be more efficient. Also, users have fewer routines to remember (three per table). Disadvantages include that the routine for updating the table will be more complex than the column-specific update routine proposed under the second option. One routine handling updates for all columns in a table requires more parameters and more complex logic.

Depending on your DBMS product, you may implement these standard maintenance routines in different ways. For example, you may code macros or programs or user exits. Potentially, the routines may access the catalog or dictionary for required parameters. Regardless of implementation, you also must construct appropriate linkages (e.g., through use of user exits) and security controls to ensure that the maintenance routines are never bypassed in favor of native, standalone DML updates.

RULE RDD6.9

Make each *standard maintenance routine table-specific*. Embed calls to *table-specific subroutines* to avoid proliferation of duplicate code.

Your goal is to modularize routines to avoid redundant code. (Redundant code carries with it associated operational and maintenance inefficiencies.)

For example, consider the school logical data model in Figure 12.5. Assume the parent delete rules for SCHOOL to COURSE, COURSE to OFFERING, and OFFERING to ENROLLMENT are *cascade*. Then the delete routine for SCHOOL should call the delete subroutine for COURSE. The delete subroutine for COURSE calls the delete subroutine for OFFERING, which in turn calls the delete subroutine for ENROLLMENT.

Alternatively, assume a *nullify* or *default* parent delete rule for SCHOOL to COURSE. In this case, the delete routine for SCHOOL must call the update subroutine for the foreign key in COURSE.

Suppose child insert rules are *dependent* for OFFERING to ENROLLMENT and *automatic* for STUDENT to ENROLLMENT. Then the insert routine for ENROLLMENT must verify existence of the appropriate OFFERING and STUDENT, and potentially must call the insert subroutine for STUDENT. In turn, the STUDENT insert subroutine must perform other validation and possibly call other subroutines based on its insert rules.

FIGURE 12.5 School logical data model.

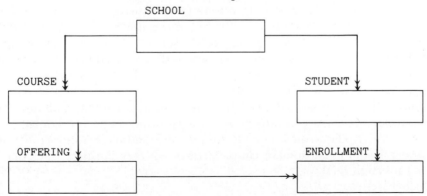

RULE RDD6.10

Establish *standard integrity audit routines* for each table (or set of related tables) to detect business rule violations.

Almost any implementation for enforcing business rules is not perfect, particularly when you code maintenance routines or rely on manual enforcement of rules. Someone may find another way to update the tables, applying incorrect or incomplete updates. To detect such violations, create routines to audit adherence to business rules. Execute these audit routines regularly.

C A S E   S T U D Y

Consider the BSNSS_PSSGR table diagrammed in Figure 12.3, the key business rules summarized in Figure 12.2, and the domain characteristics and triggering operations defined in Chapter 9 (Figures 9.5, 9.6, and 9.11). Using ANSI SQL syntax, you can define the columns in the table as follows:

```
CREATE TABLE BSNSS_PSSGR
      (PSSGR#CNTRY_NAME CHAR(25) NOT NULL,
       PSSGR#CODE CHAR(25) NOT NULL,
       BSNSS#CNTRY_NAME CHAR(25) NOT NULL,
       BSNSS#NAME CHAR(30) NOT NULL,
       TCKT_ADDRS_FLAG CHAR(1) NOT NULL,
       UNIQUE (PSSGR#CNTRY_NAME, PSSGR#CODE))
```

All columns are defined as nonnull, reflecting (1) primary key nonnull property of PSSGR#CNTRY_NAME, PSSGR#CODE, (2) child insert *dependent* and parent delete *cascade* rules governing the foreign key BSNSS#CNTRY_NAME, BSNSS#NAME (thus, the foreign key cannot be null), and (3) nonnull domain characteristic identified for TCKT_ADDRS_FLAG. The composite primary key (PSSGR#CNTRY_NAME, PSSGR_CODE) is defined to be unique.

Assume the proposed ANSI SQL extensions, as described under Steps RDD4 through RDD6, are approved, addressing primary and foreign keys, parent delete and update rules, default values, and allowable value constraints. Then several additional domain characteristics and key business rules may be enforced through DDL:

```
CREATE TABLE BSNSS_PSSGR
      (PSSGR#CNTRY_NAME CHAR(25) NOT NULL,
       PSSGR#CODE CHAR(25) NOT NULL,
       BSNSS#CNTRY_NAME CHAR(25) NOT NULL,
```

```
    BSNSS#NAME CHAR(30) NOT NULL,
    TCKT_ADDRS_FLAG CHAR(1) NOT NULL
        DEFAULT ('B')
        CHECK TCKT_ADDRS_FLAG IN ('B', 'P'),
    PRIMARY KEY (PSSGR#CNTRY_NAME,PSSGR#CODE),
    FOREIGN KEY (PSSGR#CNTRY_NAME, PSSGR#CODE)
        REFERENCES PSSGR
        ON DELETE CASCADE
        ON UPDATE CASCADE,
    FOREIGN KEY (BSNSS#CNTRY_NAME,BSNSS#NAME)
        REFERENCES BSNSS
        ON DELETE CASCADE
        ON UPDATE CASCADE)
```

The CASCADE parent delete rules implement the parent delete rules for the relationships from PASSENGER to BUSINESS–PASSENGER and from BUSINESS to BUSINESS–PASSENGER (Figure 12.2). The CASCADE parent update rule for PASSENGER to BUSINESS–PASSENGER was not explicitly identified by the user; thus, you should verify this assumption with the user. The CASCADE parent update rule for BUSINESS to BUSINESS–PASSENGER implements a triggering operation defined by the user (rule 6 in Figure 9.11). For both relationships, the syntax above implies child insert rules of *dependent*. Thus, the PASSENGER to BUSINESS–PASSENGER child insert rule of *automatic*, identified by the user (Figure 12.2) can be enforced only by ensuring that PASSENGER inserts always occur before BUSINESS–PASSENGER inserts.

What about the other triggering operations in Figure 9.11? Can they be implemented as easily using DDL? Not likely! Consider just one, rule 3 in Figure 9.11, documented as shown in Figure 12.6. DDL support for this fairly complex rule would be extremely difficult to define. Instead, let us define an insert procedure INSRT_RSVTN to be invoked whenever inserting a reservation. SQL code for this procedure follows, assuming the input values for the new reservation are defined in variables designated by the % prefixes. Numbers in the left margin reference the explanatory notes that follow.

```
(1) PROCEDURE INSRT_RSVTN (%FLIGHT#NMBR, %PSSGR#CNTRY_NAME,
                           %PSSGR_CODE, %FLT_SCHDL#DPT_DATE,
                           %CNFRMTN_NMBR, %FARE_AMT, %PYMT_CODE,
                           %ENTRY_DATE, %AGNT_NMBR)
(2) INSERT INTO RSVTN
        VALUES (%FLIGHT#NMBR,....,%AGNT_NMBR)
(3) INSERT INTO TEMPRSVTN(RSVTN_COUNT)
        SELECT COUNT(*) FROM RSVTN, BSNSS_PSSGR B1
        WHERE FLIGHT#NMBR = %FLIGHT#NMBR
        AND FLT_SCHDL#DPT_DATE = %FLT_SCHDL#DPT_DATE
        AND RSVTN.PSSGR#CNTRY_NAME = BSNSS_PSSGR.PSSGR#CNTRY_NAME
        AND RSVTN.PSSGR#CODE = BSNSS_PSSGR.PSSGR#CODE
        AND EXISTS
            (SELECT *
            FROM BSNSS_PSSGR B2
```

User Rule	Event	Entity Name	Attribute Name	Condition	Action
3. Five or more business passengers from the same company (and same country) booked on the same flight receive an additional 10% discount.	INSERT	RESERVATION	—	Increased count of RESERVATIONs for this FLIGHT*NUMBER, DEPARTURE-DATE, BUSINESS*COUNTRY-NAME, and BUSINESS*NAME is equal to 5	Apply additional 10% discount to all RESERVATIONs for this FLIGHT*NUMBER, DEPARTURE-DATE, BUSINESS*COUNTRY-NAME, and BUSINESS*NAME
	INSERT	RESERVATION	—	Increased count of RESERVATIONs for this FLIGHT*NUMBER, DEPARTURE-DATE, BUSINESS*COUNTRY-NAME, and BUSINESS*NAME is equal to 6 or more	Apply additional 10% discount to just this new RESERVATION
	DELETE	RESERVATION	—	Decreased count of RESERVATIONs for this FLIGHT*NUMBER, DEPARTURE-DATE, BUSINESS*COUNTRY-NAME, and BUSINESS*NAME is equal to 4	Increase fares on remaining RESERVATIONs for this FLIGHT*NUMBER, DEPARTURE-DATE, BUSINESS*COUNTRY-NAME, and BUSINESS*NAME by 11%

FIGURE 12.6 Triggering operation 3 from Figure 9.11.

```
              WHERE B2.PSSGR#CNTRY_NAME = %PSSGR#CNTRY_NAME
              AND B2.PSSGR#CODE = %PSSGR#CODE
              AND B2.BSNSS#CNTRY_NAME = B1.BSNSS#CNTRY_NAME
              AND B2.BSNSS#NAME = B1.BSNSS#NAME)
     (4) UPDATE RSVTN
              SET FARE_AMT = .9 * FARE_AMT
              WHERE FLIGHT#NMBR = %FLIGHT#NMBR
              AND FLT_SCHDL#DPT_DATE = %FLT_SCHDL#DPT_DATE
              AND PSSGR#CNTRY_NAME = %PSSGR#CNTRY_NAME
              AND PSSGR#CODE = %PSSGR#CODE
              AND 5 < (SELECT RSVTN_COUNT FROM TEMPRSVTN)
     (5) UPDATE RSVTN
              SET FARE_AMT = .9 * FARE_AMT
              WHERE FLIGHT#NMBR = %FLIGHT#NMBR
              AND FLT_SCHDL#DPT_DATE = %FLT_SCHDL#DPT_DATE
              AND EXISTS
                  (SELECT *
                  FROM BSNSS_PSSGR B1
                  WHERE B1.PSSGR#CNTRY_NAME = RSVTN.PSSGR#CNTRY_NAME
                  AND B1.PSSGR#CODE = RSVTN.PSSGR#CODE
                  AND EXISTS
                      (SELECT *
                      FROM BSNSS PSSGR B2
                      WHERE B2.PSSGR#CNTRY_NAME = %PSSGR#CNTRY_NAME
                      AND B2.PSSGR#CODE = %PSSGR#CODE
                      AND B2.BSNSS#CNTRY_NAME = B1.BSNSS#CNTRY_NAME
                      AND B2.BSNSS#NAME = B1.BSNSS#NAME))
              AND 5 IN (SELECT RSVTN_COUNT FROM TEMPRSVTN)
     (6) DELETE FROM TEMPRSVTN
```

1. Names the procedure and input parameters (all designated by the %
   prefix)
2. Inserts new reservation
3. Inserts into a temporary table TEMPRSVTN (predefined with one column)
   the count RSVTN_COUNT of reservations on this flight for passengers from
   the same business as the new reservation
4. Applies a 10-percent discount to the fare for just the new reservation
   when the count in (3) is greater than 5
5. Applies a 10-percent discount to the fares for all reservations selected in
   (3) when the count is exactly 5
6. Deletes row from TEMPRSVTN (to clean up for next execution of
   INSRT_RSVTN)

The procedure is complicated. In fact, the INSRT_RSVTN procedure should
incorporate all business rules pertaining to placing reservations, which cannot
be enforced by DDL or indexes (unless you choose to rely on the user for manual enforcement). For example, triggering operations 1 and 2 defined in Chapter 9 (Figure 9.11) also impact reservation inserts. Moreover, a delete procedure DLET_RSVTN is required to handle reservation cancellations. Finally,
security must be established such that these procedures are always invoked in
place of a native SQL INSERT INTO RSVTN or DELETE FROM RSVTN.

SQL for the other triggering operations defined in Figure 9.11 is dependent on product-specific implementations of date and time manipulation (or on other proposed extensions to the ANSI SQL standard). Thus, we will not address procedures for enforcing those rules here.

IMPLEMENTATION TIPS AND TECHNIQUES

Building standard maintenance routines to enforce business rules can be complex due to technical considerations. We consider just two such issues, commit logic and triggering logic.

COMMIT LOGIC. Recall from Chapter 3 the SQL COMMIT WORK and ROLLBACK WORK syntax. Implicit or explicit COMMIT/ROLLBACK logic is required to bound a transaction (sequence of SQL statements) such that the effects of all (COMMIT) or none (ROLLBACK) of the statements are reflected in the database. Your standard maintenance routines are examples of transactions requiring COMMIT/ROLLBACK logic. You must code the routines to ensure that all or none of the updates, including triggered updates, take place depending on business rule validation.

Implementing appropriate commit logic may require two routines per table per operation, or a total of six routines. For convenience, we use the following terms for these routines: insert routine, insert subroutine, delete routine, delete subroutine, update routine, and delete subroutine. (This discussion assumes you have decided to code one routine—now one routine and one subroutine—per operation (insert, delete, update) per table. Comparable guidelines apply if you elect a different implementation option, such as coding a separate update routine per column.)

The *subroutine* for each operation performs the operation on a given table and verifies successful return codes. It also calls subroutines for other related tables as appropriate. The *routine* for each operation calls the subroutine to perform the operation (and to trigger related operations) and then issues a COMMIT when the subroutine successfully completes its work.

For example, consider again the school logical data model in Figure 12.5. Assume that the parent delete rules for SCHOOL to COURSE, COURSE to OFFERING, and OFFERING to ENROLLMENT are *cascade*. You can define delete routines and subroutines to implement these rules as follows:

```
PROCEDURE DLET-SCHOOL-RTN (parameters)
     CALL DLET-SCHOOL-SUBRTN (parameters)
     COMMIT WORK

PROCEDURE DLET-SCHOOL-SUBRTN (parameters)
     CALL DLET-COURSE-SUBRTN (parameters)
     DELETE FROM SCHOOL WHERE parameters

PROCEDURE DLET-COURSE-SUBRTN (parameters)
     CALL DLET-OFFERING-SUBRTN (parameters)
     DELETE FROM COURSE WHERE parameters
```

```
PROCEDURE DLET-OFFERING-SUBRTN (parameters)
    CALL DLET-ENROLLMENT-SUBRTN (parameters)
    DELETE FROM OFFERING WHERE parameters

PROCEDURE DLET-ENROLLMENT-SUBRTN (parameters)
    DELETE FROM ENROLLMENT WHERE parameters
```

Note COMMIT WORK is issued only from the delete *routine*, after all called subroutines have completed successfully. Also note that only the subroutines actually issue DELETE commands. Not shown is the logic required for each subroutine to enforce other related business rules. For example, what is the parent delete rule for SCHOOL to STUDENT? That logic also should be implemented via the delete subroutine for SCHOOL (assuming DDL cannot enforce the rule).

TRIGGERING LOGIC. As in the previous example, business rules may *trigger* other operations, implemented by calling other subroutines. The execution logic of a given subroutine may differ depending on what *event* triggered it. Thus, the triggering event (delete of SCHOOL in the example above) must be one of the parameters passed to the subroutines (e.g., to the delete subroutines for SCHOOL, COURSE, OFFERING and ENROLLMENT). We consider two illustrations.

First, delete subroutines for tables involved in 1:1 relationships may loop endlessly unless they understand what event has triggered them. For example, assume a 1:1 relationship between SCHOOL and DEAN:

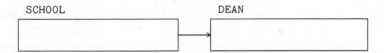

Also assume business rules dictating that, whenever one is deleted, the other related occurrence also is deleted. In other words, both parent delete and child delete rules are *cascade*. Thus, the delete subroutine for SCHOOL calls the delete subroutine for DEAN, and vice versa. An endless loop results. Instead, each subroutine must know what event (delete of which entity) triggered it and must act accordingly (either call the other subroutine or pass control back to the calling subroutine).

Second, business rules may depend to some extent on business circumstances; that is, some rules may *override* others. For instance, in the school logical data model (Figure 12.5), the parent delete rule for STUDENT to ENROLLMENT may be *restrict* when a user is attempting to delete a STUDENT. However, the *restrict* rule may be overridden by a *cascade* rule when the user is purging all rows related to a given SCHOOL. Thus, the delete subroutine for STUDENT must perform different logic depending on whether the triggering event is delete of STUDENT or delete of SCHOOL.

Note that the second example highlights potential complexities in not only implementing but also initially defining triggering operations. Subtle interrelationships may be buried in a group of business rules, involving nontrivial exception and override logic.

SUMMARY

This chapter addressed alternatives for enforcing business rules. First are rules about entities, the primary and alternate key rules. To enforce these rules, you institute mechanisms whereby you guarantee that each primary key is unique, minimal, and nonnull, and each alternate key is unique, minimal, and if appropriate, nonnull. You choose the best implementation option available, depending on the relational DBMS you will be using. Ideally, you specify PRIMARY KEY and ALTERNATE KEY via the DDL syntax. Alternatively (and more typically with today's products), you use DDL to specify NOT NULL, and either DDL or unique indexes to enforce uniqueness.

Next, you translate the insert, delete, and update rules about relationships. With many products, you must resort to custom-tailored routines or manual user procedures to enforce these rules.

Finally, you implement support for domains and triggering operations. DDL syntax probably can enforce at least some domain characteristics. More complex and less commonly encountered rules may require macros, programs, or user procedures.

You record your choices for all these steps in a data dictionary or catalog. Such documentation assists subsequent design reviews and assessment of future modifications. If accurate and complete, this documentation also can guide end users in accessing the data and in enforcing business rules that cannot be implemented effectively using the relational DBMS's automated facilities.

Steps RDD1 through RDD6 completed a translation of all information—both structure and integrity—represented in the logical data model. In fact, you could implement the relational database design at this point, and you would be assured of an accurate, consistent, comprehensive design. The database might not perform as you would like, however. It might not even support all required functionality. Next, you turn to mechanisms for tuning the design to accommodate specific processing and performance objectives.

EXERCISES

12.1 This chapter deals with translating logical data integrity into a relational implementation. List the various types of business rules that constitute logical data integrity.

12.2 List, for each type of business rule defined in Exercise 12.1, the relational implementation options in order of preference.

12.3 The chapter discusses reasons for avoiding null values. How does the logical data modeling methodology avoid null values? How does the relational translation submethodology reinforce avoiding nulls?

12.4 Suggest a modification to the logical data model diagramming technique in Part 2 to document business rules about entities. Show a sample diagram for the RESERVATION table. Refer to Figure 9.12 (p. 248) for the logical data model.

12.5 Suggest a modification to the logical data model diagramming technique in Part 2 to document business rules about relationships.

12.6 Using proposed ANSI SQL extensions, code DDL for creating the RESERVATION table. Refer to Figure 12.2 for foreign key rules, to Figure 9.12 (p. 248) for attributes, and to Figures 9.5, 9.6, and 9.11 (pp. 230, 231, 246–247) for domains and triggering operations.

12.7 Specify the logic required to implement triggering operation 5 (Figure 9.11) in an update procedure for the DISCOUNT–AMOUNT column in the CREDIT–RATING table. This rule states that any increase in discount must ripple through to all existing booked (but unused) reservations.

For extra credit: Show how this logic could be implemented as a set of routines calling subroutines which include appropriate COMMIT logic.

C H A P T E R

13 Tune by Establishing Storage-Related Access Mechanisms

Whether relational products can achieve acceptable performance has been the subject of much debate. Yet, there is nothing in the relational model that limits performance. In fact, recall from Chapter 3 that the relational model is purely an intellectual concept and is independent of performance considerations. That is, there is no correlation between the relational model and good or bad performance. Rather, performance levels are determined by a product's implementation of the relational model and by your choice of implementation options to address your application requirements.

The *relational database tuning process* tunes the preliminary relational data base design by choosing implementation options based on processing and performance requirements. Since this is the first chapter on relational database tuning, let us start by outlining five general procedures for the tuning process.

First, *determine, in conjunction with users, key characteristics of anticipated data requests (predefined and ad hoc)*. Sample key characteristics include:

1. nature of processing

    □   required operations
    □   type of selection criteria
    □   data volumes (rows searched and rows returned)

2. visibility

    □   organizational level of user
    □   relationship to day-to-day operations
    □   relationship to business opportunities

3. processing modes

- □   online (predetermined)
- □   batch (predetermined)
- □   interactive (ad hoc)
- □   peak versus nonpeak time of day

4. performance expectations

- □   execution time (response time for online and interactive requests and turnaround time for batch requests)
- □   throughput (transaction/query frequencies or input records for batch runs over a given period of time)

Second, *identify, with users, the subset of data requests that are critical.* Walk the users through the list of data requests, studying the key characteristics of each. Identify those transactions, queries, and batch runs that are critical based on importance of function, stringency of performance requirements, or visibility of request.

Third, *highlight, among the list of critical transactions, queries, and batch runs, those that may pose functionality or performance challenges.* Your product may lack support for some relational manipulation operations (e.g., union, outer join, outer union). Where such functionality is needed by critical requests, flag these requests as needing further tuning considerations. You also may be able to immediately detect at least some of the requests that may present performance problems. For instance, requests that perform n-way joins (e.g., four or five), other multitable accesses (e.g., unions or subqueries), or sorts of many rows (e.g., perhaps more than 10,000) may deserve analysis.

Fourth, *correlate critical data requests to table access.* There are two ways to do this. The first is a systematic approach. You can superimpose on your relational database diagram specific access patterns implied by each request. Although this method provides visual assistance, you do not know the access paths and options the optimizer will actually choose. A second, less rigorous approach is to list the tables and columns involved in each request (perhaps corresponding to alternative ways of formulating the request). This is the approach taken by the case study in this book.

Fifth, *consider multiple design alternatives.* Most likely, there will be several design alternatives that address your needs. Therefore, do not settle prematurely for one design alternative. Instead, be creative and open-minded in considering tuning tips and techniques. Develop a set of (perhaps two to six) design alternatives. Be prepared to prototype several of them.

Chapters 13 through 16 address a number of tuning options, proceeding from most to least desirable. Tuning options are considered more desirable when they *do not degrade favorable properties achieved by translating a high-quality logical data model* (such as correctness, consistency, and stability, stemming from a data-driven design for both structure and integrity). Also more desirable are tuning options that *are not visible to users* (i.e., users need not be cognizant of the tuning options when formulating data requests).

First, Chapters 13 and 14 address establishing *access mechanisms,* or strategies employed by a DBMS to access data within storage structures. Examples include indexes, hashes, and scans. Access mechanisms are the *most* desirable tuning options because they effect no deviations from the logical data model and they are generally invisible to users.

Chapters 15 and 16 proceed to discuss less desirable, but still effective and frequently necessary, tuning options. Such options may require deviating from the logical data model in ways that are visible to users. For example, such options may involve redefinition of tables and columns.

ROLE OF ACCESS MECHANISMS

A product's implementation of access mechanisms influences performance in a number of ways. Specifically, you must evaluate the particular access mechanisms supported by a product, and the product's ability to apply these mechanisms intelligently for efficient data access. Moreover, you influence performance by your choice of options for table access, specifically through access mechanisms you define for each table, and accompanying technical considerations you implement to improve efficiency of these access mechanisms. Chapters 13 and 14 guide you in both of these areas.

Chapter 13 discusses access approaches that influence or benefit from table storage options. These access approaches include *scanning* (sequentially inspecting many rows to identify and return a qualifying subset), *clustering* (accessing rows stored in a predefined, sorted sequence), and *hashing* (accessing rows using an algorithm that generates a random address from the value of some set of columns). Following the steps in Chapter 13, you decide on a storage structure for each table; that is, you determine whether to store the table as clustered, hashed, or nonclustered/nonhashed. You also choose techniques to maximize efficiency of data access based on the selected storage structure. Your selection of storage and access techniques for each table will, to a large extent, prioritize remaining performance challenges for which you must tune in subsequent chapters.

Chapter 14 discusses a fourth access approach: indexes. An *index* is a storage structure (distinct from the storage structure for a table) that associates each value in a given set of columns with the address of the table row containing that value in those columns. Since indexes are largely independent of table storage options, it is natural to consider adding indexes only after you determine the storage-related access approaches of Chapter 13.

THE PROCESS OF TUNING ACCESS MECHANISMS

Recall that users operate on relational data using data manipulation languages (DMLs), such as SQL. These languages do not allow users to explicitly request particular *access paths* or details of data navigation. DML syntax supports identification of only which data to access—specific tables, columns, and rows—and not of how to access the data. In this way, access paths are deliberately hidden from the user.

Technically, then, the user does not determine the access path. Instead, in most relational products, choice of access path for a particular request is made by the DBMS optimizer. The *optimizer* is an "intelligent" piece of code that analyzes various ways of performing steps necessary to satisfy a request for relational data. The optimizer chooses what it believes to be the optimal method. Usually, it evaluates a set of access alternatives in terms of estimated CPU time and number of I/O operations. The optimizer computes these estimates by studying statistics (usually in the relational DBMS catalog) about the relevant relational tables (e.g., number of rows, sequence of rows, available indexes and hashes).

Although it may seem that choice of access path is beyond your control, it is not. Only the *final* choice of access path is made by the optimizer. The database designer determines which access mechanisms are available to the optimizer in formulating an access path.

The process of establishing appropriate relational database access mechanisms has the following characteristics:

☐ It is simple
☐ It builds on general database knowledge and experience gained using other database technologies
☐ It is product-specific
☐ It is highly process- or application-driven

It is *simple* in concept because it has one focus: how to access data most efficiently (i.e., with acceptable performance, resource utilization costs, and maintenance requirements).

It *builds on experience with other database technologies* because relational access mechanisms are similar to those typically available in other DBMSs. Experience with other database technologies has highlighted benefits and drawbacks of different access mechanisms. The rules in this chapter are founded on such experience.

Establishing access mechanisms is *product-specific* as it involves choosing among access mechanisms available with a particular relational DBMS product. It requires knowledge of your product's optimizer and its use of alternative access mechanisms.

Choice of access approaches is *highly process- or application-driven* in that you must understand specific access requirements and associated performance objectives. If users plan to access data solely via predetermined requests, you probably can analyze, prioritize, and tune for these requests. When data access will be primarily ad hoc, you must make some assumptions about typical access patterns. In either case, performance objectives for different requests may call for conflicting tuning options (for instance, storing the data in different sequences). Thus, you will have to identify, analyze, and resolve performance tradeoffs.

To ensure that the optimizer has efficient access paths from which to choose, you must accomplish three subtasks:

1. *Become knowledgeable of the access mechanisms supported by your DBMS.* Take an inventory of these mechanisms. They should be documented in product reference manuals supplied by the vendor. It may be difficult to gain a true understanding of the access mechanisms, depending on the quality of product documentation. For some products, you can purchase books that describe at length access mechanisms and related storage options. You also can pursue user groups, vendor support staff, and actual product experimentation.

   Even access approaches that seem common across products (e.g., indexes) vary significantly from one DBMS to another and from one product release to another. For example, some implementations (e.g., database machines) rely on a particular hardware architecture or specialized hardware mechanisms. Others are closely integrated with the underlying operating system. Still others build on the features of particular I/O devices or controllers.

2. *Evaluate the circumstances under which your DBMS actually uses its various access mechanisms.* Existence of a hash, index, or other access mechanism does not guarantee that the DBMS will use that mechanism whenever you might expect. Is your relational DBMS "smart" enough, for example, to apply indexes in performing column-to-column comparisons (such as WHERE BONUS-AMOUNT > SALARY-AMOUNT) as well as column-to-constant comparisons (e.g., WHERE SALARY-AMOUNT > 20000)? Can your relational DBMS make use of a given access mechanism to satisfy queries involving BETWEEN or > or < operators (WHERE SALARY-AMOUNT BETWEEN 10000 AND 50000) as well as queries involving an = operator (WHERE SALARY-AMOUNT = 10000)? Documentation answering these questions may be less readily available. You may need to develop benchmarks to help you evaluate your product's behavior. The rules in this and the next chapter highlight behaviors typical of many products and thus may be helpful in the absence of adequate product documentation or experience.

3. *Concentrate on your most critical processing requests.* The optimizer's decision on how to access data in a given table may vary from one request to another; that is, the optimizer studies the DML of each request and then chooses an access path to satisfy it. It may not be practical to analyze alter-

native access mechanisms for every anticipated request. More likely, you will choose a reasonable subset of requests and tune for these. By identifying and analyzing the most critical requests, you can at least ensure availability of access paths to benefit each.

The process of establishing access mechanisms involves choosing not just *one* mechanism, but rather an optimal *set* of mechanisms facilitating several ways to access each table. During your evaluation, consider the following questions:

☐ Which access mechanisms can best benefit multiple requirements? For instance, can multiple requests effectively use the same hashing mechanism? Can a given index be expanded with an additional column to accommodate more queries?

☐ What new access mechanisms are needed? For example, do you need another index? How about storing a table in a particular row sequence?

☐ Which access mechanisms may be too costly, perhaps because they interfere with efficiency of some requests while benefiting others? For example, should you forego clustering because it degrades update processing, even though it enhances performance of retrievals? How important is the performance of updates relative to retrievals?

In general, choosing access mechanisms is a tricky task. A given access approach may appear optimal to you, but may not, in fact, be optimal for your product. Various products may choose different access paths for a given request, even if the same access mechanisms are available. In part, these choices may be due to the different strengths of various DBMSs. For example, a hardware-based database machine should optimize somewhat differently than does a mainframe software-based DBMS, which in turn should make decisions different from those made by a personal computer-based DBMS. Moreover, some products' optimizers are, indeed, "smarter" (more mature) than are others.

Recognize that optimizer theory itself is a relatively young discipline. As the discipline evolves, relational DBMS implementers will have a broader base of theory from which to draw optimizing rules. Thus, you may need to reevaluate your choices of access mechanisms as optimizer theory in general, and your product in particular, evolve.

STEP RDD7: TUNE FOR SCAN EFFICIENCY

One mechanism for accessing relational data is a scan. A *scan* is a sequential inspection of many rows for the purpose of returning to the user only rows that qualify for a given request. This chapter discusses scans first for four reasons: (1) all relational products (to our knowledge) support scans, (2) scans are simple to understand (although not necessarily simple to tune for), (3) most of your tables will be scanned on behalf of some request (whether or not scanning is what you intended), and (4) scans usually are the default access mechanism (i.e., applied in the absence of any other options).

In evaluating scan processing, you must understand when it is inefficient and when it is efficient. Scans are inefficient when many rows are inspected and only a small percentage of the rows satisfy the selection criteria. Scans are efficient when tables are small and are scanned using relatively few I/Os, when a high percentage of rows qualify for the request, or when other mechanisms (such as indexes) are too costly. The number of rows inspected, the number of I/Os incurred, and the types of requests that initiate scans depend on many factors, including the relational DBMS product, the database design, and perhaps the format of the data request. The last factor is unfortunate, since it implies that access paths may be, after all, somewhat visible to and even controlled by the user. For instance, you may find that your product optimizes some DML phrases better than it does others. To illustrate, if a query can be expressed as either a join or a subquery, with many products the join may perform better.

Surprisingly, in some products scan processing can be extremely efficient and, given appropriate circumstances, may outperform other options that intuitively seem superior. Features such as efficient blocking of table rows (reducing the number of I/Os required for a scan) and parallel processing (reducing the elapsed time associated with a scan) can significantly increase speed and reduce cost of scans.

Ask yourself two questions when assessing efficiency of scans: (1) for what tables should you promote scans? (2) what technical options can you employ to improve efficiency of scans?

Question 1: For what tables should you promote scans?

RULE RDD7.1

Encourage *scan processing* for

□   Small tables (e.g., six or fewer physical blocks)
□   Medium and large tables (e.g., more than six physical blocks) when accessed to satisfy requests for which a large percentage of rows (e.g., 20 percent or more) qualify
□   Any tables when accessed to satisfy batch or low-priority data requests, for which other access mechanisms are too costly

Most relational DBMSs scan a small table about as quickly and inexpensively as they access a particular row (in a small or large table) using some other access mechanism. Indexes, for example (as discussed in Chapter 14), typically require I/O to the index in addition to the table, and impose extra work on update operations. In general, if the DBMS can scan the entire table in five or six

I/Os, such a scan may perform similarly to index access for retrievals, and possibly better for updates.

For large tables, scans may still be efficient if a high percentage (e.g., 20 percent) of the rows satisfy the request. At first glance, 20 percent may seem a rather small percentage. However, as the "hit" ratio of qualifying rows increases, performance of other access mechanisms decreases (due to associated overhead). Obviously, the 20 percent is a guideline only. Experimentation with your product and your requests may show that 20 percent is too high or too low.

Regardless of table size, scans can be the best approach (balancing performance and cost considerations) for requests that are of low priority or can be processed overnight (i.e., in batch). The costs of other access mechanisms may not be justified for these types of requests. Of course, you must consider the size of your window for batch processing (your "night" may be only from midnight to 4 A.M.) and the relative amount of resources consumed by a full scan. For instance, you would seldom want to scan 2 million rows to retrieve one row—even if the request can be satisfied overnight!

Question 2: What technical options can you employ to improve efficiency of scans?

You may be able to improve efficiency of scans by limiting number of rows searched, or by speeding up the scan process.

LIMITING NUMBER OF ROWS SEARCHED

As much as possible, you would like to increase the percentage of rows returned per rows searched. To do so, evaluate whether you can limit the scope of a scan to a smaller set of rows, containing, of course, all qualifying, but fewer nonqualifying, rows. Begin by determining what, for your DBMS, are the boundaries that it can impose on a scan. For example, (1) must it scan a full table? (2) can it scan only part of a table? (3) might it scan rows from multiple tables?

RULE RDD7.2

Minimize *scan overhead* by limiting the number of rows searched (e.g., by clustering or partitioning).

FULL TABLE SCANS. Some products always scan *entire tables*. For example, Figure 13.1 illustrates the rows scanned in a full table scan initiated by a VENDOR query.

```
SELECT NAME,LOCATION
FROM VENDOR
WHERE LOCATION = 'New Jersey'
```

VENDOR

	NAME	LOCATION
x	Mr. Chip	New York
x	Bean, Inc.	New York
x	Mrs. Mousse	New Jersey
x	Mr. Mousse	New Jersey
x	Sancho	California
x	Freeze-It	Alaska

x designates rows scanned by DBMS

FIGURE 13.1 Full table scan.

PARTIAL TABLE SCANS. Some products allow for scanning only *part of a table*. This requires an appropriate type of storage structure. Specifically, the product supports either clustered tables, or a storage structure representing only part of a table.

A *clustered table* is a table in which rows are stored—perhaps approximately—in the sequence of values for a specified set of columns. Thus, if DML references a range of qualifying column values, the DBMS may be able to start its scan where the desired values begin and cease its scan once it has passed these values. Figure 13.2 illustrates the (smaller) span of rows searched for a VENDOR query assuming the table is clustered on the LOCATION column.

Figure 13.2 assumes that the DBMS is able to start scanning at the first qualifying row and cease scanning with the first out-of-range row. This assumption implies that a complementary access mechanism (e.g., an index) must enable direct access to the first qualifying row scanned.

An example of a *storage structure representing only part of a table* is the use of *partitions* by DB2. You can instruct DB2 to divide a given table into several partitions (separate storage structures) based on column values. For example, you can divide the VENDOR table into partitions based on values of the LOCATION column—perhaps by assigning locations beginning with A–L to one partition, and locations beginning with M–Z to a second partition. Of course, a user's DML references the VENDOR table, not its partitions. Yet, DB2 actually accesses partitions. When scanning a table that has been partitioned, DB2 may be able to limit a scan to a particular partition—if the request provides information (e.g., via columns in the WHERE clause) that identify what partitions are of interest. Figure 13.3 illustrates the (smaller) span of rows searched to satisfy

```
SELECT NAME, LOCATION
FROM VENDOR
WHERE LOCATION = 'New Jersey'
```

VENDOR

	NAME	LOCATION
	Freeze–It	Alaska
	Sancho	California
x	Mr. Mousse	New Jersey
x	Mrs. Mousse	New Jersey
x	Bean, Inc.	New York
	Mr. Chip	New York

CLUSTERED ON LOCATION COLUMN

x designates rows scanned by DBMS

FIGURE 13.2 Partial table scan due to table clustering.

a VENDOR query assuming the VENDOR table is partitioned on values of the LOCATION column.

If your product does not support DBMS partitioning (automatically managed by the DBMS), you may be tempted to segment your table (split your relational table into several, similarly structured tables). For instance, you might redefine the VENDOR table (Figure 13.1) as two tables: VENDOR–LOCA and VENDOR–LOCM, similar to the partitions in Figure 13.3. This book refers to the

FIGURE 13.3 Partial table scan due to table partitioning.

```
SELECT NAME, LOCATION
FROM VENDOR
WHERE LOCATION = 'New Jersey'
```

VENDOR   (PARTITION 1)

NAME	LOCATION
Sancho	California
Freeze–It	Alaska

LOCATIONS A–L

VENDOR   (PARTITION 2)

	NAME	LOCATION
x	Mr. Chip	New York
x	Bean, Inc.	New York
x	Mrs. Mousse	New Jersey
x	Mr. Mousse	New Jersey

LOCATIONS M–Z

x designates rows scanned by DBMS

process of splitting a table into more than one table as *segmentation* (to distinguish it from DBMS partitioning).

Admittedly, you may be able to limit the scope of scans through segmentation of tables. However, two factors argue against it: (1) requests that referenced the original table must now reference different tables, and (2) in some cases, what was formerly one request (one SQL SELECT against the original table) becomes multiple requests (multiple SQL SELECTs involving different tables) or a more complex request (multiple SELECTs and a UNION). Thus, users must be cognizant of the segmentation and may find querying the tables more complex.

Although there may be circumstances under which you are justified in segmenting a table into several tables, evaluation of the pros and cons is fairly complex. Accordingly, it is better first to consider all available tuning options that do not require deviating from your logical data model—specifically, the access approaches described in this chapter and Chapter 14. Only after exhausting these techniques and finding that you need further performance improvements should you turn to options that are visible to the user and affect query syntax (Chapters 15 and 16).

MULTIPLE TABLE SCANS. Sometimes, a relational DBMS may scan *multiple tables* even if searching for rows in only one particular table. This occurs when the DBMS interleaves rows from multiple tables within the same storage structure.

RULE RDD7.3

In general, do not store *multiple tables* within the same DBMS *storage structure*.

Storing tables in the same storage structure tends to increase the number of rows scanned for every row returned. Figure 13.4 illustrates the increased span of rows searched for a VENDOR query when the VENDOR and SUPPLY tables are stored together in one structure. Since nearly every table will be scanned for some data request, storing tables together in one storage structure usually is inadvisable.

Naturally, exceptions occasionally apply. In particular, *meaningful* interleaving of rows from several tables may enhance performance of joins. A *meaningful interleaving of rows* occurs when rows that are logically related are interleaved. The storage structure in Figure 13.4 shows a VENDOR row followed immediately by SUPPLY rows for that vendor. This interleaving may improve performance of a query joining related VENDOR and SUPPLY rows. Because such performance

```
SELECT NAME, LOCATION
FROM VENDOR
WHERE LOCATION = 'New Jersey'
```

x	Mr. Chip	New York	
x	chocolate	Mr. Chip	2 tons
x	chocolate chip	Mr. Chip	1 ton
x	Bean, Inc.	New York	
x	chocolate	Bean, Inc.	2 tons
x	Mrs. Mousse	New Jersey	
x	chocolate mousse	Mrs. Mousse	1 pound
x	Mr. Mousse	New Jersey	
x	Sancho	California	
x	Freeze-It	Alaska	

STORAGE STRUCTURE CONTAINING VENDOR AND SUPPLY TABLES

x designates rows scanned by DBMS

FIGURE 13.4 Multiple table scan.

gains are so specific to particular queries, however, the advantages of interleaving tables seldom outweigh the disadvantages.

Now, how can you speed up the scan process itself?

TUNING SCANS

RULE RDD7.4

Accelerate scan processing where feasible (product-specific) by

□   Facilitating parallel scan processing
□   Using high-speed storage devices
□   Employing high-speed scanning techniques
□   Specifying appropriate numbers and sizes of data buffers

FACILITATING PARALLEL SCAN PROCESSING. Performance of scans improves when the relational DBMS can somehow subdivide the rows that must be searched and scan these subgroups of rows in parallel. A distinctive example of such parallel processing is provided by the Teradata DBC/1012 relational DBMS. The

DBC/1012 automatically distributes rows of every table across all its disk drives and uses parallel processing to scan a table. Other products may use parallel processing when scanning a partitioned table for which partitions are stored on multiple storage devices.

USING HIGH-SPEED STORAGE DEVICES. As always, faster devices will provide quicker access to data. Relational tables (or parts of tables) that are frequently scanned are good candidates for fast devices. For example, suppose the VENDOR table is partitioned by LOCATION. Further, assume that New York vendors are stored in a partition separate from New Jersey vendors. If New York vendors are accessed more frequently, you may want to store the New York partition on a faster device. In fact, variations in access frequency may be another reason to establish partitions in the first place.

EMPLOYING HIGH-SPEED SCANNING TECHNIQUES. Some relational DBMS products employ different scanning techniques depending on the span of rows to be searched. The DBMS may use a normal-speed scan for most requests and a high-speed scan when it can determine in advance that it will need to scan large sequential blocks of data. An example is DB2 (starting with Release 2), which has both a standard scanning technique (retrieval of one block per I/O request) and a high-performance scanning technique (sequential prefetch, which allows asynchronous retrieval of many physical blocks with one I/O request). If your relational DBMS supports multiple scanning techniques, learn the circumstances under which it chooses the fastest scanning technique.

SPECIFYING APPROPRIATE NUMBERS AND SIZES OF DATA BUFFERS. Frequently, a major bottleneck in DBMS processing (particularly relational DBMS processing) is I/O. Appropriate use of buffers can reduce the number of physical I/Os. A *buffer* is an area allocated by the DBMS for temporary storage of data during, after, or even immediately before processing of queries. For instance, if the DBMS tries to access a row twice and the row is still in a buffer when the second access occurs, a second physical I/O may be avoided. Obviously, scan performance will be better if some (preferably, all) of the rows to be scanned are already available in a buffer.

For some relational DBMS products, you must specify size and number of buffers once for the entire DBMS system. Other products may allow more flexibility; for example, specifying different buffer parameters by table or even by query.

SUMMARY OF SCANNING TECHNIQUES

Scans are the most frequently employed of all relational DBMS access mechanisms. Even when you establish other access mechanisms (discussed later in this chapter and in Chapter 14), the DBMS probably will still resort to scans for many requests. Thus, always evaluate options for increasing efficiency of scans, such as table clustering, table partitioning, parallel processing, faster storage devices, prefetch or other high-performance scanning techniques, and buffer specifications. Concentrate your analysis on the largest tables and on the most critical data requests.

The remainder of Part 3 uses the terminology "table scan" to refer to any type of (full, partial or multiple) table scan (using clustering, special storage devices, parallel processing, or any other useful optimizing technique).

IMPLEMENTATION TIPS AND TECHNIQUES

To gain a better understanding of scan processing for your relational DBMS, consider three questions.

1. *What parameters should be input to scan projections?* Estimate and document CPU time, I/O time, and elapsed time for scanning a given volume of data. These estimates can be obtained in three ways: (1) paper and pencil calculations (if you or someone else understands well the technical internals of your DBMS), (2) an automated tool that simulates processing of specific requests and measures resource utilization and performance profiles, and (3) actual experimentation, monitoring, and measurement (the best, but not always a feasible, alternative—even assuming adequate measurement tools exist). To be most useful, your estimations should indicate (1) numbers of bytes or physical blocks scanned per second, (2) specifications of row width in terms of number, length and data type of columns, (3) storage specifications such as size of physical blocks and amount and distribution of free space, (4) summary of all other concurrent activity assumed or measured (e.g., is a single-user system assumed?), (5) description of resources used (e.g., CPU model, buffers, storage device types), (6) assumptions regarding how to extrapolate estimates to smaller or larger tables (e.g., is the relationship linear, exponential, or other as row width, number of rows, and number of concurrent activities change?), and (7) assumptions regarding how to extrapolate estimates to smaller or larger machines and associated resources.

2. *What tools are available for measuring and tuning scan efficiency?* Identify traces and utilities to measure processing characteristics for specific requests. Many relational products provide an EXPLAIN facility that describes access mechanisms chosen for a request. Does this facility indicate scan versus hash versus index access to each table in a data request? Does it differentiate between a normal versus faster scan (if, indeed, your DBMS has two kinds of scans)? Can you determine how many rows are searched versus how many actually qualify in satisfying the request? Can you determine how many rows of other tables are scanned if your DBMS supports

multiple tables in a storage structure? Does the EXPLAIN facility document actual measurements or projections of access paths? If projections, how accurate are they?

3. *What system resources (e.g., buffers) can affect scan performance?* Analyze how your relational DBMS retrieves data. Where does it place physical blocks retrieved by an I/O operation? Does the DBMS use buffers? Does performance of scans improve with more or larger buffers? Or, does the DBMS's buffer search algorithm degrade when there are too many buffers?

Finally, examine your database design and processing requirements. In light of the answers to the previous questions, for what tables should you tune for or even minimize scanning? Identify critical data requests that may invoke scanning of these tables. Flag these requests and tables for consideration of other access mechanisms.

CASE STUDY

Until now in the case study, you have not examined specific data requests or implications of access patterns, request frequencies, processing modes (online versus batch), or response-time constraints. You may have documented such requirements, however, as they surfaced during your discussions with users. Alternatively, someone else may have documented these requirements as part of systems design and analysis. In either case, you probably referenced such notes when building your logical data model—in search of entities, attributes, relationships, and business rules. But you have not analyzed processing requirements with regard to how to tune your relational database design.

To begin tuning, you must develop a list of processing requirements. Recall that there are four general user communities for Moon Launch Enterprise: passenger reservations agents, baggage tracking and control, space shuttle maintenance control, and gourmet chef (Philippe).

Figure 13.5 is a list of transactions and queries required for the passenger reservations agents. (How fortunate that the documentation is so complete!)

In reality, you would tune for all users. However, for the sake of simplicity, this discussion considers the passenger reservations agents only. (Other users are addressed in the exercises.)

Next, using Figure 13.5, you must identify the most critical requests from the users' perspective and tune the database to best accommodate these. Figure 13.6 depicts the most critical data requests as identified by the passenger reservations agents.

For the sake of simplicity, we tune for three transactions: T13, T14, and T33. Refer to Figure 9.12 to review the logical data model.

FIGURE 13.5 Moon Launch Enterprise, Inc., data requests for passenger reservations agents (PRA).

User	Transaction Reference Number	Process Mode	Frequency of Execution	Description
PRA	T1	online	4/yr	Add credit rating
PRA	T2	online	4/yr	Delete credit rating
PRA	T3	online	4/yr	Update credit rating
PRA	T4	online	5/day	Add business passenger
PRA	T5	online	5/day	Delete business passenger
PRA	T6	online	1/wk	Update business passenger
PRA	T7	online	10/day	Add vacation passenger
PRA	T8	online	10/day	Delete vacation passenger
PRA	T9	online	1/wk	Update vacation passenger
PRA	T10	online	1/day	Add a business
PRA	T11	online	150/yr	Delete a business
PRA	T12	online	1/mo	Update a business
PRA	T13	online	550/day	Provide a price quote for a passenger for a specific flight
PRA	T14	online	340/day	Book a reservation
PRA	T15	online	40/day	Cancel a reservation
PRA	T16	online	100/day	Reserve a special meal
PRA	T17	online	30/day	Cancel a reserved meal
PRA	T18	online	15/day	Update a reserved meal
PRA	T19	online	1/wk	Add a flight schedule
PRA	T20	online	1/wk	Update a flight schedule
PRA	T21	online	1/wk	Delete a flight schedule
PRA	T22	online	1/mo	Add a flight
PRA	T23	online	1/mo	Delete a flight
PRA	T24	online	1/mo	Update a flight
PRA	T25	batch	1/wk	List passengers for a specific business
PRA	T26	batch	1/wk	List all vacation passengers
PRA	T27	online	8/day	List all reservations for a specific flight schedule
PRA	T28	online	8/day	List passenger information for all passengers with confirmed reservations for a specific flight schedule sequenced by PASSENGER*COUNTRY-NAME, PASSENGER*CODE
PRA	T29	online	8/day	List meal information for a passenger

PRA	T30	batch	10/day	List all confirmed reservations for a specific flight schedule
PRA	T31	batch	10/day	List all unconfirmed reservations for a specific flight schedule
PRA	T32	batch	10/day	List all flight schedules for a given departure date
PRA	T33	batch	1/day	List all flight schedules that are full (confirmed and nonconfirmed) (recall: full = 100 seats) sequenced by FLIGHT–SCHEDULE*DEPARTURE–DATE, FLIGHT*NUMBER
PRA	T34	batch	1/day	List all flight schedules that are not full (confirmed and nonconfirmed)

T13: PROVIDE A PRICE QUOTE FOR A PASSENGER FOR A SPECIFIC FLIGHT

1. Verify available reservation.

   a. Read the RESERVATION table to count rows assigned to a given FLIGHT*NUMBER and each of, perhaps, several FLIGHT–SCHEDULE* DEPARTURE–DATEs (looking for counts that are less than 100).

2. Determine whether the passenger is an existing or new customer (to identify discount rate).

   a. Read the PASSENGER table via COUNTRY–NAME, CODE to determine whether the passenger already exists.
   b. Also read the BSNSS–PASSENGER or VCTN–PASSENGER table, depending on whether the passenger is booking a business or vacation reservation, to determine if the appropriate row exists.
   c. Potentially insert a PASSENGER row.
   d. Potentially insert a BSNSS–PASSENGER row. (Note the appropriate BUSINESS row must already exist, based on the key business rules— Chapter 6, Step LDM5.)
   e. Potentially insert a VCTN–PASSENGER row.

FIGURE 13.6 Critical passenger reservations requests.

Transaction	Reason for Criticality
T13, T14, T15, T16, T17, T18	Online and most frequent
T14, T20, T21, T23, T24	Critical to successful day-to-day business operations
T4, T7, T10, T19, T22, T33	Promote business growth

3. Calculate normal fare.

   a. If the reservation is for a business passenger, read the BSNSS–PASSENGER table for a specific PASSENGER*COUNTRY–NAME, PASSENGER*CODE to obtain BUSINESS*COUNTRY–NAME, BUSINESS*NAME. Then read the BUSINESS table to obtain CREDIT–RATING*CODE.

   b. If the reservation is for a vacation passenger, read the VCTN–PASSENGER table for a specific PASSENGER*COUNTRY–NAME, PASSENGER*CODE to obtain CREDIT–RATING*CODE.

   c. Read the CREDIT–RATING table for a specific CODE to obtain DISCOUNT–AMOUNT.

   d. Read the FLIGHT table for a given NUMBER to determine the STANDARD–FARE–AMOUNT.

   e. Apply DISCOUNT–AMOUNT to STANDARD–FARE–AMOUNT to calculate normal fare.

4. Advise passenger that additional discounts may be applicable (i.e., cancellation credit, business volume discount—see transaction T14) and will be calculated when the reservation is actually placed (transaction T14).

TABLE ACCESS ANALYSIS. All tables except FLIGHT–SCHEDULE and RESERVATION are accessed by their primary keys (as is typical in transaction-oriented systems). RESERVATION is accessed by a subset of the primary key, FLIGHT*NUMBER and FLIGHT–SCHEDULE *DEPARTURE–DATE to count reservations already placed for the flight. FLIGHT–SCHEDULE is not accessed at all.

T14: BOOK A RESERVATION

According to the user, this transaction assumes that availability of a reservation has already been verified; that is, transaction T13 has already been executed. Thus,

1. Flight number and scheduled departure date have been verified.
2. Passenger exists (or has been inserted) in PASSENGER table (as well as BSNSS–PASSENGER or VCTN–PASSENGER table).
3. Normal fare for passenger, applying discount based on credit rating, has been calculated.

T14 must now do the following:

4. Check PASSENGER.CANC–CREDIT–COUNT and apply 50-percent discount, if applicable, to fare amount (triggering operation 2, Figure 9.11, p. 246).

   a. Access and perhaps decrement CANC–CREDIT–COUNT in the PASSENGER table for a given COUNTRY–NAME, CODE.

    b.   Perhaps apply a 50-percent discount to the fare amount for the new reservation.

5. If applicable, apply a 10-percent discount to all RESERVATIONs held for this flight by other passengers from the same business (triggering operation 3, Figure 9.11).

    a.   Access the BSNSS–PASSENGER table by this PASSENGER*COUNTRY–NAME, PASSENGER*CODE to determine BUSINESS*COUNTRY–NAME, BUSINESS*NAME.

    b.   Access the BSNSS–PASSENGER table for all PASSENGER*COUNTRY–NAME, PASSENGER*CODE having the same BUSINESS*COUNTRY–NAME, BUSINESS*NAME.

    c.   Access the RESERVATION table by FLIGHT*NUMBER, PASSENGER*COUNTRY–NAME, PASSENGER*CODE, FLIGHT–SCHEDULE*DEPARTURE–DATE for all passengers retrieved in (b) and count qualifying RESERVATION rows.

    d.   If count in (c) is exactly equal to four, apply an additional 10-percent discount to FARE–AMOUNT for reservations retrieved in (c).

6. If applicable, apply a 10-percent discount to this RESERVATION (triggering operation 3, Figure 9.11).

    a.   If count in (5c) is greater than or equal to four, apply additional 10-percent discount to fare amount for new reservation.

7. Insert RESERVATION including calculated fare amount.

8. Check and potentially update flight status (triggering operation 1, Figure 9.11).

    a.   Read the FLIGHT–SCHEDULE table for this FLIGHT*NUMBER, DEPARTURE–DATE to determine whether STATUS–CODE is 'CANCEL'.

    b.   Potentially read the RESERVATION table to count all reservations for this FLIGHT*NUMBER, FLIGHT–SCHEDULE*DEPARTURE–DATE (or review the count already obtained by request T13).

    c.   Potentially update the FLIGHT–SCHEDULE table for this FLIGHT*NUMBER, DEPARTURE–DATE so that STATUS–CODE is 'ACTIVE'.

TABLE ACCESS ANALYSIS. The PASSENGER, BSNSS–PASSENGER, RESERVATION, and FLIGHT–SCHEDULE tables are accessed via their primary keys. In addition, BSNSS–PASSENGER is accessed by a foreign key, BUSINESS*COUNTRY–NAME and BUSINESS*NAME, to count reservations on the same flight for other passengers from the same business.

T33: LIST ALL FLIGHT SCHEDULES THAT ARE FULL

1. Read the RESERVATION table to count all rows for each FLIGHT*NUMBER, FLIGHT–SCHEDULE*DEPARTURE–DATE to determine which flights are full (have count of 100 or more reservations).
2. Return counts greater than or equal to 100, sequenced by FLIGHT–SCHEDULE*DEPARTURE–DATE and FLIGHT*NUMBER.
3. Potentially access the FLIGHT or FLIGHT–SCHEDULE tables by FLIGHT*NUMBER, DEPARTURE–DATE (depending on what other information might be included in the report).

TABLE ACCESS ANALYSIS. This request accesses all rows of one table: RESERVATION. It also potentially accesses FLIGHT or FLIGHT–SCHEDULE tables via their primary keys.

SUMMARY OF REQUIREMENTS ANALYSIS

1. These three requests (T13, T14, and T33) involve the following tables:

   □   CREDIT–RATING (4 rows)
   □   BUSINESS (3000 rows)
   □   PASSENGER (32,000 rows)
   □   BSNSS–PASSENGER (9000 rows)
   □   VCTN–PASSENGER (26,000 rows)
   □   FLIGHT (4 rows)
   □   FLIGHT–SCHEDULE (1500 rows)
   □   RESERVATION (124,000 rows)

2. All tables are accessed by their primary keys, so you need to ensure that such access is efficient.
3. Some tables also are accessed otherwise:

   □   RESERVATION—by FLIGHT*NUMBER, FLIGHT–SCHEDULE*DEPARTURE–DATE to count as many as 100 rows, perhaps for each of several DEPARTURE–DATEs (transaction T13).
   □   BSNSS–PASSENGER—by BUSINESS*COUNTRY–NAME, BUSINESS*NAME to retrieve an average of six rows, since BUSINESS : BSNSS–PASSENGER is 1 : 6 (transaction T14).
   □   RESERVATION—all rows are read to count the number of reservations for each FLIGHT–SCHEDULE*DEPARTURE–DATE, FLIGHT*NUMBER (request T33).
   □   RESERVATION—might be sorted to achieve proper output sequence for request T33.

Depending on your DBMS product and its efficiency of scans, these tables may not be large enough to pose scan performance problems. However, you may want to refer to your space calculations (from Step RDD3) to determine the number of physical blocks for each table. This will allow you to predict more accurately the performance of reading these blocks.

For this chapter, the case study presents design alternatives for IBM's DB2 and Teradata's DBC/1012, since these two products differ greatly in their implementation of the options in this chapter (scans, hashing, and clustering). The discussion assumes product releases that are current as of the time of this writing (DB2 Release 3 and DBC/1012 Release 3).

DB2 SCANS

1. *Parameters for projecting scan efficiency*–In projecting DB2 scan efficiency, your algorithms should consider at least the following variables:

   □   How many blocks are in each table? (DB2 blocks are called pages and are generally 4K bytes in length.) How are rows and free space allocated to pages?
   □   Will sequential prefetch or normal scan techniques be employed?
   □   How many blocks per second are scanned? Consider normal scan and sequential prefetch. Also consider various device types.
   □   Are you scanning full, partial, or multiple tables?
   □   How many pages must be scanned?
   □   What overhead will other DB2 processing impose? (e.g., create thread, commit, terminate thread, perhaps BIND?)

   You can project resource utilization and elapsed time for scans, based on these parameters, using paper-and-pencil calculations. You also can use the same input with an IBM internal tool called AN DB2, with assistance from your IBM representative, to predict performance of scans. Or, you can experiment and use tools available with DB2 to measure the results.

2. *Tools for tuning particular scan requests*—The DB2 EXPLAIN facility will tell you whether a scan is invoked for a given request. To determine whether a request uses normal scans or sequential prefetch, you will need a performance tool (e.g., DB2PM from IBM). The EXPLAIN facility does not specify how many pages are scanned. You may need to calculate this yourself or use a performance tool.

3. *Impact of system resources*—In general, buffers affect efficiency of DB2 scan processing, particularly for large table scans. DB2 sequential prefetch is quite efficient, and is even more so with availability of buffers.

The largest table in this case study is the RESERVATION table—124,000 rows. You may want to estimate its scan time for DB2, extrapolate to other tables, and design accordingly. You probably want to evaluate use of other access mechanisms to minimize full table scans of RESERVATION, for example to improve efficiency of transaction T13. You also might evaluate partitioning of RESERVATION (perhaps partitioning by value ranges for FLIGHT*NUMBER, FLIGHT–SCHEDULE*DEPARTURE–DATE). However, this table is probably too small to merit partitioning.

DBC/1012 SCANS

1. *Parameters for projecting scan efficiency*—The DBC/1012 uses parallel processing to speed up scans. All tables are automatically distributed across all disk storage devices (potentially hundreds of disks) within a DBC/1012 configuration. You influence distribution of rows for each table by choosing an appropriate *hash key*—to be discussed in Step RDD9. You should be able to facilitate uniform distribution of rows for each table across all disks.

   Algorithms for projecting DBC/1012 scan efficiency should consider at least the following variables:

   □ How many disks are in your DBC/1012 system? (Actually, how many database processors, or AMPs, which manage access to the disks?)
   □ For each table, how are rows distributed across disks? (If not equally, what is the largest subset of rows on any one disk?)
   □ How wide are the rows in number of bytes and columns?
   □ How many rows per disk (actually, per AMP) per second are scanned for a given row width, a given storage device type, and a given AMP processor model?
   □ What overhead does other DBC/1012 processing impose? (E.g., temporarily storing and then accessing results from the spool file?)

   You can calculate projected scan time with these parameters. Or, you can make use of internal Teradata facilities for simulating your requirements. Or, you can experiment and monitor resource utilization statistics captured in the DBC/1012 data dictionary (catalog).

2. *Tools for tuning particular scan requests*—The DBC/1012 EXPLAIN facility will project, for a given SQL query, when the DBC/1012 will perform a scan. Alternatively, actual measurements of disk I/Os and processor seconds used are captured in the data dictionary.

3. *Impact of system resources*—The DBC/1012 uses a temporary holding area, known as the spool area, for filtering all results back to users. Sufficient spool space must be available within the overall configuration to handle all concurrent requests.

Scans are very efficient in the DBC/1012 due to this product's special hardware configuration that facilitates parallel processing. However, you will still want to estimate scan time for the 124,000 rows of the RESERVATION table. If needed, you can add processors (AMPs) to your DBC/1012 configuration to improve scan performance.

STEP RDD8: DEFINE CLUSTERING SEQUENCES

Another technique in relational data access is clustering (or storing rows in a predetermined sequence based on values of one or more columns). Clustering is not really an access mechanism (as are scanning, indexing, and hashing). Rather, it is a storage technique that can facilitate access mechanisms.

This chapter discusses clustering as the second technique to evaluate when establishing access mechanisms for the following reasons:

☐ It is a technique common to most relational products, although it is not universal.
☐ It is easy to understand.
☐ It is a technique you will probably choose for most of your tables, assuming your product supports clustering (exceptions may apply if your product supports both clustering and hashing—then you typically will choose between the two for each table).
☐ It facilitates processing requirements that frequently cause performance bottlenecks: scans, sorts, and sequential processing.

Consider three major questions when evaluating usefulness of clustering: (1) which tables should you cluster? (2) on what columns in those tables should you base clustering? and (3) what technical options can you employ to improve performance and decrease costs of clustering?

Question 1: Which tables should you cluster?

RULE RDD8.1

In general, *cluster* medium to large tables (e.g., more than six physical blocks) that are any one of the following:

☐ Frequently sorted into the same sequence
☐ Frequently accessed based on selection criteria involving a range of values for a particular column or set of columns
☐ Frequently processed sequentially using the same sequence

and are

☐ Infrequently inserted or deleted
☐ Infrequently updated, where updates involve change to the columns that determine the clustering.

We shall look at each aspect of Rule RDD8.1.

Clustering reduces or eliminates sorts because rows are stored (and therefore are retrieved) in a presorted sequence. This obviously reduces cost and improves performance of any retrieval requiring rows in the predefined sequence. It also can narrow the span of scan processing, particularly for selection criteria involving a range of values (as discussed under Rule RDD7.2).

A special instance in which clustering greatly reduces the cost of requests by eliminating sorting occurs in sequential processing. *Sequential processing* is access of one row at a time in a given row sequence. Perhaps you need to access one row, perform some logic involving that row, and then access the next row in the sequence. Recall that, to define a desired sequence, the user *must* include an ORDER BY (or equivalent) clause in the data request. (That is, when you are using a relational DBMS, sequence of rows is insignificant. If a user wants the rows in a specific sequence, the user must say so via ORDER BY or equivalent.) If the table is not clustered in the ORDER BY sequence, the DBMS must retrieve all rows in the table, sort them, and temporarily store them in a "holding" area to process them in sequence. (Alternatively, an index may facilitate sequential processing—see Chapter 14.)

A similar requirement involves requests that retrieve the "first (sorted) n" rows of a table, or requests that retrieve only enough (sorted) rows to fill one or a few online screens. Frequently, for instance, a user may request retrieval of all rows in some sequence, but, after perusing the first screen or so of the response, decide to discard the rest. Here again, the user must define a sequence by specifying an ORDER BY clause (or equivalent). If the table is not appropriately clustered, the DBMS must retrieve and sort all the rows to return the first few. (Or, an index may suffice—again, see Chapter 14.)

Since it is rare to have a table for which there are no scanning or sorting requirements, in practice you should consider clustering every table. Major reasons to reject clustering are the overhead imposed on update activity (discussed later), the table size (small tables may not merit the update overhead—also discussed later), or choice of hashing over clustering (discussed as the next step—Define Hash Keys).

Of course, rows in a table can be stored in only one sequence. Therefore, you must choose the clustering order that supports the most critical or most frequent requests. If you guess incorrectly or if access requirements change, you usually can modify the clustering order at a later date. Note, however, that because clustering defines storage sequence of rows, changing the clustering order involves the DBMS's reorganizing all the rows, with consequent effects on table availability.

Sometimes you may have a need for different, conflicting clustering orders to facilitate various access requirements. Here, you might consider creating multiple copies of a table, each stored in a different sequence. Generally this is advisable only when (1) the tables are seldom updated, (2) performance is critical, and (3) policies and procedures are in place to maintain consistency across the copies.

RULE RDD8.2

Do not cluster a table if the *overhead* is detrimental to other critical processing requirements (e.g., insert/update/delete processing).

The disadvantage of clustering is that the relational DBMS usually maintains (to some extent) the clustered order. Maintaining the clustered sequence requires the DBMS to find space near logically adjacent rows when inserting new rows or when updating columns on which clustering is based. Moreover, many products accompany clustering with an index, thereby imposing additional (storage plus update) overhead.

Some products actually move existing rows to accommodate insertion or relocation of a row in the correct clustered sequence. Other products do not move existing rows. Instead, they place the new row in available free space, potentially locating the row out of sequence. Hence, clustering may begin to degenerate. As more rows get out of sequence, performance deteriorates for requests that normally benefit from clustering. Typically, you must execute a table reorganization utility to restore clustered sequence.

For some tables, the overhead of clustering outweighs its advantages. For example, if you cannot predict and accommodate free space requirements, clustering may degenerate rapidly, or the overhead of moving existing rows may be unacceptable. Perhaps, table reorganizations to restore clustering are impractical, either because the table is extremely large or because availability requirements do not allow time for even relatively short table reorganizations. Such circumstances are rare, however; generally, clustering is beneficial.

RULE RDD8.3

Do not cluster *small tables*.

The cost of clustering usually is not justified for small tables that can be scanned and sorted easily with few I/O operations. Obviously, the cost of clustering is minimized if there are no (or very few) updates of clustered columns, inserts, or deletes. Thus, extremely static small tables are a possible exception to this rule.

Question 2: On what columns in the tables should you base clustering?

RULE RDD8.4

Consider *clustering rows on columns* involved in

☐   ORDER BY
☐   GROUP BY
☐   UNION, DISTINCT, and other operations involving sorts
☐   Joins
☐   Selection over a range of values

The first four items of Rule RDD8.4 emphasize the usefulness of clustering for avoiding sorts. The requirement for sort processing is not always intuitive. Obviously, a request including ORDER BY or GROUP BY necessitates a sort if rows are not already clustered. Not so obvious, however, is that UNION and DISTINCT may require that data be sorted to remove duplicate rows.

Clustering may also enhance join performance. One way a relational DBMS may join tables is to first sort the tables on joined columns (sometimes called a *merge join*). If you are using a DBMS that implements a merge join, clustering (presorting) rows may improve join performance. Even if your DBMS does not first sort the tables (e.g., does not use a merge join, or also employs another join technique), clustering can be beneficial. For instance, when matching a primary key row with corresponding foreign key rows, fewer I/Os are needed if rows with the same foreign key values are stored together. Thus, in particular, the primary key of a parent table and the foreign key of a child table are good candidates for clustering. Of course, if the same table is both a parent and a child, and the foreign key is distinct from its primary key, you may have conflicting requirements for clustering that table. Then you must evaluate the relative priorities of requests that benefit from each clustering sequence to choose between the two.

Clustering also is recommended when rows are selected based on a range of column values (e.g., BETWEEN 10000 AND 20000). Retrieval of such rows (whether by table scan or by index access) is much more efficient when the rows are physically stored together. Fewer I/O operations are needed, since one I/O will retrieve many qualifying rows.

RULE RDD8.5

When choosing a clustering sequence, evaluate the effect of clustering on *concurrency*.

Clustering can help to isolate the effect of locking for relational DBMSs that apply update locks to more than one row, yet to less than an entire table (e.g., a lock is obtained on a physical block). For example, suppose employees in the research department receive more pay increases (i.e., incur more update activity) than do employees in any other department. Clustering the EMPLOYEE table by department will cause update locks to affect primarily transactions that access employees in the same department. However, note the tradeoffs implied: If you want to minimize the effect on transactions accessing employees from other departments, clustering by department probably is useful. On the other hand, clustering by department may slow down concurrent updates to the research department (by forcing single-threaded updates). Thus, you must carefully evaluate your goals. Are you more interested in facilitating concurrent access to departments other than the research department? Or, are you more interested in enhancing concurrent access (read and update) to the research department?

RULE RDD8.6

Consider *cross–table clustering* on primary and foreign keys to facilitate joins.

Some products allow you to cluster across tables. This was described earlier as a meaningful interleaving of rows of several tables. For example, you can cluster rows of a child table containing foreign key values near the corresponding rows of a parent table containing matching primary key values. Figure 13.4 illustrates clustering of SUPPLY rows near VENDOR rows based on matching primary and foreign key values. Such clustering can significantly improve join performance by enabling retrieval of (prematched) rows with minimal processing and I/O. It can degrade performance of other types of requests, however, since rows of both tables are scanned in search of rows for one table (see Rule RDD7.3).

When evaluating cross-table clustering, consider the overhead imposed on insert and update operations as well as the effect of such operations on clustered sequence. Inserts and updates may be expensive, since they may involve relocating or "chaining" rows from multiple (clustered) tables. Alternatively, the DBMS may enable initial loading of tables in a cross-table clustering sequence, but may not effectively maintain the clustering when performing subsequent updates or inserts.

Question 3: What technical options can you employ to improve performance and decrease costs of clustering?

RULE RDD8.7

Periodically execute *statistics-gathering utilities* on clustered tables if such utilities maintain clustering statistics used by the optimizer.

Some relational DBMS products require that you execute a utility (e.g., DB2's RUNSTATS) to make clustering information available to the optimizer. For example, until you run such a utility, the optimizer may not even be aware that a given table is clustered, that the clustering sequence has changed, or that clustering has degenerated to the point where it no longer provides performance benefits. If such is the case with your DBMS, execute the utility routinely as well as whenever you establish, reorder, or reorganize a clustered table.

RULE RDD8.8

Minimize cost of clustering through appropriate specification of *free space* and frequent table *reorganizations*.

Specify sufficient and well-placed free space to maximize efficiency of inserts and updates, to isolate (where possible) the effect of update locks, and to promote DBMS maintenance of rows in clustered sequence. Also execute table reorganizations frequently, particularly following high update activity, to rearrange rows in clustered sequence, and to redistribute free space for subsequent updates.

Watch for product restrictions that may prohibit or interfere with clustering. In DB2, for example, if you store more than one table in the same tablespace (type of storage structure), DB2 will not maintain any clustered sequence. In this case, you may effect a clustered sequence by initially loading rows in some presorted order, but subsequent inserts, updates, and deletes will cause the clustering to degenerate. This characteristic of DB2 may be another reason to avoid storing multiple tables in a DB2 tablespace (reinforcing Rule RDD7.3).

IMPLEMENTATION TIPS AND TECHNIQUES

To gain a better understanding of clustering for your DBMS (if it supports clustering), consider the following questions.

1. *What parameters should be input to sort projections?* Estimate and document CPU time, I/O time, and elapsed time for sorting a given volume of data. Indicate (1) numbers and width of rows sorted per second; (2) summary of all other concurrent activity assumed or measured (e.g., is a single-user system assumed?); (3) description of resources used (e.g., CPU model, buffers, storage device types); (4) assumptions regarding how to extrapolate estimates to smaller or larger tables (e.g., is the relationship linear, exponential, or other as row width, number of rows, and number of concurrent activities change?); and (5) assumptions regarding how to extrapolate estimates to smaller or larger machines and associated resources.

2. *What tools are available for measuring and tuning sort characteristics of particular data requests?* Identify facilities for studying sorts. Typically, an EXPLAIN facility indicates when and why a sort is performed (e.g., to satisfy ORDER BY, GROUP BY, UNION, DISTINCT, join, others). Can you determine how many rows (bytes, physical blocks) are sorted per unit of time?

3. *How does your DBMS perform sorts?* Identify, if possible, the sort algorithm used by your DBMS. Is it efficient? Can you replace it with one that is more efficient? Determine, also, what resources are required when performing a sort. Does a sort utilize buffers? Does it rely on a dataset or sort database? Is such space allocated sufficiently?

4. *How can you recognize clustering inefficiencies?* Identify facilities for recording clustering information. How will you know whether and when clustering degrades? When free space is exhausted?

Sort performance varies from product to product depending on sort mechanisms (e.g., hardware versus software) and sort algorithms. Estimate sort time for your largest tables with your DBMS. Also evaluate sort implications for critical requests involving joins, GROUP BY, ORDER BY, DISTINCT, UNIONs, range-selection criteria, or sequential processing. Assess whether clustering can reduce the sort requirements or decrease the scope of scans.

Investigate application design options that may facilitate sequential processing of clustered tables. For example, consider a transaction that reads an input record and searches for a set of matching table rows (perhaps from several tables). Sorting the input records in order of the tables' clustering sequence may increase throughput since access to the tables is sequential and "forward," thus minimizing overhead due to random disk-arm movement.

Similarly, investigate application options to improve efficiency of inserts and updates to clustered tables. For example, is it more efficient to drop the clustering sequence during mass inserts and updates and then to reorganize the table? Or, will presorting rows for insert, update, or delete processing affect efficiency of maintaining clustering?

CASE STUDY

Recall that requests T13, T14, and T33 access the following tables:

- □ CREDIT–RATING (4 rows)
- □ BUSINESS (3000 rows)
- □ PASSENGER (32,000 rows)
- □ BSNSS–PASSENGER (9000 rows)
- □ VCTN–PASSENGER (26,000 rows)
- □ FLIGHT (4 rows)
- □ FLIGHT–SCHEDULE (1500 rows)
- □ RESERVATION (124,000 rows)

Most of these tables are small and probably can be read and sorted in relatively few I/O operations. Thus, primary candidates for clustering are the RESERVATION, PASSENGER, VCTN–PASSENGER, and perhaps BSNSS–PASSENGER tables. Requests T13, T14, and T33 access only individual rows in PASSENGER and VCTN–PASSENGER and thus will not benefit from clustering of those tables.

The BSNSS–PASSENGER table may be too small to cluster. If not, or if it grows, clustering by BUSINESS*COUNTRY–NAME and BUSINESS*NAME might improve efficiency of applying volume business discounts to reservations by reducing the scope of scanning for passengers from the same business (transaction T14).

Clustering options for the RESERVATION table include:

- □ FLIGHT*NUMBER, FLIGHT–SCHEDULE*DEPARTURE–DATE (in either order) to facilitate counting reservations for request T13
- □ FLIGHT–SCHEDULE*DEPARTURE–DATE, FLIGHT*NUMBER (in that order) to facilitate counting reservations and sequencing output for request T33
- □ FLIGHT–SCHEDULE*DEPARTURE–DATE, FLIGHT*NUMBER, PASSENGER* COUNTRY–NAME, PASSENGER*CODE to cluster on the full primary key.

Of course, analysis of other requirements may suggest other clustering sequences for the RESERVATION table. For example, a query that evaluates performance of reservation agents might call for accessing RESERVATIONs by AGENT–NUMBER and might benefit from clustering by AGENT–NUMBER. Moreover, note that the RESERVATION table is frequently updated (i.e., 340 times per day for T14, 40 times per day for T15, with the possibility of multiple reservation row updates per execution). Thus, you may decide against clustering entirely. If you do cluster, appropriate free space specifications and frequent table reorganizations will be important.

Let us consider clustering options for the case study using IBM's DB2 and Teradata's DBC/1012.

DB2 CLUSTERING

1. *Parameters for projecting sort efficiency*—The DB2 sort algorithm is complicated, and sort performance does not vary linearly with the number of bytes sorted. Thus, developing sort projections usually requires simulation using AN DB2 (IBM internal tool) or experimentation.

2. *Tools for tuning particular sort requests*—The DB2 EXPLAIN facility indicates for which requests and for which requirements (uniqueness, join, ORDER BY, GROUP BY) sorts are performed. It does not, however, indicate how many rows or bytes are sorted. Thus, you may need additional analysis tools (e.g., DB2PM from IBM).

3. *Sort algorithms*—There are two DB2 sorts: its internal sort (used for sorts implied by SQL requests) and the sort used by DB2 utilities. The latter can be replaced by other sort routines. The internal sort cannot be replaced.

   Sorts are performed using DB2's temporary database. If you are performing large sorts, be sure to allocate enough space. Also, some system-installation parameters affect sort work areas.

4. *Recognizing clustering inefficiencies*—DB2 supports explicit and implicit clustering. Explicit clustering occurs when you define an index and indicate CLUSTER in its definition. Implicit clustering occurs when you define an index without indicating CLUSTER, but the data are, in fact, clustered in the sequence of the index (e.g., you sorted the input in this sequence).

   The DB2 RUNSTATS utility determines whether a table is, in fact, clustered by any of its indexes (those that are defined as CLUSTER and those that are not). You identify a table's clustering sequence by looking at statistics in the catalog after executing RUNSTATS.

   Clustering can degrade on exhaustion of free space. Check the catalog after running RUNSTATS to determine whether you need to reorganize tablespaces to restore their explicit clustering sequences.

DB2 clustering may be appropriate for the larger tables in the Moon Launch database. In particular, request T33 probably involves sorting the RESERVATION table. T13 may also involve a GROUP BY sort to count RESERVATION rows. If you cluster the RESERVATION table, allocation of sufficient free space will be important to the online SQL updates.

DBC/1012 SORTING

At the time of this writing, the DBC/1012 does not support clustering. However, we shall analyze its sort capabilities.

1. *Parameters for projecting sort efficiency*—Each database processor (each AMP) in the DBC/1012 configuration sorts the subset of rows retrieved from the disks managed by that processor. Merging rows across processors is per-

formed in hardware. Thus, elapsed time for sorting may be related to size of the largest subset of rows to be sorted on any one processor. You can influence this time by choosing a hash key that effects a uniform distribution of rows across processors (discussed in Step RDD9).

2. *Tools for tuning particular sort requests*—The DBC/1012 EXPLAIN facility indicates whether a sort is required for a given SQL query. Moreover, the data dictionary contains statistics pertaining to number of rows stored on each processor's disks for each table, a possible factor in length of sorts performed within a database processor.

3. *Sort algorithms*—DBC/1012 sorts across processors are performed via the YNET, an intelligent bus that facilitates communication among and coordination of all processors within the configuration. Sorted row subsets are presented to the YNET by each processor. The YNET then conceptually polls the processors, accepts the next row in sequence, and thereby merges the subsets. Sorted results are stored in the DBC/1012's spool area (temporary storage area) before being returned to the user.

4. *Recognizing clustering inefficiencies*—Not applicable, since the DBC/1012 does not support clustering.

Generally, the only ways to tune sorts in the DBC/1012 are to ensure uniform distribution of rows across processors by choosing an appropriate hash key and, if necessary, to add processors to increase distribution even further.

STEP RDD9: DEFINE HASH KEYS

Hashed access is another mechanism for retrieving data. *Hashed access* is the DBMS's conversion of a data value in a column or set of columns (known as the *hash key*) via some algorithm to obtain a logical address for a row in a table. A *logical address* is a number (or set of numbers) used by the DBMS to store and subsequently to locate a row of data.

A simple example is a hash algorithm that divides a column value by 100 to yield a whole-number quotient and a remainder. The hash algorithm subsequently divides the remainder by 10 to yield a second whole-number quotient. The DBMS translates the first whole-number quotient to a disk identifier. It translates the second whole-number quotient to a displacement in bytes from the beginning of the table on the disk. (Of course, it must keep track of the beginning address for the table's rows on the disk—probably managed through its space-allocation routines.) Thus, if a CUSTOMER table is hashed on CUSTOMER-NUMBER, a customer number of 525 hashes to a disk identifier of 5 (525 divided by 100) and a displacement of 2 bytes (25 divided by 10) from the beginning of the table (Figure 13.7).

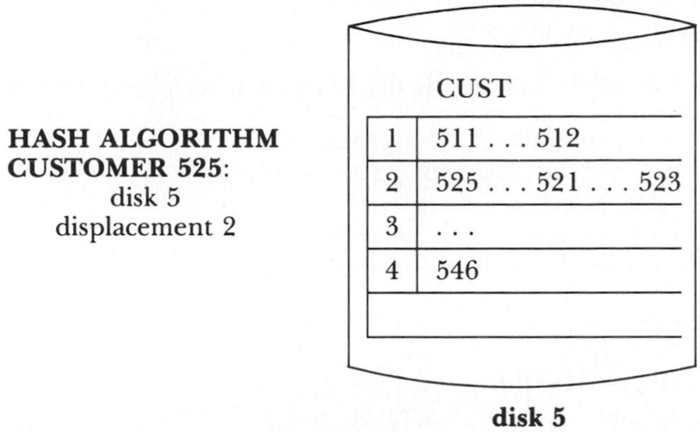

**HASH ALGORITHM
CUSTOMER 525**:
disk 5
displacement 2

	CUST
1	511 . . . 512
2	525 . . . 521 . . . 523
3	. . .
4	546

disk 5

FIGURE 13.7 Hashed access.

This chapter discusses hashed access as the third technique to consider in evaluating access mechanisms for the following reasons:

☐ It is common, although not universal to relational products.
☐ It is a technique you will probably choose for many of your tables, assuming your product supports hashing. (In products that support hashing, some require hashing for all tables. Others support both hashing and clustering; then typically you will choose between the two for each table.)
☐ It can be extremely efficient for random, direct access to individual rows.

Hashed access can be the fastest mechanism for locating a specific row. Locating the row via hashing requires CPU time to perform the hash calculation followed by direct access to the data (perhaps only one I/O operation). Of course, hashing not only facilitates access but also determines placement of rows. Therefore, you can specify only one hashing mechanism (one hash key and one hash algorithm) for a given table. Moreover, you cannot hash and cluster the same table, since clustering also determines (in this case, sequential) placement of rows. (Note that you may be able to hash, for example, a parent table and cross-cluster a child or other related table if your product supports both techniques. Refer to Rule RDD8.6 on cross-table clustering.)

As you did for clustering, evaluate three major questions when considering the usefulness of hashing: (1) which tables should you hash? (2) on what columns should you hash? and (3) what technical options can you employ to increase the usefulness of hashing?

Question 1: Which tables should you hash?

RULE RDD9.1

In general, *hash* medium to large tables (e.g., more than six physical blocks) for which you

- Frequently access individual rows in random order
- Typically specify discrete values of the same column or set of columns (known as the *hash key*) in your selection criteria
- Infrequently update values of the hash key

A DBMS can use hashing only to access individual rows based on selection criteria involving the "equals" operator and a discrete value of the hash key. Any other type of selection criteria requires that the hashed table be scanned (and perhaps sorted) in its entirety or accessed via some other coexistent mechanism (such as an index, discussed in Chapter 14). Specifically, a hash algorithm cannot be used

- To access a table based on a range of values (e.g., WHERE SALARY–AMOUNT < 10000), unless the range is expressed as a list of discrete hash key values (WHERE SALARY–AMOUNT IN (20000, 30000, 40000)).
- To reduce scope of a scan (other than to facilitate a scan of only those rows having the same hash key—when the hash key is nonunique). Since hashed rows are randomly distributed, there is no meaningful way to restrict a scan to only part of the table (involving rows with different hash keys).
- To access rows of a table in a meaningful logical sequence. Any access expecting a logical sequence of rows requires a sort.
- To access rows based on selection criteria that do not involve the hash key.
- To access rows based on selection criteria that involve only part of a (multicolumn) hash key (e.g., WHERE DEPARTMENT–NAME = 'RESEARCH' when the hash key is the combination of DEPARTMENT–NAME and EMPLOYEE–NUMBER).

These restrictions may appear extremely limiting. However, recognize that you can define a *set* of access mechanisms for each table where hashing may be only one such mechanism. For example, frequently you will add one or more indexes to a hashed table to accommodate some of the listed requirements (discussed in Chapter 14).

Recall that a given table must be hashed *or* clustered or neither, but not both. Suppose you have requirements that would benefit from hashing and requirements that would benefit from clustering. Then, you must compare the relative priorities of these requests in light of the costs and benefits of clustering versus hashing. Figure 13.8 summarizes the comparison between clustering and hashing.

Design Factors	Clustering	Hashing
Table size	medium-large	medium-large
Selection criteria	range of values	discrete values
Sequence of rows returned	sorted (ORDER BY, GROUP BY, DISTINCT, UNION, joins)	random
Number of rows returned	can be many	few
Facilitates "partial key" requests	yes	no

FIGURE 13.8 Clustering versus hashing.

Question 2: On what columns should you hash?

Determining which columns to hash may not be easy. There are two (sometimes conflicting) considerations: the effect of hashing on data distribution and the effect of hashing on performance.

RULE RDD9.2

Define hash keys and (if possible) hash algorithms that ensure a useful *distribution of data.*

Since the hash algorithm translates the hash key to a logical address, values of the hash key determine distribution of rows across addresses and potentially across storage devices. In most cases, you would like to achieve a uniform distribution of rows.

Uniform distribution across devices facilitates parallel processing of scans if supported by your product (see Rule RDD7.4). With uniform distribution of rows, each step of the parallel scanning process (each subscan) inspects approximately the same number of rows. Thus, total elapsed time for the scan is minimized. If rows are unequally distributed, total elapsed time of the scan is determined by the time required to scan the largest subset of rows.

RULE RDD9.3

In general, avoid *hash synonyms.*

Hash synonyms are hash key values that hash to the same logical address. For example, using the hash algorithm described earlier, customers 520 to 529 are hash synonyms since they hash to the same location (disk 5, displacement 2). Typically, rows representing hash synonyms are chained through pointers. Long hash synonym chains are undesirable, since the DBMS must navigate the chain to locate a specific row, thereby slowing down the process of locating that row. Imagine, also, the overhead of maintaining such chains as inserts and updates occur.

One obvious way to minimize synonyms is to avoid hashing on columns for which there are a small number of values. For example, hashing on a SEX–CODE column, the possible values of which include only 'M' and 'F', will result in many hash synonyms. Unfortunately, not all potential synonyms are so obvious, particularly if the hash algorithm is complex or if its logic is hidden from you. For example, for a given hash routine, two column values that appear to have nothing in common may hash to the same address. Always experiment with various choices of hash columns to ensure that not too many hash synonyms exist and that a useful data distribution results.

Because they have unique values, primary or alternate keys are typically good candidates for hash keys. You will still want to run tests using your product's hash algorithm on these values, however, since even unique columns can generate hash synonyms.

Some access requirements may actually benefit from hash synonyms. These include requirements that access all hash synonyms together. Consider, for example, a child table that is most frequently accessed in join operations involving a primary–foreign key match. Rows containing the same foreign key value are typically retrieved together. Defining the foreign key as the hash key will establish hash synonyms (assuming the child table is involved in a $1:N$ relationship). Retrieval of an entire chain of hash synonyms may be quite efficient if the DBMS stores synonyms in the same or adjacent physical blocks (dependent on free space specifications, uniform distribution of hash synonyms, and other factors). Thus, in this case, specification of a hash key (the foreign key of the child table) that generates synonyms can be an efficient strategy.

RULE RDD9.4

Consider hashing the column or set of columns most frequently equated to *discrete values* in selection criteria.

A table can only have one hash key, since hashing determines physical location of rows. Choose the hash key that supports the most critical or most frequent requests.

Analyze alternative hash keys carefully. Changing the hash key at a later date may be difficult, since the DBMS would have to relocate rows based on the new hash key. Some DBMSs require that you DROP and again CREATE a table to change a hash key. Other DBMSs do not require DROP and CREATE commands, but rather require a table reorganization.

RULE RDD9.5

In general, do not hash on a set of columns if a *subset* (e.g., one column of a multicolumn hash key) is frequently *referenced alone* in selection criteria. Define a clustering sequence or ordered index instead.

Recall that hashing cannot be used for selection criteria involving only part of a multicolumn hash key. For instance, if the hash key is a combination of ORDER-NUMBER and LINEITEM-NUMBER, ORDER-NUMBER alone cannot be hashed to retrieve one or more rows. Instead consider use of clustering or an *ordered index* (an index the entries of which are stored in sequence of the indexed column values—discussed in Chapter 14).

RULE RDD9.6

Avoid hashes on *frequently updated columns.*

When a hashed column is updated, the DBMS must delete the entire row and relocate that row to a new address (if the hash algorithm results in a new address). Thus, heavy updating of hashed columns is costly in performance and resource utilization.

Question 3: What technical options can you employ to increase the usefulness of hashing?

RULE RDD9.7

Test various *hash algorithms* to optimize data distribution.

It is to your advantage if your product provides a choice of hash algorithms, since one algorithm that is ideal for some data may be undesirable for other data. Some products even allow you to define your own hash algorithm (be sure you are fully cognizant of data distribution and performance implications if you develop or select your own algorithm). If you can choose among algorithms, compare the data distribution provided by each for tables to be hashed. Whether you can choose among several or are restricted to one algorithm, be sure you also experiment with various hash columns to achieve optimal distribution of rows.

RULE RDD9.8

Reevaluate *domain characteristics* (e.g., data type and length) of columns that are hash keys.

Some products restrict the length or data type of a hash key, truncate a hash key to a specified length, or convert the length or data type of a hash key to specifications accepted by the hash algorithm. These considerations can negatively affect data distribution or speed of hashed access. You may be able to accommodate such restrictions by altering the domain of your chosen hash key. For instance, rather than defining EMPLOYEE–NUMBER as CHAR(5), you might define it as INTEGER, which can be stored in fewer bytes (physical units of storage) and may be more palatable to a given hash algorithm. Alternatively, you may have to choose a different set of columns as your hash key.

IMPLEMENTATION TIPS AND TECHNIQUES

To gain a better understanding of hashing in your relational DBMS, consider the following questions.

1. *What parameters should be input to hash performance projections?* Estimate and document CPU time, I/O time, and elapsed time for hashing to a particular row of data, assuming no synonyms. You will need to know the access speed of storage devices and the overhead imposed by executing the hash algorithm. Also estimate and document the effects of hash synonyms. What is the overhead imposed on access (retrieval, update, insert and delete) by a chain of synonyms? How does the overhead vary with the number of synonyms in a chain? How does the overhead vary with amount and distribution of free space allocated to accommodate synonym chains? Can you specify free space? If so, what guidelines should apply?

2. *How does your DBMS perform hashed access?* Can you choose or develop your own hash algorithm tailored to your data values? If not, how well does the supplied routine address various types of hash keys? Are there restrictions on data type or length? Are there guidelines that help to predict number and distribution of synonyms generated for a particular hash key? Is hashing optional or mandatory for each table?
3. *What tools are available for measuring and analyzing hashed data distribution?* Identify facilities that describe or graph distribution of rows after an initial table load, table reorganization, table recovery, and insert, delete, and update activity. Do these facilities also identify hash synonyms?
4. *What tools are available for analyzing particular data requests that involve hashing?* Identify a way of verifying that a given request is invoking hashed access. Again, typically, an EXPLAIN facility provides some information.

Among your critical requests, identify those that specify discrete values in WHERE clauses to access individual rows in random sequence. These are the data requests that benefit most from hashed access.

C A S E   S T U D Y

If hashing is optional, you must determine which tables are candidates for hashing.

In general, candidate tables for hashing include those tables that are not clustered and that require more than a few I/Os to scan (e.g., are more than six physical blocks). Thus, you need to review your space calculations. Looking again at T13, T14, and T33 and making an arbitrary judgment that a physical block holds a maximum of 100 rows (you would, of course, refer to space calculations and product-specific parameters), the following tables consist of more than six physical blocks:

☐ BUSINESS
☐ PASSENGER
☐ BSNSS–PASSENGER
☐ VCTN–PASSENGER
☐ FLIGHT–SCHEDULE
☐ RESERVATION

At the time of this writing, DB2 does not support hashing in user tables. We shall discuss only DBC/1012 hashing.

DBC/1012 HASHING

1. *Parameters for projecting hash efficiency*—Hashed access to rows with no or few hash synonyms in the DBC/1012 is very efficient. Moreover, the more powerful the processor in a DBC/1012 configuration (e.g., 80386- or

80286-based processors versus 8086-based processors), the faster execution of the hash algorithm becomes.

Naturally, efficiency of retrievals and updates of individual rows decreases as the number of hash synonyms increases. Moreover, you have no control over the DBC/1012's allocation and management of free space to accommodate hash synonyms.

2. *Hash algorithm*—At the time of this writing, the DBC/1012 hashes all tables by the user-defined hash key, specified by the PRIMARY INDEX clause on the CREATE TABLE statement. (Note: Therefore, the PRIMARY INDEX clause does not define an index, as implied by the syntax. Since it specifies a hash key, it facilitates access only for selection criteria equating the entire hash key to one or more discrete values.) The hash algorithm determines on what AMP (database processor) a given row will be placed as well as where within that AMP's subset of table rows this particular row will reside.

    You cannot define your own hash algorithm on the DBC/1012, but rather must use the system-supplied algorithm. The hashing is more efficient when PRIMARY INDEX is specified on as few columns as possible and is specified as UNIQUE. Specification of UNIQUE on the PRIMARY INDEX clause alerts the system to expect at most one row to qualify for selection criteria involving a value for all of the PRIMARY INDEX columns. Thus, the system will not build an unnecessarily large spool file, as it might for a nonunique PRIMARY INDEX.

    Since the hash algorithm determines on what AMP a row is placed, specification of matching PRIMARY INDEX columns (e.g., primary–foreign key combinations) for two or more tables ensures that matching rows hash to the same AMP. You can use this property to your advantage by considering specification of matching PRIMARY INDEX columns for tables that will be joined frequently. Then, the joins can occur within each AMP, involving minimal cross-AMP communication and coordination. Note the trade-off, however: A PRIMARY INDEX on foreign key columns probably is nonunique. Generating hash synonyms may in this case improve efficiency of join requests, but may significantly impede efficiency of other requests requiring access to individual rows (and therefore requiring navigation of a chain of hash synonyms).

3. *Measuring hashed data distribution*—The DBC/1012 data dictionary maintains information describing the amount of storage occupied by each table on each AMP. You can access this information through an SQL request to obtain some idea of the uniformity of data distribution across AMPs. More specific data on hashing (for instance, actual distribution of rows by hash key and length of synonym chains) is not available without vendor help.

4. *Tools for tuning particular requests involving hashing*—The DBC/1012 EXPLAIN facility identifies when rows are accessed via the PRIMARY INDEX (i.e., via hashing).

The DBC/1012 requires a hash key for every table. If you do not explicitly identify a hash key (PRIMARY INDEX), the DBC/1012 will use the first column defined in the CREATE TABLE statement. Since the hash key determines data distribution and is the most efficient means of single-row access, you are well-advised to choose it yourself. Start by considering the primary key of each table, since the primary key is unique and typically will ensure uniform data distribution. Also evaluate your access requirements, however. If users never access a given table by way of the primary key, the primary key is probably a poor choice of hash key.

In the case study, all tables are accessed by the primary key. Thus, primary keys generally are good candidates for hash keys.

RESERVATION also is accessed by FLIGHT*NUMBER, FLIGHT–SCHEDULE* DEPARTURE–DATE to count reservations. Hashing on this combination, however, would result in synonym chains up to 100 rows long (for a full flight). Moreover, since the number of reservations per flight may vary widely, hashing on FLIGHT*NUMBER, FLIGHT–SCHEDULE*DEPARTURE–DATE may yield a nonuniform distribution of rows. Thus, hashing on the primary key probably is a better choice.

BSNSS–PASSENGER is accessed both by primary key and by BUSINESS* COUNTRY–NAME, BUSINESS*NAME. Hashing on the latter combination will yield synonym chains of six or more rows (since BUSINESS:BSNSS–PASSENGER is 1:6). Thus, for now we shall choose the primary key as a UNIQUE PRIMARY INDEX and investigate use of other options (e.g., an index—Step RDD10) for speeding access via BUSINESS*COUNTRY–NAME, BUSINESS*NAME.

Of course, other requests may suggest choice of different columns for hashing. In all cases, experiment to verify uniform distribution of rows and benchmark performance of critical requests before making a final decision.

SUMMARY

In this chapter, you evaluated three storage-related access options: scans, clustering, and hashes. You examined techniques for enhancing efficiency of each. We shall summarize when each is most appropriate.

Scans are applicable to all tables, independent of how the table is stored (e.g., clustered, hashed, or neither). Scans are particularly effective for small tables (whether retrieving a few or all rows), for larger tables when retrieving more than some percentage (e.g., 20 percent) of the rows, and for any tables when accessed by batch or low-priority data requests. Although scans can be (and probably will be) used for any type of storage structure, some storage options can significantly influence their efficiency, such as clustering, partitioning, using fast storage devices, and specifying appropriate buffers. Moreover, some relational DBMSs use techniques such as parallel processing and prefetch to make scanning efficient.

Clustering affects how tables are stored, thereby influencing efficiency of access. Clustering implies storing rows in a predefined sequence based on values of one or more columns. Clustering is particularly effective for larger tables from which rows are frequently accessed via the same sequence. Specifically, clustering avoids sorting, facilitates access based on selection criteria involving ranges, and enables efficient sequential processing. Clustering influences performance of not only scans but also possibly indexes (discussed in Chapter 14).

Hashes also affect the way tables are stored and the way they might be accessed. Thus, hashing must be chosen as an alternative to (rather than the complement of) clustering. Hashing is the conversion of values of a particular set of columns (the *hash key*) to logical addresses. Hashed access may be more efficient than other types of access because it typically entails the least I/O. However, hashed access is applicable for the narrowest range of circumstances: direct, random access to individual rows based on discrete values of the hash key. Hashed tables also can be scanned or indexed to accommodate other types of access requirements.

In Chapter 14, you evaluate addition of *indexes* to tables that also may be clustered or hashed (or neither). Indexes generally are used in concert with scanning and clustering or hashing to provide a choice of access mechanisms for each table. Remember that, for any given query, the optimizer actually chooses the access mechanisms to employ in constructing an efficient access path. Your goal is to make available an optimal set of such mechanisms so that the optimizer can perform this task effectively.

EXERCISES

13.1 Some people believe that relational processing will perform poorly because it has a tendency to invoke scans of relational tables. Comment on the performance of such scans, with emphasis on how a DBMS can have fast-performing scans, and on how a designer can influence performance of scans.

13.2 Although you provide an "optimal" access path for a specific request, under what circumstances may such a path not be selected by the optimizer?

13.3 Suppose T28 (see Figure 13.5) becomes a very high-priority requirement. The passenger information that the user wishes to see includes all columns in the PASSENGER table. Discuss some access mechanisms (scanning, clustering, hashing) that you would propose if T28 were the only or most critical request. That is, design specifically to facilitate T28.

13.4 Repeat Exercise 13.3, but this time assume that T28 is less critical than are T13, T14, and T33. In other words, reconsider your design options from Exercise 13.3 and examine how they relate to or conflict with those for T13, T14, and T33. Determine whether T28 can share tuning techniques developed for the others, whether you need to add options to accommodate T28, or whether you must sacrifice some tuning techniques that benefit T28 because they conflict with performance of T13, T14, or T33.

13.5 The user community forgot a batch requirement: T35—List all RESERVATIONs for a given reservation agent, sequenced by FLIGHT–SCHEDULE* DEPARTURE–DATE, FLIGHT*NUMBER. Assume that there are three reservation agents, each of whom places an equal number of reservations. Discuss access mechanism alternatives (scanning, clustering, hashing) to facilitate this requirement.

13.6 The user community develops a need for a new high-priority online request: T36—List all RESERVATIONs (confirmed and nonconfirmed) for a given PASSENGER, sequenced by FLIGHT–SCHEDULE*DEPARTURE–DATE, FLIGHT* NUMBER. Include PASSENGER*COUNTRY–NAME, PASSENGER*CODE, PASSENGER* LAST–NAME, PASSENGER*FIRST–NAME. Discuss access mechanisms you would propose if this were the only or the most critical request.

13.7 Repeat Exercise 13.6, but this time assume that T36 is less critical than are T13, T14, and T33. Therefore, any tuning decisions for T36 must have a minimal effect on T13, T14, and T33.

C H A P T E R

14 Tune by Adding Indexes

This chapter considers addition of indexes to your relational tables to facilitate specific performance requirements.

Indexes are separate storage structures that associate each value of one or a set of columns for a given table with a logical address for the corresponding row of the table. Figure 14.1 illustrates (a perhaps simplified version of) an index on the LOCATION column of the VENDOR table.

Figure 14.1 depicts an ordered index. In an *ordered index,* the index entries themselves are sequenced based on the values of the indexed columns. In this case, the index entries are in alphabetical sequence by state. In fact, an index may have quite a different structure. Its entries may be hashed; that is, the DBMS may hash a value of the indexed columns to access the index and from there obtain addresses of corresponding table rows. Or, the index may have a more complex tree-like structure. We consider index structures and their influence on access efficiency later in the chapter.

To our knowledge, virtually all relational products support indexed access. Some products support only one index per table; some require (at least) one index per table; but most products allow multiple indexes per table as optional access mechanisms.

Indexes typically are the most dynamic access mechanisms in that you usually can add, drop, and redefine indexes more easily than you can change a clustering sequence, redefine a hash key, or alter other parameters that affect how rows are stored. For this reason, choice of indexes may more easily be postponed to later in the design process or even after initial database implementation.

Index on VENDOR.LOCATION	
LOCATION	ROW
Alaska	6
California	5
New Jersey	3
New Jersey	4
New York	1
New York	2

VENDOR **Table**	
NAME	LOCATION
Mr. Chip	New York
Bean, Inc.	New York
Mrs. Mousse	New Jersey
Mr. Mousse	New Jersey
Sancho	California
Freeze-It	Alaska

FIGURE 14.1 Index example.

STEP RDD10: ADD INDEXES

A relational DBMS can use an index for various reasons: to avoid a table scan completely, to limit the scope of a table scan, to avoid a sort, or to avoid table access altogether.

Index access avoids a table scan when the index is used to obtain addresses for specific rows (rather than scanning the table for such rows). For example, consider the query:

```
SELECT NAME, LOCATION
FROM VENDOR
WHERE LOCATION = 'New Jersey'
```

In Figure 14.1, the relational DBMS can obtain addresses of qualifying rows 3 and 4 from the index. The DBMS can then issue I/O operations to retrieve these specific rows, thereby avoiding a scan of table rows.

Of course, I/O is required to access the index in addition to the I/O required to access corresponding rows in the table. When the sum of index I/Os plus table I/Os is less than the number of I/Os required to read the entire table (or scope of the scan—which may be more or less than an entire table), an index probably is a useful access mechanism.

An index can limit the scope of a scan if the table rows are clustered in the sequence of the indexed columns. This book refers to such an index as a *clustering index* (or *clustered index*). Given a range of qualifying values, the relational DBMS can access a clustered index to find the address of the first qualifying row, access the table at that point, and scan from there.

Some products distinguish between a clustering index and a clustered index as follows. A *clustering* index is an index that is defined using keyword CLUSTER; that is, the designer specifically wants the table rows to be stored in the sequence of such an index. Normally, only one index can be defined as a clustering index. In reality, table rows may not be stored in this sequence. This may occur if the DBMS ignores the CLUSTER clause when performing a table load and the designer does not sort the rows appropriately prior to the load. Or, it may occur if the clustering index is defined after initial load of the table and the DBMS does not automatically resequence table rows until an explicit reorganization. A *clustered* index, on the other hand, is an index the entries of which actually do correspond approximately to the sequence of table rows—regardless of whether the index is defined as CLUSTER. A statistics-gathering utility usually will identify clustered indexes. Typically a designer is interested in a clustering index (defined as CLUSTER) that is also a clustered index (table rows are actually stored in index sequence). You can have a clustering index that is not clustered or you can have a clustered index that is not clustering. This book, for simplicity, uses the terms *clustering index* and *clustered index* synonymously.

Figure 14.2 illustrates a clustered index on the LOCATION column of the VENDOR table. The table rows are stored in sequence by LOCATION, the indexed column. (In Figure 14.2, the index entries also are sequenced by LOCATION; i.e., the index also is an ordered index, the most typical structure for a clustering index. However, the index entries could be stored in some other order; e.g., they might be hashed.) To satisfy a data request for vendors in locations beginning with 'N', the DBMS can access the index, determine that the first qualifying vendor is in table row 3, begin scanning the table at row 3, and cease scanning with the first out-of-range row—in this case, at the end of the table.

Less obvious, perhaps, is the use of an index to avoid a sort. Suppose a user wishes to retrieve information about VENDORs, sequenced by LOCATION, as in

```
SELECT NAME, LOCATION
FROM VENDOR
ORDER BY LOCATION
```

FIGURE 14.2 Clustered index to limit scope of scans.

```
SELECT NAME, LOCATION
FROM VENDOR
WHERE LOCATION LIKE 'N%'
```

Clustered Index

LOCATION	ROW
Alaska	1
California	2
New Jersey	3
New Jersey	4
New York	5
New York	6

VENDOR Table

	NAME	LOCATION
	Freeze–It	Alaska
	Sancho	California
x	Mrs. Mousse	New Jersey
x	Mr. Mousse	New Jersey
x	Bean, Inc.	New York
x	Mr. Chip	New York

x designates table rows accessed by DBMS

Moreover, assume the index is ordered (i.e., the index entries are sequenced by LOCATION) but the table is not clustered by the index (thus, the table rows are not sequenced by LOCATION —refer to Figure 14.1). A relational DBMS can present the rows to the user in LOCATION sequence by employing one of two (or perhaps more) methods. The first is to scan the VENDOR rows and sort them. The second is to access VENDOR rows using the index on the LOCATION column. In Figure 14.1, by using the index, the DBMS can access the VENDOR rows in the following order: row 6, row 5, row 3, row 4, row 1, and row 2. Note that the rows of the table are retrieved in LOCATION sequence; no sort is required.

In the worst case, this second access strategy requires one I/O per VENDOR row plus I/O to read the index. The worst case assumes that there are no VENDOR table rows or index entries already in the buffer and that no two VENDOR table rows in LOCATION sequence are stored in the same physical block. Or, even if they are in the same physical block, the block is no longer in the buffer when it is needed again. The performance of such access versus scanning and sorting the VENDOR table depends on data volumes, sort algorithms, cost of reading the index, and so on. Yet, you can see that, when the entire table qualifies for the data request (as in this example), scanning and sorting the table may be more efficient than access via an index.

Suppose the query includes an additional qualifier that reduces the percentage of rows qualifying for the request. For instance,

```
SELECT NAME, LOCATION
FROM VENDOR
WHERE LOCATION LIKE 'N%'
ORDER BY LOCATION
```

Accessing the qualifying rows via an index may be more efficient than scanning all rows and sorting rows returned. In general, as the ratio of qualifying rows to rows that would be scanned decreases, access via an index becomes increasingly favorable. Frequently, testing is required to determine whether establishing an index is worthwhile. Of course, once you have established an index, the optimizer will decide (using the statistics available to it) for which requests it will actually use the index.

In some cases, indexes can be used to avoid table access altogether; that is, a relational DBMS may satisfy a request directly from the column values contained in the index without retrieving any corresponding table rows. Even when the entire index must be scanned (e.g., to satisfy a request qualified on the trailing columns of a multicolumn index), this access strategy usually is more efficient than scanning the table itself. Since the index is generally smaller (represents fewer columns) than the table, fewer I/Os are required.

With these objectives in mind, consider the following questions in evaluating where to establish indexes: (1) on which tables should you build indexes? (2) on what columns should you build indexes? and (3) what technical options can you employ to increase usefulness of indexes?

Question 1: On which tables should you build indexes?

RULE RDD10.1

In general, build *indexes* on medium to large tables (e.g., more than six physical blocks) to do either of the following:

☐ Facilitate access of a small percentage (e.g., less than 20 percent) of rows in a table
☐ Avoid table access altogether for requests involving a small subset of columns

assuming that the additional overhead imposed on updates is acceptable.

The guidelines in Rule RDD10.1 reinforce the fact that, if you are accessing a large portion of the table, a table scan probably is more efficient. (Refer to Rule RDD7.1, which addresses when to promote table scans.) You may need to reevaluate your choice of indexes as table size (number of rows or columns) increases or decreases.

RULE RDD10.2

Build *clustering indexes* to facilitate clustering of table rows (for products that require an index to accompany clustering).

Some products require that an index (called a clustering index) accompany a clustered table. The index facilitates direct access to individual rows in the table, and sequential scanning of the table can commence from there.

RULE RDD10.3

Build *ordered indexes* and specify ascending or descending (if supported by the product) to facilitate sequential or sorted access to a small percentage (e.g., less than 20 percent) of the rows.

Many products support only ordered indexes (i.e., index entries are always stored in order of the indexed columns). Other products do not support ordered indexes at all (e.g., all indexes may be hashed). If your product supports optional specification of ascending or descending ordered indexes, use it to avoid sorting a subset (e.g., less than 20 percent of the rows) of a table. Thus, use the specification to expedite queries involving range criteria, ORDER BY, GROUP BY, UNION, DISTINCT, or joins. All these criteria typically entail sorts, as discussed under the topic of clustering (see Rule RDD8.4).

Ordered indexes serve many of the same purposes addressed by table clustering. When choosing between clustering and a nonclustering, ordered index, recall that you can explicitly define only one clustering sequence per table. Thus, study your most critical access requests to choose the optimal clustering sequence. Also recall that usefulness of access via an index degrades as the number of rows that qualify for a request increases. Scanning a clustered table typically is more effective for requests that require many rows in sequence. You may find that you need to execute some sample DML, determine the number of rows returned, and then test clustered table scans versus use of nonclustering indexes.

RULE RDD10.4

If you store *multiple tables* in the same DBMS *storage structure*, establish indexes on each table to minimize inappropriate multitable scanning.

In Chapter 13, we pointed out that some products support interleaving rows of multiple tables in a single storage structure. In general, this technique is not recommended because it frequently leads to scanning multiple tables when searching for qualifying rows from one table (see Rule RDD7.3). Occasionally, however, you may have reasons to store multiple tables together (for example, for cross-table clustering on primary–foreign key combinations—see Rule RDD8.6). If you choose a multitable storage structure, consider building one or more indexes on each table in the storage structure to avoid undesirable multitable scans.

Although indexes can provide significant and varied performance advantages, these benefits are not without cost. As with all tuning mechanisms, you must weigh the improved performance for some requests against the costs, which may include degraded performance for other requests.

RULE RDD10.5

Avoid building indexes for which the *overhead* severely degrades critical processing requirements or for which the *cost* (related to index storage and maintenance) is excessive relative to the benefits. Consider

- ☐ Storage requirements
- ☐ Influence on inserts, updates, deletes
- ☐ Implications for load times
- ☐ Table reorganization performance
- ☐ Recovery times
- ☐ Backup performance
- ☐ Statistics gathering

If you remember only one fact about indexes, remember that they primarily improve performance of retrievals. In fact, they typically slow down most other processing: inserts, deletes, updates to indexed columns, and utilities.

Table inserts, deletes, and updates involving the indexed columns require maintenance to the index as well as the table. If you have strict performance requirements for insert, update, or delete processing, you may have to compromise on performance objectives for retrievals by eliminating one or more indexes.

Indexes also increase execution time for utilities such as loads (initial, mass update, or periodic refresh), reorganizations, recoveries, backups, and DBMS capture of table statistics. If you have tight windows for executing these utilities, you may need to reduce the number of indexes or temporarily drop and then rebuild indexes.

The costs of index maintenance are lower, and thus probably are acceptable, under the following circumstances: (1) the table is updated rarely, (2) the table is reorganized rarely (a consequence of low update activity), (3) the table and indexes are backed up rarely (because the table is seldom updated or because it can be reloaded from another source, if necessary), and (4) the table statistics can be established once and updated rarely (due to low update activity). Even under these conditions, however, at least two costs remain: the additional time required to build (load) the index initially, and the storage required by the index. Indexes on large tables may require substantial storage and long load times. Moreover, many small indexes may together add up to considerable storage requirements and considerable load times.

RULE RDD10.6

Do not create (nonunique) indexes on *small tables*.

In general, if the DBMS can access a table directly (e.g., by scanning the table) using fewer I/O operations than are required by indexed access to the table, the index is probably useless. It follows that small tables generally should not have indexes. For example, suppose the DBMS can scan an entire table with one I/O operation. Use of an index to retrieve a specific row will require at least two I/O operations (one for the index and one for the table—assuming neither is already in a buffer). Thus, a table scan is a better approach. Of course, the definition of "small" table is product-specific. Typically, a table that fits in five to six physical blocks does not merit indexes.

Do not, however, eliminate indexes created to enforce uniqueness (as discussed in Chapter 12—option 2 for Rule RDD6.1). Such indexes are needed to ensure data integrity regardless of their negligible contributions to performance.

Question 2: On what columns should you build indexes?

RULE RDD10.7

Consider *building indexes on columns* frequently involved in

☐   Selection or join criteria (SQL WHERE clause)
☐   ORDER BY
☐   GROUP BY
☐   UNION, DISTINCT, and other operations involving sorts

Obviously, these are the columns for which indexes may reduce scans or sorts. Remember, however, that if more than a small percentage (e.g., 20 percent) of the rows are being returned, then an index is not justified, since table scans are typically more efficient.

In evaluating use of indexes (or any other access mechanisms—e.g., clustering) to avoid sorting, consider how your DBMS generally satisfies queries entailing sorts. For instance, recall some of the following questions from Chapter 13 (when you considered clustering to avoid sorts):

☐   Under what circumstances does your DBMS perform a sort? (E.g., ORDER BY, GROUP BY, UNION, DISTINCT, join, others?)
☐   How does your product perform sorts? (E.g., using what software algorithm? Or, perhaps, what special-purpose hardware?)
☐   Can you influence the efficiency of sorts? (E.g., by substituting a more efficient sort algorithm?)
☐   What is the estimated elapsed time for sorting n rows of m length?

□ How does sort time increase with increase in number of rows? With increase in length of rows?

□ When in the selection process does the DBMS perform the sort? Before or after applying what types of selection criteria?

RDD10.8

der building indexes on *foreign key* columns.

Rule RDD10.8 is a special case of Rule RDD10.7. It highlights the importance of indexes on foreign key columns. Foreign key columns are most frequently involved in join or subquery processing. Thus, DML will typically contain WHERE clauses referencing such columns. Clustering indexes may be especially appropriate to facilitate joins (as described in Chapter 13—see Rule RDD8.4).

RULE RDD10.9

Consider building an index to encourage *index-only access* when

□ A reasonable subset of columns is required to satisfy certain requests
□ The optimizer is "smart" enough to invoke index-only access
□ Index-only access is more efficient than table access

Depending on the DBMS, index-only access can be used to retrieve data from indexed columns, to determine existence of given values in indexed columns, to aggregate (SUM, COUNT, MIN, MAX, AVG) indexed columns, and to perform calculations on indexed columns (COLUMN A + COLUMN B).

Sample requests that may (depending on the product) be satisfied through index-only access include SELECT DEPT, SUM(SALARY) FROM EMPLOYEE (may use an index built on two columns: DEPT and SALARY), SELECT NAME, SALARY + COMMISSION FROM EMPLOYEE (may use an index built on three columns: NAME, SALARY, and COMMISSION), and SELECT NUMBER, DEPT FROM EMPLOYEE WHERE DEPT BETWEEN 10 AND 20 (may use an index built on two columns: DEPT and NUMBER).

RULE RDD10.10

Consider building indexes on columns used in *built-in functions*, together with the SQL GROUP BY) columns used to aggregate the built-in functions.

Rule RDD10.10 is a special case of Rule RDD10.9. Consider the follow SQL query:

```
SELECT DEPT, AVG(SALARY) FROM EMPLOYEE
WHERE DEPT IN ('RESEARCH', 'ACCOUNTING')
GROUP BY DEPT
```

Building an index over the DEPT column would expedite accessing the rows fo research and accounting. Even better, however, may be an index on DEPT and SALARY. Perhaps the DBMS can use the index to select salaries for research and accounting and calculate the average salary by department without ever accessing the EMPLOYEE table.

RULE RDD10.11

Choose sequence of columns in a *composite* (multicolumn) *ordered index* to facilitate processing of as many types of requests as possible.

Typically, a DBMS can efficiently make use of a composite ordered index to satisfy selection criteria involving any prefix of the index (i.e., any subset consisting of leading columns). For example, given an index based on PRODUCT–GRP–CODE, PRODUCT–CODE, and COLOR–CODE (in that order), the DBMS can effectively use the index to satisfy selection criteria involving any of the following combinations:

```
PRODUCT–GRP–CODE
PRODUCT–GRP–CODE plus PRODUCT–CODE
PRODUCT–GRP–CODE plus PRODUCT–CODE plus COLOR–CODE
```

The DBMS also may be able to use the index to satisfy selection criteria involving some other subset of indexed columns; however, it must scan the index. For example, a request containing only COLOR–CODE in its WHERE clause may still use the index. In this case, the DBMS may scan the entire index in search of entries that point to table rows with the appropriate COLOR–CODE. Scanning the index rather than scanning the table may be more efficient, depending on relative size of the index versus the table and percentage of total rows qualifying for the request.

RULE RDD10.12

Evaluate ways in which the DBMS optimizer uses indexes when you choose between a *composite index* and *multiple single-column indexes*.

DBMS optimizers vary significantly in their ability to make use of composite and multiple indexes to satisfy a given request. Consider, for example, the following SQL entry:

```
SELECT NAME, ADDRESS, SALARY
      FROM EMPLOYEE
      WHERE DEPT = 'RESEARCH'
      AND SALARY > 50000
```

Options for building indexes include the following:

1. One (ordered or nonordered) index on DEPT
2. One (ordered or nonordered) index on SALARY
3. One (ordered or nonordered) index on DEPT and another index on SALARY
4. Composite ordered index on DEPT, SALARY
5. Composite ordered index on SALARY, DEPT
6. Composite (ordered or nonordered) index on DEPT, SALARY, NAME, ADDRESS

Any of these options probably will expedite access to some extent. But which is the best choice? Consider three factors. First, under option 3, can the DBMS access both indexes and join qualifying index entries to obtain table rows that meet both selection criteria? Or, will the DBMS attempt to use only one index? If so, which one? Is it making the correct choice (i.e., generating the most efficient access path)? If not, should you eliminate one of the two indexes to ensure it uses the best one? Will this elimination hurt performance of other requests that benefit from the index you are eliminating?

Second, under options 4 and 5, how many index entries must the DBMS scan to obtain qualifying addresses? For example, under option 4, how many index entries represent a DEPT value of 'RESEARCH'? Under option 5, how many index entries represent SALARY value exceeding 50000? Which index will be more efficient for satisfying this request? Suppose you build both indexes (because you have requests that can benefit from each). Will the DBMS choose the best index for a given request?

Third, under option 6, can the DBMS avoid table access altogether? What sequence of indexed columns is best, assuming you can define an ordered index? Suppose you sequence the indexed columns as follows: NAME, ADDRESS, DEPT, SALARY (perhaps to facilitate other requests qualified on NAME). Will the DBMS use this index at all (i.e., scan the index) to satisfy this query? Should the DBMS use the index for this query, or is a table scan more efficient?

You probably are beginning to appreciate that tuning by adding indexes is not as easy as perhaps initially it seemed!

RULE RDD10.13

Avoid indexes on *frequently updated columns*.

Remember that indexes impose additional maintenance overhead on inserts, deletes, and updates of the indexed columns. Thus, weigh overhead versus performance before building an index on a particularly volatile set of columns.

It is a good idea to benchmark insert, update, delete, and utility processing before and after adding an index to a table. Sometimes, an index can add hours to such processing times (depending on many factors, of course).

This is a good place to summarize what you know about effectiveness of clustering versus hashing versus nonclustered indexes. Figure 14.3 compares these three techniques.

Question 3: What technical options can you employ to increase usefulness of indexes?

RULE RDD10.14

Avoid indexes on columns with such an *irregular distribution of values* that the optimizer frequently misjudges index usefulness.

The DBMS optimizer estimates the percentage of total table rows that will be accessed using an index. This estimate assists the optimizer in determining whether to use the index or scan the table. Frequently, optimizers assume a uni-

Design Factors	Table Clustering	Table Hashing	Nonclustered Index
Table size	medium–large	medium–large	medium–large
Selection criteria	range of values	discrete values	range, discrete values, built-in functions
Sequence of rows returned	sorted (ORDER BY, GROUP BY, DISTINCT, UNION, joins)	random	sorted (if ordered index)
Number of columns returned	can be many	can be many	can be many; few for index-only access
Number of rows returned	can be many	few	few, but more than hashing
Facilitates "partial key" requests	yes	no	yes (particularly if ordered index)

FIGURE 14.3 Clustering versus hashing versus nonclustered indexes.

form distribution of data values in indexed columns. If the distribution is markedly nonuniform, the optimizer may make incorrect decisions about whether an index is efficient for satisfying particular requests.

For example, assume that the EMPLOYEE table contains 100,000 rows and the DEPT index represents 1000 distinct departments. The DBMS optimizer may conclude that, for any given department, there are approximately 100 rows (i.e., 100,000/1000). Thus, the index looks like a useful access mechanism for retrieving employee rows for a particular department (since only 100 out of 100,000 rows should be returned). If, however, 95,000 employees are assigned to the research department, accessing research employees via the index may be significantly slower than a table scan. In the worst case, indexed access could require 95,000 table I/Os plus some index I/Os.

In summary, if you know that some values for a set of columns do not fit the distribution expected by the optimizer, and these values will be specified in selection criteria, do not create an index on the columns.

RULE RDD10.15

In general, create *one to four indexes* per table, or perhaps more if the tables are rarely updated.

The number of useful indexes will vary for each table based on many factors: the DBMS product, its ability to use indexes, the relative performance of nonindexed versus indexed access, the nature of your most critical processing requests, and your specific performance requirements.

In general, more than four indexes per table are costly in terms of overhead imposed on inserts, deletes, updates, and utilities. You usually can tolerate more indexes on read-only tables, since typically storage is the only significant cost deterrent. Of course, you must analyze performance versus cost tradeoffs based on your specific requirements; we have seen as many as eight indexes on tables updated rather frequently.

RULE RDD10.16

In planning for the process of creating indexes, consider

☐   *Availability* implications for the table being accessed and perhaps for other tables or the DBMS catalog
☐   *Efficiency* implications of building the index during or after table load

A valuable characteristic of most relational DBMS products is that indexes can be added both during and after table loads. This flexibility implies that you can postpone investigation of index requirements until after data are loaded and perhaps even after queries and programs are written. Your indexes can evolve as access requirements change or become better understood.

Although you do have more flexibility with relational than with other database technologies, you would be naive to believe that no planning is needed. The magnitude of required up-front analysis depends on your particular product and user requirements. For example, consider the following (product-specific) circumstances that may occur while an index is being built:

☐   The table may be totally unavailable for other concurrent access
☐   The table may be only partially unavailable for other access (e.g., perhaps the DBMS locks each physical block in the table while building the index for rows in that block)
☐   Parts of the DBMS catalog may be unavailable for other concurrent access
☐   Building the index may take longer or require more storage space depending on whether it occurs during or after initial table load

Further, for very large tables, elapsed time for building an index can be significant, thereby magnifying these considerations.

Evaluate the importance of these questions for your DBMS and your user requirements. The answers will help to determine how much time you need to spend analyzing index requirements up front, versus in later tuning.

RULE RDD10.17

Where feasible, store indexes and indexed tables on *different storage devices.*

Typically at least two I/O operations are required to access first an index and then the indexed table. Storing the index and the table on separate storage devices minimizes delays due to device-arm movement. You also can consider placing indexes on devices that attach via cache control units to expedite index access.

RULE RDD10.18

Specify *index locking* and *index free space* options to minimize the effects of the index on concurrent processing and on updates.

Frequently, a relational DBMS locks a storage unit that is greater than one index entry and less than the entire index. For example, a product may lock an index by locking part or all of a physical block (e.g., DB2's index subpage). Since an index entry typically contains fewer bytes than does the corresponding table row (e.g., the index represents fewer columns), more index entries fit into the same physical space. Locking of the same physical unit for an index as for a table can have the effect of locking out access to many more rows (i.e., to many more index entries and consequently to many more table rows). Therefore, for frequently updated tables and indexes, choose small index locking units if supported by your DBMS. Larger locking units may be acceptable for tables and indexes that are rarely updated.

Amount and distribution of index free space significantly contribute to efficiency of updates. Moreover, a larger percentage of free space reduces the number of index entries in the same locking unit.

RULE RDD10.19

Update the *catalog statistics* by executing a utility (if supported by the DBMS) immediately after adding an index.

Normally, when you add an index to a table, the index is automatically documented in the catalog and the DBMS is immediately aware that the index exists. However, you may need to schedule a statistics-gathering utility explicitly to update the catalog with index-related information, such as number of physical blocks, amount of free space, clustering or ordering characteristics, and distribution of indexed column values.

RULE RDD10.20

Evaluate *dynamic drop and recreation of indexes* to accommodate specific processing and performance requirements.

Dropping indexes prior to an intensive period of inserts, updates, deletes, or utility processing eliminates index maintenance for those operations. Subsequently, the indexes can be rebuilt. This technique can be effective when such processing is isolated to specific time periods (e.g., quarterly, monthly, annually). It assumes a reasonably short time is required to drop and recreate the indexes. Dropping and recreating indexes for very large tables, however, may require a lot of processing time (perhaps measured in days).

In general, do not drop indexes required to maintain data integrity (e.g., indexes needed to enforce uniqueness). If the performance advantages of temporarily dropping such an index during utility processing are great, at least establish some other mechanism (e.g., disallow updates of unique columns and inserts of rows) to ensure integrity while the index does not exist.

Sometimes, an index imposes an exorbitant amount of overhead on day-to-day operations, but improves performance significantly for one less frequent processing requirement. Evaluate dynamically building the index just prior to the one processing request and dropping the index afterwards. Naturally, the time required to create and drop the index must be practical and the effect on data availability must be acceptable.

RULE RDD10.21

Establish *index names* (if supported by the DBMS) and *dictionary documentation* to convey meaning and purpose of the indexes.

Some products require that you name indexes. If possible, establish a naming standard that includes reference to columns indexed and implementation options, such as uniqueness, ordering, and clustering. Also describe reasons for and expected use of indexes in the catalog or data dictionary. Indicate the index's role with regard to (1) integrity—for instance, if the index enforces uniqueness, (2) performance—for instance, if the index facilitates join requirements, and (3) storage structures—for instance, if the index is needed to support clustering or table partitioning.

RULE RDD10.22

For DBMS products that support multiple types of *storage structures for indexes,* choose the most efficient structure based on user access requirements. Regardless of structure, also tune for efficiency of *index scans* as you did for table scans (Rules RDD7.2, RDD7.3, and RDD7.4).

As mentioned, the indexes in Figures 14.1 and 14.2 may be somewhat simplified. An index is not necessarily a linear collection of indexed columns followed by row addresses. Most likely, an index has a more complex physical structure—one that more efficiently accommodates fast access.

One common physical structure for an ordered index is a *B-tree* (binary search tree) structure. A B-tree index typically consists of several levels of indexes, where each level points to entries in a lower level. The bottommost level looks much like the simplified (linear) index diagrams; that is, it logically consists of the indexed columns followed by addresses of corresponding table rows. Access via this level alone may be rather slow if the relational DBMS has to scan the index from beginning to end. To facilitate faster access, a B-tree index enables the DBMS to read the topmost level and selectively to "jump" into lower index levels.

Consider the B-tree index in Figure 14.4. Here, the top-level index contains the highest key value of each block in the second level. The second level does the same for the third level. To access employee number 549, the relational DBMS scans only the top index block (block a), one block from the second level (block c), and finally one block from the third level (block j). Obviously, this technique requires fewer I/Os (perhaps three) than would be required to read all blocks in the bottom level (perhaps nine). Even if the relational DBMS ceases its scan of the bottom level when it finds employee 549, six I/Os may be required. Although the example appears trivial (savings of only three to six I/Os), you can see that, as the number of entries in the index (size of the bottommost

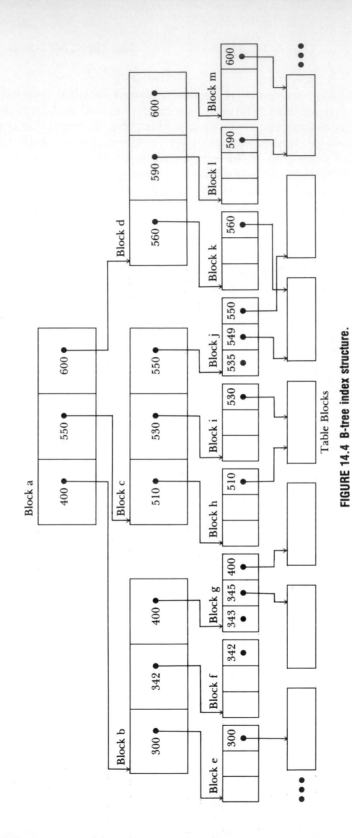

FIGURE 14.4 B-tree index structure.

level) increases, the performance improvements afforded by a B-tree structure also increase.

Another common storage technique for an index is hashing. In this case, index entries are not ordered; rather, they are stored in random order based on application of a hash algorithm to the indexed columns. The relational DBMS accesses the table by first hashing to the index, then obtaining the appropriate table row address, and finally accessing the table row.

Regardless of index storage structure, many data requests may require scanning the index. Consider, for example, an index on EMPLOYEE–NUMBER and DEPT–CODE (in that sequence). A query specifying only DEPT–CODE in its selection criteria cannot take advantage of either the layered search strategy provided by a B-tree structure or the hashed access strategy supported by a hashed structure. In either case, scanning of the table or the index is required. Scanning of the index may be faster because the index probably is smaller and can be retrieved in fewer I/Os. Of course, another factor in relative efficiency of a table scan versus an index scan is the percentage of rows qualifying for the request.

Tuning efficiency of an index scan is much like tuning efficiency of a table scan, depending on implementation options provided by the relational DBMS. Options that can limit number of index entries scanned or speed up the scanning process include

- "Clustering" the index (i.e., defining an ordered index)
- Partitioning the index
- Facilitating parallel "subscans" of the index (e.g., of index partitions)
- Allocating indexes to faster storage devices
- Facilitating DBMS use of high-speed scan techniques (e.g., DB2's sequential prefetch)
- Specifying appropriate use of buffers.

IMPLEMENTATION TIPS AND TECHNIQUES

Deciding on the most effective indexes as well as choosing among indexes and other access mechanisms (such as scanning, clustering, and hashing) can be extremely challenging. Therefore, be sure to allow adequate time for this step. Questions to help you make your decision follow.

1. *What are the various kinds of indexes that apply to your DBMS?* A product may support some or all of the indexes discussed in this chapter, as well as others. Samples include unique versus nonunique, clustered versus nonclustered, partitioning versus nonpartitioning, and multicolumn versus single-column indexes.
2. *Which index storage structures are supported by your DBMS?* Specifically, determine whether your DBMS supports more than one kind of storage structure for indexes (e.g., hashed, ordered). Different index structures may have different access characteristics.

3. *What parameters should be input to index performance projections?* Estimate and document CPU time, I/O time, and elapsed times for various types of indexed access. Also estimate performance profiles for full index scans for comparison to other design alternatives (e.g., table scans, hashes, alternative indexes).

4. *What tools are available for measuring and tuning index characteristics of particular data requests?* Identify facilities for studying index usage. Typically, an EXPLAIN facility indicates whether an index is used for a specific request. Can you also determine whether a B-tree structure has reduced access of index leaf pages? If an index is multicolumn, can you determine for what subset of columns the index is used? Can you determine how many index physical blocks are accessed? Whether index-only access occurs?

   Might indexes become inefficient as table inserts and updates occur? Can you identify when index blocks are not stored in optimal sequence (perhaps due to table inserts and updates)?

5. *What system resources (e.g., buffers) can impact index performance?* Determine where your DBMS stores index blocks as they are accessed. Are they placed in special index buffers? In the same buffers as table blocks? Have you allocated sufficient buffers?

6. *Are there index locking parameters that can be specified by the database designer?* Are there index locking parameters about which you need to be concerned? How important are they to performance and concurrency? Can they be easily modified later?

Finally, examine your database design and processing requirements. For what tables should you consider indexes? For those tables, identify insert, delete, update, and load activity in evaluating costs and benefits of indexes.

Where the overhead of index maintenance is intolerable, but indexes are still needed, investigate application alternatives. For example, can you redefine your insert and delete requirements in terms of updates? Suppose that you are storing information about placement and cancellation of customer orders every month. Assume that the index overhead of inserting and deleting rows for each customer every month is not acceptable. An alternative is to preallocate some number of rows per customer per month (provided that you can estimate fairly accurately the number of rows needed for each customer). Then, monthly, instead of inserting and deleting orders, you simply replace existing rows with new information (actually, you merely update nonindexed columns). In this way, you control the timing of index maintenance overhead.

CASE STUDY

Returning to Moon Launch Enterprise, let us evaluate index schemes to support T13, T14, and T33. Refer to Chapter 13 for a full description of these requests. Recall that they access the following tables:

- □ CREDIT–RATING (4 rows)
- □ BUSINESS (3000 rows)
- □ PASSENGER (32,000 rows)
- □ BSNSS–PASSENGER (9000 rows)
- □ VCTN–PASSENGER (26,000 rows)
- □ FLIGHT (4 rows)
- □ FLIGHT–SCHEDULE (1500 rows)
- □ RESERVATION (124,000 rows)

All tables are accessed by their primary keys. Some tables also are accessed otherwise:

- □ RESERVATION—by FLIGHT*NUMBER, FLIGHT–SCHEDULE*DEPARTURE–DATE to count as many as 100 rows when verifying availability of a reservation (transaction T13)
- □ BSNSS–PASSENGER—by BUSINESS*COUNTRY–NAME, BUSINESS*NAME to retrieve approximately six rows, since BUSINESS : BSNSS–PASSENGER is 1 : 6 (transaction T14)
- □ RESERVATION—all rows are read to determine the count of RESERVATIONs for each FLIGHT*NUMBER, FLIGHT–SCHEDULE*DEPARTURE–DATE (request T33)
- □ RESERVATION—might be sorted on FLIGHT–SCHEDULE*DEPARTURE–DATE, FLIGHT*NUMBER to achieve proper output sequence for request T33

Again, the case study addresses DB2 and DBC/1012, since these products implement indexes in different ways. Note that the discussion pertains to product releases that are current at the time of this writing (Release 3 for DB2 and Release 3 for the DBC/1012).

DB2 INDEXES

1. *Various types of indexes*—DB2 supports unique–nonunique, clustered–nonclustered, and partitioning–nonpartitioning indexes. Further, by definition, a partitioned index also is always clustered.
2. *Index storage structures*—All DB2 indexes are balanced B-tree structures. ("Balanced" implies that all bottommost pages are the same distance from the topmost page.) All index entries are ordered (ascending or descending).

    A DB2 index is stored in an index space, where an index space is a dataset (or file). Indexes are divided into physical blocks (called pages), 4K bytes in length. As for tablespaces, there are three kinds of pages for an index: header page, space map page, and index data page. Index layouts differ depending on whether the index is unique or nonunique. You will find details on storage layouts in IBM manuals and course materials.

    Interestingly, DB2 index pages have no limit to the number of entries per page, whereas tablespace pages can store a maximum of 127 rows per page. Occasionally, you may consider building a unique index on all columns of a table where the table has a very small row size to store more than 127 rows per page (within the index). A scan of such an index will involve fewer I/O operations than will a scan of the table.

3. *Parameters for projecting index efficiency*—For calculating DB2 index efficiency, analyze two questions. What are the details of a particular index's structure (e.g., key length, overhead of pointers, number of levels in the B-tree, number of lowest-level leaf pages)? What other DB2 processing overhead must be considered (e.g., create thread, commit, terminate thread, perhaps BIND)?

    An additional consideration when adding DB2 indexes is that of index recovery. At the time of this writing, DB2 recovers an index by reading the table and rebuilding the index; that is, an index cannot be recovered by restoring a copy of it and rolling forward the log. Depending on how long it takes to rebuild an index, consider carefully the potential implications of having to recover an index.

4. *Tools for tuning particular index requests*—For each request involving indexed access, you would like to determine the answers to the following questions. Are all leaf pages scanned? Is sequential prefetch invoked for the index scan? Is a subset of leaf pages scanned? How many pages are involved? Is the B-tree accessed (entailing only one I/O per level)?

    DB2's EXPLAIN facility indicates when access is via an index, as well as how many columns are used for matching in the B-tree. It does not tell you how many index pages or levels are accessed. These you must calculate, determine from the catalog, or obtain from a performance tool.

    The RUNSTATS facility updates the DB2 catalog with index information including number of pages not optimally located, number of levels, and so on. You can reorganize a DB2 index without reorganizing the corresponding tablespace.

5. *Impact of system resources*—DB2 index access uses buffers. An installation determines whether to use separate buffer pools for indexes versus tablespaces. A general recommendation is to share one large buffer pool for both table and index access.

6. *Index locking parameters*—When DB2 accesses indexes, it locks index subpages, where a *subpage* is a whole page (4K bytes) or part of a whole page. DB2 designers influence the size of index locks by specifying the number of subpages in a page for a given index. The smaller the subpage, the fewer the index entries that are locked, enabling more concurrency. You cannot change the subpage parameter with an ALTER statement, because the size of a subpage influences physical storage of the index. Thus, to change the subpage, you must drop and recreate the index.

All the tables for the case study probably should have unique indexes on primary keys (at the time of this writing, this is the only mechanism provided by DB2 to enforce uniqueness). What about access other than through primary keys?

RESERVATION is accessed via FLIGHT*NUMBER, FLIGHT—SCHEDULE* DEPARTURE—DATE to count the total number of reservations for a given flight. Since these columns are part of the primary key, the primary key index can be used for this request. Preferably, make these columns the leading columns of the index, so that DB2 can use the B-tree. If these columns are not the high-order columns of the index, DB2 may scan all leaf pages of this index. In fact, DB2 can probably use index-only access to count occurrences; that is, it need not even access the RESERVATION table to count rows for a given FLIGHT*NUMBER, FLIGHT—SCHEDULE*DEPARTURE—DATE. Since request T33 requires its output sorted by FLIGHT—SCHEDULE*DEPARTURE—DATE, FLIGHT* NUMBER, preferably define the high-order columns in this sequence and con- sider making the index a clustering index. (Note: if DB2 can satisfy this request through index-only access, perhaps you should reconsider your decision from Step RDD8 to cluster RESERVATION?)

BSNSS—PASSENGER is accessed by a foreign key (BUSINESS*COUNTRY—NAME, BUSINESS*NAME). An index here will be used to access an average of six rows (involving index I/O plus six I/Os to the table if the table is not clustered by this index). This is probably fewer I/Os than scanning 9000 rows, although the time to scan 9000 rows is probably acceptable (depending on specific response time requirements).

The BSNSS—PASSENGER table is not frequently updated (five per day for T4, five per day for T5, one per week for T6); thus overhead of index maintenance is not a major concern. The RESERVATION table is frequently updated (340 per day for T14, 40 per day for T15). Yet, the only index proposed for RESERVATION is on the primary key, needed to enforce uniqueness.

DBC/1012 INDEXES

1. *Various types of indexes*—The DBC/1012 supports unique and nonunique indexes. The syntax distinguishes between one (unique or nonunique) PRIMARY INDEX and other (unique or nonunique) INDEXes. However, recall from the case study in Step RDD9 that the PRIMARY INDEX clause actually designates the hash key for a table, and does not designate an index at all.
2. *Index storage structures*—Like tables, the entries of each DBC/1012 index are distributed across all AMPs (database processors) in the configuration to enable parallel scanning. Unique indexes are hashed on the values of the indexed columns. Thus, access via a unique index typically requires two I/Os (depending on contents of buffers and number of hash syn- onyms): first hashed access to the index, followed by direct access to the corresponding table row.

   Nonunique indexes are built within each AMP, such that index entries for all table rows stored on a given AMP also are stored on the same AMP. Consequently, index entries representing multiple occurrences of the same indexed column values typically are distributed across multiple AMPs.

We shall consider an example of a nonunique index on the DBC/1012. Suppose the VENDOR table (Figure 14.1) is hashed by NAME (i.e., PRIMARY INDEX is defined on NAME) and indexed by LOCATION (i.e., nonunique INDEX is defined on LOCATION). Two rows for vendors from New Jersey may hash to two different AMPs. Thus, each of the two AMPs has an index entry representing the LOCATION value 'New Jersey'.

Because nonunique index entries representing the same indexed column value typically occur on multiple AMPs, any access via a nonunique index requires a scan of the index. The index entries are scanned in parallel by each AMP. Thus, elapsed time for access via a nonunique index is related to the longest time required for any one AMP to scan its subset of the index and to access corresponding qualifying table rows.

3. *Parameters for projecting index efficiency*—Factors that can affect efficiency of a unique DBC/1012 index include the following:

- Occurrence of many hash synonyms for index entries (unlikely for a unique index, but possible). This circumstance would imply that long index synonym chains must be read.
- Occurrence of many hash synonyms for table rows (dependent on the hash key for the table). An index entry actually points to the starting address for a chain of table hash synonyms. Thus, this circumstance would imply that long table synonym chains must be read.
- Speed of processors and storage devices within the DBC/1012 configuration.

Factors that can affect efficiency of a nonunique DBC/1012 index include the following:

- Largest number of index entries on any one AMP—a determining factor in elapsed time for scan of the index, required for any access via the index.
- Occurrence of many hash synonyms for table rows (dependent on the hash key for the table). Just as for unique indexes, this circumstance would imply that long table synonym chains must be read.
- Speed of processors and storage devices within the DBC/1012 configuration.

Vendor assistance may be required to analyze the first two factors in either case.

4. *Tools for tuning particular index requests*—The DBC/1012's EXPLAIN facility indicates when access is via an index. You can issue the COLLECT STATISTICS statement to amass statistics regarding number and distribution of values for indexed columns. The DBC/1012 optimizer uses these statistics in choosing the access path (e.g., indexed access versus table scan).

5. *Impact of system resources*—In the DBC/1012 environment, the designer does not specify resource options (e.g., buffer pools) specific to use of indexes.

6. *Index locking parameters*—The designer has no control over DBC/1012 locking of index entries.

Analyzing the tables for Moon Launch, recall that you have already decided (Step RDD9) to hash (i.e., define a PRIMARY INDEX) on the primary key for each table. Thus, the most efficient way to access individual rows of each table will be via the primary key, since hashing is the fastest way to access individual rows. Note that, if you decide to change the hash key (PRIMARY INDEX) to something other than the primary key, perhaps to facilitate other requests), you should define another UNIQUE INDEX on the primary key to enforce uniqueness as well as to speed access.

What about the other access requirements?

RESERVATION is accessed via FLIGHT*NUMBER, FLIGHT–SCHEDULE* DEPARTURE–DATE to count the number of reservations for a given flight. Although this combination is part of the hash key, remember that selection criteria involving only part of a hash key cannot use hashed access. Since access is to a relatively small percentage of RESERVATION rows (100 out of 124,000), consider defining a nonunique index.

This design results in an index (FLIGHT*NUMBER, FLIGHT–SCHEDULE* DEPARTURE–DATE) on a subset of the hash key (FLIGHT*NUMBER, PASSENGER* COUNTRY–NAME, PASSENGER*CODE, FLIGHT–SCHEDULE*DEPARTURE–DATE). This may appear contrary to Rule RDD9.5 in Chapter 13, which recommends that you not hash on a set of columns when a subset is frequently referenced alone in selection criteria. However, Rule RDD9.5 suggests use of clustering or an ordered index instead. The DBC/1012 supports neither of these options. Thus, this design seems optimal for the DBC/1012 (based on requests analyzed thus far).

Of course, you also must evaluate impact of index maintenance on update activity for RESERVATION (340 per day for T14, 40 per day for T15). You may want to benchmark performance of T13 (retrieval) and T14 and T15 (both update) with and without the proposed index before making a final decision.

DBC/1012 indexes do not facilitate sorting because they are not ordered indexes. Thus, request T33, which involves reading and sorting all RESERVATION rows, will not benefit from an index.

Finally, BSNSS–PASSENGER is accessed by a foreign key (BUSINESS* COUNTRY–NAME, BUSINESS*NAME). You may consider a nonunique index here, containing one-sixth as many entries as the BSNSS–PASSENGER table (since BUSINESS:BSNSS–PASSENGER is 1:6). Scanning the smaller nonunique index to access approximately six table rows probably is faster than scanning the 9000-row table. However, actual scan times will depend on number of AMPs within the system (more AMPs imply shorter scan time). Updates to BSNSS–PASSENGER are relatively infrequent; thus, index maintenance probably is not a major concern. Again, benchmarking is advisable before making a final decision.

SUMMARY

This chapter addressed considerations for adding indexes to your relational tables. It specifically discussed use of indexes to facilitate performance (as opposed to ensuring integrity—covered in Chapter 12). In most cases, it is advisable to add such indexes only after you have considered storage-related access mechanisms: scanning, clustering, and hashing (discussed in Chapter 13). In this way, you are able to measure or project optimal performance prior to adding indexes, allowing you to judge more accurately whether indexes are indeed required. Such a philosophy is possible because indexes usually are easy to add or modify later in the design or implementation process. Nevertheless, there are circumstances under which you may want to evaluate the need for indexes early in the design phase, including the following:

☐   An index determines clustering
☐   An index determines partitioning
☐   Tables are large and the time to create an index is nontrivial
☐   Building of an index is extremely inefficient if the table already contains data

There are many kinds of indexes: unique–nonunique, clustering–nonclustering, and partitioning–nonpartitioning. Further, indexes can (depending on product implementation) have various storage structures, such as an ordered B-tree or nonordered hash structure.

Except when they support clustering or partitioning, indexes do not affect the way tables are stored. Indexes generally are used in concert with storage-related access mechanisms (scanning, hashing, clustering) to provide a choice of access mechanisms for each table.

In summary, indexes are most useful for medium to large tables, since small tables usually can be scanned and sorted relatively efficiently. Indexes are particularly effective in accessing a small percentage of rows (e.g., less than 20 percent) to satisfy requirements for discrete column values, for a range of column values, or for performing built-in functions on column values. If a small subset of columns is needed by a request, an index over all such columns can avoid table access altogether. Ordered indexes (indexes the entries of which are stored in ascending or descending sequence) are useful for avoiding sorts, again when retrieving a small percentage of rows.

In evaluating index effectiveness, you must first consider associated overhead due to storage requirements and to effects on insert, delete, update, and utility processing. Second, you will want to propose an indexing scheme that benefits as many types of requests as possible. In other words, you will want to share indexes among requirements where feasible, perhaps by extending a specific index to include additional columns or by altering its column sequence. You also will evaluate the possibly negative effect of indexes on other unrelated data requests. Thus, designing for indexes can challenge the creativity and analytical skills of a relational database designer and tuner.

EXERCISES

14.1 Describe two storage structures for indexes. Discuss the various ways in which the relational DBMS can access each of these index structures.

14.2 Explain how an index can avoid a sort whether or not the table rows are sequenced (clustered) by the index.

14.3 Explain why index access sometimes may perform less efficiently than a full table scan does.

14.4 Explain how the sequence of columns in a multicolumn index is important.

14.5 Suppose T28 (see Figure 13.5, pps. 378–379) becomes a very high-priority requirement. The passenger information that the user wishes to see includes all columns in the PASSENGER table. Discuss potential indexes that you would propose if T28 were the only or most critical request; that is, design specifically to facilitate T28.

14.6 Repeat Exercise 14.5, but this time assume that T28 is less critical than are T13, T14, and T33. In other words, reconsider your indexes and examine how they relate to or conflict with those for T13, T14, and T33.

14.7 The user community forgot a batch requirement: T35—List all RESERVATIONs for a given reservation agent, sequenced by FLIGHT–SCHEDULE*DEPARTURE–DATE, FLIGHT*NUMBER. Assume that there are three reservation agents, each of whom places an equal number of reservations. Discuss indexes to facilitate this requirement. Next, assume that there are many reservation agents, each of whom places approximately 3 percent of total reservations. Discuss index recommendations.

15 Tune by Introducing Controlled Data Redundancy

Up to this point, your relational tables and columns exactly mirror your logical data model. Accordingly, your relational design shares the stability and flexibility of the logical data model. It is also easily understood by users, especially if they have participated in the design or at least in the final presentation and acceptance of the logical data model. It is likely, however, that certain *performance* and *functionality* requirements are not adequately addressed by this design, even with the access mechanisms added in Chapters 13 and 14. Let us look first at performance challenges, and then at functionality limitations.

POTENTIAL PERFORMANCE INADEQUACIES

Usually, performance inadequacies result from a product's lack of efficient access mechanisms and storage structures, or from an optimizer's failure to choose the most efficient access path for a specific request. If relational products were perfect in these two areas, a relational database design that exactly mirrors a stable logical data model would not suffer from performance problems. Products are not perfect, however. Specifically, your design may provide inadequate performance (for a specific product implementation) due to the following characteristics:

□   Tables with no redundant columns except for foreign keys, reflecting a fully normalized design

□   Few, no, or somewhat arbitrary implementations of columns representing summarized or derived data (depending on the degree to which you chose to define these data in your logical data model)
□   Representation of all repeating groups as rows rather than columns, reflecting first normal form
□   One-to-one mapping between logical data model attributes and relational database design columns
□   One-to-one mapping between logical data model entities and relational database design tables

Of course, these same qualities contribute to the stability of your design. Therefore, you sometimes have to compromise stability when modifying your design to accommodate performance.

As one example, let us look at potential performance inadequacies resulting from a fully normalized design. Consider a database describing suppliers, or-

FIGURE 15.1 Supplier logical data model.

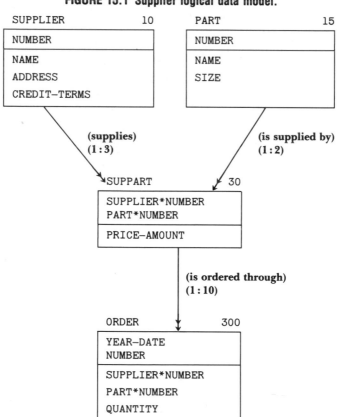

SUPPLIER NUMBER	SUPPLIER NAME	ORDER NUMBER	PART NUMBER	PRICE AMOUNT
10	ABC CO.	2	10	5.00
		16	39	29.99
		234	6	133.00
13	DEF INC.	1	54	11.49
		88	39	24.90
		174	10	4.50

FIGURE 15.2 Supplier sample report.

ders, and parts. After normalizing the data, you might develop the logical data model in Figure 15.1. It contains four entities (SUPPLIER, PART, ORDER, SUPPART), which you initially translate to four relational tables. Now, assume you need to produce the report in Figure 15.2. This report requires access to multiple tables (SUPPLIER, ORDER, SUPPART). The data manipulation language (DML) for the report must specify a join, subquery, or set of data manipulation statements where each statement references one of the tables. The size of the tables and efficiency of the database product in performing these multitable functions determine whether the request performs acceptably.

One way to improve performance is to reduce the need for multitable access. You have several alternatives. You can add duplicate columns from one table to another and thereby eliminate access to one or more tables—this procedure is discussed in this chapter. Or, you can combine several tables into one table and hence reduce the number of tables accessed—a topic of Chapter 16. In either case, you are deviating from strict compliance of the relational database structure to the logical data model. The resulting design is no longer entirely application-independent. It intentionally favors processing of some requests over others. It also may have potential integrity problems, which you must resolve through other mechanisms.

POSSIBLE FUNCTIONALITY LIMITATIONS

Likewise, you may discover that your relational database does not easily support all processing functionality. That is, it may be difficult (perhaps impractical) to produce a specific report or answer a given question. Theoretically, such functionality limitations should not occur. After all, you designed your relational database from a data-driven perspective. Why, then, should some reports or questions be difficult to address? Such limitations occur because product implementations of the relational model are not perfect.

Functionality limitations usually are due to incomplete DML support of relational operations. That is, a product may not support the operations needed to satisfy a desired request. Some common functionality limitations arise from nonexistent or inefficient support for union, outer join, and outer union operations.

You can modify your relational database design to accommodate these processing requirements. Just as in tuning for performance, however, you may have to compromise stability when tuning for functionality.

As one example, consider the supertype and subtype tables in Figure 15.3 and the report in Figure 15.4. This report involves joins of the EMPLOYEE supertype table with the LAWYER and PROFESSIONAL subtype tables and a union (vertical stack) of all resulting rows. Suppose your product's DML does not support unions! Then you must either use other DML operations to simulate a union or alter your relational database structure to eliminate the union requirement. One way to alter your relational database structure is to combine some or all of the tables (i.e., "prejoin" or "prestack" the tables). Under this option, the tables in your relational database no longer map to the entities in your logical data model in a straightforward, one-to-one manner.

STEPS FOR MODIFYING THE DATABASE STRUCTURE

This chapter and Chapter 16 address when and how to deviate from your logical data model in a responsible way. "Responsible" means that you implement such deviations only when (1) other tuning mechanisms (i.e., the access approaches discussed in Chapters 13 and 14) are inadequate, (2) you have specific requirements that benefit, (3) you implement mechanisms to minimize (or at least to assure notification of) loss of integrity or flexibility, and (4) you document adequately how and why the relational design deviates from the logical data model. The resulting relational database design is always more complex— even if it appears simpler to a particular user or processing requirement. The increased complexity results from the effects of design changes on DML, data integrity, data access, storage, performance, data availability, administration

FIGURE 15.3 Employee relational database structure.

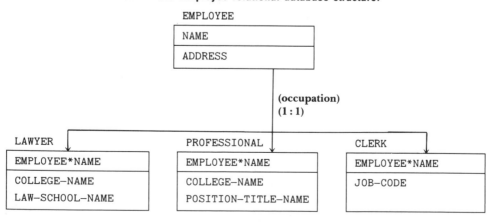

EMPLOYEE NAME	EMPLOYEE ADDRESS	EMPLOYEE COLLEGE NAME	EMPLOYEE TYPE (L = LAWYER) (P = PROFESSIONAL)
Fleming, C.	128 Main Street	Harvard	L
Meacham, K.	6 Littleton Road	Yale	L
von Halle, C.	3 Puppy Place	Fordham	P
Wollman, K.	19 Central Ave	MIT	P

FIGURE 15.4 Employee sample report.

and security, geographical distribution, and naming conventions. Therefore, carefully evaluate *all* options (not only design modifications) for addressing any remaining functionality and performance inadequacies. Your options include those in the following list.

1. *Try alternative DML syntax.* Alternative DML is the most desirable option, since it has no effect on stability of the relational database design. You can sometimes resolve functionality problems by using a series of DML statements to simulate an unsupported operation. Likewise, you may be able to address performance problems by rephrasing DML to enable the optimizer's selection of a more efficient access path.

2. *Complement the DML with other programming or processing techniques.* For example, if your product is inefficient at sorts, you may call on external sort routines. In place of implicit sorts invoked by relational DML clauses (e.g., DISTINCT, ORDER BY, GROUP BY), you may retrieve rows without specifying these clauses, store the rows in a sequential file, and invoke an outside (high-performing) sort routine. Other requirements may necessitate coding and calling procedures to perform functions not supported by your relational product. For instance, you may effect a union by retrieving rows from several relational tables and inserting them into a relational table or sequential file.

3. *Modify the relational database structure such that it no longer conforms to your logical data model.* The previous two options are more closely related to application design than to database design. If those two options are inadequate or inappropriate, your final choice is to revise your relational database design. Modifications that cause your relational database design to deviate from the logical data model are the focus of this and the next chapter. Specifically, you can

   □ Add duplicate data—*Step RDD11*
   □ Redefine columns—*Step RDD12*
   □ Redefine tables—*Step RDD13*

Here and in Chapter 16, we present these three steps for modifying the relational database design in a deliberate sequence, beginning with techniques that are least disruptive to the logical data model and proceeding to more drastic measures. First, Step RDD11 selectively duplicates data by adding "extra" columns or rows. At the same time, it adds compensatory mechanisms (e.g., additional insert/delete/update rules and triggering operations) to ensure continued integrity of data values. Steps RDD12 and RDD13 in Chapter 16 redefine columns and potentially rearrange entire tables. They do so, however, only by applying well-understood transformations from the logical data model, again accompanied by additional integrity mechanisms to preserve consistency of data values.

You are unlikely to apply these three steps in strictly this sequence. Rather, you will study your critical data requests and identify your particular performance and functionality challenges. Then you will evaluate and choose the set of column and table modifications that best address your needs.

STEP RDD11: ADD DUPLICATE DATA

You can add duplicate data to your logical data model in the form of duplicate columns or duplicate rows. First, we consider duplicate columns, typically the more useful form of duplicate data. We return to the topic of duplicate rows at the end of this step.

A *duplicate column* is the representation of an attribute at least twice (although possibly not in exactly the same form) in one or more tables in your database design. So far, the only duplicate columns in your relational database are foreign keys. Foreign keys are *necessary* duplicate columns. In the logical data model, they represent relationships between entities. In the relational database, they relate one table to another.

There are four other kinds of duplicate columns. None are necessary, but any may be useful in tuning. These are columns that (1) are *exact copies* of existing columns (in addition to existing foreign keys), (2) are *summarized or derived* from existing columns, (3) represent *repeating groups* that originally appeared as rows (rather than columns) in the table, or (4) are *contrived substitutes* for existing columns.

DUPLICATE COLUMNS: EXACT COPIES OF EXISTING COLUMNS

The process of adding columns that are exact copies of existing columns is one example of denormalization. Denormalization is the "undoing" of the normalization process. It does not, however, imply omission of the normalization process. Rather, *denormalization* is the process whereby, after defining a stable, fully normalized data structure, you selectively introduce duplicate data to facilitate specific performance requirements.

Types of columns that replicate existing columns include:

☐   A column that is a nonkey column from a parent or ancestor (where an *ancestor* of a table is one of the following: a parent table, a parent's parent table, a parent's parent's parent table, and so on)

- □ A column that is a nonkey column from the child or parent of a 1 : 1 relationship
- □ A column that is the primary key of an ancestor, not contained in the primary key of an immediate parent—that is, an "unnecessary" foreign key

RULE RDD11.1

Consider *duplicating* one or a few nonvolatile *columns* from a parent, ancestor, or one-to-one child table to expedite table lookups in frequent or critical requests.

We shall consider an example of each type of copied column.

DUPLICATE NONKEY COLUMN FROM PARENT OR ANCESTOR. Figure 15.5 shows sample value listings for two tables in the ice-cream parlor database: SUPPLY and VENDOR. The VENDOR table is a parent of SUPPLY. (You know VENDOR is a parent because of the foreign key VENDOR*NAME in the SUPPLY table). Copying the LOCATION column into the SUPPLY table duplicates a parent nonkey column. Figure 15.6 illustrates the resulting SUPPLY table. The (DD) notation designates VENDOR%LOCATION as duplicate data. Requests for SUPPLY information, requiring a VENDOR table lookup solely to obtain vendor location, now can be satisfied by accessing only one table (SUPPLY).

FIGURE 15.5 Normalized VENDOR **and** SUPPLY **tables, sample value listings.**

VENDOR

NAME (PK)	LOCATION	STATUS	CONTACT
Mr. Chip	New York	active	Mary
Bean, Inc.	New York	inactive	Joe
Mrs. Mousse	New Jersey	active	Sue

SUPPLY

FLAVOR*NAME (PK, FK1)	VENDOR*NAME (PK, FK2)	WEEKLY-VOLUME-AMOUNT
chocolate	Mr. Chip	2 tons
chocolate mousse	Mrs. Mousse	1 pound
chocolate	Bean, Inc.	2 tons
chocolate chip	Mr. Chip	1 ton

SUPPLY

FLAVOR*NAME (PK, FK1)	VENDOR*NAME (PK, FK2)	WEEKLY-VOLUME-AMOUNT	VENDOR%LOCATION (DD)
chocolate	Mr. Chip	2 tons	New York
chocolate mousse	Mrs. Mousse	1 pound	New Jersey
chocolate	Bean, Inc.	2 tons	New York
chocolate chip	Mr. Chip	1 ton	New York

FIGURE 15.6 SUPPLY **table with duplicate column.**

Ignore, for the moment, the naming convention (involving a % character) for the duplicate column. Suggestions for naming conventions are addressed at the end of this step.

Consider the amount of duplicate data introduced by copying the LOCATION column into the SUPPLY table. First, vendor location appears in two tables instead of one. Second, a particular vendor location occurs many times in the SUPPLY table if that vendor supplies many flavors. In other words, the SUPPLY table is no longer in third normal form.

DUPLICATE NONKEY COLUMN FROM ONE-TO-ONE CHILD OR PARENT. Figure 15.7 illustrates two other tables in the ice-cream parlor database: FLAVOR and BIN. FLAVOR is the parent of BIN in a 1 : 1 relationship. (You know FLAVOR is the parent because of the foreign key FLAVOR*NAME in the BIN table). The relationship represents the fact that, in the storeroom, each flavor is kept in one bin, and each bin holds one flavor.

FIGURE 15.7 Normalized FLAVOR **and** BIN **tables, sample value listings.**

FLAVOR

NAME (PK)	COLOR
chocolate	brown
chocolate chip	white
chocolate mousse	brown

BIN

NUMBER (PK)	SIZE	LOCATION	FLAVOR*NAME (FK, AK)
1	1 ton	aisle 1	chocolate
2	1 ton	aisle 2	chocolate chip
3	0.5 ton	aisle 2	chocolate mousse

FLAVOR

NAME (PK)	COLOR	BIN%SIZE (DD)
chocolate	brown	1 ton
chocolate chip	white	1 ton
chocolate mousse	brown	0.5 ton

FIGURE 15.8 FLAVOR **table with duplicate column.**

Copying the SIZE column into the FLAVOR table (Figure 15.8) duplicates a nonkey column from the child. If you also copied the COLOR column into the BIN table, you would be duplicating a nonkey column from the parent. Either type of duplication makes more data available via access of a single table.

In the case of a 1 : 1 relationship, the data redundancy is limited to storing the same column in two tables. It does not imply multiple occurrences of the duplicated column in either table. Both tables are still in third normal form (i.e., there are no redundancies among rows of either table).

"UNNECESSARY" FOREIGN KEYS. Figure 15.9 illustrates a logical data model relating the SCHOOL, COURSE, PROFESSOR, and CLASS entities.

FIGURE 15.9 School logical data model.

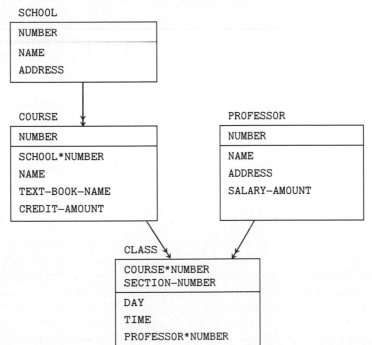

Suppose a user wishes to determine the school that offers courses taught by a specific professor. The user must access the CLASS table (to determine classes taught by the professor) and the COURSE table (to determine the school that offers these classes). Alternative SQL requests include a subquery using IN:

```
SELECT DISTINCT SCHOOL*NUMBER
FROM COURSE
WHERE COURSE.NUMBER IN
(SELECT COURSE*NUMBER
FROM CLASS
WHERE PROFESSOR*NUMBER = X)
```

a subquery using EXISTS:

```
SELECT DISTINCT SCHOOL*NUMBER
FROM COURSE
WHERE EXISTS
(SELECT *
FROM CLASS
WHERE CLASS.PROFESSOR*NUMBER = X AND
CLASS.COURSE*NUMBER = COURSE.NUMBER)
```

and a join:

```
SELECT DISTINCT SCHOOL*NUMBER
FROM COURSE, CLASS
WHERE CLASS.PROFESSOR*NUMBER = X AND
CLASS.COURSE*NUMBER = COURSE.NUMBER
```

A denormalization alternative is to duplicate the SCHOOL*NUMBER column in the CLASS table. Then SCHOOL*NUMBER in the CLASS table is an "unnecessary" foreign key, representing the primary key (NUMBER) of an ancestor (SCHOOL). The duplicate column is an unnecessary foreign key because it can be obtained by relating the child (CLASS) to its parent (COURSE) (and perhaps to some higher ancestors—not applicable here). Thus, adding SCHOOL*NUMBER to the CLASS table violates third normal form. (Violation of some normal form is evident because the same value for SCHOOL*NUMBER is repeated in the CLASS table for every occurrence of a given COURSE*NUMBER.) Now, however, rather than performing joins or subqueries, you can obtain the (duplicate) data as follows:

```
SELECT SCHOOL*NUMBER
FROM CLASS
WHERE PROFESSOR*NUMBER = X
```

Duplicate columns impose costs. First, extra *storage* is needed to hold the duplicate data. Obviously, the amount of storage depends on the length of the duplicated column and the number of rows and tables to which the column is copied. Second, enforcement of *data integrity* is more complex. You must define new triggering operations, ensuring that column inserts and updates are synchronized across all tables in which the duplicate column appears. Third, user *DML* (in programs or ad hoc commands) should reference the appropriate (most efficient) copy of the duplicate column. Thus, the user assumes some responsibility for optimizing access paths.

These costs increase with the extent of data redundancy and the volatility of duplicated columns. For instance, if a request references a number of columns from each of several tables, duplicating those columns probably is too costly. Moreover, if you are referencing only a few rows in a lookup table, such that duplicating a column eliminates only a few I/Os, the cost of duplicating the column probably outweighs the benefit. Finally, if you are accessing highly volatile columns, the maintenance costs probably argue against duplication.

___

RULE RDD11.2

Specify the *domain of a copied column* to be consistent with that of the source column.

___

Since the original and duplicate columns have the same business meaning, their domains should be consistent (at least in data type and length). Deviation will cause potential confusion. Are the columns really the same? Moreover, deviation can affect processing functionality and performance. Will the DBMS perform comparisons and joins on these columns if data types and lengths differ? Will it do so efficiently?

DUPLICATE COLUMNS: DERIVATIONS OF EXISTING COLUMNS

Although summarized or derived columns are not *exact* duplicates of existing columns, they represent a more subtle way of storing duplicate data. During logical data modeling, you probably defined some derived attributes based on importance to the user. Your initial translation of the model into a relational database (Chapter 11) established columns for those derived attributes. We now evaluate whether storing these or other derived columns is desirable.

Examples of summarized or derived columns include columns that sum another column over a number of rows (e.g., total volume of ice cream supplied by a supplier), columns that are a count of rows in a table (e.g., total students enrolled in a class), columns representing a calculation over multiple columns (e.g., salary plus commission), and columns reflecting a more complex calculation (e.g., the standard fare amount from the case study).

Consider the SUPPLY table in Figure 15.5. The attribute called WEEKLY–VOLUME–AMOUNT denotes the amount of an ice-cream flavor supplied by a vendor. Summing the column for each flavor yields the total amount of each flavor received by the ice-cream parlor each week. You might store these derived data as a column in the FLAVOR table as shown in Figure 15.10.

FLAVOR

NAME (PK)	COLOR	SUPPLY%SUM—WEEKLY—VOLUME—AMOUNT (DD)
chocolate	brown	4 tons
chocolate mousse	brown	1 pound
chocolate chip	white	1 ton

FIGURE 15.10 FLAVOR **table with summarized or derived data.**

The new column (SUPPLY%SUM—WEEKLY—VOLUME—AMOUNT) does not appear in any other table. Thus, you are not storing the *exact* same column twice. Yet, you are indirectly storing duplicate data because the column is derived from other existing data.

RULE RDD11.3

Consider adding columns *derived* from existing, nonvolatile *columns*

- ☐ To reduce multitable access
- ☐ To improve performance of frequent or critical requests involving calculations (by performing the calculations in advance)
- ☐ To circumvent DML limitations that prevent expressing the derivation in DML

In the example, storing SUPPLY%SUM—WEEKLY—VOLUME—AMOUNT in the FLAVOR table obviously avoids access to the SUPPLY table. A request for flavor name, color and sum of weekly volumes no longer involves two tables (SUPPLY, FLAVOR).

Performance of a derivation depends on complexity of the calculation, the number of tables involved, and the number of rows accessed (more specifically, the number of I/Os). By selectively storing derived data, you not only reduce multitable accesses, but also control timing of calculations. For example, because you have stored the sum of the WEEKLY—VOLUME—AMOUNT from the SUPPLY table in the FLAVOR table, you no longer need to recalculate this sum whenever it is needed. Instead, you calculate it only when you populate the FLAVOR.SUPPLY%WEEKLY—VOLUME—AMOUNT column. In this way, you can schedule the calculation for nonpeak times so as not to jeopardize performance of critical requests.

Storing summarized or derived columns is especially useful when you cannot easily express a calculation using your product's DML. For example, you may be unable to express some required calculations in terms of supported built-in functions, or some calculations may require complex recursive process-ing. Thus, you must use a programming language to perform the calculations dynamically or to do so prior to storing the calculated values in a table as dupli-cate data.

RULE RDD11.4

Use special *naming conventions* to denote columns that are copied or derived from exist-ing columns.

Copied or derived columns introduce special integrity considerations. Therefore, use naming conventions to denote duplicate columns, similar to conventions used for foreign keys. After all, foreign keys are themselves a form of controlled duplicate data. For example, as for foreign keys, include as a pre-fix the name of the source table, followed by a special character to denote du-plicate columns. For duplicate columns that are exact copies of nonkey columns, use a special character different than that used for foreign keys. For duplicate columns that are also "unnecessary" foreign keys (i.e., refer to pri-mary keys of nonimmediate ancestors), perhaps retain the foreign key special character (e.g., *). In both cases, keep the remainder of the name the same as the name of the source column. Following this convention, Figure 15.6 depicts the duplicate vendor location column in the SUPPLY table as VENDOR%LOCATION to denote it as a non–foreign-key duplicate column.

Naming conventions for derived columns are not so straightforward. Derived columns may represent calculations over many columns from many ta-bles and are therefore difficult to name. At minimum, consider use of a special character (e.g., %) in the name to denote a derived column.

Consider creating synonyms for both copied and derived columns so that users need not remember the special naming conventions. The conventions are intended for database designers, database administrators, and data administra-tors. Users appreciate more intuitive synonyms. Your product may support syn-onyms through a CREATE SYNONYM syntax or through creation of views (Chap-ter 17).

RULE RDD11.5

Document copied and derived columns in the *data dictionary* or catalog, with reasons for the duplication.

Usually, relational catalogs do not automatically denote columns as representing duplicate data. Therefore, you need standards for capturing such information. Include designation of source tables and columns, particularly if not obvious from the column name. For derived columns, also include the underlying derivation algorithm.

RULE RDD11.6

Enforce *consistency* of source and copied or derived columns by

☐ Permitting users (and programs) to update only the source (not the copied or derived) columns
☐ Establishing triggering operations on the source columns that automatically cascade updates to all copied or derived columns

Adherence to this rule ensures that you always synchronize values of the source column with the copied or derived columns. Note that these triggering operations can be implemented using any of the options for enforcing attribute business rules discussed in Chapter 12.

Are there exceptions to Rule RDD11.6? Of course there are. Let us consider just one. It may be more efficient or convenient to update the duplicate columns before the source columns, for example if the source columns reside in a different database or are offline when an online update takes place. In this case, you might allow updates to the duplicate columns, probably triggering update of the source columns. The triggering operation might involve a time lag before cascading the update to the source columns.

DUPLICATE COLUMNS: REPRESENTING REPEATING GROUPS

Following the principles of first normal form (Chapter 8), your logical data model and therefore your preliminary relational database design contains no repeating groups. More exactly, your design represents all repeating groups as rows rather than columns.

Occasionally, violating first normal form by storing repeating groups across columns is an effective tuning option. For example, consider a COURSE–ASSIGNMENT table containing prices charged by instructors for teaching courses. Figure 15.11 illustrates one possible implementation, in which the repeating group INSTRUCTOR*NAME, PRICE (occurring multiple times per course) is stored as multiple row occurrences. Figure 15.12 illustrates the repeating group stored as three pairs of columns.

We shall consider the pros and cons of each implementation.

COURSE—INSTRUCTOR

COURSE*CODE (PK, FK1)	INSTRUCTOR*NAME (PK, FK2)	PRICE
RC101	James	2500
RC101	Smitty	1500
RC201	James	6000
RC301	Kendall	10000
RC101	Kendall	1000
RC201	Kendall	2000

FIGURE 15.11 COURSE—INSTRUCTOR **table with repeating group as rows.**

REPEATING GROUP AS ROWS (FIGURE 15.11). There are two advantages to this approach. The first is the ease with which you can express many DML operations. Adding an instructor for a course involves a simple insert of a new row. Deleting an instructor for a course involves a simple delete of a row. Applying built-in functions to INSTRUCTOR*NAME or PRICE is relatively straightforward because built-in functions operate down rows of a given column. For example,

```
SELECT AVG (PRICE)
FROM COURSE—INSTRUCTOR
WHERE COURSE*CODE = 'RC101'

SELECT COUNT (INSTRUCTOR*NAME)
FROM COURSE—INSTRUCTOR
WHERE COURSE*CODE = 'RC201'
```

Other types of queries also are generally straightforward. As an example, a request for courses and instructors charging prices below a certain amount can be constructed as follows:

```
SELECT COURSE*CODE, INSTRUCTOR*NAME, PRICE
FROM COURSE—INSTRUCTOR
WHERE PRICE < 6000
```

The second advantage is the ease with which you can tune performance. Use of indexes, hashing, or clustering to satisfy search criteria involving

FIGURE 15.12 COURSE—INSTRUCTOR **table with repeating group as columns.**

COURSE—INSTRUCTOR

COURSE—CODE (PK)	INSTR1 (FK1)	PRICE1	INSTR2 (FK2)	PRICE2	INSTR3 (FK3)	PRICE3
RC101	James	2500	Smitty	1500	Kendall	1000
RC201	James	6000	Kendall	2000	null	null
RC301	Kendall	10000	null	null	null	null

INSTRUCTOR*NAME or PRICE is straightforward, because each is one column in the table.

There are also three disadvantages. First, you potentially increase storage. Storage must accommodate duplication of COURSE*NUMBER for every professor qualified to teach the course. As the number of professors for each course increases, the storage overhead increases. Second, you may experience performance problems due to row volumes. Because there is one row per instructor of a course, the number of rows in the table may be quite large. For example, assume there are 500,000 instructors, each of whom offers an average of five courses. The table would contain 2.5 million rows. Table loads, reorganizations, recoveries, or scans may take too long using a specific DBMS product. Third, formatting reports showing multiple instructors in the same row is complex. A comparison of one instructor's course prices to those of another instructor requires joining the table to itself if the user wishes to see the prices in one row. This may be tricky SQL, and may not perform well. A sample SQL query is

```
SELECT A.COURSE*CODE, A.INSTRUCTOR*NAME, A.PRICE,
       B.INSTRUCTOR*NAME, B.PRICE
FROM COURSE-INSTRUCTOR A, COURSE-INSTRUCTOR B
WHERE A.COURSE*CODE=B.COURSE*CODE AND
A.INSTRUCTOR*NAME = 'James' AND
B.INSTRUCTOR*NAME = 'Kendall'
```

Moreover, comparing all instructor prices for a specific course (where "all" is a varying number depending on the course) is more difficult since you cannot specify a varying number of self-joins.

REPEATING GROUP AS COLUMNS (FIGURE 15.12). There are three advantages to the approach. First, you have potentially less storage. COURSE*NUMBER is stored only once for every three instructors for a given course. Second, you may improve performance by storing fewer rows. There are fewer (although, wider) rows than in the original design. This may improve performance of loads, reorganizations, recoveries, or scans for a specific product. Third, you increase the ease of formatting some reports showing multiple instructors in the same row. Comparing instructor prices by course and formatting the prices into one row on a report are fairly easy (if all instructors are, indeed, in one row in the table):

```
SELECT COURSE*CODE, INSTR1,PRICE1,
       INSTR2,PRICE2,
       INSTR3,PRICE3
FROM COURSE-INSTRUCTOR
```

However, comparing course prices for two particular instructors is not so easy. What columns do you qualify (INSTR1, INSTR2, or INSTR3) to find the prices charged by two particular instructors (James and Kendall)? Moreover, if more than three instructors teach the same course, multiple rows per course are re-

COURSE-INSTRUCTOR

COURSE* CODE (PK)	ROW- NUMBER (PK)	COURSE- NAME	INSTR1 (FK1)	PRICE1	INSTR2 (FK2)	PRICE2	INSTR3 (FK3)	PRICE3
RC101	1	Math	James	2500	Smitty	1500	Kendall	1000
RC101	2	Math	Woods	2500	Johnson	1500	null	null
RC201	1	Science	James	6000	Kendall	2000	null	null
RC301	1	English	Kendall	10000	null	null	null	null

FIGURE 15.13 COURSE-INSTRUCTOR **table with repeating group as columns and rows.**

quired. Then comparing all or selected instructor prices for a course can be extremely complex.

The approach also has three disadvantages. The first is potentially wasted storage. The design in Figure 15.12 implies that a COURSE typically has three qualifying instructors. Courses with fewer than three instructors will have nulls or default values in some of the columns. Courses with more than three instructors will need more than one row. Moreover, if courses can have more than three instructors, an additional column (e.g., ROW-NUMBER for row number within COURSE*CODE) must be defined as part of the primary key (since COURSE*CODE no longer uniquely identifies a row). Worse, any other (nonrepeating) nonkey columns (e.g., COURSE-NAME) become redundant across rows (Figure 15.13).

The second disadvantage is the complexity of expressing many DML operations. Adding instructors for a course is complicated. Is there room in an existing course row for the new instructor? Further, use of a load utility to add instructors probably is infeasible due to the processing logic required. Because load utilities usually outperform DML insert processing, this disadvantage can be important.

Deleting instructors may be even more complex. Which column contains the existing instructor? Do you set it to null? A default value? Shift other instructors around? If all other instructor columns in the row are set to nulls or default values, do you delete the row?

You cannot easily apply built-in functions across columns—that is, across INSTR1, INSTR2, INSTR3 or across PRICE1, PRICE2, PRICE3. If courses have an arbitrary number of rows, each containing up to three instructors, averaging the prices for a given course is complex.

Other types of queries are not straightforward. For instance, to list courses and instructors charging prices below a certain amount requires a UNION operation:

```
SELECT COURSE*CODE, INSTR1, PRICE1,
    FROM COURSE-INSTRUCTOR
    WHERE PRICE1 < 6000
UNION
```

```
SELECT COURSE*CODE, INSTR2, PRICE2
    FROM COURSE-INSTRUCTOR
    WHERE PRICE2 < 6000
UNION
SELECT COURSE*CODE, INSTR3, PRICE3
    FROM COURSE-INSTRUCTOR
    WHERE PRICE3 < 6000
```

The third disadvantage is the potential complexity of business rules. In the COURSE-INSTRUCTOR table, the repeating group contains a foreign key (INSTRUCTOR*NAME) that becomes three foreign keys (INSTR1, INSTR2, INSTR3) when stored as three repeating columns. Just as instructor updates are hard to express in DML, INSTRUCTOR to COURSE-INSTRUCTOR insert/delete/update rules are hard to specify when instructor is a columnar repeating group. You must customize all such rules; for example, cascade a delete to the appropriate column (which varies on a row-to-row basis within COURSE-INSTRUCTOR), or verify that an insert does not result in a redundant instructor name in the same row.

Even worse, suppose you need multiple rows to accommodate more than three instructors per course (as in Figure 15.13). Then you need additional business rules to ensure that the same row number is not repeated for a given course and to synchronize the now redundant nonkey columns (COURSE-NAME in Figure 15.13) across multiple rows for the same course. You also must ensure that inserts do not result in redundant instructor names for the same course even across different rows.

FIGURE 15.14 Customer monthly revenues with repeating group as rows.

CUSTOMER

CUSTOMER*NUMBER (PK)	MONTH (PK)	REVENUE-AMT
10	jan	1000
10	feb	500
10	mar	1500
10	apr	6000
10	may	10
10	jun	3000
20	jan	3000
20	feb	10
20	mar	6000
20	apr	1500
20	may	500
20	jun	1000

In the COURSE–INSTRUCTOR example, storing the repeating group down rows rather than across columns probably is the better solution. The INSTR1, INSTR2, and INSTR3 columns have exactly the same meaning and are accessed independently of one another. In other words, instructors are added, updated, and deleted independently, and there is no rationale for labeling any given instructor "first" (INSTR1), "second" (INSTR2), and so on. Similarly, PRICE1, PRICE2, and PRICE3 have the same meaning and are accessed independently.

What if INSTR1, INSTR2, and INSTR3 have slightly different meanings? Suppose there are always exactly three instructors per course: a senior instructor, a junior instructor, and a trainee. What if users qualify most queries by specific reference to senior instructor, junior instructor, or trainee? In this case, the advantages may outweigh disadvantages of storing the "repeating group" across columns. In fact, the "repeating group" is no longer a repeating group, since each INSTR*n* column has a different meaning and is accessed independently of the others.

RULE RDD11.7

Consider storing *repeating groups across columns* rather than down rows when

☐ The repeating group contains a fixed number of occurrences, each of which has a different meaning, or
☐ The entire repeating group is normally accessed and updated as one unit (i.e., individual occurrences are seldom updated, retrieved or involved in selection criteria)

A special case of Rule RDD11.7 involves time-dependent data. *Time-dependent data* frequently take the form of a repeating group, each occurrence of which is associated with a particular time value. For example, Figure 15.14 illustrates a CUSTOMER table of monthly revenues. The table contains six rows per customer to represent revenues for 6 months. If there are numerous customers (e.g., one million), the table becomes quite large (e.g., 6 million rows). If you increase the number of months per customer, you multiply the number of rows.

An alternative is Figure 15.15: storing the 6-month repeating group across columns in a row. In this alternative, you may even choose not to store values for MONTH because the definition of a revenue column conveys the month (e.g., JAN–AMT). Thus, not only the number of rows, but also the total volume of data are reduced, due to storing a given CUSTOMER*NUMBER only once and MONTH not at all.

What happens to the design in Figure 15.15 if you increase the number of months per customer? You have several choices. You can increase the number

CUSTOMER

CUSTOMER*NUMBER (PK)	JAN–AMT	FEB–AMT	MAR–AMT	APR–AMT	MAY–AMT	JUN–AMT
10	1000	500	1500	6000	10	3000
20	3000	10	6000	1500	500	1000

FIGURE 15.15 Customer monthly revenues with repeating group as columns.

of columns to correspond to the number of months (e.g., 18 columns for 18 months). You can allow multiple rows per customer, each storing 6 months of data (e.g., three rows per customer for 18 months). Then you must also define an additional column (e.g., ROW–NUMBER for row within CUSTOMER*NUMBER) as part of the primary key (because CUSTOMER*NUMBER no longer uniquely identifies a row). Finally, you can define more than one table (e.g., three), each storing a fixed number of months of data (e.g., 6 months per table).

The first alternative applies Rule RDD11.7. The third applies Rule RDD11.7 and then *vertically segments* the table into three tables by dividing it into three subsets of columns (advantages and disadvantages are discussed in Chapter 16). The second alternative essentially defines a repeating group of 6 months (rather than 1 month) and stores the repeating group down rows, with all the advantages and disadvantages previously discussed.

In summary, it is frequently appropriate to store time-dependent data across columns rather than down rows because the number of values (and, therefore, columns) is fixed, and the different values have clearly different meanings.

DUPLICATE COLUMNS: CONTRIVED SUBSTITUTES FOR EXISTING COLUMNS

A *contrived substitute column* has no business meaning of its own. Rather, it is contrived (by the database designer) as a substitute for one or more existing columns solely to alleviate performance or functionality problems.

The most common use for a contrived substitute column is to replace long primary and foreign keys.

RULE RDD11.8

Consider *contriving* a (shorter) *column to substitute for a primary key* and all associated foreign keys when the primary key

- ☐ Is very long (in bytes)
- ☐ Is comprised of many columns
- ☐ Cannot effectively be indexed or hashed

A very long primary key, appearing in many tables as a foreign key, requires a lot of space. Consider the real estate tables in Figure 15.16. Assume PROPERTY.ADDRESS can be up to 50 bytes, and the PROPERTY table lists 2000 rental properties. Further, assume each property is rented an average of 10 times. Thus, storing the foreign key PROPERTY*ADDRESS in the RENTAL table requires 2000 × 10 × 50 bytes—a large amount of storage. Moreover, long primary and foreign keys may lead to poor performance of utilities, scans, joins, and so on for a specific product implementation.

An alternative is to contrive a shorter, substitute primary key, as illustrated in Figure 15.17. Redefine the original (longer) primary key as an alternate key. Replace all referencing foreign keys with the shorter substitute column.

Multicolumn primary keys also may pose problems. Suppose the primary key of PROPERTY in Figure 15.16 consisted of five columns (STREET–NUMBER, STREET–NAME, CITY–NAME, STATE–CODE, ZIP–CODE). Every table related to the PROPERTY table would contain a five-column foreign key. Moreover, queries about PROPERTY must reference all five columns to retrieve a specific row. Even worse, joins across tables must specify comparison operators across all five columns. Such queries are not only tedious but also error-prone, since omitting a column from the selection criteria will yield incorrect results.

For multicolumn keys, you have four alternatives:

1. Create views defining multicolumn joins and selection criteria (relieving users and developers of such responsibility).

FIGURE 15.16 Real estate tables with long primary/foreign keys; sample value listings.

PROPERTY

ADDRESS (PK)	RNTL–AMT
111 Millburn Ave., Glendale NC	1500
245 Bob White Way, Richardson NC	2000
84 Prospect St., Orange FL	1800

RENTAL

PROPERTY*ADDRESS (PK, FK)	START–DATE (PK)	RENTER
111 Millburn Ave., Glendale NC	7/1/88	Kimball
111 Millburn Ave., Glendale NC	8/1/88	Morris
111 Millburn Ave., Glendale NC	9/1/88	Williams
245 Bob White Way, Richardson NC	8/1/88	Robinson
245 Bob White Way, Richardson NC	9/1/88	Thomas
84 Prospect St., Orange FL	7/1/88	Williams

PROPERTY

NUMBER (PK)	ADDRESS (AK)	RNTL—AMT
1	111 Millburn Ave., Glendale NC	1500
2	245 Bob White Way, Richardson NC	2000
3	84 Prospect St., Orange FL	1800

RENTAL

PROPERTY*NUMBER (PK, FK)	START—DATE (PK)	RENTER
1	7/1/88	Kimball
1	8/1/88	Morris
1	9/1/88	Williams
2	8/1/88	Robinson
2	9/1/88	Thomas
3	7/1/88	Williams

FIGURE 15.17 Real estate tables with substitute primary/foreign keys; sample value listings.

2. Create views establishing synonyms for the concatenation of composite primary and foreign keys.
3. Redefine the composite primary key as one column. (Typically, this option is not desirable. Refer to reasons that originally led you to define it as multiple attributes in the logical data model and as multiple columns during translation to a relational database design—specifically Rule RDD2.2, Chapter 11).
4. Contrive a substitute column to serve as the primary key. Redefine the original (longer) primary key as an alternate key. Replace all referencing foreign keys with the shorter substitute column.

Finally, composite or long primary keys can pose a problem when product limitations prevent indexing or hashing the primary key (e.g., perhaps indexes or hashing algorithms can handle only a limited number of columns or characters). For these keys, you have two alternatives: redefine the primary key as one (perhaps shorter) column or contrive a substitute column.

RULE RDD11.9

Instead of replacing a primary key by a contrived substitute, consider redefining an *alternate key as the primary key.*

Recall that originally you selected the primary key over other candidate keys for business reasons. Perhaps the primary key was more intuitive to users, or was referenced by the majority of users. However, if the primary key is the cause of problems, choosing an alternate key may be preferable to contriving a new, arbitrary substitute.

When you replace a primary key, whether by a contrived substitute column or by a (previously defined) alternate key, redefine all related foreign keys to reference the new primary key. Consistent use of the same columns as foreign keys will simplify user access of the tables (users need not remember different ways to relate the same parent table to other child tables) and automated support for referential integrity (you have a consistent set of primary/foreign key references). In some cases, you also may want to copy the original primary key as duplicate data in child tables (applying Rule RDD11.1). This option may reduce or eliminate multitable access if users continue to reference the original primary (now alternate) key.

In summary, this step provided guidelines and examples pertaining to four types of duplicate columns: (1) exact copies of existing columns, (2) derivations of existing columns, (3) columns to represent repeating groups, and (4) contrived substitute columns.

At the beginning of the step, we made reference to introduction of duplicate rows. We turn to that topic now.

DUPLICATE ROWS

A *duplicate row* is the representation of an entity occurrence at least twice (although possibly not in exactly the same form) in one or more tables in your database design. So far, you have *no* duplicate rows in your relational database. Each table represents a distinct business entity, and each row in a table is uniquely identified by a primary key.

Duplicate rows may be of three types: (1) exact copies of existing rows, (2) derivations of existing rows, and (3) contrived substitute rows.

You may introduce *exact copies of existing rows* into the same or different tables. Two exact copies of a row *in the same table* are seldom if ever useful—in fact, they destroy the uniqueness property of the primary key.

RULE RDD11.10

In general, do not allow *exact copies of rows* in the same table.

One example where you might be tempted to permit duplicate rows in the same table is in a transaction log table, as illustrated in Figure 15.18. This table

TRANSACTION

INPUT-PARAM1	INPUT-PARAM2	INPUT-PARAM3
red	34	Jones
blue	45	Smith
red	34	Jones
green	11	Thomas
blue	13	Wood

FIGURE 15.18 Transaction log table with potential duplicate rows.

captures data values for transactions as they occur. The table rows are always processed in aggregate—for example, a user may count transaction occurrences, sum transaction statistics, or perhaps pass an entire set of input parameters to a batch-processing job. There is no "natural" primary key of the table; duplicate rows seem possible. Yet, you should contrive a primary key for the table, perhaps some combination of date, time, and sequence number. Doing so provides a way of verifying that each row is unique and that no row is an inadvertent duplicate insert.

Exact copies of rows *across multiple tables* are possible only when the tables have exactly the same columns. Currently, you have no such tables in your design. Duplicate rows across multiple tables may be advantageous if you implement horizontal segmentation in Chapter 16—splitting the rows of a table into two or more tables.

Derivations of existing rows entail either defining derived columns in other or in new tables, or defining columns in the same table to have a special meaning for specified rows. An example of *derived rows in a different table* is storing counts of one table's rows in another table. This involves defining one or more (duplicate) columns in the second table to hold the derived data. Using the supplier database (logical data model in Figure 15.1), an example is creating

FIGURE 15.19 SUPPLY **table with derived rows.**

SUPPLY

FLAVOR*NAME (PK, FK1)	VENDOR*NAME (PK, FK2)	WEEKLY-VOLUME-AMOUNT
chocolate	Mr. Chip	2 tons
chocolate mousse	Mrs. Mousse	1 pound
chocolate	Bean, Inc.	2 tons
chocolate chip	Mr. Chip	1 ton
chocolate	TOTAL	4 tons
chocolate mousse	TOTAL	1 pound
chocolate chip	TOTAL	1 ton

an ORDER—COUNT table, depicting the total number of orders for each supplier. The ORDER—COUNT table contains columns SUPPLIER*NUMBER and ORDER%COUNT—BY—SUPPLIER. Thus, this alternative equates to defining duplicate (derived) columns, but such columns appear in a separate table.

An example of *derived rows in the same table* is use of particular primary key values to flag rows containing the sum of column values for other rows in the same table. For instance, in the ice-cream parlor database, the SUPPLY table might include the sum of WEEKLY—VOLUME—AMOUNT by flavor in rows with a vendor name of 'TOTAL' (Figure 15.19). This technique generally is not recommended.

RULE RDD11.11

Avoid storing *rows derived from existing rows* within the same relational table, because such derived rows destroy the association of every column with exactly one domain.

Derived rows within the same table violate the rule of associating each column with exactly one domain (including one meaning). In Figure 15.19, the VENDOR*NAME column has two meanings. It either depicts the name of a vendor or it is a special flag (e.g., 'TOTAL') with a different meaning. Likewise, WEEKLY—VOLUME—AMOUNT also has two meanings. Sometimes it is the weekly amount of a flavor supplied by a vendor. At other times, it is the total amount of a flavor supplied by all vendors. Derived rows within the same table significantly complicate manipulation of rows and columns via relational operators. For example, counting all (nonaggregate) rows of the SUPPLY table in Figure 15.19 would involve excluding the duplicate (aggregate) rows. Accordingly, this tuning option is seldom (if ever) recommended.

Contrived substitute rows are "extra" rows that facilitate a specific access requirement. Usually substitute rows are added to overcome a shortcoming in a product's implementation of a relational manipulation operator. A common example is the insertion of "extra" rows to facilitate simulating the outer join operation.

ACCOMMODATING OUTER JOINS

Recall from Chapter 3 that an *outer join* is a join that returns not only rows containing matching values for the joined columns, but also nonmatching rows from any one or more of the tables. Many relational products do not directly support the outer join (at least in earlier product releases). Instead, you may

SUPPLIER NAME	PART NAME
Davis Co.	bolt
Tojas, Inc.	bolt
– – – – –	bumper
– – – – –	wheel
J&JS, Inc.	– – –

FIGURE 15.20 Supplier/part report involving outer join.

have to accommodate outer join requirements by simulating the outer join using alternative DML syntax or by modifying your relational database structure.

As an example of an outer join requirement, assume you need to produce the report in Figure 15.20 from the supplier logical data model (Figure 15.1). This report lists the names of suppliers and the names of parts they supply. The report includes suppliers who supply no parts (i.e., suppliers not associated with parts in the SUPPART table). It also includes parts with no suppliers (i.e., with no SUPPART rows). Thus, producing the report entails the outer join operation. More specifically, producing the report entails two one-way outer joins: the outer join of SUPPLIER and SUPPART (including nonmatching rows from SUPPLIER) and the outer join of PART and SUPPART (including nonmatching rows from PART).

Your DBMS may not support an outer join operation. Thus, we describe several DML alternatives for simulating the outer join.

OPTION 1 FOR OUTER JOIN SIMULATION: UNION WITH NOT EXISTS SYNTAX. For our example, this option requires three SELECT clauses. The first retrieves matching (joined) rows. The second two retrieve nonmatching rows (excluded by the first join). The UNION stacks the results of the three SELECT clauses.

```
SELECT DISTINCT SUPPLIER.NAME, PART.NAME
FROM SUPPLIER, PART, SUPPART
WHERE SUPPLIER.NUMBER = SUPPART.SUPPLIER*NUMBER
AND PART.NUMBER = SUPPART.PART*NUMBER
UNION
SELECT DISTINCT '– – – – –', PART.NAME FROM PART
WHERE NOT EXISTS
        (SELECT * FROM SUPPART
        WHERE SUPPART.PART*NUMBER = PART.NUMBER)
UNION
SELECT DISTINCT SUPPLIER.NAME, '– – – ' FROM SUPPLIER
WHERE NOT EXISTS
        (SELECT  * FROM SUPPART
        WHERE SUPPART.SUPPLIER*NUMBER = SUPPLIER.NUMBER)
```

OPTION 2 FOR OUTER JOIN SIMULATION: UNION WITH NOT IN SYNTAX. Some products do not support the EXISTS operator. In this case, you can use the following syntax to perform the same functions as in option 1.

```
SELECT DISTINCT SUPPLIER.NAME, PART.NAME
FROM SUPPLIER, PART, SUPPART
WHERE SUPPLIER.NUMBER = SUPPART.SUPPLIER*NUMBER
AND PART.NUMBER = SUPPART.PART*NUMBER
UNION
SELECT DISTINCT '- - - - - ', PART.NAME FROM PART
WHERE PART.NUMBER NOT IN
     (SELECT PART*NUMBER FROM SUPPART)
UNION
SELECT DISTINCT SUPPLIER.NAME, '- - - ' FROM SUPPLIER
WHERE SUPPLIER.NUMBER NOT IN
     (SELECT SUPPLIER*NUMBER FROM SUPPART)
```

OPTION 3 FOR OUTER JOIN SIMULATION: INSERT INTO TEMPORARY TABLE. Many products also do not support the UNION operator. In that case, neither option 1 nor option 2 will work as is. Instead, use the SELECT syntax from option 1 or 2, but insert the results of each SELECT into a temporary table. Specifically:

1. Create a temporary table to hold SUPPLIER.NAME and PART.NAME.

```
CREATE TABLE TEMPOUTJOIN
     (SUPNAME...,
     PARTNAME...)
```

2. Retrieve matching rows by joining SUPPLIER, SUPPART, and PART (first SELECT clause of option 1 or 2) and insert them into the temporary table.

```
INSERT INTO TEMPOUTJOIN (SUPNAME,PARTNAME)
     SELECT DISTINCT SUPPLIER.NAME, PART.NAME
     FROM SUPPLIER, PART, SUPPART
     WHERE SUPPLIER.NUMBER = SUPPART.SUPPLIER*NUMBER
     AND PART.NUMBER = SUPPART.PART*NUMBER
```

3. Retrieve nonmatching rows from SUPPLIER and PART (using NOT IN or NOT EXISTS as in the last two SELECT clauses of option 1 or 2) and insert them into the temporary table.

```
INSERT INTO TEMPOUTJOIN (SUPNAME, PARTNAME)
     SELECT '- - - - -', PART.NAME FROM PART
     WHERE PART.NUMBER NOT IN
          (SELECT PART*NUMBER FROM SUPPART)
INSERT INTO TEMPOUTJOIN (SUPNAME,PARTNAME)
     SELECT SUPPLIER.NAME, '- - -' FROM SUPPLIER
     WHERE SUPPLIER.NUMBER NOT IN
          (SELECT SUPPLIER*NUMBER FROM SUPPART)
```

4. Retrieve all rows from the temporary table for return to the user.

```
SELECT DISTINCT SUPNAME, PARTNAME FROM TEMPOUTJOIN
```

5. Delete all rows from (or drop) the temporary table (to clean up for the next execution).

```
DROP TEMPOUTJOIN
```

OPTION 4 FOR OUTER JOIN SIMULATION: INSERT INTO A SEQUENTIAL FILE. This option is similar to option 3. Instead of creating a relational table to hold the interim results, you create an ordinary (nonrelational) file.

Depending on your DBMS product, there undoubtedly are other DML variations that can achieve the effect of an outer join. Sometimes, all these DML options either are not supported by the product or are unacceptably slow or costly. In this case, you may consider introducing duplicate or "extra" (other-

FIGURE 15.21 Facilitating the outer join by adding rows.

SUPPLIER

NUMBER (PK)	NAME	ADDRESS	CREDIT—TERMS
21	Davis Co.	OH	30 days
98	Tojas, Inc.	FL	60 days
142	J&JS, Inc.	NV	10 days
0	null	null	null

PART

NUMBER (PK)	NAME	SIZE
6	bolt	.75 in
5	bolt	1.00 in
2	bumper	3.00 ft
3	wheel	26.00 in
0	null	null

SUPPART

SUPPLIER*NUMBER (PK,FK1)	PART*NUMBER (PK,FK2)	PRICE—AMOUNT
21	6	1.00
98	6	.55
21	5	1.50
142	0	0
0	2	0
0	3	0

wise unnecessary) rows or columns to effect an outer join with an ordinary (inner) join operator (i.e., the SQL WHERE `tablel.columnl = table2.column2` syntax). Option 5 involves adding extra rows to the joined tables, so that, in effect, all rows do match.

OPTION 5 FOR OUTER JOIN SIMULATION: ADDING EXTRA ROWS. You can facilitate the outer join in Figure 15.20 by adding rows to SUPPART to represent parts with no suppliers and suppliers with no parts. Represent the nonexistent supplier or part numbers in these rows by default values as in Figure 15.21. Moreover, establish rows for the default values in the SUPPLIER and PART tables. Then joins will automatically include "nonmatching" parts and suppliers since, actually, now they all match.

RULE RDD11.12

To effect an *outer join,* consider *adding rows* to the joined tables, so that, in effect, all rows match. However, do so only after evaluating DML alternatives for simulating an outer join, such as

☐   UNION, NOT EXISTS syntax
☐   UNION, NOT IN syntax
☐   Insert into temporary table
☐   Insert into nonrelational file

After adding the extra rows to SUPPLIER, PART, and SUPPART, you can produce the SUPPLIER/PART report in Figure 15.20 using the following SQL syntax:

```
SELECT SUPPLIER.NAME, PART.NAME
FROM SUPPLIER, PART, SUPPART
WHERE SUPPLIER.NUMBER = SUPPART.SUPPLIER*NUMBER
AND PART.NUMBER = SUPPART.PART*NUMBER
```

In fact, if you want a report that excludes "nonmatching" rows (suppliers with no parts and parts with no suppliers), you must code extra logic:

```
SELECT SUPPLIER.NAME, PART.NAME
FROM SUPPLIER, PART, SUPPART
WHERE SUPPLIER.NUMBER = SUPPART.SUPPLIER*NUMBER
AND PART.NUMBER = SUPPART.PART*NUMBER
AND SUPPART.SUPPLIER*NUMBER <> 0
AND SUPPART.PART*NUMBER <> 0
```

If there are a lot of "nonmatching" rows, option 5 for simulating an outer join may entail adding a lot of extra rows (e.g., to SUPPART in Figure 15.21). In this case, option 6 may be preferable.

OPTION 6 FOR OUTER JOIN SIMULATION: CONTRIVING SUBSTITUTE COLUMNS. Option 6 adds one column and potentially one row to each table involved in an outer join. For example, in Figure 15.22, several columns and rows have been added to SUPPLIER, PART, and SUPPART.

First, to facilitate the outer join of SUPPLIER and SUPPART,

☐   SUPPART–JOIN–FLAG column is added to SUPPLIER. SUPPART–JOIN–FLAG is set to 'X' for rows with no matching SUPPART row. Otherwise, SUPPART–JOIN–FLAG is null.

FIGURE 15.22 Facilitating the outer join by contriving substitute columns.

SUPPLIER

NUMBER (PK)	NAME	ADDRESS	CREDIT–TERMS	SUPPART–JOIN–FLAG (JF)
21	Davis Co.	OH	30 days	null
98	Tojas, Inc.	FL	60 days	null
142	J&JS, Inc.	NV	10 days	X
0	null	null	null	null

PART

NUMBER (PK)	NAME	SIZE	SUPPART–JOIN–FLAG (JF)
6	bolt	.75 in	null
5	bolt	1.00 in	null
2	bumper	3.00 ft	X
3	wheel	26.00 in	X
0	null	null	null

SUPPART

SUPPLIER*NUMBER (PK,FK1)	PART*NUMBER (PK,FK2)	PRICE– AMOUNT	SUPPLIER–JOIN FLAG (JF1)	PART–JOIN– FLAG (JF2)
21	6	1.00	null	null
98	6	.55	null	null
21	5	1.50	null	null
null	0	null	X	null
0	null	null	null	X

□   SUPPLIER–JOIN–FLAG column is added to SUPPART. SUPPLIER–JOIN–FLAG is set to null for all existing SUPPART rows.

□   One new row is added to SUPPART. SUPPLIER–JOIN–FLAG in this new row is set to 'X' (to enable joining this row to any "nonmatching" SUPPLIER row, which likewise has SUPPART–JOIN–FLAG set to 'X'). SUPPLIER* NUMBER in the new row is set to null (*not* to a default value! See explanation below). Any other columns in this new row which may be referenced in a join operation are set to the default value for the respective column. For instance, in Figure 15.22, PART*NUMBER in this new row is set to 0. Any columns in the new row that will never be joined can be set to either nulls or default values.

□   If necessary, one new row is added to every other table to which SUPPART might be joined, representing the default value of the joined column. Thus, in Figure 15.22 a new row is added to the PART table containing the default value of 0 in the PART.NUMBER column and containing nulls or default values in every other column. (Note: Such columns *must* be set to default values rather than nulls if they, too, might be joined; likewise, those default values must correspond to default value rows in the joined tables—see Rule RDD6.6.)

Second, to facilitate the outer join of PART and SUPPART,

□   SUPPART–JOIN–FLAG is added to PART. SUPPART–JOIN–FLAG is set to 'X' for rows with no matching SUPPART row. Otherwise, SUPPART–JOIN–FLAG is null.

□   PART–JOIN–FLAG is added to SUPPART. PART–JOIN–FLAG is null for all existing SUPPART rows.

□   One (additional) new row is added to SUPPART. PART–JOIN–FLAG in this new row is set to 'X' (to enable joining this row to any "nonmatching" PART row, which likewise has SUPPART–JOIN–FLAG set to 'X'). PART* NUMBER in the new row is set to null (*not* to a default value). Likewise, any other join flag columns in this row (such as SUPPLIER–JOIN–FLAG) are set to null. Any other columns in the new row which may be referenced in a join operation are set to the default value for the respective column. For instance, in Figure 15.22, SUPPLIER*NUMBER in this new row is set to 0. Any columns in the new row that will never be joined can be set to either nulls or default values.

□   If necessary, one new row is added to every other table to which SUPPART might be joined, representing the default value of the joined column. Thus, in Figure 15.22 a new row is added to SUPPLIER containing the default value of 0 in the SUPPLIER.NUMBER column and containing nulls or default values in every other column. (Note: Such columns *must* be set to default values rather than nulls if they, too, might be joined; likewise, those default values must correspond to default value rows in the joined tables—see Rule RDD6.6.)

RULE RDD11.13

To effect an *outer join,* consider *contriving columns* to substitute for the joined columns in nonmatching rows. (This will include nonmatching rows in the result.) Do so in preference to adding extra rows (Rule RDD11.12) when the number of extra rows is excessive. However, consider DML alternatives (see Rule RDD11.12) first.

The SQL request to retrieve matching and nonmatching parts and suppliers is as follows:

```
SELECT DISTINCT SUPPLIER.NAME, PART.NAME
FROM SUPPLIER, PART, SUPPART
WHERE (SUPPLIER.NUMBER = SUPPART.SUPPLIER*NUMBER
    OR SUPPLIER.SUPPART-JOIN-FLAG = SUPPART.SUPPLIER-JOIN-FLAG)
AND (PART.NUMBER = SUPPART.PART*NUMBER
    OR PART.SUPPART-JOIN-FLAG = SUPPART.PART-JOIN-FLAG)
```

Each row returned by the SQL request meets one and only one of the following criteria sets:

1. SUPPLIER.NUMBER = SUPPART.SUPPLIER*NUMBER
AND

PART.NUMBER = SUPPART.PART*NUMBER

These are the rows that match (i.e., there are matching rows in SUPPLIER, SUPPART and PART because the suppliers supply parts, and the suppliers and parts exist in the SUPPLIER and PART tables).

2. SUPPLIER.SUPPART-JOIN-FLAG = SUPPART.SUPPLIER-JOIN-FLAG = 'X'
AND

PART.NUMBER = SUPPART.PART*NUMBER = 0

These are the suppliers with no matching supplier number in SUPPART (because they supply no parts).

3. PART.SUPPART-JOIN-FLAG = SUPPART.PART-JOIN-FLAG = 'X'
AND

SUPPLIER.NUMBER = SUPPART.SUPPLIER*NUMBER = 0

These are the parts with no matching part number in SUPPART (because they are not supplied by any supplier).

Notice that any row in SUPPART has a null value *either* in SUPPLIER*NUMBER or in SUPPLIER-JOIN-FLAG. Likewise, each row in SUPPART has a null value *either* in PART*NUMBER or in PART-JOIN-FLAG. This ensures that particular SUPPLIER and SUPPART rows can be joined on either supplier number or the join flag. Similarly, particular PART and SUPPART rows can be joined on either part number or the join flag. This fact is due to the relational model property that nulls are not considered equal (or unequal) and thus never produce a match in a join. (In fact, if your product does otherwise, the outer join solution outlined here will not work for you!) This is an example when nulls are useful and are *not* easily replaced by default values. If you prefer default values over nulls for your join flag columns, you must establish different default values for each side of a join flag pair so that they do not produce a join match. For instance, default values for SUPPLIER.SUPPART–JOIN–FLAG and SUPPART. SUPPLIER–JOIN–FLAG must be different. That is, in Figure 15.22, the value in SUPPLIER.SUPPART–JOIN–FLAG for "matching" suppliers (suppliers 21, 98, and 0) must not be the same as the value in SUPPART.SUPPLIER–JOIN–FLAG for those suppliers (21, 98, and 0). Otherwise, those suppliers' rows will match with SUPPART not only on supplier number, but also on the join flag. Likewise, default values for PART.SUPPART–JOIN–FLAG and SUPPART.PART–JOIN–FLAG must be different.

Note the new notation used in the relational table diagrams in Figure 15.22:

JF (or JF*n*)   join flag, or column contrived as a substitute join column for "nonmatching" rows

A final option for simulating an outer join is to combine the tables into one table reflecting the results of an outer join. This option is addressed in Chapter 16.

The outer join is just one example of a functional requirement that may not be adquately supported by your product's DML. Other functional limitations, specific to your product, also may require introduction of controlled redundant ("extra") data or even modification of the database structure (Chapter 16). Thus, adding duplicate columns or rows may be motivated by functional inadequacies, performance problems, or a combination of both.

IMPLEMENTATION TIPS AND TECHNIQUES

In evaluating whether and where to introduce duplicate data, proceed as follows. The first six tips and techniques involve copies and derivations of existing columns.

1. *Identify critical requests involving multitable access.* Study proposed DML in search of joins, subqueries, unions, or multiple DML statements.
2. For each multitable access request, *identify table accesses for which denormalization would be too costly.* These are accesses that involve many columns in multiple tables or columns that are frequently updated.
3. *Evaluate costs and benefits of selective denormalization for the remaining multitable accesses.*
4. *Consider the effects of your proposed denormalization options on other requirements.*
5. *Review your logical data model for derived attributes.* Evaluate whether to store these derived attributes, considering performance implications and DML functionality limitations.

6. *Review proposed DML and programming code for additional candidate derived columns.* Evaluate tradeoffs of storage versus dynamic calculation.

The seventh technique concerns representing repeating groups.

7. *Evaluate row versus column representation of repeating groups that have a fixed number of occurrences, each with a different meaning—particularly time-dependent data.* Where users refer to the need for "arrays" (frequently implying different meanings for particular occurrences), consider storing such repeating groups as columns.

The eighth relates to contriving substitutes for existing columns.

8. *Examine "large" primary keys, particularly those referenced by foreign keys in many tables.* Calculate the impact on storage and performance. Consider contriving substitute columns.

The final technique concerns outer joins or other functions not adequately supported by the DBMS.

9. *Identify requirements for functions (such as the outer join) that are not supported adequately by your product.* Evaluate alternative DML syntax versus introduction of duplicate rows or columns to accommodate these requirements.

C A S E   S T U D Y

Let us evaluate where controlled duplicate data might be useful in the Moon Launch passenger reservations database. As in earlier chapters, focus primarily on requests T13, T14 and T33. Refer to the case study in Chapter 13 for a full description of these requests.

First, identify critical requests involving multitable access. Of the three requests, only T13 and T14 access multiple tables.

Second, identify table accesses that are difficult to avoid.

T13—PROVIDE PRICE QUOTE FOR A PASSENGER FOR A SPECIFIC FLIGHT

The RESERVATION table is accessed to determine whether there is an available reservation (i.e., to count existing reservations for a flight). You may instead consider storing the count of reservations as a derived column in the FLIGHT–SCHEDULE table.

The PASSENGER table is accessed to determine whether the passenger is an existing passenger with Moon Launch Enterprise. Because this is a check for existence (hence, to preserve integrity), it cannot be avoided.

The BSNSS–PASSENGER and VCTN–PASSENGER tables are accessed to determine whether the passenger booking the reservation is known as a business or vacation passenger (depending on the kind of reservation being placed). This access cannot be avoided unless a duplicate column denoting vacation or business passenger is stored in PASSENGER.

The BSNSS–PASSENGER, BUSINESS, VCTN–PASSENGER, and CREDIT–RATING tables are accessed to obtain CREDIT–RATING.DISCOUNT–AMOUNT. You might consider storing an exact copy of this column in the BUSINESS, BSNSS–PASSENGER, and/or VCTN–PASSENGER tables.

The FLIGHT table is accessed to determine the standard fare amount; this cannot easily be avoided.

T14—BOOK A RESERVATION

PASSENGER is accessed to determine and perhaps decrement the PASSENGER.CANC–CREDIT–COUNT; therefore, this access cannot be avoided.

BSNSS–PASSENGER is accessed to determine the BUSINESS*COUNTRY–NAME, BUSINESS*NAME of the passenger placing the reservation; this access, therefore, cannot be avoided unless these columns also are stored in PASSENGER.

BSNSS–PASSENGER also is accessed to obtain all other passengers from the same BUSINESS*COUNTRY–NAME, BUSINESS*NAME. You might consider duplicating these columns in RESERVATION.

RESERVATION is accessed to count the number of reservations on this flight for other passengers from the same business. You might consider storing this count per flight per business in the FLIGHT–SCHEDULE table.

RESERVATION also is accessed to insert a new reservation and potentially to further discount the fares for reservations for other passengers from the same business. These accesses cannot be avoided.

FLIGHT–SCHEDULE is accessed to update the FLIGHT–SCHEDULE.STATUS–CODE. Thus, this access cannot be avoided.

The third task is to evaluate selective denormalization.

T13—PROVIDE A PRICE QUOTE FOR A PASSENGER FOR A SPECIFIC FLIGHT

For T13, there are three types of table accesses that potentially can be avoided: (1) RESERVATION table to count reservations for a given scheduled flight, (2) VCTN–PASSENGER and BSNSS–PASSENGER to determine if the passenger is known as either (depending on the kind of reservation being placed), and (3) VCTN–PASSENGER, BSNSS–PASSENGER, BUSINESS, and CREDIT–RATING tables to determine DISCOUNT–AMOUNT.

First, how can you eliminate the dynamic count of reservations? You have two options: store RESERVATION–COUNT by FLIGHT*NUMBER, DEPARTURE–DATE in the FLIGHT–SCHEDULE table, or store FLIGHT–FULL–FLAG in the FLIGHT–SCHEDULE table indicating whether the flight is full. Storing RESERVATION–COUNT probably is preferable to storing FLIGHT–FULL–FLAG. With storage of RESERVATION–COUNT, updates to the RESERVATION table trigger simple additions to or subtractions from this column. If, instead, you store FLIGHT–FULL–FLAG, many RESERVATION updates would require recounting existing reservations to determine whether a new reservation fills the flight.

On the other hand, dynamic calculation of RESERVATION–COUNT involves only one table (RESERVATION table), can be expressed using the SQL built-in COUNT function, and may access only 100 or fewer rows (since a full flight has 100 reservations)—assuming appropriate access mechanisms are in place to avoid a full table scan. If the RESERVATION table is clustered by FLIGHT*NUMBER and DEPARTURE–DATE, obtaining these rows may require only one I/O (depending on row size, buffer size, and potential index I/O). Because of the high volume of RESERVATION updates, however, you may decide not to cluster RESERVATION. In that case, accessing up to 100 rows may involve a table scan or perhaps index plus corresponding table I/Os. If these options are unacceptable, consider storing RESERVATION–COUNT in the FLIGHT–SCHEDULE table. The storage space needed is minimal (perhaps an integer value for each of 1500 FLIGHT–SCHEDULE rows). However, the many updates to the RESERVATION table must now also access and update this new column.

What about storing columns in PASSENGER indicating whether the passenger is known as a BSNSS–PASSENGER or VCTN–PASSENGER? Doing so saves access to only one row per execution of T13 (by primary key) to the BSNSS–PASSENGER or VCTN–PASSENGER table. Thus, these duplicate columns may not be worth the overhead.

What about duplicating CREDIT–RATING.DISCOUNT–AMOUNT in any combination of BUSINESS, BSNSS–PASSENGER or VCTN–PASSENGER? The CREDIT–RATING table is extremely small (four rows). Thus, duplicating DISCOUNT–AMOUNT will save very few I/Os (perhaps only one or even none, depending on buffer contents, per T13 execution). Also note that you anticipate relatively frequent changes in the DISCOUNT–AMOUNT schedule (transaction T3). Therefore, duplicating the column probably is not beneficial.

T14—BOOK A RESERVATION

Table accesses that can potentially be avoided include BSNSS–PASSENGER, to determine the BUSINESS*COUNTRY–NAME, BUSINESS*NAME of the passenger placing the reservation; BSNSS–PASSENGER, to obtain other passengers from the same business; or RESERVATION, to count reservations on this flight for those passengers.

Access to BSNSS–PASSENGER for BUSINESS*COUNTRY–NAME, BUSINESS*NAME for the passenger placing the reservation involves access to only one row per T14 execution. Thus, the overhead of denormalizing these columns may not be warranted.

How might you expedite (that is, avoid access to BSNSS–PASSENGER or RESERVATION for) the count of reservations on this flight for other passengers from the same business? Alternatives include the following:

1. Create a new table with primary key FLIGHT*NUMBER,
   FLIGHT–SCHEDULE*DEPARTURE–DATE, BUSINESS*COUNTRY–NAME, and
   BUSINESS*NAME. Store the count in this table. You must update this table
   whenever you add or cancel a reservation for a business passenger.
2. Add the count by business to the FLIGHT–SCHEDULE table. Then the primary key of FLIGHT–SCHEDULE becomes FLIGHT*NUMBER, DEPARTURE–
   DATE, BUSINESS*COUNTRY–NAME, and BUSINESS*NAME. The table is no
   longer normalized because STATUS–CODE is determined by only part of the
   primary key (FLIGHT*NUMBER and DEPARTURE–DATE). Thus, STATUS–CODE
   contains redundant data across rows of the table.
3. Store, in the RESERVATION table, the BUSINESS*COUNTRY–NAME, BUSINESS*
   NAME for each BSNSS–PASSENGER who has a reservation. Reservations for
   VCTN–PASSENGERs would contain nulls or default values in these columns.
   You can then count reservations per business without accessing the
   BSNSS–PASSENGER table. You also can discount fares (if appropriate) for
   other passengers on this flight from the same business without ever accessing the BSNSS–PASSENGER table (not true of options 1 and 2).

These pose a variety of tuning options for T14, which are addressed in the Exercises.

The fourth task is to consider the effects of your proposed denormalization
options on other requirements. Consider request T33, which lists all flights that
are full. Suppose you decide to store a derived total RESERVATION–COUNT by
flight in FLIGHT–SCHEDULE (in tuning for T13, as discussed above). An index on
RESERVATION–COUNT might be useful for T33, but only if: FLIGHT–SCHEDULE
has enough rows to merit an index, typically only a small percentage of flights
are full, and the overhead of maintaining the index (due to RESERVATION table
updates) is acceptable.

If the output of T33 includes only FLIGHT*NUMBER and DEPARTURE–DATE,
you may evaluate instead adding RESERVATION–COUNT to the unique primary
key index for the FLIGHT–SCHEDULE table to facilitate index-only access. However, in either case, scanning the 1500 rows of FLIGHT–SCHEDULE may be
equally efficient.

The fifth task is to review your logical data model for derived attributes.
Referring to Figure 13.7, you see that RESERVATION.FARE–AMOUNT is flagged as
a derived attribute in the logical data model. However, recall that, after applying the discount due to a passenger's accumulated cancellation credit (based on
PASSENGER.CANC–CREDIT–COUNT—see triggering operation 2, Figure 9.11), you
can no longer derive the fare from other existing columns. Thus,
RESERVATION.FARE–AMOUNT, although derived, is not really redundant and
must be stored.

The sixth task is to review proposed DML and programming code for additional candidate derived columns. For this case study, you do not have access to
proposed DML (although, in reality, you may).

FLIGHT* NUMBER (PK, FK1)	DEPARTURE- DATE (PK)	ROW- NUMBER (PK)	STATUS- CODE	BSNSS* CNTRY- NAME1 (FK2)	BSNSS* NAME1 (FK2)	BSNSS% COUNT1 (DD)	BSNSS* CNTRY- NAME2 (FK3)	BSNSS* NAME2 (FK3)	BSNSS% COUNT2 (DD)
115	10/5/87	1	active	USA	ABC Co.	4	Canada	DEF Co.	1
115	10/5/87	2	active	Holland	GHI Co.	11	null	null	null
224	11/1/87	1	active	Germany	Tools, Inc.	7	null	null	null
115	12/1/87	1	active	Germany	Bolts, Inc.	0	Spain	Bolts, Inc.	54

FIGURE 15.23 Modified FLIGHT–SCHEDULE table with columnar repeating group.

The seventh task is to evaluate row versus column representation of repeating groups with a fixed number of occurrences. There are no obvious repeating groups having a fixed number of occurrences. There also are no time-dependent data, since the model reflects current information only—not historic information.

What about the modified FLIGHT–SCHEDULE table proposed in option 2 (or the similar proposal in option 1) for tuning request T14? You might consider representing reservation counts by business across columns. This alternative, illustrated in Figure 15.23, probably is undesirable for several reasons. First, an arbitrary number of businesses may place reservations on any given flight. Thus, the repeating group has an arbitrary number of occurrences. To accommodate these occurrences, you must add rows and another column (ROW–NUMBER) to the primary key. Because of the multiple rows per flight, STATUS–CODE is redundant across rows. Moreover, nulls or default values may appear in some rows. Finally, business rules for enforcing integrity become complicated due to the repeating foreign key columns, the appearance of nulls or default values, and the redundant STATUS–CODE column.

The eighth task is to evaluate "large" primary keys. The largest primary key is in the RESERVATION table. However, no foreign keys reference this primary key; thus, a contrived substitute column would not save space. Moreover, many accesses to RESERVATION are by partial primary key (FLIGHT*NUMBER, FLIGHT–SCHEDULE*DEPARTURE–DATE). For these requirements, a substitute column would not even simplify access.

The final task is to evaluate outer join requirements or other requests affected by the functional limitations of the DBMS. Requests T13, T14, and T33 do not involve an outer join.

SUMMARY

This chapter provided insight into realistic requirements for implementing relational databases where such databases do not comply exactly with underlying logical data models. These requirements revolve around *performance* or *functionality* inadequacies that exist in spite of and sometimes because of the stability of your initial relational database design.

Before turning to the guidelines in this and the next chapters, you should consider other alternatives, including establishing appropriate storage-related access mechanisms, adding indexes, experimenting with alternative DML syntax, and complementing your DML with other programming or processing techniques (e.g., non-SQL code, sort routines, user exits) if appropriate based on the nature and scope of the database project.

When these alternatives fail or are not appropriate, you can evaluate selective introduction of controlled data redundancy to accommodate your requirements. Most frequently, you may add duplicate columns to expedite frequent or critical lookup requests, to improve efficiency or performance of requests involving calculations, to simplify access to or perhaps to improve efficiency of repeating groups, to substitute for a long primary key and thereby simplify access or improve efficiency, or to overcome functionality limitations such as lack of an outer join operator. Less frequently, you may introduce "extra" rows to facilitate special functional requirements such as an outer join.

Such modifications, however, add complexity by affecting at least storage, naming conventions, data access, DML, performance, and data integrity. Thus, when resorting to such options, carefully evaluate pros and cons. Apply the rules in this chapter to minimize inadvertent destruction of the stability, flexibility, and integrity characterizing your logical data model.

EXERCISES

15.1 List at least five tuning options you should exploit prior to modifying compliance of your relational database structure to your logical data model.

15.2 What are five disadvantages of a relational database structure that does not conform exactly to an underlying logical data model?

15.3 Typically, you modify the relational database structure to facilitate *performance* or *functionality* requirements that cannot be accommodated in other ways. List at least three examples of performance requirements and three examples of functionality requirements that may benefit from structural modifications.

15.4 List four types of duplicate columns, describe the circumstances under which each is useful, and explain the associated advantages and disadvantages.

15.5 Evaluate duplicating BUSINESS*COUNTRY−NAME and BUSINESS*NAME in the RESERVATION table to expedite counting reservations per business and discounting fares (when appropriate) for other passengers on the same flight and from the same business (option 3 for tuning request T14 in the case study). What tuning techniques can you employ with this option to further increase efficiency of T14?

15.6 Evaluate storing flight reservation counts by business either in FLIGHT−SCHEDULE or in a new table (options 1 and 2 for tuning T14 in the case study). How do these options compare to option 3, evaluated in Exercise 15.5?

16

Tune by Redefining the Relational Database Structure

Steps RDD12 and RDD13 are the final steps in tuning your relational database design, except for addressing some special design challenges discussed in Chapter 17. Step RDD12 selectively redefines columns. Step RDD13 evaluates the rearrangement of entire tables. In some cases, these changes make mapping your design back to an underlying logical data model rather complex. They may affect the stability that results from a comprehensive, high-quality logical design, and the formulation of DML requests by users and programmers.

The design changes proposed in this chapter frequently are visible to users, particularly if users are familiar with the logical data model. Moreover, the changes often require definition and enforcement of new business rules to preserve data integrity. Thus, these techniques are not recommended for casual implementation. Rather, consider Steps RDD12 and RDD13 only to address performance and functionality problems that remain after you have exhausted the techniques suggested in earlier steps.

STEP RDD12: REDEFINE COLUMNS

Step RDD11 proposed addition of duplicate columns to improve performance or to overcome functionality limitations. Duplicate columns represent additions rather than actual changes to the logical data model. Step RDD12 proposes slightly more significant changes: defining columns to be different from the corresponding logical data model attributes. Some differences might be changes in domain characteristics. For instance, a particular product might not

475

support the data type or length defined for an attribute in the logical data model. Such domain differences are highly product-dependent. This chapter considers two general column deviations from the logical data model: reevaluating storage of long columns and selectively redefining foreign keys to reference alternate rather than primary keys.

REEVALUATING STORAGE OF LONG COLUMNS

Long columns usually contain textual data. Sample long columns include descriptions, memos, and miscellaneous notes. From a business perspective, defining such information as one column is logical, since it represents one data element to the user. Therefore, until now you have probably defined single columns to store textual data as depicted in Figure 16.1, perhaps assigning to the columns a maximum length (e.g., CHAR(500)) or a variable length (e.g., VARCHAR(500)).

Such textual columns can present funtionality and performance challenges. For instance, frequently a user may want not only to *equate* such columns to exact values, but also to *search* such columns for the occurrence of given character strings (e.g., WHERE EMPLOYEE.ADDRESS LIKE '%NJ%'). Your product may not support all the functional capabilities required to search columns in this way. Moreover, performance of queries involving these search functions may be less efficient than is matching on exact values. Finally, long or variable-length columns frequently waste a significant amount of storage associated with occurrence of nulls, default values, or values that are shorter than maximum length. This wasted space can lengthen the time for table scans and utility processing. Even if no space is wasted, the presence of long columns may significantly lengthen scans or utility processing as compared to the time that would be required to process only the nontextual (shorter) columns in a table.

Assessing these functionality or performance problems may lead you to redefine the textual columns as multiple shorter columns or as columns isolated to a separate table.

FIGURE 16.1 Textual data as one long column.

EQUIPMENT

NUMBER (PK)	NAME	PRICE	DESCRIPTION (500 characters)
10	phone	175	portable, pushbutton, collapsible antenna, radio
3	walkie talkie	75	cordless, two components, collapsible antenna, range 750 feet
15	deluxe phone	80	nonportable, dial, rhinestone digits, flowered base, night light

EQUIPMENT

NUMBER (PK)	NAME	PRICE	DESCRIPTION (25 characters)
10	phone	175	portable, pushbutton
3	walkie talkie	75	cordless, two components
15	deluxe phone	80	rhinestone, night light

FIGURE 16.2 Textual data limited to a shorter column.

RULE RDD12.1

Evaluate redefining a *long or variable-length textual column* as one of the following:

☐ Short column of abstracted text
☐ Long column in a separate table
☐ Short column in the existing table plus a long column in a separate overflow table
☐ Multiple occurrences (rows) of fixed-length columns in a separate table

Consider each design alternative:

☐ *Redefine a column as a short column of abstracted text.* This implies limiting textual columns to a reasonable length. (Perhaps users will accept storage of the first 80 characters, or perhaps they can develop 80-character abstracts.) See Figure 16.2.

☐ *Store a long column in a table of its own, separate from other columns.* This may not be efficient if users always access the textual data with other columns. (For more discussion of segmenting tables into multiple tables, see Step RDD13.) See Figure 16.3.

☐ *Store only the first n characters or a short abstract in the table.* Create a separate table for rows that require more characters. See Figure 16.4.

☐ *Divide the text into subsets (e.g., 80-character lines) and store multiple rows per each occurrence of text in a separate description table.* An example is given in Figure 16.5.

Any of these alternatives may be appropriate, depending on your users' access requirements, users' willingness to truncate or abstract the text, and DBMS support for special text data types and text-processing functions.

SELECTIVELY REDEFINING FOREIGN KEYS

Until now, all foreign keys in your design reference primary keys. Thus, the same set of attributes is always used to identify a row in a table, no matter from where it is referenced.

EQUIPMENT

NUMBER (PK)	NAME	PRICE
10	phone	175
3	walkie talkie	75
15	deluxe phone	80

EQUIPMENT–DESCRIPTION

EQUIPMENT* NUMBER (PK, FK1)	DESCRIPTION (500 characters)
10	portable, pushbutton, collapsible antenna, radio
3	cordless, two components, collapsible antenna, range 750 feet
15	nonportable, dial, rhinestone digits, flowered base, night light

FIGURE 16.3 Textual data stored in a separate table.

You may find that some requests involve multitable access (e.g., joins) solely to retrieve alternate key columns from tables referenced by foreign keys. There are two ways to eliminate such access: You can copy the alternate key columns as duplicate columns into the referencing tables (see Rule RDD11.1), or you can replace the foreign key (originally referencing the primary key) with an alternate key such that the joins are no longer required.

FIGURE 16.4 Textual data stored across two tables.

EQUIPMENT

NUMBER (PK)	NAME	PRICE	SHORT–DESCRIPTION (25 characters)
10	phone	175	portable, pushbutton
3	walkie talkie	75	cordless, two components
15	deluxe phone	80	rhinestone, night light

EQUIPMENT–DESCRIPTION

EQUIPMENT*NUMBER (PK, FK1)	LONG–DESCRIPTION (500 characters)
10	collapsible antenna, radio
3	collapsible antenna, range 750 feet
15	nonportable, dial, rhinestone digits, flowered base, night light

EQUIPMENT

NUMBER (PK)	NAME	PRICE
10	phone	175
3	walkie talkie	75
15	deluxe phone	80

EQUIPMENT–DESCRIPTION

EQUIPMENT*NUMBER (PK, FK1)	LINE–NUMBER (PK)	DESCRIPTION (35 characters)
10	1	portable, pushbutton
10	2	collapsible antenna, radio
3	1	cordless, two components
3	2	collapsible antenna, range 750 feet
15	1	nonportable, dial
15	2	rhinestone digits, flowered base
15	3	night light

FIGURE 16.5 Textual data stored as multiple rows.

RULE RDD12.2

Consider selective *redefinition of foreign keys* to reference alternate rather than primary keys when

□ Such redefinition eliminates multitable access and improves performance of critical requests
□ Referenced alternate keys do not allow nulls
□ Referential integrity still can be enforced

Consider the school logical data model in Figure 16.6. SCHOOL is related to both COURSE and STUDENT via foreign keys referencing its primary key, SCHOOL* NUMBER. Suppose, however, that the most frequent access to the STUDENT table is to list attendance rosters including school name, student name and student address (as in Figure 16.7). Requirements involving the COURSE table, on the other hand, typically include SCHOOL*NUMBER, treating it as part of a composite course identification code. Thus, a database design facilitating more efficient production of attendance rosters would replace the foreign key in STUDENT (SCHOOL*NUMBER) with the alternate key of SCHOOL (SCHOOL*NAME), as shown in Figure 16.8. This design is possible only if SCHOOL.NAME (in the SCHOOL table) is

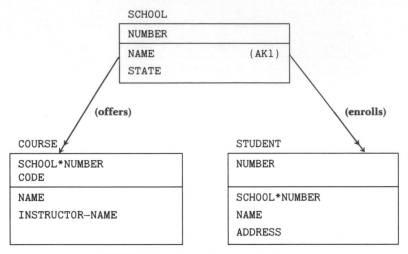

FIGURE 16.6 School logical data model.

never null (at least for all schools enrolling students). If SCHOOL.NAME is null for a particular row in SCHOOL, that SCHOOL row cannot be related (via SCHOOL* NAME) to any STUDENT rows.

Redefining foreign keys to reference alternate keys has two negative implications. First, it increases complexity for users. Users must remember when to relate tables through alternate/foreign keys versus primary/foreign keys. For instance, in Figure 16.8, users must know that SCHOOL and COURSE are joined on SCHOOL*NUMBER, and SCHOOL and STUDENT are joined on SCHOOL*NAME. Second, it involves potential loss of automated referential integrity mechanisms. Depending on your product, DDL syntax may automatically enforce some referential integrity rules—but perhaps only for foreign keys that reference the primary key of a table. Enforcing relationships rules for foreign keys that reference alternate keys may require less desirable implementation options (i.e., other than DDL). Thus, evaluate redefinition of foreign keys carefully and be

FIGURE 16.7 School attendance roster.

School Name	Student Name	Student Address
Princeton	Tom Chase	Burlington, VT
Columbia	Bill Maynard	Atlanta, GA
Barnard	Lisa Gordon	San Francisco, CA
SMU	Casey Adams	Phoenix, AZ

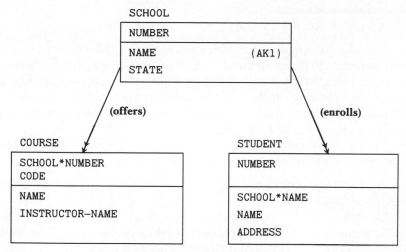

FIGURE 16.8 School relational database with a redefined foreign key in STUDENT.

sure the performance advantages for specific requests outweigh the disadvantages.

IMPLEMENTATION TIPS AND TECHNIQUES

Spend some time analyzing the attributes in your logical data model and the columns in your relational database design. Consider redefining columns under the following circumstances:

1. *Are any attributes defined with structural domain characteristics (i.e., data types and lengths) that your DBMS does not support (or does not support efficiently)?* If so, evaluate product-specific implications of defining the columns differently.
2. *Are there columns that are equal to or longer than 25 characters?* If so, treat these as long textual columns and consider the alternatives for storing text. In particular, look for a natual way of subdividing such columns. For example, can the data in a COMMENTS column be subdivided by date or by person? Can data in a MISCELLANEOUS NOTES or ITEM DESCRIPTION column be dissected into pages and lines and thus stored as several rows in a table rather than as one large row?
3. *Are there frequent or critical requests that use foreign keys to relate multiple tables solely to obtain alternate keys?* If so, evaluate pros and cons of selectively redefining some foreign keys to reference alternate keys. Would the same users have to relate tables via primary/foreign keys in some cases and alternate/foreign keys in other cases? Are there any implications for referential integrity?

C A S E   S T U D Y

Let us revisit the passenger reservations database for Moon Launch Enterprise.

First, are any attributes defined with structural domain characteristics (i.e., data types and lengths) that your DBMS does not support (or does not support efficiently)? For the case study, assume that all data types are supported adequately, with the exception of very long or variable-length columns. There do not appear to be any variable-length columns.

Second, are there columns that are equal to or longer than 25 characters? There are three types of columns that qualify as long columns:

☐ Names (BUSINESS.COUNTRY-NAME, BUSINESS.NAME, PASSENGER.COUNTRY-NAME, PASSENGER.FIRST-NAME, PASSENGER.LAST-NAME, PASSENGER.MIDDLE-NAME). There is no natural way to divide these columns into smaller subsets. In fact, you have already dissected passenger name into FIRST-NAME, LAST-NAME, MIDDLE-NAME, and TITLE-NAME.

☐ Addresses (BUSINESS.BILLING-ADDRESS, PASSENGER.ADDRESS). You might consider dividing these into component columns (STREET-NUMBER, STREET-NAME, TOWN-NAME, STATE-NAME, ZIP-CODE). However, storing all or part of the addresses in a separate table increases multitable access and degrades efficiency. Since the addresses are not extremely long, probably you should leave them as defined in the logical data model.

☐ Code (PASSENGER.CODE). This column is 25 characters. There is no natural way to divide it into smaller subsets. It probably makes little sense to store it in a separate table, especially since it serves as a primary and foreign key. If it were too long to be an efficient key, you would have considered contriving a substitute column in Step RDD11.

Third, are there frequent or critical requests that use foreign keys to relate multiple tables solely to obtain alternate keys? The only alternate key is CONFIRMATION-NUMBER in the RESERVATION table. However, there are no foreign keys that reference the RESERVATION table. Thus, the option of selectively redefining foreign keys to reference alternate keys is not applicable.

STEP RDD13: REDEFINE TABLES

Deviations from your logical data model are most obvious when relational tables do not directly correspond to logical entities. Such discrepancies occur when you eliminate tables, duplicate tables, segment one table into several tables, or combine several tables into one table.

Elimination of tables involves very minor deviations from the logical data model. More precisely, elimination of tables implies narrowing the subset of the logical data model represented by the relational database design at this time. Obviously, you can add tables later.

Duplication of tables introduces data redundancy into the relational database. Such duplication requires new business rules and adds complexity, but does not otherwise degrade stability of your database.

Segmentation of a table into several tables destroys the 1 : 1 relationships between entities and tables. However, resulting tables are still in third normal form (if you apply appropriate rules for segmentation). Thus, although you increase complexity of your design and may need additional business rules, typically there is little or no other effect on stability. Further, frequently you can logically recreate the underlying entity by defining views that join or union the segmented tables.

Combining tables is more likely to result in tables that violate third normal form. Thus, additional business rules are critical for ensuring data integrity. Moreover, stability may deteriorate in the sense that your design may no longer be as easily extended to accommodate new requirements.

In applying any of these techniques, you alter your design to favor certain application requirements to the detriment of others. Thus, you consciously reduce the sharability of the database to improve its support for specific application functionality or performance requirements.

ELIMINATING TABLES

The first tuning possibility is to eliminate (choose not to create) some tables that are not really required. Probably, you identified such tables (entities) to represent business concepts or to add clarity to the logical data model. However, such tables may appear superfluous in your database design based on known information requirements.

RULE RDD13.1

In general, *eliminate* (choose not to create) *tables* that

- [ ] Add no new information
- [ ] Are not referenced by any (known) data requests

Tables add no new information when they have no nonkey attributes and their primary keys appear in child tables. You may have addressed this circumstance already by consolidating entities in your logical data model (Rule LDM6.15, Chapter 7). If you did not, however, evaluate now eliminating such tables.

For example, consider the category relationship illustrated in Figure 16.9. The PRODUCT supertype table adds no new information to the database. You

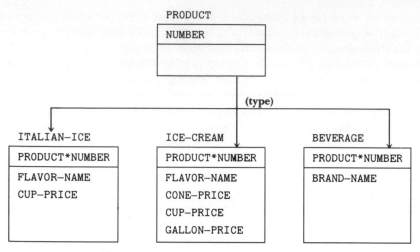

FIGURE 16.9 Ice-cream parlor product tables.

FIGURE 16.10 Ice-cream parlor sale tables.

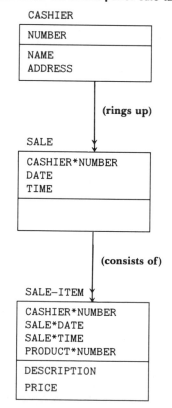

can access all PRODUCT numbers by unioning the subtype tables. Thus, you may eliminate the PRODUCT table. Of course, if your DBMS does not support the UNION operation and if you require access to all PRODUCT numbers together, you may have to simulate the UNION via other DML or create the PRODUCT table after all.

Consider a second example, shown in Figure 16.10. This model represents CASHIER, SALE, and SALE–ITEM. However, the SALE table contains no nonkey attributes. It adds no new information since you can obtain SALE information from SALE–ITEM (i.e., the primary key of SALE appears in SALE–ITEM). Thus, eliminate the SALE table from the database. You can always add it later if the user defines new nonkey attributes that logically belong in the SALE entity.

You also may have tables (entities) that include nonkey attributes that are never referenced by user requests. For instance, these tables may contain information not required until implementation of subsequent applications or phases. Wait to create such tables until they are needed, because requirements may change, necessitating design changes.

ADDING DUPLICATE TABLES

Sometimes, you may add entire tables that duplicate columns from existing tables. Three types of duplicate tables are possible: (1) tables comprising a subset of columns from one or more existing tables, (2) tables comprising a subset of rows from one or more existing tables, and (3) tables containing only columns that are summarized or derived from columns of one or more existing tables.

RULE RDD13.2

Consider adding *duplicate* (subset or derived) *tables:*

☐   To expedite frequent or critical requests
☐   To enable testing of new or ad hoc requests
☐   To facilitate requests involving only summarized or derived data

Duplicate tables containing a *subset of columns* from existing tables may be useful when your original tables contain "wide" rows—either many bytes or many columns. If critical or frequent requests reference only a small subset of those columns, you can consider duplicating them in another new table. Imagine, for example, a SUPPLIER table containing 1300 bytes in each row, when most requests need only 100 of those bytes. You may consider duplicating the 100 bytes in their own table. On the other hand, a better solution may be to *vertically segment* the table into two tables: one with 100 bytes and the other with the remaining 1200 bytes. We discuss this option in the next section.

Duplicate tables that contain a *subset of rows* from existing tables are more common and may be extremely useful for expediting access to very large tables (e.g., millions of rows, multiple gigabytes). The sheer volumes of such large tables may result in intolerable processing times for some requirements. You may consider duplicating a subset of rows in another table to expedite frequent or critical queries that reference only the subset. For example, if the most typically accessed rows of a SUPPLIER table are rows for a small number of preferred suppliers (perhaps 100 out of 2 million), you may consider duplicating these 100 suppliers in their own table. Perhaps a better alternative, however, is to *horizontally segment* the rows into two or more tables—one with 100 rows and the other with the remaining 1,999,900 rows—discussed in the next section.

Tables containing a subset of rows from existing tables are useful for testing requests that eventually will involve large data volumes. Frustration is magnified in an ad hoc environment when, after waiting a long time for the results of a request, users discover logic errors in their DML. Perhaps the result is incorrect (i.e., the users inadvertently asked for something other than what they wanted) or incomplete (i.e., the request requires additional parameters or selection criteria). Consider providing a set of smaller "test" tables—perhaps consisting of 3 percent of the rows from the large tables. Users and programmers can experiment against these subset tables to ensure that the request is correctly formulated. In this way, users access the large tables only when they are satisfied with the command formulation.

The third type of duplicate table contains only *derived/summarized columns*. You can even develop relational databases that consist totally of derived tables—for instance, providing roll-up data for a decision-support application or executive information system. Such a database may bear little resemblance to the detailed logical data model, because users are interested solely in summary information. Yet, developing a detailed logical data model is necessary for understanding the derivation of the summarized information and its relationship to other, perhaps source, databases.

For example, consider a PHONE-CALL entity as it might be defined by a telephone utility:

```
PHONE-CALL
┌─────────────────────────────┐
│ START-DATE                  │
│ START-TIME                  │
│ ORIG-AREA-CODE              │
│ ORIG-EXCH-CODE              │
│ ORIG-LINE-NUMBER            │
│ TERM-AREA-CODE              │
│ TERM-EXCH-CODE              │
│ TERM-LINE-NUMBER            │
├─────────────────────────────┤
│ CALLER*BILLING-NUMBER       │
│ DURATION-TIME               │
│ RATE-AMOUNT                 │
│ CALL%BILLING-AMOUNT    (d)  │
└─────────────────────────────┘
```

MONTHLY-BILL

CALLER* BILLING- NUMBER	MONTH-NAME	BILLED-AMOUNT	ORIG- AREA- CODE	TERM- AREA- CODE
132	Jan	130.00	201	212
132	Jan	65.00	201	916
156	Feb	76.00	617	914

ANNUAL-SMMRY-BILL

ORIG-AREA-CODE	TERM-AREA-CODE	BILLED-AMOUNT
201	212	150000.00
212	201	500000.00
617	201	16000.00
201	408	95000.00

FIGURE 16.11 Summarized phone call relational database, sample value listings.

This entity provides detail on the duration, rate, and billing number for every telephone call (identified by date and time of call placement, originating telephone number, and terminating telephone number). The entity also includes a derived attribute representing the amount billed for the call (derived by applying the rate to the duration).

Actual tables representing this information might be defined as in Figure 16.11. The MONTHLY-BILL table aggregates amounts billed by billing number, month, originating area code, and terminating area code. This table facilitates fast access to customer billing information for a customer service center responding to certain customer inquiries. It may even present the most detailed level for storing data; as telephone calls are placed, the system capturing data may automatically aggregate them into the MONTHLY-BILL table. If so, MONTHLY-BILL is not a duplicate table. ANNUAL-SMMRY-BILL, on the other hand, is a duplicate table summarizing data to an even higher level, by originating and terminating area codes for 12 months for all billable customers. ANNUAL-SMMRY-BILL is useful to benchmark proposed rate structures.

RULE RDD13.3

Treat columns in duplicate tables as *duplicate columns*. Specifically, apply Rules RDD11.5 and RDD11.6

- □ To document the duplicate columns in the data dictionary or catalog (Rule RDD11.5)
- □ To permit update of only the source (not the duplicate) columns (Rule RDD11.6)

□   To establish triggering operations on source columns to automatically cascade updates to duplicate columns (Rule RDD11.6)

Duplicate tables introduce the same complexities that arise with duplicate columns, because essentially such tables involve addition of many duplicate columns. New business rules must be defined to ensure synchronization of source and duplicate columns.

SEGMENTING TABLES

Segmenting tables is defining multiple tables to represent one entity in the logical data model. Do not confuse segmenting with partitioning, which is mapping one table into multiple physical storage structures, automatically managed by the DBMS (Chapter 13). When you partition a table, users and programmers are for the most part unaware of the partitioning, because they continue to formulate DML referencing only one table. When you segment a table, typically at least some if not all users are aware of the segmentation, because it results in more than one table. Specifically, users must know which rows and columns are assigned to which table (segment), and they must reference the correct table (segment) names in their DML.

Partitioning, then, represents a *physical* distribution of a table; you still define only one relational table. Segmentation is a *logical* distribution of an entity; you define more than one relational table. Recall also from Chapter 13 that you have already considered, and perhaps have implemented, partitioning. When partitioning is not available or is insufficient, you may now consider segmenting.

There are two ways to segment a table: horizontally (into groups of rows) and vertically (into groups of columns). Further, you can segment one table both horizontally and vertically into any number of new tables. Segmentation can provide a number of advantages:

□   *Performance*—Segmented tables are smaller and faster to scan. If you can limit scans to only one or a subset of table segments, performance improves.

□   *Data availability*—In a multiuser environment, locking at the row, block, or table level may impede concurrent access to the same table. Segmenting a table into separate tables may reduce locking contention. A user accessing one table (e.g., one segment) is less likely to affect access of another user to a separate table (e.g., separate segment).

   Utility processing such as backup, restore, or reorganization may make an entire table unavailable for other processing, depending on the DBMS. Segmentation into several tables may reduce the impact on concurrency in that, while you perform utility processing on one table (or segment), the other tables (and segments) are still available for user access.

□   *Administration and security*—Segmentation can facilitate assigning adminis-

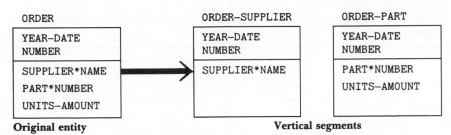

FIGURE 16.12 Sample vertical segmentation.

trative or security responsibilities based on entity subsets. Assume, for example, that each department owns, controls, or administers its departmental data. Segmenting one EMPLOYEE table into a set of departmental employee tables is conducive to establishing an administrator (space or security manager) for each table segment.

An alternative is to define views on subsets of a table, where such views support administrative and security requirements. However, views can introduce their own problems, as discussed in Chapter 17. Moreover, views may not be able to address all requirements—for instance, managing space allocation. Segmenting a table into more tables may be the better solution.

☐ *Geographical distribution*—Segmentation also can enable distributing subsets of a table to different nodes of a network.

The advantages of segmentation are not free. We discuss vertical and horizontal segmenting in more detail, with corresponding disadvantages.

SEGMENTING TABLES VERTICALLY. *Vertical segmentation* is splitting a table into multiple tables by assigning some columns (including the primary key) to one table and the remaining columns (also including the primary key) to another table. Conceptually, think of vertical segmentation as drawing vertical lines down the rows of a table to split it into several groups of columns, and then adding the primary key columns to each group.

Figure 16.12 illustrates vertical segmentation of an ORDER entity. One segment contains supplier information (SUPPLIER*NAME) for an order, and the other segment contains details about parts on an order (PART*NUMBER and UNITS—AMOUNT).

RULE RDD13.4

Consider *segmenting a table vertically* into separate tables if different users consistently access specific subsets of *columns* in the table. Consider not doing so if either of the following:

□   Other frequent or critical requests would reference multiple table segments
□   Update processing would span table segments

If groups of users consistently access well-defined subsets of columns in a table, segmenting the table vertically can provide the advantages we listed previously: improved scan performance, increased data availability, perhaps more decentralized administrative or security responsibilities, and potential geographical distribution. However, recall that the logical data model represents all such columns (attributes) in one table (entity) for *business* reasons, whereas vertical segmentation separates these columns for *access* reasons. Therefore, vertical segmentation carries with it the following disadvantages:

□   *Performance*—Although vertical segmentation improves performance for some requests, performance for other requests, requiring access to multiple segments, may deteriorate. Such access will involve joins, subqueries, or multiple DML statements.

□   *Visibility to users*—Users or programmers requiring access to multiple table segments must refer to multiple tables in DML. They will need to specify joins, subqueries, or multiple DML statements. (You may be able to mask the segmentation from many users by defining views that join the vertical segments—see Chapter 17.)

□   *Data integrity*—Update of columns spread across several segments (tables) will be more complex, especially because usually you cannot update views involving joins (see Chapter 17). Insertion and deletion of rows also will be more complex when columns of the rows reside in different tables.

   All segments of vertically segmented tables should have the same primary key. You must enforce primary key properties in each table segment. Moreover, all of the table segments are related to one another via 1 : 1 relationships. Thus, you must define and enforce new foreign keys with associated insert/delete/update rules.

□   *Storage*—Storage requirements will increase because each primary key value will be stored multiple times—once for each row in each table segment. Moreover, typically products assign each table to a different storage structure (e.g., file). Thus, extra storage may be required for control information associated with additional storage structures.

□   *Naming conventions*—You will need to choose names for the new tables. Try to choose a name for each that reflects the original entity as well as the subset of columns represented in the segment. In the previous example, the ORDER table became two tables named ORDER–SUPPLY and ORDER–PART corresponding to the original ORDER table and describing information particular to each segment (SUPPLY and PART).

Product restrictions may mandate vertical segmentation of a table. For example, a product may limit the number of columns or bytes per row of a table. Moreover, product-specific efficiency considerations may make vertical segmentation desirable. You may want to define row sizes such that one or a group of rows closely matches the size of a physical block (or other unit of storage) to optimize I/O efficiency. If original row sizes are too large or do not match block sizes, vertical segmentation can adjust row sizes.

RULE RDD13.5

In general, when segmenting a table vertically, store the *primary key* in every segment but each *nonkey column* in exactly one of the segments.

Storing the primary key in every segment is necessary to identify each row and enable relating rows of multiple segments. On the other hand, duplicating nonkey columns in multiple segments involves redundant data and associated integrity rules to avoid data inconsistency. Of course, after segmenting a table, you may decide *selectively* to introduce duplicate nonkey columns to enhance performance for particular access requests (Rule RDD11.1). In this case, consciously weigh the tradeoffs and, as appropriate, define and enforce additional insert/delete/update rules (Rule RDD11.6).

RULE RDD13.6

When segmenting a table vertically, include *every row in each segment* to avoid the need for outer joins.

Invariably you will have some requirements for data in multiple segments. Accommodating such requirements may involve joins matching primary keys across segments. Any row appearing in one but not all table segments will be excluded from the results unless you specify (or simulate) an outer join.

Thus, preferably avoid an outer join requirement by ensuring that every row in one segment corresponds to matching rows in all other segments. Moreover, maintain this correspondence by defining and enforcing *cascade* or *restrict* parent and child delete rules and *automatic* or *dependent* parent and child insert rules. (Note, of course, that you cannot define all of the delete rules as *restrict* or all of the insert rules as *dependent*—you would never be able to delete or insert any rows!)

Occurrence of a row in one segment and not in all others implies that some columns permit null values. Yet, if you have avoided nulls earlier by defining supertypes and subtypes or at least by assigning default values, you will automatically be in compliance with Rule RDD13.6.

SEGMENTING TABLES HORIZONTALLY. *Horizontal segmentation* is splitting a table into multiple tables by assigning a subset of rows to one table and the remaining rows to another table. Conceptually, think of horizontal segmentation as drawing horizontal lines through the columns of a relational table to split it into several groups of rows.

Figure 16.13 illustrates horizontal segmentation of an ORDER entity. Here, one segment contains orders for part numbers less than or equal to 100 and another segment contains orders for part numbers over 100. Both segments have exactly the same columns. Thus, the basis for horizontal segmentation is indicated only by descriptions of the tables (which should be recorded in your data dictionary) or perhaps by the table names.

RULE RDD13.7

Consider *segmenting a table horizontally* into separate tables if different users consistently access specific subsets of *rows* of the table. Consider not doing so if either of the following:

☐   Other frequent or critical requests would reference multiple table segments
☐   Update processing would span table segments

Horizontal segmentation also can provide the advantages described earlier: improved scan performance, increased data availability, perhaps more decentralized security or administrative responsibilities, and potential geographical distribution. However, you implement horizontal segmentation for *access* reasons, thereby deviating from strict compliance with the *business* definitions em-

FIGURE 16.13 Sample horizontal segmentation.

ORDER	ORDER–PARTS–TO–100	ORDER–PARTS–FROM–101
YEAR–DATE NUMBER	YEAR–DATE NUMBER	YEAR–DATE NUMBER
SUPPLIER*NAME PART*NUMBER UNITS–AMOUNT	SUPPLIER*NAME PART*NUMBER UNITS–AMOUNT	SUPPLIER*NAME PART*NUMBER UNITS–AMOUNT

Original entity   **Horizontal segments**

bodied in the logical data model. Therefore, horizontal segmentation has the following disadvantages:

- *Performance*—Some requests may require access to multiple horizontal segments. These requests will involve UNIONs or separate DML statements and may suffer in performance.
- *Visibility to users*—Users or programmers requiring access to multiple table segments must refer to multiple tables in DML. They will need to specify UNIONs or multiple DML statements. (You may be able to mask the segmentation by defining views that UNION the horizontal segments *if* your product supports the UNION operation in views—see Chapter 17.)
- *Data integrity*—Horizontal segmentation also can add complexity to update processing and enforcement of associated data integrity. Are insert, delete, and update routines defined for each segment? Do you implement the common logic as a set of subroutines, invoked by maintenance routines for each segment? Or do you define one set of routines that handle all the segments and dynamically determine which table to update?

   Each segment of a horizontally segmented table should have the same primary key. You must enforce primary key rules for each. Moreover, no two rows in different (as well as the same) horizontal segments should have identical primary key values. This is a new business rule that you should enforce.
- *Storage*—Horizontal segmentation does not involve additional storage for data, because every row is stored in exactly one segment. However, products typically assign each table to a different storage structure (e.g., file). Thus, extra storage may be required for the control information associated with additional storage structures.
- *Naming conventions*—You will need to name each resultant table. Again, choose names that reflect the original table plus describe the basis for segmentation. In the previous example, the ORDER table was horizontally segmented into the ORDER–PARTS–TO–100 and ORDER–PARTS–FROM–101 tables. The name of each segment incorporates the original ORDER table name and also conveys the logic of the segmentation.

Product restrictions may mandate horizontal segmentation of a table, although they typically do not. A product may limit the number of rows or maximum storage for a table. An example would be a restriction that rows of a table cannot occupy more than one disk volume.

RULE RDD13.8

In general, when segmenting a table horizontally, store *each row in exactly one* of the segments.

Storing the same row in two tables introduces duplicate data and potential data inconsistencies. If your users consistently access specific *overlapping* subsets of rows, you may choose to duplicate selected rows across multiple horizontal segments. However, then you also must implement maintenance routines ensuring synchronization of updates across segments. In general, the costs of such duplicate rows outweigh the potential benefits.

RULE RDD13.9

When segmenting a table horizontally, include *all columns in each segment* to avoid the need for outer unions.

Again, if you have avoided null values in your design, compliance with Rule RDD13.9 (as with Rule RDD13.6 for vertical segmentation) should be automatic. If, however, some columns permit nulls, and all rows of a particular horizontal table segment contain null values in a given column, be wary of the decision to exclude that column for the one segment. Doing so may complicate requests requiring unions of multiple segments unless you can specify (or simulate) an outer union. Recall from Chapter 3 that an *outer union* is the vertical stacking of tables to include even those columns from one table that have no counterpart in another table. Few relational products today support the outer union. Thus, avoid such requirements by ensuring that all segments of a horizontally segmented table have the same columns.

COMBINING TABLES

The final option for redefining tables is to combine some of them. As in segmentation, you have two ways of combining tables: horizontally and vertically. Further, in your final design, any one table can be the result of combining any number of tables horizontally or vertically. Combining tables can provide the following advantages:

☐ *Performance*—Performance may improve for requests that access one combined table rather than multiple smaller tables.
☐ *Simplicity of access*—Single (combined) table access may be simpler than multitable access, reducing the need for joins, unions, subqueries, and multiple DML statements.
☐ *Functionality*—Combining tables sometimes can accommodate requirements for relational functions not supported by a particular DBMS, such as a union or an outer join.

COMBINING TABLES HORIZONTALLY. *Horizontal combining of tables* is the selective merging of tables having the same primary or alternate key. Conceptually, think of horizontal combining as concatenating columns of multiple tables that have the same identifier and therefore describe the same or closely related entities.

If you followed a comprehensive logical data modeling methodology (such as the one in Part 2), you have few tables that are candidates for horizontal combining. With the exception of supertypes and subtypes or other entities with truly distinct business meanings, you merged entities having the same primary key into one entity and thereby into one table (see Rule LDM6.12, Chapter 7). (Of course, if by chance you have not already merged such entities, now is a good time to do so.) Thus, at this point any tables with the same primary key are consciously defined as separate tables, either: (1) because they are viewed by users as logically distinct entities (e.g., supertypes and subtypes), or (2) as a result of segmentation to accommodate access requirements (earlier in this step).

RULE RDD13.10

Consider *combining tables* that

☐ Represent entities involved in 1 : 1 relationships
☐ Are frequently referenced together by users
☐ Are infrequently referenced separately

assuming the effect on performance, data availability, and storage is acceptable.

For example, consider the PAYCHECK and PAYSTUB entities related through a 1 : 1 relationship in Figure 16.14. They might be combined as illustrated in the relational table diagram, also in Figure 16.14.

Combining such tables appears to simplify the relational database design (e.g., results in fewer tables), but in fact it does not. Combining tables for *performance* reasons (because users frequently access them together) when the tables are *logically* different entities adds complexity with associated disadvantages:

☐ *Storage*—Suppose the rows of the original tables do not correspond in exactly a 1 : 1 relationship (i.e., there are some parent table rows with no related child table rows, or vice versa). Then columns that are not common to both original tables will now have occurrences containing null or default values, requiring extra storage.

☐ *Data integrity*—If the original tables participated in different relationships,

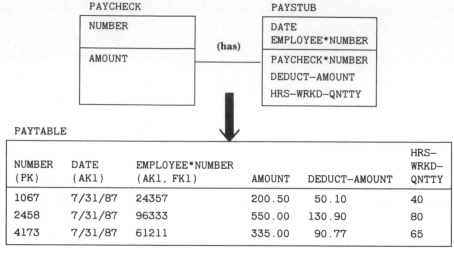

FIGURE 16.14 Sample combining of 1:1 entities into one relational table.

insert/delete/update rules for relationships between the new table and other tables may be more complex.

If the two original tables did not share the same primary key (refer to PAYCHECK and PAYSTUB in Figure 16.14), you must now choose one primary key for the new combined table. This may not be an easy choice. Depending on the insert/delete/update rules, you may have occurrences of one entity without corresponding occurrences of the other and vice versa (e.g., can you have a PAYCHECK without a PAYSTUB? Might you also have a PAYSTUB without a PAYCHECK?) Yet, you must define a primary key so that it will never be null.

Where you have columns that are not common to the tables being combined, you may need additional business rules (for example to manipulate nulls or default values). Where columns are common to all tables being combined, you must merge business rules and perhaps resolve resulting conflicts (e.g., insert/delete/update rules or triggering operations may differ).

☐ *Naming conventions*—You will need to choose a name for the new table. Try to choose a name that reflects all originating tables or reflects the original table accessed most often. Perhaps you can assign to the new table one of the original table names, and make other table names synonyms.

☐ *Performance*—Presumably, you combine tables to improve performance (by reducing multitable access), because users frequently access such tables together. Remember, however, that the combined table is larger than each of the original tables. Therefore, you may inadvertently degrade concurrent access or table scan performance for requests needing only columns that were originally in one table.

□   *Data availability*—You may also decrease overall availability of data in the combined table. That is, requests against one entity may impact (via locking) access to another entity because both entities are represented in one table. Utilities, likewise, may impact access to multiple entities. For instance, if you recover the table to a particular point in time, multiple entities will be recovered to that point (because they are all in one table). While you reorganize the table, access to several entities may be restricted.

RULE RDD13.11

Consider *combining subtype tables* that share the same supertype if the subtypes

□   Have similar columns
□   Are involved in similar relationships
□   Are frequently accessed together
□   Are infrequently accessed separately

assuming the effect on performance, data availability, and storage is acceptable.

This rule is similar, but not identical, to the logical data modeling rule for combining subtypes (Rule LDM6.13, Chapter 7). However, there are two important differences. In logical data modeling, you never consider access requirements, and you combine subtypes with the *same* attributes and relationships (because their business definitions are the same). In relational database tuning, you consider combining subtypes with *similar* attributes and relationships based on user access patterns. That is, if users consistently access the subtypes together, reducing multitable access by combining the subtypes into one table may have significant performance and ease-of-use benefits. Naturally, you must weigh these benefits against the disadvantages we have outlined.

Let us evaluate combining subtypes within the ice-cream parlor database (Figure 16.15). Suppose the database contains a supertype table PRODUCT with subtype tables ITALIAN–ICE, ICE–CREAM, and BEVERAGE. Further, the BEVERAGE table has two subtypes: DIET and NONDIET.

The subtype tables ITALIAN–ICE and ICE–CREAM might be candidates for combining because they have similar columns and the same relationships. On the other hand, these tables may not be accessed together frequently. Customers may more typically ask "What flavors of ice cream do you have?" or "What flavors of ice do you have?" They may be less likely to ask "What flavors of ice and ice cream do you carry?" Thus, advantages of combining these tables may not override the inherent costs.

Probably, you would be even less inclined to combine BEVERAGE with ITALIAN–ICE and ICE–CREAM. The BEVERAGE subtype has totally different

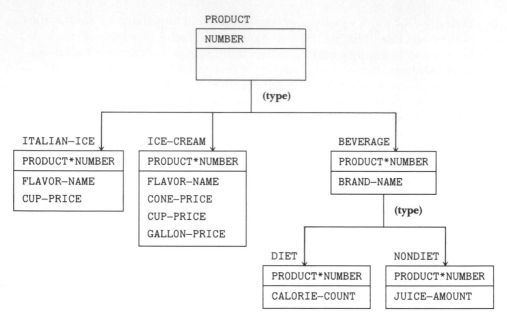

FIGURE 16.15 Ice-cream parlor database.

columns than ITALIAN–ICE and ICE–CREAM. BEVERAGE also is involved in different relationships (i.e., with its subtypes). However, you might combine BEVERAGE's subtypes, DIET and NONDIET.

Several options for combining the subtypes are illustrated in Figure 16.16. Option 1 combines ITALIAN–ICE and ICE–CREAM. Option 2 combines DIET and NONDIET. Option 3 combines ITALIAN–ICE, ICE–CREAM, and BEVERAGE. You can see that Option 3 wreaks the most havoc because it introduces numerous discrepancies with the logical data model and adds significant complexity in terms of null column values and changes to insert/delete/update rules. Clearly, you must study your access requirements to understand pros and cons of any of these combinations.

RULE RDD13.12

Consider *combining a supertype table* with (typically all of) its subtype tables if

- ☐ Users usually access the supertype and subtypes together
- ☐ Users infrequently access the supertype and subtypes separately
- ☐ The effect on performance, data availability, and storage is acceptable

Rule RDD13.12 is similar but not identical to the logical data modeling rule for combining supertype and subtype entities (Rule LDM6.14, Chapter 7). There are important differences, however. In logical data modeling, you combine a supertype and subtype when the subtype *spans* the supertype (i.e., for every subtype occurrence, there also exists a supertype occurrence). Thus, you do not introduce complications involving null values or business rules that apply to some but not all occurrences of the combined entity. Also in logical data modeling, you never consider access requirements. In relational database tuning, you evaluate access requirements. Based on those requirements, you may choose selectively to merge supertypes and subtypes even when they are logically different entities. Naturally, you will do so only when the benefits for specific access requirements clearly outweigh the costs.

Note that, if a supertype has more than one subtype, merging the supertype with only one subtype establishes the combined table as the supertype (i.e., as parent of all the remaining subtypes). This combination can significantly complicate relationship business rules. For instance, if the combined subtype and an uncombined subtype are mutually exclusive, relationship rules must restrict relating the uncombined subtype to a combined supertype row when the combined row also represents a combined subtype row. In general, therefore, combining a supertype with one or a few subtypes is less useful than combining a supertype with all subtypes.

Consider the ice-cream parlor database (Figure 16.15) once more. You might consider merging the DIET and NONDIET subtypes with their supertype BEVERAGE, particularly if you already decided to merge the two subtypes (option 2 in Figure 16.16). You may even merge the PRODUCT supertype with all of its subtypes, thereby replacing all tables in Figure 16.15 with one conglomerate table. Figure 16.17 illustrates both options. You can see that the latter option may be an extremely drastic measure. For instance, nearly every column may be null, so rules must be defined to determine exactly when nulls are valid and when they are not. Morever, insert/update/delete rules for relationships to or from the one combined table are probably extremely complex. Finally, the combined table is significantly larger than is any one of the original tables, potentially degrading scan performance.

On the other hand, what if users always (or nearly always) reference all these tables together? Then combining the tables may offer significant benefits in terms of improved performance and simpler DML. Once again, *analysis of specific access requests is paramount* in deciding whether or how to combine tables (as in making *any* database tuning decision).

COMBINING TABLES VERTICALLY. *Vertical combining of tables* is the selective merging of parent tables into their child tables. Conceptually, think of vertical combining as drawing the columns from a parent table down into the child. Rows in the combined table have a 1:1 correspondence to the rows in the original child table. However, rows of the new combined table are wider, to accom-

Option 1

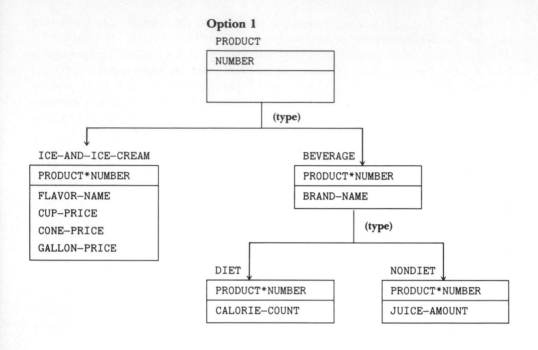

Option 2

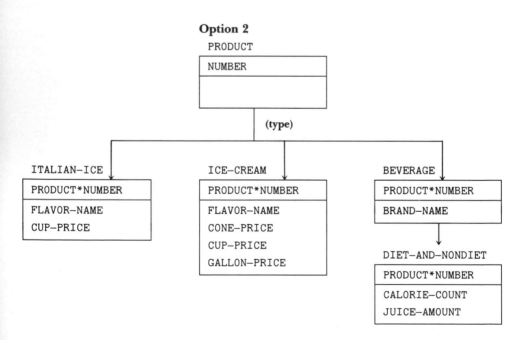

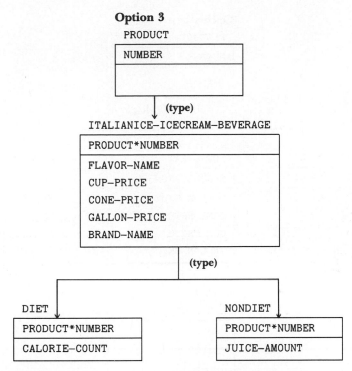

FIGURE 16.16 Ice-cream parlor database, combining subtype tables.

modate columns from the original parent table. The primary key of the combined table is the primary key of the original child table. It follows that vertical combining is valid only when every row in the original parent table is associated with at least one row in the original child table (since the primary key of the combined table cannot be null).

RULE RDD13.13

Consider *combining a parent table* with a child table if

☐ Every parent row is associated with at least one child row
☐ Users often reference the parent table with the child
☐ Users infrequently reference one without the other
☐ The effect on performance, data availability, and storage is acceptable

Consider the VENDOR and SUPPLY tables from the ice-cream parlor database. Assume all requests involving VENDOR or SUPPLY information always require access to both tables. You might eliminate the need for accessing the two tables by combining them, as shown in Figure 16.18.

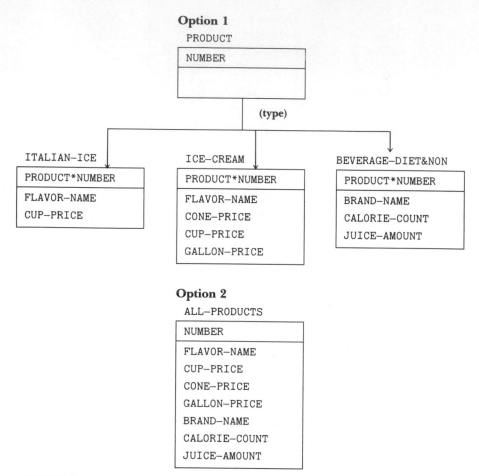

FIGURE 16.17 Ice-cream parlor database, combining supertype and subtype tables.

Rule RDD13.13 for combining parent and child tables resembles the logical data modeling rule for merging parent and child entities (Rule LDM6.15, Chapter 7). There are important differences, however. In logical data modeling, you combine a parent and child only when the parent contains no nonkey attributes. Thus, you avoid introducing redundant data (nonkey attributes from the parent that will now appear in multiple combined parent/child rows). Also, in logical data modeling, you never consider access requirements.

Note the subtle difference between combining tables and Step RDD11, in which you add duplicate data. In Step RDD11, you *selectively copy* columns (e.g., LOCATION) from the parent (VENDOR) to the child (SUPPLY), but you retain the

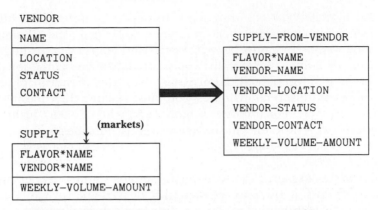

VENDOR

NAME
LOCATION
STATUS
CONTACT

(markets)

SUPPLY

FLAVOR*NAME
VENDOR*NAME
WEEKLY-VOLUME-AMOUNT

SUPPLY-FROM-VENDOR

FLAVOR*NAME
VENDOR-NAME
VENDOR-LOCATION
VENDOR-STATUS
VENDOR-CONTACT
WEEKLY-VOLUME-AMOUNT

FIGURE 16.18 Combining the VENDOR **and** SUPPLY **tables.**

parent table. In Step RDD13, you *move all* columns from the parent to the child, and then eliminate the parent (VENDOR) table entirely. You can, of course, logically recreate the VENDOR table by defining a view:

```
CREATE VIEW VENDOR AS
SELECT DISTINCT VENDOR-NAME, VENDOR-LOCATION, VENDOR-STATUS, VENDOR-CONTACT
FROM SUPPLY-FROM-VENDOR
```

You need to specify DISTINCT because of potential multiple occurrences of each vendor in the combined SUPPLY-FROM-VENDOR table.

Disadvantages of vertically combining tables include the following:

☐ *Storage*—The table formed by merging a parent table into a child table contains duplicate data. You are duplicating all column values for each parent occurrence across all associated child occurrences in the new table. In Figure 16.18, all vendor information is stored redundantly with each flavor supplied by the vendor. The combined table (SUPPLY-FROM-VENDOR) is no longer in third normal form.

Moreover, suppose the original child table had rows with no related parent rows. Now you require additional storage in the combined table for columns with null or default values.

☐ *Data integrity*—New business rules are required to maintain consistency of redundant data values. For instance, in Figure 16.18, triggering operations must ensure that any updates of VENDOR-NAME, VENDOR-LOCATION, VENDOR-STATUS, and VENDOR-CONTACT ripple through all SUPPLY-FROM-VENDOR rows for the affected vendor. In general, all insert/ update/delete rules defined for the original (now erased) relationship (e.g., the original relationship from VENDOR to SUPPLY) must be incorporated into new business rules governing values of the new combined table

(SUPPLY–FROM–VENDOR). Moreover, business rules defined for other relationships involving one of the combined tables (e.g., the relationship from FLAVOR to SUPPLY) must be reevaluated and adjusted accordingly.

☐ *Naming conventions*—Naturally, you must choose one name for the combined table. Moreover, if the original tables used identical column names to represent different attributes, you must rename the columns in the combined table. For instance, if both VENDOR and SUPPLY included DATE columns (with different meanings), you must rename those columns in the combined SUPPLY–FROM–VENDOR table (e.g., to VENDOR–DATE and SUPPLY–DATE).

☐ *Performance*—Again, although combining tables improves performance for some requests, it also may inadvertently degrade performance for other requests by lengthening table scan time or by degrading concurrent access.

☐ *Data availability*—Similarly, availability of both (combined) entities may be affected by access or utilities involving either one.

Combining a supertype with all its subtypes might be viewed as either horizontal combining of tables (concatenation of columns) or vertical combining of tables (drawing parent columns down into the child tables). Supertype–subtype combinations can be somewhat more complex than other parent–child combinations because the supertype may be simultaneously (and perhaps nonredundantly) merged into multiple subtypes, each corresponding to a subset of the supertype. Consider another example of supertype–subtype combining that points out some special implications of this tuning technique.

Let us extend the ice-cream parlor model to include TOPPINGs. The parlor serves liquid toppings (e.g., chocolate syrup, hot fudge, caramel) and dry toppings (e.g., chocolate sprinkles, almonds, coconut). For each liquid topping, you record whether it is to be served warm or at room temperature.

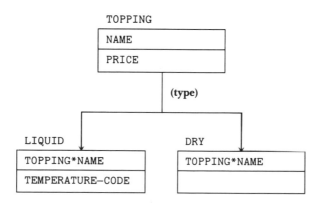

You can combine the TOPPING table with each of its subtype tables, producing the following two tables:

```
LIQUID-TOPPING            DRY-TOPPING
┌──────────────────────┐  ┌──────────────────────┐
│ NAME                 │  │ NAME                 │
├──────────────────────┤  ├──────────────────────┤
│ TEMPERATURE-CODE     │  │ PRICE                │
│ PRICE                │  │                      │
└──────────────────────┘  └──────────────────────┘
```

Rows from the original TOPPING table are selectively combined with rows from *either* the LIQUID *or* DRY tables to form *two* new combined tables: LIQUID-TOPPING and DRY-TOPPING. Thus, accessing *all* information originally contained in the TOPPING table now requires access to two tables: LIQUID-TOPPING and DRY-TOPPING. It follows that, whereas supertype–subtype combining may improve performance for requests accessing both supertype and subtype, it may significantly degrade performance of access to all rows of the supertype alone.

Moreover, logical recreation of the TOPPING table through a view definition requires the UNION operation, as in

```
CREATE VIEW TOPPING AS
SELECT NAME, PRICE
FROM LIQUID-TOPPING
UNION
SELECT NAME, PRICE
FROM DRY-TOPPING
```

Unfortunately, many relational database products, at least in their earlier versions, do not support the UNION operation in a view definition. This restriction may be a compelling reason not to combine a supertype with its subtypes (when they are multiple) in the first place.

ACCOMMODATING THE OUTER JOIN THROUGH TABLE REDEFINITION

Chapter 15 discussed six options for accommodating the outer join, involving alternative DML syntax, adding extra rows such that all rows "match," and contriving substitute columns to facilitate joining "nonmatching" rows. This chapter presents one more option for simulating an outer join—combining the tables involved in the outer join.

OPTION 7 FOR OUTER JOIN SIMULATION: COMBINING TABLES. Consider an insurance database where you have information about insurance policies in one table and corresponding claims against some subset of policies in another table. A logical data model is shown in Figure 16.19.

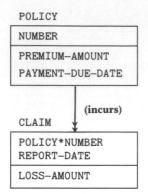

FIGURE 16.19 Insurance logical data model.

corresponding claims against some subset of policies in another table. A logical data model is shown in Figure 16.19.

To produce the report in Figure 16.20 containing policies both with and without claims, you need an outer join. If your DBMS does not explicitly support outer join DML syntax, an alternative is to combine the two tables vertically into one table, as shown in Figure 16.21.

RULE RDD13.14

To effect an *outer join*, consider *combining the tables* into one table. However, do so only after evaluating other alternatives for simulating the outer join, such as

- □   UNION, NOT EXISTS syntax
- □   UNION, NOT IN syntax
- □   Insert into temporary table
- □   Insert into nonrelational file
- □   Adding extra rows so that in effect all rows "match" (Rule RDD11.12)
- □   Contriving substitute columns to facilitate joining "nonmatching" rows (Rule RDD11.13)

You can then produce the report in Figure 16.20 through the following SQL query:

```
SELECT POLICY-NUMBER, PREMIUM-AMOUNT, REPORT-DATE, LOSS-AMOUNT
FROM POLICY-CLAIM
ORDER BY POLICY-NUMBER, REPORT-DATE
```

POLICY NUMBER	PREMIUM AMOUNT	REPORT DATE	LOSS AMOUNT
123	200.00	1/5/84	120.00
123	200.00	2/5/84	300.00
123	200.00	4/27/84	100.00
234	250.00	1/6/85	900.00
457	500.00		
487	120.00		
879	400.00	7/7/84	1200.00

FIGURE 16.20 Sample insurance report.

The option of physically combining tables to effect an outer join compares to other alternatives discussed in Chapter 15 as follows:

☐ Any of the alternatives functionally satisfies a requirement for an outer join.

☐ Combining the tables results in the simplest DML to effect an outer join (since it involves single-table access only).

☐ Combining the tables also typically contributes the most toward improving performance of the outer join and some other types of requests that formerly involved multitable access. Now such requests may no longer require multitable access at all (unlike in any of options 1 through 6, described in Chapter 15).

☐ On the other hand, combining the tables may cause the greatest degradation in performance of requests originally involving rows from only one of the now-combined tables. Such requests may now require longer table scans and more complex data integrity rules.

☐ Combining the tables may negatively impact storage and data availability (as discussed generally for combining tables) to a greater degree than do the other alternatives.

FIGURE 16.21 Combined POLICY **and** CLAIM **tables.**

POLICY—CLAIM

POLICY—NUMBER REPORT—DATE
PREMIUM—AMOUNT
PAYMENT—DUE—DATE
LOSS—AMOUNT

IMPLEMENTATION TIPS AND TECHNIQUES

This step discussed options for eliminating, adding, segmenting, and combining tables. Implementation tips and techniques to consider for each of these options follow.

ELIMINATE TABLES

1. *Identify tables that are all key.* If they are parents to other tables, they add no new information, and they are candidates for removal.
2. *Identify, from your list of transactions, queries, and so on, tables that are never referenced.* These, too, are candidates for removal.

DUPLICATE TABLES

1. *Identify tables that have wide rows.* Are there critical requests that access only a subset of such columns? If so, you may want to create a duplicate table containing these columns (or perhaps to postpone your decision until you investigate vertical segmentation).
2. *Identify very large tables for which a subset of rows may be helpful in testing DML requests.* If a table consists of millions of rows and if sample requests are easily tested against a small percentage of rows, you may want to create a duplicate subset table (e.g., with 3 percent of the rows).
3. *Identify very large tables for which a subset of rows are frequently accessed by critical requests.* Consider duplicating the subset of rows in a separate table to expedite these requests (or postpone your decision until you investigate horizontal segmentation).
4. *Study DML and output formats for frequency of* GROUP BY *or other forms of aggregations.* Analyze the columns in the GROUP BY or aggregation. Is there a pattern? For example, do users consistently reference data aggregated over a given column, such as DEPARTMENT*NUMBER, AREA–CODE, GEOGRAPHICAL–LOCATION–CODE? If so, consider implementing a summarized table in addition to, or even in place of, the detailed table.

SEGMENT TABLES

1. *Review user views comprising your logical data model to determine whether there are groups of users who consistently access only subsets of columns or rows in a table.* When you developed these user views, you already divided the user community into subsets—perhaps by function, location, access needs, or security. Review the user views to determine whether different user views contain groups of attributes that describe the same entity yet are mutually exclusive (except for the primary key). If so, the corresponding table may be a candidate for vertical segmentation. Also determine whether different user views indicate different volumes for the same entity. Perhaps each

user view represents a mutually exclusive subset of occurrences of the entity. If so, you may want to consider horizontal segmentation for the corresponding table.

2. *Within each user view, determine whether there are any natural subsets of users who consistently access subsets of columns or rows.* For example, if a user view represents the needs of one division, are there departments within the division and do the users in each department require access to mutually exclusive subsets of rows or columns? Study sample queries, if available. Determine whether various user groups always specify the same column subsets or whether particular users always use the same WHERE clause. These circumstances may cause you to consider vertical or horizontal segmentation.

COMBINE TABLES

1. *Identify critical queries requiring joins or subqueries.* Do they involve entities of 1 : 1 relationships? Do they involve subtypes and supertypes? Do they involve a large number of rows (or specifically, many I/Os) or many tables (e.g., more than four)?
2. *Identify the need for unions or outer unions.* Does your product support these operations? Does it support union in a view? Do the unions involve subtypes? Are the subtype tables large or are there many of them?
3. *Identify requirements for outer joins.* Does your product support the outer join? If not, how does combining the tables compare to other outer join options discussed in Chapter 15?
4. *Identify processing requests involving multiple DML statements.* Are they required to verify data integrity? Will combining tables provide more benefits than disadvantages?

C A S E   S T U D Y

Let us return to the Moon Launch passenger reservations database to evaluate redefinition of the database structure. Consider the logical data model (Figure 9.12—page 248) and the list of transactions (Figure 13.5—pages 378–379).

ELIMINATING TABLES

The first task is to identify tables that are all-key. The passenger reservations database has no such tables.

The second task is to identify tables that are never referenced. Let us assume that only requests T13, T14, and T33 will be implemented first (to test feasibility of the entire system). After reviewing the descriptions of these requests in Chapter 13, you see that the requests reference all tables. However, you also need to review the tuning decisions made in Chapter 15 to determine whether denormalization has eliminated requirements to access some tables.

In Chapter 15, the case study proposed the following as potential tuning options:

☐ Storing RESERVATION–COUNT in the FLIGHT–SCHEDULE table to eliminate dynamic recounting of all reservations for a scheduled flight
☐ Storing the count of reservations by business for a given flight in a separate table, either FLIGHT–SCHEDULE or a new table
☐ Expediting the count of reservations by business by storing BUSINESS*COUNTRY–NAME, BUSINESS*NAME in the RESERVATION table

Each of these options avoids access to tables (i.e., to the RESERVATION table to count reservations or to the BSNSS–PASSENGER table to identify passengers from the business in question). Yet, access to the tables is still needed for other processing (e.g., retrieving other information associated with RESERVATION, obtaining TICKET–ADDRESS–FLAG from BSNSS–PASSENGER). Thus, these tables cannot be eliminated.

ADDING TABLES

The first task is to identify tables that have wide rows. There are really no tables with exceptionally wide rows. The table with the most columns is RESERVATION. Row size is approximately as follows:

FLIGHT*NUMBER	4 BYTES
PASSENGER*COUNTRY–NAME	25 CHARACTERS
PASSENGER*CODE	25 CHARACTERS
FLIGHT–SCHEDULE*DEPARTURE–DATE	6 CHARACTERS
CONFIRMATION–NUMBER	4 BYTES
FARE–AMOUNT	4 BYTES
PAYMENT–CODE	1 BYTE
ENTRY–DATE	6 CHARACTERS
AGENT–NUMBER	4 BYTES
BUSINESS%COUNTRY–NAME (duplicate data)	25 CHARACTERS
BUSINESS%NAME (duplicate data)	<u>30 CHARACTERS</u>
	134 BYTES

This is probably not a wide row. (Wide rows, depending on the product, may be rows exceeding 600 bytes.)

The second task is to identify very large tables for which subsets of rows may be helpful in testing DML requests. There is no table large enough to justify a separate table for testing DML requests.

The third task is to identify very large tables for which subsets of rows frequently are accessed by critical requests. The largest table is the RESERVATION table, which may or may not pose performance problems (depending on your product, of course). Inspection of critical transactions (T13, T14, T33) does not highlight frequent access to specific row subsets of the the RESERVATION table. On the other hand, looking at other transactions that access the RESERVATION table, you notice that two requests access confirmed reservations:

T28 (8 per day online)

T30 (10 per day batch)

One request accesses unconfirmed reservations:

T31 (10 per day batch)

The following requests access both:

T27 (8 per day online)

T32 (10 per day batch)

T33 (1 per day batch)

T34 (1 per day batch)

You might consider duplicating confirmed reservations in a separate table to facilitate T28 and T30. Doing so is probably not desirable, however, because there are so many RESERVATION inserts and updates that would impact the duplicate table as well.

The fourth task is to study DML and output formats for frequency of GROUP BY and other forms of aggregations. The most critical transactions require the following aggregations:

☐ RESERVATION table by FLIGHT*NUMBER, FLIGHT–SCHEDULE*DEPARTURE–DATE or a range of departure dates to count reservations

☐ BSNSS–PASSENGER table by BUSINESS*COUNTRY–NAME, BUSINESS*NAME to retrieve all passengers for a business, *or* (if you duplicate columns in RESERVATION) RESERVATION by FLIGHT*NUMBER, FLIGHT–SCHEDULE* DEPARTURE DATE, BUSINESS%COUNTRY–NAME, BUSINESS%NAME to count reservations for a business

An additional, derived table storing RESERVATION–COUNT to facilitate the first requirement would have as primary key FLIGHT*NUMBER, FLIGHT–SCHEDULE*DEPARTURE–DATE—exactly the primary key of FLIGHT–SCHEDULE. Thus, storing a derived RESERVATION–COUNT in FLIGHT–SCHEDULE (technique suggested in Step RDD11) is more logical.

An additional, derived table storing BUSINESS–RESERVATION–COUNT to facilitate the second requirement would have as primary key FLIGHT*NUMBER, FLIGHT–SCHEDULE*DEPARTURE–DATE, BUSINESS*COUNTRY–NAME, BUSINESS* NAME. This option also was suggested in the case study in Chapter 15 (option 1 for tuning T14). You evaluated its usefulness in Exercise 15.6.

SEGMENTING TABLES

The first task is to review each user view comprising your logical data model to determine whether groups of users consistently access only a subset of columns or rows in a table. Refer to your solutions for the exercises in Part 2 to review other user views for Moon Launch Enterprise. This task is for the ambitious reader!

The second task is to determine whether, within the passenger reservations user view, there are any natual subsets of users who consistently access subsets of columns or rows. Focus on the RESERVATION table, because it is the largest and perhaps is the only table that may merit segmentation. Recall the mix of requests that access confirmed versus unconfirmed reservations (listed under *Adding Tables*). This mix may suggest horizontally segmenting the RESERVATION table into tables for confirmed and for unconfirmed reservations. But, what is the ratio of confirmed to unconfirmed reservations? Assume most reservations (e.g., 80 percent) are unconfirmed, since passengers typically request a reservation and reserve the right to cancel or change it. Then only 20 percent of the rows are confirmed reservations. Segmenting the tables will expedite transactions accessing only confirmed reservations (T28 and T30)—particularly when such transactions are online (T28).

You must, however, consider that many updates to the RESERVATION table imply frequent deleting and inserting rows from one table to another to change from unconfirmed to confirmed status. Also, four transactions (T27, T32, T33, T34) request both confirmed and unconfirmed reservations, thereby implying a union or multiple DML statements. Finally, other tuning techniques (clustering, indexing, and so on) may yield acceptable performance without segmentation.

COMBINING TABLES

Because you do not have DML to study, you are unable to pinpoint specific occurrences of joins, subqueries, unions, outer joins, outer unions and other multitable access. However, by studying the list of transactions in Figure 13.5, you can gain a fairly good understanding of requirements for multitable access and can design accordingly.

We look again at the critical transactions. T13 (provide a price quote) needs to relate (via join, subquery, or separate DML statements)

    PASSENGER and BSNSS-PASSENGER
    PASSENGER and VCTN-PASSENGER
    BUSINESS, CREDIT-RATING, and BSNSS-PASSENGER
    VCTN-PASSENGER and CREDIT-RATING

T14 (book a reservation) needs to relate

☐   RESERVATION and BSNSS-PASSENGER   (if BUSINESS*COUNTRY-NAME,
                                             BUSINESS*NAME are not dupli-
                                             cated in RESERVATION)

□ FLIGHT–SCHEDULE and RESERVATION   (if RESERVATION–COUNT is not stored in FLIGHT–SCHEDULE)

T33 (list full flights) accesses only one table.
    Options for combining tables include the following:

1. Combine the BSNSS–PASSENGER and VCTN–PASSENGER subtypes, or merge PASSENGER with each, or (most likely) combine PASSENGER, BSNSS–PASSENGER, and VCTN–PASSENGER into one table. Implications of the last option include:

   □ You will need an additional attribute flagging a PASSENGER row as a business, vacationing, or business and vacationing passenger.
   □ For rows representing business and not vacationing passengers, CREDIT–RATING*CODE will be null (or a default value), since CREDIT–RATING*CODE is stored in BUSINESS.
   □ For rows representing vacationing and not business passengers, BUSINESS*COUNTRY–NAME, BUSINESS*NAME, and TICKET–ADDRESS–FLAG will be null (or a default value).
   □ Relationships from BUSINESS and CREDIT–RATING must have customized business rules, since they can occur only for particular types of (business or vacationing) passengers.

   The performance benefits for T13 are probably not worth these costs, as you already decided when you chose not to add passenger type flags to PASSENGER in Chapter 15.
2. Merge CREDIT–RATING with BUSINESS and/or VCTN–PASSENGER. Then updating the credit rating schedule (transaction T3) affects many more than the four rows in the CREDIT–RATING table. Probably the performance benefits for T13 are not worth the costs (as you also already decided when you chose not to duplicate DISCOUNT–AMOUNT in BUSINESS or VCTN–PASSENGER in Chapter 15).
3. Combine BUSINESS with BSNSS–PASSENGER. CREDIT–RATING*CODE and BILLING–ADDRESS will have redundant occurrences in the resulting table. Additional storage will not be excessive (since BUSINESS : BSNSS–PASSENGER is 1:6). The effect on BUSINESS updates (T12) will not be major since such updates are relatively infrequent (once per month). Savings (in determining CREDIT–RATING.DISCOUNT–AMOUNT) is only one I/O per execution of T13. On the other hand, other requests also typically access BUSINESS and BSNSS–PASSENGER together. Thus, this tuning option may be desirable.
4. Combine RESERVATION and BSNSS–PASSENGER. These tables are frequently accessed separately as well; thus, the tuning options in Chapter 15 (duplicating data) probably are more appropriate.
5. Combine FLIGHT–SCHEDULE and RESERVATION. These tables also are fre-

quently accessed separately. Moreover, storing RESERVATION–COUNT in FLIGHT–SCHEDULE (evaluated in Chapter 15) is probably a more effective technique.

SUMMARY

This chapter presented two additional tuning steps to accommodate *functionality* and *performance* challenges not already addressed by techniques in previous steps. These final tuning steps can result in a relational database that no longer strictly conforms to the logical data model.

In Step RDD12, you evaluate the need to alter original column definitions. You do so to overcome product-specific restrictions (e.g., lack of support for certain domain characteristics), to store long or variable-length columns more efficiently, and to selectively redefine foreign keys to reference alternate rather than primary keys. Product-specific limitations are not addressed by this chapter, but should be obvious for your DBMS.

Alternatives for representing long or variable-length columns can make access to such columns more efficient or less restrictive. These alternatives include defining such columns as shortened or abstracted columns, long columns in a separate table, short columns in original table with overflow in additional table, and multiple occurrences of fixed-length columns (e.g., by page and line number) in a separate table. Choosing among these alternatives involves evaluating access requirements, functionality and performance characteristics of the DBMS, and ease with which such columns can be divided into smaller pieces.

Selectively redefining foreign keys to reference alternate keys can expedite critical or frequent requests involving multitable access solely to obtain an alternate key. This technique requires restricting null values in the alternate key (at least for rows corresponding to foreign keys in the referencing table).

In Step RDD13, you evaluate rearranging entire tables by eliminating some tables, adding duplicate tables, segmenting a table into more than one, or combining tables into one. You eliminate tables if they add no new information to your database or are never referenced.

Sometimes you may add duplicate tables that are subsets or derivations of existing tables. These "extra" tables can expedite performance of requests that require only the subsetted or derived rows. Or, the tables may be used for testing requests that will eventually execute against very large tables.

Segmenting a table into separate tables also may facilitate access requirements targeted at subsets of columns or rows. Horizontally segmenting a table (assigning whole rows to resultant tables) or vertically segmenting a table (assigning column sets to resultant tables) enables tailoring of scan and utility performance and may increase concurrent access. However, some requests may consequently have to access multiple tables versus one. Such requests will involve more complex DML and may perform less efficiently. Moreover, performing updates and enforcing business rules across segments may be more complex.

Combining tables may improve performance of requests involving multitable access or may accommodate functionality limitations (e.g., lack of outer join or union support). You can combine tables horizontally by merging tables with the same primary key. Or, you can combine tables vertically by merging parent and child tables. However, enforcing data integrity may be more complex, because tables may no longer be normalized and columns may contain more null or default values.

In summary, because redefining columns and tables causes your database design to deviate from your logical data model, consider such alterations with care. Evaluate the negative as well as positive implications and plan accordingly.

EXERCISES

16.1 List at least five ways of modifying your relational database structure so that tables do not correspond directly to logical entities. Also, discuss how each approach influences the stability of the relational database design.

16.2 Discuss the various types of duplicate tables and describe situations in which each may be useful.

16.3 If you segment a table horizontally, how can you recreate the original logical entity?

16.4 If you segment a table vertically, how can you recreate the original logical entity?

16.5 If you combine two entities into one entity, how can you recreate the original logical entities?

16.6 Suppose the first implementation phase for the Moon Launch Enterprise database is concerned only with implementation of a customer information file. Thus, the first phase will implement information relating only to passengers and not to reservations, flights, meals, and so on. Discuss design options from this chapter that may be useful.

16.7 Assume that Moon Launch Enterprise has two kinds of reservation agents: agents dealing exclusively with business passengers and agents dealing solely with vacationing passengers. Discuss design alternatives.

16.8 The passenger reservations agents are requesting an enhancement to the system. They would like the system to issue and mail flight tickets automatically for all confirmed reservations. The following is a (partial) modified logical data model.

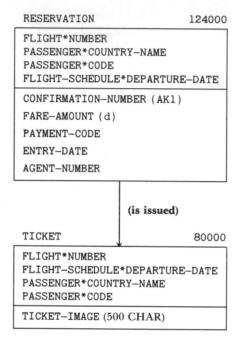

Suggest potential modifications to the TICKET primary key. Also make recommendations regarding storage of TICKET–IMAGE.

17 Special Design Challenges

This chapter presents a number of miscellaneous design topics. None is integral to the relational database design methodology in that not one represents a step that you must perform to design your relational database. However, each topic discusses issues that warrant consideration in your design or implementation strategy.

Provide for access through views discusses effective use of views to promote data independence, simplicity of access, productivity, and security. However, overuse or mismanaged use of views can create significant problems. This section proposes a strategy for defining views to maximize their usefulness and to minimize their disadvantages.

Establish security addresses mechanisms for responding to security requirements. Of course, each relational product has its own internal facilities for providing security. Thus, this section highlights typical security requirements and use of facilities common to most relational DBMS products—views and data control language (DCL).

Cope with very large databases examines special considerations for design of tables of several million rows or more. The section also summarizes techniques included in the design methodology that are particularly critical when dealing with such large data volumes.

Assess and accommodate change recognizes that the design of relational databases, like nonrelational databases, must change over time due to evolving user requirements and technology. This section helps in planning for and implementing such changes. It aids in distinguishing between changes that may be significant (may affect users or data availability) and changes that are probably minor.

Anticipate relational technology evolution assesses near- and far-term expectations for relational DBMS product developments. Emphasis is on how the design steps and guidelines in this book assist in developing relational databases that will keep pace with evolving technology.

Since each of these topics represents a collection of design techniques rather than an actual design step, the rules in this chapter are simply numbered sequentially as RDDT.*n* (for Relational Database Design Technique—Rule *n*).

PROVIDE FOR ACCESS THROUGH VIEWS

All of the design steps in this book focus on designing *base relational tables*, where base tables correspond to stored data structures. Recall from Chapter 3 that, in fact, there is a second type of relation known as a view. A *view* is a logical window depicting the result of relational operations applied to one or more base tables or other views. A view, like a base relation, is a two-dimensional structure of rows and columns, since relational operations applied to rows and columns always yield rows and columns. A view appears to the user to be (for the most part) equivalent to a base table. Users specify operations against views just as against tables. Typically, users are unaware of whether they are accessing views or base tables.

Let us consider an example of a view. Suppose the ice-cream parlor database includes a SUNDAE table, as illustrated in Figure 17.1. The SQL that defines this table is

```
CREATE TABLE SUNDAE
      (FLAVOR*NAME CHAR(20) NOT NULL,
       TOPPING*NAME CHAR(20) NOT NULL,
```

FIGURE 17.1 SUNDAE **base table.**

SUNDAE

FLAVOR*NAME (PK, FK1)	TOPPING*NAME (PK, FK2)	SIZE–CODE (PK)	PRICE–AMOUNT
vanilla	hot fudge	large	1.90
vanilla	hot fudge	small	1.25
chocolate	chocolate	large	1.90
chocolate	chocolate	small	1.25
caramel	butterscotch	large	2.10
chocolate chip	hot fudge	large	2.10
chocolate	butterscotch	small	1.25

FAVORITES

TOPPING	SIZE	PRICE
chocolate	large	1.90
chocolate	small	1.25
butterscotch	small	1.25

FIGURE 17.2 FAVORITES view.

```
SIZE-CODE CHAR(5) NOT NULL,
PRICE-AMOUNT DECIMAL(3, 2) NOT NULL,
UNIQUE (FLAVOR*NAME, TOPPING*NAME, SIZE-CODE))
```

SQL for the FAVORITES view in Figure 17.2 is

```
CREATE VIEW FAVORITES
    (TOPPING, SIZE, PRICE)
    AS SELECT TOPPING*NAME, SIZE-CODE, PRICE-AMOUNT
    FROM SUNDAE
    WHERE FLAVOR*NAME = 'chocolate'
```

Users issue relational operations (e.g., SQL commands) against FAVORITES, as in:

```
SELECT * FROM FAVORITES

SELECT TOPPING, PRICE
    FROM FAVORITES
    WHERE PRICE < 1.50
```

Note that there is no additional storage for data values associated with a view. Data values are stored in only the base tables. Moreover, views always reflect current data values, because views are materialized by applying the view definitions to the base tables at the moment of user access. A view definition can include any syntax that is valid in a retrieval (SQL SELECT) operation. Thus, view definitions can incorporate

☐ Arithmetic expressions (column1 + column2 * column3)
☐ Built-in functions (SUM(column1), COUNT(column2))
☐ Selection criteria (WHERE column1 > value1)
☐ Boolean operators (OR column2 = value2)
☐ Joins (SELECT ... FROM table1, table2)
☐ Unions (SELECT ... UNION SELECT ...)
☐ Nested SELECTs (WHERE EXISTS (SELECT ...))

Of course, specific DBMS products may place restrictions on use of some of these functions in a view definition. For instance, some products restrict use of UNION in views. Regardless, views are clearly a very powerful relational construct.

RULE RDDT.1

Allow users to access data only through *views*. Do not permit users to access *base tables* directly.

By funneling user access through views, you provide a large degree of *data independence*. You insulate users from changes that you might make to the underlying base table structures. For instance, you can add columns, drop columns, redefine data types, resequence columns in a table, or rename columns, with no effect on a user accessing data through views, provided that the original view definition is still valid or that you alter the view definition to appropriately reference the modified table definition. This advantage of using views is so important that you should *always* employ views for access.

In addition to providing data independence, views can be used for the following purposes:

☐ *Simplify data retrieval for end users.* Views can be defined to join several tables, to perform calculations, or to select specific rows and columns. Frequently, these operations require complex DML. Specifying them as part of a view definition significantly reduces the syntax a user or programmer must learn or code.

☐ *Improve productivity for users and programmers.* Views enable defining once calculations or built-in functions that are commonly used in many queries or programs. Subsequently, requests reference the view and further refine selection criteria by qualifying rows and columns selected from the view.

☐ *Define synonyms for tables, columns, and derived data.* Views allow for definition of synonyms by which users and programs can reference tables (actually views) and columns. Moreover, since views can include columns representing expressions, views provide the ability to name the results of expressions via the view's column names.

☐ *Enable access authorizations and restrictions.* Recall from Chapter 3 that you secure access to data in relational databases through SQL GRANT and REVOKE commands (or the equivalent). Such commands restrict users to specific functions on selected tables, views and columns. For example,

```
GRANT SELECT ON SUNDAE TO TOM
GRANT SELECT ON FAVORITES TO CANDY
GRANT UPDATE (PRICE) ON SUNDAE TO BOB
GRANT INSERT, DELETE, UPDATE ON FAVORITES TO JOHN
REVOKE UPDATE (PRICE) ON FAVORITES FROM JOHN
```

By defining views, you can effectively authorize and restrict access to specified rows and columns of one or more tables. Based on the examples above, Candy can retrieve only the TOPPING, SIZE, and PRICE columns in rows where FLAVOR*NAME = 'chocolate' (as in the definition of the FAVORITES view).

Overuse of views, however, can create problems. Specifically, unmanaged view definition can cause the following:

- □ *Proliferation of views*—Defining a different view for every access requirement leads to an overabundance of views to maintain and manage. For instance, an organization with 20 users accessing five tables can easily generate hundreds of views.
- □ *Proliferation of data names*—Each view may define its own view and column names. If every view has different names (and, obviously, every view must have at least a different view name, even if column names are standardized), users may access the same data via many different names, resulting in confusion.
- □ *Proliferation of programs*—Program logic involving data that can be accessed via multiple views must be built to handle the different views. For instance, suppose multiple views are defined against a PAYCHECK table to restrict access to rows by department. That is, a RESEARCH–PAY view includes only PAYCHECK rows where DEPT–NAME = 'Research', a MANUFACT–PAY view includes only rows for the manufacturing department, and so on. Then a generalized paycheck query would have to access RESEARCH–PAY, MANUFACT–PAY, or some other view depending on the rows being accessed and, of course, on the authorization level of the user issuing the query. Either you must develop multiple transaction modules, one for each view, or you must parameterize the query to accept or even determine the appropriate view name. In the latter case, the transaction also must formulate query syntax by incorporating the correct view name at execution time—a functional capability supported by some but not all relational DBMSs.
- □ *Functional limitations associated with particular views*—Relational DBMSs prohibit updates through many if not all views. This restriction is due not only to product implementations but also to the logical limitations of views. That is, some update operations yield ambiguous results when applied through views, as discussed in Chapter 3. Thus, users may, perhaps unexpectedly, find they can execute some but not all functions through a particular view, and they may not understand why.

Your goal is to use views to maximize usefulness and minimize maintenance headaches and user confusion.

RULE RDDT.2

Create one *master view* for each table and build all other views on the master views (i.e., not directly on the base tables).

A *master view* is a view that includes every column and every row from one base table. A master view of the SUNDAE table is

```
CREATE VIEW SUNDAES—MASTER
      AS SELECT FLAVOR*NAME, TOPPING*NAME, SIZE—CODE, PRICE—AMOUNT
      FROM SUNDAE
```

This view contains all columns (by explicitly specifying them in the SELECT clause) and all rows (by the absence of a WHERE clause) from the SUNDAE table.

Because master views look exactly like base tables, they have no theoretical update restrictions, although some products may impose restrictions nevertheless. Assuming your product does not impose its own limitations, you should be able to perform all DML operations (select, update, insert, delete) against master views just as against base tables. Thus, you can require that all accesses occur through master views or views built on top of master views. Should you later change a base table, users accessing the master views will be largely unaffected unless, of course, an access requirement is logically affected by the change—for example, the access involves a column that is dropped.

Users and programmers probably will think of master views as base tables. Thus, employ master view and column naming standards that are useful in accommodating shared data access across many different requirements. Names for views and columns in views need not include all technically oriented conventions applied to names of tables and columns in tables. For instance, view names may not include designation of version number or test or production status. Moreover, column names in views may be shorter for convenience in access, whereas column names in tables tend to be somewhat long for descriptiveness in design.

RULE RDDT.3

Create views on master views as needed to simplify or restrict *read-only* access.

Views simplify access by screening complex syntax from the typical user or programmer. For instance, views can rename columns (establish synonyms), join two or more tables, perform calculations on columns, or reorder columns.

Views that simplify user access also may be used to restrict access; however, they are primarily useful for restricting read-only access due to limitations on updates through views.

RULE RDDT.4

Build the *standard maintenance* (insert, update, and delete) *routines* and the *integrity audit routines* to access master (or potentially more restricted) views rather than base tables.

Master views allow you to control the timing and consequences of changes in table structures. For example, if your maintenance and audit routines access master views rather than base tables, you can test changes to the base tables (e.g., addition of new columns or reordering of existing columns) without affecting enforcement of integrity for existing update processes. When and if appropriate, you can redefine both the master view and the standard maintenance and integrity audit routines to reference the change (e.g., a new column) in the underlying table.

RULE RDDT.5

Name and document views in the *data dictionary* or catalog.

Views are defined primarily to facilitate user access. Make the view and column names user-friendly and easy to remember. Your product also may support explicit syntax for defining synonyms, which are useful when multiple users share the same view or when users prefer cryptic, abbreviated names to expedite DML coding.

Include the view definitions (e.g., SQL SELECT statements) in the data dictionary to provide descriptive detail as well as a means of view recreation, if necessary. Also record information such as creator or owner, synonyms, test or production status, version or copy, master view designation, and associated maintenance and integrity audit routines (if applicable—i.e., in the case of a master view).

Views are a principal mechanism in the relational model for restricting access to data. However, because of the problems described, views may be insufficient as security mechanisms.

ESTABLISH SECURITY

Generally, you use views and DCL (GRANT and REVOKE commands) to secure access to relational data. Views define the granularity (specific columns or rows) of data being secured. GRANT and REVOKE commands specify the functions that particular users can perform against particular views or tables, or, in the case of updates for some products, specific columns of tables or views.

RULE RDDT.6

Where feasible, enforce user security through *master views* or through second-level *security views* defined on the master views.

If you are restricting or authorizing access to an entire table, specify GRANT and REVOKE commands on *master views*. This technique retains data independence established by defining master views in the first place. If you need more selective security controls at the column or row level, define a second level of *security views* on top of the master views (Figure 17.3). For example, allow access to an EMPLOYEE master view to users who should access all rows and all columns. Define one second-level security view for access to NAME, ADDRESS, and DEPT–CODE. Define another second-level security view for access to NAME, DEPT–CODE, and SALARY–AMOUNT.

Use these second-level security views with GRANT and REVOKE commands to *control* access. Define more selective user views on top of the security views to *simplify* access or to improve productivity. As long as you define appropriate security restrictions against the second-level security views, you can make the top-

FIGURE 17.3 Hierarchy of views to simplify, control, and protect data access.

	EMPRESEARCH view	EMPDEPTSAL view
User Views (Simplify Access)	NAME / ADDRESS / DEPT–CODE = 'RESEARCH'	NAME / DEPT–CODE / SUM–SAL–BY–DEPT

	EMPGENERAL view	EMPRESTRICT view
Security Views (Control Access)	NAME / ADDRESS / DEPT–CODE	NAME / DEPT–CODE / SALARY–AMOUNT

	ALLEMPLOYEES view
Master View (Protect Data Independence)	NAME / ADDRESS / DEPT–CODE / SALARY–AMOUNT

	EMPLOYEE table
Base Table (Store Data)	NAME / ADDRESS / DEPT–CODE / SALARY–AMOUNT

level user views available to everyone (i.e., GRANT ALL ON userview TO PUBLIC). Since all accesses to user views must pass through the security views, the security views effectively control access.

RULE RDDT.7

Consider creating a *user authorization table* to control access to row subsets by user ID.

A common security requirement is to restrict access to particular rows of a table based on the user ID invoking access. For instance, access to rows of the EMPLOYEE table in Figure 17.3 might be restricted by department. Only specified users are granted access to the EMPLOYEE table at all, and each of those users is permitted access only to rows corresponding to employees in the user's respective department. One way to accommodate this requirement is to define a different security view for each departmental subset of rows. If the EMPLOYEE table includes rows for 50 departments, you will define 50 views. Managing and maintaining all these views can be an administrative nightmare. Moreover, design of program logic becomes complex. To satisfy the same request against each view, do you create separate programs—one per view? What if there are many such requests? Or, can you create one program that determines (somehow) at execution time which view it needs?

An alternative is to create a *user authorization table* that associates user IDs with column values for rows authorized for access by that user ID. Figure 17.4 illustrates such a user authorization table for the EMPLOYEE table (or actually, for the ALLEMPLOYEES master view). Now you can define an *authorization view* joining the master view for the user authorization table and the master view for the base table. Include in this joined authorization view only rows that match the invoking user ID. For instance,

```
CREATE VIEW MY-DEPT
     AS SELECT NAME, ADDRESS, DEPT-CODE, SALARY-AMOUNT
     FROM ALLEMPLOYEES, USERAUTHEMP
     WHERE USERAUTHEMP.USER-CODE = USER
     AND ALLEMPLOYEES.DEPT-CODE = USERAUTHEMP.EMPLOYEE*DEPT-CODE
```

Here USER represents a product-specific keyword designating the ID of the user accessing the view. Thus, any users with read access to MY-DEPT can see only those ALLEMPLOYEES rows to which their ID is authorized access via the USERAUTHEMP table.

USERAUTHEMP master view

USER-CODE (PK)	EMPLOYEE*DEPT-CODE (PK, FK)
TOM	R1
TOM	R2
CANDY	B11
BARB	C02
MIKE	D14
MIKE	T01
CHRIS	S34
CASEY	T15

ALLEMPLOYEES master view

NAME (PK)	ADDRESS	DEPT-CODE	SALARY-AMOUNT
Smith	FL	R2	50000
Jones	FL	R2	25000
Thomas	AZ	S34	34000
Woods	NJ	R1	15000
Green	NJ	D14	74000
Williams	CA	S34	20000
Kimball	CA	T15	36000
Seid	NY	C02	89000

FIGURE 17.4 User authorization table controlling access to ALLEMPLOYEES.

You also can represent the authorization view as a subquery:

```
CREATE VIEW MY-DEPT
     AS SELECT NAME, ADDRESS, DEPT-CODE, SALARY-AMOUNT
     FROM ALLEMPLOYEES, USERAUTHEMP
     WHERE DEPT-CODE IN
          (SELECT EMPLOYEE*DEPT-CODE FROM USERAUTHEMP
          WHERE USER-CODE = USER)
```

You can use the same user authorization table to restrict access to other related tables (e.g., to the PAYCHECK table, related to the EMPLOYEE table) by relating master views for such tables to the authorization view (e.g., by relating the ALLPAYCHECKS master view to MY-DEPT, which relates ALLEMPLOYEES and USERAUTHEMP).

When considering a user authorization table, evaluate performance of views involving a join or subquery. If performance of both is poor, consider techniques for eliminating the join or subquery, such as the following:

1. Selectively denormalize by copying the column value that determines access authorization (such as DEPT–CODE in the EMPLOYEE table) into other related tables (such as PAYCHECK). This reduces joins or subqueries needed to verify access authorization to those tables. A join or subquery involving the user authorization table is still required, however—unless you also employ the next tuning technique (option 2).
2. Selectively denormalize by copying the USER–CODE column from the user authorization table (e.g., USERAUTHEMP) to the restricted tables (e.g., EMPLOYEE or PAYCHECK). This is useful primarily when only one USER (or at most a small fixed number of USERs) can access each row so that only one (or perhaps a few) duplicate column is added to each table.
3. Physically combine the user authorization table with the restricted tables (e.g., merge the USERAUTHEMP and EMPLOYEE tables). This is similar to option 2, but actually eliminates the user authorization table. It involves the same restrictions as option 2.
4. Create separate security views for each security requirement, instead of creating a user authorization table.
5. Handle row-level security through program logic. The program can access a user authorization table, so that security changes do not require changes in program logic but rather require inserts, deletes, or updates to the user authorization table.

As a reminder, multitable views (involving joins or subqueries) are generally useless for restricting update access due to product limitations or theoretical update ambiguities. Thus, to restrict row-level update access, you will need techniques that do not involve multitable views—for example, options 2 through 5.

RULE RDDT.8

When using *standard maintenance routines* to enforce integrity, grant appropriate user access to the routines and prohibit use of native DBMS update commands.

Following the design methodology in this book (Chapter 12), you probably have designed a set of standard maintenance routines to enforce integrity rules not supported by standard DDL syntax. You must ensure that users always perform updates by invoking the maintenance routines rather than by issuing native DBMS update commands.

Effecting appropriate security controls is critical to your implementation scheme for enforcing integrity. In fact, if a particular implementation mechanism is not compatible with your security requirements, choose a different implementation mechanism! For example, suppose that with your DBMS any user who invokes a macro (set of predefined DML statements) must be authorized to issue any of the DML commands contained in the macro. Users are then able to bypass the macro by issuing native DML. Thus, macros are not an appropriate mechanism for enforcing integrity rules. Instead, you must rely on other mechanisms, such as user exits or program code (again, depending on your DBMS's implementation of security features).

Figures 17.5 and 17.6 summarize implementation options for the most common security requirements.

RULE RDDT.9

In a production environment, generally restrict access to *base table definitions* and *storage structure specifications* to designated database administrators. If users are permitted to create their own (e.g., temporary) tables, isolate such user definitions to their own space or even their own databases.

Limit authorization for modifying table structures, including such functions as CREATE/ALTER/DROP TABLE, CREATE/DROP INDEX, allocation of space, and establishing user IDs. Performing these functions requires technical expertise. If users need to create tables (e.g., to create and drop tables serving as user workspaces), consider assigning such tables to their own user-specific databases to minimize possibility of inadvertent destruction of tables accessed by other users. Of course, you may be able to relax such restrictions in a test environment if you can isolate the effects of potential modifications to a particular test database or other test area.

Ideally, the designers or implementors of a database structure (when they are not also users) should be authorized to create, drop, and modify the structure but not to see the contents (data values) therein. Unfortunately, some DBMS products do not distinguish between access to a database structure and access to the values within the structure. If such is the case with your product, *restrict privileges for modifying database structures* to one or a few designers. This practice does not eliminate security exposures, but at least limits them to desig-

Security Requirements	Use of Views	Use of GRANT Command
1. Read access to all rows and columns of a table	Master view of the table	GRANT read access ON view TO each user or group as needed
2. Read access to subset of columns	Second-level security views	GRANT read access ON views TO each user or group as needed
3. Read access to subset of rows	Second-level security views	GRANT read access ON views TO each user or group as needed
	Master view of the table related to master view of a user authorization table through	GRANT read access ON authorization view TO PUBLIC or GRANT execution ON authorization program TO PUBLIC
	☐ authorization view involving join and SELECT WHERE column = USER ☐ authorization view involving subquery and SELECT WHERE column = USER ☐ duplicate columns in table with authorization view involving SELECT WHERE column = USER ☐ authorization program performing SELECT WHERE column = USER	
4. Read access to subset of columns and rows	Combinations of options 2 & 3	

FIGURE 17.5 Read-only security requirements; common implementation techniques.

nated people. Also *maintain an audit trail* of all activities performed by people authorized to modify data structures, if these people can view or update sensitive database contents. This practice again does not eliminate exposures, but reduces them by enabling repercussions should privileges be abused.

Depending on your requirements and on the facilities provided by your DBMS, administration of security privileges may be highly centralized or decentralized or a combination of both. A popular scenario entails centralized control

Security Requirements	Use of Views	Use of Native Updates versus Standard Maintenance Routines	Use of GRANT Command
1. Update access to all rows and columns of a table	Master view of the table	With native DML updates	GRANT updates ON view TO each user or group as needed
		With standard maintenance routines	Do not permit native DML updates through view. GRANT execution ON maintenance routines TO each user or group as needed
2. Update access to subset of columns	Master view of the table	With standard maintenance routines (required for this option)	Do not permit native DML updates through view. GRANT execution ON maintenance routines TO each user or group as needed
	Second-level security views	With native DML updates	GRANT updates ON views TO each user or group as needed
		With standard maintenance routines—separate routine for each view, one routine but different compiled versions for each view (product-specific option—e.g., supported by DB2), or one routine that dynamically determines appropriate view	Do not permit native DML updates through views. GRANT execution ON maintenance routines TO each user or group as needed

3. Update access to subset of rows	Master view of the table	With standard maintenance routines (required for this option)	Do not permit native DML updates through view. GRANT execution ON maintenance routines TO each user or group as needed
	Second-level security views	With native DML updates	GRANT updates ON views TO each user or group as needed
		With standard maintenance routines (involving same alternatives as option 2)	Do not permit native DML updates through views. GRANT execution ON maintenance routines TO each user or group as needed
	Master view of the table, master view of a user authorization table, and authorization view relating the two (assuming DBMS allows updates through that join/subquery view)	With native DML updates	GRANT updates ON authorization view TO PUBLIC
		With standard maintenance routines	Do not permit native DML updates through views. GRANT execution ON maintenance routines TO PUBLIC
	Master view of the table and master view of a user authorization table (assuming DBMS prohibits updates through join/subquery view relating the two)	With standard maintenance routines (required for this option) that verify access authorization through SELECT WHERE column = USER	Do not permit native DML updates through views. GRANT execution ON maintenance routines TO PUBLIC
4. Update access to subset of columns and rows	Combinations of options 2 and 3		

FIGURE 17.6 Update security requirements; common implementation techniques.

of the more sensitive and more technical tasks, such as creating databases, specifying storage options, and authorizing access to shared tables. Less sensitive or less technical activities, such as creating and authorizing access to personal databases and creating or dropping temporary tables or workspaces, may be more decentralized. Of course, in a test environment, all security administration and, indeed, security itself may be much more loosely controlled, even to the extent that all developers and perhaps all users perform nearly any function. Typically, when a database is moved into production the user function assumes principal responsibility for security administration.

COPE WITH VERY LARGE DATABASES

The definition of a "very large database" is, of course, dependent on capabilities and limitations of a given relational DBMS. This section considers a very large relational database (VLRDB) to be one in which at least one table contains several million rows, or where at least one table contains multiple gigabytes of data. (Gigabytes are a better measure of table volumes since they represent row *size* as well as row *count*.)

Common examples of systems involving very large data volumes occur in these domains:

☐ *Insurance industry*—capturing information about insurance policies, premiums, payments, losses, and claims for millions of policy holders over many geographical locations

☐ *Financial services industry*—depicting customer information along with historical records of individual financial transactions, such as transfers of funds from one account to another

☐ *Telecommunications industry*—recording local and long-distance telephone calls for millions of customers, including billing and receivables information

☐ *General mass marketing*—tracking nationwide mailing lists along with brochures and pamphlets sent to individual addresses over several months

Five general issues often are magnified by very large volumes of data in relational or nonrelational databases: performance of retrievals, throughput, insert and delete processing, checkpoint and restart considerations, and utility scheduling.

PERFORMANCE OF RETRIEVALS

Data retrieval from VLRDBs may be especially slow due to scans and sorts of large data volumes.

RULE RDDT.10

Tune performance of *data retrieval* from a *VLRDB* by

- ☐ Selecting appropriate access mechanisms
- ☐ Implementing sample tables
- ☐ Implementing summarized tables

Tuning techniques used for all relational tables (as discussed in previous chapters) can not only speed up but may determine feasibility of long-running retrievals against VLRDBs. Specifically, you should *select appropriate access mechanisms;* proper choice of indexing and clustering can reduce or even eliminate long sorts and scans. *Implement sample tables;* sample tables representing 2 to 5 percent of the full data volume can expedite testing of new and ad hoc queries by users and developers. *Implement summarized tables;* creation of summarized tables can convert a very long-running request to a very short and simple (perhaps one-row) access.

THROUGHPUT

Very large transaction volumes (e.g., hundreds or thousands of transactions per second) cause throughput to be a critical factor in database design. Such large transaction volumes are certainly not unique to systems with large data volumes, nor do systems with large data volumes necessarily imply large transaction volumes. Yet, often the two occur together. Consider, for example, a financial services database representing millions of customers, where each customer has potentially several investment accounts and activates daily deposits, withdrawals, and transfers of monies. The volume of transactions per second is commensurate with the number of customers. Moreover, timely accommodation of the high transaction and data volumes may translate into significant effects on business profit and loss.

RULE RDDT.11

Facilitate maximum *throughput* against a *VLRDB* by appropriate

- ☐ Choice of locking options
- ☐ Clustering
- ☐ Table partitioning or segmentation
- ☐ Commit processing
- ☐ Segmentation of updates

CHOICE OF LOCKING OPTIONS. Small locking granularity maximizes concurrency by minimizing not only table but also index locking, which is particularly important during update processing. In fact, it is probably intolerable to invoke table-level locking for updates to extremely large tables! On the other hand, large locking granularity can be effective for read-only tables by reducing the overhead associated with locking.

For very high transaction volumes, you might try to contrive row sizes and storage parameters such that a related set of rows fits exactly within one lockable unit. If you fit all information for a customer in a financial services database (e.g., all transactions for a given customer's accounts) into one lockable unit (e.g., one physical block), locks on that unit may not affect processing of other customers. You may even try forcing related rows into a single lockable unit by careful and creative use of free space or by definition of dummy (meaningless) columns to fill extra space. Obviously, this solution has its drawbacks, such as excess storage requirements. Yet, the increase in concurrency, and hence in throughput, may be worthwhile.

CLUSTERING. Use clustering to minimize contention due to locking by concurrent transactions. For instance, in a financial services system, consider clustering (perhaps all tables) by customer number. This technique can reduce contention among requests pertaining to different customers, since generally different customers are in different lockable units.

TABLE PARTITIONING OR SEGMENTATION. Use partitioning or segmentation to minimize contention. For example, partitioning customer-related tables by brokering agent increases concurrency of requests and utilities accessing customers of different brokering agents. Note that partitioning and segmentation generally enhance concurrency more than does clustering. With clustering, related rows are stored together, but related and unrelated rows are probably stored in the same physical data structure. Partitioning or segmentation implies physical boundaries between unrelated rows. Rows for one brokering agent are not stored in the same physical data structure (e.g., file) as are those for another.

COMMIT PROCESSING. Issue frequent commits to release locks quickly, especially update locks, thereby freeing up table resources for subsequent access. Frequent commits are especially important in large-volume systems to avoid deadlocks. A deadlock occurs if two requests are each waiting for resources held by the other request. Neither request can proceed. In a deadlock situation, typically the relational DBMS abends (aborts) one request. If your requests are very long-running (e.g., several hours), such abends can be extremely expensive due to the time required to rerun the request. Of course, small locking granularity, clustering, partitioning, and segmenting also help to reduce the probability of deadlock.

SEGMENTATION OF UPDATES. Segment large numbers of batch updates into smaller groups such that each group accesses different table partitions, segments, or ranges of key values (where the value sequences correspond to table clustering). For example, segment large batches of financial transactions by brokering agent and execute the segments concurrently. If relational tables also are segmented or partitioned by brokering agent, each group of transactions accesses a different segment or partition, thereby only slightly, if at all, affecting each other.

INSERT AND DELETE PROCESSING

Inserts or deletes of millions of rows may perform poorly due to overhead of logging, locking, commit processing, index maintenance, and so on.

RULE RDDT.12

Tune mass *insert processing* against a *VLRDB* by

□   Using a load utility
□   Disabling logging
□   Temporarily dropping and subsequently recreating indexes

Load utilities usually outperform DML inserts, because the former are designed to handle mass rather than individual row inserts. Fortunately, some load utilities can be used not only to initially populate a table, but also to refresh a table totally (DB2 LOAD REPLACE), to add new rows to an existing table (DB2 LOAD RESUME) and perhaps even to update existing rows (DBC/1012 BULK LOAD).

Some load utilities always append rows to the end of a table, ignoring available free space within the table and disregarding clustering sequence. In such cases, schedule a table reorganization soon after the load to recluster rows and to redistribute free space.

Sometimes, you can disable logging during a load to further hasten the update process. Be sure to follow with a backup utility to ensure adequate recovery.

Index maintenance can slow loads and updates substantially. Evaluate the effect of dropping indexes prior to mass row inserts or updates and recreating the indexes thereafter. If the number of inserts or updates is large enough, dropping and recreating the indexes may be faster than maintaining them during the table updates.

RULE RDDT.13

Tune mass *delete processing* against a *VLRDB* by partitioning and segmenting.

If your DBMS does not support partitioning, consider segmenting large tables so that delete requirements can be implemented through DROP and CREATE table statements. For example, create one CUSTOMER–TRANSACTION table for each month. To purge the oldest month, simply drop the oldest table and create a new one for the new month. Of course, you must evaluate the effect of dropping and recreating tables on existing views, synonyms, security controls, and so on. You also must consider the complexity of processing logic to access segments that are constantly being dropped and created (e.g., which table is accessed when?).

If your DBMS supports partitioning (automatically managed by the DBMS), consider creating partitions so that mass delete requirements become partition drop and reload requirements (e.g., DB2, Release 3, LOAD REPLACE partition). However, also evaluate the time required to rebuild any indexes that span partitions.

CHECKPOINT AND RESTART CONSIDERATIONS

You may have requests that have long execution times due to access of large data volumes. Consider the effects of potential abends and consequent restarts.

RULE RDDT.14

For *VLRDBs*, ensure that long-running requests can be *recovered* and *restarted* within reasonable timeframes.

The terms "checkpoint" and "restart" refer to the ability to start DBMS processing from a "consistent" point reached previously by all affected user transactions. Typically, a DBMS does not checkpoint activities until completion of the execution of a DML statement. Recall that a single DML statement may entail long-running scans, index access, sorts, and so on. Therefore, if the request (or system) fails during execution of the statement, processing must restart from the beginning (which for a VLRDB can involve hours of scanning and sorting).

To avoid such restart delays, dissect extremely long-running DML statements into multiple "shorter-running" DML statements, perhaps saving the results of each statement in a relational table or sequential file. For example, consider the retrieval of a set of information for all customers. You might divide this request into several similar requests, each one retrieving the information for a subset of customers. Of course, this technique implies knowledge of how much execution time each DML statement requires, so that you can divide the overall request into "equal" pieces. Moreover, this technique may result in slower execution of the request when no restart is required, since the request now involves multiple DML statements rather than one.

UTILITIES

Utility processing against VLRDBs may require excessive time.

RULE RDDT.15

Accommodate *utility processing* against a *VLRDB* by

☐ Encouraging parallel utility execution
☐ Taking advantage of partial utilities
☐ Scheduling statistics-gathering utilities only as needed
☐ Assessing recovery times

Partition or segment large tables into sizeable chunks to accommodate shorter and parallel executions of backups, reorganizations, and recoveries. Evaluate circumstances that influence whether such utilities can execute in parallel. For example, can you execute two recoveries on two partitions of a table at one time? If not, you may choose to segment rather than partition a table to enable parallel recovery. Can you execute two recoveries on two tables in the same database at the same time? If not, you may choose to assign segmented tables to different databases to accommodate parallel recoveries.

If possible, alternate full backups with partial backups, where a partial backup copies only physical blocks that have changed since the last full or partial backup. Partial backups can execute more quickly than full backups do. Where feasible, evaluate use of partial reorganizations (e.g., per partition) for the same reasons.

Minimize frequency of utilities that update catalog statistics. If there are few row inserts and few column updates that might influence effectiveness of access strategies (i.e., few updates to columns that are indexed, clustered, or hashed), catalog statistics should seldom need updating. Or, if table refreshes result in rows having roughly the same characteristics as the old rows (e.g., distribution of values for indexed or hashed columns are similar), you may not need to update the catalog statistics for the table.

Also assess the time to recover a VLRDB and associated indexes. Such recoveries can require days or weeks. Is this tolerable? How can you reduce the recovery times? Should you execute more frequent backups? Should you consider off-line recovery utilities, table segmentation?

In summary, VLRDBs and commensurately high transaction volumes are no longer an anomaly in relational database environments. However, feasibility depends on many factors: specific access and performance requirements, characteristics of utility processing, design options supported by a given product, and creativity and skill level of the designer.

ASSESS AND ACCOMMODATE CHANGE

Most databases (relational and nonrelational) are not static objects. They contain data values and relationships that vary with time. Reports, queries, and transactions operating against a database provide point-in-time snapshots of these changing values. The structures modeled by databases also change over time. For example, a business may develop new products, acquire new subsidiaries, or implement changes in its manufacturing processes. These changes may affect not only values of data within the database but also definitions of columns, tables, and rules associated with tables.

Many of these changes are relatively easy to implement due to the flexibility of relational technology. Others are more difficult and affect existing programs and user views despite facilities provided by relational environments.

Your challenge is to understand the planning and implementation associated with making changes in a relational environment. This section addresses those objectives for three types of relational database changes: dropping, adding, and changing objects.

DROPPING OBJECTS

The term *drop* refers to the action of deleting an object and its definition or description from the facilities managed by the DBMS. For example, if a user drops a relational table (e.g., via an SQL DROP command), all rows of the table plus the table definition in the catalog (columns, creator, and so on) are deleted. Objects that you can drop typically include databases, tables, columns, indexes, views, and synonyms. However, the specific objects that can be dropped are different in each product.

You may need to drop relational objects for two reasons: (1) you no longer need the object, or (2) you need to modify the object in such a way that you must drop and redefine it.

RULE RDDT.16

Be cognizant of the structural modifications that require *dropping, redefining,* and *recreating* existing objects (product-specific).

Modifications that may (depending on the DBMS product) require dropping and recreating a relational table include change in data type and length; disallowance of null values for a column; addition of column; drop of column; change in default value; partitioning, segmenting, or combining existing tables; change in hash routine or columns to be hashed; change in clustering sequence; and change in other specifications affecting table storage (e.g., assignment of tables to storage structures).

In most relational products, you can perform drop and recreate operations using online facilities. However, the time required for the operations may be excessive, and impact on existing users may be nontrivial. Some DBMSs lock other objects in the catalog while performing a drop operation, thereby affecting users who would not expect to be affected. Thus, you must carefully plan and schedule such operations.

In some relational products, the drop of one relational object results in the simultaneous drop of all related objects with no notification to the person issuing the drop command or to anyone else. For example, dropping a view may result in automatic drop of all views built on that view as well as all security privileges referencing those views. In other products, dropping a relational object may not cause the drop of related objects. Still other relational products do not permit a user to drop a relational object unless the object has no dependent objects. The user must explicitly drop all dependent objects prior to dropping the target object.

In any case, before dropping an object, you will want to understand implications of the drop. What other objects will also be dropped or will become invalid? Be sure to reference the catalog before you drop the object to obtain a list of related objects.

RULE RDDT.17

Determine the *effect* that *dropping* a relational object will have on existing relational objects, applications, and users.

The DBMS catalog denotes objects that the DBMS considers to be related or dependent. For example, if you drop a SALARY table, the DBMS may recognize views and indexes as dependent objects. However, in the absence of DBMS referential integrity support, the DBMS will not know that the DEDUCTION table is implicitly dependent on the SALARY table through foreign keys and insert/delete rules. Therefore, it is your responsibility to ensure that dropping an object does not damage the integrity of your database.

RULE RDDT.18

Notify users prior to dropping an object.

Notifying users before dropping an object alerts them to the consequences and may even surface an unforeseen consequence.

RULE RDDT.19

In environments where object drops automatically cascade to dependent objects or where objects cannot be dropped until all dependent objects have been dropped, establish mechanisms or procedures for *identifying* and subsequently *recreating* such dependent objects.

You may be dropping an object only to turn around and create another, similar object, perhaps to implement changes that you could not apply to the original object. In addition, you may need to restore erroneously dropped objects. If the DBMS automatically drops all dependent objects (or if you have to drop them before dropping the target object), you will need a means of recreating the dependent objects as well. Therefore, ensure that you maintain copies of the DDL to create all objects.

To restore dropped objects, not only must you have access to the DDL, but also you will need appropriate authority to recreate the object definition and to restore the object contents (where applicable—e.g., to restore the table). You also will need copies of related DCL (Data Control Language) so that you can reestablish dropped access privileges.

ADDING OBJECTS

In general, adding objects to a relational database is a simple operation. Objects that can be added (e.g., via an SQL CREATE command) usually include databases, tables, indexes, views, and synonyms. You will need to consider naming conventions and ownership, security, and authorization implications. For tables, indexes, or (product-specific) databases, you also will need to calculate space requirements. Finally, you must enforce any integrity rules pertaining to relationships among existing and new objects.

RULE RDDT.20

When adding a table, identify its *relationships* with existing tables and enforce associated *integrity rules*.

All steps in designing relational tables also apply to adding new ones. You must identify and enforce primary keys, foreign keys, insert/delete rules, domain rules, and triggering operations. For foreign and primary key support (insert/delete rules), you may need to modify maintenance routines for existing related tables.

CHANGING OBJECTS

Changing existing objects may be more complex than adding new objects, due to the effects on existing programs and users. Changes can be of two types: changes in physical representation and changes in logical structure. Changes in *physical representation* involve underlying storage structures (e.g., changes to space allocation, indexes, locking, and buffering). Such changes also may affect row placement (e.g., changes in clustering sequence, hashing mechanism, or assignment of rows across nodes in a distributed environment). Changes in *logical structure* involve objects visible to users (tables, views, columns) and integrity rules. Sample logical changes include adding columns, dropping columns, renaming objects, redefining primary keys, and combining or segmenting tables.

RULE RDDT.21

Make structural database changes as *transparent* as possible to existing users and applications.

Typically, DBMSs enable modification of at least some physical storage options without affecting the logical structure or contents of the database. Thus, many physical changes are easily implemented without users being cognizant of them at all.

Frequently, products are less successful in effecting logical changes transparently. That is, if *you* alter the logical structure of the database, *you* are responsible for making the change transparent (where feasible) to existing users. When adding new columns, you can create a view that does not include the new columns to simulate the original table. In fact, if all DML requests reference columns explictly by name (Rule RDD3.2), the new column will be transparent to existing requests even without a new view. Dropping a column is more difficult to hide; generally, you must modify the programs, queries, and so on that referenced the original column. Of course, if you drop a duplicate (copied or derived) column, you can simulate it for existing programs and queries through views. If you rename a table, view, or column, you can preserve the original name by defining views or synonyms—or, better yet , use views or synonyms to define the new names.

RULE RDDT.22

Use synonyms or views to *rename* objects (instead of using a RENAME command).

Views can be useful in hiding many types of structural changes from existing users. For instance, if you decide to vertically segment a table, you can simulate the original (combined) table through a view involving a join of the segments. If you horizontally segment a table, you may be able to simulate the original (combined) table through a view involving a union of the segments (assuming your product supports unions in views—some products do not). If you combine two tables, you can simulate the original tables through views involving appropriate selection criteria.

In all cases, you are less likely to be able to hide structural database changes from access requests that involve inserts, deletes, or updates. First, such requests are more likely to be affected logically by the changes in structure or business rules. Secondly, views—your chief mechanism for insulating users from change—are frequently not effective in the case of update requests. Recall that most views involving joins cannot be updated. Moreover, different columns, different business rules, new occurrences of nulls and default values, and so on may require new logic in insert/update/delete routines.

Sometimes there also are other, more subtle implications (such as unforeseen effects on performance, storage, or availability) to consider when implementing structural database changes. A common example is the perhaps unexpected consequences of adding a column via an SQL ALTER command.

RULE RDDT.23

When adding columns, consider implications with respect to *domains* and *sequencing of columns* within a table.

Typically new columns must permit null or default values because, when first created, the column values are empty.

Moreover, usually relational DBMS products place new columns logically to the right of existing columns. Thus, the command SELECT * displays new columns to the right of all others. Depending on DBMS space management, however, new columns may not be physically adjacent to original columns. For instance, they may be placed in available free space and "chained" through "pointers" to other columns in the same row. Performance implications of such suboptimal row storage can be significant.

If either of these implications—the occurrence of null or default values or the rightmost (and perhaps nonadjacent) column positioning—is undesirable, you may want to add the column by dropping and recreating the entire table. In this way, you can explicitly restrict occurrence of nulls and specify column positioning.

PLANNING CHANGES

Having discussed dropping, adding, and changing relational objects, let us consider some general guidelines for planning structural database modifications.

RULE RDDT.24

Document all design changes in the *data dictionary*. Include a description of the original design, the changed design, and the reason for the change.

Just as you recorded all aspects of the original database design in a data dictionary, you should record any changes to that design. You may even keep a history of old definitions. Such documentation is important if you need to re-store a database structure to the way it was before a change. The documenta-tion may also assist in evaluating future design changes.

RULE RDDT.25

Create a *scenario* for incorporating changes before attempting to implement them.

Even when the resulting change should be transparent to users (e.g., in the case of physical storage changes), creating an implementation scenario assists in analyzing the effects and reducing risk. In particular, an implementation sce-nario may highlight perhaps unforeseen implications of the change process it-self—for instance, effect on availability of the object being changed and of re-lated or even unrelated objects. Specify a scenario detailing object additions, drops, changes, and reloads. Identify procedures for redefining objects (where is source DDL?), loading data (where is source data?), and changing mainte-nance routines. Highlight availability implications, required access to other ta-bles (i.e., to validate business rules), sort requirements, back-up requirements, and approximate schedule.

We present sample scenarios for three changes. Typically the most compli-cated changes involve dropping objects; thus, each of the selected examples di-rectly or indirectly includes a drop operation.

EXAMPLE 1: ADD A NEW TABLE. Suppose the ice-cream parlor database contains in-formation about each ice-cream parlor and the employees who work in it. After initial database implementation, the user decides to assign employees to partic-ular cash registers within each parlor (Figure 17.7).

A sample scenario for the change is as follows:

1. Create the REGISTER table.
2. Add the REGISTER*NUMBER column to the EMPLOYEE table.
3. Drop the PARLOR*NUMBER column from the EMPLOYEE table.
4. Modify the business rules (e.g., insert routine) for the EMPLOYEE table to include the new column and exclude the dropped column.
5. Implement insert, delete, and update rules for the REGISTER table.
6. Modify the business rules (e.g., delete routine) for the PARLOR table to re-late to the REGISTER table rather than to the EMPLOYEE table.
7. Modify existing views, as appropriate. If users or applications expect to see PARLOR*NUMBER as part of EMPLOYEE, you will need to create a joined view. Verify that existing users will not try to update this view.

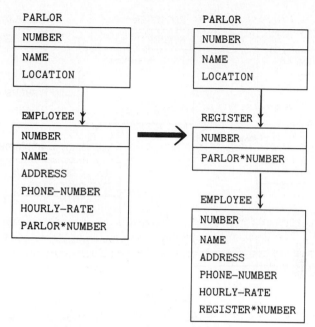

FIGURE 17.7 Proposed modification 1.

8. Load the REGISTER table.
9. Update the EMPLOYEE table with appropriate REGISTER*NUMBER values.

Consider this scenario in a DB2 environment. Step 3 requires dropping and recreating the EMPLOYEE table because DB2 does not support dropping columns through an SQL ALTER TABLE statement. Since you must drop the EMPLOYEE table, you may want to incorporate Step 2 when redefining the table to specify positioning and nullability of the REGISTER*NUMBER column. Step 7 implies recreating existing views, with associated drop and recreation of all dependent views, because DB2 does not support modifying existing views.

EXAMPLE 2: ADD OR CHANGE A RELATIONSHIP. Assume the user decides that each employee may work at more than one register. Thus, the relationship between REGISTER and EMPLOYEE changes from $1:N$ to $M:N$, as shown in Figure 17.8.

A sample scenario for the change is as follows:

1. Create the ASSIGNMENT table.
2. Drop the REGISTER*NUMBER column from the EMPLOYEE table.
3. Modify the business rules (e.g., insert and delete routines) for the REGISTER and EMPLOYEE tables to relate to the ASSIGNMENT table and to remove references to one another.
4. Implement insert, delete, and update rules for the ASSIGNMENT table.

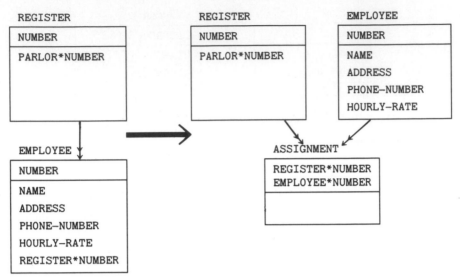

FIGURE 17.8 Proposed modification 2.

5. Make view changes as appropriate. Where users and applications previously expected one REGISTER per EMPLOYEE, now they may see many ASSIGNMENTs. Thus, programs and queries also may need to be changed.
6. Load the ASSIGNMENT table.

EXAMPLE 3: CHANGE A NONKEY COLUMN TO A FOREIGN KEY. Suppose the ice-cream parlor stores ice cream in various refrigerators. Thus, for inventory control you record, for each flavor, the storage location (refrigerator and bin number), how much is currently in stock (on-hand amount), and at what level a reorder should be initiated (reorder amount). Subsequently, the equipment-maintenance personnel decide to track refrigerator repair and maintenance activity. Thus, as indicated in Figure 17.9, REFRIGERATOR becomes an entity. REFRIGERATOR*NUMBER becomes a foreign key in FLAVOR.

A sample scenario for the change is as follows:

1. Create the REFRIGERATOR table.
2. Change the name of the REFRIGERATOR–NUMBER column in FLAVOR to comply with naming standards for foreign keys. Use synonyms or views to preserve the original column name.
3. Modify the business rules (e.g., insert routine) for the FLAVOR table to support the new foreign key.
4. Implement insert, delete, and update rules for the REFRIGERATOR table.
5. Make view changes, as appropriate.
6. Load the REFRIGERATOR table.

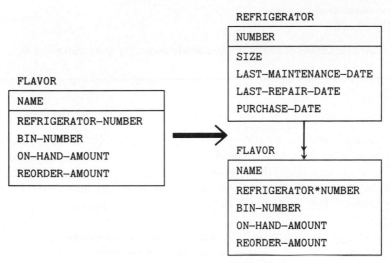

FIGURE 17.9 Proposed modification 3.

7. Verify that REFRIGERATOR*NUMBER values in FLAVOR are consistent with rows in the REFRIGERATOR table.

ANTICIPATE RELATIONAL TECHNOLOGY EVOLUTION

Whereas crystal balls are unreliable tools, the theoretical foundation that underlies relational technology enables projecting commercial enhancements with some confidence. You can expect to see improvements such as these:

☐ Improved support for integrity rules within the relational model (referential integrity, domains, and so on)
☐ Increased optimizer intelligence
☐ Reduction of functional limitations (enabling outer joins, updates through theoretically updatable views, and so on)
☐ Hardware and software advances (improved I/O subsystems, more database machines, operating system enhancements)
☐ Intelligent data dictionaries
☐ Distributed processing and distributed data

Timeframes for these improvements are difficult to predict and will vary with product implementations. Timing will depend in part on evolution of industry standards (e.g., ANSI SQL), vendor resources for research and development, user persistence in demanding these improvements, and market competitiveness.

Even with so many unknowns, you can make certain assumptions and design accordingly.

RULE RDDT.26

Assume relational DBMS products will eventually *automate* enforcement of most *business rules.*

For starters, assume relational technology will evolve to automate enforcement of additional business rules (domains, insert/delete rules, and so on). Domain characteristics (e.g., data types, uniqueness, range-checking) are already enforced in part by all products. Aspects of referential integrity (i.e., rules restricting foreign key values) are also or will soon be supported by many relational products.

Facilitate future migration to such improved integrity features by thoroughly documenting all business rules and employing consistent, shared enforcement mechanisms in the meantime. A systematic strategy for enforcing rules now will not only protect data integrity but also simplify migrating to more automated support in the future.

RULE RDDT.27

Assume relational DBMS products will evolve to support all *relational operations.*

Common functional limitations of today's relational products include inadequate support for union, outer join, outer union, and other operations. Where appropriate, consider alternatives for simulating such missing functionality. Preferably, resort to other DML combinations that simulate and can eventually be replaced by the missing operators. In some cases, you may modify your relational database design to compensate for today's missing functionality. If so, as functionality enhancements arrive, consider revising your relational database structure to comply more closely with your logical data model.

RULE RDDT.28

Assume relational DBMS products will improve in *performance.*

Users and vendors are just beginning to understand performance challenges and solutions for relational systems. Hardware and software breakthroughs will continue to reduce performance limitations. Even more important, a growing understanding of the usefulness and applicability of relational technology (e.g., in information centers, decision support systems, and transaction-based applications) will focus ongoing research.

The design approach in this book proposes that you translate a logical data model as directly as possible to a relational implementation, including integrity support. The methodology encourages infrequent deviation from the logical data model—only under specific circumstances, to meet particular functionality or performance objectives. As relational product performance improves, it should be relatively easy for you to identify design options to "undo" such deviations. That is, as products automate better performance, there will be less need for selective denormalization, segmenting or combining of tables, and so on to meet performance objectives. Thus, you will be able to evolve your design to approximate your logical data model more closely and still achieve acceptable performance. In this way, you will increase the stability, flexibility, and maintainability of your database while continuing to meet all functionality, integrity, and performance requirements.

SUMMARY

It has been the authors' experience that relational technology can very successfully address a wide range of business needs. However, such success is more likely when the design team is equipped with effective tools and an open, positive attitude toward applying new technology. One of the most valuable tools is a relational database design methodology, consisting of step-by-step procedures, guidelines or rules of thumb, and implementation examples. Such a methodology instills confidence by clarifying the process, techniques, and options along the way. Our hope is that this book serves as a foundation for building such confidence.

A P P E N D I X

Exercise Solutions

CHAPTER 5

5.4 BSNSS–PASSENGER and VCTN–PASSENGER would constitute a category. Thus, there would be one squared-off arrow connecting PASSENGER to BSNSS–PASSENGER and to VCTN–PASSENGER, as shown here:

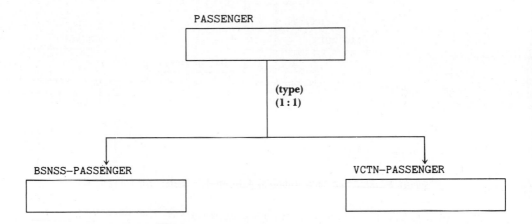

5.5 There would be a new box called TICKET and a 1:1 relationship arrow from RESERVATION to TICKET. A cardinality ratio (1:1) (assuming most reservations result in issuance of a ticket) and the number of TICKET occurrences (less than 124,000, the annual number of reservations) also would be added.

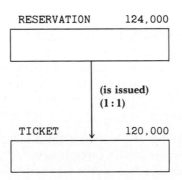

5.6

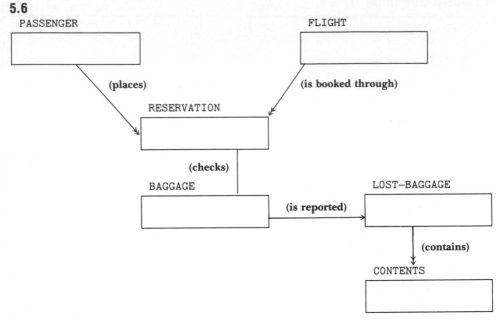

Baggage tracking and control logical data model; Steps LDM1 and LDM2.

Of course, you also should create associated data dictionary entries and design documentation.

You do not have enough information to show entity volumes or relationship ratios. You should prompt the user for this information.

Note that LOST–BAGGAGE is a subtype of BAGGAGE. It is required because Moon Launch records baggage value and contents only when the baggage is reported lost.

CHAPTER 6

6.3 Update rules for foreign keys must be consistent with relevant insert and delete rules. Consider that update of a foreign key is similar to delete and reinsert of the child entity in a relationship. If the foreign key also is a primary key in the same entity, then the update also is similar to delete and reinsert of a parent entity for any relationships having that entity as parent. Thus, the foreign key update rule must

- ☐ Incorporate the insert rule governing valid insert of the entity as child for the relationship defined by the foreign key.
- ☐ Potentially (if the foreign key also is a primary key) incorporate any delete rules governing valid delete of the entity as parent within one or more relationships.

❑   Incorporate any other relevant validation criteria, not addressed by insert/ delete rules. For example, there may be criteria governing valid delete of the entity as child or valid insert of the entity as parent within one or more relationships. (You may be wondering why the key business rules discussed thus far do not address this possibility. Key business rules cover the most frequently encountered integrity constraints: those governing insert of a child or delete of a parent entity. Other types of business rules, discussed in Chapter 9, address less frequently encountered constraints.)

In the Moon Launch Enterprise case study, what do you know about a foreign key update rule for the attribute PASSENGER*CODE in BSNSS– PASSENGER?

❑   It must incorporate the *automatic* child insert rule for PASSENGER *type* BSNSS–PASSENGER.
❑   Since PASSENGER*CODE also is part of the primary key for BSNSS– PASSENGER, the update rule also must incorporate the *restrict* parent delete rule for BSNSS–PASSENGER *places* RESERVATION.
❑   It probably also includes other logic. For instance, whenever you update BSNSS–PASSENGER.PASSENGER*CODE, you probably want to delete the PASSENGER with the old CODE and to create a new PASSENGER with the new CODE (sort of a child delete rule combined with a child insert rule). Chapter 9 specifically addresses the need for child delete as well as insert rules in the case of subtypes.

6.4 The introduction of international passenger code raises the issue of whether it becomes the primary key of PASSENGER.

❑   If it does, it must be propagated as the foreign key in child entities (BSNSS–PASSENGER, VCTN–PASSENGER, RESERVATION). Moreover, PASSENGER.COUNTRY–NAME and PASSENGER.CODE must be designated an alternate key in the PASSENGER entity.
❑   If it does not, international passenger code becomes an alternate key in PASSENGER.

6.5 The rules are

❑   Insert rule—*dependent* (RESERVATION must exist to issue TICKET)
❑   Delete rule—*no effect* (TICKET remains in existence even though RESERVATION has been canceled)

Of course, you will not want to allow passengers holding tickets for canceled reservations to board the plane! Thus, you may want to record the canceled status as another attribute in TICKET (*customized* delete rule). Or, you may just require that the ticket agent check whether the RESERVATION still exists before allowing a passenger to board.

6.6

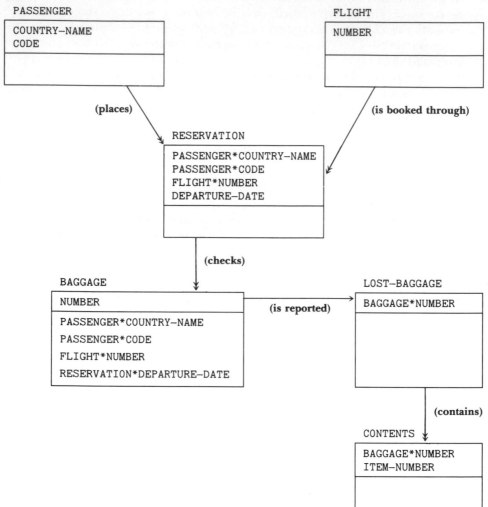

Baggage tracking and control logical data model; Steps LDM3 and LDM4.

Parent	Child	Child Insert Rule	Parent Delete Rule
PASSENGER	RESERVATION	automatic	restrict
FLIGHT	RESERVATION	dependent	customized
RESERVATION	BAGGAGE	dependent	customized
BAGGAGE	LOST–BAGGAGE	dependent	cascade
LOST–BAGGAGE	CONTENTS	dependent	cascade

Baggage tracking and control insert/delete rules; Step LDM5.

Note that the rules for the first two relationships (PASSENGER *places* RESERVATION and FLIGHT *is booked through* RESERVATION) stem from the information provided in the passenger reservations user view. We should check with the baggage clerks to be sure that these rules are consistent with their view of the business.

Also note that the *cascade* delete rule for the BAGGAGE *is reported* LOST–BAGGAGE relationship is dictated by Rule LDM5.5 for supertype–subtype relationships.

CHAPTER 7

7.4 Total number of reservations is derived by counting occurrences of the RESERVATION entity for a given flight number and date. Currently, there is no entity in the logical data model with a primary key composed of flight number and date. Thus, to represent total number of reservations, you would have to create a new entity as follows:

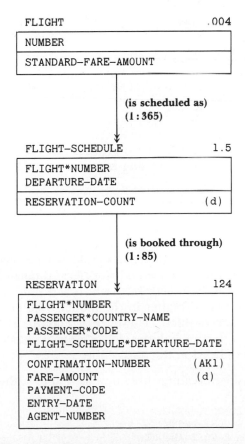

Note that under this scenario, DEPARTURE–DATE becomes a foreign key in RESERVATION. Also, the relationship cardinalities change to reflect the new entity.

7.5 Under a uniform credit-rating scheme, CREDIT–RATING*CODE should be placed in PASSENGER and removed from BUSINESS and VCTN–PASSENGER. The relationships CREDIT–RATING *is granted to* BUSINESS and CREDIT–RATING *is granted to* VCTN–PASSENGER are replaced by one relationship, CREDIT–RATING *is granted to* PASSENGER.

7.6 A baggage tracking and control logical data model program is illustrated on the following page. You should have added at least the following nonkey attributes, based on the user view description:

```
PASSENGER.NAME
PASSENGER.ADDRESS
PASSENGER.PHONE–NUMBER
FLIGHT.DESTINATION–NAME
LOST–BAGGAGE.DESCRIPTION–TEXT
LOST–BAGGAGE.VALUE–AMOUNT
CONTENTS.DESCRIPTION–TEXT
CONTENTS.VALUE–AMOUNT
BAGGAGE.CANCEL–FLAG
```

Also, you should have defined LOST–BAGGAGE.VALUE–AMOUNT as the value of the *baggage only*, excluding its contents, to avoid redundant or partially derived data.

Finally, if any attributes seem misplaced to you, retain your questions until Chapter 8. The Exercises in Chapter 8 provide you with an opportunity to verify—or to correct—your solution using *normalization* techniques.

CHAPTER 8

8.4 The data element called CALORIES should not be placed with RESERVED–MEAL, since RESERVED–MEAL then would violate third normal form. (CALORIES is determined by MEAL*NUMBER–SPECIAL, which is a nonkey attribute). Instead, CALORIES should be placed higher in the model. The next candidates include VEGET–MEAL and SEAFOOD–MEAL. However, if Philippe records calories for *all* meals, you want to record calories for STANDARD–MEAL also. In this case, CALORIES should be placed in the MEAL entity.

8.5 You might consider creating three new attributes within MEAL:

```
ENTREE–WHOLESALE–COST–AMOUNT
SALAD–WHOLESALE–COST–AMOUNT
DESSERT–WHOLESALE–COST–AMOUNT
```

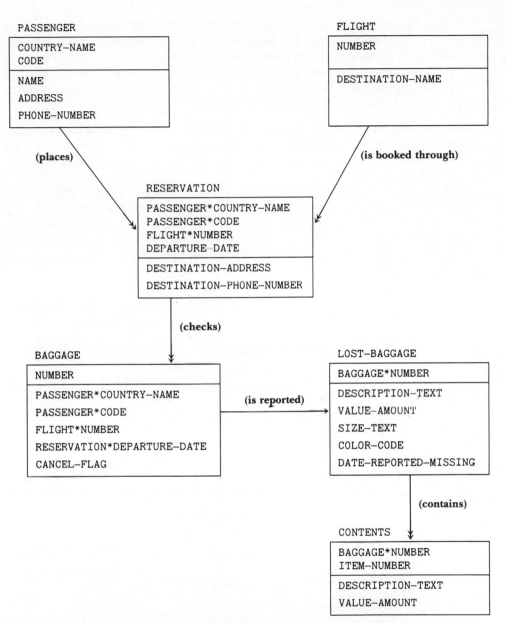

Baggage tracking and control logical data model; Step LDM6.

However, then MEAL would no longer be in third normal form (since ENTREE-NAME determines ENTREE-WHOLESALE-COST-AMOUNT, and so on). Thus, create three new entities: ENTREE, SALAD, and DESSERT. In each of these new entities, record the primary key (ENTREE.NAME, SALAD.NAME, and DESSERT.NAME, respectively). Also record wholesale cost within each new entity.

Note that ENTREE*NAME, SALAD*NAME, and DESSERT*NAME become foreign keys in MEAL. Thus, there are new key business rules to be determined. In addition, depending on usefulness to the user, you may choose to represent related costs (e.g., price of meal to passenger, or total cost of meals stocked on a flight) as derived attributes in other entities, such as MEAL, STANDARD–MEAL, VEGET–MEAL, SPECIAL–MEAL, RESERVED–MEAL, FLIGHT–SCHEDULE.

8.6 In the baggage tracking and control user view, you established a *customized* delete rule for the RESERVATION *checks* BAGGAGE relationship (Exercise 6.6). This rule says that, whenever you delete a RESERVATION due to passenger cancellation, you turn on the CANCEL–FLAG in associated BAGGAGE occurrences.

This design causes CANCEL–FLAG to *appear redundant* in BAGGAGE. (Since CANCEL–FLAG can be determined by the primary key of RESERVATION, why is it not moved up to be an attribute of the parent RESERVATION entity instead?) However, the business rule directs you to "denormalize" and to place CANCEL–FLAG in BAGGAGE, so that you can delete RESERVATION and not lose cancellation data about associated BAGGAGE.

Alternatively, you could place CANCEL–FLAG in RESERVATION. Then cancellation of a reservation should *not* cause delete of RESERVATION but rather should flag RESERVATION as canceled. This design would be more consistent with normalization principles, but would change the meaning of the RESERVATION entity to encompass canceled as well as active reservations. Thus, it would alter business rules and transaction specifications.

You will have a chance to reconsider these questions when you tune your design based on processing considerations in Part 3. Processing considerations may cause you to favor one alternative over the other.

CHAPTER 9

9.4 A sample domain hierarchy is as follows:

General Domain

NAME

data type: character
length: 35 or less
format: embedded blanks and punctuation
allowable values: a-z, 0-9, foreign language letters, punctuation marks
meaning: name

Entity-Independent Domain

BUSINESS–NAME

general domain: NAME
length: 30 or less
meaning: name of business

Entity-Specific Domains

BUSINESS.NAME

independent domain: BUSINESS–NAME
allowable values: (PK component)
uniqueness: nonunique
null support: nonnull

```
BSNSS-PASSENGER.BUSINESS*NAME
```
independent domain: BUSINESS-NAME
allowable values: (FK component)
uniqueness: nonunique
null support: nonnull
meaning: name of business that employs this
    passenger

Entity-Independent Domain

```
LAST-NAME
```
general domain: NAME
length: 20 or less
meaning: last name of individual

Entity-Specific Domain

```
PASSENGER.LAST-NAME
```
independent domain: LAST-NAME
uniqueness: nonunique
null support: nonnull
meaning: last name of passenger

9.5 Triggering operations for PASSENGER.FIRST-RESERVATION-PENDING-FLAG
are as follows:

User Rule	Event	Entity Name	Condition	Action
On passenger's first reservation, turn off flag	INSERT	PASSENGER	if not also inserting RESERVATION	set PASSENGER. FIRST-RESERVATION-PENDING-FLAG to 'Y'
	INSERT	RESERVATION	if FIRST-RESERVATION-PENDING-FLAG = 'Y' in associated PASSENGER entity	set PASSENGER. FIRST-RESERVATION-PENDING-FLAG to 'N'

9.6

Attribute Name	Data Type, Length, and Format	Allowable Values	Meaning
PASSENGER.PHONE-NUMBER	numeric 10 digits mask: nnn-nnn-nnnn	–	passenger's home telephone number
RESERVATION. DEPARTURE-DATE	date mask: cc/yy/mm/dd	calendar date in the range 1980–1990	flight departure date of reservation
BAGGAGE.NUMBER	numeric 3 digits mask: zzn	range: 1–999	identification number for baggage, generated by system

**Baggage tracking and control logical data model; Step LDM8, entity-independent domain
characteristics.**

Attribute Name	Uniqueness	Null Support	Default Value	Entity-Specific Meaning and Allowable Values
PASSENGER.PHONE-NUMBER	N	Y	-	-
RESERVATION.DEPARTURE-DATE	N	N	-	(PK component)
BAGGAGE.RESERVATION*DEPARTURE-DATE	N	N	-	(FK component)
BAGGAGE.NUMBER	Y	N	-	(PK)
LOST-BAGGAGE.BAGGAGE*NUMBER	Y	N	-	(PK), (FK)

Baggage tracking and control logical data model; Step LDM8, entity-specific domain characteristics.

Note that you need not define entity-independent domain characteristics for foreign key attributes, because they are already defined for the corresponding primary keys.

User Rule	Event	Entity Name	Attribute Name	Condition	Action
1. Delete LOST-BAGGAGE after 90 days	UPDATE	system variable	current date	current date = LOST-BAGGAGE.DATE-REPORTED-MISSING + 90 days	delete LOST-BAGGAGE
2. Add $3 to RESERVATION.FARE-AMOUNT for each BAGGAGE in excess of 2 occurrences	INSERT	BAGGAGE		COUNT(BAGGAGE) associated with this RESERVATION > 2 after insert operation	RESERVATION.FARE-AMOUNT= RESERVATION.FARE-AMOUNT + 3
	DELETE	BAGGAGE		COUNT(BAGGAGE) associated with this RESERVATION ≥ 2 after delete operation	RESERVATION.FARE-AMOUNT= RESERVATION.FARE-AMOUNT - 3

Baggage tracking and control logical data model; Step LDM9, triggering operations.

Note the business rules imply the need for the following attributes:

LOST-BAGGAGE.DATE-REPORTED-MISSING

RESERVATION.FARE-AMOUNT (d)

RESERVATION.FARE-AMOUNT is a derived attribute based on the standard fare for the flight (FLIGHT.STANDARD-FARE) and the number of baggage pieces checked (as well as any applicable discounts).

CHAPTER 10

10.4 The conceptual schema for Gran's Grocery Store must be extended to incorporate the new entities, relationships and attributes defined in the payroll logical data model. The only entities already in the conceptual schema that are affected by the new logical data model are FROZBIN, SHELF, and TRANSACTION.

First, FROZBIN and SHELF become children in relationships to a new conceptual schema AISLE entity:

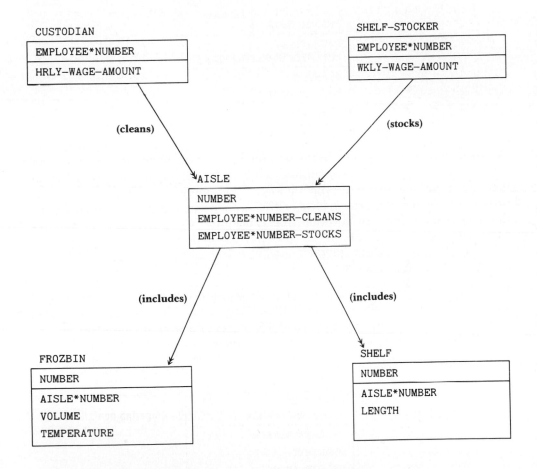

CUSTODIAN

EMPLOYEE*NUMBER
HRLY-WAGE-AMOUNT

SHELF-STOCKER

EMPLOYEE*NUMBER
WKLY-WAGE-AMOUNT

(cleans)

(stocks)

AISLE

NUMBER
EMPLOYEE*NUMBER-CLEANS
EMPLOYEE*NUMBER-STOCKS

(includes)

(includes)

FROZBIN

NUMBER
AISLE*NUMBER
VOLUME
TEMPERATURE

SHELF

NUMBER
AISLE*NUMBER
LENGTH

AISLE was not previously represented in the conceptual schema because it had no nonkey attributes. (It was solely an aggregation of entities FROZBIN and SHELF). When AISLE is added to the conceptual schema, AISLE*NUMBER in FROZBIN and SHELF assumes the role of a foreign key.

Second, CHECKER–NUMBER in the conceptual schema TRANSACTION entity is renamed to EMPLOYEE*NUMBER–CHECKER, as a foreign key reflecting a relationship to the new conceptual schema CHECKER entity:

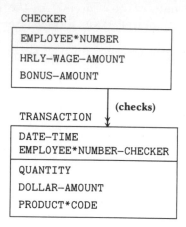

CHECKER

EMPLOYEE*NUMBER
HRLY–WAGE–AMOUNT
BONUS–AMOUNT

(checks)

TRANSACTION

DATE–TIME
EMPLOYEE*NUMBER–CHECKER
QUANTITY
DOLLAR–AMOUNT
PRODUCT*CODE

No changes are required in the payroll logical data model because it has no conflicts with the existing conceptual schema. Moreover, the mappings from the conceptual schema to the payroll logical data model are extremely straightforward: they are primarily selects of the appropriate conceptual schema entities and relationships. In addition, the conceptual schema AISLE entity is renamed to AISLE–ASSIGNMENT in the payroll logical data model, and the conceptual schema AISLE.NUMBER attribute is similarly renamed to AISLE–ASSIGNMENT.AISLE–NUMBER.

10.5 (1) Gran's purchase of another cash register will require addition of a REGISTER–NUMBER attribute to the TRANSACTION entity. Moreover, the combination of DATE–TIME and REGISTER–NUMBER becomes a second candidate key. If you choose this combination to be the new primary key, you have the following:

TRANSACTION

DATE–TIME	(AK1)
REGISTER–NUMBER	
CHECKER–NUMBER	(AK1)
QUANTITY	
DOLLAR–AMOUNT	
PRODUCT*CODE	

Since this change affects the primary key of TRANSACTION and any related foreign keys, and since the modified logical data model correctly represents the business even before Gran buys a second cash register, it probably is desirable to modify the logical data model now.

(2) One nonkey attribute (N/S–FLAG) must be added to both the FROZBIN and the SHELF entities to accommodate Cecilia's requirement:

FROZBIN

NUMBER
AISLE–NUMBER
N/S–FLAG
VOLUME
TEMPERATURE

SHELF

NUMBER
AISLE–NUMBER
N/S–FLAG
LENGTH

Since the effect is minor, it makes little difference whether you incorporate the change now into the logical data model or merely note it in the data dictionary.

(3) Gran will require one additional attribute (DATE–SHIPPED) in the SHIPMENT entity, plus perhaps renaming of the SHIPMENT.DATE attribute to SHIPMENT.DATE–RECEIVED for clarity:

SHIPMENT

PRODUCT*CODE ORDER*DATE DATE–RECEIVED
QUANTITY DATE–SHIPPED

Now, what about the primary key of SHIPMENT? Is it possible to receive two shipments for the same order on the same date (perhaps shipped on different dates)? If so, the primary key shown is not sufficient to identify entity occurrences. What about the combination of PRODUCT*CODE, ORDER*DATE, DATE–RECEIVED, and DATE–SHIPPED as primary key? Is it possible to receive on the same date multiple shipments for the same order, also shipped on the same date? If so, you may need a different primary key altogether—perhaps PRODUCT*CODE, ORDER*DATE, and the vendor's shipment code.

Since this change affects both the primary key of SHIPMENT and the name of an existing attribute (SHIPMENT.DATE), it may seem desirable to reflect the change in the logical data model now. However, inclusion of a new attribute like vendor's shipment code in the primary key requires that a value of that attribute always be present. Thus, you may be unable to implement this change if Gran is not yet ready to change her business operation to begin recording this shipment data.

10.7

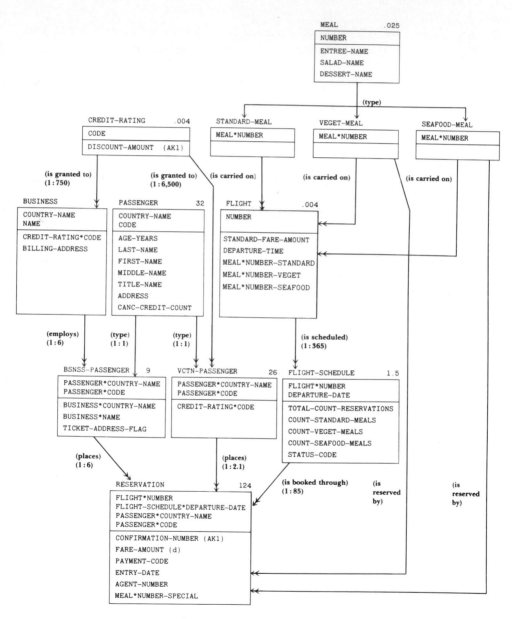

Entity Volumes: Annual averages in 000s

Moon Launch composite reservations/meals logical data model; Step LDM10.

Steps in combining the Moon Launch meal assignments and passenger reservations user views are as follows:

- Merge the FLIGHT and FLIGHT-SCHEDULE entities as well as the relationship from FLIGHT to FLIGHT-SCHEDULE.
- Merge the PASSENGER entities, noting that the primary key of PASSENGER is COUNTRY-NAME plus CODE. It seems Philippe incorrectly identified the primary key as CODE alone. Also note that NAME from Philippe's user view is eliminated as redundant with LAST-NAME, FIRST-NAME, MIDDLE-NAME, and TITLE-NAME from the passenger reservations view.
- Correct the foreign key in RESERVED-MEAL from PASSENGER*CODE to PASSENGER*COUNTRY-NAME plus PASSENGER*CODE (as a result of merging the PASSENGER entities).
- Merge the RESERVATION and RESERVED-MEAL entities, which now share the same primary key. Similarly, merge the relationships FLIGHT-SCHEDULE *is booked through* RESERVATION and FLIGHT-SCHEDULE *has booked* RESERVED-MEAL.
- Eliminate the PASSENGER *reserves* RESERVED-MEAL relationship. Now that RESERVED-MEAL is merged with RESERVATION, this relationship is redundant with the (PASSENGER *type* BSNSS-PASSENGER, BSNSS-PASSENGER *places* RESERVATION) and (PASSENGER *type* VCTN-PASSENGER, VCTN-PASSENGER *places* RESERVATION) relationship chains.
- Incorporate all other entities and relationships.
- Incorporate or resolve entity volumes and relationship cardinality ratios. (Note that Philippe has provided insufficient information to determine some of these numbers.)
- Union or reconcile key business rules, domains, and triggering operations. (You can ignore this step since, luckily for you, Philippe has also neglected to define his business rules.)

The composite logical data model diagram is shown on page 564.

CHAPTER 11

11.4 A logical data model for data dictionary information about tables might be constructed as on page 566.

Note that TABLE-VERSION represents an actual table implementation. Thus, the relational DBMS name for a table is assumed to include four components: user ID of the table creator (perhaps implied as a prefix), logical table name, status code (as in production or test), and version number (perhaps with a default of 0). Details specific to an implementation (such as resident processor or scheduled/actual date of production release) are stored in TABLE-VERSION.

ENTITY-TABLE-MAPPING contains details regarding entity-to-table transformations. The double-headed arrows indicate these transformations may be *M:N*. Such transformations are discussed in Chapters 15 and 16.

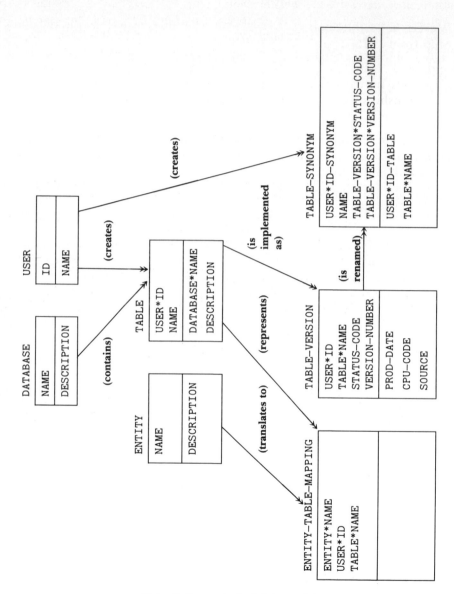

Data dictionary logical data model.

Finally, the diagram indicates that synonyms can be created by users who are not the creator of the associated table. Thus, TABLE–SYNONYM includes two foreign keys: USER*ID–SYNONYM representing the creator of the synonym, and USER*ID–TABLE, TABLE*NAME, TABLE–VERSION*STATUS–CODE, TABLE–VERSION*VERSION–NUMBER, representing the associated table (including its creator and version identification). If your DBMS does not permit the creators of a table and its synonyms to be different, your logical data model will represent other relationships. Note that the foreign key representing TABLE–VERSION is part primary key and part nonkey.

11.6 A possible diagramming technique for relational tables is to extend the logical data modeling conventions presented in Part 2 as follows:

☐   Keep boxes to represent relational tables
☐   Replace logical entity and attribute names with relational table and column names
☐   Keep arrows and names representing relationships for clarity
☐   Keep entity volumes and relationship cardinality designations for clarity
☐   Add dashed lines around boxes to indicate database boundaries. Label the dashed lines with database names
☐   Add table-locking parameters in parentheses following table names
☐   Allow the sequence of columns in the diagram (top to bottom) to indicate sequence of columns in the table (left to right) (Note: this approach assumes that the primary key attributes are the leftmost columns in the table.)
☐   Add dataset (file) names for each table under the box representing the table

A diagram for the Moon Launch passenger reservations tables is shown on page 568. It is based on several assumptions:

☐   All tables are assigned to one database. (Possible motivations for defining multiple databases are explored in Exercises 11.7 and 11.8).
☐   Each table is assigned to its own dataset (as we shall recommend in Chapter 13). Our dataset naming convention assigns the first two letters (ML) to designate the database (MNLAUNCH), the next letter (P) to designate test versus production status, and the final five letters to designate a table.
☐   Table and column naming conventions adopt the guidelines suggested for DB2 in the case study.
☐   Sequencing of columns follows the guidelines provided in the case study for DB2; namely, nullable columns follow nonnullable columns, and variable-length columns follow fixed-length columns.
☐   Locking parameters refer to DB2's options for locking, discussed in the case study. Most of the tables will be updated frequently and online (as discussed further in Chapter 13); thus, lock size ANY is specified. Updates to the CRDT_RTNG and FLIGHT tables are less frequent and can be scheduled when there is little other concurrent activity; thus, lock size TABLESPACE is specified.

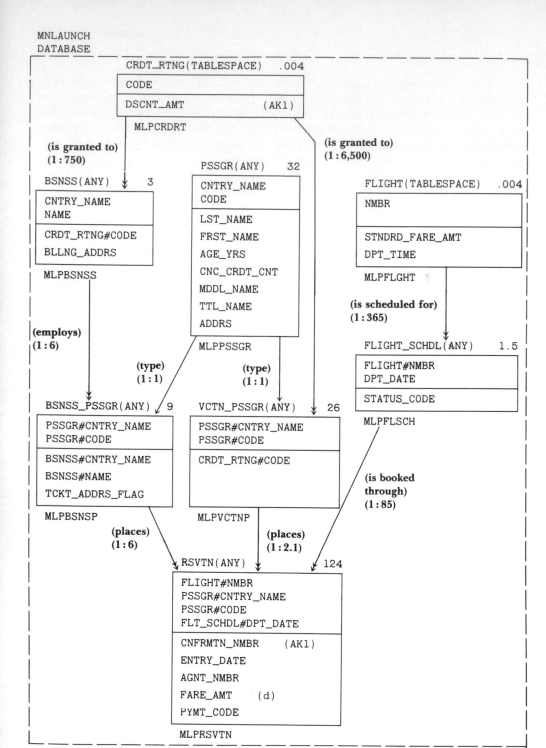

MNLAUNCH
DATABASE

CRDT_RTNG(TABLESPACE)   .004

| CODE |
| DSCNT_AMT   (AK1) |

MLPCRDRT

(is granted to)
(1:750)

(is granted to)
(1:6,500)

PSSGR(ANY)   32

BSNSS(ANY)   3

| CNTRY_NAME |
| NAME |
| CRDT_RTNG#CODE |
| BLLNG_ADDRS |

MLPBSNSS

| CNTRY_NAME CODE |
| LST_NAME |
| FRST_NAME |
| AGE_YRS |
| CNC_CRDT_CNT |
| MDDL_NAME |
| TTL_NAME |
| ADDRS |

MLPPSSGR

FLIGHT(TABLESPACE)   .004

| NMBR |
| STNDRD_FARE_AMT |
| DPT_TIME |

MLPFLGHT

(is scheduled for)
(1:365)

FLIGHT_SCHDL(ANY)   1.5

| FLIGHT#NMBR DPT_DATE |
| STATUS_CODE |

(employs)
(1:6)

(type)
(1:1)

(type)
(1:1)

BSNSS_PSSGR(ANY)   9

| PSSGR#CNTRY_NAME PSSGR#CODE |
| BSNSS#CNTRY_NAME BSNSS#NAME TCKT_ADDRS_FLAG |

MLPBSNSP

VCTN_PSSGR(ANY)   26

| PSSGR#CNTRY_NAME PSSGR#CODE |
| CRDT_RTNG#CODE |

MLPVCTNP

MLPFLSCH

(is booked
through)
(1:85)

(places)
(1:6)

(places)
(1:2.1)

RSVTN(ANY)   124

| FLIGHT#NMBR PSSGR#CNTRY_NAME PSSGR#CODE FLT_SCHDL#DPT_DATE |
| CNFRMTN_NMBR   (AK1) |
| ENTRY_DATE |
| AGNT_NMBR |
| FARE_AMT   (d) |
| PYMT_CODE |

MLPRSVTN

Entity Volumes: Annual averages in 000s

Relational table diagramming technique.

11.8 Your DBMS (like DB2) may facilitate performing or administering maintenance activities against tables grouped by database. For instance, you may establish database administrators with responsibility for executing (or for authorizing execution of) backup, recovery, and reorganization utilities against all tables within a given database. Alternatively, you might group tables into databases based on table size and associated time required for utility processing. For instance, you might ensure that all tables within a database are similar in size. Then you can "stop" the entire database, initiate utilities to run in parallel against each table within the database, and be reasonably confident that the utilities will all complete in approximately the same timeframe. Or, if your DBMS prohibits parallel execution of utilities against tables within the same database, you may split across different databases tables that you want to backup or recover in parallel.

CHAPTER 12

12.4 You can show entity business rules and associated enforcement techniques on the relational database diagram

☐ By placing primary key attributes above a horizontal line (as in the logical data model diagram)

☐ By designating alternate key attributes with (AKn) (as in the logical data model diagram)

☐ By following primary and alternate key names with codes designating implementation mechanisms—for instance, PK to denote DDL PRIMARY KEY syntax, AKn to denote DDL ALTERNATE KEY syntax for the nth alternate key, NN to denote DDL NOT NULL syntax, Un to denote DDL UNIQUE syntax for the nth unique attribute group, UIXn to denote the nth unique index, SMR to represent an automated standard maintenance routine, or ME to indicate manual enforcement by users

A sample diagram for the RESERVATION table builds on the diagram from Exercise 11.6 (refer to its solution) as follows:

```
RSVTN(ANY)                          124
┌─────────────────────────────────────────┐
│ FLIGHT#NMBR              U1,NN           │
│ PSSGR#CNTRY_NAME         U1,NN           │
│ PSSGR#CODE              U1,NN            │
│ FLT_SCHDL#DPT_DATE       U1,NN           │
├─────────────────────────────────────────┤
│ CNFRMTN_NMBR  (AK1)      U2              │
│                                          │
│ ENTRY_DATE                               │
│                                          │
│ AGNT_NMBR                                │
│                                          │
│ FARE_AMT  (d)                            │
│                                          │
│ PYMT_CODE                                │
└─────────────────────────────────────────┘
  MLPRSVTN
```

This diagram indicates compliance with existing ANSI SQL standards to enforce primary and alternate key properties: namely, specification of UNIQUE for the primary and alternate keys (designated by U1 and U2, respectively) and NOT NULL (designated by NN) for the primary key. Note that a code of U alone to represent UNIQUE is insufficient since you must be able to denote uniqueness of attribute groups (i.e., composite primary and alternate keys). Other coding designations in the RSVTN diagram were explained in the solution to Exercise 11.6.

As an example of a product-specific design, the following diagram illustrates implementation of the RESERVATION table using IBM's DB2 relational DBMS.

```
RSVTN(ANY)                              124
┌──────────────────────────────────────────┐
│ FLIGHT#NMBR                  UIX1,NN       │
│ PSSGR#CNTRY_NAME             UIX1,NN       │
│ PSSGR#CODE                   UIX1,NN       │
│ FLT_SCHDL#DPT_DATE           UIX1,NN       │
│                                            │
│ CNFRMTN_NMBR    (AK1)        UIX2          │
│ ENTRY_DATE                                 │
│ AGNT_NMBR                                  │
│ FARE_AMT    (d)                            │
│ PYMT_CODE                                  │
└──────────────────────────────────────────┘
  MLPRSVTN
```

This diagram indicates use of unique indexes (UIX1 and UIX2) to enforce uniqueness of the primary and alternate keys.

12.5 You can show relationship business rules and associated enforcement techniques on the relational database diagram

- [ ] By labeling each relationship on the diagram with a number or name—as on the logical data model diagram
- [ ] By providing a legend that associates each relationship with codes for corresponding business rules and enforcement mechanisms

A sample diagram of the BSNSS–PASSENGER *places* RESERVATION relationship follows on page 57. This diagram assumes an extended ANSI SQL implementation. Parent delete and update rules (abbreviated PD and PU) of *restrict* and child insert and update rules (CI and CU) of *dependent* are implied by the ANSI SQL PRIMARY KEY and FOREIGN KEY DDL syntax (or, perhaps, are explicitly enforced through ON DELETE RESTRICT and ON UPDATE RESTRICT syntax). In fact, the child insert and update rules are redefined from *automatic* to *dependent*, so they can be enforced through ANSI SQL DDL (as suggested in the case study). Other key business rules, not enforceable through DDL, might be enforced through standard maintenance routines or manual enforcement procedures, and would be coded as such (e.g., SMR (routine–name) or ME).

```
BSNSS_PSSGR(ANY)                       9
┌─────────────────────────────────────────┐
│ PSSGR#CNTRY_NAME            U1,NN         │
│ PSSGR#CODE                 U1,NN         │
├─────────────────────────────────────────┤
│ BSNSS#CNTRY_NAME              NN          │
│ BSNSS#NAME                    NN          │
│ TCKT_ADDRS_FLAG                          │
└─────────────────────────────────────────┘
  MLPBSNSP
```

(R6—places)
(1:6)

```
RSVTN(ANY)                            124
┌─────────────────────────────────────────┐
│ FLIGHT#NMBR                 U1,NN        │
│ PSSGR#CNTRY_NAME            U1,NN        │
│ PSSGR#CODE                 U1,NN        │
│ FLT_SCHDL#DPT_DATE          U1,NN        │
├─────────────────────────────────────────┤
│ CNFRMTN_NMBR   (AK1)        U2           │
│ ENTRY_DATE                               │
│ AGNT_NMBR                                │
│ FARE_AMT   (d)                           │
│ PYMT_CODE                                │
└─────────────────────────────────────────┘
  MLPRSVTN
```

Relationship Rules

Relationship	Business Rule	Enforcement Mechanism
R6	PD—*restrict*	DDL
R6	PU—*restrict*	DDL
R6	CI—*dependent*	DDL
R6	CU—*dependent*	DDL

12.6 Extended ANSI SQL DDL to create the RESERVATION table is as follows:

```
CREATE TABLE RSVTN
    (FLIGHT#NMBR SMALLINT NOT NULL
        CHECK FLIGHT#NMBR IN (1,2,3,4),
    PSSGR#CNTRY_NAME CHAR(25) NOT NULL,
    PSSGR#CODE CHAR(25) NOT NULL,
    FLT_SCHDL#DPT_DATE CHAR(8) NOT NULL,
    CNFRMTN_NMBR INTEGER,
    ENTRY_DATE CHAR(8) NOT NULL,
```

```
AGNT_NMBR SMALLINT NOT NULL,
FARE_AMT DECIMAL (6,2),
PYMT_CODE CHAR(2) NOT NULL
     DEFAULT ('C'),
PRIMARY KEY (FLIGHT#NMBR,
              PSSGR#CNTRY_NAME,
              PSSGR#CODE,
              FLT_SCHDL#DPT_DATE),
FOREIGN KEY (FLIGHT#NMBR,
              FLT_SCHDL#DPT_DATE)
     REFERENCES FLIGHT_SCHDL
     ON DELETE RESTRICT
     ON UPDATE RESTRICT,
FOREIGN KEY (PSSGR#CNTRY_NAME,
              PSSGR#CODE)
     REFERENCES PSSGR
     ON DELETE RESTRICT
     ON UPDATE RESTRICT)
```

Note we assume that key business rules governing the relationship FLIGHT–SCHEDULE *is booked through* RESERVATION are the same as those originally specified by the user for FLIGHT *is booked through* RESERVATION (Figure 12.2). Recall that the entity FLIGHT–SCHEDULE was added later in the logical data modeling process (Chapter 9); thus, the relationship FLIGHT *is booked through* RESERVATION was replaced by relationships from FLIGHT to FLIGHT–SCHEDULE and from FLIGHT–SCHEDULE to RESERVATION.

Also observe that we must redefine the foreign key PASSENGER*COUNTRY–NAME, PASSENGER*CODE in RESERVATION to reference one entity PASSENGER rather than either of two entities BSNSS–PASSENGER or VCTN–PASSENGER. The ANSI SQL standard does not easily support a foreign key that may, depending on occurrence, reference either of two parent tables. Suppose you defined RSVTN's foreign key PSSGR#CNTRY_NAME, PSSGR#CODE twice: once to reference BSNSS_PSSGR and once to reference VCTN_PSSGR. How could the DBMS automatically enforce child insert rules of *automatic* (or of *dependent*)? That is, into which table (BSNSS_PSSGR or VCTN_PSSGR) should the DBMS automatically insert a row (or in which table should it check for existence of a row)?

The extended ANSI SQL syntax shown does *not* address:

☐ DATE data types (and domain enforcement) for FLT_SCHDL#DPT_DATE and ENTRY_DATE.

☐ *Customized* parent delete rule for the FLIGHT–SCHEDULE *is booked through* RESERVATION relationship (when a flight is canceled, associated reservations are flagged, so that notices can be mailed out). The RESTRICT rule prevents use of DML DELETE or UPDATE commands to delete a FLIGHT–SCHEDULE entity or update its primary key when it has associated RESERVATIONs. In addition, however, you need a standard maintenance routine to invoke the *customized* rule when attempting to delete FLIGHT–SCHEDULEs with associated RESERVATIONs.

☐ Child insert rule of *automatic* for the PASSENGER *places* RESERVATION relationship. Instead, the rule is redefined as *dependent*—implied by the ANSI SQL standard for all child insert and update rules.

☐ Any of the triggering operations associated with RESERVATION. They must be enforced through standard maintenance routines.

12.7 The logic to update the DSCNT_AMT column from the CRDT_RTNG table, when passed input parameters %CODE, %DSCNT_AMT, can be specified as follows:

    a.   If new %DSCNT_AMT is lower than old DSCNT_AMT from CRDT_RTNG WHERE CODE = %CODE, go directly to (d)

    b.   Identify all RSVTN rows WHERE FLT_SCHDL#DPT_DATE = today or later, for either VCTN–PSSGR WHERE CRDT_RTNG#CODE = %CODE, or BSNSS–PSSGR associated with BSNSS WHERE CRDT_RTNG#CODE = %CODE

    c.   Update FARE_AMT for all RSVTN rows identified in (b) by dividing FARE_AMT by old DSCNT_AMT from CRDT_RTNG table WHERE CODE = %CODE, and multiplying FARE_AMT by new %DSCNT_AMT

    d.   Update CRDT_RTNG table with new %DSCNT_AMT WHERE CODE = %CODE

For extra credit, you may have identified the following chain of routines and subroutines:

```
PROCEDURE UPDT_CR_DSCNT_RTN (parameters)
      CALL UPDT_CR_DSCNT_SUBRTN (parameters)
      COMMIT WORK

PROCEDURE UPDT_CR_DSCNT_SUBRTN (parameters)
      SELECT rows FROM RSVTN
            WHERE FARE_AMT should be updated
      CALL UPDT_RSVTN_FAREAMT_SUBRTN (parameters) to update identified
            RSVTN rows
      UPDATE CRDT_RTNG
            SET DSCNT_AMT = %DSCNT_AMT
            WHERE CODE = %CODE

PROCEDURE UPDT_RSVTN_FAREAMT_SUBRTN (parameters)
      UPDATE RSVTN
            SET FARE_AMT = parameters
            WHERE parameters
```

CHAPTER 13

13.3 Table accesses for T28 are as follows:

☐ RESERVATION is accessed by FLIGHT*NUMBER and FLIGHT–SCHEDULE*DEPARTURE–DATE (to identify rows for a given flight) and CONFIRMATION–NUMBER (to include only rows with valid confirmation numbers). T28 retrieves a maximum of 100 RESERVATION rows since 100 reservations constitute a full flight.

☐   PASSENGER is accessed by its primary key to obtain all passenger information for passengers holding confirmed reservations on a given flight. T28 retrieves a maxium of 100 PASSENGER rows because 100 passengers constitute a full flight.

Output for T28 is sequenced by the PASSENGER table's primary key—COUNTRY–NAME and CODE.

SCAN OPTIONS. The tables probably are too small to merit partitioning. Depending on your DBMS, however, you may be able to use buffers, high-speed storage devices, or other options to improve scan efficiency.

CLUSTERING. Clustering RESERVATION by FLIGHT–SCHEDULE*DEPARTURE–DATE, FLIGHT*NUMBER (in either sequence), and CONFIRMATION–NUMBER will facilitate retrieving rows for confirmed reservations on a given flight. In fact, because there are a maximum of 100 reservations for a scheduled flight and because 100 reservations may all fit in one physical block, including CONFIRMATION–NUMBER in the clustering sequence may be unnecessary. Furthermore, clustering by FLIGHT–SCHEDULE*DEPARTURE–DATE, FLIGHT*NUMBER (in either sequence), and PASSENGER*COUNTRY–NAME, PASSENGER*CODE (in that sequence) will avoid the need for a sort of the output for T28.

T28 also retrieves all PASSENGER rows for a given flight. There probably is no set of columns that enables clustering such rows together. Suppose, however, that most reservations on any flight tended to be from the same country. Then clustering PASSENGER by COUNTRY–NAME or by COUNTRY–NAME plus CODE would effect approximate clustering by flight. Moreover, clustering PASSENGER by COUNTRY–NAME plus CODE and clustering RESERVATION by FLIGHT–SCHEDULE*DEPARTURE–DATE, FLIGHT*NUMBER, PASSENGER*COUNTRY–NAME, plus PASSENGER*CODE may increase efficiency of a join of RESERVATION with PASSENGER. That is, T28 will retrieve RESERVATION rows for a scheduled flight in sequence by the PASSENGER primary key. A relational DBMS may more efficiently join such presorted RESERVATION rows to a PASSENGER table whose rows are also in this sequence.

HASHING. RESERVATION is not a good candidate for hashing. Hashing by FLIGHT*NUMBER, FLIGHT–SCHEDULE*DEPARTURE–DATE (in either sequence) would result in long synonym chains (100 rows) and potential nonuniform distribution of rows. Hashing on CONFIRMATION–NUMBER would also be of no use to T28 since T28 retrieves a range of confirmation numbers (any nonnull, for example) and hashing does not facilitate this kind of access.

T28 will benefit from hashing PASSENGER on its primary key because the primary key is unique and access is by discrete primary key values. If your relational DBMS supports hashing and clustering, you may want to benchmark both alternatives for the PASSENGER table.

DB2 SOLUTION. Cluster RESERVATION by its primary key—FLIGHT*NUMBER, FLIGHT–SCHEDULE*DEPARTURE–DATE, PASSENGER*COUNTRY–NAME, and PASSENGER*CODE. Cluster PASSENGER by COUNTRY–NAME and CODE to facilitate a join of RESERVATION with PASSENGER. Do not partition the tables because both are small.

DBC/1012 SOLUTION. Choose a hash key for RESERVATION by evaluating transactions other than T28. Allow T28 to scan RESERVATION—at least until you investigate indexes in Chapter 14. Hash PASSENGER on its primary key.

13.4 Refer to the solution for Exercise 13.3 for a review of table accesses for T28. That solution recommended the following tuning techniques, assuming T28 were the most important requirement: cluster RESERVATION by primary key, and cluster or hash PASSENGER by primary key.

Clustering RESERVATION by primary key is consistent with clustering recommendations for T13, T14 and T33 as long as the clustering columns are sequenced as follows: FLIGHT–SCHEDULE*DEPARTURE–DATE, FLIGHT*NUMBER, PASSENGER*COUNTRY–NAME, PASSENGER*CODE. This sequence of clustering columns facilitates sequencing output for T33, counting RESERVATION rows for T13, retrieving RESERVATION rows by primary key for T14, retrieving rows for confirmed reservations on a flight for T28, joining RESERVATION and PASSENGER rows for T28, and sequencing output for T28. If your DBMS does not support clustering at all, T28 will have to scan RESERVATION, and you may proceed with whatever other access mechanisms (e.g., hashing) you have chosen for T13, T14 and T33 (at least until you consider indexes in Chapter 14). If your DBMS supports both hashing and clustering, clustering is probably a better choice, since RESERVATION rows are accessed and sorted by both full and partial primary key values for T13, T14, T33 and T28.

Hashing or clustering PASSENGER by primary key is consistent with tuning recommendations for T13, T14, and T33. If your DBMS supports hashing and clustering, you may want to benchmark both alternatives.

DB2 SOLUTION. Cluster RESERVATION by its primary key in the sequence FLIGHT–SCHEDULE*DEPARTURE–DATE, FLIGHT*NUMBER, PASSENGER*COUNTRY–NAME, PASSENGER*CODE. Cluster PASSENGER by its primary key in the sequence COUNTRY–NAME, CODE. Because both tables are small, you need not partition them.

DBC/1012 SOLUTION. Hash RESERVATION and PASSENGER on their full primary keys. Rely on table scans for partial key access as required by T28, at least until you investigate indexes in Chapter 14.

13.7 T36 accesses the RESERVATION table by PASSENGER*COUNTRY–NAME, PASSENGER*CODE (foreign key that is part of the primary key). T36 also accesses the PASSENGER table by its primary key to retrieve FIRST–NAME and LAST–NAME. Output is sequenced by FLIGHT–SCHEDULE*DEPARTURE–DATE, FLIGHT*NUMBER.

T36 and other requests cause RESERVATION to be accessed and sorted by full and partial primary keys. Thus, clustering is probably your best choice. There are at least five clustering alternatives:

1. FLIGHT*NUMBER, FLIGHT–SCHEDULE*DEPARTURE–DATE (in either sequence) for counting RESERVATION rows by T13
2. FLIGHT–SCHEDULE*DEPARTURE–DATE, FLIGHT*NUMBER (in that sequence) to sequence the output for T33 and T36 and to facilitate counting RESERVATION rows by T13
3. FLIGHT*NUMBER, FLIGHT–SCHEDULE*DEPARTURE–DATE, PASSENGER* COUNTRY–NAME, PASSENGER*CODE (in any sequence) for primary key access by T14 and other transactions
4. FLIGHT–SCHEDULE*DEPARTURE–DATE, FLIGHT*NUMBER, PASSENGER* COUNTRY–NAME, PASSENGER*CODE (in that sequence) to facilitate primary key access, partial key access by flight for counting of rows by T13, and sequencing of output for T33 and T36
5. PASSENGER*COUNTRY–NAME, PASSENGER*CODE, FLIGHT–SCHEDULE* DEPARTURE–DATE, FLIGHT*NUMBER (in that sequence) to facilitate primary key access, partial key access by passenger for T36, and sequencing of output for T36

Given the assumption that the online transactions (T13 and T14) have higher priority than the batch requests (T33 and T36), option 4 appears to provide the greatest combination of advantages.

If your DBMS does not support clustering, hashing RESERVATION on the full primary key is likely your best choice. This will improve performance of T14. Other requirements must resort to table scans and sorts—at least until you consider indexes in Chapter 14.

Access to PASSENGER for T13, T14, T33 and T36 always involves discrete rows based on primary key values. Thus, hashing on the primary key is an optimal solution. If your DBMS does not support hashing, clustering on the primary key is the next choice.

DB2 SOLUTION. Cluster the RESERVATION table by FLIGHT–SCHEDULE* DEPARTURE–DATE, FLIGHT*NUMBER, PASSENGER*COUNTRY–NAME, PASSENGER*CODE (in that sequence). Cluster the PASSENGER table by its primary key—COUNTRY–NAME, CODE. Do not partition the tables—both are small.

DBC/1012 SOLUTION. Hash the RESERVATION table by its primary key to facilitate T14. Rely on table scans of RESERVATION for T13, T33, and T36—at least until you consider indexes in Chapter 14. Hash the PASSENGER table by its primary key.

CHAPTER 14

14.5 Table accesses for T28 are as follows:

☐ RESERVATION is accessed by FLIGHT*NUMBER and FLIGHT–SCHEDULE* DEPARTURE–DATE (to identify rows for a given flight) and CONFIRMATION– NUMBER (to include only rows with valid confirmation numbers). T28 retrieves a maximum of 100 RESERVATION rows, since 100 reservations constitute a full flight.

☐ PASSENGER is accessed by its primary key to obtain all passenger information for passengers holding confirmed reservations on a given flight. T28 retrieves a maximum of 100 PASSENGER rows because 100 passengers constitute a full flight.

Output for T28 is sequenced by the PASSENGER table's primary key— COUNTRY–NAME and CODE.

Refer to the solution for Exercise 13.3 for a discussion of scanning, clustering, and hashing options to facilitate T28. We will assume you choose the options recommended in that solution for DB2 or for the DBC/1012. Here we consider indexes to complement those options.

DB2 SOLUTION. From the solution to Exercise 13.3, assume you decide to cluster RESERVATION by its primary key—FLIGHT*NUMBER, FLIGHT–SCHEDULE* DEPARTURE–DATE, PASSENGER*COUNTRY–NAME, and PASSENGER*CODE. Thus, you need a clustered index on these columns. You also may consider adding CONFIRMATION–NUMBER to the index to allow for index-only access. In this way, the relational DBMS can determine whether a reservation is confirmed without retrieving the row from the table. Furthermore, sequencing CONFIRMATION– NUMBER between FLIGHT–SCHEDULE*DEPARTURE–DATE and PASSENGER* COUNTRY–NAME in the index key will ensure that all index entries for confirmed reservations for a given flight are stored together.

Also, from the solution to Exercise 13.3, assume you decide to cluster PASSENGER by its primary key—COUNTRY–NAME, CODE. Thus, you need a clustered index on these columns.

DBC/1012 SOLUTION. From the solution to Exercise 13.3, assume you decide to hash the PASSENGER table on its primary key. Hashing RESERVATION on FLIGHT*NUMBER, FLIGHT–SCHEDULE*DEPARTURE–DATE (in either sequence) is undesirable because it would result in long synonym chains (100 reservations per scheduled flight) and potential nonuniform row distribution. Thus, consider adding an index into the RESERVATION table on FLIGHT*NUMBER, FLIGHT– SCHEDULE*DEPARTURE–DATE. This index will be used to retrieve up to 100 rows and is probably considerably more efficient than is a full table scan of 124,000 rows (depending, however, on the DBC/1012 configuration). You may also consider adding CONFIRMATION–NUMBER to this index.

14.6 Refer to the solution for Exercise 14.5 for a description of table accesses for T28. Also refer to the solution to Exercise 13.4 for a discussion of scanning, clustering, and hashing options to accommodate the mix of requests T13, T14, T28, and T33. We will assume you choose the options recommended in that solution for DB2 or for the DBC/1012. Here we consider indexes to complement these options.

DB2 SOLUTION. From the solution to Exercise 13.4, assume you decide to cluster RESERVATION by its primary key, sequencing the clustering columns as follows: FLIGHT–SCHEDULE*DEPARTURE–DATE, FLIGHT*NUMBER, PASSENGER*COUNTRY–NAME, PASSENGER*CODE. Thus, you will need a clustered index on those columns. You also may add CONFIRMATION–NUMBER to the index to allow for index-only access for T28. However, you should make CONFIRMATION–NUMBER the lowest-order column in the index to facilitate primary-key access for the more critical requests (T13, T14, and T33).

Also, from the solution to Exercise 13.4, assume you choose to cluster PASSENGER on its primary key. Then, you need a clustered index on those columns as well.

DBC/1012 SOLUTION. From the solution to Exercise 13.4, assume you decide to hash PASSENGER and RESERVATION on their full primary keys. Consider adding an index into the RESERVATION table on FLIGHT–SCHEDULE*DEPARTURE–DATE, FLIGHT*NUMBER to facilitate access by T13 and T28. You also may consider adding CONFIRMATION–NUMBER as the lowest-order column of the index to facilitate access by T28.

CHAPTER 15

15.5 Duplicating BUSINESS*COUNTRY–NAME and BUSINESS*NAME in RESERVATION enables counting the reservations on a given flight for passengers from a particular BUSINESS and discounting the fares of such passengers without accessing the BSNSS–PASSENGER table. Tuning techniques that you can employ with this option include the following:

   a.   Cluster RESERVATION by the combination FLIGHT–SCHEDULE*DEPARTURE–DATE, FLIGHT*NUMBER, BUSINESS*COUNTRY–NAME, and BUSINESS*NAME to eliminate scanning of RESERVATION to satisfy T14. This technique is consistent with earlier recommendations to cluster RESERVATION on FLIGHT–SCHEDULE*DEPARTURE–DATE, FLIGHT*NUMBER (Chapter 13) to optimize processing of requests T13 and T33.

   b.   Add an index to RESERVATION on the combination of FLIGHT–SCHEDULE*DEPARTURE–DATE, FLIGHT*NUMBER, BUSINESS*COUNTRY–NAME, BUSINESS*NAME. If the index is a clustering index, this technique incorporates the first technique described. Passengers from a given business with reservations on a particular flight can be counted via index-only access. The index also speeds access to RESERVATION rows for those passengers to discount their fares.

c. Add BUSINESS*COUNTRY—NAME, BUSINESS*NAME to the unique index on the primary key of RESERVATION (FLIGHT—SCHEDULE*DEPARTURE—DATE, FLIGHT*NUMBER, PASSENGER*COUNTRY—NAME, PASSENGER*CODE). This technique accomplishes the same objectives as technique b and enables enforcing primary key uniqueness. Consider defining the index as a clustering index and sequence columns in the index definition as follows: FLIGHT—SCHEDULE*DEPARTURE—DATE, FLIGHT*NUMBER, BUSINESS*COUNTRY—NAME, BUSINESS*NAME, PASSENGER*COUNTRY—NAME, PASSENGER*CODE. Access to RESERVATION rows to discount fares for passengers from the same business requires fewer I/Os due to clustering (as in technique a). On the other hand, access qualified by primary key values entails scanning of the index, since the primary key columns do not comprise the higher-order columns of the index. Thus, to determine the optimal sequence of clustering columns, you must weigh importance and frequency of different types of requests and efficiency of (perhaps partial) index scans versus direct index access.

Technique c appears to be the best choice, because it incorporates most benefits of techniques a and b.

15.6 Precalculating and storing flight reservation counts by business in FLIGHT—SCHEDULE or in a new table appears to reduce the number of rows that T14 must access dynamically. Consider the following points:

☐ There are 1500 FLIGHT—SCHEDULE rows. Approximately one-half of the reservations (say, 40) on each flight are for business passengers. Since most businesses fly six or fewer passengers in a year, any given flight is likely to have passengers from well over seven businesses. Suppose only 10 businesses are represented on an average flight (an extremely conservative estimate). The number of rows in the new or modified FLIGHT—SCHEDULE table, after adding counts by business, is $1500 \times 10 = 15,000$. Scanning the table to find the row with a particular count implies scanning an average of 7500 ($1/2 \times 15,000$) rows. Access of BSNSS—PASSENGER to obtain the same information implies scanning 9000 BSNSS—PASSENGER rows and accessing an average of six RESERVATION rows by the primary key (FLIGHT—SCHEDULE*DEPARTURE—DATE, FLIGHT*NUMBER, PASSENGER*COUNTRY—NAME, PASSENGER*CODE) for values corresponding to rows obtained from BSNSS—PASSENGER.

☐ Adding an index to BSNSS—PASSENGER on BUSINESS*COUNTRY—NAME, BUSINESS*NAME (as suggested in Chapter 14) enables direct access to business passengers from the same business—thus, you will access six rows on average rather than scan 9000 rows. In addition, assuming an index on the primary key of RESERVATION, an average of six accesses to corresponding RESERVATION rows are required. On the other hand, adding an index to the modified FLIGHT–SCHEDULE table (or to the new table) on FLIGHT*NUMBER, DEPARTURE–DATE, BUSINESS*COUNTRY–NAME, BUSINESS*NAME enables direct access to the one required row. Such an index also eliminates the need to access RESERVATION unless fares for existing passengers must be revised.

In both cases, savings in I/O and consequent performance improvements gained by storing reservation counts by business are not tremendous. The gains must be balanced against the costs: implications for integrity enforcement rules, overhead added to processing of RESERVATION inserts and updates, and additional storage requirements. In contrast, option 3 for tuning T14 (discussed in Exercise 15.5) provides similar (perhaps somewhat lower) savings in I/O by eliminating access to BSNSS–PASSENGER while requiring access of (on average) six RESERVATION rows for a given business and flight. Costs imposed by option 3 are lower, since duplicating BUSINESS*COUNTRY–NAME and BUSINESS*NAME can be handled during RESERVATION inserts and updates with minimal added overhead. Thus, option 3 seems the most desirable tuning option of those evaluated for request T14.

CHAPTER 16

16.6 To accommodate initial implementation of passenger information only, you can probably eliminate the following tables from the Moon Launch passenger reservations database:

```
FLIGHT
FLIGHT–SCHEDULE
RESERVATION
```

If you do not plan initially to store a schedule of credit-rating discounts, you also may eliminate the CREDIT–RATING table and consequently the VCTN–PASSENGER table (which contains CREDIT–RATING*CODE as its only nonkey column). If you do not plan initially to store information about businesses, you may eliminate the BUSINESS table. Eliminating the BUSINESS table may enable you to eliminate the BSNSS–PASSENGER table, unless business passengers may still have billing addresses that differ from their home addresses—in which case BUSINESS–BILLING–ADDRESS may be stored in BSNSS–PASSENGER. If you eliminate CREDIT–RATING, VCTN–PASSENGER, and BUSINESS but cannot eliminate BSNSS–PASSENGER, you may choose to merge BSNSS–PASSENGER with PASSENGER, allowing BUSINESS–BILLING–ADDRESS to be null or to default to a value meaning "not applicable" for rows representing vacation passengers.

16.7 If Moon Launch Enterprise distinguishes between business and vacationing passenger reservations agents, many of the processing requirements undoubtedly deal exclusively with one or the other type of reservation. Thus, you may decide to segment the RESERVATION table horizontally into two tables. This segmentation will shorten table scan times, increase data availability, and perhaps allow for more decentralized administrative responsibilities. On the other hand, both segments must be related to the FLIGHT-SCHEDULE table. Thus, requirements that involve counting, listing, or otherwise accessing all reservations for a flight will necessitate more complex DML and might be slower to process (or, on the contrary, might be faster to process if the DBMS is able to access the two table segments simultaneously).

You also may consider horizontal segmentation of the PASSENGER table into two tables. Recall, however that the same passenger may fly both on business and on vacation; thus, such a passenger will have rows in both segments. Additional business rules will be required to maintain data consistency across redundant rows. If you segment PASSENGER nevertheless, each segment will be a supertype with exactly one subtype spanning the supertype. Thus, you probably also will combine BSNSS-PASSENGER and VCTN-PASSENGER with their respective (segmented) supertypes.

16.8 The primary key of TICKET, comprising four columns, also is a foreign key referencing RESERVATION. Thus, joins of RESERVATION and TICKET must equate four columns—a potentially unwieldy DML syntax. Simpler DML and reduced storage requirements might be achieved by redefining the foreign key in TICKET to reference the alternate key (CONFIRMATION-NUMBER) of RESERVATION. This option requires that tickets are issued only for confirmed reservations. (Is this a reasonable business assumption?)

TICKET-IMAGE is a long textual column. It may be inefficient to search for the occurrence of a given character string (e.g., how many tickets include the character string 'ISSUE-DATE: 05/01/88'). It also may waste storage (if different tickets actually require different amounts of text) and slow performance of table scans and utility processing.

TICKET-IMAGE probably contains multiple types of textual data; for instance, it may include the name under which the ticket is issued, address, destination(s), payment information, or special services requested. Thus, one design alternative is to redefine TICKET as a table perhaps 60 characters long with composite primary key RESERVATION*CONFIRMATION-NUMBER, TEXT-TYPE-CODE (designating type of textual data), and LINE-NUMBER (within text type). Then, each occurrence of TICKET-IMAGE would be stored as approximately 10 (perhaps more) rows of the new table.

BIBLIOGRAPHY

American National Standards Institute. *Database Language SQL,* Document ANSI X3.135–1986. New York, NY: American National Standards Institute. Also available as International Standards Organization Document ISO/TC97/SC21/WG3 N117.

American National Standards Database Committee. *Database Language SQL Addendum-2* (working draft), Document X3H2-86-61. Washington, D.C.: American National Standards Institute (May 1986). Also available as International Standards Organization Document ISO/TC97/SC21/WG3 N143.

Appleton, Daniel S. "Business Rules: The Missing Link." *Datamation.* Newton, MA: The Cahners Publishing Co., A Division of Reed Publishing USA (October 15, 1984).

Appleton, Daniel S. "Law of the Data Jungle." *Datamation.* Newton, MA: The Cahners Publishing Co., A Division of Reed Publishing USA (October 1983).

Appleton, Daniel S. "Rule-Based Data Resource Management." *Datamation.* Newton, MA: The Cahners Publishing Co., A Division of Reed Publishing USA (May 1, 1986).

Brown, Robert G. *Logical Database Design Techniques.* Mountain View, CA: The Database Design Group, Inc., 1982.

Brown, Robert G. "Referential Integrity Checking and SQL." Proceedings—69th Meeting of GUIDE International. Anaheim, CA: Database Design Group, Inc., (March 15–20, 1987).

Codd, E. F. "Relational Database: A Practical Foundation for Productivity." *Communications of the ACM 25,* No. 2. New York, NY: Association for Computing Machinery, Inc. (February 1982).

Codd, E. F. "A Relational Model of Data for Large Shared Data Banks." *Communications of the ACM 13,* No. 6. New York, NY: Association for Computing Machinery, Inc. (June 1970). Reprinted in *Communications of the ACM 26,* No. 1 (January 1983).

Date, C. J. *A Guide to DB2.* (Second Edition). Reading, MA: Addison-Wesley Publishing Company, 1988.

Date, C. J. *A Guide to the SQL Standard.* Reading, MA: Addison-Wesley Publishing Company, 1987.

Date, C. J. *An Introduction to Database Systems.* Volume 1 (Fourth Edition). Reading, MA: Addison-Wesley Publishing Company, 1986.

Date, C. J. *An Introduction to Database Systems.* Volume 2. Reading, MA: Addison-Wesley Publishing Company, 1983.

Date, C. J. *Relational Database: Selected Writings.* Reading, MA: Addison-Wesley Publishing Company, 1986.

Durell, William R. *Data Administration: A Practical Guide to Successful Data Management.* New York: McGraw-Hill Book Company, 1985.

Elmasri, Ramez, James Larson, and Shamkant Navathe. "Integrating User Views in Database Design." *IEEE Computer,* Vol. 19, No. 1, (January 1986).

Fleming, Candace C. "DBC/1012 Teradata Corporation." *Data Base Management.* Pennsauken, NJ: Auerbach Publishers, Inc. Article number 26-10-02, 1987.

IBM Corporation. Miscellaneous *DB2* reference manuals. San Jose, CA: IBM Corporation, (1986–1987).

Loomis, Mary E. S. "Data Modeling—The IDEFIX Technique." IEEE, Proc. 1986 Phoenix Conference on Computers and Communications. Phoenix, AZ (March 26–28, 1986).

Loomis, Mary E. S. "Logical Data Modeling—A Step Toward Integration." IEEE, Proc. COMPINT '85—An International Conference on CIM and Databases. Montreal, Canada (September 8–12, 1985).

MUST Software International. *NOMAD2 Reference Manual.* Volumes 1 and 2. Wilton, CT: U3S International Ltd. (July 1987).

Shaw, Phil. "Referential Integrity in ISO-ANS SQL: Status and Plans." Proceedings - 69th Meeting of GUIDE International. Anaheim, CA: IBM Corporation, (March 15–20, 1987.)

Teradata Corporation. Miscellaneous *DBC/1012* reference manuals. Los Angeles, CA: Teradata Corporation, (1986–1987).

von Halle, Barbara. "DB2 IBM Corporation." *Data Base Management.* Pennsauken, NJ: Auerbach Publishers, Inc. Article number 26-10-04, 1987.

von Halle, Barbara. "Eliminating Ugly Surprises in the DB2 Environment." *Computerworld,* Vol. XXI, No. 37. Framingham, MA: CW Publishing/Inc. (September 14, 1987).

von Halle, Barbara. "The Taming of DB2." *Database Newsletter,* Vol. 13, No. 4. Boston, MA: Database Research Group, Inc. (July/August 1985).

Wiorkowski, Gabrielle and David Kull. *Designing for DB2 Performance.* Reading, MA: Addison-Wesley Publishing Company, 1988.

INDEX OF DESIGN RULES

BUILDING A LOGICAL DATA MODEL
CHAPTER 5
Step LDM1: Identify major entities.

1.1 Name, define, diagram and document *entities,* p. 90.

Step LDM2: Determine relationships among entities.

2.1 Name, define, diagram and document *relationships,* p. 96.

2.2 Classify relationships as *one-to-one (1:1)* or *one-to-many (1:N).* Reduce *many-to-many (M:N)* relationships, p. 100.

2.3 Reclassify *complex relationships* as entities, p. 103.

2.4 Eliminate *redundant relationships,* p. 105.

2.5 Establish 1:1 relationships between *supertypes* and *subtypes* and between *supertypes* and *categories,* p. 106.

2.6 Represent *1:N bill-of-materials* relationships and reduce *M:N bill-of-materials* relationships, p. 109.

CHAPTER 6
Step LDM3: Determine primary and alternate keys.

3.1 Choose one *primary key* for each entity, p. 116.

3.2 Identify *alternate keys* for each entity, p. 116.

Step LDM11: Integrate with existing data models.

11.1 *Integrate databases* by comparing and defining mappings among the underlying logical data models, p. 284.

11.2 Evolve the *business conceptual schema* by integrating and incorporating each new logical data model, p. 285.

11.3 Identify the *mappings* between each logical data model and the business conceptual schema, p. 286.

Step LDM12: Analyze for stability and growth.

12.1 Incorporate and document *changes that are imminent, significant and/or probable,* p. 293.

BUILDING AND TUNING A RELATIONAL DATABASE

Chapter 11

Step RDD1: Identify tables.

1.1 Identify one *table* for each entity, p. 306.

1.2 Name and document each table in the *data dictionary,* p. 307.

Step RDD2: Identify columns.

2.1 Identify one *column* for each attribute, p. 311.

2.2 Do not define *multiple attributes* as one column, p. 312.

2.3 Name and document each column in the *data dictionary,* p. 313.

2.4 *Diagram* tables, columns, implementation options, p. 315.

Step RDD3: Adapt data structure to product environment.

3.1 Define *sequencing of columns* to optimize storage utilization and performance, p. 318.

3.2 Require users and programs to *explicitly name columns* in a query or insert, p. 318.

3.3 Allocate *primary* space to contain the entire table, p. 320.

3.4 Allocate *free* space to accommodate row inserts, updates that may occur after table load or reorganization, p. 320.

3.5 Assign to one *database* tables representing related entities, p. 321.

3.6 Consider assigning sets of tables to *separate databases,* p. 321.

3.7 *Name* each database, p. 322.

3.8 Document databases in the *data dictionary,* p. 322.

3.9 Set *database locking* parameters to lock the least amount of data for the shortest duration, p. 323.

CHAPTER 12

Step RDD4: Design for business rules about entities.

4.1 Enforce logical properties of the entity's *primary key*, p. 329.

    option 1: DDL
    option 2: Domain Definition Techniques

4.2 Enforce logical properties of *alternate keys*, p. 332.

    option 1: DDL
    option 2: Domain Definition Techniques

4.3 Document primary and alternate keys in the *data dictionary*, p. 332.

Step RDD5: Design for business rules about relationships.

5.1 Enforce *business rules* about *relationships*, p. 334.

    option 1: DDL
    option 2: Triggering Operation Implementation Techniques

5.2 Document foreign keys in the *data dictionary* and techniques used to enforce them, p. 336.

Step RDD6: Design for additional business rules about attributes.

6.1 Enforce *business rules* about *attributes* (domains and triggering operations), p. 340.

    option 1: DDL
    option 2: Unique Indexes
    option 3: Standard Maintenance Routines
    option 4: Manual Enforcement

6.2 Document in the *data dictionary* business rules about attributes and techniques used to enforce them, p. 345.

6.3 Do not permit *null values* for any column, p. 349.

6.4 Favor use of *default values* over null values, p. 349.

6.5 *Automate* assignment of *default values*, p. 350.

6.6 Establish a primary key occurrence for a *foreign key default value*, p. 350.

6.7 Establish special mechanisms to ensure correct execution of *aggregate operations* involving *default values*, p. 350.

6.8 Enforce business rules about tables and columns through *standard maintenance routines*, p. 351.

6.9 Make each *standard maintenance routine* table-specific, p. 353.

6.10 Establish *standard integrity audit routines* for each table (or set of tables), p. 354.

CHAPTER 13

Step RDD7: Tune for scan efficiency.

7.1 Encourage *scan processing* when appropriate, p. 369.

7.2 Minimize *scan overhead*, p. 370.

CHAPTER 17

Tuning Techniques.

INDEX